JAPAN IN TRANSITION

JAPAN IN TRANSITION

FROM TOKUGAWA TO MEIJI

EDITED BY MARIUS B. JANSEN
AND GILBERT ROZMAN

Princeton University Press
Princeton, New Jersey

PUBLISHED BY PRINCETON UNIVERSITY PRESS, 41 WILLIAM STREET, PRINCETON, NEW JERSEY 08540
IN THE UNITED KINGDOM: PRINCETON UNIVERSITY PRESS, GUILDFORD, SURREY

LIBRARY OF CONGRESS CATALOGING IN PUBLICATION DATA WILL BE FOUND ON THE LAST PRINTED PAGE OF THIS BOOK

ISBN 0-691-05459-2

THIS BOOK HAS BEEN COMPOSED IN LINOTRON SABON

CLOTHBOUND EDITIONS OF PRINCETON UNIVERSITY PRESS BOOKS ARE PRINTED ON ACID-FREE PAPER, AND BINDING MATERIALS ARE CHOSEN FOR STRENGTH AND DURABILITY
PRINTED IN THE UNITED STATES OF AMERICA BY PRINCETON UNIVERSITY PRESS, PRINCETON, NEW JERSEY

DESIGNED BY LAURY A. EGAN

CONTENTS

LIST OF FIGURES AND MAPS vii

LIST OF TABLES viii

ACKNOWLEDGMENTS xi

1. Overview BY MARIUS B. JANSEN AND GILBERT ROZMAN 3

PART ONE: ADMINISTRATION

Introduction to Part One BY MARIUS B. JANSEN 29

2. The Central Government BY ALBERT M. CRAIG 36
3. The Ruling Class BY MARIUS B. JANSEN 68
4. From Domain to Prefecture BY MICHIO UMEGAKI 91
5. Local Administration: The Example of Awa-Tokushima BY ANDREW FRASER 111

PART TWO: ORGANIZATIONS

Introduction to Part Two BY D. ELEANOR WESTNEY 133

6. Buddhism: The Threat of Eradication BY MARTIN COLLCUTT 143
7. The Military BY D. ELEANOR WESTNEY 168
8. Education: From One Room to One System BY RICHARD RUBINGER 195
9. The Press BY ALBERT A. ALTMAN 231
10. Shipping: From Sail to Steam BY WILLIAM D. WRAY 248

PART THREE: CITIES AND POPULATION

Introduction to Part Three BY GILBERT ROZMAN 273

11. Population Changes BY AKIRA HAYAMI 280

12. Castle Towns in Transition BY GILBERT ROZMAN 318

13. The Edo-Tokyo Transition: In Search of Common Ground BY HENRY D. SMITH II 347

PART FOUR: RURAL ECONOMY AND MATERIAL CONDITIONS

Introduction to Part Four BY KOZO YAMAMURA 377

14. The Meiji Land Tax Reform and Its Effects BY KOZO YAMAMURA 382

15. The Rural Economy: Commercial Agriculture, By-employment, and Wage Work BY OSAMU SAITŌ 400

16. Grain Consumption: The Case of Chōshū BY SHUNSAKU NISHIKAWA 421

17. The Material Culture: Stability in Transition BY SUSAN B. HANLEY 447

ABOUT THE CONTRIBUTORS 471

INDEX 475

FIGURES AND MAPS

FIGURES

8.1	Elementary School Enrollment Rates, 1873-1905	212
10.1	Mitsubishi Administrative Structure, 1882	260
11.1	Population Trends of Aizu *Han* and Yonezawa *Han*, 1680-1850	293
11.2	Age Composition in Japan, December 31, 1886	297
11.3	Age Composition in Japan, December 31, 1908	302
11.4	Comparison of Population Change, by Region, 1822-1846 and 1872-1885	303
11.5	Population Trends in Kōzuke-Shimotsuke and Bingo-Aki Areas, 1822-1885	309
11.6	Age Components in Kōzuke-Shimotsuke and Bingo-Aki Areas, 1885	310
11.7	Crude Birth and Death Rates in Kōzuke-Shimotsuke and Bingo-Aki Areas, 1877-1885	311
11.8	Sex Ratio Trends in Kōzuke-Shimotsuke and Bingo-Aki Areas, 1750-1885	313
12.1	Domain Production and Castle-Town Population, 1875	331
13.1	Population Change in the Edo-Tokyo Transition, 1820-1920	356
13.2	Edo-Tokyo Sex Ratios, 1820-1920	366
13.3	Native-Born Population in Edo-Tokyo, 1830-1920	368
15.1	Nonfarm Households and Cash-Crop Production, 26 *Gun* of Osaka Prefecture, 1870s and 1880s	415

MAPS

11.1	The Shifting Demographic Center of Gravity, 1720-1893	292
11.2	Population Change in Japan, 1822-1846 (Except 1834-1840)	299
11.3	Population Change in Japan, 1872-1885	300
12.1	Urbanization in Japan by Region, 1875	327
16.1	Chōshū (Later Yamaguchi *Ken*)	424

TABLES

4.1	Amalgamation of Domains into *Ken* Jurisdiction, 1871	92
4.2	Voluntary Liquidation of Domains, 1870/71	101
5.1	Local Tax Expenditures in Tokushima, 1890	112
6.1	The Reduction of Buddhism in Early Meiji	162
7.1	Military Organization Changes in Seven Nagano-Prefecture Domains, 1850-1870	175
8.1	Elementary School Enrollment Rates in Selected Prefectures, 1874-1894	213
8.2	Income Sources of Public Elementary Schools, 1873-1881	216
8.3	Number of Middle Schools, 1877-1879	219
8.4	Number of Middle Schools, 1879-1887	224
10.1	Regional Distribution of Steamships, by Prefecture, June 1887	267
11.1	Population Growth and Per Capita Agricultural Production, 1872-1885	307
11.2	Population Indices for Kōzuke-Shimotsuke and Bingo-Aki Areas, 1884	312
12.1	Chronology of Reforms Affecting Japanese Cities, 1859-1889	319
12.2	Distribution of Cities, by Size, Late Tokugawa–1886	323
12.3	Populations of Former Castle Cities, 1875	325
12.4	Regional Levels of Urbanization, 1875	328
12.5	Regional Distribution of Cities, by Size, 1875	329
12.6	Taxes, Stipends and City Populations for Large Domains, Late Tokugawa	332
12.7	Regional Variations in Castle-City Growth, 1883	335
12.8	Percentage of Samurai in the Urban Population, 1883	342
14.1	Model Calculations of Land Value, 1873	389
14.2	Post-Reform Mean Prefectural Effective Tax Rate	390
14.3	Post-Reform Changes in Tax Burden, by Prefecture	395
15.1	Social Class of Population Engaged in Side Activities in Four Yamanashi Villages, 1879	412
15.2	Sericulture among Tenant Farmer Households and Their Side Activities in Four Yamanashi Villages, 1879	413

16.1 Output and Supply of Grain in Chōshū/Yamaguchi, 1840s and 1887 426
16.2 Supply of "Grain" by *Saiban* in Chōshū, 1840s 428
16.3 Possible Consumption of Rice by Commoners in Chōshū, 1840s 434
16.4 "Grain" Consumption in Chōshū/Yamaguchi, 1840s and 1887 435
16.5 Caloric and Nutritional Intake Per Capita Per Day from Staple Foods in Chōshū/Yamaguchi, 1840s and 1887 436
16.6 Caloric and Protein Intake in Japan, 1874-1892 437
16.7 Caloric and Nutritional Intake Per Capita Per Day from Military Rations, 1883 439
16.8 Comparison of Staple Food Proportions in Chōshū/Yamaguchi, 1840s and 1886-1887 443
17.1 Number of Shops in Tokyo, 1881, 1891, and 1900 459

ACKNOWLEDGMENTS

This book is the product of two workshops and a conference that were held in 1981 and 1982 to examine aspects of Japan's transformation in the middle decades of the nineteenth century. It was our hope to add social science and quantitative analysis to the study of a period previously treated largely in terms of political and diplomatic history.

One workshop met at the Lake Wilderness Conference Center of the University of Washington, from August 30 to September 2, 1981, and a second at the Quail Roost Conference Center of the University of North Carolina, from September 3 to 6 of the same year. The conference that followed brought members of both groups together at White Sulphur Springs, West Virginia, from August 9 to 13, 1982.

In addition to the authors of the papers that follow, a number of colleagues made important contributions to workshops and conference alike. Professors William G. Beasley, of the University of London's School of Oriental and African Studies, and Bernard S. Silberman, of the University of Chicago, sent initial papers but were not able to attend. Professors William B. Hauser (University of Rochester), Stephen Vlastos (University of Iowa), and James Leavell (Clemson University), as well as Elizabeth Allan, a graduate student at Princeton University, proposed problems; and Professor James W. White, of the University of North Carolina, contributed throughout every stage of the project. In addition, Professors John W. Hall (Yale University) and Thomas M. Huber (Duke University) participated in workshop discussions.

We are grateful to all, particularly to our colleagues from Australia, Japan, and Israel who came so far and contributed so much. We acknowledge the help of the Social Science Research Council, which provided funds in the early stages of our planning, and especially that of the Japan–United States Friendship Commission, whose grant made the conference and project possible. Miriam Brokaw and her associates at Princeton University Press provided the editorial assistance and enthusiasm that made the Press our automatic choice as publisher. We are also fortunate that Charles Purrenhage of the Press gave a great deal of his time to the professional copyediting of our complex manuscript, and that Thomas Schalow prepared the index.

M.B.J.
G.R.

Princeton, 1984

JAPAN IN TRANSITION

CHAPTER 1

OVERVIEW

BY MARIUS B. JANSEN AND GILBERT ROZMAN

This is a book about the changeover from Tokugawa (1600-1868) to Meiji (1868-1912) in nineteenth-century Japan. It was a transition from early modern (*kinsei*) to modern (*kindai*), as the Japanese put it; from late-feudal to modern institutions, as many historians have described it, from shogunal to imperial rule, and from isolation to integration in the world economy. Most accounts treat it chiefly in its political dimension, focusing on the events associated with the return of power to the throne. The Meiji Restoration, the central event of that transition, thus serves as its symbol. Too frequently it also serves to shield the student from the longer and deeper process of revolutionary social change that was underway and that gave the Restoration its significance in world history. In their totality, the changes with which these chapters are concerned constituted a profound transformation of Japanese society. But it was one long in taking shape, and its future outlines were never as clear to those who led as their subsequent recollections seemed to indicate.

It is easy to be taken in by the rhetoric of the Meiji leaders, most of it produced long after the state had taken form—a rhetoric that implies an unchanging vision and a steady purpose. In fact, vision and purpose were in process of definition throughout the period of transition. The general outlines of a country that would be able to compete with other countries were in the leaders' minds, but the shape and individuality of its institutions—even its political institutions—were in question for several decades. Kido Takayoshi's discovery of the uses of the 1868 Charter Oath during his visit to Washington in 1872 provides a case in point. Later generations would point to that document as a blueprint, and in recent years it has even been credited with containing the germ of the liberal Constitution of 1947; but at the time it was issued, as Michio

Umegaki shows in Chapter 4, the Oath was designed as reassurance for daimyo and leading samurai. Even Kido, who had contributed to its formulation, was startled by his realization of its future utility.

The changes Japan experienced in the middle decade of the nineteenth century had profound consequences for the world state system, the world economy, and world history. A country that had been decentralized, with rule divided among some 260 hereditary authorities (daimyo) who ruled their domains, was transformed into a centralized, unitary state. A society in which roles and aspirations had been limited by hereditary designations of status threw off class restrictions to construct a meritocracy based on educational achievement. An undeveloped country, dependent on the product of premodern agriculture and a complex land tax paid in kind by village communities, launched changes based on individual ownership, monetarization, and commercial integration and diversification to inaugurate industrialization.

Treaties with Western countries, negotiated under duress, opened major ports to foreign presence and goods. Acute consciousness of dangers to national sovereignty forced military changes that replaced hereditary warriors with conscript soldiers and enabled Japan, by century's end, to regain its sovereignty and threaten that of its neighbors. In numerous ways, cataclysmic changes transformed a way of life long isolated from the rest of the world. Glaring inconsistencies with the needs of a modern society were swept away. The enactment and implementation of the reforms that did this are the subject of many of the chapters that follow.

The Organization of This Book

Part One is concerned with the often traveled but still inadequately understood terrain of administrative change. Our coverage ranges from an overview of the changes in central government to a case study of the structure and costs of local government in the Meiji period. Chapters center on the transformation of the ruling class, the crucial decision to abolish the domains in 1871, and the consequences of that decision in one domain. Together these chapters document the political aspect of Meiji centralization in administration.

Part Two is a study of the transformation of some of the most important and diverse organizations in Japan. Of the many areas that might have been selected, our authors have chosen to examine five types of organizations: 1) Buddhist religious organizations, which had been closely linked to the Tokugawa order; 2) military organizations, which, as a primary concern of Meiji leaders, led the way in institutional innovation;

3) the educational system, which developed the human resources to staff all organizations; 4) the press, which quickly became the principal means of communication between the leaders and the public; and 5) shipping, one of the primary arenas of competition between new and old types of commercial organization. The dramatic changes in these organizations in the short space of a decade or two reveal how profound the transformation of Japan was. They show, in the case of education, how quickly a rationalized and uniform system could take hold or, in the case of shipping, how readily foreign technology could be adopted with state support. The transformation of many types of organization reflects the active role of the Meiji government in centralizing without dominating and mirrors the intensely competitive setting of the Meiji environment.

The rapid expansion of social science methods in historical studies of Japan makes possible the use of statistical records to examine the course of Japan's nineteenth-century transition in Parts Three and Four. Here we show the promise of linking the Tokugawa and Meiji periods through detailed statistics that are now available for each. The merging of statistical and descriptive analysis is especially important for a book on nineteenth-century Japanese history for three reasons: the ever wider availability of historical statistics; the need for objective bases for judgments that too often are based on normative assumptions; and the recent growth of interest among Japanese scholars in specialized statistical methods.

We are fortunate to have as contributors to this volume three scholars who exemplify this new trend in Japan: Akira Hayami, Shunsaku Nishikawa, and Osamu Saitō.[1] The chapters in Part Three analyze population and urban data; in addition, there is a separate study of the transition in Tokyo (Edo), Japan's largest city and the seat of both the Tokugawa shogunate and the Meiji central government. Part Four focuses on the land tax reform, labor use, and grain consumption as determined from local records. The final chapter explores the penetration of Western living standards into Japan. To an altogether astonishing degree, given the importance of the issue for evaluation of the impact of the Restoration, the land tax reform—though clearly the central administrative device for transforming feudal dues into modern taxes—has hitherto been treated in generalities that emphasize burden more than incentive, tenancy more than the freedoms that came with fee simple possession, and village decline more than growth and diversification. The deflation of 1881-1885 has been taken as symptomatic of a much deeper malaise. Kozo

[1] Unlike other Japanese names throughout this book, our contributors' surnames follow their given names because they here write in English.

Yamamura raises important doubts about such conclusions, and all our authors show the need for careful analysis that long-accepted generalizations require when quantifiable data can be found.

It is not surprising that the bulk of historical scholarship concerned with the changes of which we speak has concentrated on the political experimentation of early Meiji, and the democratic movement of the 1880s. Foreign policy disputes that intersected with these—the approach and challenge of the West, the nature and impact of unequal treaties, and the issue of Korean policy—have also received their due.

Much less in evidence, whether in Japanese or English, is research that offers a broad perspective on changes in central and local administration, on the transformation of diverse organizations, on changes in demography and the structure of cities, and on continuities and discontinuities in rural life and the standard of living. New currents in social science analysis are now being widely applied in Japanese studies, but these essays are among the first to bring them to bear on the transition from Tokugawa to Meiji. For more than two decades, one of the most productive areas of research in Japanese studies has been the study of dynamism within Tokugawa society. Surprisingly, however, many findings about changing conditions in the last century of the Tokugawa era have yet to be incorporated into interpretations of modern Japan. The bridge needed to link the premodern and the modern across the second half of the nineteenth century remains unbuilt. Here we begin the construction of such a bridge.

Transition, Restoration, or Revolution?

Our studies had their origin in a concern with the deeper sort of change that was occurring as the late Tokugawa and early Meiji shifts took place. Change in class relations was in progress long before the status restrictions were abolished, and it accelerated as the tumultuous years of crisis that followed the coming of Perry put a premium on ability. The domains of the Tokugawa political system had become drawn together owing to joint concern with stability, the interchange of goods, and migration patterns. Official concern with the adequacy of food and popular well-being produced impressive compilations of statistical evidence long before the events of the Restoration. Demographic and urban patterns, which varied by place and time, were transforming the human map of Japan long before Meiji centralization.

It is this transition, rather than the Restoration, that is our theme. But how is it to be delimited? Tides of change vary from measure to measure, and only political decisions provide convenient benchmarks for a programmed survey. Since the early 1930s Japanese historians, in their search for the inception of the Meiji state, have often defined that administration in terms of Marxist categories of absolutism, and they have tended to begin their survey in the 1830s and 1840s. Their reasoning was that the economic reforms and administrative tightening of those (Tempō) years led to increased control in the hands of feudal administrators. Domain monopolies, and greater central control in the hands of shogun and daimyo, seemed to prepare a generation for the integrated and structured trends that lay ahead. The transition years were judged to extend until the 1880s, when political institutions were in place; thereafter, the Matsukata fiscal program produced a countryside dominated, as historians put it, by a landlord-capitalist alliance directed by bureaucrats in the interest of a Meiji "absolutism."

More recent scholarship is less firm about the significance of the Tempō era and the definition of Meiji absolutism. The reforms mounted by the shogunate failed to achieve their purpose, though programs inaugurated by some of the major domains proved more successful in bolstering local economies. The foreign problem was looming larger by the 1840s, but no real response to it came before Perry's arrival in 1853. If there was something new about the Tempō period, it was the growing consciousness that a problem existed in the combination of economic distress and military weakness, an awareness that resulted in unsuccessful attempts to strengthen the Tokugawa center. But those attempts proved not only ineffective but even counterproductive, for domain reforms more nearly strengthened the periphery against the center. Nor can it be shown that reform followed a straight (or even winding) line from Tempō on. The Meiji leaders were born in the Tempō years, to be sure, and by the turn of the century they were being derided by their juniors as the "old men of the Tempō era." Their years of conditioning and experience, however, came well after Tempō.

For most purposes our transition is best defined in terms of the three decades that began with the coming of Perry and ended with the institutionalization of "modern" trends in administration, production, organization, and settlement in the 1880s. In this book we follow the Japanese convention of referring to the years 1853-1868 as *bakumatsu*, or the end of the *bakuhan* system, i.e. the political order defined by the Tokugawa *bakufu* and the 260-odd *han* (domains). We use "early Meiji" for the 1870s and "mid-Meiji" for the 1880s. The changes that were deliberate found their point of origin in the crisis of foreign policy presented by the appearance of Perry's flotilla. Political and administrative moves can be most clearly dated, and so we begin with them. These provided the framework for a program of defensive modernization to restore the national sovereignty that had been threatened by unequal treaties. Japan's inability to prevent that damage, it seemed to many, could be traced to the lack of institutions able to control and centralize effectively. Incipient central institutions, though initially obscured by an apparent decline in central authority, undermined the pattern of decentralization. Without this preparation for economic and administrative integration, Japan's nineteenth-century transition clearly would not have been so speedy or successful.

We have taken the decades from the 1850s to the 1880s as pivotal to this transition. The foreign crisis became acute with the coming of Perry. It intensified with the opening of the ports in the 1860s, and determined the course of official westernization in the 1870s. Its "solution," in the form of full recovery of national sovereignty through reform of the unequal treaties, required the full length of the Meiji period, but it was in sight by the 1880s and negotiated by 1894. Local autonomy, which had actually been strengthened by the weakening of the shogunate in the 1860s, survived the Restoration and came to an end only in 1871; as late as 1884 the daimyo were rewarded with titles of peerage. Samurai activism and terrorism reached a high in the 1860s, and it required a full decade of Meiji rule before the loss of warrior-class economic and social privileges was sealed by the failure of the Satsuma Rebellion in 1877. New institutions of centralization and rationalization of local government developed gradually. The new regime began with the Tokugawa lands, most of which were retained as heartland of the new "imperial" authority; it extended its sway cautiously over daimyo lands in 1871, and then began a process of experimentation that was completed only with the establishment of institutions of local government in the late 1880s and promulgation of the constitution in 1889.

Much Japanese writing has met or avoided the problem of classification by resort to the term "Restoration." This is by no means an empty word, for it is expressed with orthography different from that employed for the cyclical, though ultimately futile, efforts to revive dynastic health in China (restorations rendered as *chūkō* in Japanese). *Ishin* carries with it ideas of linking change and renewal, and can serve to signify revolutionary or comprehensive change. In both loyalist and non-Marxist historiography, however, it becomes inseparably linked with the return of power to the sovereign. That was what constituted the centerpiece of what Meiji statesmen referred to with satisfaction at the end of their careers as "the great work of Restoration" (*ishin no taigyō*). Consequently, we find it inadequate to convey the depth and variety of social change with which we deal in this book; and although the term can well accommodate revolutionary social change, it does not convey that meaning for most readers.

One might then concentrate on the depth of those changes to describe our period as one of "revolution." Many scholars, among them Professor Kuwabara Takeo, do so,[2] and write persuasively of the Meiji Revolution. Yet there are important contrasts to be made between the Tokugawa-Meiji transition on the one hand and the great world revolutions on the other. We shall return to these contrasts below and feel that "revolution" exaggerates the political element involved, describing Japan poorly in that regard. Ultimately it fits our needs little better than "Restoration."

We therefore prefer to speak of "transition." The word comes with fewer presuppositions and expectations, and permits a better treatment of developments on both sides of the great political turnover of 1868.

Studies of the Tokugawa-Meiji transition must, of course, identify what it was that changed. A few decades constitute a short time span for the observation of changes in the lives of people, especially in the absence of devastating wars, large-scale migration across national borders, or massive foreign trade. Formal institutions were reordered, but we should not expect to find the pervasive transformations of local conditions that mark the literature on modernization or imperialism. Nevertheless, if the concept of transition is to have meaning beyond the political sphere, there must be evidence of significant and widespread change.

Our second task has thus been to explain the process of change in the 1860s and 1870s. Most of the chapters that follow are organized chronologically; they discuss, where appropriate, the timing of major reforms and the variations in their implementation across Japan.

Our third task is to explain why conditions changed as they did. What were the respective roles of leaders, national policies, and local initiatives? To what extent were changes a continuation of trends already present during the second half of the Tokugawa era? What were the ramifications of such key decisions as the abolition of domains and the land tax reform for many areas of daily life?

The fourth objective is to link these studies to comparative work on the emergence of modern societies elsewhere in the world. Such an effort is clearly beyond the scope of this book's individual chapters, which have had to cope with the demands of the first three tasks in very brief compass, but we do attempt to address these wide-ranging concerns in the introductions to each of the main parts of the book. The introductions draw together the conclusions of the chapters that follow, within the context of what is known about the transition period and with an eye to the

[2] Kuwabara Takeo, *Japan and Western Civilization: Essays on Comparative Culture* (Tokyo: University of Tokyo Press, 1983).

questions that might emerge in comparative analysis. That task will have to continue with the cooperation of specialists on other countries.

Important contrasts can be made between the Tokugawa-Meiji transition, on the one hand, and the transitions associated with state building in Western countries, as well as the experiences of the great revolutions in Russia and China, on the other. In England, the United States, and most other Western countries, the process of change was more gradual, and the role of the state was generally secondary. Japan's transition offers at least four sharp contrasts to these Western experiences:

1) In Japan the role of the state in initiating changes and guiding the transformation of society was much greater. State reforms were a primary force in bringing on change.
2) In Japan the consciousness of foreign experience played a central role. The deliberate borrowing of models from the West in an effort to "catch up" operated as a powerful influence on the course of change.
3) Given the state's active role and the importance of foreign models, Japanese society became more centralized in relation to its level of development than had been the case in the West.
4) In Japan the transition in state building, organizational formation, and way of life was greatly compressed.

While attention has been lavished on the great revolutions that set the course of most thinking and writing about the character of modern transformations, Japan's less wrenching nineteenth-century transition has been little analyzed, and then mostly in narrow political terms. Like the Marxist revolutions, Japan's transition brought a fundamental change in a way of life. But because Japan's experience was also different, it deserves to be clearly distinguished as a path to modern transformation. In the absence of an ideological literature or an elaborate vision of the future, reform in Japan was more groping and more pragmatic. There are also at least four contrasts that should be made between Japan's transition and those of countries that underwent Marxist revolutions:

1) The violence that contributed to overthrowing the old order did not involve large numbers of the disadvantaged in Japan, and it was seldom directed against those with privilege or property. Rather, social equals were pitted against each other. Samurai armies from four domains in the southwest met resistance from the armies of other domains in the northeast.
2) The central event in Japan, the Meiji Restoration of 1868, symbolizes the reassertion of traditional authority—in the person of the emperor—rather than its overthrow or effacement.

3) The events of 1868 resulted in virtually no big losers (the new Tokugawa family head was resettled in a large domain carved out of former shogunal lands) and little in the way of spoils to the winners (if one excepts the imperial family and its branches) or to members of particular social classes or strata. The "victorious" southwestern domains would themselves soon become economic backwaters.
4) Although representatives of domains on the "losing" side were temporarily disadvantaged in the decades that followed, individuals were free to draw on all assets of family and personal background, without stipulated restrictions or priorities weighted according to previous social class or political commitment.

The changes we discuss were ultimately revolutionary in their impact on Japanese society, and they led to a Japan that altered radically the international balance of power. But they were not revolutionary in the sense of a social and political upheaval so great that it led to overturn of the social order. Class animosities were present in many forms; there were innumerable instances of urban and rural insurrection and protest, of rural notables' irritation with urban samurai administrators, and of lower-samurai resentment of the privileges of their superiors. Disorders continued for more than a decade after the Restoration, as rural notables found the new bureaucrats sent to rule them little to their taste or as change came more slowly than hoped. Samurai resentment flared in a series of rebellions, of which the last and greatest came in 1877. Nevertheless, there were no popular uprisings large enough to cause samurai armies to shift allegiance, and no movement of samurai discontent crossed the traditional bounds of regional separatism and loyalty. In comparative terms of world history, the Tokugawa-Meiji transition, conflict-ridden as it was in its Japanese context, was nonetheless remarkably smooth.

There were remarkably few losers and winners in the Tokugawa-Meiji transition. The last of the shoguns was forced to retire as head of his house, but he continued to be treated with the greatest of respect. In 1880 his court titles were returned to him; subsequently, he was given the highest rank in the new peerage, and was even singled out as an ideal choice for prime minister in one newspaper poll. His successor as head of the Tokugawa house served as president of the new House of Peers. Such leading Tokugawa statesmen as Katsu Kaishū and Enomoto Takeaki, men who were responsible for major setbacks to the imperial armies in the Restoration War, received high posts in the Meiji government. But again, if there were few losers, there were also few winners. The sovereign and his relatives experienced a dramatic shift in status, but they paid for this by being forced into military uniforms and careers as symbols of the new era. The court nobles whose prestige was vital to the new regime usually counted for little in its deliberations. Satsuma and Chōshū leaders were disproportionately numerous in the new government, but both Satsuma and Chōshū, as well as Saga, produced samurai rebellions that were put down ruthlessly. The first governor assigned to Chōshū was a former Tokugawa vassal. The samurai class, which provided virtually 100 percent of the Restoration movement's leadership, dominated the early government, but its members also paid the highest price in loss of income, perquisites, and honor. The leaders of that class, the former daimyo, were pushed aside—the most eminent into affluence, but a good many into genteel poverty.

Our generalization holds for geographic areas, as well. The Restoration domains that led in the events of 1868 were not the recipients of special consideration, except with reference to concern for security and disorder. Members of their ruling strata who served in the central government knew their old fellow revolutionaries too well to trust them very far. Tani Kanjō had his agents monitor the activities of Itagaki Taisuke in Tosa; Kido Takayoshi saw to it that dissent was crushed in his native Chōshū; and Ōkubo Toshimichi personally took command of the campaigns to crush the Satsuma Rebellion. Nor did it end there. The special advantages that Satsuma had with respect to the China trade through its control of the Ryūkyūs, the vigorous coastal trading that Chōshū could tap for income, and the regional monopolies that helped Tosa stockpile arms and play a national role—these were not inherited by the successor territorial administrations in Kagoshima, Yamaguchi, or Kōchi prefectures. They lost their political importance in the Meiji settlement and became economic backwaters. The efforts of the Meiji regime were concentrated at the center. The Tokugawa capital of Edo, after some years of slump, re-emerged with greater strength as the national capital of Tokyo. For the first decade and more of Meiji, the Restoration domains, indeed most of remote Japan, probably contributed more to the center than they received from it.

A final criterion, once advanced by R.R. Palmer to measure revolutionary zeal, is expropriation and/or flight into exile. Neither was a factor in the Restoration shift. The Tokugawa ruling class held land in stewardship and lacked any kind of base from which to protest. It is probably a measure of Japanese insularity that exile was unknown. That has in train, of course, another important factor: winners and losers realized that disruption and violence would benefit only Japan's foreign rivals. With the last shogun's decision to surrender his powers as with the new government's relative mildness in treating its recent rivals, the specter of foreign gain was never distant, and it served to moderate thoughts of vengeance. This was in considerable contrast to the readiness of domains and *bakufu* in late Tokugawa times to demand and surrender the heads of high retainers as proof of sincerity.

For all these reasons, the transition in nineteenth-century Japan has not fired the imagination of students of comparative social change. It has seemed to lack the breathtaking political drama of impoverished masses taking to the streets, of aristocrats being liquidated by guillotine or gun. There was no grand design for delivering mankind from injustice and creating an ideal social order in advance of the rest of the world. We realize that our chosen term, transition, is unlikely to evoke the sensation of far-reaching and cataclysmic change. We prefer this term not because we think that the complex of changes during this period was of little importance in world history, but because we want to accentuate a perception of gradual change, of a bridge between two periods, that stands in contrast to much of the literature on revolution. The Japanese experience teaches us that without the explosion of revolution at the top, without massive change in the circumstances of life below, a radically different social structure can materialize. The past lives on and affects the new order, but this does not prevent the dismantling of that order, the expropriation of the privileges and incomes of the old elite, an organizational revolution, and profound reform of institutions and rules that restricted the opportunities of ordinary people. Nevertheless, none of this can be allowed to obscure the fact that the events with which this book deals marked a decisive juncture in world development and constituted the formative period of modern Japanese history.

Centralization: The Essence of the Transition

The transition from Tokugawa to Meiji was one of three that set the course of Japan's development in recent centuries. The Tokugawa victory in 1600 signaled the reunification of a country long divided by warfare. It re-established social order on the basis of political fragmentation; it systematized Tokugawa hegemony over the military houses and social stability on the basis of fixed hereditary classes; and it ushered in two and a half centuries of peace characterized by economic growth, urban culture, and a startling rise in literacy. Japan's most recent transition came with the emergence of modern political institutions and accelerated economic growth after World War II. The Tokugawa-Meiji transition was the product of the first and helps explain the third of these periods of dramatic change. It is the key link, vital to an understanding of social change from the seventeenth century to the present.

Each of these transitions brought an order more centralized than the one before. Each, though symbolized by political events—unification in 1600, restoration in 1868, defeat in 1945 and reconstruction—was the product of incremental changes that played themselves out on timetables which differed from one social indicator to another. There was not an abrupt turn from an ossified "Tokugawa" to a dynamic "Meiji"; and although some alternatives, like continued Tokugawa rule, were ruled out, there was not a sudden change in the nature of discourse, but a transition. Recent scholarship makes clear the rich and continually changing tapestry of social change in Tokugawa Japan; by the nineteenth century, formal restrictions laid down by early rulers were circumvented and inappropriate. But there was also the drag of a longstanding tradition. Even in the political sphere, as writers in this book show, the Tokugawa downfall left a vacuum that was at first concealed only by slogans. The Meiji change did not come overnight and, in fact, continued over such a long period that many Japanese scholars prefer to divide the period into decades instead of taking it up as a unit.

The real import of the changes that transformed Japanese society over a few decades needs to be considered in international perspective. With remarkably little demonstration of foreign military and economic superiority, the Japanese were prodded into abandoning many of the most basic principles and organizations of their government and economy. With little large-scale violence or class struggle, a consensus was reached on the need for centralization and on the sacrifices of group interests to achieve it. The goals of national prosperity and strength were quickly accepted in popular consciousness. Major reforms that established a new social order were adopted and fully implemented within a short time of their original conception. These are the features that stand out in Japan's rapid transformation from Tokugawa to Meiji.

The chapters that follow try to show how this was possible. At the risk of oversimplification, we can single out four persistent explanations that appear again and again. First, Japan already possessed a remarkably solid foundation for modern reforms. Its high levels of literacy and urbanization and its extensive economic integration were important assets for change. Second, many of the changes were anticipated by developments of the late Tokugawa. Third, the attitudes of Japanese elites were relatively homogeneous and amenable to considerable reorganization and centralization. Finally, some of our authors who deal with rural life point to stability in conditions of daily life, a stability that may have provided a context in which families felt secure enough to accept substantial change in other areas. In short, the Japanese people—influenced by conditions developed earlier, by recent changes, by a world view supportive of centralization, and by stability in basic conditions of life—accepted with remarkable ease a radical restructuring of their central institutions. We find this message repeated in the chapters that follow on the principal Meiji reforms and organizational changes.

During the nineteenth century most societies experienced the need to centralize. Japan was no exception; its problems were in fact clear to most of the literate. How could the multiple foreign threats of military expansion, trade, and cultural diffusion be countered without centralization? The need for a national military force and a unified government was readily perceived. It is also clear that in Japan, as in most countries, formidable barriers stood in the way. Even where a powerful premodern state existed, the dual task of transforming it, in order to facilitate adoption of advanced technology, and of organizing its population in new ways was not an easy one.

The personalized nature of control at all levels of society was invariably a major problem. Again, Tokugawa Japan was no exception. Evident were paternalistic landlord-tenant bonds, the personal authority of lords and rulers, and other manifestations of individual dependency within communities and localities. Moreover Japan, unlike China, was characterized by three institutions clearly inimical to modern forms of centralization: 1) division into feudal domains, without a true national government; 2) lord-vassal relations within the samurai elite; and 3) the rigid separation of social classes. A centralized modern state requires, to a large extent, direct rule from the national capital and impersonal methods of control applied uniformly to all groups.

Japan also had important advantages. Its historical memory included eras of national unification under imperial rule, some of which had known creative and successful periods of nation building on the basis of mainland models. The Tokugawa centuries had served to institutionalize seclusion in the minds of Japan's military rulers so firmly that the forced opening of the country had a traumatic impact, making it seem critical to develop a more rational and responsive administrative order. The luxury of a parcelized, hereditary, and leisured administrative class could not long survive the arrival of what was perceived as real danger from abroad. The foreign threat and arrival next served to diminish regional consciousness at the same time that it seemed to justify the exercise of regional discretion in response to that danger. Samurai began to respond to such impulses in relative disregard of conventional morality and loyalty. The decline of feudal order brought temporary confusion, but it also presaged an understanding of the need for greater unity.

To some degree that understanding preceded the foreign presence. In late Tokugawa times the shogunate showed an awareness of the fact that it lacked adequate controls over the movements and activities of its vassals and people. It was concerned about conspicuous consumption in violation of sumptuary laws, migration out of farming areas, and village activities that deprived it of agricultural surpluses. One response was to tighten control in its own territories. Early-nineteenth-century reforms led to efforts to rationalize village structures into larger units and to limit the activities of youth groups. A few decades later, the Tempō reforms tried to consolidate shogunal holdings around major cities for more effective control. As the problems of control in many areas became more and more apparent, the shogunate also became reconciled to less stringent regulations with respect to merchant guilds.

After the coming of Perry, new requirements of defense and foreign relations produced additional bureaucratic offices. This does not seem to have been difficult in a structural sense. In the Chinese administrative structure, which was a rationally balanced expression of a bureaucratic state dominated by an emperor, the addition of central offices to accommodate new foreign relations required the evidence provided by disaster and crisis. The Tokugawa administrative structure, on the other hand, was never fully rationalized; it had grown according to need, in response to existing problems, and had always been conceived as supplementary to the formal, though ineffective, hierarchy that remained in place in Kyoto. Consequently it was relatively easy to add the offices required for new functions such as foreign affairs (*gaikoku bugyō*), a Western-style army (*rikugun bugyō*), and a Western-style navy (*kaigun bugyō*).

The early Meiji government inherited these difficulties. Foreign policy, finance, and military force constituted its three chief problems. Foreigners had to be protected, peasants constrained, and samurai mollified. Officials who dealt with foreigners emerged as major figures in the new structure, and posts dealing with them, such as prefectural governorships at the new treaty ports, assumed particular importance because of the numbers of foreigners in Kobe and Yokohama. In finance, plans for revenue were requisite to progress on every other front.

Administrative centralization was perhaps the most visible and important consequence of the Meiji Restoration. As these chapters show, it was achieved on a trial-and-error basis by leaders who began without a fixed plan. But they did have a fixed sense of need, and that produced an astounding record of unification within a decade. High levels of centralization would have to wait for the development of professionally trained and specialized bureaucracies, advanced communications, and intense urbanization. These did not exist in Japan until the end of the century, but the transition decades saw steady progress toward centralization.

Administrative centralization came in stages and eventually took three main forms: 1) rule in the name of the emperor as the unifying central authority; 2) direct administration through a unified central bureaucracy and the establishment of a hierarchy of offices that linked the center to the localities without sharing power; and 3) equality of the population before the state through universal conscription, the abolition of samurai status, and the stipulation of uniform rights.

Meiji centralization was not without cost. It involved the control of local leadership, and this was done with loss of variety and initiative. The Tokugawa village had been governed and taxed as a unit, and village notables were the pivot of local control. They remonstrated with authorities in case of need and, on occasion, led protests to protect their status and position. Arrangements and requisitions were to some degree negotiable. Samurai authority, which operated from castle towns and rural posts, was dependent on village cooperation. Meiji uniformity saw balance as competition and a threat. The new government began with the old Tokugawa domains (*tenryō*), the first areas to come under the control of the new regime. Long disarmed, lightly garrisoned, and highly commercialized, the *tenryō* areas had profited from special treatment and opportunity to work out a relatively moderate rate of taxation and support. In early Meiji, outside governors and "foreign" troops from other domains sometimes used these areas as object lessons in enforcing uniformity of treatment and administration. The new government, however, was also the beneficiary of Tokugawa institutions; protests rarely crossed Tokugawa class or *han* lines. Had the discontented samurai of Kyūshū joined together, for instance, and had farmers from a sufficiently large area joined together with or without the support of disgruntled samurai, the government might not have been able to enforce its will.

With the suppression of samurai opposition there came a new and potentially more disruptive stage of popular participation. The "movement for freedom and people's rights" (*jiyū minken undō*), though it began as an expression of samurai dissatisfaction, spread to village leaders in the 1880s and evoked a vigorous demand for effective participation in national politics and policies. This seemed clearly undesirable to administrators accustomed to associating organization with rebellion. The government countered with promise of a constitution to be drawn up under its own auspices, meanwhile suppressing popular movements of protest that had been sparked by agricultural depression and the rigid structure of the newly uniform tax and debt provisions. This, too, brought obvious cost; it stripped the local elite of their intermediary role and to a large degree extinguished their political initiatives. New powers for a central Ministry of Home Affairs, exercised through police bureaus in prefectural governments, culminated in a pattern of local police posts in 1886-1887 that made it possible for the central government to penetrate local society uniformly and effectively.

By the end of the 1880s a highly centralized administrative system was in place to guide Japan's modern course. In comparative administrative terms, this was an extraordinary achievement. China struggled without an effective political structure well into the twentieth century. A homogeneous island people, sharing a common political heritage, the Japanese had had a deeply rooted foundation for concerted action. Tokugawa political consolidation had demonstrated the advantages of overcoming fragmentation without carrying centralization to an extreme that would have drawn attention to its drawbacks. Additionally, the Tokugawa ruling class lacked a proprietary interest in land and thus was less able to resist a process that stripped it of its power and income. Years later, the absence of adequate checks on administrative concentration of power would lead to the militarism of the 1930s and 1940s; in the context of the nineteenth century, however, that concentration helped meet a dangerous challenge from abroad.

The changes that accompanied the implementation of capitalism in the countryside were part of the Meiji reorganization. Abolition of the domains made possible individual ownership and specific, predictable tax rates on parcels of land rather than on villages as entities. Distribution of ownership certificates, the adoption of a fixed rate of taxation, and issuance of samurai bonds made it possible to prepare for internal war against samurai dissidents. With the entry of Matsukata Masayoshi into the Ministry of Finance, in 1881, a program of fiscal orthodoxy brought an end to government spending to achieve instant industrialization; sale of government industries and adoption of austerity measures combined with inflexible tax rates to plunge the countryside into a depression which dominates conventional treatments of the land settlement. Discontent also surfaced in connection with the democratic movement of that decade. By the time the 1880s had run their course, village society had changed considerably. Local tax rolls showed a significant decline in numbers qualifying for the franchise, tenancy rates had risen, and planners were speaking of the need to restore the local government they had earlier tried to restrain.

The speed of organizational centralization under the leadership of the Meiji government is particularly striking. Contributors to Part Two discuss changes in diverse types of organizations. The successful reorganization of the military, discussed by D. Eleanor Westney, was convincingly demonstrated by victories over China in 1894-1895 and Russia in 1904-1905. William Wray focuses on the conversion to modern shipping organizations, an important feature of Japan's effective response to the penetration of its domestic market by foreign business concerns. Richard Rubinger analyzes an organizational development in education that probably has no equal in the world: the expansion and rationalization of schooling in two decades to a point at which a universal system was rapidly being approached. Government ministries led the way in the centralized development of new organizations throughout the country. Even in areas that lacked an indigenous tradition, as Albert Altman shows in his discussion of the press, there were examples of rapid and widely diffused expansion. Perhaps the state's capacity to control Japanese society is nowhere more in evidence than in the area of religion, described in Martin Collcutt's chapter on Buddhism. The state encouraged a rejection of institutional Buddhism so extreme that it almost constituted as Alan Grappard has put it, a "cultural revolution."

Political representation provided an additional organizational context for Meiji Japanese. In the Tokugawa political structure the domains were substantially autonomous, and the *bakufu* provided no means of representation for national affairs. Staffed by hereditary vassal (*fudai*) houses, it systematically excluded even collaterals, to say nothing of the major "outside" (*tozama*) lords. The greatest of the daimyo were as a result without influence in national politics. The crisis that followed the coming of Perry saw the *bakufu* consult its vassals, and that act of 1853 can be said to begin a process of wider representation. In the early 1860s some daimyo began to propose a form of power sharing between court and *bakufu* in which they would have a part, and by late Tokugawa a form of conciliar structure was being discussed. The shogun's resignation of his titles and powers in 1867 was made in the mistaken assumption that he would emerge as first among equals in whatever form of collegial structure succeeded the *bakufu*. Echoes of such assumptions dominated the discussion of councils that survived into the early months of the Restoration government. But by the time the military campaign against the northeast succeeded in the summer of 1869, those echoes had died.

Other forms of representation, however, did develop. In 1875 a Council of Local Officials was convened. Impromptu prefectural assemblies began meeting after 1873, and a formal structure of prefectural assemblies was finalized in 1890. In that year the Meiji Constitution, promised in 1881, was implemented. With electorates determined by tax qualifications, the new structure of political representation relied upon the support of local landholder taxpayers. The electorate that selected the membership of the first Imperial Diet (1890), restricted to males able to pay a direct national tax of 15 yen, included approximately 500,000. Curiously, this was very nearly equal to the number of samurai family heads who had made up the political elite at the beginning of the transition period, though the overlap in family identities was not high.

The Charter Oath had pledged a search for "wisdom throughout the world," and in 1871 some fifty of the government's leaders set out on a world tour. Their search for institutions and procedures helped to initiate a selective utilization of foreign advisers and examples. In Washington, the travelers hired Commissioner of Agriculture Horace Capron; in Tokyo, French and German jurists and English educators would work side by side. Industrial technology seemed to find England in the lead, and the administrative example of the unitary state seemed to point to France. In time the Prussian and German examples of limited constitutionalism, a centralized military, and local government came to the fore. Throughout the initiative, the timetable and the direction were Japanese. The twin goals of limited participation and central government control were balanced in an effort to build a society that would be recognizably modern in inspiration but Japanese in form.

The search for social order and uniformity in procedure also required consideration of law. The Meiji government began with the promulgation of codes that were closely modeled on those of China; but these bore little relevance to Japanese practice and were soon ignored. Next, the comprehensive perfection of the French civil code attracted government planners. The French code was translated in the 1870s, a French jurist was employed as counselor in the 1880s, and a code for Japan was ready by 1890. Its promulgation was delayed when a battle broke out between the traditionalists, who argued the moral superiority of the traditional family system, and the reformers. In the final code, promulgated in 1898, the government adopted the paternalist, male-dominated samurai household system as the norm for all Japanese. Hence, a pattern that had begun in the Tokugawa years as class-specific, buttressed by Confucian values, finally became an ideal type for the family code of imperial Japan.

In one additional respect the transition century can be said to have come full circle by 1890. In 1790 Matsudaira Sadanobu, the author of the *bakufu*'s Kansei reforms, determined to bring an end to the diversity of Confucian teachings that had characterized the eighteenth-century flowering of scholarship. His ban on heterodox teachings decreed that the structured Neo-Confucian synthesis of Chu Hsi was to be the only source of moral education in the *bakufu* academy. A somewhat "Chinese" emphasis on ability led to examination requirements for appointment to political office within the samurai class. Later, other domains followed the *bakufu* lead; in addition, education in some samurai academies became more open to ability without reference to class and rank. In the early Meiji years, with the diffusion of Western learning, the diversity of teaching was so great that by the 1880s Motoda Eifu, the emperor's Confucian tutor, was urging his eminent student to call for a return to moral education. Midway in the 1880s the government's program of crash westernization was creating an atmosphere in which Christianity, Western thought, and Western fads were alarming Japanese conservatives. The product of this alarm was the 1890 Imperial Rescript on Education, which pronounced loyalty and filial piety to be the center of Japanese education. Thereafter, subtle pressures against Christianity, the addition of courses on ethics (*shūshin*) to the public school curriculum, and the provision of uniform national textbooks all became expressions of the authorities' desire for a congruence in outlook and values, one that was echoed in each of the organizational contexts in which Japanese found themselves.

In their search for a central image for those values, the Meiji leaders instinctively turned to the symbolism of a ruling house described as coeval with the land. It was a symbol that had developed and grown in the course of eighteenth-century historicism and cultural-ethnic nationalism. The passion of the political debate that was sparked by the appearance of the West intensified activists' commitment to the image in *bakumatsu* times, and the urgency of a unifying symbol in the early Meiji found leaders making constant use of the boy sovereign in proclamations, promises, and processions throughout the country. As institution building began in earnest in the 1880s government leaders like Itō Hirobumi reflected soberly that in the absence of a vital tradition of national religion comparable to the ties that bound Western nations together, Japan had no alternative to centering its institutions around the Imperial House. "If there is no cornerstone," Itō wrote, "politics will fall into the hands of the uncontrollable masses, the government will become powerless and the country will be ruined. . . . [T]he state must not lose the use of the administrative power. . . . Thus in our country the one institution which can become the cornerstone of our constitution is the Imperial House."[3]

As a result, the sovereign became the cornerstone of every institution—through the Rescript on Education, the school system; through the Rescript to Soldiers and Sailors, the armed forces; through administrative ties and precepts, the police. As the emperor's name and words became associated with every advance and ultimately with the national victories over China and Russia, his picture came to hang in almost every home. By the end of the century, educators, philosophers, and moralists were seeing in this symbol the guarantor of a national character dominated

[3] Quoted in Joseph Pittau, S.J., *Political Thought in Early Meiji Japan, 1868-1889* (Cambridge: Harvard University Press, 1967), p. 177.

by diligence, loyalty, and self-sacrifice, as well as a safeguard against social radicalism. The Imperial House with its branch families can thus be seen as a conspicuous "gainer" in the sense that its authority was considered sacrosanct, its security buttressed with impressive holdings in land and industrial equities. Yet, at the same time, its sacrifice of freedom was equally impressive, for a "cornerstone" could not be allowed to shift. Surrounded with the aura of divinity and powerless before the powerful who spoke in its name, the royal house paid a high price for its lonely majesty "above the clouds."

Change in Town and Country

During the transition the population of Japan was in excess of 30 million. It was spread across roughly 60,000 villages and more than 1,000 towns and cities. Administrative reform led to revisions in political boundaries, and organizational growth introduced new types of associations into the lives of millions of people in scattered communities. As the cities of Japan became more integrated, regional variations were gradually reduced.

The chapters by Akira Hayami and Gilbert Rozman stress regional variation across Japan, distinguishing eastern from western Japan. The former consists of central and northeastern Honshū island, including Tokyo. The island of Hokkaidō began to be developed only in the Meiji period, and its small population is usually excluded from regional comparisons. For the most part, the eastern regions were more dependent on agricultural production and, thus, more vulnerable to bad weather. Large castle towns supported by heavy taxation did not become very diversified commercial centers. Although some regions, as Osamu Saitō shows, benefited in the early Meiji from the rapid spread of sericulture and silk reeling, and though Yokohama prospered as a foreign trade center, most of the northeast remained less commercialized. Western Japan, on the whole closer to large urban markets, enjoyed a more favorable climate for cash crops; there, peasant by-employments and small-town commercial expansion created a diversified economy. These regions were most easily drawn into an increasingly centralized economy.

Edo, renamed Tokyo in 1868, was Japan's largest city and was closely integrated with Osaka. In most respects it belongs with "developed" regions of the country. Yokohama's emergence as a leading treaty port brought greater prosperity to the South Kantō region. Henry Smith's chapter shows how Edo/Tokyo, which lost population with the abolition of the system of alternate residence of daimyo in the 1860s, gained in political significance with the emperor's move from Kyoto at the end of the decade, as well as how it fared in the period of transition. Centralization meant an ever expanding role for Tokyo as the nation's first city.

Early-eighteenth-century Japan had been very urbanized for a premodern society. That level of urbanization remained little changed in the mid-nineteenth century, however, and by then Japan had been surpassed by several Western societies. Nonetheless Tokyo was a huge city; except for a span of barely one decade in the 1860s and 1870s, it supported a million people or more. Osaka and Kyoto were cities of several hundred thousand residents each. No less important in the overall city system were the approximately two hundred castle towns, some of which were small settlements of perhaps 1,000 inhabitants while others were populous cities of 50,000 or even 100,000. This longstanding and widely dispersed foundation of cities helped make possible the centralization of Meiji Japan. A great city like Edo gave the new Meiji leadership a communications and commercial node with long experience as the administrative center of the country. Remarkably evenly distributed castle towns, which had been purposefully built up to bring together nonagricultural functions, offered the necessary links to local areas for the work of administrative centralization.

Continuities remained, of course, in conditions of daily life, especially in diet and housing. Yet even in the countryside, as Susan Hanley shows, important changes were beginning to take place. The monochrome scenes and life style that Tokugawa sumptuary laws enforced were beginning to give way. *Shōji*, once restricted to the main houses, were common, the paper often salvaged from school use. In time, houses with better light could be divided into rooms; they could support several braziers of charcoal for family use and permitted the first steps toward privacy in the lives of different generations. Food tastes would broaden, though the mainstay continued to be a high level of grain consumption, as shown by Shunsaku Nishikawa.

Before and After

The transition that this book describes was anticipated in Tokugawa and it extended into Meiji; an examination of two points in time, taken at the beginning and end of the process, would highlight the vastness of the changes that Japan experienced. No summary of the elements in early-nineteenth-century Japan that contributed to its subsequent modernization can be allowed to overlook those many aspects of Tokugawa society which could not possibly be reconciled with the needs of national strength in a nineteenth-century context.

In 1853 Japan was divided into some 260 domains, each with its own army, its own government, its own hereditary military elite, and often its own currency. These domains were the constituent units of the *bakuhan* system. Those domains which led the Restoration movement were large and powerful, but the vast majority were postage-stamp principalities. The military houses were vassals of the shogun, and the threshold for daimyo status was an area assessed at 10,000 *koku* of rice income. A very rough concordance of food productivity with population would give us a population of some 30 million; the smallest principality, then, might have as few as 10,000 inhabitants. In so limited a setting, local autonomy meant a highly unrationalized, expensive, and administrator-intensive government in the hands of the hereditary samurai class. At the highest levels, great daimyo were lords of creation; at the lowest levels, however, petty samurai eked out a miserable living that was made only slightly tolerable by incongruous assertions of honor, name, and duty, symbolized by a special style of hair and dress and by the two swords.

A Japanese who might have left with Perry, as one famous nationalist tried to do, and who returned three decades later would have found his country profoundly altered. A single governance and source of authority had replaced hundreds of daimyo; the lines of political authority and social order had been simplified and rationalized. A legally undifferentiated citizenry had replaced the social strata of military, farmer, artisan, and merchant, distinguished by privileges, duties, and appearance. The former communal village, which largely ruled itself and paid land dues as a unit, had given way to a system of individual ownership, individual taxation, and national education. Everywhere authority was becoming more visible and present. Instead of running its own affairs at minimal cost to daimyo government, a village was now expected to contribute toward the upkeep of national and prefectural offices, bureaus, and schools. Conscription was beginning to acquaint the villager with a larger world and with new customs and instruments. Local administrative and financial disputes, which would have been the subject of negotiation and compromise in late Tokugawa times, no longer required group negotiation; government administrators and the armed forces were in a position to force compliance. By the 1880s, the diffusion of police posts throughout the countryside brought Japan the most effective centralization it had ever known. What had been done locally and informally was now done nationally and regionally by specialists, at greater financial cost and with much stronger sanctions. Japan was becoming a modern state.

It is possible to make a further point about chronology and mood. The events of the decade preceding the Restoration prompted a consciousness of crisis and of peril that evoked furious discussion and courageous (often reckless) action from the young men of that era. The early Meiji decades were a period of optimism marked by a sense of starting over and doing away with "evil customs of the past," as the Charter Oath put it. To many it seemed that men of ability would very soon be able to regain equality for their country. The slogan, *bummei kaika* (Civilization and Enlightenment!) indicated that mood. In the 1880s consciousness seems to have changed once more. The young remained buoyant, and Tokutomi Sohō's *Shin Nihon no seinen* [Young men in the New Japan] spoke for such optimism. But in the same period, government fears and economic depression snuffed out the prospects for a genuine liberal movement led by ordinary Japanese. The newly formed political parties declared themselves dissolved in 1884, returning to the fray a few years later chiefly to criticize the government for its delay in securing equality in international relations. Frustration, irritation, and disillusion were replacing the buoyant optimism of an earlier day. A new administrative structure was taking shape. The new political elite was firmly in the saddle, and the romantic expectations of a few years earlier no longer seemed as relevant. Nation building was proving to be a slower, more demanding, and more costly process than had seemed likely in the first bloom of enthusiasm for the modern. This, too, suggests that the late 1880s are where a study of the transition should end.

By middle and late Meiji all children, not just some, trooped off to uniform public schools; there they learned the new national hymn of loyalty, its lyric drawn from a *Kokinshū* poem, selected by a committee of scholars, and harmonized by a German bandmaster. More often the children sang the tunes of Stephen Foster, adroitly adapted to conform to Japanese mode. They bowed to the imperial picture, and stood to hear their principal read the Imperial Rescript on Education. Indeed, education was becoming the key to success in life. Army service was beginning to make peasant boys aware of ruler and country. Those too poor to buy exemptions were socialized by life in army barracks or navy ships. Japan was becoming a "nation in arms," something its leaders saw as necessary for survival in the international jungle.

Agricultural conditions and economic opportunity were combining to accelerate a move to the cities, where simple, low-technology industries were providing employment opportunities for young people. Everywhere, town and village alike, Tokugawa patterns of self-government, under appointed or traditional leaders and elders, were being replaced and regulated by uniformed police, whose short swords hung as reminders of the effort the government was making to instill pride in them as imperial servants. In most of Japan, administrative changes were serving to weaken the domain consciousness of Tokugawa times; prefectural regiments of soldiers appeared to keep the public order. The Home Ministry appointed town and village heads, and local assemblies provided notables with opportunity to participate in larger things. Taxation, once a communal responsibility, was now the individual's affair, and the legal and social position of the landowner was steadily strengthened as a result.

The larger part of the once proud samurai were recognizable as such no longer: hair, clothing, and deportment had changed, and gone were the no-longer-legal swords. A fortunate minority conserved their pride in administrative jobs and in the army or police, but with the exception of entry into military academies (where status origin was recorded into the interwar years) samurai standing was losing its meaning. By the 1890s, in popular writing, *shoshi* meant "gentleman" and no longer "samurai," just as *kuni* signified "Japan" instead of "province."

Japan had become a country, rather than a collection of domains. Its borders had been firmly drawn to the south with the incorporation of the Ryūkyūs, in Tsushima with the abandonment of a station at Pusan, and in the north with the full incorporation of Hokkaidō and the Kuriles. The Japanese, so long divided by status, had become a people. The dynamism of tradition, harnessed, and supported by new techniques of nation building, had changed the balance of forces in Northeast Asia. Japan would soon change that balance in the Pacific and, later, in the larger world.

PART ONE

ADMINISTRATION

INTRODUCTION TO PART ONE

BY MARIUS B. JANSEN

The theme that best sums up the administrative changes of the transition decades is that of centralization. The Japan that awaited the coming of Perry's flotilla in 1853 had some 260 units of political administration, each with its own capital, its own bureaucracy, its own army, and its own taxation system. Each was headed by a daimyo, of whom the shogun was the greatest and most powerful, so powerful that all others were required to spend alternate years in attendance upon him at his capital city of Edo, where they resided in estates allotted to them. The political order of that day was characterized by its extreme diversity, for while most discussions of daimyo and domains focus upon the major actors and territorial units, only sixteen daimyo administered domains of 300,000 *koku* or more. Five of these were Tokugawa family members or collaterals, and the other eleven were *tozama*, or "outside," daimyo. The vast majority were closer to the 10,000- *koku* threshold of daimyo status, however, and thus were the lords of minuscule geographic districts with populations between 10,000 and 50,000 and burdened with administrative, ritual, and military costs that strained the abilities even of gifted samurai bureaucrats. This system called for rationalization and rearrangement, and only the fear that the hereditary ruling class had of losing its prerogatives stood in the way.

Administrative reforms of the late Tokugawa decades included several attempts to move toward greater centralization. In the Bunsei reforms of the early nineteenth century the *bakufu* tried to tighten control over its own lands, and in the Tempō reforms of 1841 the minister Mizuno Tadakuni attempted to add to this by measures to call in petty realms within the urban heartland of the Tokyo and Osaka plains. Opposition from hereditary Tokugawa vassals, reinforced by the hostilities aroused by simultaneous measures affecting commerce and urban life, defeated his efforts. Less than a decade after the coming of Perry, shogunal administrators moved in this direction once again. Although shogunal control over the Tokugawa vassals weakened with relaxation of the system of alternate attendance in 1862, *bakufu* administration of the *tenryō*, as *bakufu* lands were called, saw steps toward greater centralization and efficiency. In its final years the *bakufu* relied increasingly upon professional, rather than daimyo, administrators. Especially after the political disasters of the struggle with Chōshū, described by Albert Craig, it improved the administrative machinery, modernized its military levies, and even moved in the direction of a non-samurai, Western-trained armed force.

The great *tozama* daimyo also took steps in this direction. As their leaders tried to gain strength for the political crisis they saw approaching, they took steps to build military and economic strength that had the effect of increasing bureaucratic direction over many forms of activity. Chōshū and Tosa supervised trade, and Tosa established a trading firm for local specialties like indigo that became the nucleus of the great Meiji shipping firm of Mitsubishi (as William Wray notes later in this book). Satsuma increased the command sector of its economy by establishing firm control over sugar, in which it had a virtual monopoly, and over commodities available from China through Okinawa. In each case these measures increased state control over areas that had functioned under the relatively tolerant indifference of samurai administrators, and in each case they suggested a more ambitious and purposeful exercise of official intitiative.

The victory of the "imperial" armies—as the Satsuma, Chōshū, and Tosa forces styled themselves in the 1868-1869 Restoration War against their Tokugawa and northeastern opponents—made further steps in this direction likely. These were most imminent with respect to the Tokugawa lands that had been seized: to return them to their original stewards would have negated the gains of the war, while to re-create the pattern of diversified administration in new and friendly hands would have been seen as a retrograde, selfish step that would give the lie to talk of sovereign and nation. Moreover, it would have diminished the political strength of the combatants, who needed to husband their unified force for future emergencies. Consequently the Tokugawa *tenryō* was not returned to Tokugawa or pro-Tokugawa hands, nor was it parceled out to Restoration or pro-Restoration daimyo; instead, it was set aside as imperial domain and constituted as the heartland of what would gradually become a national unit.

Albert Craig's discussion of the emergence of the central government traces this process. However essential and inevitable in retrospect, he reminds the reader, contemporaries did not by any means view it as certain. Even the leaders moved step by step, as they gradually became aware of the logic of successive moves, spurred in good measure by fear of destructive regional and clique loyalties within the old structure, and by the need to provide a new vision of nation to replace the limited vision of loyalty to *han* and daimyo.

A major stumbling block for such a move was the existence of the ruling samurai class, the subject of the Jansen essay. In retrospect, the very cost of the hierarchical structure of special privilege doomed it in the eyes of administrators who had to struggle with the costs of military and economic modernization, but such considerations prevailed only gradually. The Restoration government, led as it was by samurai from powerful *han* that gloried in their strength and in their distinctive past, was torn by conflict on this point; it found itself obligated to samurai loyalties, yet forced to redirect them in a national pattern. To be sure, it was helped by the fact that the Restoration War had permanently weakened—indeed, all but destroyed—the potential of the central and northeastern domains. The Restoration *han* of the southwest presented both danger and opportunity in this regard. Nowhere were expectations higher or opportunities so plentiful. The decade that was dominated by the disestablishment of the samurai class thus resulted in the most basic sort of conflicts, in which recent colleagues organized troops to conquer and hunt down their friends. Ōkubo Toshimichi personally led the search for Etō Shimpei, and a national army still importantly Satsuma in its makeup put down the great Satsuma Rebellion of Saigō Takamori.

It is nevertheless well to remember that one cannot judge the samurai class by its most vigorous and most militaristic sector; Saigō was a symbol of the heroic, old-style samurai, but many were not like him. Regional loyalties also ruled out any sort of cohesive, multiregional opposition, and samurai hostility across boundaries was as great as samurai hostility toward the government's modernization policies. It is a sign of the times that very few made any attempt to defend special privilege or support for samurai in the absence of convincing proof of their utility in the building of a strong Japan. Even Saigō, as head of the caretaker government in the early 1870s, had lent his name and prestige to plans for drastic cuts in samurai support. Although the leaders did not so articulate, and could not see their way into the future, one suspects that an inner logic or presentiment, made up of their growing knowledge of the West and of Japan's weakness relative to the expansive West, provided a predisposition for the decisions that were made. They themselves had risen by merit, and they had known the frustration and inefficiencies of a system based on hereditary attribution.

Michio Umegaki focuses on the decision to abandon the *han* and fashion prefectures as units of national administration. It is symptomatic of the post-Restoration days that this key decision, from which all others followed, is so difficult to document and follow. To be sure, Japan did not yet have an orderly governmental system; there were no memoranda arguing the benefits of the move, no debates, and no explanatory proclamations. Instead one finds a handful of leaders groping toward it, often by indirection, keenly aware that the very suggestion of their move could be denounced as disloyalty and contribute to explosive violence. One comes to speak again of predisposition: the need of an emerging government to refute charges of regional bias; the Restoration memory of the earlier movement, explicitly designed to restore the "antiquity" in which the court functioned as central government a millennium before. Moreover, the Restoration leaders knew that, among major countries, only Japan was so divided, so parceled out, and so inefficient. However clear these predispositions may appear in retrospect, they were less so to contemporaries; and the scale and speed of the great achievement, for which surviving Meiji leaders congratulated themselves to the end of their days, remain startling.

The great merit of the chapter by Andrew Fraser, with which this section concludes, is its concise and practical illustration of the way these changes affected residents of a single area, the *han* of Awa, which became modern Tokushima. It was not an area that figured large in Restoration history; neither enemy nor friend of the new regime, it was thus an area in which territorial and administrative continuity permits close comparison with conditions before and after the Restoration. The reader sees here the practical effects of moves toward administrative rationality. There are economies of scale, as well as cost-effective moves that lead to standardization of administration, the amalgamation of units of control, and experimentation with types of division and allocation. Because the samurai were off the land, and because everything could be subsumed under the twin goods of antiquity and liberation, the Meiji government did not need to pillory a landlord class as its enemies or march in its troops to take possession. Initially, at least, its chief interest was in the maintenance of public order and the regular collection of taxes. The Awa countryside remained quiet, and one has the impression of a population that bore with changes and designations, confident that in the end the basic design would be recognizable by those who had known what went before.

In other parts of Japan, the late 1860s were years of rural insecurity and agrarian discontent made worse by the levies that accompanied mobilization and civil war. Rumors of impending change and betterment were frequently fueled by promises of tax relief put out by the new "imperial" forces as they marched against northeastern domains. The diversity of local conditions and complaints made the early Meiji years a period of tension that required administrative caution as the government felt its way along. In the Tokugawa lands in Nagano prefecture, the inhabitants of a lightly taxed area organized to demand and receive assurances of further tax reform shortly after the political change. They were at first successful, but after force became available the promises were withdrawn by the central government. A harsh repression followed in which 112 were imprisoned, 477 exiled, and 28 executed. Most were small and medium farmers, but members of the local elite who had helped lead the demonstrations were also involved and were subsequently enshrined as local deities.[1] In Aizu, the center of opposition to the "imperial" armies, the collapse of traditional samurai authority in a setting of rural distress produced demands for more effective self-government from villagers who resented the domination of the local economy by the traditional village elite. The victorious troops who garrisoned the domain made little attempt to protect the headmen or punish the attackers, since the village leaders were performing their duties of tax collection satisfactorily.[2]

The Japan Sea *han* of Shōnai, the subject of a recent book by William Kelly,[3] experienced a more remarkable series of events. There the ruling family was, for its adherence to the Tokugawa cause, punished by replacing the daimyo with his younger brother, who was assigned first to Akita and later to Iwaki as "governor." Both moves were resisted and ultimately blocked through vigorous lobbying in Tokyo by senior retainers and by the large landholding Homma family. Their efforts included subsidies to villagers bearing petitions to Tokyo and, more effectively, negotiations with the Finance Office for huge loans and gifts from the Homma. The next stage of local protest was directed against the traditional elite, which remained in power, and included complaints that the legislation for cash payments in the 1873 land tax reform was being ignored.

Of Kawasaki, next door to Yokohama and Tokyo and at the very center of government concern, Neil Waters writes that "through all the

[1] Elcuk Esenbel Tüzeren,"Takaino Village and the Nakano Uprising of 1871" (Columbia University Ph.D. diss., 1981), sees the incident as a continuation of traditional communal protests and a direct response to Meiji centralization.

[2] Stephen Vlastos, "*Yonaoshi* in Aizu," in Tetsuo Najita and J. Victor Koschmann, eds., *Conflict in Modern Japanese History: The Neglected Tradition* (Princeton: Princeton University Press, 1982), pp. 164-176. Vlastos concludes that "the goals of the movement in Aizu were political as well as economic, but the boundaries of the movement reflected the particular close interests of peasants with small or marginal holdings." The consciousness of those who took part, he says, was limited to the village.

[3] William W. Kelly, *Deference and Defiance in Nineteenth-Century Japan* (Princeton: Princeton University Press, 1985).

paper changes of this confusing decade, local leadership . . . remained virtually unchanged. It was dominated by the same people . . . all of whom owed their regional influence to a combination of wealth, personal ability, and positions in the Edo period."[4]

The conclusion that follows from these local studies is that administrative centralization usually had to be carried out in a pattern of compromise, and that regional and local leaders whose wealth and influence were important to the new government usually managed to retain a good deal of their influence after the exit of their immediate samurai authorities. Until it had the power to coerce and the knowledge to inform, the Meiji government stepped carefully and kept regularity of income as its first priority.

In time, the process of standardization and centralization meant an inexorable increase in the power of the state over its parts. As Professor Fraser shows, the process was accompanied by an increase of professionalization in which tasks previously done by the community were gradually delegated to specialists in the new jobs of security, administration, and education. Such officials looked to the central power that had qualified them for their tasks, and local constraints and sanctions were of diminishing importance in the execution of their tasks. It is Professor Fraser's conclusion that the costs of modernization bore heavily on the countryside as local and prefectural taxes increased. This is a topic which both Kozo Yamamura and Susan Hanley turn to later in this book. For now, we may observe that while the monetary contribution became heavier than it had been, it was more specific and thus more limited at the same time that it seemed more burdensome. Fiscal burdens began to replace the nonmonetary obligations that the community had enforced before. At the same time, the farmers' taxes were now pulling those who paid them into a larger, national consciousness instead of sustaining a nonproductive samurai class in castle towns.

A final point—one that deserves more treatment than it usually receives—is that the Meiji government, in its eagerness for local support, tried to channel local enthusiasm for participation in local government and taxation. In the years after 1871 a large number of regional assemblies (made up of local notables and former samurai) sprang up, submitting petitions and, in some cases, taking governmental action on such matters as local constabularies and public works. Once the government had firmly set the boundaries of its new prefectures and installed its major tax, education, and conscription reforms, it issued in 1878, as one of three

[4] Neil L. Waters, "Local Leadership in the Kawasaki Region from Bakumatsu to Meiji," *Journal of Japanese Studies*, vol. 7, no. 1 (Winter 1981), p. 76.

laws for local administration, a set of Regulations for Prefectural Assemblies. These called for elective assemblies to deliberate on local budgets under the authority of appointive prefectural governors. Imperfect as these arrangements might seem, they provided a framework for continued influence by local notables in public affairs as well as experience to be drawn on by the Imperial Diet that would meet in 1890.[5] From an early point, representation was seen as a necessary part of centralization.

[5] James L. McClain, "Local Politics and National Integration: The Fukui Prefectural Assembly in the 1880s," *Monumenta Nipponica*, vol. 31, no. 1 (1976), pp. 51-75, concludes that "the prefectural assembly system contributed to the relatively harmonious transformation of Japanese society during the early Meiji period."

CHAPTER 2

THE CENTRAL GOVERNMENT

BY ALBERT M. CRAIG

> No great historical event is better calculated than the French Revolution to teach political writers and statesmen to be cautious in their speculations; for never was any such event, stemming from factors so far back in the past, so inevitable yet so completely unforeseen.
>
> ALEXIS DE TOCQUEVILLE

> Any event, once it has occurred, can be made to appear inevitable by any competent journalist or historian.
>
> JOSEPH PULITZER

Was the Meiji Restoration inevitable? Could it have happened otherwise than it did? Might some random act of human will have made a difference? Or does the very idea of inevitability include the random factor, error, and the indeterminacy of human decisions? At one level of discourse the resolution of the question may be metaphysical. But it can be phrased in a homelier fashion: do vital events sometimes hinge on decisions so individual that no social science could ever predict them, or even explain them systematically after the fact?

Consider the situation in Chōshū toward the end of 1864. *Bakufu* armies were camped on its borders. They represented an inexorable force that could invade and occupy the hapless domain at will. Within the domain the radical loyalist militia were still intact, but control of the government and the daimyo had passed into the hands of the conservatives. The conservative government had capitulated to the *bakufu* forces, executing the loyalist military commanders who had led the earlier Chōshū attack in Kyoto and sending the heads of the three responsible domain elders to the *bakufu* headquarters in Hiroshima. In this most precarious situation, and with the odds stacked against them, Takasugi Shinsaku and Itō Hirobumi led militia units in an attack on the conservatives in the domain's Shimonoseki offices. The *bakufu* commander,

Tokugawa Keishō, on learning of this attack, proposed using troops from his own domain of Owari to subjugate the loyalist militia. The conservative government of Chōshū assured him that it could handle the rebels with regular domain troops. Keishō accepted the assurances and, without waiting to see the outcome, disbanded the *bakufu* armies. There ensued a civil war in Chōshū from which the loyalist troops who played so large a role in the Restoration emerged victorious.

But how delicately balanced was the issue! If the conservatives had accepted the use of Owari troops, or if Keishō had waited just a few weeks longer to make sure of the outcome, the conservatives would have been able to consolidate their grip on Chōshū. This would have removed Chōshū from Restoration politics as effectively as Mito had been removed earlier by the victory of its conservatives after an internal split. Then what would have happened? Would Satsuma have been able to carry on alone? Unlikely. Would it have joined with Tosa and Saga? Would a Restoration have occurred along the lines envisaged by the more moderate *kōbu-gattai* forces? Or would Tokugawa Keiki's reforms have had a chance? Might the *bakufu* have gone on to modernize Japan—a possibility Honjō Eijirō suggested long ago?

How would de Tocqueville have responded to the above? He would certainly not have denied the freedom of the individual act. His central argument in *The Old Regime and the French Revolution* was in favor of freedom and against that equality which, destroying freedom, leads to despotism. He might have argued, however, that there are constant factors at work over any considerable period of time and that these, despite the outcome of particular situations, would conduce to a similar historical result. His notion of the inevitable has to do with such constants. Whether historical constants are that efficient in correcting for random human actions, and whether we can adequately identify the constants, is a complex matter. The advantage of proceeding as if they are, and as if we can, is that it permits the rational analysis of history. As much as possible, this is the approach I use in this chapter.

The Last Years of the Shogunate

Was there a central government in Tokugawa Japan? If there was, it was the *bakufu*. It established such national policies as seclusion and the Edo hostage system, directly governed Japan's major cities, and administered the laws that controlled the imperial court, temples, and shrines as well as the external relations of the domains. Some have argued that the totality of these controls represented a centralism akin to European monarchies of the age. The problem with this argument is that within the system of *bakufu* controls the 260-odd domains were largely autonomous in the administration of their internal affairs. They had their own vassals, armies, domain laws, courts, economic policies, etc. That is to say, just those functions which we usually view as essential to central government were dispersed among the domains, including, of course, the *bakufu* governance of its own giant domain.

Domain governments were staffed by hereditary samurai vassals. To follow the usage current at the time, the samurai were divided into *shi* and *sotsu*, and those into many further grades. Virtually all officials were *shi*. The higher *shi* were well-do-do, the aristocrats of the society, and naturally held the more important posts. Together with the daimyo, they maintained goals and set policies. Middle and some lower *shi* served beneath them as officials. *Sotsu* and rear vassals, the "lumpen-samurai" of the age, were domain soldiers or at times servants of the higher-ranking *shi*. But during the early nineteenth century the situation had begun to change. Middle-ranking samurai often became involved in policy making. The distinction between policy making and bureaucratic roles had begun to blur.

The early-nineteenth-century changes were the consequence of a creeping bureaucratization that had begun more than a century earlier. It centered on the evolution of bureaus within domain governments. As education spread, their procedures became more and more determined by precedents and handled by paperwork. The competency of the bureaus was extended into matters that had been private. Men with education sought official advancement. Financial crises became more frequent, leading domain governments to seek out men of ability. Cliques formed within domain governments or among those eligible for high office; they often contended, one supporting the status quo and another advocating reforms. By the early nineteenth century there was in many domains a two-platoon system of bureaucratic government. Whether the defensive or offensive team was sent in would depend on the times and on who had the ear of the daimyo. In any case, education, the rise of bureaus, and the politicization of middle officials were important Tocquevillean constants in the political process of Japan. They provided a context for what would follow.

Bakufu *Clique Politics, 1853-1858*

Until 1853 Japan was a world unto itself. The word "country" (*kuni*) applied not to Japan but to the domains. The arrival of Perry made

Japanese aware that Japan was their *kuni.* It also made them aware as never before of foreigners, gunboats, and distant alien lands. The removal of the battleship armor of seclusion left them feeling vulnerable and exposed. If national politics depends on a national consciousness of self, then both were enormously heightened at this time.

The particular events leading to the new politics are well known. Perry came in 1853, demanded a treaty of friendship, and left, promising to return the following year. "Will he return?" the *bakufu* officials asked themselves. He did and he renewed his demands. He was willing to use force—he might have interdicted the coastal trade on which Edo depended—so the treaty was signed. In the course of the negotiations the *bakufu,* uncertain about an act that so sharply contravened its own tradition, asked the daimyo and court for their opinions. It expected strong support, but received a mixed response: some domains replied with samurai bravado; others with timidity, or with hopes for trade, or with fanciful talk of expansion across the seas. The court gave its approval. In arriving at these opinions, daimyo consulted their elders (*karō*), who discussed the question with samurai officials. At the court, nobles discussed how they should answer. The initiation of discussions on national policy outside the councils of the *bakufu* broke a taboo and called into being a new kind of high-level public opinion.

For the first five years after 1853, however, it is easier to talk of what did not change. Daimyo still journeyed to Edo every second year, accompanied by a contingent of retainer-officials. In Edo politics remained at the daimyo level. Decisions within the *bakufu* were made as usual by councils of hereditary (*fudai*) daimyo who occupied a position in the *bakufu* comparable to high-ranking samurai in the domains. "Outside" (*tozama*) daimyo were able to exert only a minor influence, and that by allying themselves with cliques within the *bakufu.* There has been a tendency among historians to depict late Tokugawa daimyo as incompetents. Some were; but others, by Tokugawa if not Meiji standards, were surprisingly able.

In the domains, too, government changed little. Some domains did nothing except as required by the *bakufu.* Others carried out reforms, mostly of the late Tokugawa type—Confucian in inspiration and aimed at restoring domain finances. Military reforms also became more important, extending a trend that had begun after the Opium War. The demand for men of talent increased; some domains created new posts in Western studies. In some domains, where reformist cliques contended with conservative cliques for control of the government, the immediate effect of the early treaties was to strengthen the position of the former. Yet, until 1858 there is little evidence of a major break with tradition.

The Reimposition of Shogunal Despotism, 1858-1860

The change came in 1858 with the signing of the commercial treaty. To grasp what happened next, we must digress briefly to look at the imperial institution. Japan's imperial institution, another Tocquevillean factor, contrasts sharply with the parallel institution in China.

In China the emperor-ruler was always closely bound up with the state he ruled. But his relationship to Heaven was tenuous since its mandate might be withdrawn, bringing the dynasty to an end. This might be schematized as follows:

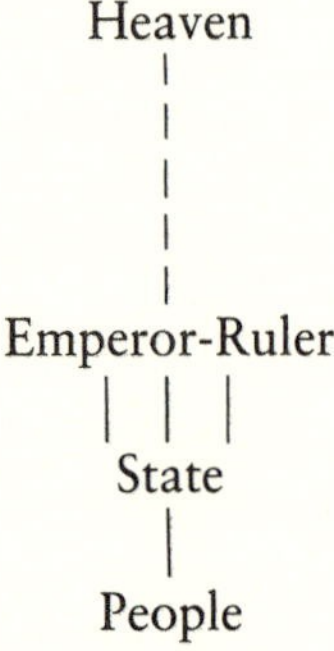

Perhaps the line between the state and the people should also be dotted since it was the people who acted for Heaven when the mandate was taken away. In the Chinese conception there was no possibility of using the emperor against the state.

In Japan the relationships were different. The single-dynasty, Sun-line emperors were closely bound up with Heaven and possessed a nonretractable mandate. During the Edo period a few writers went so far as to say it was the heavenly emperors who gave the mandate to the ruler-shogun. Since the tie to Heaven was so close and since, as in China, the actual holders of power did change, the tie between the emperor and the state was necessarily tenuous. To express this diagrammatically:

In this schema Heaven was not simply the Confucian Heaven but was also the abode or the collective designation of the Shinto deities from one of whom the imperial line was descended. The unit made up of Heaven and the emperor was the ultimate source of political legitimacy. Beneath this unit was the ruler, in Tokugawa times the shogun, who was tightly connected to the state. Because the emperor was so far removed from the apparatus of government, most Japanese were able to tolerate the situation in which the emperor was a prisoner, as Herschel Webb put it, in "an area about the size of the deck of a large modern aircraft carrier."[1] But it created a jarring anomaly for thinkers steeped in Chinese Confucian doctrines. One or two questioned the relationship, but most, if they faced it at all, found ingenious rationalizations for it. As a practical matter, so long as other institutions held firm, the Tokugawa grip on the emperor was secure and his religious authority was routinized within the system.

This easy tolerance for Japan's peculiar institution ended abruptly when, in 1858, the United States consul Townsend Harris persuaded the *bakufu* to sign a commercial treaty despite court disapproval. This was a mistake on the part of the *bakufu*. However theoretical the shogun's subordination to the emperor may have been, this "disobedient act" shivered the foundations of *bakufu* legitimacy, opening the way for a new kind of politics outside the formal framework of government and at a lower level of samurai society. Among younger samurai there was an outpouring of pro-emperor (*sonnō*) sentiments and the beginning of anti-*bakufu* agitation. The key figures in these political movements were charismatic teachers, men like Aizawa Seishisai and Fujita Tōko in Mito

[1] Herschel Webb, *The Japanese Imperial Institution in the Tokugawa Period* (New York: Columbia University Press, 1968), p. 129.

or Yoshida Shōin in Chōshū. Few such teachers survived the Restoration, but the movements they initiated were important factors in *bakumatsu* politics.

The *bakufu* responded to what it saw as subversion by abandoning its early gestures in the direction of consultation and reverting to its traditional autocracy. It carried out a purge in 1858-1859, punishing and even executing its samurai critics and forcing dissident daimyo to abdicate. For a time the purge was effective. But when the chief councilor responsible for it was assassinated by samurai loyalists, the *bakufu* swung toward compromise, marking the start of a new period.

*Domain Action on a Court-*Bakufu *Axis, 1861-1868*

The system of controls administered by the *bakufu*, as noted earlier, was another key variable in the Tokugawa political system. One gauge of the progress of the Restoration movement was their step-by-step dismemberment. The process began with Perry's breaching of seclusion. The second step was the *bakufu* request for the domains' opinions. Then came the 1858 court-*bakufu* rift, followed by the emergence of domains as mediators in 1861 and the end of the Edo hostage system in 1862. After that, the process speeded up and changes occurred too rapidly to enumerate. As the controls ended, the domains emerged as autonomous actors.

It is puzzling that several domains acted when others did not. Some were small, lacked leadership, or had troubled finances. But more might have acted than did. In any event, the first to act was Chōshū, which in 1861 nominated itself as mediator between court and *bakufu*. We will help you patch up your differences, its emissaries seemed to say to both the *bakufu* and the court when, in fact, they were creating a role in national politics for their own domain. Then Satsuma sallied forth, challenged Chōshū with a policy slightly more favorable to the court, and usurped its role. Not to be outdone, Chōshū dropped its earlier policy, adopted that of its loyalist faction, and replaced Satsuma as upholder of the court. These years marked the heyday of the loyalist movement in Japan: parties of pro-emperor samurai were formed in every domain, political assassinations were rife, and "Expel the Barbarian" became a popular slogan. These were also the years in which the *bakufu* and its allies seemed subject to a paralysis of will.

The first phase of domain action ended in the summer of 1863, when Satsuma, which had been outmaneuvered in the diplomatic game, joined with Aizu to seize the court in a military coup. This inaugurated a second phase characterized by armed struggles. Diplomacy and negotiations continued on every hand, but it does not misrepresent to say that every turning point between 1863 and 1868 depended on a military action:

1863	The English bombard Kagoshima. Satsuma responds by purchasing Western weapons.
1864	Chōshū attempts a countercoup in Kyoto. Two-thirds of the city burns. Chōshū is declared an "enemy of the court."
1864	Chōshū attempts to expel the barbarian, firing on foreign ships at Shimonoseki. A four-nation fleet bombards Chōshū's Shimonoseki forts and spikes its cannon. Chōshū steps up its purchase of Western weapons.
1864	First *bakufu* expedition against Chōshū; Chōshū submits.
1864/65	Civil war in Chōshū; loyalists win.
1866	Second *bakufu* expedition against Chōshū; *bakufu* army trounced.
1868	Satsuma and Chōshū, joining forces, defeat *bakufu* army at Toba-Fushimi. Shogun and *bakufu* troops leave western Japan.

The most striking feature of the above events is how so few with so little could do so much to so many. About a quarter of Japan was in the *bakufu* domain; the rest of the country was divided among the 260 daimyo domains. Even allowing for sporadic support from lukewarm allies, and granting that Chōshū and Satsuma were big, they were still a very small part of the whole. There are complicated answers to this question, but in simple military terms the answer is that they developed armies that no foe could withstand. At the Battle of Toba-Fushimi in 1868, for example, a *bakufu* army three times the size of the Sat-Chō contingents was forced to flee in disarray.

Trotsky wrote in 1930 of the "law of uneven development," of what happens, for example, when machine guns are introduced into a peasant society.[2] Something similar happened in Japan during the 1860s when Minié and Spencer rifles, products of the nineteenth-century industrial West, were introduced into Japan's late "feudal" society—a society at a wholly different technological level. The Minié rifle was vastly superior to the old blunderbuss: it could be reloaded quicker; it shot farther, and with far greater accuracy. Spencer breechloaders purchased from American merchants were, in turn, capable of about ten times the rate of fire of the Minié. Apparently Sat-Chō troops at Toba-Fushimi had both Miniés and Spencers, while the *bakufu* troops had old-fashioned weapons and some Miniés.

[2] Leon Trotsky, *The Third International after Lenin* (New York: Pioneer Publishers, 1936), pp. 18-24.

Weapons, though, are not the whole story. Ideology and morale played a part. Chōshū and Satsuma rifle companies were associated with the loyalist position. They saw their cause as righteous and fought with a fervor not matched by their reluctant foes. Another factor was Chōshū's desperate situation. Torn by a civil war in 1864-1865, its very existence threatened by the second *bakufu* expedition in 1866, Chōshū had its back to the wall. Just as the molecular structure of chemicals may be transformed by high temperatures and great pressures, so was Chōshū society remolded by events for which there was no Tokugawa precedent. Reforms were carried out that went far beyond the earlier reformist tradition. The irregular militia were organized as rifle companies, with recruitment of commoners and greater attention to ability. Itō Hirobumi as a samurai was the lowest of the low, yet he quickly rose to command such a unit. After each victory—in the domain civil war and then against the second *bakufu* expedition—further reforms weeded out incompetents and improved the troops in the direction of Western military practice. Ōmura Masujirō played an important role in these changes. In time, the irregulars became the regular domain army, but one very different from the old feudal groupings. By the time of Toba-Fushimi the army had also been blooded: it was accustomed to battle and led by experienced commanders. Satsuma was not subject to comparable pressures. Whether its troops were as efficient as those of Chōshū before the wars of 1868-1869 is not clear.

From the mid-1860s the question within Chōshū and Satsuma was who could control these new troops, so vastly more potent than the traditional, "feudal" soldiery. The answer was a handful of middle-ranking samurai: Kido, Ōkubo, Saigō, and their associates. Their ties to the commanders of the new rifle companies and to loyalists in other domains, as well as their connections with court nobles dating back to the early 1860s, thrust them upward within the decision-making apparatus of their domains. Especially in Chōshū, where there was no Shimazu Hisamitsu and where civil war had discredited the conservatives, this group was virtually supreme. The subsequent victory of these domains in the larger civil war within Japan propelled these leaders, willy-nilly, into a commanding position at the court in Kyoto early in 1868. Events had moved faster than consciousness.

The Early Meiji Years

In May of 1868, Edo was handed over to the imperial forces without a struggle. The outcome of the earlier battle at Toba-Fushimi had convinced the last shogun that resistance was futile. Western Japan was quiet. Its domains had acknowledged the government of the emperor. They watched and waited. Most were unconvinced that the new government would endure. In July the ardently pro-Tokugawa or anti–Sat-Chō domains of the northeast rose in rebellion. Central government in Japan was at a two-century low.

Where was the base of the new court government during the late summer of 1868?

1) The new government itself was in Kyoto. A simple framework of offices had been erected, but the officials had nothing to govern except the city of Kyoto and its immediate environs. There was, for example, a "Ministry of Finance." Its primary job, however, was to scour the countryside and cities, exacting "special contributions" for support of the government army. The Kyoto government consisted of the emperor, Iwakura, Kido, and a pool of nobles, daimyo, and samurai.
2) The main outpost of the Kyoto government was the Chinshōfu, or military headquarters, located in Edo. This was run by Ōkubo and Sanjō with the aid of Ōmura, Etō, and others, In major respects the Chinshōfu, not the Kyoto court, was the actual heart of government. It was the command center for the military campaigns in the northeast, and it administered the *bakufu* domain, the only lands directly under "imperial" control. Sanjō, Ōkubo, and their cohorts replaced the shogun and councils of the old *bakufu*, but they retained the existing apparatus of Tokugawa officials. For some months in 1868, officials in Kyoto who issued orders but did little work resented the primacy of the Chinshōfu, whose officials worked long hours and paid little heed to the orders emanating from Kyoto.
3) The main base of the new central government was the armies fighting in the northeast. Other domains also sent troops, but casualty lists make abundantly clear the core role of Sat-Chō troops. The field commanders of these armies would become the pillars of the new state after the fighting ended.
4) Finally, there were the domains of Satsuma and Chōshū (as well as Tosa and Saga). These were left in the hands of associates of the leaders who had moved on to Kyoto and Edo. These stay-at-home associates coexisted uneasily with the still powerful daimyo and elders. They secured the home bases of the new regime.

The new government, then, was strung out geographically from the southwest to the northeast, almost the length of Japan, with a loose and untested hegemony over an even more varied array of daimyo states.

To say that central government was at a two-hundred-year low is not to say that the social or legal order had collapsed. The self-rule characteristic of Tokugawa government lasted through the transition. The domains, for example, continued to manage their affairs during the interim between the collapse of the *bakufu* and the consolidation of the new government. Or, where domain government became less competent because of military or political turbulence, district and village administration usually continued unimpeded. In the larger towns, even when *bakufu* intendants had fled, ward self-government by townsmen continued. Throughout the 1860s and early 1870s—with a few perturbations—taxes were collected, records were kept, samurai were paid their stipends, and the public order was maintained. Local authority remained intact and was seen as legitimate throughout the transition. Despite occasional uprisings at the local level, there was nothing like the Great Fear of revolutionary France.

During the Restoration period, Chōshū could be Chōshū and Satsuma could be Satsuma just because so many other domains were inactive yet stable. It was a great boon to the new government that it did not immediately have to assume responsibility for all of Japan, a task for which it was ill-prepared. It could proceed slowly, step by step, confident that in the meantime most of the minimal functions of government would be performed. Had the daimyo states and local administrative structures collapsed, the difficulties in building a new order would have been of a far greater magnitude.

At the same time the autonomy of the domains constituted the greatest obstacle in the path of the new government. How could it transfer power from these other bodies to itself? Even the armies that fought in the northeast, though called the "government army" (*kangun*), were in fact domain troops. For the new leaders to use the military might of the domains to transfer political and then military power from the domains to the central government was social engineering of a very high order.

Military Consolidation and Liberalism, 1868-1869

The formal structure of government underwent several transformations during the first year and a half: from the Three Offices of January 1868, to the Three Offices and Seven Departments of early February 1868, to the Three Offices and Eight Bureaus of late February 1868, to the Eight Offices of the "June Constitution" (which lasted for more than a year). The highest posts went to nobles and daimyo. But the formal table of organization only imperfectly mirrored the realities of political power. The samurai leaders, especially those of Chōshū and Satsuma, called the shots. In many regards the configuration of political power that had emerged in late-*bakumatsu* Chōshū and Satsuma continued on during the early Meiji years.

The key figures were Ōkubo and Kido. They were the leaders of their respective domain cliques within the central government. They controlled the emperor through Iwakura and Sanjō. They controlled their domains through officials who had stayed behind: Kido, with greater ease since few men of power were left in Chōshū; Ōkubo, with difficulty since he had to contend with both Shimazu Hisamitsu and Saigō. Finally, they controlled the domain armies through their commanders. An anecdote told by Maeda Renzan illustrates the balance between actual power and formal organization during the early months at the Kyoto court. When deliberations were held, the nobles and daimyo sat on the elegant tatami inside the palace while the samurai councilors, without court rank, sat on rough, circular straw mats on the gravel outside. "Yet those who discussed policy were mainly the councilors, so the nobles crowded out onto the palace veranda to participate in the talk. A funny sight!"[3]

During the early months, while the government army moved against the remaining shards of the ancient regime—the alliance of thirty-one northeastern domains and the *bakufu* naval forces that had fled to Hakodate in Hokkaidō—the policies of the court were extremely circumspect. Government leaders feared that other domains with longstanding ties to the Tokugawa house might join the northeastern alliance or coalesce into a neutral bloc and withdraw their passive backing from the government. To prevent this, they adopted an open or even liberal guise as if to say to the domains, "We will share power with you." Influential daimyo were given high posts in the government. The Charter Oath with its vague promises of representative government, fairness, and openness was sworn to before the gods by the emperor, nobles, daimyo, and officials.[4]

A new structure of government (Seitaisho) with a threefold separation of powers was promulgated in June 1868. Its legislature had two houses: the upper was stocked with appointed officials; the lower, having only advisory powers, contained representatives sent by the domains. This was a gesture, at least, in the direction of domain representation, although it fell far short of a council of daimyo under the emperor—the form of

[3] Maeda Renzan, *Seihen monogatari* (Tokyo: Kokumin taimususha, 1920), p. 32.

[4] Sometimes too much is made of the Charter Oath. While in the United States with the Iwakura mission, Kume Kunitake in a conversation with Kido, made a reference to the Charter Oath sworn by the emperor before the gods. Kido, an author of the Oath, responded, "What is this about the emperor swearing an oath before the gods?" Kume replied, "The five-article Charter Oath." Kido suddenly clapped his hands and said: "That's right. There was such a thing. Do you recall what it was?" Tanaka Akira, *Meiji ishin*, vol. 24 of *Nihon no rekishi* (Tokyo: Shōgakkan, 1976), pp. 56-57.

government envisaged by the *kōbu-gattai* movement prior to 1868. In addition to the façade of power sharing, the new government paraded the emperor about the country as a visible symbol of its legitimacy and of its national character. When the emperor traveled to Edo between November 1868 and January 1869, he was accompanied by an entourage of 2,300 persons. Messengers were sent to shrines along the way to announce his coming. Rewards and alms were distributed to filial children, chaste wives, the old, and the unfortunate. A great festival was held in Edo. The cost of this trip was almost one-fifth of the new government's regular budget for 1868![5]

But when the last northeastern domain of Aizu surrendered in October 1868, the government began to move away from power sharing. It abolished the Legislature (Giseikan), merging it with the Executive Office (Gyōseikan). This left the domain representatives in the lower house without an upper house to advise.[6] Then in December the government issued orders (*hanji shokusei*) to the domains to set up three new executive posts at the top of their government to replace those held by elders or other high retainers. The court government, in effect, was claiming a voice in the internal organization of domain governments. The court hoped that the daimyo would fill the posts with men sympathetic to itself. Some did and some did not. Then, in March 1869, the new leaders from Chōshū, Satsuma, Tosa, and Saga persuaded their former daimyo to petition the court to accept the return of their lands and people. "Return" in this context meant that domains would no longer be held as independent fiefs, but would be subject to central government administration. The petition was a trial balloon. The reaction was all the new leaders could have hoped for: protests were few, and some daimyo, hoping to jump on the bandwagon, submitted similar petitions. The fact that many important daimyo held high positions in the new government may have allayed fears within the domains with respect to how much the central government would actually interfere in their internal affairs.

By April of 1869 it was clear that the *bakufu* naval forces at Hakodate, the last overt resistance to the new government, could not hold out much longer. This realization triggered a new round of actions by the central

[5] Ibid., p. 171. The cost was 778,060 yen.

[6] Once having established the principle of representation, the government could not abandon it completely. But each successive manifestation became weaker. The 1868 Kōgisho could not initiate legislation; it could only respond to inquiries handed down by the Dajōkan. It was followed by the Shūgiin, which mainly discussed reforms in the domains. In 1869 its members were sent home to help implement reforms. In 1871 the Shūgiin was placed under the Sain. In 1873 it was abolished, and two years later the Sain itself was replaced by the Genrōin.

government. In April the government (Dajōkan) was moved from Kyoto to Tokyo, ending the anomaly of divided rule. The move was opposed by most nobles, whose influence was greater in Kyoto. In June, two days after the *bakufu* forces at Hakodate surrendered, the government held an election as provided for under the June Constitution. The election was like musical chairs by ballot: only the top three grades of officials had the right to vote, and they voted to determine which of their number would remain in government. The results were dramatic. The number of senior councilors dropped from twenty to three, junior councilors from sixteen to six. Daimyo and nobles were the hardest hit. Until this time, high offices had been pools of people too influential to leave outside government. The completion of military consolidation made it safe to push them aside.

In July 1869 the government "accepted" the petitions of the four daimyo and ordered all daimyo to return their lands and people (*hanseki hōkan*) to the court. Since all daimyo were reappointed as governors of the areas over which they had been feudal lords, the immediate effect of the order was imperceptible; however, the change in their status provided the rationale for the stream of orders subsequently issued to the domains by the central government.

The 1869 Imperial Government

The process of centralization between 1868 and 1871 can be viewed as an intricate dialectic between actions to strengthen the central government and actions to subordinate the domains. A reform promoting the efficiency of the central government enabled it to advance a step in asserting its authority over the domains. An extension of authority over the domains, in turn, permitted yet another reform at the center. Thus the new offices established in the domains in December 1868 prepared the way for the election in the central government in June 1869. This led to the acceptance of petitions for the "return of lands and people," and that, in turn, led to a new reform at the center—the establishment in August 1869 of offices modeled on those of ancient Japan. Since the forms and nomenclature of this government continued until the establishment of a cabinet system in 1885, it is worth noting several of its features.

One feature was the use of religion as a bulwark of state authority. Since the emperor was the lineal descendant of the Sun Goddess and the high priest of Shinto, and since the emperor had been the focus of the Restoration movement, even under the earlier June Constitution there had been a ministry-level Office for Shinto Affairs. It had encouraged the movement to separate Shinto shrines and Buddhist temples. For example, shrines dedicated to the Great Boddhisattva Hachiman were rededicated to the Great [Shinto] God Hachiman. But in the 1869 government reorganization, this office was raised in status to become the highest in the state, superior even to the Council of State (Dajōkan).[7] This gave the new government a slightly theocratic cast during the years from 1869 to 1871, just when the domains were still ruled by their daimyo-governors and the authority of the center most needed bolstering. A slogan at the time was "Unity of Religion and Politics" (*saisei itchi*). In fact this high religious office had little power, and after the abolition of the domains in 1871 it again became a ministry (Jingishō) beneath the Council of State. In 1872 it became a Ministry of Religion, less narrowly devoted to the interests of Shinto, and in 1877 it was further downgraded, becoming a bureau in the Home Ministry.

A second feature of the 1869 reorganization was the emergence for the first time of a fairly strong government at the center. Another slogan of the day was "Personal Rule by the Emperor" (*tennō shinsai*), which in practice meant that all decisions were made by a handful of leaders in the Council of State. Few traces remained of the earlier power sharing. Within the Council of State there was an uneasy balance between nobles and samurai. All major decisions had to be ratified by the emperor. The few remaining nobles hung onto their positions by controlling access to the emperor and the ratification process. The council was headed by Minister of the Right Sanjō Sanetomi, who was assisted by Iwakura Tomomi, and four other *dainagon*. Beneath these nobles were the samurai councilors, the actual decision makers. At first there were four, Ōkubo of Satsuma, Hirosawa Saneomi and Maebara Issei of Chōshū, and Soejima of Saga; the following year these were joined by Kido, Ōkuma, and others. Beneath the Council of State were the ministries. Each was headed by a daimyo or noble, aided by a samurai vice-minister. The actual lines of power in the new government ran from the samurai councilors to the samurai vice-ministers.

A third feature of the 1869 government was the conscious return to the forms and nomenclature of the Nara court, an age when emperors sometimes ruled. Like the use of Shinto, this move was designed to increase the prestige of the central government. Initially there was some

[7] Office names are hard to translate. The ministry-level office concerned with Shinto in the 1868 government was the Jingikan. In that government the executive, the legislature, and the various ministries were all called *kan*. But in the 1869 government, only the Jingikan and Dajōkan (Council of State) were *kan*; the ministries were *shō*. The usual English translation for the Jingikan of the Nara period is "Office of Deities." This does not sound right for the Meiji, so I have used "Office for Shinto Affairs."

confusion. Shibusawa wrote afterward that when the new government structure was first promulgated, officials rushed out to secondhand bookstores to buy copies of the commentaries on the Taihō code (*Ryō no gige*) so they would know what the new office titles meant. Along with their new titles, high officials also received new, noble-sounding family names. Taira, Minamoto, and Fujiwara blossomed at the court like flowers after a spring rain. Ōkubo became Fujiwara Ason Toshimichi, Ōkuma became Sugawara Ason Shigenobu, and Itō, who had begun as a lowly *ashigaru* (foot soldier), became Shu Ochi no Sukune Hirobumi. With what titillation must they have gazed upon their names in the *Register of Officials*! Even the clothing worn by the councilors at certain court ceremonies was dictated by the new ethos. High-ranking samurai officials were required to dress as nobles; and all, including nobles, were required to wear swords. Saigō after joining the government, is said to have despaired of ever wearing his robes correctly. On one occasion the Saga samurai Etō Shimpei, late for a ceremony, dashed into the court uncapped by an *eboshi*—a small, black, silly-looking hat that perches forward on the head. A noble asked him, "Where is your hat?" Etō retorted, "Where are your swords?" Both hastened out for the proper accouterments.[8]

Parallel to the new office titles, another Nara-inspired innovation was a system of nine court ranks with upper and lower grades. These made possible equivalences across organizations—between, for example, a Ministry of Finance official and a colonel in the army. Officials with the same rank and grade received the same pay. This was the start of a systematization that continued thereafter as a permanent feature of Japanese bureaucracy. But the immediate effect was to upset existing social statuses. In the new system of ranks, a samurai vice-minister was equal to the daimyo-governor of a great domain, and both were outranked by the samurai members of the Council of State. This gave rise to some tension and much humor. Saigō, who had been accused by Shimazu Hisamitsu of being self-seeking, refused both high office and the third-rank upper grade because it would have made him superior to his daimyo. On one occasion, the Saga daimyo addressed a former vassal who had become a councilor of state familiarly as "Soejima" without the polite *san*, the equivalent of "Mr." Soejima protested, saying: "Soejima is at present an official of the court and should be addressed, therefore, with the proper etiquette." His daimyo responded with elaborate sarcasm: "Well, then, Lord Soejima!" On another occasion, Lord Yōdō of Tosa asked an official if he were not by birth a lowly *ashigaru*. Kido, who was

[8] Kume Kunitake, *Kume Hakushi kyūjūnen kaikoroku* (Tokyo: Waseda University Press, 1934), vol. 2, pp. 182-183.

present, rebuked Yōdō, saying that to inquire into the previous status of a ranking official of the Finance Ministry was inexcusable. Yōdō's reaction was like that of the Saga daimyo. He addressed the man as "Teacher" and had him sit in the place of honor. The official stuck to his guns and won the exchange with his reply: "Though I am unworthy and have no accomplishments, in one area, the handling of money, I probably am slightly more experienced than Lord Yōdō."[9]

The Completion of Political Consolidation, 1869-1871

Even after the formal "return of lands and people," the central government proceeded slowly in extending control over the domains. Early communications were often requests for information. The domains gradually became accustomed to responding. Then orders were issued to do this and not do that. Report the domain's income and population, report any debts owed to foreigners, maintain a certain number of troops according to domain income; do not borrow from foreign governments, do not print domain currency, and so on. The orders made it clear that the authority of the central government extended to the domains and that the daimyo-governors were no longer autonomous rulers over their domains. But nothing substantial changed: the first year after the "return" might be called the period of paper initiatives.

The government leaders were not satisfied with this state of affairs. It is clear from their letters that they wished to take stronger measures. But they feared the reaction in the domains, especially the reaction of the domain armies of Chōshū and Satsuma (and of these two, especially Satsuma).

In the case of Chōshū, its victorious armies were reorganized into four battalions late in December 1869. The best troops were kept, but the old, the wounded, the poorly trained, and the less disciplined members of the famous old militia were discharged. Filled with the consciousness that it was they who had restored the emperor, and resentful at being discharged when they had expected to be rewarded, about one or two thousand of these ex-soldiers rose in rebellion and seized the Chōshū government offices in Yamaguchi. Kido, visiting the domain at the time, was attacked and only barely escaped. Saigō heard of the incident and counseled leniency. Kido, however, used the new battalions to crush the dissidents. It is interesting that the battalions were willing to move against their former comrades, given the existing high level of friction between the privileged officers (all samurai) and the strictly disciplined rank and

[9] Maeda, *Seihen monogatari*, pp. 33-34.

file (mixed samurai and commoners). The leaders of the uprising were harshly punished.

It was while putting down the dissidents that Kido wrote to Ōkuma:

> The domains, relying on military force, are establishing independent bases, exactly as if they are little kingdoms [*shōtenchi*]. With this our goal of progress will not be realized. Therefore today's urgent duty is to sweep away domain practices and firmly establish the military axis without which nothing can be carried out.[10]

However strong Kido's sentimental attachment to his old domain, he would brook no opposition. He had become completely an official of the central state and was bent on strengthening it. The failure of the revolt in Chōshū, coupled with the exodus of its most able leaders to Tokyo, broke the back of any vestige of autonomy in that domain. There was another flare-up of resistance in 1876, Maebara's Hagi Rebellion, but it, too, was easily suppressed.

The situation in Satsuma was wholly different; it remained autonomous and a thorn in the side of the new government until 1877. The samurai population of Satsuma was larger, with rural as well as castle-town samurai. After 1869 its leaders carried out reforms that transformed the domain from a hierarchical, late-feudal state into a lower-samurai military state. High-ranking vassals had their stipends cut while others were left unchanged. Men of ability were appointed to office. Army units were formed both in Kagoshima and local areas, and army commanders were put in charge of local government. The revenues of the Shimazu daimyo were separated from those of the domain government. In short, a new state was constructed in Satsuma, one that represented the interests of its victorious returned soldiery. Many able army commanders stayed in the domain, and with them stayed Saigō, the darling of the Restoration armies.

To proceed further against the many domains, the government had to ensure itself of the backing of Satsuma and Chōshū, the two domains possessing effective military power. And so, to remove from the domains the nuclei about which dissident sentiments might coalesce, Ōkubo and Kido journeyed to their respective domains in January 1870 and tried to persuade Shimazu Hisamitsu, Saigō, and the Chōshū daimyo to come to Tokyo. The trip was a complete failure. Hisamitsu, who had opposed the "return of lands and people" and disliked the new upstart government, stayed at home. So did Saigō. The Chōshū daimyo went docilely

[10] Tanaka Akira, *Bakumatsu no Chōshū* (Tokyo: Chūkō shinsho, 1965), p. 173.

to Tokyo, waited patiently for four months, and when nothing happened, returned home.

This left the government at such an impasse that for the next year it could do little; in some respects, the difficulties that had dogged it grew worse. Other nobles were jealous of Sanjō and the low-ranking Iwakura. Antiforeign feelings continued to run high. *Shishi* activists who had fought to expel the barbarians were incensed that the new government outdid even the *bakufu* in truckling to the foreign powers. A number assaulted foreign diplomats: Bizen troops clashed with British soldiers, and Tosa samurai attacked French sailors at Sakai. In each case the government severely punished the samurai. Assassinations continued, but now the targets were the new government leaders who before 1868 had been on the side of the assassins. Yokoi Shōnan was assassinated in February 1869 by samurai opposed to relations with foreign countries; Ōmura Masujirō was killed at the end of the same year by fellow Chōshū samurai critical of his westernizing policies; and Hirosawa of Chōshū was slain early in 1871. Kido and Ōkubo, as well, were seen as traitors by many in their domains.

Even more ominous was the continuing animosity between the leading domains. Ōkubo, aware of the danger, wrote a long position paper in January 1870:

> If we measure strength today, Satsuma and Chōshū are more powerful than the court. The two domains do not use their power on behalf of the court but store it up within their borders. . . . This is why the court is so weak. Some argue that the court can get along without the two domains, but that is shortsighted. Others argue that the customs and character of Satsuma and Chōshū are like fire and ice: to join them forcibly can have only ill effects. To this I say, his argument may have a grain of truth, but it reveals a lack of sincere love of country. Satsuma and Chōshū are the foundation stones of the imperial country; its life depends on them. If they do not cooperate, its life will be shortened. Since last year, discord has arisen time and time again between the two. Today the situation is worse than ever. . . . True patriots grieve and malcontents break into smiles. Street-corner gossip, needless to say, is not worthy of our attention, yet doubts and suspicions have arisen among the people, and one hears that not a few are plotting for a change of government. . . . If at present the imperial country faced no foreign threat, a few internal disturbances would be no cause for alarm.[11]

[11] *Ōkubo Toshimichi monjo* (Tokyo: Nihon shiseki kyōkai, 1928), vol. 3, pp. 355-357. In this chapter, I focus on the internal dynamics of the formation of the central government.

But such is not the case, Ōkubo concludes. The insatiable foreign powers watch for an opportunity to fatten themselves on Japan, so "Sat-Chō unity is today's urgent duty." In February 1870, Sanjō wrote to Iwakura:

> Observing the situation in the east and west, I feel that the present is a truly difficult time. The outcome of the Restoration depends on the next three or four or five months. It is vital that officials exert themselves to the maximum. If we are fortunate enough to overcome the danger, then, just as the ground hardens after rain, a time of stability will arrive. But for a while the divine land will be at peril.[12]

Dissension, however, continued. In April 1870 Sasaki Takayuki, a samurai of Tosa, wrote in his diary:

> Lord Iwakura has spoken with me several times on secret matters. If, later on, a person unfamiliar with today's conditions came to know of this, he would wonder why Iwakura spoke privately with an unimportant person like me instead of with men of power like Ōkubo or Kido. The reason is that Chōshū and Satsuma distrust one another. Of the Saga contingent, Ōkuma is on Chōshū's side, Soejima on Satsuma's. Of my countrymen from Tosa, Gotō is the most closely allied with Kido, and Itagaki has a similar leaning. Hirosawa [of Chōshū] is for fairness, but does not like Satsuma. Ōkubo, too, is fair on the whole, but from before the Restoration he has had a tendency to worry constantly about Chōshū. Because this situation prevails, Sanjō and Iwakura are greatly worried. They avoid talking with persons from Satsuma, Chōshū, and Saga, and speak secretly with me instead.[13]

A week or so later, Sasaki made another entry in the same vein:

> Since the beginning of this year, Kido has not come to Tokyo. He tends to be difficult. When he returns, he will no doubt voice his dissatisfactions. Hirosawa and others worry. Saigō, too, has withdrawn to Kagoshima. The powerful do just as they please, leaving the central government to fend for itself. Sanjō and Iwakura worry greatly over the friction between Satsuma and Chōshū. Only Ōkubo can be relied on; without him we could not carry on. In Tosa, too,

But I agree with Ōkubo's point. Foreign pressure did not end with the cracking of the eggshell of seclusion. It continued, and Japanese awareness of it grew stronger. It certainly acted as a powerful constraint on the freedom of the new government of which I speak in my conclusion.

[12] Ōtsuka Takematsu, ed., *Iwakura Tomomi kankei monjo*, vol. 4 (Tokyo: Nihon shiseki kyōkai, 1930), pp. 36-47.

[13] Tsuda Shigemaro, *Meiji Seijō to shin Takayuki* (Tokyo: Jishōkai, 1928), p. 179.

> Gotō and Itagaki express only discontent. As the top domain official, Itagaki is prone to resist the central government. The troubles of these days are beyond description.[14]

Furthermore, there were struggles for power within the government itself. To give but one example, in September 1869 two ministries, Finance and Civil Affairs, were joined. The head of the new ministry was a daimyo, but real power was in the hands of Vice-Minister Ōkuma and a host of extremely talented younger officials, including Itō, Inoue Kaoru, Shibusawa, and Maejima Hisoka. The new ministry was difficult for the Council of State to control—it was too progressive for mossbacks from Satsuma, and it had too much power—so, less than a year later, it was again broken up into two separate ministries. The details are complicated, but the main story line is one of clique struggles and disagreements over goals.

During 1870, in short, momentum was lost; it was not a good year for the new government. The one positive development was the order issued to the domains in October to reform their governments, military forces, budgets, samurai stipends, daimyo house finances, etc. But even this order was asking the domains, in effect, to do to themselves what the central government was too weak to do to them. Its implementation varied from domain to domain. In some, there were few substantial changes. In others, pro-Restoration samurai gained high office for the first time—men who would never have come to power without outside support and who were thus beholden to the central government.

The impasse facing the government was resolved in January 1871, when Iwakura was appointed as imperial messenger and sent to Chōshū and Satsuma with imperial rescripts ordering their daimyo as well as Saigō to Tokyo. Iwakura was accompanied by Ōkubo and by Yamagata and Kawamura of the Army Ministry. This tactic proved effective. Unable to resist a direct order from the emperor, Hisamitsu gave Saigō permission to leave the domain and promised that he himself would go to Tokyo in the spring, after he recovered from an illness. The Chōshū daimyo also agreed to go. The mission then went on to Tosa, where it conferred with Itagaki Taisuke. Like Saigō, Itagaki was a military commander who had become the chief executive officer of his domain.

In April, probably as a consequence of these talks, the government ordered the three domains of Satsuma, Chōshū, and Tosa to send 10,000 troops to Tokyo to constitute an imperial guard. Saigō, Kido, and Itagaki were sent back to their domains from Tokyo to expedite the matter. Arriving in Tokyo between April and June, these troops became the first central government army.

[14] Ibid., p. 183.

Also in April, the central government was strengthened by the appointment of Sanjō as the great minister of state, Iwakura as minister of the right, and Saigō, Kido, Itagaki, and Ōkuma (representing the four leading domains) as councilors of state. Ōkubo, deferring to Saigō, stepped down to become the minister of finance, the first samurai to become titular head of a ministry.

Reorganized, and with troops of its own, the government moved forward rapidly. On July 2 it tested the waters by taking action against the Fukuoka domain on a charge of counterfeiting. The daimyo-governor was dismissed from his post, and the five highest officials, all members of that domain's pro-emperor clique, were executed. There was no outcry of alarm from other domains; so two weeks later, fifty-six daimyo, who had been summoned to Tokyo, were told by the emperor that their domains would be taken from them and made into prefectures. Griffis, in Fukui, wrote that the news came as a "thunder-bolt" or a "political earthquake."[15] At the time of the "return of lands and people," the four leading daimyo had been consulted in advance. This time they were not, and even Iwakura was apparently told of the decision only at the last minute. In all, 261 domains were abolished. Added to prefectures formed earlier out of *bakufu* lands, this came to a total of 302 prefectures and 3 administrative cities. Later in the year, little prefectures were absorbed by their larger neighbors, leaving 72 prefectures and 3 cities. The former daimyo-governors were retired and required to live in Tokyo.

Samurai were appointed as the new governors, each accompanied by an outside staff of officials. Only in Satsuma and one other, unimportant domain were samurai of that domain appointed as governors. Chōshū's new governor came from Shizuoka, a former *bakufu* domain. This reform marked a shift to a truly centralized state. Some historians have called it the "second Restoration."

A month after the domains were abolished—in the usual pattern of alternation between changes in local areas and changes at the center—another reform took place at the center. The most notable change was that nobles and daimyo, with the exceptions of Sanjō and Iwakura, were relieved of their posts. Japan is sometimes said to like figurehead government; but, apart from the emperor, a remarkable feature of the early Meiji years is how rapidly the reality of rule by a small group of samurai overtook the forms that had been instituted immediately after the Restoration. Another change, presaging perhaps a turn toward the West, was the disappearance of the Fujiwaras, Tairas, and Minamotos from

[15] William Elliot Griffis, *The Mikado's Empire* (New York: Harper & Brothers, 1908), vol. 2, p. 526.

the government. Ōkubo went back to being plain old Ōkubo, Itō to being Itō, and so on.

Thus, by midsummer of 1871, the work of centralizing governmental authority in Japan was complete: a single monolithic bureaucracy stretched downward from a handful of decision makers with authoritarian powers, through ministries headed by samurai ministers, to prefectures with appointed governors, and then to the districts and villages, or cities and wards. Despite the burden of inept nobles, decorative daimyo, domain jealousies, personal antipathies, the ever present peril of assassination, and unrelenting foreign pressures, the men of Meiji had been able to use the power of the domains to destroy the domains. If one compares Japan in 1871 with, say, Germany after its unification, Japan was far more unified and centralized. In part this was because Japan was already more centralized before unification began. In part it is because Japan's unification was national and imperial, not a one-area-centered unification of the Prussian type. Despite the prominence of Chōshū and Satsuma, it aimed at universality.[16]

Further Developments, 1871-1890

The administrative transition from the Tokugawa to the Meiji was virtually complete by the summer of 1871. All of the autonomous political structures of the old regime had been liquidated or transformed and, with the single exception of the Satsuma domain, had been brought under the control of the Restoration government. So confident were the new leaders in what they had wrought that more than half of them, including Iwakura, Ōkubo, and Kido, went blithely off to Europe and America for a year and a half. What leader could do this today? The only precaution they took after installing Saigō, Itagaki, and Ōkuma in a caretaker government was to extract written promises that no new initiatives would be taken during their absence. Events proved that they had been a bit overconfident, but not irretrievably so.

The 1873 Crisis

Of new initiatives taken despite the promise not to, none was more dangerous than the plan for an expedition against Korea. The occasion was the unwillingness of Korea—which saw itself as a younger-brother

[16] One must distinguish between the old domains and those who came from them. One piece of evidence is the rapidity with which Yamaguchi, Hagi, and Kagoshima sank into prefectural obscurity. Visiting them today we ask, "Can these be the towns from which such a storm arose?"

kingdom of the Chinese empire—to recognize the imperial character of Japan's Restoration. The plan was supported by the stay-at-home officials with the exception of Ōkuma. Saigō in particular zealously championed the expedition as a means of renewing the pride of samurai soldiers. The expedition was opposed by the members of the mission, who had come home convinced that Japan was too weak to engage in a foreign adventure that might provoke the Western powers. The opposition was led reluctantly by Ōkubo and Kido and assisted by Itō. The struggle over this issue laid bare the fault lines within the government. It ended with victory for those who had seen at first hand the strength of the West and who gave the highest priority to internal development.

The resolution of the 1873 crisis led to changes in the central government. One such change was a decrease in the number of top leaders. Saigō, Itagaki, Gotō Shōjirō, Etō Shimpei, and Soejima all quit when the decision went against them. It can be argued that this "sloughing off" was an important part of early political development, and that those who left were less suited to the work of state building. The leaders who remained were too few to staff all of the top posts, so councilors of state were for the first time permitted to hold concurrent ministerial portfolios. The terminology remained that of Nara, but what resulted closely resembled a cabinet system. Ōkubo had wanted such a system in 1871 but had been blocked by Iwakura, who felt that the power of samurai councilors in control of ministries would undercut his own. The period from 1873 to 1878 is sometimes called the era of "Ōkubo despotism." Certainly Ōkubo was the most powerful figure within the collective Sat-Chō leadership.

The Social Revolution from Above, 1873-1878

In 1873 central government finances faced two problems. The first was that the land tax, the main source of government revenue, was paid two-thirds in kind and only one-third in cash. Budgetary planning was difficult when the greater part of that revenue consisted of grain, which fluctuated in value according to the market. The second problem was that the government had to pay out almost a third of its revenue as samurai stipends, an obligation incurred when the domains were made over into prefectures in 1871.

The solution to the first problem was to convert the land tax into a monetary tax. This was a gigantic and expensive bureaucratic endeavor that involved surveying all of the land in Japan and assessing its value. It was a reform that directly affected the vital interests of more than 80 percent of Japan's population and required delicate and complex negotiations at the local, district, prefectural, and national levels, with thousands of persons participating. The task was not completed until 1878. Overall, the new taxes were somewhat lighter than those collected during the Tokugawa era. Some areas that had been lightly taxed saw their taxes increase, however, and land taxes in Japan remained heavier than those in Korea or China. That such a reform could be undertaken within a decade of the Restoration says something about the level of stability and authority achieved by the new government. In the course of the reform, farmers were issued land certificates making the land their private property, though where the land had been alienated, the title went to the landlord and not to the tenant. Selling grain to pay taxes dramatically increased the money economy's penetration of the village. Paying in money meant that Japanese farmers benefited from the inflation of the late 1870s, but suffered during the deflation of the mid-1880s.

The solution to the second problem was the formation of a conscript army, beginning in 1874, and the abolition of the samurai in 1876. Where the daimyo had been handsomely compensated for their loss of position, the samurai were paid off in long-term bonds at a very reduced rate. The majority, unable to make the transition, ended up impoverished. What is interesting historically is how little resistance these measures aroused. A sprinkling of small uprisings occurred during the mid-1870s, virtually all in southwestern domains (such as Saga, Kumamoto, or Chōshū) that had played roles in the Restoration movement; and there was the serious 1876-1877 rebellion in Satsuma, the one domain never brought under central government control. Had these rebellions occurred before the completion of political consolidation or the formation of a conscript army, the consequences might have been disastrous. As it was, the consequences were short-lived.

The intent of the two reforms was primarily financial, but the effect was a social revolution. The late Tokugawa peasantry became, mostly, a class of small farmers. The samurai class, which had ruled Japan for centuries, was destroyed. In these measures can be seen the same blend of toughness and caution that had characterized the Meiji leadership of the 1868-1871 era. Indeed, the very fact that we can periodize the early Meiji years into an era of political consolidation and one of social revolution from above reveals the skill with which the leaders proceeded: not until all the bureaucratic levers were in their hands did they move against the powerful samurai and farming classes.

The 1881 Crisis

By 1878 Ōkubo, Kido, and Saigō, the triumvirate of the Restoration, were all dead. There followed a three-year interim during which it was unclear who would take their place. During this time, new problems emerged: intractable inflation, budget controversies, disagreement over foreign borrowing, a scandal in Hokkaidō, and increasingly importunate party demands for constitutional government. Each policy issue became entangled in a power struggle of which the principals were Ōkuma and Itō. Ōkuma lost and was expelled from the government along with his followers. Whereas those who left the government after the 1873 crisis had been less suited to state building than those who remained, the same cannot be said of the protagonists in 1881. Ōkuma was basically the same type of enlightened bureaucrat as Itō; if anything, he was a shade more progressive.

Itō's victory was the affirmation of Sat-Chō rule against a Saga outsider. Itō never quite became an Ōkubo, but he did assume the key role within the collective leadership of Japan during the 1880s. As in 1873, the resolution of the crisis led to some reorganization within the central government. It also determined the direction of the next decade—the adoption of a deflationary monetary policy, the avoidance of foreign borrowing, and the kind of constitution that would be drawn up for Japan.

The Conservative Eighties

During the 1870s the government had been the chief agency for social change in Japan. It had been more progressive, one can argue, than the samurai political parties. Within the range of positions represented by the samurai parties, some, imbued with resentment over the loss of samurai status, were closer to samurai rebels than to those building the new state. Some of the articles in 1876 party newspapers were these: "Overthrow Oppressive Government," "Assassinate Tyrannical Officials," "A Murderous Spirit [*sakki*] is the Basis for Establishing the Country," and "Freedom Must be Bought with Fresh Blood."[17]

During the 1878-1881 interim the situation changed. The failure of the Satsuma Rebellion demonstrated the futility of insurrection. The establishment of prefectural assemblies in 1878 legitimated political parties, leading to an influx of tax-paying farmers. And just as the parties were changing, the government turned away from reform and set about building institutions to preserve what it had achieved. In particular, having promised a constitution within ten years, the government wanted an institutional order that would hedge in the power of the parties in the lower house of a future parliament. Thus, a nobility was created to stock

[17] Tōyama Shigeki, *Meiji ishin* (Tokyo: Iwanami shoten, 1951), p. 330.

the future House of Peers. A Western-style cabinet system was begun in 1885. Laws were enacted to insulate the bureaucracy from political meddling. The imperial household was endowed with great wealth so that it would never have to go, hat in hand, to the Diet for its expenses.

Finally, the Meiji Constitution itself, as if inscribed on tablets of gold, was given by the emperor to the Japanese people. These measures, intended as they were to conserve the power of the Meiji revolutionaries, mark the final step in the formation of the Meiji central government.[18]

Conclusion

Earlier on, I noted the dual character of the domains after 1868: they posed an enormous threat to the frail, new, court government but, at the same time, gave it a considerable advantage in that they remained stable, orderly, and integrated local governments. They took care of themselves until the new central government had time to put its own affairs in order.

The same problem of local autonomy and what it meant in Restoration history may also be viewed through comparisons with other countries. First, we frequently ask why "feudal" Japan in the mid-nineteenth century was able so rapidly and effectively to build a modern state when "bureaucratic" China stumbled and fell into warlordism and disarray. The premises of such a question, however, will not stand up to scrutiny. Japan may have been partially feudal in 1600, but by the mid-nineteenth century it was something else. Perhaps it can be described as quasi-feudal at the top and bureaucratic at the bottom. China was just the opposite, bureaucratic at the top and something quite different at the bottom.

In China, that is to say, the trunk of bureaucratic government extended from the court at the center down to the offices of the district magistrates. But bureaucracy stopped at the *yamen* of the magistrate. Below it was a shifting equilibrium involving the *yamen*, gentry, and village leaders. That this equilibrium was nonbureaucratic in nature is reflected in the fact that it was the gentry who rebuilt the local order after the Taiping Re-

[18] I see the 1880s as a turn to conservatism. But the question is admittedly complex. Certainly the period from 1873 to 1878 was the most despotic; it had to be to carry out the social revolution. Government leaders like Kido lamented the necessity. After the samurai issue was settled and Satsuma pacified, the need became less pressing. In November 1877 Inoue Kaoru wrote to Ōkubo: now that the "great reforms" are done, he argued, "some of the authority of the center can be given to local areas so that a gulf will not emerge between the government and the people." *Ōkubo Toshimichi kankei monjo*, vol. 1 (Tokyo: Yoshikawa kōbunkan, 1965), p. 194. The turn to conservatism in the 1880s did not undo the post-1877 relaxation; it did not, for example, undo prefectural assemblies, but aimed at establishing extraconstitutional checks on future Diet powers.

bellion. After the dynasty came to an end in 1911, the nonbureaucratic equilibrium broke down. The gentry became landlords who looked to warlords for the preservation of order. In terms of the availability of local bureaucratic organizations, Sun Yat-sen's description of Chinese society as "a sheet of loose sand" is not amiss. When attempting to build a nation, local market networks are no substitute for local governments.

Japan, in contrast, had no bureaucratic trunk linking the *bakufu* with the regional states. Daimyo were vassals, not officials, of the shogun. *Bakufu* officials administered the controls over the domains but did not administer the domains themselves. Yet, within a domain (which, if large, might have a population of a quarter million) there was a bureaucracy—a three-tiered administration from castle town to district to village. Bureaucracy in Japan, in other words, began at the very level at which it ended in China. Between 1854 and 1868 the *bakufu* and its controls were swept away, but the regional bureaucratic building blocks—some small and some the size of a Chinese district—remained intact. However talented Ōkubo and his colleagues may have been, they would not have been able to build on sand.

A comparison with prerevolutionary France reveals a second facet of domain autonomy. The vital question for de Tocqueville was the degree of de facto centralization that had occurred in France even before the Revolution. He distinguished between two types of regional states within the old order, *pays d'état* and *pays d'élection*. Both received intendants sent by the Royal Council. But the *pays d'état*, and particularly Languedoc, were not so tightly controlled by their intendants as the *pays d'élection*. De Tocqueville based his thesis—that France had already become administratively centralized before the Revolution—on the *pays d'élection*.[19]

With this thesis in mind, we look at Japan and immediately wonder whether the outside (*tozama*) domains were not parallel to the *pays d'état*, and the hereditary (*fudai*) domains parallel to the *pays d'élection*. But further consideration inevitably leads to the conclusion that the parallels do not apply. Tokugawa Japan was fundamentally different. Instead of having intendants sent by the *bakufu* to govern the domains, in Japan the lords of the regional domains journeyed to Edo to govern the *bakufu*. The hereditary lords constituted the Japanese equivalent of the Royal Council.

Thus, in terms of the balance between center and periphery, Japan

[19] Alexis de Tocqueville, *The Old Regime and the French Revolution*, trans. Stuart Gilbert (New York: Doubleday, 1955). For the arguments on this point see pt. 2, chap. 2; pt. 3, chap. 7; and the appendix.

represented a much earlier "stage" of development. Harold Bolitho has argued that the primary concern of the hereditary lords was for their domains, not for their posts in Edo.[20] But it was just their position as members of the ruling council of the *bakufu* that gave them the power to watch over and safeguard the interests of their domains. They could check any extension of "monarchical" authority. To be sure, the hereditary lords administered the *bakufu* laws that governed all domains. They were not averse to keeping the large outside domains in their place. But the institution of the *bakufu* was not akin to the powerful central bureaucracies developed by European monarchies during the seventeenth and eighteenth centuries. From this perspective, the Meiji government with its nonfeudal bureaucracy represented a fundamental break with the past.

A second factor I would like to touch on again was the vital role of the new military. Its backing enabled the court government first to bring the regional states under control, and then to turn the old society topsy-turvy without provoking a Thermidor. In 1600, Ieyasu had rewarded and put into positions of power those who had supported him at the Battle of Sekigahara. In 1868, the Meiji court government did the same with the young military commanders who held its fate in their hands. The extraordinarily large number of such commanders—Saigō, Ōmura, Itō, Hirosawa, Itagaki, Maebara, Kawamura, Kabayama, Yamada, Ōyama, Yamagata, and the rest—among the officials of the new Meiji government was not accidental. A largely civilian interpretation of the Restoration is probably mistaken.

Most of the commanders were young, low-ranking samurai with stipends and salaries but no land. They were usually of the same class background as their troops. Their social background helps explain some of their policy positions; for example, they held little brief for feudal landholdings. But to interpret their actions solely in terms of their social origins would be to succumb to the fallacy of the petrified prescription. By 1867 or 1868 these commanders already had moved some distance from their origins. Saigō, for example, had begun as a poor castle-town samurai, but after the 1867 battle of Toba-Fushimi he became a national leader. Listen to Saigō's description of the situation; his obvious satisfaction is not at all diminished by his use of the objective third person:

> Fighting began, and once reports of victories began to arrive, the atmosphere at the court changed from fear and doubts [about the wisdom of cooperating with the anti-*bakufu* forces] to voices of

[20] See Harold Bolitho, *Treasures among Men: The Fudai Daimyo in Tokugawa Japan* (New Haven: Yale University Press, 1974), introduction and epilogue.

rejoicing. Earlier on, Saigō and Ōkubo had been viewed as snakes and scorpions and no one would go near them, but now they are plagued by a constant stream of courtiers asking for interviews.[21]

Saigō is especially interesting because, despite his national prominence, in the end he was unable to break with his past. The greatest crisis the Meiji government ever faced was when Saigō and his fellows left the government in 1873. But he was also exceptional in this regard. Most of the former commanders never looked back—except in bouts of nostalgia which were not uncommon.

Finally, I want to emphasize the freedom of the new government, the extent to which it was not bound by the past. One reason for this freedom is the factor we have just considered: the new government came to power after an internal war and with military forces so powerful that all other sources of influence seemed weak in comparison. Another reason is that, beyond the goal of restoring the emperor, there was no agreement as to what kind of government or what kind of society would be built. Instead, many ideas and models jostled for attention. Some domains had wanted a council of daimyo. Others had proposed institutions based on Western parliamentary practices. These influenced the "June Constitution" of 1868. Hisamitsu of Satsuma wanted a council of elders like that of Hideyoshi. The appeal of a return to a Nara-style government can be seen in the government actually established in 1869. New ideas also entered from the West. Meiji leaders recognized early on that the West contained within it a variety of models.

At a more concrete level, what can be said of models can also be said of policies. Meiji leaders disagreed not only regarding the pace of change, but also on its direction. There was no single vision of a new polity, much less a blueprint. On the question of how to handle the domains, for example, one can see what Edwin O. Reischauer has called the "pragmatic outlook" of the leaders. After the abolition of the domains in 1871, Kido wrote in his diary:

> Three years ago, observing the situation, I wished to destroy the 700-year-old feudal system, to make the domains into administrative units [*gunken*], to unify gradually the nation's strength and to develop its human talents. . . . I discussed this with a number of my comrades, but only one agreed with me. So there was nothing to do but to use stratagems and carry out the policy. . . . First we abolished fiefs within the *bakufu* domain, returning the land to the court. In this way the duty [*meibun*] of the domains of the court was made

[21] Katsuta Magoji, *Ōkubo Toshimichi den* (Tokyo: Dōbonkan, 1910), p. 406.

> clear. Gradually Ōkubo of Satsuma and others responded, and we finally were able to accomplish the "return of lands and people." But people saw me as the author of this, controversies arose, and not a few argued that I should be assassinated. Many from Chōshū, too, vilified me, and even among my comrades there were many disputations.[22]

But this entry is self-serving. "Imperial rule," as it emerged in 1868, did not require that the domains be abolished. Kido had little patience with Satsuma conservatives. He may have made the leap from domain official to court official more speedily than most. But even then, if we look at his letters and diary during the 1868-1871 period, it is quite clear that he only gradually progressed toward his 1871 position.

Early on, Kido wrote of his attachment to Chōshū. Then little by little he began to change. By October 1868, he wrote of difficulties with those in Chōshū who did not understand what the court government was trying to do. Toward the end of the year, he had become mildly critical of the domains, writing: "Each [domain] wants to make its own mountain higher," when what is needed is for all to line up in a Mount Fuji–like unity. These sentiments were accompanied by sketches of two bonsai, one with tiny jagged peaks and the other with the domains aligned shoulder to shoulder to form a single volcanic cone.[23] A few months later, Kido wrote to Ōmura expressing some bitterness:

> The domains talk only of rewards for service; they are more arrogant than in the days of the *bakufu*. In proportion to their strength, they raise their selfish demands at the court. They speak noisily of their duty to the court, but for most it ends just as talk. Looking at the overall situation, I see no signs of behavior appropriate to supporting the imperial country for ten thousand generations; instead they have fallen into a pattern of pursuing only their own self-interest: they look for wrong in others, they are jealous of ability in others, they become angry at the faults of others. It is sometimes said that the Japanese are narrow by nature, but I do not think it is this alone; it is also the result of the decay of moral principles [*daidō*].[24]

It was also at this time that Kido explicitly described the domains as the enemies of the court: "We are surrounded on four sides by many little

[22] Tsumaki Chūta, ed., *Kido Takayoshi nikki*, vol. 3 (Tokyo: Nihon shiseki kyōkai, 1933), pp. 65-66.

[23] Tsumaki Chūta, ed., *Kido Takayoshi monjo*, vol. 3 (Tokyo: Nihon shiseki kyōkai, 1930), pp. 174-175.

[24] Ibid., pp. 231-232.

bakufu."[25] By the early summer of 1869, in another letter to Ōmura, he wrote despairingly: "If only the court had two or three domains as loyal to it as Aizu was to the *bakufu*."[26] Kido's views on policy, then, were not prefabricated during the years of the Restoration movement, but slowly evolved in response to post-Restoration circumstances.

The multiplicity of models, the openness of options, and the might of their military gave the Meiji leaders an unusual awareness of freedom. They knew that it was up to them to chart Japan's future course. In 1869 Shibusawa felt frustrated and wanted to quit the Finance Ministry, but Ōkuma persuaded him to remain. Ōkuma's words reflect the Japanese style of administration and contain as well a bit of theater and a bit, perhaps, of blasphemy, but they also convey his special sense of mission and freedom:

> Ōkuma listened silently as I spoke. When I stopped speaking, he suddenly asked whether I knew the words: "O myriad gods, aid me according to your divine plan." I was taken aback at the eccentricity of the question, but replied that I knew them—they were the words of a Shinto prayer. I waited to see what he would say next. Drawing closer to me, he said: "In Japan at present the *bakufu* has been overthrown and imperial government restored. But that alone does not mean that our obligation has been discharged. Our duty [now] is to advance further and build a new Japan. For this reason [I say that] those who are participating in the planning of the new government are the myriad gods. The gods have gathered together and are now in the midst of discussing how to proceed in building the new Japan. It is not only you who does not know where to start. No one does. The discussion begins now. The most urgent task is to seek men of wisdom and talent and appoint them to office. . . . Since you were selected deliberately as one of these myriad gods to perform this great work, please exert yourself to the utmost."[27]

[25] Albert M. Craig, "Kido Kōin and Ōkubo Toshimichi: A Psychohistorical Analysis," in Albert M. Craig and Donald H. Shively, eds., *Personality in Japanese History* (Berkeley: University of California Press, 1970), p. 297.

[26] Tsumaki, *Kido Takayoshi monjo*, vol. 3, p. 349.

[27] *Shibusawa Eiichi denki shiryō*, vol. 2 (Tokyo: Shibusawa Eiichi denki shiryō kankōkai, 1955), p. 239.

CHAPTER 3

THE RULING CLASS

BY MARIUS B. JANSEN

The Tokugawa-Meiji transition transformed the complex social strata established in the sixteenth and seventeenth centuries into a simplified and rationalized social order suitable for the modern capitalist state that would emerge in the twentieth century. It was a transformation made under pressure—in the perception that foreign danger required more effective management of human and material resources—and it was accompanied by a good deal of uncertainty and violence. Most discussions have stressed the speed, relative ease, and "success" of the program that was pursued, and they have tended to neglect the strains that accompanied it. Emphasis on speed risks the assumption that there was a settled blueprint for action; emphasis on success overlooks the elements of irrationality that survived with the creation of a new aristocracy. The Meiji changes resulted in a social order less encumbered by ascriptive patterns of class than any that Japan had ever known, and vindictive measures directed against the old elite were remarkably absent. Yet, although those changes greatly simplified privilege, they also led to new forms of privilege that lasted until the reforms which followed World War II.

PERIODIZATION

The crisis brought by Perry politicized literate society. President Fillmore's letter to the shogun was followed by shogunal letters to the daimyo requesting advice; and the daimyo in turn sought the counsel of their advisers and administrators. Within four years the court, which had first warned the *bakufu* to be careful about coastal defense in 1846, was instructing the shogun to consult daimyo opinion more carefully. Knowledge of the court's displeasure with the treaty negotiated by Harris in

1858 led to the Ansei purge of dissidents, and that violence brought counterviolence against the *bakufu*'s first minister, Ii Naosuke, in 1860. The foreign crisis proved damaging to the legitimacy of the shogun as "barbarian-subduing commander." As his inability to subdue the foreigners became clear, lower-ranking samurai—acting with the knowledge of their superiors or deserting their posts to join terrorist bands outside the boundaries of their domains—began to fashion new criteria for legitimacy and loyalty. The rigid standards of loyalty that had been maintained throughout centuries of a closed political order now began to give way. Samurai indiscipline remained a problem for the successor Meiji government, which ordered the freewheeling activists to return to their authorities after the proclamation of Restoration.[1] The problem would not be fully solved until the new regime prevailed in the great samurai revolt, the Satsuma Rebellion of 1877.

The politicization that weakened the lord-vassal bonds within the samurai ranks extended to other classes, as well. Many village headmen and rural samurai had grown impatient about their subordination to the upper samurai of the castle town, and numerous Restoration activists sprang from these ranks. As Tokugawa rule gave way to a new "imperial" government, still staffed by samurai, the rhetoric of loyalism and of "people's rights" came to take on new meaning in opposition to the new government. By the end of the 1880s, the terminus of this chapter, institutions of local government tapped the abilities of local leaders; prefectural assemblies prepared the way for a national legislature, and in 1889 the Meiji Constitution ushered in a cautious constitutionalism that set the course of political development until Japan's defeat in 1945.

The period under discussion was thus one of redefinition and, in some measure, devolution that had its beginnings in the 1860s. In addition to the devolution of power and politicization downward, this period saw "lateral" politicization of an elite that had been denied influence by the Tokugawa settlement. Tokugawa house rules and tradition had kept collaterals (*shimpan*) and even branch houses (*gosanke*) locked off from central government decisions, which were the preserve of the principal hereditary vassals (*fudai* daimyo). So too with the great "outside" (*tozama*) daimyo of the southwest and northeast, who had great honor but little role. In a functional sense these daimyo were, as Conrad Totman has put it,[2] lower samurai. The politics of the 1860s also included efforts to bring such forces to the center in a series of schemes collectively known

[1] Haga Noboru, *Bakumatsu shishi no seikatsu* (Tokyo: Yuzankaku, 1982), p. 38.

[2] Conrad Totman, *The Collapse of the Tokugawa Bakufu* (Honolulu: University Press of Hawaii, 1980), pp. xvi-xvii.

as *kōbu-gattai*. None of these was successful, but together they destroyed the monopoly that Tokugawa traditionalists held on high office, with the result that the shogunate itself came to be held by Hitotsubashi Keiki (Yoshinobu), a son of the branch-house daimyo of Mito. The daimyo involved in this move tried to assert themselves in collusion with court nobles who were even more removed from political influence. These efforts, too, proved unsuccessful in the 1860s, but they had the effect of politicizing the court, dividing it, and drawing from it figures who, like Iwakura and Sanjō, would prove mainstays of the Meiji government.

As the political crisis deepened, men of modest rank found it possible to rise in influence. In Tosa a middle-ranking samurai like Gotō Shōjirō rose to *karō* status, and late Tokugawa reforms were dominated by minor daimyo and *hatamoto*. All this was accompanied by agreement that the times required "men of ability." At the end of the decade, criticism of entrenched privilege could go as far as Sakamoto Ryōma's advocacy of the substitution of elections for appointment within feudal ranks; he and others spoke with scorn about pampered feudal aristocrats who "do not feel the winter's wind and neither know nor care if people are dying of starvation and cold."[3]

No part of late Tokugawa politics was more striking than the growth of respect for court and sovereign. This shift, too, was inextricably related to perceptions of danger from abroad, although it can be granted that the re-emergence of the sovereign in late Tokugawa times would have been impossible without a base in legitimacy and aura that was far advanced by the time the foreign danger actually appeared.[4] But the court's authority and assertiveness increased with the reality of that danger, for it gave point and immediacy to the philosophical underpinnings of anti-Tokugawa and antiforeign thought. Gradually Kyoto came to replace Edo as the center of national politics; not once did the last shogun, during his brief incumbency, feel able to leave the Kyoto-Osaka area for Edo.

The order Japan achieved in the 1880s, at the other end of this period, owed much to the talismanic role of emperor and court. By 1890, the parliament had been established; a representative system selected its lower house, while the upper house was drawn from the newly established aristocracy. A period of "absolutism," essentially rule by fiat in the name of the imperial totem, had prepared the way for a "capitalist" Japan.

[3] Marius B. Jansen, *Sakamoto Ryōma and the Meiji Restoration* (Princeton: Princeton University Press, 1961), p. 340.

[4] Nagahara Keiji, "Zenkindai no tennō," *Rekishigaku kenkyū*, no. 467 (April 1979), and Bitō Masahide, "Sonnō-jōi shisō," in *Iwanami kōza Nihon rekishi*, vol. 13 (Tokyo: Iwanami shoten, 1977).

"Antiquity," in the form of the ancient Council of State (Dajōkan) that had been reinstituted in 1868, was replaced by the "modernity" of the cabinet system of 1885. An era of investigation and experimentation, which began with the first mission to the West in 1860, to ratify the Harris Treaty, and continued through the ever larger "learning missions" that followed, came to an end with the promulgation of imperial orthodoxy in politics and education in 1890. These decades had important connotations for status, privilege, and class. The ideal of "One Sovereign, Ten Thousand Subjects" had evened out the multiple hierarchies of Tokugawa days.

The Tokugawa Elite

The Tokugawa structure of political privilege was one of great complexity. Legitimacy lay with the court, where the sovereign linked the present with the semihistorical past and where a hereditary aristocracy traced its roots almost as far back. Matters of governance, however, were the preserve of the shogun, who, as supreme hegemon and head of the military houses, delegated responsibility to his vassals. Those vassals, the 260-some feudal lords, were for the most part symbols of an authority that was increasingly more abstract and distant, and they let their samurai retainers carry out the administrative duties. No one below the sovereign held authority by anything approximating personal right. Samurai administrators could be replaced at a daimyo's whim, and most daimyo at the shogun's displeasure; the exact nature of the shogun's authority posed a problem that occupied the best political minds of the eighteenth century. Was the "ruling class," then, made up of the nonfunctioning *tennō* and his nobles, or of the warrior status group that had become separated from its lands and prerogatives during the early Tokugawa years? These ambiguities probably made it somewhat easier to dispose of much of this structure in the 1870s.

Japan's elite system contained two distinct hierarchies, those of court and camp. The Kyoto "court" consisted of the nobles (*kuge*) who surrounded the sovereign (*tennō*). In the Japanese context it is difficult to think of either without the other, though in the abstract there is no reason why a modern state could not have kept the sovereign while scuttling the nobility. Postwar Japan was forced to do exactly that.

Kuge families numbered 137; in Restoration times the addition of quasi- and collateral branches brought the number to 148. This large group, its residences clustered around the sovereign's palace, was subdivided into three major rankings of prestige and income.

The top rank, *sekke*, was made up of the Konoe, Kujō, Ichijō, Nijō, and Takatsukasa families. Heads of these five houses qualified for appointment as "chancellor" (*kampaku*) and "regent" (*sesshō*) in the classical bureaucratic structure. They were the wealthiest of the nobles, drawing their support from lands producing between 1,500 and 2,860 *koku* of rice. Their daughters were often selected as imperial consorts, and most of the other noble houses were attached to them in some sort of filiation. The *sekke* were the Kyoto establishment. They had worked with shogunal ministers for centuries, and in the politics of the 1860s they tended to be cautious and side with their Tokugawa counterparts. The next group was made up of nine families, designated as *seika*, followed by three more set apart as *daijin*. Income and honor dwindled rapidly: *seika* held income from lands rated at 300 to 700 *koku*; *daijin* still less, though they too qualified for ministerial posts in the mummified bureaucratic structure that had survived from Heian times. Below these strata were three lower ranks, many without "income lands" of their own and supported from the land set aside for the throne by the Tokugawa.[5]

This structure, even more than the most prestigious groups of warrior families, was rigid and closed. Of the 137 major houses, Webb points out, 128 belonged to or claimed descent from five medieval lineages, 96 of them from the Fujiwara. With stratification came the rather mechanical assignment of rank and office. But since the offices were honorary and the ritual of court life could not fill the time of so large a group, restricted income and a secluded social role made for a life concentrated on petty concerns. Income was often supplemented by house specialties (*kagyō*) of teaching, and licensing others to teach, the cultivated arts. *Kuge* sons were important in the Buddhist hierarchy, and central to *monzeki* temples having court connections. Court life, however, did not provide much preparation for practical politics, and Restoration-period daimyo often sneered at the impracticality and inexperience of the "long sleeves" (*nagasode*), probably with some justification. *Kuge* participation in late Tokugawa politics was for the most part restricted to a few nobles, such as Iwakura Tomomi and Sanjō Sanetomi, of less than top rank, although Restoration activists did manage from time to time to involve others in the politics of violence.

The sixteenth-century unifiers had faced the problem of utilizing the court's prestige without risking its meddling in politics. Nobunaga, Hideyoshi, and Ieyasu began by using imperial rank and prestige, went on to

[5] Herschel Webb, *The Japanese Imperial Institution in the Tokugawa Period* (New York: Columbia University Press, 1968), p. 90ff., discusses the *kuge* stratification.

forbid court interference with the military houses, and ended by resigning their court offices and transferring them to their intended successors.[6] Ieyasu, the only unifier with time to complete his plans, betrothed his granddaughter Kazuko to the sovereign Go Mizunoo when she was only seven; as a result Hidetada, the second shogun, was father-in-law to the *tennō* and grandfather of the empress Meisho. But this was temporary convenience and did not become a pattern. Thereafter, the two lines stayed clear of each other until the shogunate, needing support and solidarity, arranged for the marriage of Kazu no Miya to the young shogun Iemochi in 1860. Attempts to use this lady as a bridge to Kyoto at the end of the shogunate proved fruitless.

The complexity of the court and *kuge* pattern was outdone by that of the military houses. The Tokugawa unification had been brought about by leagues of daimyo over whom the shogun, though hegemon, was not absolute. Within the Tokugawa ranks, family tradition and loyalty were reflected in distinctions between branch houses (*gosanke, gosankyō*), collaterals (*shimpan*), and hereditary vassals (*fudai*); the great outside houses (*tozama*), who submitted after Sekigahara and Osaka, controlled large domains. The vast majority of feudal lords, however, held petty domains that kept them near the 10,000-*koku* threshold of daimyo status. The seating in the Edo ceremonial halls, when resident lords paid homage to the shogun, reflected the correlation of power, prestige, and status. Lords of provinces and lords of quasi-provincial rank were followed by lords of castles and lords of quasi-castle rank, and their immense estates at the capital showed their wealth. But there was also an inverse correlation of regional power with access to office in the central Tokugawa councils, which were staffed by house vassals. As Totman has put it, "the greatest daimyo were not permitted to participate in bakufu decision-making regardless of whether the great lord were himself a related (*shimpan*) daimyo . . . or an outside (*tozama*) daimyo," and as a result the most powerful and prestigious barons were simultaneously functionally disenfranchised.[7] This arrangement was not challenged until the Bunkyū reforms of 1862, and the changes made at that time proved disastrous for shogunal primacy and feudal discipline.

The few hundred families discussed so far were symbols more than they were wielders of authority, for administration was carried out by samurai retainers of the daimyo. Here, too, rank and status had no necessary correlation with well-being, since their meaning lay within the

[6] Asao Naohiro, "Shogun and Tenno" (trans. M.B. Jansen), in J.W. Hall, Nagahara Keiji, and K. Yamamura, eds., *Japan before Tokugawa* (Princeton: Princeton University Press, 1982).

[7] Totman, *The Collapse*, pp. xvi-xvii.

context of the domain and its resources. Many a great lord's vassal enjoyed income and standing superior to that of a petty *fudai* daimyo, while that daimyo's vassal could know genuine poverty. Watanabe Kazan, a senior official of the 13,000-*koku* Tawara domain, eased his poverty by selling his paintings. Yet that same artist-official, because Tawara was a Tokugawa house, exerted influence on national affairs greater than that of a *tozama* vassal with many times his income.

Striking as these inequities could be, they were eclipsed by those within domains, where distinctions between "upper" and "lower," or *shi* and *sotsu*, were so great that they put the very notion of a "ruling class" in question. Sendai had thirty-four ranks, Yamaguchi fifty-nine, and Fukuzawa's memoirs of Nakatsu speak of "one hundred." In *Kyūhanjō* (1877) Fukuzawa's emphasis was on the unbridgeable gulf between upper and lower samurai. There had been, he wrote, a few cases in which men had crossed the barrier of income, status, and culture that separated the two, but probably "not more than four or five during the whole period of 250 years. A lower samurai might therefore aspire to promotion within his own class, but he would no more hope to enter the ranks of the upper samurai than would a four-legged beast hope to fly like a bird." In Nakatsu, men of lower rank had to prostrate themselves before those of higher rank, and even a casual encounter on the road would involve removal of footgear and prostration in the dust. "The lower samurai were thus very ill-versed in literature and other high forms of learning, and not unnaturally came to have the bearing and deportment of humble workmen," while their superiors, "their manners . . . naturally elegant and aristocratic . . . could be considered most cultured and refined gentlemen." By the nineteenth century, Fukuzawa went on, there was no little amount of bad feeling between the two groups. In 1863 there had been a plot to murder the chief minister. Had this come a century earlier, "the culprits would certainly have been immediately arrested. But as it was, the spirit of the times made it impossible that they should be apprehended, [and] public opinion was eventually appeased by the temporising measure of dismissing the Chief Minister."[8]

The irrationality of this elite system was so obvious as to be visible to anyone concerned about developing national strength; but it was the upper reaches of the system, rather than the whole structure, that usually

[8] *Kyūhanjō* has been translated by Carmen Blacker in *Monumenta Nipponica*, vol. 13 (1958). It forms the basis of numerous discussions of the samurai rank system. Professor Shunsaku Nishikawa, however, adds a note of caution, suggesting that Fukuzawa was so impressed by these unbridgeable distinctions precisely because he had crossed them by marrying an upper-rank samurai's daughter and may, as a result, have exaggerated them. (Personal communication.)

came in for criticism. Advocacy of a search for "men of ability" became code language for ousting the highborn few from their sinecures; "one ruler over all" telegraphed the importance of eliminating the crazy quilt of domain separateness and class privilege; and "a single decision center" meant trimming the power of the multiple hierarchies in order to streamline decisions and focus resources. Nineteenth-century Japan witnessed steps toward a rationalization of the extremes of the system. The Kansei reforms of the 1790s brought increased educational opportunities for non-samurai and for lower samurai in some *han* schools. The military crisis of the post-Perry years brought experimentation with mixed units that included commoners as well as samurai; and at the end of Tokugawa rule, *bakufu* administrators were working toward a money tax on vassals that was to be used to pay commoner soldiers. Without the sweeping centralization measures of the Meiji government, however, it would surely have been difficult to implement such reforms on more than a piecemeal basis.

Despite the complexity of this elite structure, there was one important thing that characterized all its elements and that is essential to an understanding of the speed with which the system was changed. None of the elite had a proprietary interest in land. It might be said of the sovereign that the entire realm was his, but that amounted to saying that no given part was more his than any other part. The court had delegated rule to the shogun, but the shogun allocated income lands to the court and the nobles. Everyone was prepared to admit that the land and its inhabitants were not his own. "As for sovereignty," agreed the last shogun, in a communication to foreign representatives at the height of his distress with the new Meiji government, "it lies with the Mikado."[9] And the southwestern daimyo would soon take the lead in returning their registers to the throne, with the explanation that "the land where we the undersigned dwell is the Sovereign's land; the people over whom we rule are his people. Why should we privately own them?"[10] It was universally agreed that the daimyo held land as stewards and not as owners. As for ordinary samurai, few had rural roots; most had experienced a change from fief to stipend as early as the seventeenth century.[11] Even where samurai still had fiefs, they held them as stewards for their lords. This constituted an immense difference between Japan and Europe, where the

[9] Quoted by U.S. Minister van Valkenburgh, in M.B. Jansen, "Japan Looks Back," *Foreign Affairs*, vol. 47, no. 1 (1968).

[10] Quoted in W.G. Beasley, *The Meiji Restoration* (Stanford: Stanford University Press, 1972), p. 331.

[11] In 1690-1691 "only about one-sixth of the domains still maintained the custom by which samurai held fiefs in land." Ibid., p. 21.

landed classes were very sure of what was their own. As a result of that difference, concludes a recent comparison of Japan and Germany, a process that required several centuries in Prussia could take place in Japan in little more than a decade. None of the former daimyo emerged as major landholders in the Meiji records; and when they were incorporated into a new nobility, the most frequent argument against this was that they did not represent a true landed interest.[12]

The Restoration

The first four years of the Meiji government, 1868-1871, constitute a period of improvisation and hesitation that had important consequences for the status structure. Japan was in a remarkably "open" situation; its leaders were cautious and uncertain, and they did their best to avoid any confrontation that might antagonize or alarm the privileged strata. Pronouncements were worded with deliberate ambiguity, and they were intended to reassure. Thus the Charter Oath of April 1868 stressed that "all classes, high and low" would be able to achieve their "just aspirations," but nothing was said about the makeup or retention of such classes. There were vague statements about following the norms of justice; "council chambers" would be established, but nothing was said about how they would be made up. The regime was distancing itself from the "monopolist" and "selfish" practices for which it had reproached its predecessor. But all statements had room for the perpetuation of the early-modern elite structure. Any suggestion of radical change received short shrift. Notice boards were repainted to tell the commoners to go about their business as before. Activists were thanked for their contributions and told to return to their domain authorities, and enthusiasts who had waged psychological warfare with sweeping promises of reduced or canceled taxes were dismissed and sometimes punished harshly.[13]

The Tokugawa and holdout houses in the northeast had to be punished for their resistance: the principal Tokugawa figures were ordered into retirement, the last shogun was ordered into Shizuoka, and all Matsudaira houses were ordered to revert to their original names. Financial assess-

[12] Suzuki Seiko, "Kazokusei o meguru jakkan no mondai," *Nihon shi kenkyū*, no. 3 (1980), p. 37, provides a thoughtful comparison between the Prussian and Meiji systems and emphasizes landholding as a critical difference.

[13] Haga, *Bakumatsu*, p. 41. Michio Umegaki, "After the Restoration: The Beginning of Japan's Modern State" (MS, p. 168), relates the scorn with which Sagara Sōzō, and then Takezawa Kunimitsu, were fired: "ignorant of the very art of governing society, you simply offered petty charity in order to please the local people."

ments were levied against forty-one domains that had been guilty of assisting rebellion, some of them so severe that the domains were unable to pay despite efforts by their retainers to cooperate by selling their possessions and even their swords.[14] The domain of Aizu—which had been singled out for particularly harsh military treatment with the siege of Wakamatsu—was virtually destroyed through division, its retainer corps scattered. Matsudaira Katamori, the "Protector of Kyoto," who had given Restoration leaders so much trouble, was trusted with "no more responsible office for the rest of his life than chief priest of the Tokugawa shrines at Nikko."[15]

Yet these same steps can be seen as moderate. The houses were not extinguished, but their heads replaced. Most sixteenth-century losers had met worse fates. Indeed, one remarkable thing about the Boshin War is that the daimyo emerged unscathed; it was retainers who atoned through suicide. At Wakamatsu the "Tiger Band" of adolescent samurai sacrificed themselves to a man when they saw the flames of their castle, not realizing that it had been torched on the command of their superiors, but Katamori survived to put on priestly robes. Sengoku daimyo had done things differently.

The new government's decision to retain most shogunal territory was of the greatest significance. That territory might have been parceled out to the Restoration fiefs; but, by retaining it, the government guaranteed that the new "imperial" patterns would become a model for the country, as the shogunal lands had been for earlier centuries.

Late in 1868, daimyo were ordered to make their administrations uniform. Domain administrative matters and budgets were to be kept separate from those of the daimyo house. Uniform terminology was to be adopted for senior posts, which were to be filled by men selected for ability rather than for rank only, and each domain was to assign one official to a consultative assembly at the capital. The determination to rationalize patterns of local administration was unmistakable.

In 1869 the daimyo of Satsuma, Chōshū, Tosa, and Saga—the Restoration centers—petitioned the court to accept the return of their registers. Accepting this, the court appointed the former daimyo as governors, set aside one-tenth of their former income for their use, and ordered further standardization of administrative methods. "Governors" needed rank, so daimyo and *kuge* were now declared *kazoku* and given special legal status. Another relic of the Tokugawa structure ended when the

[14] Fukuchi Shigetaka, *Shizoku to shizoku isshiki* (Tokyo: Shunjūsha, 1956), pp. 61-64.

[15] Harold Bolitho, "Aizu, 1853-1868," in *Proceedings* of the British Association for Japanese Studies, vol. 2 (London: 1977).

daimyo were ordered to withdraw those vassals, families, and assets which remained in Edo-Tokyo to their home provinces. All were invited to submit proposals for further reform to the Tokyo assembly. Meanwhile, significant portents of future decisions could be seen in developments throughout the southwestern domains. In Satsuma, samurai stipends were reduced sharply; in Saga, announcements of office for "men of ability" were made; in Chōshū, the official structure was revised, stipends were lowered, status subdivisions within the samurai class were simplified, and samurai were permitted to enter agriculture or commerce. And in Tosa, sweeping reforms anticipating the abolition of hereditary status divisions were announced. In the autumn of 1870 the central government ordered reforms in domain government that included abolition of the numerous categories of *han* in favor of a simple division into "big," "middle," or "small," according to rice yield.

From this it was only a step to the abolition of the domains altogether, and they were integrated into prefectures in 1871. Now the central government found itself responsible for the identification and support of the former privileged class. The complex structure of samurai military rank was changed: middle-level and higher samurai were declared *shizoku*; those below, *sotsuzoku*. A year later, any officials who did not already qualify were incorporated into the *shizoku* category. Subsequently the rank of *sotsuzoku* was abolished; hereditary members were advanced to *shizoku*, and single-generation members merged with commoners (*heimin*). It is not difficult to imagine the difficulties of definition that accompanied this process of regulation from the center. The 1871 registration law (*kosekihō*) made it a matter of economic survival for thousands. Were standards more stringent in "unfriendly" areas of northeastern Japan than in the Restoration centers of the southwest? Were samurai service records sufficient for this?

Whatever the case, the new government had made some important decisions. The bottom layer of the military status group, into which entrance and exit had long been possible and in which well-being was lowest, had been cast off to find its way with the commoners. Commoners in turn had been allowed to take surnames (1870) as well as ride horses (1871), and were included in the registration legislation system established in 1871. Upon the abolition of the domains in the fall of 1871, commoners were also allowed to travel freely. One month later (tenth month, 1871) intermarriage between status groups was permitted; farmers were free to cultivate crops of their choice; and *eta* and *hinin*, the subcaste status categories, were raised to commoner status.[16] At the

[16] Among many surveys, Fukuchi, *Shizoku*, stands out for its clarity.

higher levels of social status, daimyo and *kuge* had been merged into the category of *kazoku*, and sword-bearing, office-worthy samurai retained as *shizoku*. The central government now paid their stipends.

From Stipends to Bonds

The disestablishment of the samurai class has received close attention from historians, and probably presents the fewest problems. The documentary record is particularly full; for, anxious about the loyalty of the former administrative class, the government conducted extensive surveys to guide it in measures of aid and relief as counters to samurai opposition.[17] H.D. Harootunian has drawn on Japanese scholarship for two articles that provide a succinct summary of the process of disestablishment,[18] and W.G. Beasley concludes his study of the Restoration with a judicious evaluation of the principal steps in that disestablishment.[19]

The phenomenon of a samurai-dominated government setting about on the ruin of fellow samurai nevertheless remains a problem full of interest for the historian. It is true that many, perhaps most, of the Meiji leaders had known much frustration as middle or lower samurai in years when the power of decision lay with their superiors, but there is no intrinsic reason why promotion to superior status might not have made them think better of the status system. They knew just how shadowy claims to samurai status could be at the lower levels, where entrance and exit were frequent, and one could expect them to be careful about definitions of status. Yet, even that would not suffice to explain the decision that the samurai could not be maintained as a status group.

In explaining that decision, one should probably put a good deal of weight on the military experience of the 1860s. Samurai pride went poorly with the routine and discipline necessary for modern armed forces; peasant recruits had been obedient and shown endurance, and were more easily led, than samurai. These considerations seem to have been the basis for the *bakufu*'s drift toward commoner-soldiers. Perhaps international examples counted for much, particularly knowledge of how ordinary

[17] *Meiji zenki zaisei keizai shiryō shūsei*, vol. 8, contains the basic sources; Fukaya Hakuji, *Ka-shizoku chitsuroku shobun no kenkyū* (Tokyo: Yoshikawa kōbunkan, 1973), and Fukuchi, *Shizoku*, which gives particular attention to Morioka and Tokugawa domains, are excellent studies.

[18] Harry D. Harootunian, "The Economic Rehabilitation of the Samurai in the Early Meiji Period," *Journal of Asian Studies*, vol. 19, no. 4 (1960), and "The Progress of Japan and the Samurai Class, 1868-1882," *Pacific Historical Review*, vol. 28, no. 3 (1959).

[19] Beasley, *The Meiji Restoration*, pp. 379-390.

French citizens had affiliated with the national cause in the Franco-Prussian War. Itagaki would later contrast that war with the siege of Aizu, at which farmers came down from the hills to sell fruit to both sides during lulls in the fighting. The American Civil War does not seem to have made a comparable impression; late Tokugawa Japanese, who had just discovered a Washington who, as Nakaoka Shintarō put it, had raised an army to drive out the barbarians,[20] were not ready for Lincoln. It is also true that the rhetoric of late Tokugawa days, with its emphasis on "ability" rather than "birth," operated to the disadvantage of permanent status provisions. But cost was surely the most compelling argument of all.

As might be expected, it was easier (and necessary) to begin with the Tokugawa lands that had been retained by the new government. In 1870 the government divided former *bakufu* retainers into twenty-one grades (the lowest three designated *sotsu*, the others *shizoku*) with a drastically reduced scale of income; but before long rations were set without particular reference to former stipends, and within the year monetary rewards were offered those who resigned their commissions.[21]

Once the government found itself responsible for all samurai salaries, steps had to be taken to cut entitlements in order to pay for the needs of modernization. Early measures combined reductions in salary with the introduction of functional criteria. At the same time, a new system of uniform designations of rank incorporated local officials into a hierarchy that included the central bureaucracy.[22]

Umegaki notes that even the Saigō caretaker government came to the conclusion, while the Iwakura mission was abroad, that samurai costs had to be cut. Yoshida Kiyonari was sent to Washington D.C. to secure agreement for proposals to cut stipends by one-third and to terminate all stipends within six years. Yoshida carried with him a personal letter from Saigō Takamori to Ōkubo Toshimichi urging that "we must not miss this opportunity"; Saigō's proposals, however, met with angry rejection by Kido and Iwakura, who thought them far too severe.[23] It would take more time to convince government leaders that there was no point in supporting men who could be doing useful work. Such stipends had always been predicated upon the samurai's inability to do anything remunerative, and Kido argued with Yoshida that "they are not the only ones to be blamed"; all Japanese shared responsibility for this state of

[20] Jansen, *Sakamoto*, p. 251.

[21] Fukuchi, *Shizoku*, p. 65. The same work, pp. 203-215, discusses the subsequent fate of Tokugawa samurai.

[22] Umegaki, "After the Restoration," p. 183.

[23] Ibid., pp. 244-245.

affairs. Even after it became clear that "all Japanese" could no longer bear such a burden, Kido was among those who advocated retention of the *shizoku* designation even though financial benefits might have to be discontinued. Office salaries, theretofore supplemental to hereditary income, began to eclipse the much-reduced hereditary stipends in importance. Ability began to outdraw birth. The *shizoku/sotsu* distinction of 1869 also brought a good deal of readjustment in income, making it possible to begin to reward persons of local eminence and importance by moving them up to *shizoku* status once the *sotsu* distinction was given up. In Tosa, for instance, many *sotsu* who had been *gōshi* and *shōya* found themselves promoted to *shizoku*. In 1871 *shizoku* were permitted to enter agriculture, commerce, or industry without sacrificing their status; at the same time, distinctions of dress and hair were abolished.

Providing stipends, at any level, for a half million samurai, proved onerous. Early in 1872, Finance Ministry officials proposed seeking a foreign loan to apply against greatly reduced stipends, the remainder to be covered by transferable bonds. Even a reform bureaucrat like Kido thought this far too drastic and grossly unfair. Once the Iwakura mission had returned from Europe (1873), and the government had decided against military action in Korea, however, the discussion resumed, this time with proposals for taxing stipends. Later in 1873, this idea was paired with an option to exchange stipends for cash, at an amount to be determined by capitalizing the stipend at six years' worth for most samurai; one-generation stipends were to be capitalized at four years. A graduated tax on stipends was installed.

In 1874, optional commutation was encouraged for large stipends; the following year all stipends were converted to cash, and in 1876 the government decreed compulsory commutation of remaining stipends. Interest-bearing bonds (at 5 percent) were now issued against large stipends, which were capitalized at between five and seven and one-half years' income; lower incomes were capitalized at fourteen years' income, at 7 percent interest. As a result, notes Beasley, the government's samurai burden was cut by 30 percent, and a solution of what remained was in sight.[24]

As was to be expected, these years marked the high point of samurai discontent in the southwestern fiefs, where expectations had been highest. Violence culminated in the Satsuma Rebellion. Nevertheless, generations of tutelage in scorn for money, advantage, and profit kept samurai from expressing their grievances in terms of concern for income. There was indignation against the 1876 ban on swords, outrage over the failure to

[24] Beasley, *The Meiji Restoration*, p. 389.

avenge insults from Korea, and a sense of betrayal at the rapid course of change along Western lines, but little explicit complaint about livelihood and income. *Shizoku* consciousness, bounded by domain and lord, also kept the revolts from becoming national or even regional. "We are Tosa men," was Hayashi Yūzō's response to suggestions that he and his fellow malcontents join Saigō.[25]

Within domains, furthermore, rank consciousness lived on. In 1877, after Saigō's failure had shown that the past was dead, Fukuzawa concluded his reminiscences of Nakatsu by saying that the "delusion of birth and lineage has been wiped out and the upper samurai no longer flaunt their rank before the lower samurai. . . . [T]hey know that today such arrogance will only invite harm and ridicule." But he was too honest to leave it there, and went on to admit that "upper samurai . . . tend to regard their old feudal status as the permanent, fixed standard, and the present system of equal rights as only a passing incident. They tend to look on the lower samurai rather as though they had lent them something." At meetings, he noted, seats were still "arranged in the order of the old scale of stipends and social rank"; upper and lower samurai of Nakatsu did not intermarry, for "upper samurai . . . regard such marriages with secret disgust. Neither have the lower samurai any wish for such marriages. On the contrary, they flatly reject them, saying that anyone brought up in an upper-samurai family, whether man or woman is of no use at all in practical life, and that marriage with such a person would mean an end of any future hopes of making a living."[26]

The speed of these changes was so great that one's only surprise is that they did not produce more turbulence. Thousands must have felt cheated. Ardath Burks quotes an Okayama edict of 1871, at the beginning of the process: "some say that the lower-salaried shizoku will be ordered to return to farms or go into business. Some are annoyed, but we will never take such steps."[27] What were two-sworded men to do when their government betrayed them so blandly? Had the *shizoku* possessed land and followers, as many did in Satsuma, it could well have been more difficult for the government.

From *Kazoku* to Peers

Almost none of the Meiji leaders seem to have doubted the need to retain a special elite. No doubt the use of the *tennō* dictated this; a ruling family

[25] Fukuchi, *Shizoku*, p. 111ff., discusses the problem of samurai revolts and separatism.

[26] *Kyūhanjō* (fn. 8, above).

[27] Ardath Burks, "Administrative Transition from *Han* to *Ken*: The Example of Okayama," *Far Eastern Quarterly*, vol. 6, no. 3 (May 1956).

presumed the presence of princes, and princes required a supporting cast. Thus, resurrection of the court brought with it status for the *kuge* and, with them, for the daimyo. The need for consensus and a demonstration of gratitude to the former lords argued for such a social policy. So did international example. Almost all the Western countries known to the Meiji leaders had peerages. Aoki Shūzō, who was studying in Berlin when the Iwakura mission reached that city, argued the importance of a peerage with Kido.[28] But there were problems, as well. European peerages represented landed classes. Japan's could not, but the government still felt the need for a buffer against political radicalism. As the Movement for People's Rights rose in popularity in the 1880s, it became clear to government leaders that a parliamentary upper house made up exclusively from *kuge* and daimyo would be a poor match for a lower house dominated by more politically conscious *shizoku*, and with that realization came the conclusion that the old aristocracy would have to be augmented by recruits from below. The result of all this, the Meiji peerage, was a curious structure that incorporated the old nine-grade system of court ranks among the *kuge*, secured social prestige for former daimyo, and made provision for outstanding leaders among the *shizoku* coalition that ran the government. The old court grades (of Chinese origin) survived alongside the new patents of nobility, and they outweighed those titles in social precedence. To these hereditary groups the House of Peers added lifetime places for imperial appointees, including scholars, honored for exceptional national service; seven-year elective terms for large taxpayers chosen, as were peers, from among their own numbers; and, later, members elected from within the Imperial Academy.

The edicts that abolished the title of shogun in 1868 had also brought an end to those of *kampaku* and *sesshō* at court, and this forecast a restructuring of the *kuge*. When the daimyo surrendered their registers to the court in 1869, they were merged with the old aristocracy in a new privileged status termed *kizoku*. Two years later, with the abolition of domains, the term was changed to *kazoku*, a word previously reserved for part of the old nobility. With the daimyo initially appointed as governors of their domains, and the entire group included in the new registration law, free choice of occupation seemed possible. A fraction of former *kokudaka* income was reserved for each house, but in the 1876 commutation of pensions this was converted to money. With the abolition of domains, the daimyo were ordered to take up residence in Tokyo; the *kuge* were first encouraged and then instructed to follow suit, and by 1877 the nobles, old and new, were equally on the government's rolls in Tokyo. To ensure compliance, most of the Kyoto residences were pulled

[28] Suzuki, "Kazokusei," p. 28.

down, and the old *kuge* were the subject of imperial pronouncements urging them to cooperate in modernization and even to study abroad. Some forty of them had already done so.

In 1874, agitation for an elective assembly began, and in the following years problems of internal order made it natural to consider ways in which the *kazoku* might serve the national purpose. Several informal groups that had been formed were used as the nucleus of a new structure, the Kazoku Kaikan, which was set up in 1874 under the leadership of Iwakura and Sanjō. Until its functions were taken over by the Peers' Division of the Imperial Household Ministry, set up in 1882, this organization ordered the internal affairs of the nobility. They were divided into twelve, then into six, ranks. With structure came control. Members of the aristocracy were required to secure approval for marriage. So, too, were field-grade army officers after the Takehashi Mutiny in 1879, and navy officers after 1885.[29]

For a time it remained unclear whether provision for former samurai should be made in the peerage. Kido, shortly before his death in 1876, advocated incorporating all *shizoku* into the peerage at the lowest rank. Arguing from international example and Japanese tradition, he suggested that members of this "fifth rank" be qualified for imperial bureaucratic appointments. Iwakura, too, in memoranda of 1876 and 1881, saw merit in reserving one house of parliament for former samurai, with the express purpose of rebuilding and restoring their sense of dignity and service. Within less than a decade after the issuance of bonds to former samurai, however, their economic and social status had sunk so far that such proposals were quite impractical. Only a select few, those who had served the government most faithfully, would be incorporated into the nobility, in a newly created fifth rank (*danshaku*, usually translated "baron").[30]

The story of Itō Hirobumi's progress toward final institutional incorporation of the new aristocracy is a familiar one. As he wrote Itō Myoji in 1881, "The creation of a peerage is an indispensable device for fortifying the position of the Imperial House."[31]

By the Peerage Law of July 1884, *kazoku* were supplemented by newly created peers. When the peerage was abolished after World War II, 913 houses had been so designated. The two highest ranks were entitled to hereditary seats in the House of Peers; other ranks selected representatives

[29] Iwai Tadakuma, "Seiritsuki kindai tennōsei to mibunsei," *Nihon shi kenkyū*, no. 3, 1980, pp. 10-11.

[30] Ibid., p. 14.

[31] Quoted in Donald H. Shively, "The Japanization of Middle Meiji," in D.H. Shively, ed., *Tradition and Modernization in Japanese Culture* (Princeton: Princeton University Press, 1971).

by internal vote. Utilizing conventional translations for the Japanese rank terms (which Itō reluctantly took from Chinese precedent), we may list the patents issued:[32]

Prince	11 daimyo	7 *kuge*
Marquis	24 daimyo	9 *kuge*
Count	73 daimyo	30 *kuge*
Viscount	325 daimyo	91 *kuge*
Baron	74 daimyo	0 *kuge*
	507 daimyo	*137*

On the occasion of the Peerage Law the court awarded monetary gifts by rank. Counts received 35,000 yen, viscounts 20,000, and barons 10,000. The court had earlier given merit gifts, as well. Sanjō and Iwakura received 5,000-*koku* awards; the young daimyo Yamauchi Toyonori of Tosa was granted 100,000 *ryō* after he took up residence in Tokyo as ordered in 1871.[33] Surely his counterparts from Satsuma and Chōshū did not fare worse. Special status privileges were reserved for the top branches of the new peerage; family alliances with the imperial family were limited to the top rank (the former *sekke* and *seika*, the Tokugawa and Tokugawa branch houses, and a few major daimyo families), while "newly created" aristocrats were specifically excluded. The same restrictions and opportunities prevailed for ladies-in-waiting.

The peers were enjoined to be diligent in educating themselves. As Richard Rubinger points out in Chapter 8, the Gakushūin, or Peers' School, was the first educational institution provided for by the new government. Peers' political powers, which gave them control over the upper house of the parliament and substantial control of the Imperial Household Ministry (through access to the throne), were extensive.

It is not an exaggeration to say that many Japanese saw the new aristocracy as a contradictory step in the process of modernization. Many resented, as Kita Ikki put it in the 1920s, Itō's importation of the remnants of a medieval European social structure into a modernizing Japan. The House of Peers was never popular and, from the first, posed a problem for leaders anxious for further political change. But the institution did have one unforeseen effect. It speeded the decline of samurai consciousness, which became meaningless in the face of the new privileged stratum. This is tellingly shown in the popular acclaim of Prime Minister Hara in

[32] Fukuchi, *Shizoku*, p. 313. Iwai, "Seiritsuki," gives a different total, identifying 483 former *kazoku* (including branch families) and 83 newly created peers for a total of 566, but without the details of rank shown here.

[33] *Kōchi ken shi, Kindai* (Kōchi ken, 1970), p. 4.

1918 as a "Great Commoner," although his Morioka feudal rank (*karō*) had been considerably higher than that of the new peers created by the Meiji government.

Were the peers also a major economic power? E.H. Norman, basing himself upon the work of Hirano Gitarō, saw them as a new plutocracy created by the Meiji state, and wrote of their ability to buy large tracts of government land and to invest in new industries and banks.[34] Iwai Tadakuma's examination of the evidence leads to more cautious conclusions.[35] The greatest feudal barons, he grants, became and remained very wealthy, thanks to bonds scaled to their earlier income. Maeda of Kaga, the daimyo whose holdings were second only to those of the Tokugawa shogun, received bonds worth 1,131,062 yen, which at 5 percent interest would have given him an annual income of 56,553 yen. But daimyo payments varied widely. *Kazoku* payments in bonds averaged 60,000 yen, which at 5 percent would yield a modest 3,000 yen. (One might note that foreign teachers such as William Griffis and L.L. Janes, at approximately 4,000 yen per year, were in this category.) Most *kuge* (although they had fewer retainers clustering around them) were lucky to match small daimyo in income; Sanjō and Iwakura probably received about the same as median-level daimyo. Peers were furthermore fortunate in that the government leadership considered it important to protect their finances from error or failure. Iwakura worked for the creation of the Fifteenth National Bank, which was based on the capitalized pensions of peers, and in 1881 the National Railways were established as a desirable investment for them. The Fifteenth Bank (1877), capitalized at 17,820,000 yen, had 484 investors, all *kazoku*; the next-largest bank was capitalized at 2,440,000 yen. In 1886 the Hereditary Peerage Finance Law placed peerage fortunes under the protection of the Imperial Household Ministry, thus adding a special privilege to peerage status. Many of the larger lords were also able to retain the services of their former domain financial authorities.

Daimyo and *kuge* claims to land were for the most part swept away by the new centralization, although some managed to retain upland

[34] *Japan's Emergence as a Modern State* (New York: Institute of Pacific Relations, 1946), p. 99.

[35] Iwai, "Seiritsuki," p. 16ff. See also discussion in Fukuchi, *Shizoku*, p. 311ff. The Fifteenth Bank provides a good example of the relaxation of government control and protection over time. The bank began as a *kazoku* venture under Imperial Household Ministry protection; its first officers, Mōri and Tokugawa. In 1897 the bank became a private enterprise, its shares available to nonpeer purchasers. It merged with the Kobe and Kawasaki banks in the crisis that followed World War I and, owing to bad loans to Kawasaki Shipyards and Suzuki Lines, was absorbed by the Bank of Japan in 1927. *Nihon rekishi jiten* (Tokyo: Kawade shobō, 1960), vol. 10, p. 94.

acreage. By and large, however, any land they owned they had to buy, and figures show that not one among the aristocrats was in the 1,000-*chōbu* category as a major landowner. In an 1889 list of taxpayers who reported annual incomes of 30,000 yen or more, almost one-half (twenty-six out of sixty) were former daimyo, and two were former *kuge*. Mōri Motonari of Chōshū, whose bond payment had been 1,107,755 yen, invested with particular success, standing third in the country with his income of 173,164 yen.[36]

Clearly, special payments and bonds concentrated a significant amount of capital in the hands of the aristocracy at a critical time of economic development. With access to advice and adequate capital, the nobility stood a better chance of retaining and adding to their fortunes than the former samurai, who had less to lose and lost it on their own—and very rapidly at that. Nevertheless, the aristocrats overall were by no means a new plutocracy. More than a few, finding it impossible to maintain their status, resigned their patents, which could be restored if income stood at 500 yen per year. The genteel poverty of the aristocrat was a common image, and among the new aristocrats, Itagaki Taisuke's poverty was well known.

Conclusion

What, then, became of the Tokugawa ruling class in the transition years? What sort of change was there in the makeup of the men who led Japan?

The early years of Meiji saw frequent changes in political institutions. The government began by making extensive use of the old ascriptive elite—Princes of the Blood, court nobles, and daimyo—in the highest posts. As the central government began to take shape, its samurai leaders found it possible and necessary to take formal responsibility themselves. The abolition of domains and their amalgamation into prefectures in 1871 marked a decisive turn. From the proclamation of Restoration to June 1868 the administrative structure was crowned by the so-called Three Offices, presided over by a Prince of the Blood. *Gijō*, the next most honorific post, went to eleven *kuge*, fourteen daimyo, and one Shinto priest. Below them, *sanyo* included forty-six *kuge*, five daimyo, forty-eight samurai, and another Shinto priest. In June 1868 the Seitaisho restored the ancient Council of State (Dajōkan), a structure that survived until the inauguration of the cabinet system in 1885. Daimyo and *kuge* remained visible, but their numbers declined as samurai retainers began

[36] Iwai, "Seiritsuki," p. 18ff.

to move up in the hierarchy. After 1871, virtually all the administrative bureaus were in the hands of former samurai.

The initial use of Princes of the Blood (a practice that was repeated in 1945 when the decision to end the war was communicated to field commanders) testifies to the symbolic importance of an important member of the previous elite, the youthful Mutsuhito. For commoners, samurai, and daimyo alike, it was easier to survive these shifts because of the continuity of the sovereign—better to change hierarchies than to abandon hierarchy altogether. The early Meiji years saw the emperor sent off on great tours of the country, acquainting him with his realm and his people with him, and justifying change in the name of continuity.

The growing dominance of samurai/*shizoku* in governmental positions continued into the mid-Meiji decades, although the appointment of former *shizoku* to lower ranks of the new nobility in the 1880s often makes it difficult to distinguish them from their erstwhile betters. But top bureaucrats (*chokunin*, or imperial appointees) of the Meiji period were overwhelmingly former *shizoku* or new *kizoku*. The key figures were those who were promoted to the *kizoku* peerage from *shizoku* ranks. Of the Meiji senior statesmen (*genkun* or *genrō*) all were in this category. Of the ninety-six men appointed to the Privy Council, all were or became peers, but only six had been such before 1884. In this bureaucratic musical chairs, 259 cabinet appointments (to eighty-three men) included only 12 appointments to men who were not peers, two of whom (Hoshi Tōru and Komatsubara Eitarō) were commoners. Fourteen appointments went to six men who were peers before 1884, and 233 to sixty-eight men who were or would become peers. Clearly, former *shizoku* took over the aristocracy and dominated the political process.[37]

This is made all the more evident if one notes that "new" peers dominated the House of Peers, as well. If the argument for adding new blood to the aristocracy was the need to match the vigor and acumen of the *shizoku*-dominated Lower House, then the tactic proved sound. In the first Diet, Iwai points out, 252 were to be seated: 10 Princes of the Blood, 135 peers, 61 imperial appointees, and 45 large taxpayers. But the Princes of the Blood did not attend, and high-ranking peers who were qualified for Imperial Household Ministry or Privy Council jobs resigned their seats, thus increasing the weight and importance of the new peers, the ones who were also the most interested.

Of course there is a difference between a "closed" peerage, which monopolizes high office, and an "open" peerage dominated by leaders

[37] Fukuchi, *Shizoku*, p. 310, and chart and commentary in Iwai, "Seiritsuki," pp. 15-16, 24.

who rewarded themselves and their followers with titles of rank. *Shizoku* origin, while initially required, was by no means sufficient. The Meiji political elite harbored a regional bias toward the southwestern domains that had led in the Restoration. They recruited widely in their search for support, but the first-generation leaders were drawn from Satsuma and Chōshū. This concentration provided the basis for in-group cooperation, with a high congruence of experience, values, and self-interest. Similar bonds characterized the high command of the armed services, whose leaders were generously rewarded with peerage titles after the victories over China and Russia.

A useful examination of continuity and change within the political elite has been provided by Takane Masaaki, who analyzed samples of the national leadership in the years 1860 (207 men), 1890 (202 men), 1920 (331 men), 1936 (393 men), and 1969 (445 men) against variables of inherited status, political career of the father, regional origin, and educational level.[38] Takane found little overlap at either end of his survey; only two individuals (including the emperor!) made the transition from 1860 to 1890. In two periods, however, 1890-1920 (15 men) and 1920-1936 (23 men), the continuity was considerably higher.

The 1860 elite were young (in their forties), had inherited privilege and office, and thus showed a high degree of continuity with the previous generation. The 1890 sample, however, represented the Restoration mobility; only 13 percent of its members (as opposed to 64 percent for 1860) represented such continuity. The 1920 sample maintained this same percentage of 13. For the most part, cases of continuity were represented by members drawn from the nobility; "hardly any of the sample members born into either samurai or commoner families had powerful fathers."

Predictably, the 1890 sample found the Restoration domains providing 50 percent of the former samurai and 30 percent of the entire sample. "Since the population of the four *han*-clique domains comprised only 7 percent of the total population in 1890," observes Takane, "these domains enjoyed a fourfold representation among the elite proportionate to their numbers, reflecting the strength of their *han* cliques. Further, they were concentrated in the higher bureaucratic positions and in the military elite. *Han*-clique members occupied about 50 percent of the

[38] Takane Masaaki, *Nihon no seiji eriito: kindaika no sūryō bunseki* (Tokyo: Chūō kōron, 1976), revision of a University of California–Berkeley Ph.D. diss., published in English as *The Political Elite in Japan: Continuity and Change in Modernization* (Berkeley: University of California Press, 1981). The data cited can be found on pp. 66-67, 21, 75, 85, 93, and 86 of the 1981 work. For reservations on the larger structure of Takane's argument, however, see the review by Bernard S. Silberman in the *Journal of Japanese Studies*, vol. 10, no. 1 (Winter 1984), pp. 256-258.

higher bureaucratic posts, including bureau chief and higher posts." But that dominance was of relatively brief duration; by 1920, the percentage had fallen to 13 (15 percent if new peers are included). The Tokyo area, which had dominated before 1890, regained its ascendancy by 1920 and retained it thereafter.

It is clear that *shizoku* or samurai status remained advantageous; urban life, educational opportunity, and high achievement expectations combined to make it so. Takane concluded that "ascriptive factors of feudal status influenced political status as late as 1936."[39]

Historians have long agreed that in the Meiji transformation the top elements of the old ruling class were set aside in favor of lower-ranking members of that class, who devised institutions under which they, in turn, were replaced by a meritocracy based on education. One must add that the first generation provided, through the new peerage, Privy Council, and Imperial Household Ministry, institutions that preserved for their followers special places from which they could resist further institutional change.

That said, it is necessary to remind ourselves of the radical nature of the changes in the leadership group. Under the Tokugawa institutions, the new holders of power would have remained completely without influence in national policy. The success with which the old elite was utilized, and then set aside, is what makes the Meiji transformation unusual. Some of the elements that combined to make it possible have been suggested above: the old elite lacked a landed base, and was aware of the diminishing economic viability of the Tokugawa territorial divisions; there was general fear that devolution and disorder would benefit foreign powers; the imperial symbol legitimized the new hierarchy.

The changeover was accompanied by a fair amount of violence and terror, between 1860 and 1877; but the struggle was between contenders for power, not between contenders for and holders of power. Samurai violence was reserved for other samurai, not for daimyo. At the highest level, the new regime found itself able to relate to the old elite, to reward and honor it, and even to absorb the Tokugawa house and branch families into the highest of aristocratic ranks. Finally, the samurai class was so large that it provided a very generous pool of applicants and talent. As its members were scattered throughout Meiji society, they enriched the leadership of the Movement for People's Rights, education, and the press, as well as providing the political troublemakers and assassins who dogged the modernizers' steps.

[39] Takane, *The Political Elite*, p. 61.

CHAPTER 4

FROM DOMAIN TO PREFECTURE

BY MICHIO UMEGAKI

In the late summer of 1871, the 260-odd *han* were declared abolished. William Griffis, who was in Fukui, described the reaction of samurai to this turn of events: they were stunned by what appeared to them to be a reversal of post-Restoration developments.[1] *Haihan chiken*, as historians term the event, deprived the daimyo of their powers and summoned them to Tokyo. Yamagata Aritomo would later refer to it as "a second Meiji Restoration." The domains were subjected to a series of mergers that, within a few years, reduced the number of administrative units to fifty. By the end of 1871, none but the largest of the *han* had retained any semblance of their former boundaries. As shown in Table 4.1, nine of the new prefectures comprised eight or more former domains each. The long tradition of dispersed political power under Tokugawa dominance had come to a sudden end through a single act of the new central government, although it was not, as yet, more powerful than the old one had been. *Haihan chiken* had radical consequences for the political order, and yet there was no resistance.

The Restoration government, claiming to be responsive to the "nation," next began to replace the daimyo with a system of prefectural government. The modernization of the military, the establishment of a national education system, the reform of the land tax, and many other changes examined in this book were all linked to this pivotal event. *Haihan chiken* was followed by a massive effort to transform Japan into a modern state.

The period that preceded *haihan chiken*, however, had seemed to indicate a dissipation rather than an acceleration of the momentum for change; the governing authority of the court had seemed to be contracting rather than expanding. In fact, *haihan chiken* appeared to be highly

[1] William Griffis, *The Mikado's Empire* (London: Harper & Brothers, 1912), p. 518.

TABLE 4.1
Amalgamation of Domains into *Ken* Jurisdiction, 1871

No. of Former Domains Incorporated	No. / Names of *Fu* and *Ken*	
0-1	26	Kōchi (Tosa), Myōdō, Kumamoto, Okayama, Yatsushiro, Obi, Kagoshima (Satsuma), Hiroshima, Tottori, Hamada, Hamamatsu, Shizuoka, Yamanashi, Kanazawa, Nanao, Shinkawa, Kanagawa, Iruma, Tokyo, Sendai, Wakamatsu, Nihonmatsu, Oitama, Morioka, Mizusawa
2-4	25	Nagasaki, Mitsuma, Fukuoka, Matsuyama, Kagawa, Uwajima, Hōjō, Yamaguchi, (Chōshū), Sakai, Osaka, Nagahama, Ōtsu, Hyōgo, Wakayama (Kii), Nagoya (Owari), Watarae, Mimizu, Chikuma, Asuba, Tsuruga, Tochigi, Ashigara, Saitama, Sakata, Yamagata
5-7	14	Imari (Saga), Kokura, Ōita, Kyoto, Anotsu, Nagano, Niigata, Kashiwazaki, Ibaraki, Imba, Utsunomiya, Iwasaki, Akita, Hirosaki
8-10	8	Fukatsu, Nara, Niiharu, Nukada, Shikama, Toyo'oka, Gifu, Gunma
11 or more	1	Kisarazu

SOURCE: *Chihō enkaku ryakufu* (Tokyo: Naimushō toshokyoku, 1882).

unlikely until immediately before it was carried out. It will be seen that the liquidation of the daimyo houses was not an inevitable consequence of the demise of the *bakufu*. On the contrary, restoration of imperial rule and the civil war that followed had created conditions that seemed unfavorable for the alteration of the old order. Given this background, it is important to examine how the crucial decision was made to abolish the *han* and establish prefectures directly under the central government.

Restoration and Civil War

Imperial rule was declared restored on January 3, 1868. There followed the Restoration War between the "imperial" forces of Satsuma, Chōshū, Tosa, and a few other southwestern *han*, on the one hand, and the northeastern *han* that resisted, on the other. Yet, the sudden political ascendancy of the imperial court should not be allowed to obscure the fact that the Tokugawa house retained its daimyo status, though under new leadership and at the cost of a great deal of its territory. This tolerance for the "enemy of the throne" developed shortly after the fall of Edo in summer 1868 while fighting continued to the north. Behind this moderation was the court's calculation as to the effects harsher treatment of the Tokugawa house might have on Tokugawa loyalists.[2] Apart from that, however, it revealed an important implication for the old political order and its beneficiaries, the daimyo houses. It was a signal that the demise of the shogunate did not contradict the continuation of the daimyo houses.

This turn of events was consistent with the closing phase of late Tokugawa politics. The final years of the shogunate had seen the Tokugawa acting more as a regional territorial power than as the national government, suggesting the possibility that the former might survive the latter. This development was gradual, and it was concealed by the widespread use of the slogan *sonnō-jōi* (Revere the Emperor, Expel the Barbarians) by those who were critical of the *bakufu* for its inability to fend off Western encroachment on Japan. Ironically, though, it gradually became possible for Tokugawa supporters to resort to the same language.

Sonnō-jōi had provided legitimacy for those who fled their domains to work with like-minded individuals from other areas at the center. The *sonnō-jōi* cause had led such men to deeds of violence and terrorism for immediate political ends, and it inspired in them a sense of proximity to the imperial throne, which they regarded as the ultimate source of sanction for political action. Yet, the incompetence of the *bakufu*, strikingly apparent after its wasteful punitive campaigns against Chōshū, only deepened the sense of crisis. Foreign affairs, *jōi*, began for many to loom larger than internal differences.

The focus on the foreign issue, however, made it possible for some Tokugawa supporters to resort to the language of *jōi* as well. They wanted to prevent the antiforeign issue from hardening into a determinedly anti-Tokugawa movement, and they were able to exploit this cause to support

[2] There seems to be no definite account of how the new fief for the Tokugawa was set at 700,000 *koku*. On the one hand, Iwakura Tomomi, for example, believed that "even if the fief were to be set at 2,000,000 *koku*, resistance by the house's vassals would be unavoidable." *Iwakura Tomomi kankei monjo* (Tokyo: Nihon shiseki kyōkai, 1929), vol. 3, pp. 513-517. On the other hand, there was also a more general sort of consideration for the problem of uprooting the samurai, as a consequence of such extreme measures as the outright confiscation of the pro-Tokugawa daimyo fiefs. See Kido Takayoshi's letter to Ōmura Masujirō on November 17, 1868, in *Kido Takayoshi monjo* (Tokyo: Nihon shiseki kyōkai, 1929), vol. 3, p. 155.

the shogun, asserting that his aim was to avoid polarization in a time of crisis. Tokugawa supporters argued that *bakufu* and court needed to be, and could be, integrated, and that the former represented the latter. In the process, *sonnō-jōi* no longer isolated them as much as it once had.

One indication of these trends was the increasing use of the term *kakkyo*, "independent campaigns," reflecting a growing competition among the military houses reminiscent of pre-Tokugawa days. It indicated rejection of the Tokugawa hegemony, but not necessarily elimination of the Tokugawa house from the competition itself. Tokugawa Yoshinobu's resignation as shogun on November 9, 1867, was in a sense a formal declaration of Tokugawa participation in the competition; and the restoration of imperial rule made the Tokugawa the equal of the daimyo houses of Satsuma, Chōshū, Tosa, and other domains. Thus, the condemnation of the Tokugawa as "enemy of the throne" did not follow from the fact that its heads had served as shoguns. Rather, there was a fear that the Tokugawa, still the largest and most powerful of the daimyo houses, might be rewarded and praised for self-demotion and emerge as victor in the *kakkyo* competition. Activists who had engineered the Tokugawa downfall considered it of critical importance to head off such a possibility.

It was in this context that Satsuma and Chōshū leaders adopted the metaphor of *gyoku* (jewel) for the emperor, calculating that with the "jewel" in their possession they would be able to block the Tokugawa. Subsequent maneuvers were designed to create the illusion that all actions and pronouncements were sanctioned by the *gyoku*.[3] Yoshinobu's failure to discredit this claim was ensured by his defeat at Toba-Fushimi; thereafter, he could be clearly identified as an "enemy."

The Restoration War that followed was not so much a challenge to the military houses as a struggle for victory in the *kakkyo* competition. Most daimyo saw the court's condemnation of the Tokugawa house as dangerous only in that it might be extended to Tokugawa supporters. They countered this by hurriedly disassociating themselves from the last shogun, and then by working to limit his punishment and condemnation. Most daimyo simply declared their allegiance to the court. Even for domains that had been closely involved in Yoshinobu's efforts to regain the *gyoku*, there were still ways to escape inclusion in his condemnation. Thus the Matsudaira (Takamatsu) wrote the court apologizing for the fact that their retainers had fought for Yoshinobu at Toba-Fushimi. They had had no choice, the letter explained, for they had found themselves locked in place, marching alongside troops from Aizu, the strongest To-

[3] Kido Takayoshi's letter to Shinagawa Yajirō, December 17, 1867, in *Kido Takayoshi monjo*, vol. 2, pp. 336-340.

kugawa supporter. The apology was strengthened by sending the court the heads of two high-ranking Matsudaira retainers who had commanded the Takamatsu troops on that day.[4]

Once the survival of the daimyo houses seemed sure, many daimyo began to urge relaxation of the punishment intended for Tokugawa Yoshinobu and his supporters. The last shogun might have been in error, they argued, but he had in fact abdicated his powers, making the Tokugawa house equal with the others. Then, even after it was clear that the Tokugawa house would be maintained, some continued to request similar leniency for the Matsudaira of Aizu, which faced extinction for its resistance to the "imperial" armies.[5] Thus, while the Restoration War brought home the finality of a change in the central government, it also contained a countertheme: equality of all military houses before the imperial court. Most daimyo houses were convinced that their places in the new, court-centered order would be similar to those they had known in the shogun-centered order.

The Charter Oath

Immediately after the declaration of Restoration, a formal announcement of the "new" political order was dictated by several needs. One was the Restoration leaders' desire to reassure the military houses that they would survive the Tokugawa fall. It was also important to stress that the actions of the new government had the sanction of the imperial court, and that they were in fact carrying out the sovereign's will. Furthermore, the leaders needed to strengthen their case for financial support from leading merchant-financiers whose resources were vitally important for the war effort.[6]

It was equally important for the government to establish its credibility with respect to foreign affairs. In Kobe (February 4, 1868) and Sakai (March 8, 1868), actions by units of Okayama and Tosa against foreigners had created a crisis of confidence at the very time that the new government was trying to establish itself. Its leaders had to prove that they could maintain order, protect foreign privileges and interests, and

[4] *Fukkoki* (Tokyo: Tokyo teikoku daigaku, 1929), vol. 1, p. 486; *Dajōkan nisshi*, no. 12 (1868), in Hashimoto Hiroshi, comp., *Ishin nisshi* (Tokyo: Meicho kankōkai, 1966), vol. 1, bk. 1, pp. 22-23.

[5] See, for example, *Chūgai shimbun gaihen* (vol. 1, no. 13), in *Meiji bunka zenshū* (Tokyo: Nihon hyōronsha, 1929), vol. 13, p. 343; and Kido Takayoshi's letter to Ōkubo Toshimichi on July 23, 1868, in *Kido Takayoshi monjo*, vol. 3, pp. 113-116.

[6] See the entries for December 7, 1867, January 17, 1868, and January 25, 1868, in *Date Munenari zaikyō nikki* (Tokyo: Nihon shiseki kyōkai, 1916), pp. 617-619, 651, 681.

override domain authorities claiming exclusive power over the lives of retainers who had been involved in the violence. Eventually, settlements were brought about between the new government and the foreign powers. A score of men responsible for the violence were permitted "honorable" suicides—but not without frantic efforts on the part of government leaders, who had to negotiate with representatives of foreign governments *and* representatives of daimyo houses.[7]

One last reason for a formal government statement of intent was perhaps most compelling of all. The course of events had inevitably increased the importance of the Restoration *han* of the southwest, and their eminence seemed to discredit the claim that all military houses were equal before the court. Suspicions were rife among court nobles that "either Chōshū or Satsuma will propose a new shogun."[8] Consequently, the Charter Oath of April 6, 1868, had a vital task to achieve. It had to establish the authority of the court and simultaneously emphasize the collective support of all military houses, in order to offset the preponderant weight of Chōshū and Satsuma.

The very general language of the Oath reflected these requirements. The first of the five articles—"deliberative assemblies shall be widely convoked, all matters shall be decided by public discussion"—was particularly important in its implications for the future retention of the military houses. In the Oath, "public discussion" was placed within a general context of political participation. However, two men who had submitted proposals put it more specifically: Yuri Kimimasa, in *Giji no tai'i*, contrasted "public discussion" with "private discussion," while Fukuoka Takachika, in *Kaimei*, explained "public discussion" as an "assembly of feudal lords." "Public," in effect, meant a realm, however fictitious, in which "private deliberations" of smaller groups would have no place.[9] Several months later, when a proclamation explaining the Restoration was needed for newly conquered territories in northern Japan, "public" was defined as "court nobles, feudal lords, and men of samurai rank from all areas," who were to be convened as "deliberative assemblies so that all matters can be decided by public discussion."[10]

The 1869 petition for the return of *han* registers to the court (*hanseki*

[7] See Ishii Takashi, *Meiji ishin no kokusaiteki kankyō* (Tokyo: Yoshikawa kōbunkan, 1966), pp. 757-762, 799-809.

[8] Higashikuze Michitomi, *Chikutei kaikoroku ishin zengo* (Tokyo: Hakubunkan, 1911), pp. 254-255.

[9] See Fukuoka Takachika, "Gokajō goseimon to seitaisho no yurai ni tsuite," in Kokka gakkai, ed., *Meiji kensei keizai shiron* (Tokyo: Kokka gakkai, 1918), pp. 1-45; and Ōkubo Toshiaki, "Gokajō no seimon ni kansuru kōsatsu," *Rekishi chiri*, vol. 88, no. 2 (1957), pp. 65-91.

[10] Dajōkan, *Hōrei zensho*, no. 603 (1868).

hōkan) was a further extension of this effort to equalize the daimyo houses before the court. The petition was prompted by awareness among some Restoration leaders that there was an emerging trend in some military houses to remain isolated from each other and aloof from the court. Kido Takayoshi would later refer to this as the beginning of multiple "mini-*bakufu*."[11] There was little in the wording of the petition that would be disturbing to the daimyo. Kido went back to Chōshū in order to work for the idea with his daimyo in the autumn of 1868. He did incur animosity from among his fellow Chōshū retainers, but that was chiefly because of his absence from the Restoration War in the north, and the feeling that he was putting national affairs ahead of Chōshū affairs.[12]

The petition itself may not have been controversial, but for the rest of the daimyo, who quickly followed suit, what mattered was that the petition had come from the four southwestern Restoration domains. Shortly after the petition was submitted, a memorandum written by a samurai in Tanakura *han*, Iwaki, pointed out that "even those southwestern domains having meritorious Restoration records have presented this virtuous petition; should not we, guilty as we are [of once having sided with the emperor's enemy], have initiated this petition ourselves?"[13] The thing to note here is the sense of competition, and the fear of being outmaneuvered once again by the southwestern domains. Okayama *han*, in its petition, was quite direct in insisting that the gist of the *hanseki hōkan* petition had long been under discussion, and that it was surprised to have the Restoration *han* come in earlier.[14] The majority of the daimyo had come on board by July, and their petitions all followed the form of the original petition.

At the same time, few seem to have thought that *hanseki hōkan* threatened the military houses. The petition stated that "we respectfully return our fiefs to the court." Then came an important passage that the court "should give what should be given and take what should be taken away" from the military houses.[15] Thus, while this did honor the authority of the court above that of the military houses, it seemed to make clear that such authority did not contradict the continued existence of the military houses. Kido Takayoshi, after the original petition had been submitted, wrote in his diary that it should provide an everlasting foundation for

[11] Kido Takayoshi's letter to Ōmura Masujirō, mid-February 1869, in *Kido Takayoshi monjo*, vol. 3, p. 231.

[12] See the entries for June 4, 1868, and August 6, 1868, in *Kido Takayoshi nikki* (Tokyo: Nihon shiseki kyōkai, 1932), vol. 1, pp. 26, 56-57.

[13] *Chūgai shimbun*, no. 5 (1869), in *Meiji bunka zenshū*, vol. 13, p. 379.

[14] *Dajōkan nisshi*, no. 9 (1869), in Hashimoto, *Ishin nisshi*, vol. 2, bk. 1, p. 26.

[15] Ibid., p. 25.

the "three hundred military houses."[16] All the petitions were acknowledged and accepted by the court on July 25, 1869. Technically, the daimyo were now court-appointed governors of their domains.

There is additional evidence that few participants saw this as a serious blow to daimyo rule. While the petitions were being submitted, a lively debate was going on among the representatives that daimyo were supposed to maintain at the national capital.[17] The *kōshi*, as they were called, were debating the relative merits of central (*gunken*) rule and feudal (*hōken*) divisions. As the debate progressed, *gunken* became hard to distinguish from *hōken*. Those endorsing *gunken* numbered 80, and those who were for *hōken* came to a little over 110. One group of *gunken* advocates urged that all lands should be made public property under the emperor and that laws should "originate from one source." In order to manage this, it was suggested that "there be *fu* in large provinces, and that small ones be governed by adjacent *fu*," and that the minimal size for *ken* should be 100,000 *koku* in productivity, ten times the traditional threshold for daimyo status. But they went on to argue that governors of *fu* and *ken* should be "furnished from among the daimyo" or their ranking retainers. For another group that supported the central-government principle of *gunken*, daimyo were to become governors of *fu* and *ken*, which would be renamed large, medium, and small domains. Domains would be "entrusted" to daimyo, and the daimyo office would be "hereditary." Finally, one group straddled the issue completely, suggesting that Japan would be best governed if one-third of the country were set aside as imperial territory, under a *gunken* system, and the rest left under the present *hōken* arrangement. In effect, this would have maintained the essence of the Tokugawa settlement, under which one-fourth of the land had been the *bakufu*'s *tenryō*, with the rest divided up among the daimyo. Thus, few saw *hanseki hōkan* as any kind of death blow to daimyo rule.

From Daimyo to Official

During and after these events, meanwhile, changes taking place in the new central government and in the daimyo territories contributed significantly to the complacency with which the country accepted the *haihan chiken* decision in 1871. At the center, the way in which the new government honored daimyo and court nobles with honorific titles, while

[16] *Kido Takayoshi nikki*, vol. 1, p. 183, entry for March 11, 1869.

[17] See *Kōgisho nisshi* (1869), in Hashimoto, *Ishin nisshi*, vol. 7, bk. 1, pp. 195-200.

keeping them far removed from the major problems it faced, provided an indication of what lay ahead.

The first institutions by which the court tried to organize its new political role (January 3, 1868) were called the Sanshoku: the Three Offices of *sōsai* (president), *gijō* (senior councilors), and *sanyo* (junior councilors). The structure gave way on February 10, 1868, to the Seven Departments (*shichika*), augmented to eight (*hakkyoku*) on February 25. Four months later (June 11, 1868), the Seitaisho retained the number of departments and ministries, but reduced the number of officials. After *hanseki hōkan* (August 15, 1869), the Council of State (Dajōkan) replaced all this with councilors (*sangi*) and ministers of the left and right.

These frequent changes indicate a good deal of experimentation, but daimyo and court nobles were giving way to samurai in positions that mattered. Under the first structure (Sanshoku), slightly over a hundred men entered the central government. As changes in bureaucratic structure continued, fewer "new" men entered, and of them a far smaller percentage were daimyo or court nobles. Moreover, the great majority of the daimyo and nobles who came in under the first structure were without ministerial responsibilities. They were there for prestige and legitimacy. Restoration activists, who came in as *chōshi* (court appointees), soon dominated the emerging ministries. Among these samurai, allegiance to the central government was expected to outweigh allegiance to their own daimyo. If the Restoration made the daimyo constitutionally equal to one another before the court, the new category of imperial servants began to give domain retainers, recruited as *chōshi*, equal standing with daimyo before the court.

The preponderance of *chōshi* in the new government is readily discernible from listings in *Hyakkan rireki*, the two-volume career records of new government officials during the first decade after the Restoration. Of the 366 samurai in the listing, 122 were *chōshi*. (Some, such as Kido Takayoshi, Ōkubo Toshimichi, and a few others, were also *sanyo*.) Considering that the *chōshi* system ceased to exist within a little over a year and a half (it was abolished on August 4, 1869), the preponderance was remarkable: in fact, 109 out of the 122 became *chōshi* before the end of 1868. Despite the internal friction arising from the fact that these samurai were serving more than one "overlord,"[18] *chōshi* in effect created a pool of administrative talent for the new government. On the other hand, daimyo served primarily as a symbol of unity between the court and the military houses.

[18] See, for example, the entry for May 2, 1869, in Sasaki Takayuki's diary, *Hogohiroi* (Tokyo: Tokyo daigaku shuppankai, 1973), vol. 4, p. 36.

The new government, which professed to observe the autonomy of the military houses, instituted no central administrative office for the domains, and the Ministry of Home Affairs confined its jurisdiction to the territories that had been seized from the Tokugawa.[19] The daimyo in the central government were concentrated in offices of little consequence for the domains or for the relationship between the court and the domains. The new government was thus largely limited to its own "imperial" territory. Most tangible signs that the new government was trying to make its presence felt outside its own boundaries were met by indifference or hostility. For example, central-government paper currency, *dajōkan-satsu*, was less popular and less used than the many domain currencies—even in Tosa, Okayama, and Awa, whose daimyo and retainers were occupying high offices in the new government. Sasaki Takayuki's efforts to recruit fellow-Tosa retainers for a central office, the Justice Ministry, were countered by their criticism of him for serving more than one lord. Sasaki confessed: "It just does not please the men at home to argue for the improvement of the new government."[20]

There were also some advantages in the government's restriction to its own territory. The new government constituted no threat to the military houses, and this helped protect the men in government from more suspicion and criticism from their fellow retainers. In turn, the men in the government began to deepen their allegiance to the new center, and that allegiance began to surpass loyalty to their daimyo. Furthermore, the disappearance of the domains was to require no corresponding change in the central government.

Outside the imperial territories, on the other hand, some domains began trying to liquidate themselves voluntarily prior to *haihan chiken*. The daimyo who made this decision (see Table 4.2) had little in common. There was the pro-court Tsuwano *han* as well as the pro-Tokugawa Morioka *han*. There was Nagaoka *han*, which had staged something of a one-domain war against the superior imperial armies. Included, too, were Takasu *han*, with a large samurai population burdening its treasury (369 samurai per 1,000 *koku*) and, at the opposite pole, Yoshii *han*, with only 51 per 1,000 *koku*. Perhaps many of the military houses would have taken such action sooner or later, even without *haihan chiken*. In most domains, the timing for this step was related to financial exhaustion, worsened by the strain of Restoration mobilization and warfare, and made insoluble by a renewed sense of traditional loyalty and autonomy that had been tested and strengthened by the war and by the threat of

[19] Sashihara Yasuzō, *Meiji seishi*, in *Meiji bunka zenshū*, vol. 2, pp. 24-27.

[20] Tsuda Shigemaro, *Meiji seijō to shin Takayuki* (Tokyo: Jishōkai, 1928), pp. 184-185.

TABLE 4.2
Voluntary Liquidation of Domains, 1870/71

	Productivity	Revenue	Population
Fukumoto (1/13/1871)	10,573	3,204	166
Morioka (8/6/1870)	130,000	68,580	—
Mariyama (10/11/1870)	10,000	4,950	64
Marugame (5/16/1871)	51,512	33,120	218
Nagaoka (11/15/1870)	24,000	10,500	783
Ōmizo (July or August 1871)	20,000	6,730	132
Sayama ((1/27/1870)	10,000	5,470	—
Takasu (2/11/1871)	30,000	6,630	369
Tadotsu (5/11/1871)	10,000	7,400	170
Tatsuoka (7/2/1871)	16,000	5,140	127
Tsuwano (7/9/1871)	43,000	30,753	138
Tokuyama (7/2/1871)	40,010	21,410	193
Yoshii (1/27/1870)	10,000	2,160	51

SOURCES: Ōtsuka Takematsu, *Hansei ichiran* (Tokyo: Nihon shiseki kyōkai sōsho, 1928), vols. 1 and 2; *Dajōkan nisshi*, in Hashimoto Hiroshi, comp., *Ishin nisshi* (Tokyo: Meicho kankōkai, 1966).

NOTE: Productivity = agricultural output in *koku*; Revenue = domain revenue in *koku*; Population = samurai population per 1,000 *koku* of domain revenue. The dates, except for Mariyama and Tadotsu, are when the central government received the request for self-liquidation. For Mariyama and Tadotsu, the dates are when these domains submitted their requests for self-liquidation.

condemnation. These considerations led most domain officials to try to meet their crises with their own resources; many domains responded by reducing samurai stipends and reclaiming land. The inadequacy of such steps compelled the domain bureaucracies to reduce the sphere of administrative activity. They began to turn away from the management of territory and to concentrate on the administration of the daimyo households and their most important constituency, the retainer corps. Domain bureaucracies were, in some sense, on the verge of becoming private organizations.

For its part, the new central government still honored domain autonomy and, through administrative guidelines issued on August 2, 1870, and October 4, 1870, made only hesitant steps to assert its control. These set out broad requirements of uniform administration and, distinguishing between public (domainwide) administration and private (daimyo household) concern, directed that 10 percent of *han* revenue be set aside for the latter. As one unanticipated result, domain officials spontaneously reduced the stipends of their house's principal vassals.[21]

As the financial crisis deepened, there were more and more instances in which domain leaders tried to abdicate their responsibility. In some areas, house vassals were encouraged to return to agriculture in order to lessen the burden of samurai stipends. Increasing numbers of domains informed the central government of their inability to repair deteriorating castles, and presumably defense needs were not being met.[22] Several military houses made direct requests for relief. In response to one such request, the government suggested that the Tsuruta (formerly Hamada) *han* turn to domains headed by houses related to its daimyo.[23] Then, by the end of 1870, domains had begun requesting permission to divert for public use the 10 percent of revenue nominally set aside as daimyo maintenance. Kumamoto led in this, and twenty-seven other cases are recorded in the *Dajōkan nisshi*.[24] Thus, despite their mutual isolation, the domains were beginning to consider their tax revenues as "public" property whose use had to be sanctioned by the new central government. Equally important, the daimyo household itself, long the center of *han* concern, was no longer so immune to the disruptive impact of financial crisis.

[21] See *Chitsuroku shobun enkaku gaihyō*, vol. 8 of *Meiji zenki zaisei keizai shiryō shūsei* (Tokyo: Meiji bunken shiryō kankōkai, 1963), pp. 310-387, for the cases of thirty-seven domains.

[22] *Ishin shiryō kōyō* (Tokyo: Ishin shiryō hensan jimukyoku, 1939), vol. 10, passim, particularly for 1870 and 1871, before the *haihan chiken*.

[23] *Dajōkan nisshi*, no. 82 (1869), in Hashimoto, *Ishin nisshi*, vol. 2, bk. 1, p. 223.

[24] For the Kumamoto *han* report, see *Dajōkan nisshi*, no. 38 (1870), in Hashimoto, *Ishin nisshi*, vol. 2, bk. 2, pp. 124-125.

At the last, a few domains worked out ways of avoiding the admission of collapse by proposing mergers with larger, related houses. The Mariyama *han* (Sakai, 10,000 *koku*) merged with Obama on September 19, 1870; Takasu (30,000 *koku*) with Owari on February 11, 1871; and Tokuyama (40,000 *koku*) with Chōshū on July 2, 1871. The other members of the "bankrupt" group agreed with Yoshii (10,000 *koku*), which petitioned the new government: "public expenditures have grown larger and larger; there are no conceivable ways to meet the crisis, and the people's cries for relief fill the air; we humbly request the imperial government to extend its rule over us."[25] In exchange for *han* self-liquidation, the government was to guarantee that the daimyo would continue to receive the equivalent of one-tenth of his domain revenue from the central treasury. Samurai stipends for the retainers were also to be continued. Clearly, few domains were in a position even to contemplate resistance to a decision by the new government to abolish them.

The Final Decision

The chain of events that culminated in the decision to end the military houses, then, was far from linear, and contemporaries were some time in coming to see its logic. As late as 1870, Kido Takayoshi observed that "for the time being, the court will have to establish itself independently within the resources of the 8,000,000 *koku* [of Tokugawa territory]."[26]

Uncertainty, however, did not end a sharp competition on the domain level that was reminiscent of the intrigues of *bakumatsu* politics. One incident late in 1870—a Satsuma contingent left the capital without explanation after an imperial review of troops from Satsuma, Chōshū, Tosa, and Saga—led to immediate suspicion that Satsuma was preparing to pursue hegemonic ambitions. The incident and the response to it focused attention on a larger problem: the movement of troops, even those from "loyal" domains, was outside the court's ability to command. Moreover, efforts to strengthen the shaky foundation of the new government might, as its leaders were well aware, produce the unwelcome effect of even greater reliance on the very domains that were suspected to harbor hegemonic ambitions. Thus, for many months after *hanseki hōkan*, there was an increasing sense both of crisis and of an inability

[25] *Dajōkan nisshi*, no. 113 (1869), in Hashimoto, *Ishin nisshi*, vol. 2, bk. 1, pp. 301-302.

[26] By "for the time being" Kido meant "ten, fifteen, or twenty years." Kido's letter to Sanjō Sanetomi on September 15, 1870, in *Kido Takayoshi monjo*, vol. 4, pp. 103-104.

to do anything about it. As Ōkubo Toshimichi put it: "the threat to the foundation of the imperial state is more pressing now than a year ago."[27]

The course of action followed by Ōkubo Toshimichi in this period illuminates the narrow path that leaders in the central government had to tread to improve its status. Ōkubo was from Satsuma, a domain perpetually suspected of hegemonic ambitions, and also was fully aware of his unpopularity at home because of his service to the central government. On the one hand, in a diary entry, he recorded his plea for a resurrection of intense commitment to the imperial cause—if necessary, through Satsuma alone.[28] At the same time, his acts needed to be carefully calculated to show deference to Kido, the Chōshū man who expressed suspicion of Satsuma, and no less to Shimazu Hisamitsu, the de facto lord of Satsuma who voiced the frustration of *han* samurai at being slighted by the new government. Nor was the issue of constitutional equality among the military houses the least of Ōkubo's concerns. Ōkubo repeatedly expressed his fears concerning the consequences to the new government if it were habitually to rely on Satsuma or Chōshū "whenever it faces difficulties."[29]

There were three ways whereby leaders might improve the foundation of the new government: a one-*han* approach, a multi-*han* approach, and an approach that observed the constitutional equality of all the military houses. The choice hinged more on a process of elimination than on a weighing of merits. The first was too risky, implying as it did the deepening of divisions among the major domains; the last had already proved ineffective. The second approach at least provided the possibility of reinforcing the coalition that had brought about the demise of the Tokugawa: it had always been a few *han* such as Satsuma, Chōshū, and Tosa that set things in motion, leaving the rest to follow suit.[30]

The result was the agreement on the so-called *sanpan kenpei* of January 1871, which created a 10,000-man Imperial Guard with troops provided by Satsuma, Chōshū, and Tosa. For the leaders of the central government, the decision was meant to restore the harmony that had united those domains in their overthrow of the Tokugawa and to develop a unified front within the new government. As such, the move would still fall short

[27] Ōkubo Toshimichi's letter to Shinnō Tateo on October 25, 1869, in *Ōkubo Toshimichi monjo* (Tokyo: Nihon shiseki kyōkai, 1928), vol. 3, pp. 304-305.

[28] Entry for September 27, 1870, in *Ōkubo Toshimichi nikki* (Tokyo: Nihon shiseki kyōkai, 1927), vol. 2, p. 124.

[29] Ōkubo Toshimichi's letters to Iwakura Tomomi on September 29, 1870, and October 29, 1870, in *Ōkubo Toshimichi monjo*, vol. 4, pp. 10-11, 45-46.

[30] For example, Ōkubo Toshimichi's "Kihan no sai dōshi ni wakachishi ikensho," January 19, 1870, in *Ōkubo Toshimichi monjo*, vol. 3, pp. 348-358.

of challenging the existing order. Indeed, Saigō Takamori, the figure in Satsuma upon whom successful mobilization of the Satsuma troops depended, did not regard the agreement as an instrument with which to destroy the military houses.[31] So, too, with Itagaki Taisuke, who played a similar role in Tosa, and with other Tosa leaders at home: the decision that Tosa would join the agreement was seen as a move to prevent Satsuma and Chōshū from achieving a political monopoly.[32] For those outside the three-*han* nexus, however, especially for the court nobles, the new Imperial Guard suggested the possibility that they were declining in importance. Power and influence seemed likely to depend on the ability to contribute troops. "The three houses seem to become more and more influential," wrote Iwakura Tomomi to Sanjō Sanetomi on May 23, 1871; "may this not lead to great harm some day?"[33] But while these men were defending the principle of equality among the military houses, the architects of *sanpan kenpei* were disturbed by the realization that their new unity would leave the court nothing to fall back on if that unity should be lost.[34]

It was at this juncture that a *fourth* possibility emerged: the strengthening of the new government not on the basis of a coalition of the southwestern domains, but by an act that would render that coalition altogether unnecessary. Such a possibility seems not to have occurred to those who engineered and implemented the *sanpan kenpei.*

Documents detailing the formulation of this realization are limited; security, and danger, may enter into this. But the impetus for the final resolution seems to have come from Inoue Kaoru and a few other lower-echelon Chōshū men in the central government. These men, who included Yamagata Aritomo and Torio Koyata, had some important things in common. They had all risen to their high positions, from relative obscurity in the samurai bureaucracy, thanks to the fluidity of late Tokugawa politics at a time when the importance of social origin was reduced. Further, their realm of action since that time had been with the new government, either at its center or in administrative posts in the former Tokugawa territories, especially at the open ports which were so vitally important for foreign relations. In these respects they differed from men like Kido or Ōkubo or Itagaki, who were leading *han* officials preoccupied with high-level politics and with unity. Furthermore, Chōshū's experience

[31] *Ōkuma bunsho* (Tokyo: Waseda daigaku shakai kagaku kenkyūjo, 1958), vol. 1, pp. 5-7.

[32] See, for example, *Tani Tateki ikō* (Tokyo: Seikensha, 1912), vol. 1, p. 209.

[33] In *Iwakura Tomomi kankei monjo*, vol. 5, p. 55.

[34] Kido Takayoshi's letter to Sanjō Sanetomi and Iwakura Tomomi on April 15, 1871, in *Kido Takayoshi monjo*, vol. 4, pp. 196-197.

in Restoration politics had been longer and more violent than that of other domains, and it had alerted these men to the fact that the growth of standing armies in Chōshū was far beyond the capacity of the domain treasury to maintain.[35] Thus, for them, the termination of the military houses was desirable both from a personal and a managerial point of view.

The policy to terminate the domains seems to have surfaced among these men in mid-August.[36] Inoue Kaoru, Yamagata Aritomo, and a few others quickly saw the soundness of the policy. This still left, however, the task of lobbying for it with the more powerful members of the government, Kido Takayoshi, Saigō Takamori, and Ōkubo Toshimichi. The policy was received cautiously by these powerful men. Approached by the men of Chōshū, Saigō's concern was whether or not they had informed Kido of the policy. Likewise, Kido was relieved when told by his lieutenants that Saigō had already been approached. Not until a week or so before the abolition of the domains does one find the first use of the term *haihan* in Kido's diary. By and large, the policy elicited more fear of a hostile reaction than it did disagreements as to its desirability. Though the limited availability of documents leaves the issue of explicit disagreements something of a puzzle, fears of resistance seem to have been overcome by the realization that no single domain could resist the allied forces of Satsuma, Chōshū, and Tosa—all of which had arrived in Tokyo by the beginning of July.

It is particularly noteworthy that those who had voiced reservations about the monopoly that the three domains exerted through their preponderance of military strength played no role in this final act to strengthen the new imperial government. Iwakura Tomomi, the most important of the court nobles in the government, was not even told about the decision until a few days before *haihan chiken* was to be implemented (August 29, 1871). His response was to try to maintain the fiction of equality among the military houses by diffusing the central role played by Satsuma, Chōshū, and Tosa. He wrote, in "Procedure for the Announcement of the Liquidation of the Feudal Houses," that Owari, Fukui, and Kumamoto were equally instrumental in the decision.[37] On the other hand, one consequence of *haihan chiken* quickly became obvious to Saigō

[35] See, for example, Inoue Kaoru's letter to Kido Takayoshi on November 10, 1869, urging the reduction of the size of Chōshū's army, in *Segai Inoue-kō den* (Tokyo: Naigai shoseki, 1933), vol. 1, pp. 389-390, and his recollections as quoted in *Kōshaku Yamagata Aritomo den* (Tokyo: Yamagata kai, 1933), vol. 2, pp. 131-133.

[36] *Kōshaku Yamagata*, vol. 2, pp. 124-140.

[37] Quoted in Asai Kiyoshi, *Meiji ishin to gunken shisō* (Tokyo: Ganshōdō, 1939), pp. 288-289.

Takamori and Itagaki Taisuke, whose weighty presence had formerly been felt by the central government. Once it ceased to rely on the coalition of the major military houses, the government was no longer so responsive to Saigō and Itagaki. Their popularity among the domain troops was now more a private and personal phenomenon. Their desire to make the Restoration government responsive to them once again would move them to cooperate in the debate over waging war on Korea in 1873. Saigō's career was to end four years later in the abortive rising of Satsuma samurai, while Itagaki pursued other measures in the Movement for People's Rights that he launched in 1874.[38]

Haihan chiken, important as it was to the foundation of the Restoration government, nonetheless fell short of providing an alternative to the conditions that had brought it about. In conclusion, a few observations are appropriate; these have to do with the assumptions and developments that dictated the creation of *fu* and *ken* as effective units of regional administration.

There was, first of all, a concern with administrative efficiency and rationality. Leaders were concerned to make sure that, whatever the intermediate institutions between locality and center, people and emperor, those institutions should be as few as possible and as responsive to central direction as possible. Thus, the reductions in the number of units through mergers of *fu* and *ken*, a process that went on for several years, and the reductions in the number of official posts allocated to each new locality, were logical. The new units would come to have an average of sixty positions each, in contrast to the days of samurai rule with its top-heavy layer of military rulers. Moreover, the concern with "efficiency" went far beyond a simple preoccupation with numbers. It was also important to help the populace rise above its "old provincial" orientation. One step was to avoid appointing "native" samurai to top prefectural posts. According to the *Fu-ken shiryō* of the mid-1870s nearly all top prefectural officials were recruited from outside their areas. Not even Chōshū escaped this rule: a former Tokugawa retainer, Nakano Goichi, was installed as its first governor. Steps were also taken to integrate prefectural officials into the overall governmental organization. The system of ranks for *fu* and *ken* officials (inaugurated December 10, 1871) integrated the upper echelons of prefectural officials according to the same ranking scale adopted for central government officials. Court ranks performed a similar function: the prefectural governors were given court rank of lower fourth

[38] In "After the Restoration: The Beginning of Japan's Modern State" (MS), I discuss at some length the origin and consequences of this alienation of Saigō and Itagaki.

class (*juno shii*), which was usually reserved for medium-high officials in the central offices.

Leaders of the new government did their best to hold to a middle line, and they did not allow advocates of "efficiency" to streamline the structure more than they thought wise. There were some who advocated reducing intermediate units to the absolute minimum. A Finance Ministry official, for instance, argued in an 1872 memorandum that "it is . . . imperative to abolish the *ken* and divide the country into five or six districts where branch offices of the central government can be set up, so that the working of the entire [administrative] system can be improved and cost reduced."[39] Caution in this matter was probably reinforced and rewarded by the tendency of some of the new governors to think of their prefectures more or less as private domains, in which they could practice traditional approaches of humane and benevolent rule in tandem with the new form of government. This was, as one would expect, most often the case with governors who had become accustomed to thinking of themselves as equal to their central government colleagues during the freewheeling activist days of the past.[40]

On the other hand, the flood of institutional reforms that followed *haihan chiken* made it necessary for the new government to retain intermediate institutions. Furthermore—in the absence of familiarity with the localities, and with small staffs—the governors found themselves forced to delegate some responsibility to individuals, interests, and institutions that had not been formally incorporated into the governmental structure. This requirement in turn made local notables conscious of the possibility of making government responsive to their demands. In other words, the balance generated by the pressure on the new rulers to expand the new role of government coincided with the desire of the ruled to see a measurable expansion of political participation.

A catalyst for joining these two opposing pressures was the creation within the prefectures of special districts (*ku*) and their officials. These districts were invented in order to implement a national census (the Household Residence Registry) ordered on May 22, 1871, and expected to begin a year later. They were to be terminated upon completion of the census survey. At first the local authorities were given a great deal of leeway on how to draw up the new districts and where to recruit the *ku* officials. The result was the use of existing villages and townships, combinations of which made up *ku*, and the extensive recruitment of *ku* officials from what may be broadly termed the traditional community

[39] *Ōkuma bunsho*, vol. 1, pp. 186-187.

[40] Kikegawa Hiroshi, *Jichi gojūnen shi* (Tokyo: Ryōsho fukyūkai, 1955), p. 19.

elite of non-samurai status. Then, following *haihan chiken* and its aftermath, prefectural officials began to call upon *ku* officials for purposes other than the one for which they had initially been recruited.

In particular, the complexities and costs involved in the land tax reform (1873-1881) broadened the role of the *ku* officials. Well-informed in community affairs and well-connected among the villagers, *ku* officials were often indispensable to the prefectural authorities who were responsible for the land surveys. For the farmers, fearful of an increase in their tax burden, *ku* officials represented virtually the only way to make known their demands and interests. It is thus no surprise that *ku* officials were often caught in a crossfire of criticism—from the prefectural authorities, who viewed them as leaders of resistance to the reform, as well as from the villagers, who sometimes viewed their actions as unjust to the farmer.

The emerging importance of *ku* officials represented a significant change in local politics. The fact that they could aid or hinder the reform led some prefectural authorities to devise formal measures to have them represented in prefectural politics. Such measures, in turn, prompted *ku* officials (and the community leaders they represented) to press for more. By 1875, there were seven prefectures with assemblies of elected members (often from the ranks of the *ku* officials), and twenty-three more had assemblies with a mixed membership of elected and appointed members.[41] The debate in the Tokyo Governors' Conference, held in 1875, was particularly significant. When the participating governors acknowledged that *ku* officials were above, but not categorically different from, those still outside the formal boundary of government, this was just one step away from proposing a systematic movement toward broader participation.[42]

Ōkubo Toshimichi was cognizant of these developments. In 1878 he wrote to propose a new mode of local administration that would include popularly elected prefectural assemblies:

> If we provide a measure for opening popular assemblies, all the responsibilities for mistakes, wrongdoings, drawbacks as well as merits [attendant upon prefectural administration] must inevitably rest with the assemblies and the local populace; and even the slightest discontent toward the central government will be minimized.[43]

Ōkubo was acutely aware of the need to expand the authority of the Restoration government throughout the new *fu* and *ken*, as he was of

[41] *Chihōkan kaigi nisshi*, in *Meiji bunka zenshū*, vol. 4, p. 313.

[42] For the debate, ibid., pp. 314-322.

[43] Quoted in Kikegawa, *Jichi gojūnen shi*, p. 46.

the disruptive impact that an excessively rapid expansion could have upon the populace. For him, dispersion of power among the new political strata was the solution to both problems. The central government was no longer isolated, and the prefectural institutions were the key to ending its isolation.

Haihan chiken thus stands as a turning point in the Tokugawa-Meiji political transition. It brought to an end the sway of the military houses, which had seemed to survive the demise of the *bakufu*. It was a response to intractable and specific problems facing individual domains after the Restoration War: financial crisis and administrative irrationality had rendered meaningless the survival of the individual *han*. Within the national setting of competitive *han* politics dominated by the Restoration *han*, *haihan chiken*, product of the search for cooperative action by the Restoration *han*, also imposed on them steps that would give the lie to charges of hegemonic ambition. Finally, the need of new, "outside" prefectural authorities to establish contact and to work out cooperation with their populations caused those authorities to institutionalize the role of local notables in prefectural assemblies. Eventually, the terms "public" and "assemblies," which had been reserved for the traditional samurai elite in 1868, took on meaning for non-samurai, local notables who would take seats in the future assemblies.

CHAPTER 5

LOCAL ADMINISTRATION: THE EXAMPLE OF AWA-TOKUSHIMA

BY ANDREW FRASER

The transformation of local administration between 1860 and 1890 was one of the major achievements of modern Japan. In these thirty years some 260 domains, differing widely in size and complexity, were regrouped into three metropolitan cities and forty-two prefectures more or less uniform in population and administrative structure. Within them, cities, urban and rural districts, towns and villages were established as standard units, each with offices, elected assemblies, schools, and police posts conforming to national standards laid down by the central government.

I have selected the province of Awa-Tokushima as an example of local transition. In 1860 it was the heart of a large domain formally rated at 250,000 *koku*. Several times amalgamated with its neighbors after 1871, the province became a separate Tokushima prefecture in 1880. Along with a dozen or so large domains that survived basically unchanged as prefectures, Awa-Tokushima provides a useful example of administrative continuity, in contrast to other prefectures put together from as many as twenty-four previous domains. In population (660,000), and in production, Awa-Tokushima comes close to one-fiftieth of the national total. In statistics of all kinds it is thus comparatively easy to handle, and the figures given in this chapter can usefully be related to the national scene.

In 1860 Awa was one of the rich, stable domains of central Japan seeking to avoid both domination from Edo and civil war either for or against the *bakufu*, the cloak beneath which powerful domains at the extremities sought to conceal their drive toward national leadership.

Comparatively free of samurai rebellion and farmer uprisings, Awa-Tokushima was a province in which the transformation of local administration proved relatively uneventful. As late as 1890, significant variations existed between prefectures, despite two decades of constant effort toward standardization. Local governors were allowed considerable latitude in the application of central orders, and each prefecture had its own peculiarities, but Awa-Tokushima can nonetheless be regarded as broadly representative of local administration over the nation as a whole.

While tracing changes in administrative structure, I also relate them to costs, in at least a general way. The problem of costs imposed strong restraints on structural change and required important political concessions to allay local opposition. The main body of this chapter selects seven key areas of local administration which between them absorbed the greatest proportion of local taxes (see Table 5.1), or which had the most important political, social, and economic implications.

Boundaries and Units

From the outset of the Meiji regime, the central government was busy reorganizing the territories of the defunct *bakufu* into urban and rural prefectures. On the abolition of the domains, in 1871, the whole nation was divided into three metropolitan cities and seventy-three prefectures. Savings in administrative costs could be made if the number of prefectures were reduced, and ambitious plans were drawn up to widen local boundaries to comprise large groups of provinces (*shū*).[1] The number of pre-

TABLE 5.1
Local Tax Expenditures in Tokushima, 1890
(%)

	Police / Prisons	Administration	Education	Public Works	Other
Prefecture	40	30	10	10	10
Community	—	35	32	24	9

SOURCES: For prefecture, Tōkyō keizai shimpōsha, *Meiji Taishō zaisei shōran* (Tokyo: Tōkyō keizai shimpōsha, 1929), table 526; for community, Kikegawa Hiroshi, *Meiji jichi seido no seiritsu katei* (Tokyo: Tōkyō shisei chōsakai, 1957), p. 72.

[1] *Kensei shi hensankai shūshū monjo mokuroku*, item 715, and *Watanabe Tokujirō ke monjo*, vol. 1, item 5 (Kensei shiryōshitsu, National Diet Library, Tokyo). Also, Ōshima

fectures was successively reduced to a low of thirty-six in 1876, when fourteen of them (including Awa-Tokushima, then named Myōdō prefecture) were abolished and amalgamated with neighbors. By 1880 the government had decided that the traditional province (*kuni*) was the best unit for prefectural boundaries; larger provinces formed a single prefecture, smaller ones were grouped two or three to a prefecture. By 1890, the number of prefectures had risen to forty-three as various provinces recovered their administrative independence. Awa-Tokushima was one of the first to do so, in 1880. The inability of prefectural assemblymen from different provinces to agree on local taxes, wide differences in local customs, and poor communications were the major considerations in this decision.[2]

Within the province, the next traditional subdivision was the district (*gun*). In 1860 there were ten such districts in Awa province, by no means uniform in area or population. In 1872 all Japanese districts were replaced as administrative units by large and small sections (*daiku* and *shōku*) in an ambitious attempt to standardize local administration at the subprefectural level. In the case of Awa-Tokushima the district survived in new guise as the large section until 1878, when a return was made to the traditional towns and villages as administrative units. At the same time, the government ordered the districts to be revived as branches of the prefectural office. By 1883 the government had defined the district head (*gunchō*) as a regular official paid from the national treasury, and the district office then became an important center of local administration. In order to cut costs, groups of two or three of the smaller districts in Awa province were placed under a single head, but in 1888 the government, probably as a preparatory step toward the new district assemblies set up in 1890, ordered that no districts were to be amalgamated. Thus in 1891 Tokushima prefecture once again consisted of ten districts, each with its own office and assembly. Like the province, the district survived despite early attempts to supersede it.

Amalgamation was more successful at the town and village level. In 1860 Awa province had five rural towns (*gō machi*) with populations of 1,000 to 3,000 or more, plus a dozen or so larger villages singled out as ports or post stations. Over the rest of the province there were some six hundred villages, most having about 800 inhabitants but many smaller ones having 200 or so. After 1868, the domain attempted to amalgamate these into numbered units (*ban*) at an average of ten wards or villages

---

Tarō, "Nihon chihō gyōzaisei no keisei to kōzō," pt. 2, *Shakai kagaku kenkyū*, vol. 9, no. 2 (August 1957), pp. 52-53.

[2] See *Kōbunroku 1878 Fuken*, 2A 10 kō 2379, item 7, and *1880 Naimushō*, 2A 10 kō 2854, item 18 (Kokuritsu kōbunshokan, Tokyo).

to a unit. When they were reorganized into small sections (*shōku*) the scale was doubled to about twenty wards or villages to a unit. The small section was abolished in 1878, but on the initiative of the prefectural governor, whose express purpose was to cut costs, a "registry unit" (*kibetsu*) consisting of five or more wards or villages was formed in Awa province. By 1890 these *kibetsu* had been replaced by a total of seven towns (*machi*) and one hundred eleven villages (*son*), with a minimum of rearrangement. Thus, the amalgamations that in 1888 caused so much trouble in other provinces had been anticipated in Awa by almost a decade.

In 1860 the castle town Tokushima, in addition to its samurai quarters, comprised about forty wards, varying a great deal in size but averaging around 800 inhabitants. These, like the wards in the towns and villages, were successively reorganized into numbered units, small sections, and *kibetsu* between 1868 and 1879. In 1890, after government orders that all towns of more than 10,000 inhabitants be classed as cities (*shi*), some twenty-nine wards and eight neighboring villages were amalgamated to form Tokushima City (population 60,000, roughly one-tenth the population of the prefecture).

Unlike the prefectures and districts, the traditional wards and villages were thus considerably widened in administrative scale between 1860 and 1890. Even so, they continued to survive as informal subunits (*aza*, *buraku*), and the plans of government leaders to pool their common property failed in the face of ingrained local particularism.[3] While Japan looked to Prussia as a model in so many aspects of local administration, it ended up with prefectures much smaller than the Prussian provinces but having much larger towns and villages.

Taxation

In 1860 the tax system in Awa, as elsewhere in Japan, was riddled with inconsistencies and anomalies.[4] The system was complicated by the fact that senior retainers held at least one-third of the province in subdomain. Many villages thus had to apportion their domain taxes among several

[3] See Fujita Takeo, *Nihon chihō zaisei seido no seiritsu* (Tokyo: Iwanami shoten, 1941), pp. 173-176. In 1911 only one-fifth of all town and village property in Tokushima prefecture was owned by the legally established bodies. See Tokushima ken shi hensan iinkai, *Tokushima ken shi*, 6 vols. (Tokushima: Tokushima ken shi hensan iinkai, 1964-1967), vol. 5, pp. 119-120.

[4] Ikeuchi Motokazu, *Kaikoroku*, 3 vols., MS (Tokushima kenritsu toshokan), vol. 2, p. 15.

collecting agents. Despite these complexities, however, domain officials and local heads had developed a high level of practical expertise in tax assessment and collection.[5] After 1871, leaders admitted that the policy of posting officials to localities other than their own had led to some decline in these standards.[6] Tax payment in money or against vouchers (*sashigami*) was widespread in Awa province; together with the detailed tax registers kept by local heads, this provided a platform for the radical Meiji advance from tax-in-kind, assessed on communities, to tax-in-money, paid by individuals.

Between 1868 and 1871 all Awa subdomains were abolished and efforts were made to regularize taxes. The domain also planned to impose export taxes, but it was hamstrung by government restrictions on local trading organizations in the interests of its own banking and commercial companies.[7] In 1870 the domain had to suspend tax payment in paper money because of the prevailing financial chaos.

After the Restoration, both the central government and the domains announced that taxes were to remain at current levels. When the domains were replaced by prefectures in 1871, the first steps were taken toward land tax reform—again with promises that the purpose was to rationalize the tax burden, not to increase it on a national basis. From 1872 to 1873, abortive attempts were made to issue certificates of land ownership,[8] followed by the land tax reform of 1874-1881, which is discussed by Kozo Yamamura elsewhere in this book.[9] Only a few aspects of special relevance to this chapter need be noted here.

The cost of land survey, borne largely by the farmers themselves, was well over $500,000 in Awa.[10] Some, but by no means all of this, appears in community budgets of the mid-1870s. Further, the central government's allotment of a rice price to each province after area and yield had been calculated caused consternation among local heads when the price for Awa was announced in 1876. The chief secretary of the prefecture was dismissed in 1878 for arbitrarily attempting to cut the land tax

[5] Amō Ioe, *Ikeda chō shi* (Tokushima: Ikeda chō yakuba, 1962), pp. 1124-1125.

[6] Fukushima Masao, "Meiji rokunen no chihō kaidō to chiso kaisei," *Tōyō bunko kenkyū kiyō*, vol. 18 (March 1959), p. 42.

[7] Kannō Watarō, *Nihon kaisha kigyō hassei shi no kenkyū* (Tokyo: Iwanami shoten, 1931), pp. 167-168.

[8] Fukushima Masao, *Chiso kaisei* (Tokyo: Yoshikawa kōbunkan, 1968), pp. 98-100. For Awa, see also Tokushima shi shi henshūshitsu, *Tokushima shi shi*, 2 vols. (Tokushima: Tokushima shi kyōiku iinkai, 1973-1976), vol. 2, pp. 344-345.

[9] A major study by Fukushima Masao, *Chiso kaisei no kenkyū* (Tokyo: Yōhikaku, 1962), points out regional variations in previous land tax burdens, pp. 465, 470-471.

[10] Ibid., pp. 481, 484.

assessment by 5 percent, and the governor also resigned in protest.[11] Finally, although the government had promised reductions in land tax as commercial taxes increased, as well as resurveys every five years, it reneged when these promises came due in the early 1880s.

The new central land tax became the standard for the prefectural tax, which in 1876 was not to exceed one-fifth of it, a limit raised to one-third in 1880. Meanwhile, prefectural governments and communities levied their own taxes on land, supplementing this as far as possible by business and household taxes. In 1872 numerous traditional taxes such as the corvée (*buyakugin*) were abolished and replaced by the business tax (*eigyōzei*) and household taxes (*nikkawari, kosūwari*). After 1878 various kinds of business taxes were reserved for the new prefectural tax (*chihōzei*), weakening the tax base of the communities. In addition, the central government imposed new national taxes after 1880 on sake brewing and tobacco. By 1881, as a national average, the prefectural tax was drawn chiefly from land (65%), then household tax (22%), and finally business tax (13%). Left with small resources for land and business tax, most communities turned to household levies (*kobetsuwari*) as the major source of their tax income.[12]

These changes were masked for a few years by the inflation of the 1870s, but the deflationary 1880s posed problems throughout Japan. By 1890 the situation had improved again with a rise in commodity prices and a marked improvement in the volume of commercial activity. But even if we allow for such alleviating factors as more equitable tax collection, greater productivity resulting from the abolition of internal barriers, as well as improved communications and a flourishing export trade, taxes were probably still heavy by 1860 standards.

Local Administration

In 1860 the top local heads were the *ōdoshiyori* of the castle town and the *yotō shōya* of the districts. Serving under the *machi bugyō* or *gundai* of the domain office, they were drawn from the richest merchants and farmers, and enjoyed samurai status. There were in all about thirty such men, each with his own staff of secretaries, clerks, and constables. While supervising all important matters of administration, they had a direct

[11] *Shinagawa Yajirō kankei monjo mokuroku*, shorui no bu, item 919 (Kensei shiryōshitsu, National Diet Library, Tokyo). Also, Arimoto Yoshishige, *Hompō chiso no enkaku* (Tokyo: 1914), p. 99.

[12] Ōshima Tarō, "Nihon chihō gyōzaisei no keisei to kōzō," pt. 1, *Shakai kagaku kenkyū*, vol. 8, nos. 5 and 6 (March 1957), pp. 34-40, points out inequitable results.

responsibility to transmit and enforce domain orders to the ward and village heads (*machi toshiyori* and *shōya*) within their area of jurisdiction. Within each community, the leading householders and farmers formed a kind of council to advise and assist the ward or village head. Termed *goningumi* (but not to be confused with the neighbor pledge-groups of the Kantō provinces and elsewhere), they usually numbered from two to eight, depending on the population and wealth of the community. All these men were either directly appointed or confirmed in their posts by the domain office.

The domain made a modest yearly contribution of a few hundred *koku* to the *ōdoshiyori* and *yotō shōya*, but otherwise they and their juniors in the administrative hierarchy recouped their expenses from community taxes. By Meiji standards, these were modest. For example, local heads used their own homes as offices, meeting at temples and inns for wider conferences. On one occasion, the domain had to order that village underofficials be treated with more respect, which suggests that their status and salaries were low.

For principal-domain tax collection and subsidiary administrative functions, there were also offices (*daikansho*) at three or four outlying towns or post stations in the 1860s. When all subdomains were abolished after 1868, the domain set up four local offices (*minseisho*) for handling justice, commercial products, and water control in addition to taxation. Although abolished in 1871 along with the domain, such local offices were revived in 1878 as district offices (*gun yakusho*) under heads appointed by the prefectural office. This reaching out by local administration into the districts was an important part of the Meiji transformation, with increased costs that will be noted below.

Between 1868 and 1878 the titles of local heads changed almost yearly, as the domain and subsequent prefectural governments attempted to increase their standing and widen the scale of local administration. While ordering that local heads must be ranked above ordinary samurai in social status, the government often reiterated that they were not to be regarded as regular officials—no doubt to ensure that they continued to be paid from local taxes. The government also sought to raise their salaries, ruling in 1872 that they were to be paid at standard rates, increased by 30 percent if local conditions allowed. Salaries ranged at this time from 120 yen per annum for large-section heads (*daiku chō*) down to 12 yen per annum for the heads of small villages. In 1874 the salaries of local heads and staff in Awa province amounted to 30,022 yen; the cost of local offices, 12,271 yen. By 1876, these figures had risen to 41,000 and 22,000 yen, respectively.

When the new prefectural tax (*chihōzei*) was set up in 1878, it was ruled that the salaries of local heads and staff were to be paid from it—no doubt for greater security of payment, since prefectural tax had legal enforcement, which community tax at this time did not. Office expenses however, were to be paid from community tax (*kyōgihi*). That same year, new district offices were set up; their heads, staff, and office expenses were all to be paid from the prefectural tax. The cost of this was offset in Awa province by amalgamation of the smaller districts under a single office and by the *kibetsu* system, which from 1878 to 1880 reduced the number of town and village heads as noted.

Nevertheless, government orders continued to prescribe higher salary scales for community officials, and as the quantity of delegated business required to be handled by local offices rose, so did expenses. By 1881 the cost of the Tokushima district offices was 40,000 yen, and the salaries of community heads and underofficials amounted to 75,000 yen—all told, 30 percent of the prefectural budget. Nationally, the cost of offices averaged 15 percent of the community budget,[13] but this was to double in the next decade.

The government made great efforts after 1881 to reduce the cost of local administration, keeping a tight rein on salaries and office expenses. The nationwide amalgamation of towns and villages in 1888 aimed at cutting costs; and the new self-government system of that year sought to increase the number of nonsalaried community posts, beginning with the town and village heads. District office expenses in Tokushima prefecture had now been cut to 34,000 yen and the salaries of community heads and clerks to 71,000 yen, but between them they still absorbed nearly 30 percent of the prefectural tax.[14] The eight district offices were employing 180 men, the two hundred thirty town and village offices 579. In 1890 the number of district employees was further reduced to 153; but the city, town, and village offices were now employing more than 800 men. Office expenses had now risen to 35 percent of community tax.

Central leaders and prefectural governors often expressed regret at the amount of delegated business (especially the preparation of statistical reports) imposed on community offices, but this proved a necessary part of the Meiji transformation. By and large, the traditional urban and rural upper class continued to dominate town and village administration, which, at 30 percent of prefectural tax and 35 percent of community

[13] Kikegawa Hiroshi, *Meiji jichi seido no seiritsu katei* (Tokyo: Tōkyō shisei chōsakai, 1957), p. 72.

[14] Yearly salaries of village heads rose as follows: 1870, 18-24 yen; 1875, 48-120 yen; 1884, 72-240 yen. The average yearly salary of village clerks in the 1880s was 50 yen.

tax, was the largest single item in the total local tax burden of Tokushima prefecture during 1889.

Police and Prisons

Tokushima castle town certainly had a common prison in 1860, but its extent and capacity are not known. A dozen or so domain officials handled police business in the castle town itself; in the districts, police inspectors (*gō metsuke*), appointed from men of the village-head class, operated under the control of the domain office. These inspectors had full samurai status and wide powers to investigate and report legal infractions of all kinds, including those of local heads. They were assisted by a number of lesser officials (*dōshin*). But most routine policing in the towns and villages was performed by watchmen (*ban hinin*) hired according to local needs. Of the lowest social status, these men were allowed twice a year to solicit gifts from house to house as a means of support.[15]

A further guarantee of law and order was provided by the militiamen (*gō teppō* and *machi teppō*) that were increasingly fostered by the domain after 1840 as a counter to the threat of foreign incursions. By 1860, many wards and villages had perhaps half a dozen such men, armed with guns and enjoying minor privileges such as exemption from the corvée, but unsalaried.[16]

Domain budgets for 1868-1871 suggest that expenditure on police and prisons was very modest by later standards. In 1870 the Criminal Justice Department of Awa domain drew 150 *koku* (about 500 yen) and its policemen (*hobōyaku*) about 1,700 yen. In that year seventy people (sixty-eight men, two women) were sentenced to imprisonment. They were employed inside the prison on woodworking, washing, and weaving or on outside work such as roadsweeping, for which they received a small daily wage. In 1871 the domain spent 541 yen on prisons. The judicial

[15] For good accounts of Awa-domain police arrangements, see Tokushima ken keisatsu shi hensan iinkai, *Tokushima ken keisatsu shi* (Tokushima: Tokushima ken keisatsu shi hensan iinkai, 1968), pp. 212-213; Tadokoro Ichita, *Hinotani son shi* (Tokushima: Hinotani son yakuba, 1936), pp. 39-41; Mihara Takeo, "Meiji jidai Tokushima ken keisatsu no hensen," *Awa gakkai kyōdo kenkyū happyōkai kiyō*, nos. 6, 7, and 8 (August 1961), p. 87.

[16] No roster of local militiamen has survived for Awa province; but at a guess, based on such clues as reductions in *sotsu* enrollment from 1868 to 1871 and the number of military guns in private hands (2,756 in 1882), the province had about 3,000 militiamen, distributed between six hundred or so towns and villages. On the use of local militia under village-head officers to counter farmer uprisings in the 1860s, see Watanabe Nobuo, "Bakumatsu no nōhei to nōmin ikki," *Rekishi*, vol. 18 (1959), pp. 35-50.

system of Meiji Japan, modeled on Western legal codes and standards, was to prove much more expensive than that of the domain regime with its prompt and economical punishments such as banishment, loss of status, house arrest, handcuffing, and whipping.

In 1872, at a time of massive reductions in local posts of all kinds, the police establishment of Awa province numbered about one hundred men. For the next year or so, costs remained at the level of 1,500 yen in salaries and 500 yen for prisons. Meanwhile, communities continued to hire police constables of their own under various titles. Two farmer uprisings in 1870 and 1873, involving several hundred rioters, were put down after hiring volunteer constables, probably from the local militia class, suggesting that the latter was still an important guarantee of law and order.

The establishment of the Home Ministry in 1874 marks the first step toward the creation of a national police force. The government was now anxious to upgrade the status of policemen, paying them higher salaries and allowing them to bear arms, while discouraging communities from hiring constables of their own. The local militia had been disbanded by 1871, and henceforth the new army garrisons were to provide the ultimate means of control in cases of local disturbance.

Until 1878, police costs in the prefectures were drawn about evenly from community tax (*mimpi*) and various kinds of official subsidy (*kampi*);[17] but from this year on, only building expenses were paid by the government. Henceforth, salaries and other expenses were paid from the new prefectural tax (*chihōzei*). In 1880, Tokushima prefecture had a police establishment of 18 inspectors and 336 constables deployed in five stations and forty-seven branch stations, and drawing 46,000 yen from prefectural tax. By 1890, the number of policemen had risen to 442; they were now deployed in ten stations, ten branch stations, and nearly one hundred outstations—virtually one police post to each town and village. Expenses had risen to 63,000 yen annually.

A new prison was constructed in a converted domain warehouse by 1873, and a separate prison workshop by 1881. In 1885 the prefectural assembly approved construction of a new prison building, which was completed in 1889 largely by the work of the prisoners themselves. By this time there was also a small branch prison in one of the outlying districts. In 1890, the cost of these prisons—as with police expenses, required to be paid from prefectural tax—amounted to around 65,000 yen. Prisons were now costing more than police, for as the Meiji legal

[17] Yamamoto Kazuo, *Nihon keisatsu shi* (Tokyo: Shōkadō shoten, 1934), pp. 332-333. Also, *Tokushima ken keisatsu shi*, pp. 598-602.

system took final shape the number of prisoners rose—in Awa, from 736 in 1882 to 1,500 in 1890,[18] guarded by two hundred officials of all kinds.

The government was very proud of its new police force, with its much higher levels of education, training, and social status.[19] By 1890, standards of prison discipline, work, and educational opportunities had also greatly improved.[20] The ordinary policeman or prison warder, earning around 150 yen annually, was certainly much better paid than his 1860 counterpart. Police and prisons were now taking up 40 percent of the prefectural budget, its largest single item. It was not until 1899, after further increases in costs, that the central government took over all prison expenses when the lower house of the Diet approved an increase in the land tax.

Education

The chief educational institution in the 1860s was the Awa domain school. With six professors and sixty or so pupils, this school taught Western studies, classics, and medicine. Situated on the castle grounds, it was the direct forerunner of the Meiji middle, normal, and medical schools of Tokushima City. Next were the district schools (*gō gakkō*) set up in four or five rural centers after 1840 as part of the domain mobilization program. Headed by stipended samurai, these schools taught classics and military arts to the children of local worthies, but were small in scale, usually having two or three teachers and thirty or so pupils.[21] The three middle schools set up after 1879 in district centers, each with about thirty pupils, can be regarded as their short-lived successors. (They were abolished in 1885 to reduce costs.) The majority of schools, however, were either *kajuku/shijuku*, at which a single teacher taught classics to well-connected pupils, or *terakoya*, where children learned basic writing and arithmetic. These schools averaged about fifty pupils and were in many cases the direct forerunners of Meiji primary schools. In the 1860s there were 37 *shijuku* and 432 *terakoya* in Awa province, a total of 469 schools attended by some 24,000 pupils (roughly

[18] On average, one-tenth of prison inmates were women, and one-third of all prisoners were awaiting trial or sentence. For national policy on prisons and its effect on local finance, see Nakajima Nobutora, *Dai Nihon chihō zaisei shi* (Tokyo: 1915), pp. 21-22, 52-53.

[19] Takahashi Yūsai, *Meiji keisatsu shi kenkyū*, 2 vols. (Tokyo: Reibunsha, 1960-1961), vol. 1, pp. 12-13.

[20] Shinshū Honganjiha Ōtaniha Honganji, *Nihon kangoku kyōkai shi*, 2 vols. (Tokyo: Shinshū Honganjiha Ōtaniha Honganji, 1927), vol. 2, pp. 1517-1520, 1536-1537, 1542.

[21] Tokushima ken kyōikukai, *Tokushima ken kyōiku enkaku shi* (Tokushima: Tokushima ken kyōikukai, 1920); Ishikawa Ken, *Nihon shomin kyōiku shi* (Tokyo: Tōkō shoin, 1929).

20,000 boys, 4,000 girls).[22] Over 20 percent of Awa children were attending school of some sort. Both the *shijuku* and *terakoya* were funded entirely from pupil fees, estimated in the reminiscences of one local head to have been around 15 sen per annum in terms of Meiji currency.[23]

Between 1868 and 1871, further efforts were made to promote education, but in 1871 all domain schools were abolished. The former daimyo, senior retainers, and a wide range of local worthies now gave land, buildings, and money to transform the domain and private schools into primary schools of the kind stipulated by the government. In 1873 there were 479 primary schools in Awa province, many of them still classified as private. By 1880, the number of primary schools had dropped to 458, but there was now at least one to each *kibetsu* group of town wards and villages. Only 2 private schools still remained, a decline signaled in 1878 by the failure of Tokushima worthies to maintain an independent academy teaching foreign languages and law. With the drive to reduce costs in the 1880s, the number of primary schools fell further—to 355 by 1890. There was now a single middle school, a normal school, and a medical school, all situated in the city of Tokushima.

In 1878, Awa schools were receiving an annual subsidy of 15,000 yen from the Education Ministry. The total income of the four hundred or so government schools was 129,042 yen, of which 7,525 yen (6%) were recovered from pupil fees, averaging 12 sen per capita.[24] After 1880 the government cut all subsidies for local education. Henceforth the Tokushima middle, normal, and medical schools were funded from the prefectural tax (25,000 yen per annum, or 10 percent of the budget). By 1885, income from pupil fees had fallen to 1,709 yen per annum (1 percent of costs, an average of 2 sen per pupil), but the government was now determined that costs should be recovered as far as possible from this source. Between 1886 and 1890, annual income from pupil fees rose to 24,832 yen (20 percent of costs, an average of 30 sen per pupil).[25] The government insisted that communities must bear the full burden of their own primary schools,[26] and by 1890 (on top of pupil fees) education still took up 32 percent of the average community budget.

[22] Ōsaka Toshio, "Kinsei Tokushima han ni okeru kyōiku no tenkai katei," *Tokushima kenritsu Wakimachi kōtō gakkō kiyō*, no. 5 (March 1979), p. 23.

[23] Ikeuchi, *Kaikoroku*, vol. 1, p. 200; Miyata Takezō, *Horieshō shi* (Tokushima: Horieshō son yakuba, 1918), pp. 63-67.

[24] Sasamori Takeshi, *Meiji zenki chihō kyōiku gyōsei ni kansuru kenkyū* (Tokyo: Kōdansha, 1978), p. 352 insert; Kaigo Tokuomi, *Inoue Kowashi no kyōiku seisaku* (Tokyo: Tōkyō daigaku shuppankai, 1968), p. 102.

[25] Sasamori, *Meiji zenki chihō kyōiku*, p. 361, and shiryō 5, p. 352 insert.

[26] Fujita, *Nihon chihō zaisei seido no seiritsu*, p. 170.

That education costs were a crippling burden on many communities is evident from the numerous cases of primary schools being singled out for destruction in farmer uprisings, and from the despairing comments of government officials like Inoue Kowashi and Mori Arinori on the miserable state of local education in the late 1870s.[27] Much of the increased cost of education was owing to teachers' salaries, which rose progressively in response to government orders. In 1890 the 357 teachers of Tokushima prefecture were paid a total of 73,000 yen, about 60 percent of total education expenditure. The average primary school teacher was now earning 100 yen a year, certainly more than his 1860 counterpart.

Meanwhile, progress had been made in raising school attendance, from 25,000 in 1868 to more than 50,000 in 1890. In Awa, nearly 60 percent of school-age boys and 20 percent of girls were now attending school. However, it was not until 1900, after further rises in costs, that school attendance rose to over 90 percent.

Comparing educational change between 1860 and 1890, one can point first to economies of scale. Very generally, the number of schools had been reduced by one-third, and the number of pupils per school trebled. As for costs, in 1870 the domain budgeted 4,000 *koku* (about 15,000 yen) for the domain and district schools;[28] compared with the 25,000 yen per annum spent after 1880 on the prefectural normal, middle, and medical schools, the cost of higher education had nearly doubled. If we add to the costs of primary schools in community budgets the equivalent sum received from pupil fees, the town or village school was by far the largest public investment made by most Meiji communities.

Public Works and Disaster Relief

Under the Tokugawa regime, public works were handled in the following ways. The *bakufu*, as the prototype central government, levied the domains from time to time for public works within its territories. By 1860 the Awa domain met such demands by levies on rich farmers and mer-

[27] Tsuchiya Tadao, *Meiji zenki kyōiku seisaku shi no kenkyū* (Tokyo: Bunkyō tosho, 1962, repr. 1968), p. 105; Egi Chiyuki, *Egi Chiyuki ō keireki dan*, 3 vols. (Tokyo: Egi Chiyuki ō den kankōkai, 1933), vol. 1, pp. 33-46. For Mori, *Japan Weekly Mail*, January 12, 1889, trans. from *Tōkyō nichi nichi shimbun*, December 7, 1888. Also see Inoue Kowashi denki hensan iinkai, *Inoue Kowashi den*, 6 vols. (Tokyo: Kokugakuin daigaku toshokan, 1966-1967), vol. 1, p. 98.

[28] Tokushima shi shi hensanshitsu, *Tokushima shi shi*, 3 vols. (Tokushima: Tokushima shi shi hensanshitsu, 1973-1983), vol. 2, p. 682.

chants, rewarding them with samurai status and other privileges. Major public works within the domain were carried out by levies apportioned among the districts on the basis of their tax assessments and corvée registers. Finally, towns and villages carried out their own public works, either individually or jointly, by levies made at their own discretion after appropriate consultations. Disaster relief was provided from reserve granaries (*gisō*) and by tax cuts, amounting in very severe years to as much as half of domain income.

Upon abolition of the domains in 1871, the government took over all reserve granaries, diverting their funds to finance public works, police, and schools.[29] The government now had the final responsibility for relief in major disasters; an attempt, in 1873, to define this responsibility gave way quickly to ad hoc grants and confused regulations for delayed tax payment.[30] Meanwhile, prefectures and communities continued to manage public works from their own taxes, appealing to the Home and Finance ministries for subsidies in major undertakings. Amounts spent in public works by communities varied considerably from place to place and from year to year, but throughout the 1870s and 1880s these averaged around 25 percent of the budget. After 1880, when the prefectural tax rose to equal the community tax, most prefectures spent from 10 to 40 percent of their yearly budget on public works.[31]

In 1877 the government ruled that if a given village lost the whole of its crop in a natural disaster all tax for that year was to be remitted, but would have to be repaid in installments over the next ten years. If the loss were one-half or more, proportional remissions were to be granted (and repaid over five to ten years). No tax remission was to be given if the loss were less than half.[32] In 1880 this system was replaced by a Disaster Savings Law (*bikō chochiku hō*). The government contracted to put aside 1.2 million yen per annum for the next twenty years; this money would accumulate in a central fund. At the same time, prefectures were required to put aside a sum—equivalent to 10 percent of the yearly budget—that would accumulate in a fund of their own.[33] The government was concerned to guarantee its own tax income against demands for

[29] In Awa province, the reserve granary funds amounted to 18,910 yen, plus 17,353 yen in a relief fund for fishermen. See *Kōbunroku*: *Fuken keikyō 1873*, 2A 9 kō 998, item 3 (Kokuritsu kōbunshokan, Tokyo). The total gain to the government was estimated at 1.5 million yen. See P. Mayet, *Agricultural Insurance in Organic Connection with Savings-Banks, Land-Credit, and the Calculation of Debts* (London: S. Sonnenschein, 1893), p. 265.

[30] Mayet, *Agricultural Insurance*, p. 265.

[31] Tōkyō keizai shimpōsha, *Meiji Taishō zaisei shōran* (Tokyo: Tōkyō keizai shimpōsha, 1929), table 526.

[32] Mayet, *Agricultural Insurance*, pp. 268-269.

[33] Ibid., pp. 271-280, 287-290, 297-302.

disaster relief and, in March 1884, reiterated that the land tax was on no account to be increased or decreased according to good or bad harvests.[34]

In the late 1870s the government was spending up to 1 million yen a year on public works, but announced in 1880 that no further subsidies would be granted. Nevertheless, it continued to give selective subsidies, in particular to promote trunk roads, bridges, and harbor works as part of a national drive to improve communications. In 1885 such subsidies were amounting to about 500,000 yen a year, with equivalent sums in government grants for disaster relief.[35]

The cost of the Meiji system was heavy for the localities. Even with government grants, prefectures often had to raise loans to pay for disaster relief,[36] and in 1890 the government reneged on its 1880 promise (to put aside 1.2 million yen) and quietly dropped this provision from the revised Disaster Savings Law of that year.[37]

Tokushima prefecture was not fortunate in its subsidy grants. Between 1885 and 1889 the Home Ministry spent 242,827 yen on Yoshino River control, but all work was suspended for several decades when the new dikes broke under heavy floods, with loss of life and much damage to property. In road construction, the prefecture petitioned in 1885 for a 1:2 subsidy to link up with the Kōchi-Takamatsu trunk road, but it was granted only a 1:3 subsidy on the grounds of lower priority. Even when the full subsidy was granted for road construction, the burden on the favored localities remained heavy.[38] Unlike some prefectures, where economic advantage or military strategy prompted the government to construct railway lines, Tokushima had to finance railway development with private capital after 1890. Its expenditure of 10 percent of prefectural tax and 25 percent of community tax on public works, while not as much as administration, police/prisons, and education, was still one of the four major local burdens.

Elected Assemblies

Election to town and village offices was by no means unknown in pre-Meiji times. Especially in the Kantō provinces, the election by villagers of representatives (*hyakushō dai*) to look after their interests in dealing

[34] *Chiso jōrei*, March 15, 1884, cl. 2.

[35] Ariizumi Sadao, *Meiji seiji shi no kiso katei* (Tokyo: Yoshikawa kōbunkan, 1980), pp. 139-143.

[36] Nakajima, *Dai Nihon chihō zaisei shi*, pp. 71-72.

[37] Mayet, *Agricultural Insurance*, p. 387.

[38] Ōshima, "Nihon chihō gyōzaisei," pt. 1, pp. 81-84.

with local heads was a well-established custom.[39] The town and village assembly (*yoriai*), attended by all independent household heads, had become an almost universal feature of community life by 1860. As part of its mobilization program, Awa domain after 1850 encouraged communities to select and employ able men in their offices. Throughout the province, as in many others, a new class of independent medium and small farmers had begun to challenge the traditional local heads in their role as tax assessors and managers of community funds.[40]

The Meiji regime was characterized from the outset by a strong interest in the representative assembly as an instrument of government. Many domains set up elected assemblies of various kinds between 1869 and 1871, but there is no record that Awa-Tokushima did so. In 1870, elections were certainly held for all of Tokushima's ward officials.[41]

After 1871 the chief motive behind government encouragement of elections to local offices was the urgent need to employ men of ability and good reputation, men capable of handling new forms of administration and enforcing government orders, many of which were bound to be unpopular. On the other hand, in most localities only the urban and rural upper class was literate and experienced enough to manage affairs, while the traditional community assemblies with their concern for consensus often proved an obstacle to the reform measures ordered by the government.[42] Most government leaders were agreed that at a time when local taxes were rising, the common people had to be allowed greater participation in financial affairs and some redress against the arbitrary decisions of local heads.[43]

[39] For an account of electoral practices in *bakufu* villages, see *Ōmori Shōichi monjo*, MS, vol. 13, in Tokugawa shi gōson seido taiyō (Shisei semmon toshokan, Tokyo). For a Wakayama example of electing ward heads, see Hayashi Tadasu, *Nochi wa mukashi no ki* (Tokyo: Jiji shimpōsha, 1910), p. 8.

[40] Inada Masatsugu, *Meiji kokka keisei katei no kenkyū* (Tokyo: Ochanomizu shobō, 1977), pp. 286-292. For Awa, Kondō Tatsurō, *Yamashirotani son shi* (Tokushima: Yamashirotani son yakuba, 1975), pp. 270-272, 463-465; Hiraoka Yoshiyasu, *Hiraoka Harunosuke den* (Tokushima: 1975), pp. 76-77.

[41] Tokushima ken, *Awa han minsei shiryō*, 2 vols. (Tokushima: Tokushima shiryō kankōkai, 1916, repr. 1968), vol. 1, pp. 296-297; vol. 2, p. 1495.

[42] The government's dilemma on this issue led it to instruct local officials in 1869 that "when holding assembly with the common people, it is necessary that the popular view (*shūron*) adopt proper proposals. If the majority is followed and the minority rejected, this will give rise to the evil of confusion." See Ōshima Tarō, "Nihon chihō gyōzaisei," pt. 2, p. 45. On discontent with the traditional assemblies often expressed by local governors, see R.E. Ward, *Political Development in Modern Japan* (Princeton: Princeton University Press, 1968), p. 229.

[43] Itō Hirobumi to Ōkubo Toshimichi, June 13, 1877, in Nihon shiseki kyōkai, *Ōkubo Toshimichi monjo*, 10 vols. (Tokyo: Yoshikawa kōbunkan, 1969 reprint), vol. 8, pp. 270-271. Inoue Kowashi also had much to say on this issue; see *Inoue Kowashi den*, vol. 1, p. 98ff. and pp. 114-115, 165-166.

The result of these dilemmas was a very confused period of experiment with local elections and assemblies between 1871 and 1878. In Awa province, regulations for the election of section heads were issued in 1873, and for section, town, and village heads in 1875. A prefectural assembly with elected delegates was also held in 1874. At this time it was left to the local communities to decide for themselves whether or not to elect their heads. In the one recorded instance of such an election in Awa province, all the section and village heads stepped down but they were voted back to their former posts.[44]

In 1875 the Assembly of Local Governors, held in Tokyo, resolved that it was still too early for elected assemblies to be promoted at the town and village level and that, as a general rule, local assemblies should be composed of community heads. In 1876 the governor ordered that in Awa province all town and village heads would henceforth be appointed by the prefectural office, which suggests that the earlier regulations for election had not worked well. Fearful of landlord dominance of the land tax reform at a time of widespread farmer uprisings, the government stipulated around this time that three or four popular representatives (*jimmin sōdai*) were to be elected by each town and village to participate in the survey work. A firsthand account of this survey work in Awa province recalls that only one of the popular representatives could write with any ease and none could use an abacus, thus leaving practically all the work to a member of the village-head class.[45] Such ineptitude on the part of the popular representatives in the land tax survey was noted in many other provinces.[46]

In 1878 the government made up its mind on the issue of local elections and prefectural assemblies. Suffrage was to be limited to adult male taxpayers, at the rate of 5 yen per annum to elect and 10 yen per annum to be elected. These assemblies were to debate and approve a yearly budget for items paid from the new prefectural tax (*chihōzei*), limited in 1876 to one-fifth of land tax but increased to one-third in 1880. The electoral qualifications for prefectural assemblies restricted membership to the richer merchants and farmers.[47] At the same time, the communities were allowed to draw up regulations for town and village assemblies and to elect their own heads. These assemblies were to debate and approve

[44] Ikeuchi Motokazu, *Kaikoroku*, vol. 1, pp. 98-99.

[45] Ibid., pp. 171, 174.

[46] Arimoto Masao, *Chiso kaisei to nōmin tōsō* (Tokyo: Shinseisha, 1968), pp. 265-269.

[47] *Tokushima ken shiryō*: *1881 Tokushima ken no rekishi*, MS, vol. 2 (Naikaku bunko, Tokyo). Of a total population of 609,318 persons, 23,669 could elect and 11,805 could be elected. Electors included 1,309 *shizoku*, 20,483 farmers, 203 artisans, and 1,674 merchants; those able to be elected included 729 *shizoku*, 10,174 farmers, 72 artisans, and 830 merchants. For national figures, see Kikegawa, *Meiji jichi*, pp. 89-90.

yearly budgets for items paid from community tax (*kyōgihi*). No limits were prescribed for this tax, but it remained at the same level as the prefectural tax, mainly because of the constant increase in delegated business required to be handled by community offices. It was left to the towns and villages to define the electoral qualifications of their own assemblies; for the nation as a whole, some 6 million adult males had voting rights in community assemblies by the early 1880s.[48]

This situation lasted until 1884. Then, under pressure from the Movement for People's Rights, and in a mood of disappointment over the quality of many elected community heads, the government ruled that town and village heads were again to be officially approved.[49] The governor of Tokushima prefecture promptly issued an order that town and village heads would henceforth be directly appointed by the prefectural office, and that they were to act as chairmen and control the agenda of their assemblies.[50] These were crisis years, however. By 1888 the government was once again anxious to restore election to community headships on the basis of new voting qualifications for town and village assemblies (and for the city assemblies to be set up in 1890). Following the Prussian model, electoral rights for community assemblies (which in turn elected one of their members as head) were restricted to male adults paying at least 2 yen per annum in total national taxes (*kokuzei*), either direct (*chokusetsu kokuzei*), prefectural (*chihōzei*), or community (*kuchōsonzei*; after 1890, *shichōsonzei*). Electors in the upper bracket (i.e. those who paid an annual community tax above the median) elected half the assembly members (eight to thirty in number); those in the lower bracket elected the other half. This two-tier system ensured that the higher taxpayers held at least half the seats in order to prevent domination by the larger number of taxpayers in the lower bracket.

Electorates varied greatly from community to community, but in most Awa-Tokushima examples the ratio of upper to lower voters was about 1:5. In the case of the cities set up in 1890, the electorate was divided into three brackets, with even more extreme disparities. In the first election to the Tokushima City assembly of that year, for example, the three brackets (each electing ten members) numbered as follows: upper, 56; middle, 420; lower, 2,165. In 1890 a total of 4 million men had voting

[48] Kikegawa, *Meiji jichi*, p. 75. In 1882, Tokushima-prefecture community assemblies comprised 77,109 electors and 71,513 able to be elected; most independent-household heads, then, had the right to vote.

[49] For government discontent with the elected heads, see Haraguchi Kiyoshi, *Meiji zenki chihō seiji shi kenkyū*, 2 vols. (Tokyo: Hanawa shobō, 1972-1974), vol. 2, pp. 231-232; Sasamori, *Meiji zenki*, p. 368.

[50] *Ōmori Shōichi monjo*, vol. 17.

rights in community assemblies, 2 million fewer than in 1880. As a national average, about 50 percent of male adults had voting rights; since land tax was still the chief national tax, this means that most villages had a noticeably higher percentage of voters than towns or cities.

Finally, the government set up new district assemblies (*gunkai*) in 1890, each having from fifteen to forty members. Every town and village assembly in the district put up one member, while resident landowners worth 10,000 yen or more provided one-third of the members. These assemblies, chaired by the district head, handled a yearly budget of about 10,000 yen spent mainly on public works and education.[51] In some districts there were no large landowners, or too few to make up one-third of the assembly, but the provision for their participation wherever possible again demonstrates the government's basic principle: to link assembly membership and electoral rights to property and taxes.

The cost of elected assemblies was not great, since membership was honorary and meetings were held for only a few weeks each year, but their importance is obvious. By debating and approving yearly budgets for items paid from local taxes, they provided an effective check on wasteful expenditure and did much to quell the hostile suspicions of taxpayers toward the traditional community heads and their immediate Meiji successors. In downgrading the voting power of the lower taxpayers and excluding the poor, the government ensured that many a town or village after 1890 had a balance of power very much like that of 1860 in spite of the new electoral system.

Conclusion

An itemized account of local administration such as the one above requires some sort of chronological perspective. Very generally, the first period of 1860-1868 was one of exhortation to higher standards, but with very little achievement. On top of the grave political uncertainties of the time, Awa faced a paralyzing crisis in domain finance, further aggravated by severe floods and crop failures. Between 1868 and 1871, the domain took the first positive steps toward administrative reform, prompted by the orders and example of the central government. Reform proceeded apace in the 1872-1877 period, accompanied by stabilized commodity prices and rising local taxes, which caused considerable rural

[51] In 1899, while abolishing the one-third membership of large landowners, district assemblies were elected by taxpaying qualifications: 3 yen per annum to elect, 5 yen per annum to be elected. For district assembly budgets in Tokushima prefecture for 1903, see *Ōmori Shōichi monjo*, vol. 37, p. 58.

unrest over much of the nation. From 1878 to 1881, the government, its income much reduced by inflation, increased local taxes under tighter prefectural control. The deflation of 1882 to 1885 then pushed the localities to the point of exhaustion, while the government had to impose even stronger controls to subdue the burgeoning Movement for People's Rights. By 1886, the government had achieved the twin goals of redeeming its paper currency and placing its armaments program on a firm footing. Thus it could afford to relax its hold on the localities and devote its attention to formulating a new self-government system for them. This took final shape in 1890.

PART TWO

ORGANIZATIONS

INTRODUCTION TO PART TWO

BY D. ELEANOR WESTNEY

Japan in the 1870s embarked on one of the most remarkable organizational transformations of the nineteenth century. In less than a decade, Japan witnessed the inauguration of new national systems of central and local administration, primary schools, police, postal communications, telegraph offices, and law courts; a national army and navy; banks, factories, newspapers, railways, chambers of commerce, and joint-stock companies. The emergence of new organizations modeled explicitly on those of the major Western powers dominated the processes of transformation, but by no means monopolized them. Existing organizations continued to operate in many sectors, and in some cases even increased in number, while new organizations emerged which combined elements of both the old and the new. The rapidity and diversity of this organizational change and its importance for Japan's subsequent development raise numerous questions that have yet to be explored systematically. What was the pattern of organizational development in various sectors of society? From where were the resources for the new organizations drawn? How did the various emerging organizations interact? What affected the rate of change after their initial establishment?

As social structures for coordinating and controlling the activities of many individuals, formal organizations are indispensable elements of the development of the nation-state, the application of the new technologies of the Industrial Revolution, the expansion of communications and transportation networks, and the growing specialization and differentiation of social roles. The far-reaching significance of the great rise in the number, size, and importance of large-scale formal organizations is reflected in the label "the organizational revolution," coined by Kenneth Boulding.[1] Like the Industrial Revolution which is its conceptual analogue, the

[1] Kenneth E. Boulding, *The Organizational Revolution: A Study in the Ethics of Economic Organization* (New York: Harper & Brothers, 1953). There have been almost as many definitions of "formal organization" as there have been organizational studies. Among the most commonly cited variables are formal criteria of membership; specified goals; a

Organizational Revolution consists everywhere of the same fundamental processes. New formal organizations emerge to take over the performance of activities previously carried out in the context of other social structures—the family, the community, and other less specialized organizations—and to perform entirely new functions. Societies vary greatly, however, with respect to the timing of this transformation, its pace, and the sequence in which organizations emerge and grow in different sectors.

Each of the five chapters in this section focuses on one organizational sector. Three of these sectors—the military, shipping, and education—had been characterized by considerable organizational development in the Tokugawa period, but in the second half of the nineteenth century they witnessed the emergence and rise to dominance of new organizations inspired by those of the West. One sector, the press, had no functional equivalent in the Tokugawa period, and its emerging organizational forms were products of the Meiji environment. Institutional Buddhism, already challenged in late Tokugawa and identified with the Tokugawa political order, faced serious problems of survival. It illustrates the problems of adaptation faced by old organizations in a period of rapid transition.

The pace and the patterns of change exhibit great variation across these five sectors, but common themes can be identified. All five sectors witnessed sudden and dramatic changes as well as less obvious, continuous, incremental development. All five were characterized by organizational disintegration as well as by organizational growth—by the decline or elimination of certain types of organizations as well as by the expansion and emergence of others. All five exhibit continuities with the past as well as discontinuities; of necessity, organizations in all five sectors drew on the resources—human, material, financial—developed in the Tokugawa period, and all actively tried to generate new resources to meet the challenges of change.

A number of developments in the Tokugawa period had raised considerably the level of human and economic resources in Japanese society: the spread of education, the extension of commercial development to the rural areas, high levels of urbanization, and the growing density of communications and transport networks. The level of organizational development itself was very high for a preindustrial society, and because of the Tokugawa political system, organizations were widely dispersed throughout the country. Each domain supported a large samurai bureaucracy and encouraged the development of commercial organizations

formally delineated hierarchy of authority; formally defined organizational roles, accompanied by allocation of the resources deemed necessary to perform them; standardized and performance-oriented criteria of recruitment and promotion; and rules of procedure for record keeping, communications, and task performance.

within its own boundaries. The large merchant houses of the great urban centers increased in scale and in formalization over time; except for state administration, they were the largest organizations in the society. Equally important in terms of the dissemination of organizational experience, however, were the smaller artisan and merchant units, which spread to the towns and even to the rural areas during the second half of the Tokugawa period, and the largely self-administering village "corporate units." All this contributed to an increase in what Arthur Stinchcombe has dubbed the "organizational capacity" of the society.[2] Organizational change was, however, extremely slow, both because of the institutional constraints imposed on administration and commerce by the *bakuhan* system and because of the low level of incentives for change. Three of the principal spurs to organizational innovation—technological changes, competition from other types of organizations, and new functional demands—were limited by the relative isolation of the Tokugawa environment through the 1840s. These were provided by the arrival of the Westerners in the 1850s.

Contact with the Western nations exposed the Japanese to a wide range of new material technologies as well as new social technologies—that is, new organizational models. It also introduced direct competition between Japanese organizations and Western entrepreneurs in transport, trade, and commerce. The realization of the full extent of the Western challenge was gradual, extending into the 1870s. The Tokugawa system was, however, immediately confronted with new functional demands not provided for by existing institutional arrangements: the negotiation and enforcement, on a national level, of diplomatic and commercial treaties; the defense of Japan's territory against the superior military forces of the Western powers; and finally, after the opening of the ports in 1859, trade with Western merchants. The first two demands were the primary areas of pressure in the 1850s and 1860s, and both were focused on the organizational structures of the state.

The initial response to these new demands was the establishment of new organizations on existing models: the creation of the office of the *gaikoku bugyō*, to handle relations with the foreign powers, is an early example. This response in the 1850s was gradually augmented by a resort to Western models to handle these tasks, often at the demand of the foreign powers themselves. By the late 1860s, with the increasing awareness of the scale and scope of Western institutions, there began to emerge a broader acceptance of a range of new tasks and of new organizational

[2] Arthur Stinchcombe, "Social Structure and Organization," in James March, ed., *Handbook of Organizations* (Chicago: Rand McNally, 1965), p. 143.

forms to handle their performance. The way for the emergence of such new organizations on a national scale was opened by the abolition of the domains in 1871, and by 1890 there were few organizations in the major Western nations that did not have their counterparts in Japan.

In the establishment of these new organizations, the government acted—as Stinchcombe put it—as an "organization-creating organization." It did not just set up a number of organizational systems that remained under its control: it also set up organizations that were initially under its direct control, but that were released when they reached a certain stage of development, and it provided resources for the development of still other organizations, which were (at least formally) autonomous. The foundations for this role were laid in the Tokugawa period, when the shogunate and the domains both established organizations such as the domain schools, the domain monopolies, and the communications systems, and fostered the development of formally autonomous organizations such as the merchant guilds (*kabunakama*).

In the 1850s and the 1860s, the organization-creating roles of the *bakufu* and the domains expanded primarily in the area of the military and military manufacture. By the mid-1860s, the *bakufu* showed signs of expanding its role. It was considering the establishment of a joint Japanese-French trading company, the licensing of a private telegraph company, and a new postal system—foreshadowing, in fact, at least on paper, the activist role of the Meiji government in the 1870s, although the *bakufu* fell before these plans could be realized. The new Meiji government expanded the organization-creating role of the center somewhat, although limited resources and internal uncertainty constrained it considerably. Outside the military and communications systems, the new government fostered the development of trading-and-exchange companies that were at least formally autonomous. Local governments, both prefectures and domains, also played organization-creating roles. The high degree of local autonomy that characterized the *bakuhan* system was diminished only slightly in the first years of the Meiji period, and the role of local governments in organization formation seems actually to have expanded. The multiplicity of administrative units—many with longstanding traditions of organization creation and with strong networks of communications with the political center—seems to have provided the spur of competition to organizational development, less in terms of a drive for original innovations than in terms of an eagerness to monitor and emulate centrally initiated structures.

The abolition of the domains in 1871 ushered in nearly a decade of the most broad-ranging introduction of new organizational forms in Japan's history. The 1870s also marked the high point of the government's role as an organization-creating organization. We say "the government"; more accurately, this role was played by the individual ministries or, in some cases, by bureaus within the ministries, acting throughout the 1870s with considerable independence.

Whatever the range of individual motivations marshaled in the service of these ambitious programs, the institutional impetus was clear: to end the system of unequal treaties, to transform Japan into a "civilized" nation that would be accepted as an equal by the Great Powers. The institutions that were set up to accomplish these goals were consciously based on Western models drawn, in this decade, largely from France, Great Britain, and, to a lesser extent, the United States.[3] The selection of models tended to be cumulative: that is, the choice of an organizational model from one society increased the likelihood that the same society would serve as a source for further models. One reason for this has to do with language. A model applied in one area was a training ground that provided Japanese with scarce language resources which could be transferred to other areas. Perhaps more important, the application of a model opened channels of communication with officials in the foreign country and provided networks of personal contact. These facilitated further emulation of that country's institutions in other fields—either related, as when Etō Shimpei was persuaded by the French advisers working on legal codes to jettison his early preference for the English police system, or unrelated, as when the British adviser hired to help in the construction of lighthouses was asked to assist in setting up the telegraph system.

The cumulative nature of organizational models is most evident in the pervasiveness of the French influence in governmental systems: first in the army; then in the organizations set up by the Justice Ministry, the Education Ministry, and later the Home Ministry. These French models were all national systems, involving much centralization of control despite the reliance on local financing; a large and carefully recruited central bureaucracy with highly standardized training; and wide spatial dispersion of subunits, linked by an extensive system of internal communications.

None of these was present in Japan in the early 1870s. The problem of establishing the new system was exacerbated by the fact that none of the organizations' recruits had any firsthand experience with the new

[3] A clear distinction should be drawn between the very large number of countries from which the Japanese drew foreign advisers and teachers, and the much smaller range of countries from which they drew their organizational models. In the 1880s, German models joined French, English, and American ones as major influences, particularly in state subsystems and higher education.

forms, and in the 1870s very few individuals had even had an opportunity to observe them in operation in Western countries. The new organizations adopted very similar means of coping with the problem of inadequate resources, especially information resources. There was a heavy reliance on translated materials; even when individuals were sent abroad to study the model firsthand, they were expected to return with piles of materials on regulations and structure that could be translated and circulated. As a result, there was a strong focus on creating the formal system (the positions, titles, responsibilities, and rules of procedure), which explains the emphasis on terminology and titles in the enormous volume of governmental regulations.

Equally important was a longer-range strategy for expanding the information resources of the new organizations: the establishment of schools and training facilities to equip the members with needed technical and organizational skills. The number of ministries and bureaus to set up such facilities is at once a symptom of the serious problems they encountered and a measure of the autonomy they enjoyed. Eventually these various programs were incorporated into specialized institutions of higher education, under the jurisdiction of the Education Ministry, contributing to the Meiji emphasis on training government officials.

Financial resources were also in short supply, and the energies of top administrators in the new system were largely directed toward obtaining funds from the central government. The strategy to which most resorted, in the face of financial scarcity, was to establish the formal center of the system for the entire country, creating districts and criteria for the density and size of future organizational subunits. The Education Ministry, for example, established a system of school districts; the Postal Bureau, postal districts; the Justice Ministry, judicial districts; the Home Ministry, police districts; the army, military districts—each one independent of the others. The reluctance to use already established local grids probably reflected a fear of local autonomy. The actual organizational system was instituted first in Tokyo; it was then gradully extended to the rest of the country (usually beginning with Osaka and Kyoto), using personnel who had gained their training in Tokyo. Before the 1880s, all the organizational systems were rather highly developed in Tokyo and the major urban centers, but had yet to penetrate effectively into most of the nation. The formal commitment to such penetration, however, was built into the control structures of the organizations.

Until 1878, when the so-called Three New Laws formalized the structures, resources, and responsibilities of local government, the extension of the new systems depended heavily on the support of local leaders. In many parts of Japan, local notables financed the construction of local primary schools and post offices, and in some they also paid for the construction of police posts. This made for considerable regional variation in organizational development, which was most rapid in those regions having an active prefectural government, active local notables, and a high level of existing organizational resources.

The 1880s provide a marked contrast to the previous decade with respect to the state's role in organizational development. These were years not of the creation of new organizations, but of the modification, consolidation, and expansion of the organizational systems set up before 1878. The army's switch in 1878 from the French to the German model was the first of a series of reorganizations and adjustments of the various state subsystems, including the police in 1881, 1884, and 1886; the school system in 1879, 1880, and 1886; the banking system in 1882; the central government ministries in 1881 and 1885; and local government in 1888. All these reorganizations involved increasing differentiation and specialization, increasing centralization of coordination and control, and greater spatial dispersion and penetration into society. This was made possible by the development of national communications networks, through the telegraph and postal systems, and by the skillful use of human resources developed in the previous decade. Effective control over the governmental systems passed from men whose personal knowledge of these systems had been derived from brief observation tours in the West to men who had worked in the administration of the new organizations during the 1870s, often under the tutelage of foreign advisers (whose numbers were sharply reduced); some had studied abroad for a year or more. The level of organizational skills and knowledge possessed by such men was considerably higher than that of the previous generation; and, since their numbers were far greater, they were much less thinly spread.

A prototypical case of the changing patterns of government is that of the police. In the 1870s, although the National Police Bureau had formal jurisdiction over the police of the entire country (except Tokyo, which followed the French model in having an autonomous police agency responsible directly to the home minister), its role was largely confined to issuing standards and guidelines that were to be enforced in the prefectural police force. Actual control over police appointments, and therefore over police development, was vested in the prefectural governors. As a result, wide variations in the scale and the caliber of the prefectural forces persisted. In 1881 the creation in the prefectural governments of a new senior police position, whose incumbent was to be appointed directly by the home minister, gave the center direct control over police administration for the first time. Central control and standardization were enhanced in 1884 by the establishment of a police training school in each prefecture, with centrally set curricula and instructors who were graduates of the National Police Officers Training Institute.

Finally, in 1886-1887, a radical revision of the pattern of dispersion for police posts dramatically increased the penetration of the organization into Japanese society. A network of one- and two-man posts dispersed throughout the countryside achieved a remarkable increase in the scope of police penetration without an expensive increase in manpower. In Miyagi prefecture, for example, the number of police posts had increased gradually from 38 in 1878 to 83 in 1886; by 1888, there were 383. The standardized training in the prefectural police schools was a critically important part of the control structure that made this system work, but equally important was the infrastructure of communications—the telegraph and postal systems—which had come of age in the mid-1880s and linked the widely dispersed posts with the administrative centers. As a result, the police became highly visible and effective agents of the central government at the community level, enforcing public health regulations, conscription laws, and codes of legal behavior.

The balance sheet of costs and benefits resulting from the emerging state systems can be drawn up in many ways. Growing centralization and standardization raised the general resource levels of the society and widened the range of opportunities for many individuals throughout Japan. Those who value the regional diversity and local initiatives of the 1870s, however, point out that these processes also undermined the role of the regionally based, multifunctional groups that had been developed in those years to involve local notables in the encouragement of industry and education. The growth of local administration and of routinized, centrally controlled channels of investment, education, and agricultural and industrial improvements played as great a role in altering the social functions of the local elites as it did in opening new channels of mobility for their offspring. In emphasizing the importance of the state role in organization creation, therefore, we should not ignore its less positive aspects. The erosion of certain kinds of nongovernmental organizations was only one aspect of this. In his chapter, Richard Rubinger points out the narrowing range of educational alternatives. Albert Altman investigates a more sinister aspect when he discusses the negative impact of the state's increasingly effective regulation of the press. In that sector and elsewhere, the state acted as an "organization-constraining organization." Martin Collcutt shows how the state reduced the institutional role of Buddhism. The restrictions put on the founding of newspapers and the curbs on public meetings and on the development of political parties are additional examples of this area of state activity.

In positive as well as negative ways, then, the state was the principal influence in the environment of nearly every type of organization that emerged in the private sector. The state shaped the organizational structures of commerce and finance; it provided the infrastructures of communications and transport; it frequently provided financial subsidies; and its role as information broker—encouraging the expansion of the nation's base of knowledge, particularly of Western models and technical skills—was of immeasurable importance.

The patterns of interorganizational mobility that characterized the 1870s and 1880s had a profound effect on the diffusion of knowledge across systems, both within the government and in the private sector. For all organizations, the early shortage of information resources created a great demand for the services of that small group of people who had access to Western organizational information. Shibusawa Eiichi is perhaps the most dramatic example: he is credited with a key role in the establishment of more than 500 enterprises. The rapid emergence of new organizations and their steady expansion once established also generated a very high demand for men with administrative expertise. The relatively high level of interorganizational mobility within the government owed much to such demand factors; it was also facilitated by the absence of formal, qualification-based recruitment criteria. Personal networks were important tools for gaining office or promotion, and men tended to move with their patrons—or, if the patron was particularly powerful, to be appointed to new systems in order to give their patrons a measure of indirect influence. The uniformity of ranks across all governmental subsystems facilitated such transfers. So did the fluidity of governmental control structures: as control over an organizational system (say, the police or the postal system) shifted from ministry to ministry, its personnel went with it.

There was also considerable movement between the government and the private sector during this period. With very few exceptions, such movement was from the government into the private sector; this was hardly surprising, given the more advanced development of governmental systems with respect to size and scope. But the growing exclusiveness of Meiji politics played a major part: men who felt that their policies were overlooked, or their careers blocked by Satsuma-Chōshū dominance, often left to pursue careers in private education and business. Thus, the clique politics so castigated by political commentators was in many cases a boon to the private sector.

Japanese society in the 1860s, the 1870s, and the 1880s was undergoing enormous changes. The organizations that emerged in or survived through these years had to adjust to strong pressures pushing them toward internal changes—in their patterns of coordination and control, their methods of acquiring resources, even the functions they performed. Those organizations, however, were themselves agents of change, contributing to the rapid metamorphosis of society: socializing their members and often their clientele to new patterns of behavior; generating rising levels of resources for other organizations; and, in most cases, increasing the level of national integration economically, politically, or culturally.

Between 1850 and 1890 the organizational landscape of Japan was transformed to an extent that was probably unmatched in any other nation of the era. Led by state structures that developed more standardization and centralization than the European systems which were their models, Japan's organizational revolution drew on resources and skills that, in retrospect, were already observable in Tokugawa Japan (although few of the Westerners who arrived on Japanese shores in the 1850s would have recognized that potential). But this by no means made Japan's transformation inevitable; those resources and skills were amplified and changed in a massive program of organization creation in the 1870s and a major restructuring of organizations in the 1880s. The organizational capacity that has received so much attention in the light of Japan's contemporary economic success is nowhere more evident than in its nineteenth-century transformation.

CHAPTER 6

BUDDHISM: THE THREAT OF ERADICATION

BY MARTIN COLLCUTT

Many Buddhists believed that the political upheavals of the late Tokugawa period, the intrusion of the Western powers, and the vigorous pro-Shinto policies of the new Meiji government had brought Buddhism face to face with the most severe crisis in its long history in Japan. The Pure Land Buddhist priest Fukuda Gyōkai (1806-1888), for instance, was very pessimistic about the prospects for Buddhism:

> At the present, provincial temples are being destroyed; people are withdrawing their memberships and this causes temple revenues to decline; priests are gladly returning to secular life. Although there is no demand to destroy Buddhism there probably has been nothing to compare with this situation in the fourteen or fifteen centuries during which Buddhism has been in Japan. In my opinion there will be an Imperial Rescript eradicating Buddhism within five to seven years.[1]

To Fukuda, and to millions of Japanese who were sympathetic to Buddhism, the political transition from Tokugawa to Meiji had brought for Buddhism not merely a crisis of transition from one regime to another, but a crisis of survival. The crisis was epitomized in two slogans of the day: *shinbutsu bunri* (Separation of Shinto Deities, *Kami*, and Buddhas) and *haibutsu kishaku* (Eradication of Buddhism). This chapter will examine the meaning of these two phrases and assess some of the quantitative as well as descriptive evidence of their impact on Buddhism in the late Tokugawa and early Meiji periods.

[1] Quoted in Kishimoto Hideo, *Japanese Religion in the Meiji Period*, trans. John F. Howes (Tokyo: Ōbunsha, 1956), p. 111.

The Tokugawa Period

The intellectual and institutional squalls that whipped Buddhism in early Meiji did not come out of a cloudless sky. Widespread anti-Buddhist intellectual attitudes and the policies of several domains during the Edo period provided models for the early Meiji drive for the separation of Shinto from Buddhism and for the severity of the surge of local efforts to eradicate Buddhism.

The large Buddhist institution enjoyed a protected and privileged position in Tokugawa society. The cost of that privilege was compliance. The lives of temples and their monks and nuns were closely regulated by *bakufu* codes and domain ordinances. Still, compliance brought tangible benefits. In its determination to eradicate Christianity, the *bakufu* used Buddhist temples as centers of compulsory religious registration. Buddhism was thus firmly entrenched as an established religion and as a religious arm of the system of political controls. As Buddhism extended its religious, social, and political influence during the seventeenth century, temples were able to count on increased lay support. Although the great medieval temples had been stripped of much of their landed wealth in the wars of the fifteenth and sixteenth centuries, and by the unifying policies of Oda Nobunaga and Toyotomi Hideyoshi, many temples still enjoyed secure (if reduced) incomes from donations and land grants confirmed either by the *bakufu* or by domain administrations. Whether the closely regulated but generally comfortable and privileged position of Tokugawa-period Buddhism led to the high degree of clerical laxity and spiritual torpor that is suggested by many contemporary and modern critics is open to question. Intellectually, however, there is no doubt that Buddhism was on the defensive throughout the Tokugawa period.

Rejection of Buddhism was a powerful current in Tokugawa intellectual history. Most Edo-period samurai intellectuals reacted against Buddhism with varying degrees of antipathy. Throughout that period, the most vigorous intellectual currents were flowing away from Buddhism, toward Confucianism, Confucian Shinto, pure Shinto, "national learning," or Dutch and Western studies. Buddhism was attacked from all of these positions, and Buddhist apologists were hard pressed to justify either their privileged place in Tokugawa society or the spiritual utility of Buddhism in an increasingly rationalist and nationally conscious intellectual climate.

Early in the period Hayashi Razan, Yamazaki Ansai, Nakae Tōju, and Kumazawa Banzan, in their efforts to liberate Confucian teachings from Buddhist influence, advocated an alliance of Confucian ethics and Shinto devotion against Buddhism. At the same time, from the Shinto side,

Watarai Nobuyoshi was urging a Shinto-Confucian synthesis as a way of freeing Ise Shinto from Buddhist contamination. In Edo, Yoshikawa Koretaru and his successors, as hereditary Shinto ritualists for the *bakufu*, were advocates of pure (*yuitsu*) Shinto. They rejected the traditional Shinto-Buddhist syncretism (*honji suijaku*) and called for the severance of Shinto from Buddhism. Koretari had the support of such daimyo as the Tokugawa of Kii, the Maeda, and the Hoshina.

During the eighteenth and nineteenth centuries, scholars advocating "national learning" (*kokugaku*), mounted an increasingly determined attack on both Confucianism and Buddhism. Residual Pure Land Buddhist elements have been detected in Motoori Norinaga's thought; but he frequently wrote that the success of Buddhism and Confucianism in Japan, and the association of Shinto with Buddhism through dual Shinto (*ryōbu shinto*), had brought demotion for the *kami* and for Japan's native beliefs. Likewise, Hirata Atsutane, sometimes supported his nativist fulminations with reference to Buddhism; but, at bottom, he was the most vehement, emotional, and aggressive critic of Shinto's contamination by, and subordination to, Buddhism. Hirata's followers were numerous and influential in many domains. It was his ideas that provided much of the fuel for assaults aimed at the reduction or eradication of Buddhism. Other bitter critics of Buddhism included reformers and loyalists of the later Mito school, men such as Aizawa Seishisai and Fujita Tōko.[2]

There were, of course, a few thinkers like Ishida Baigan or Ninomiya Sontoku who were favorably disposed toward Buddhism and who continued to advocate versions of the syncretic ideal of "Unity of the Three Creeds." Most intellectuals, however, attacked Buddhism as an alien and irrational creed—or criticized the protected and privileged place of the Buddhist institution in Tokugawa society, the excessive number and wealth of its temples, their exactions on the peasantry and townspeople, the strain they imposed on domain treasuries, the unruliness of True Pure Land or Nichiren devotees, and the idleness and immorality of bonzes.

Not all thinkers were consistently anti-Buddhist, and not all criticism implied a call for the disestablishment or destruction of Buddhism. Some clerics defended their beliefs with restatements of traditional arguments for the utility of Buddhism; others urged and led reform movements. Although samurai were generally unsympathetic, Buddhism continued to enjoy a large measure of official protection and popular support. Many new temples were established in the seventeenth and eighteenth centuries, and numerous Buddhist texts were published in Kyoto, Osaka, and Edo.

[2] Intellectual criticisms of Buddhism in the Tokugawa period are detailed in Tsuji Zennosuke, *Nihon bukkyō shi, kinsei 4* (Tokyo: Iwanami shoten, 1970), pp. 1-404.

But calls for reform were always in the air, and these became more strident as the sense of national crisis and national awareness mounted.[3]

The political authorities were not unresponsive to these criticisms of Buddhism. In the mid-seventeenth century several domains, following *bakufu* example, tightened their control over Buddhism and gave greater prominence to Shinto.

In Okayama domain the daimyo, Ikeda Mitsumasa, advised by Kumazawa Banzan and responding to *bakufu* calls for restrictions of Buddhist temple building and tightening up of the Christian-surveillance system, enforced a two-pronged religious reform in 1666. More than half the Buddhist temples in the domain—598 out of 1,035—were abolished and some four hundred monks and nuns laicized. Most of these returned to agriculture and farmed their temple lands; some became Shinto priests. The other prong of Mitsumasa's religious reform policy was the promotion of Shinto and Confucianism within the domain. He ordered that registration at temples (*tera-uke*) be replaced by registration at shrines (*shinshoku-uke*), thus giving Shinto, at least while he lived, a more central place in the life of the domain.[4]

In Aizu domain the daimyo, Hoshina Masayuki, a student of Neo-Confucianism and of Yamazaki Ansai, had little sympathy for Buddhism. He pursued a policy of gradual but determined containment of Buddhism. In 1654, monks and nuns were required to secure official approval before taking the tonsure. From 1666 he ordered the abolition of all temples built within the past twenty years as well as those which were no longer active. Six temples were abolished immediately as a result of this order, and others followed.[5]

Tokugawa Mitsukuni of Mito domain, also in response to *bakufu* requests for a tightening of control over Buddhism, instituted a purge of Buddhism and planned a Shinto revival. Tamamuro Fumio's research has

[3] It is now commonplace in modern scholarship to characterize Tokugawa-period Buddhism as corrupt or moribund. This assessment echoes the negative criticisms made in the nineteenth century by Japanese, who often were ideologically hostile to Buddhism themselves, or by Western observers inclined to view Buddhism as an obstacle to Christian missionary success in Japan. While it is impossible to deny that institutional Buddhism in the Tokugawa period had lost much of its earlier vitality, it is important to remember that there were some dedicated priests, enthusiastic believers, and attempts at spiritual reform. This more positive side of Buddhism was evident, for instance, in the stimulus provided by the introduction of Ōbaku Zen and its popularization by Hakuin and Bankei, as well as by the scholarly contribution of monks like Jiun Sonja, and in the spontaneous support for Buddhism seen in the popularity of pilgrimages, temple festivals, and Buddhist literature.

[4] Tamamuro Fumio, *Shinbutsu bunri* (Tokyo: Kyōikusha, 1977), pp. 57-58.

[5] Tamamuro Taijō et al., eds., *Nihon bukkyō shi* (Kyoto: Hōzōkan, 1967), vol. 3, pp. 62-63.

shown that out of 2,377 temples in the domain in 1666, 1,098 were abolished or amalgamated. The temples singled out for closure were those with few sponsors (*danka*), those with ill-qualified monks, and those which conducted esoteric rituals (*kitō*) but did not offer funeral rites for their parishioners. Some land may have reverted to the domain, but much of it seems to have been reallocated to surviving temples or to laicized monks to be farmed. Temple sponsors were likewise reallocated to surviving temples. Mitsukuni also planned shrine reforms aimed at the elimination of Buddhist influence: the use of Buddhist titles for *kami*; the elevation of Shinto priests (*kannushi*) to control of shrines; and the abolition of shrines, such as those dedicated to Hachiman, having a strong Buddhist coloration.[6]

These seventeenth-century religious reforms in Mito, Okayama, and Aizu were certainly severe and brought protests from Buddhist clerics inside the domains and in the principal metropolitan temples of the various sects. On the whole, however, reforms took their cue from *bakufu* policy and could be justified as a necessary rationalization or as an elimination of dead wood. It is difficult to say how many temples or monks were "too many" for a community to support, but prior to the reforms of 1666 the five hundred or so villages in Mito were supporting more than 2,000 temples, an average of 4 temples per village. If the average population per village was about four hundred people, then each temple had a *danka* support base of only one hundred people, or about twenty-five families. This was a heavy burden for the domain and its villagers. In cutting the number of temples to an average of 2.3 per village, domain officials could argue that their policies were reasonable. Displaced monks and nuns do not seem to have been harshly treated, and there is little indication of uncontrolled destruction of property or images. In the long run, the determination of daimyo like Tokugawa Mitsukuni or Ikeda Mitsumasa to restore Shinto to independence and supremacy in the spiritual life of the domain was probably the greatest cause for concern on the part of Buddhist leaders.

In the late Edo period, Buddhism was also subjected to purges in some domains. Coming as they did at a time of domestic and foreign crisis and generally being part of domain self-strengthening reforms, these attacks on Buddhism went beyond administrative tidying to spoliation, destruction, and elimination of Buddhism.

In Mito, Tokugawa Nariaki, advised by Aizawa Seishisai and Fujita Tōko, extended the religious reforms begun by Mitsukuni. From 1843,

[6] Tsuji Zennosuke et al., eds., *Meiji ishin shinbutsu bunri shiryō* (Tokyo: Tōkyō shoin, 1925-1929), vol. 3, pp. 590-605; Tamamura, *Shinbutsu bunri*, pp. 23-57.

190 temples were abolished, most of them esoteric centers, and 121 of these were destroyed. Their monks were laicized and encouraged to return to agriculture. Nariaki ordered the confiscation of temple bells and bronze objects to be used for cannon. Mixed Shinto-Buddhist shrines were converted to pure Shinto sanctuaries, and the shrine monks (*shasō*) attached to many of them were obliged to return to lay life or become Shinto priests. Temples attached to shrines (*jingūji*) and Yamabushi centers were abolished. As in the Okayama domain in the seventeenth century, temple registration was abandoned in favor of shrine registration, and Shinto funeral rites were adopted. Although the second wave of Mito religious reforms did not affect nearly as many temples as the reforms of Mitsukuni, they had a sharper, more destructive edge. Nariaki, Fujita, Aizawa, and other young Mito samurai detested Buddhism and were intent not merely upon tighter regulation of Buddhism, or separation of Buddhism from Shinto, but upon destruction of Buddhist images and suppression of Buddhist teaching. The severity of Nariaki's policies naturally produced a sharp reaction among Buddhist clerics and traditionalist samurai officials. In the seven-count indictment made by the *bakufu* against Nariaki when he was placed under house arrest in 1844 were two items reflecting on his religious policy: that he had destroyed temples and forcibly converted the Tōshōgū into a pure Shinto shrine.[7]

Kamei Koremi, the daimyō of Tsuwano domain, was a reformer who sent some of his domain's young samurai to study in Edo and Osaka and who promoted Dutch studies and Shinto in the domain. From the 1850s, his closest advisers were *kokugaku* scholars like Ōkuni Takamasa and Fukuba Bisei, both of whom were followers of Hirata Atsutane. A purge of Buddhism was set in motion in 1864. As in other domains where anti-Buddhist measures were taken in this period, the rationale was a blend of Shinto supremacist thought and economic advantage in the name of domain strengthening. Buddhism was criticized as a distorted teaching, unworthy of samurai and misleading to the people. The Buddhist institution was castigated as an economic drain on the domain and its population, monopolizing lands that would otherwise produce annual tax revenues and bleeding the people through donations. Monks and nuns, it was asserted, no longer practiced their religion but were ignorant and idle, devoted only to ease and ostentation. The religious reforms in Tsuwano affected samurai most immediately. The daimyo family temple was abolished and its holdings confiscated. Other temples were encouraged to amalgamate, and monks and nuns were laicized. Surviving temples

[7] Tsuji et al., *Shinbutsu bunri shiryō*, vol. 3, pp. 605-723; Tamamuro, *Shinbutsu bunri*, pp. 72-118.

were forbidden to repair derelict buildings other than the main hall, or to gather crowds and conduct public ceremonies such as those for the Obon festival. Shinto funeral rites were ordered to be adopted by members of the daimyo's family and by all samurai. Although Tsuwano was a small domain, it is particularly significant because Kamei Koremi and Fukuba Bisei became senior officials of the Ministry of Rites in the Meiji government and were thus able to enforce their anti-Buddhist policies on a national scale.[8]

Satsuma domain maintained stringent religious policies throughout the Tokugawa period. In addition to enforcing the *bakufu*'s proscriptions of Christianity and the Fuju Fuse branch of the Nichiren school of Buddhism, Satsuma enforced a local ban on True Pure Land Buddhism. When Shimazu Nariakira became daimyo in 1851, he set in motion reform policies aimed at strengthening the domain economically and militarily. Buddhist temples were one target for his reform efforts. Followers of Hirata Atsutane were strong in Satsuma, and Nariakira may also have been influenced by recent Mito attacks on Buddhism. He planned to expropriate temple bells and statues, to be made into cannon as a first step in a policy of suppressing Buddhism. After his death in 1858, his ideas were kept alive by young samurai who submitted a proposal to the domain authorities in 1865 to the effect that "monks only talk and eat. Young ones can bear arms, and the older ones can make themselves useful as teachers, farmers, or merchants. Buddhist ritual objects can be made into weapons and the funds from the domain treasury that now go to support temples (an estimated 65,000 *koku*) can be better used supporting impoverished samurai."[9] A contemporary survey revealed that there were some 4,470 shrines in Kagoshima domains, 1,066 temples, and 2,964 monks.[10] It is not clear how far the purge had proceeded by 1868, but the domain government had certainly begun closing or amalgamating temples, confiscating statues, bells, and gongs, defrocking monks and nuns, and eradicating traces of Buddhism from Shinto shrines. In Satsuma the acquisition of temple wealth was clearly a powerful motive in the suppression movement, but the attack was also fueled by the arguments of Shinto advocates that Buddhism was an alien and distorted creed, inimical to the interests of Shinto, the domain, and the country.

Like Satsuma, Chōshū saw domain-inspired attacks on Buddhism in the 1840s and 1860s. From 1842, Murata Seifū, as part of his effort to restore domain finances and to promote and centralize Shinto within the

[8] Tsuji et al., *Shinbutsu bunri shiryō*, vol. 5, pp. 808-840.

[9] Ibid., vol. 4, p. 1035.

[10] Ibid., vol. 4, pp. 1036-1038.

domain, enforced a purge of Buddhism and an amalgamation of Shinto shrines. According to Miyake Arinori, 9,666 temples, shrines, Pure Land halls, and hermitages were abolished and 12,510 Buddhist images destroyed.[11] In the turbulent 1860s there was another outburst of anti-Buddhist sentiment in Chōshū. This time the upsurge was largely ideological. It did not involve an attack on Buddhist property or personnel, but it did call for the separation of Shinto from Buddhism and the promotion of Shinto in the religious and intellectual life of the domain. This movement was in step with the growth of loyalist sentiment in Chōshū and was spearheaded by Shinto priests. That it did not develop into an all-out attack on Buddhism of the kind made in Satsuma was probably owing to a greater degree of popular support for Buddhism in Chōshū and to the active role played by Buddhist priests in Chōshū militia units.[12]

The Meiji Restoration Era

The overthrow of the *bakufu* and the seizure of power by the new leadership promised religious and institutional, as well as political, changes. Buddhism was on the defensive, in a state of intellectual and institutional siege. The Restoration brought no respite. If anything, the prospect grew darker. Buddhism had been integrated into the Tokugawa system of social controls. To the extent that Buddhism was viewed as a protégé of the *bakufu*, anti-*bakufu* rhetoric could quickly spill over into anti-Buddhist sentiment. The downfall of the *bakufu* left Buddhism exposed and vulnerable to the whims of an unsympathetic new regime. Loyalist, pro-Shinto, anti-Buddhist rhetoric was running high in many parts of the country. Reform efforts, hitherto conducted piecemeal within individual domains, could now be coordinated on a national scale. The Satsuma and Chōshū leaders, who had known *shinbutsu bunri* in their domains, were intent on promoting Shinto beliefs that would contribute to a strengthened imperial ideology. They had little sympathy for Buddhism and put the making and enforcement of religious policy in the hands of Shinto advocates some of whom, like Kamei Koremi and Fukuba Bisei of Tsuwano, were dedicated to, and experienced in, the reduction of Buddhism. Moreover, Iwakura Tomomi and several other influential nobles in the imperial court, which had been brought more prominently

[11] Miyake Arinori, "Bakumatsu Chōshū han no shūkyō seisaku," in Kawai Masaharu, ed., *Setonaikai chiiki no shūkyō to bunka* (Tokyo: Yūzankaku shuppan, 1976), p. 233.

[12] Kitagawa Ken, "Bakumatsu Chōshū han ni okeru shinbutsu bunri no tenkai," *Yamaguchi ken monjokan kenkyū kiyō*, no. 7 (n.d.), pp. 67-94.

into political life, were also eager to promote Shinto and demote Buddhism.

By its own claims, the new government did not seek to eradicate Buddhism, *haibutsu kishaku*. Its declared policy was rather one of separating Shinto from Buddhism, *shinbutsu bunri*. Certainly, in the volatile political situation of the Restoration, any overt attempt at a total suppression of Buddhism might have provoked further local opposition and contributed to increased political instability. The leaders, however, were indifferent or unsympathetic to Buddhism and immediately sanctioned a religious policy that, on the one hand, continued the *bakufu* proscription of Christianity and, on the other, aimed at the rapid disentanglement of Shinto from Buddhism, the total elimination of Buddhist influence from shrines, the elevation of Shinto to primacy as a national creed, and (from 1871) the disestablishment of Buddhism and the confiscation of temple lands and property. This policy was shaped and pushed through by pro-Shinto factions in the court and government, using organs of the Department (later Ministry) of Rites (Jingikan), staffed by Shinto priests.

While Shinto was being elevated and represented at the very highest levels of government as part of the ideology of the new Meiji state, Buddhism was accorded only lowly representation through an office in the Department of Home Affairs. Neither the opinions of Buddhist leaders nor those of the local population were solicited in the making of the early phases of religious policy. Thus, although Buddhism was critically affected by the religious reforms of the government, Buddhist leaders for several years had no say in the making of those policies and no effective political channel through which they could criticize them.

Although the declared government policy was one of *bunri* rather than *haibutsu*, the patently anti-Buddhist tone of the early regulations, their sweeping application, and the rigor and suddenness with which Buddhism and Shinto were to be wrenched apart seemed to many people to signal the beginning of a concerted government attack on Buddhism. In domain bureaucracies, and under local officials of the Meiji government in villages, shrines, and temples in many parts of the country, the line between *bunri* and *haibutsu* was quickly crossed. While government ordinances repeatedly deplored acts of destruction, the government did little to contain them or to punish the perpetrators. It is, of course, important to remember that the political situation in the late 1860s and early 1870s was still extremely volatile, that central authority was hesitant, and that the domains still maintained considerable autonomy.

The religious policy of *shinbutsu bunri* was enforced through regulations and memoranda issued by the Council of State (Dajōkan) and drafted in the Department of Rites. There was a stream of these regulations beginning early in 1868, within weeks of the Restoration. Among them, those most important in defining basic government policy were issued in the third month of 1868. On the seventeenth day, an instruction from the Office of Rites (Jingi Jimukyoku) to all shrines ordered that, in the interests of restoration (*ōsei fukko*) and the elimination of longstanding religious abuses, all bonzes serving as shrine priests (*bettō* or *shasō*) were to be laicized.[13] The intent here was that Buddhist priests attached to shrines and *jingūji* would either move to Buddhist temples or let their hair grow, adopt secular dress, and live as laymen or be reordained as Shinto priests.

On the twenty-eighth day of the same month, an instruction to all shrines from the Office of Rites ordered that Buddhist titles such as Gongen or Gozu Tennō were no longer to be applied to Shinto divinities (*kami*) or to the sacred objects that represented them (*shintai*), that Buddhist icons were not to be used as *shintai*, and that all Buddhist statues and ritual objects were to be removed from shrine precincts.[14] This order was aimed at eliminating all taint of Buddhism from Shinto shrines and at ending more than a millennium of the kind of syncretism expressed in *ryōbu shinto* or *honji suijaku* thought. It was, in effect, a mortal blow at what had become the prevalent syncretic expression of Japanese religion. Although the separation edicts did not call for the destruction of Buddhist property, they were widely interpreted as heralding or condoning attacks on Buddhism, especially in domains where pro-Shinto groups were strong and in those shrines and *jingūji* whose Shinto priests had long resented the superior status of Buddhist shrine monks.

These basic regulations were followed by a stream of memoranda—reiterating and detailing the official policies, clearing the imperial court of all tincture of Buddhism, and promoting Shinto funeral services and shrine registration. From 1871 through 1872 the government turned from separation to disestablishment of Buddhism. The economic strength of the Buddhist institution was undercut by the abolition of the old networks of lay sponsors (*danka*) and by the confiscation of temple lands. Its social position was reduced by the abolition of ranks and titles for the Buddhist clergy. Far from enforcing the traditional standards of Buddhist clerical life as taught in the *Vinaya*, the government issued regulations permitting monks and nuns to grow their hair, to eat meat, to return to lay life, and to marry. Many temples were closed and some schools of Buddhism were forced to amalgamate or disband.[15] Even if all these orders were not always enforced to the letter, their cumulative impact was severe.

[13] Tsuji et al., *Shinbutsu bunri shiryō*, vol. 1, p. 82.

[14] Ibid.

[15] Shibata Dōken, *Haibutsu kishaku* (Tokyo: Kōronsha, 1978), pp. 91-100.

Thus, while disclaiming any deliberate policy of eradication, the new government enforced religious policies that sharply reduced the remaining material vitality of Buddhism and transformed its role in the religious, political, and social life of the nation. As a result, Buddhism was reduced from its established primacy in the Tokugawa religious world to a very subordinate role in the early Meiji social order. This did not necessarily mean that support for Buddhism among the mass of the population had been quenched or even seriously reduced. It was very clear to all Japanese, however, that Buddhism was being downgraded and subjected to a potential lethal attack.

The Administrative Machinery of Separation

Four government agencies were responsible for the articulation of the *shinbutsu bunri* policy of the Meiji government during its first decade. For simplicity, they can be grouped in pairs. The Department, or Ministry, of Rites (the Jingikan or Jingishō) and its satellite, the Office of Proselytizers (Senkyōshi) were basically hard-line, all-Shinto organizations. The Ministry of Rites and Education (Kyōbushō) and its satellite, the Office of the Great Teaching (Daikyōin), which replaced the Jingishō in 1872, were less militant organizations into which Buddhist clergy were co-opted, but in which the drive was still very much toward the promotion of Shinto as the spiritual core of a new imperial ideology.[16]

The Jingikan was established early in 1868 out of an earlier Office of Rites as one of seven departments under the Dajōkan. The expressed motive for the creation of the Jingikan was to achieve a "union of rituals and government," *saisei itchi.* In government changes during 1869, following the ancient *ritsuryō* bureaucratic model, the Jingikan was set formally above the Dajōkan. In 1871, in another bout of administrative reforms, its title was changed to Jingishō (Ministry of Rites). From 1868, the Jingikan was given control over all shrines and Shinto priests—thus replacing the looser control hitherto exercised by the Yoshida and Shirakawa schools of Shinto priests—as well as the oversight of Buddhist temples. The government's determination to promote a remodeled Shinto as both a national creed and a buttress for imperial authority, together with its eagerness to regulate the future development of Buddhism and Christianity, made the Jingikan, although nominally responsible only for

[16] For a more detailed discussion of the administrative mechanisms of *shinbutsu bunri*, see Yasumaro Yoshio, *Kamigami no Meiji ishin* (Tokyo: Iwanami shoten, 1980), pp. 119-130, and Toyoda Takeshi, *Nihon shūkyō seido shi no kenkyū* (Tokyo: Daiichi shobō, 1973), pp. 191-216.

Shinto rituals and the maintenance of imperial mausolea, the pacesetter in religious policy formulation. With so much of Shinto and Buddhism intertwined, policies formulated in the Jingikan inevitably affected Buddhism.

The Office of Proselytizers (Senkyōshi) was set up within the Jingikan in 1869. The task given to its Shinto propagandists was to explain and justify *shinbutsu bunri* policies in villages and towns throughout the country, to promote Shinto as national creed and imperial ideology, and to counter Buddhism and Christianity. The agenda for the Senkyōshi was provided by the Edict for the Promulgation of the Great Teaching (*daikyō senpu*), issued early in 1870. This stressed "unity of ritual and government" and blended reverence for *kami*, country, government, and the imperial house.

By 1872 some of the Meiji leaders, Etō Shimpei and Saigō Takamori among them, were clearly having doubts about the wisdom of the aggressive and exclusively pro-Shinto policies advocated by the Jingishō. In many parts of the country, *shinbutsu bunri* had degenerated into despoliation of Buddhist property. Buddhist leaders of all schools (especially Hōshū Kōson, Shimaji Mokurai, and Daishū Tetsunen of Honganji) appealed to the government to moderate its policies and to incorporate Buddhists into the formulation of religious policy. While the officials of the Jingishō and the Office of Proselytizers had been very zealous in arousing the opposition of Buddhists, they had been less successful in providing a theoretical and spiritual content for the "Great Teaching" of Restoration Shinto and in spreading it among the people. The situation was made more difficult and urgent for the government by demands from the Western powers that the prohibition against Christian missionary activity be lifted. To some leaders, the threat of a Christian resurgence in Japan was a greater menace to the country than tolerance of the old evil of Buddhism. Some Buddhists were quick to argue that Buddhism alone or in concert with Shinto would serve as a bulwark against unwanted Christian intrusion.

The new Ministry of Rites and Education (Kyōbushō) was intended to meet these various difficulties. It would, it was hoped, continue to promote Shinto as the "Great Teaching" but harness Buddhist clerics as well as Shinto priests to the task. Some 4,000 Shinto priests and 3,000 Buddhist priests were licensed as instructors under the Kyōbushō.[17] The incorporation of Buddhists could be expected to take away some of the

[17] Yoshida Kyūichi, *Nihon kindai bukkyō shi kenkyū* (Tokyo: Yoshikawa kōbunkan, 1964), pp. 81-149. According to Yoshida, p. 147, the number of licensed instructors grew rapidly until, by 1880, they exceeded 100,000, of whom the great majority were Buddhist priests.

sting of *shinbutsu bunri*. And it would perhaps counter the likely infiltration of Christianity by emphasizing a stronger and more concerted doctrinal approach. The inclusion of Buddhist priests under the Kyōbushō may have acted as a brake on some destructive excesses, but the foundation of this renamed ministry did not bring an end to *shinbutsu bunri*, disestablishment of Buddhism, or *haibutsu kishaku* outbursts.

At first, the promise to involve Buddhist priests in the Kyōbushō seemed to many Buddhist leaders to offer the possibility of defusing the attacks on Buddhism and of providing a chance for institutional recuperation by cooperation with the very vaguely defined ideals of the "Great Teaching" as embodied in the Three Injunctions:

> Revere the *kami* and love the country.
> Clarify heavenly reason and the Way of humanity.
> Revere the emperor and respect court directives.[18]

On the basis of these injunctions, Buddhist leaders could have had few grounds for hoping that Buddhism would have a significant role within the "Great Teaching." However, the chief temples of the various schools had appealed to the government in mid-1872 to set up an office within the Kyōbushō in which Buddhist priests could be trained for their new proselytizing mission. The idea was picked up and expanded upon by Etō Shimpei and Kyōbushō officials.

The Daikyōin was set up in the temple of Zōjōji in Tokyo. "Medium" and "small" branches were established in prefectures, shrines, and temples throughout the country. The aim was to build up a nationwide network of centers for the inculcation of the "Great Teaching" as a national creed and for the popularization of the political aims of the Restoration. These centers were to be staffed by instructors having a talent for winning an audience. Besides Shinto and Buddhist priests, Confucian scholars, Kabuki actors, and popular entertainers were recruited as instructors. From the point of view of the Buddhist clergy, the whole idea of the Daikyōin turned into a fiasco. Zōjōji was decked out like a Shinto shrine and provided with Shinto images, regalia, and torii. Shinto as well as Buddhist priests were in training in the Daikyōin, and the first batch of 300 Buddhists there soon found that they were being subjected to Shinto indoctrination and used as Shinto propagandists. They were obliged to wear the stiff caps of Shinto priests on their shaven heads and to say prayers and make offerings before the shrine. Although Buddhists were thus involved in the dissemination of what was to be a new national religion, this state creed made no provision for the teaching

[18] Tsuji et al., *Shinbutsu bunri shiryō*, vol. 1, p. 282.

of Buddhism. Buddhist priests found that their preaching was to be confined to the Three Injunctions, as detailed in two sets of eleven and seventeen topics—all of which stressed the primacy of Shinto and the imperial line, or the virtues of the reform-minded policies of the Meiji government. In practice, of course, Buddhist priests found ways of advocating Buddhism, and even the complementary character of the Buddhas and *kami*, while discussing the various topics. This, however, ran counter to the intent of government policy.[19]

The Assault on Buddhism

The *shinbutsu bunri* policies of the Meiji government were aimed most directly at the elimination of Buddhist influence from shrines and the separation of shrines from Buddhist temples. Some of the most destructive attacks on Buddhism occurred in shrines and *jingūji* throughout the country as Shinto priests and their local supporters shook off what they saw as the centuries-old yoke of Buddhist domination. The following examples of *haibutsu* incidents will give some sense of the scope and character of these attacks.

Hardly were the *shinbutsu bunri* laws announced than a band of more than fifty armed men, led by the Shinto priest Jūge Shigekuni, burst into the Hie shrine at the foot of Enryakuji and burned hundreds of sutras and statues.[20] In Ise, the governor of the Watarai district, Hashimoto Jitsuryō, allied with the priests of the Ise shrines and enforced *haibutsu*. Prior to the imperial visit to Ise in 1869 it was ordered that all Buddhist buildings and statues be cleared from the district in which the shrines were located and that only Shinto ritual practices should be permitted in the area. Several hundred temples were closed, some of them destroyed by Shinto priests, their monks returned to agriculture, and their statues and sutras burned or sold.[21] The government's instruction that the title of Boddhisattva was no longer to be used in reference to Hachiman, and that the divinity should be treated strictly as a Shinto *kami*, led to *haibutsu* outbursts in many Hachiman shrines throughout the country. At the Tsurugaoka Hachiman in Kamakura, the Iwashimizu Hachiman in Kyoto, the Usa Hachiman in Kyūshū, and in many other centers, Buddhist shrine priests were laicized and sometimes assaulted. Buddhist statues were dragged out of shrines and desecrated, burned, or sold, and Buddhist

[19] Fujii Sadafumi, "Kyōdōshoku haishi no yōin," *Shintōgaku*, no. 86 (August 1975), pp. 1-24.

[20] Tsuji et al., *Shinbutsu bunri shiryō*, vol. 1, pp. 679-684.

[21] Tamamuro, *Shinbutsu bunri*, pp. 148-154.

buildings were destroyed.[22] In Nikkō, by 1871, the eighty or so monks from the Tōshōgū had all moved to other temples, taking with them much of the Buddhist regalia.[23] In the Suwa Jinja, some of the Shinto shrine priests were *kokugaku* scholars, and there had been a festering tension between them and the Buddhist priests at the shrine. When the *shinbutsu bunri* edicts were announced there was some destruction, and Buddhist priests were forced either to leave or to become Shinto priests.[24]

Events similar to those outlined above occurred in shrines all over Japan. In many shrines and *jingūji*, Buddhist features were so pervasive, and so closely intertwined with Shinto elements through centuries of syncretism, that it was extremely difficult to disentangle them either by government fiat or by violence. This was particularly true of Shugendō, or mountain asceticism, in which the divinities were an all-but-inseparable blending of *kami* and Buddhas. Regardless of the fact that traditional religious practice would thereby be vitiated, separation of Shinto and Buddhism was enforced at such great sacred mountain centers of Japan as Haguro, Hakusan, Hōki, Ōmine, and Sado.

Yamabushi were given the choice of becoming Shinto priests, joining Tendai or Shingon temples, or returning to lay life. Buildings and objects having a Buddhist taint were attached to other temples or destroyed. Syncretic divinities such as Zaō Gongen were renamed and treated as purely Shinto figures.[25]

In the early Restoration period, a number of domains continued to enforce *shinbutsu bunri* policies with great severity. In some of these domains, pro-Shinto officials seized the initiative and the result was destruction. The three domains most active in the Restoration—Satsuma, Chōshū, and Tosa—all continued to enforce policies drastically reducing Buddhism. In Satsuma in 1869 it was ordered that only Shinto observances be permitted within the domain. According to national census data, by 1872 all Buddhist temples (1,066) had been abolished, their monks laicized, their temple holdings confiscated for military expenses, and many of their statues, sutras, and ritual objects destroyed.[26] In Tosa, followers of Hirata Atsutane were charged with the enforcement of *shinbutsu bunri*. Shinto ceremonies were adopted, and some 439 out of a

[22] Shibata, *Haibutsu kishaku*, pp. 125-128.

[23] Tamamuro et al., *Nihon bukkyō shi*, vol. 3, p. 280.

[24] Shibata, *Haibutsu kishaku*, pp. 127-128.

[25] Ibid., pp. 129-147; Yasumaro, *Kamigami no Meiji ishin*, pp. 145-162.

[26] According to the national census data for the years 1871-1876, not a single Buddhist temple is known to have survived in Satsuma. This coincides with the account given in Kuroita Katsumi, ed., *Kagoshima ken shi* (Tokyo: Kondō shuppansha, 1939), vol. 3, pp. 643-662. See also Tsuji et al., *Shinbutsu bunri shiryō*, vol. 4, p. 1053.

total of 615 temples were abolished and their monks laicized.[27] Chōshū was less thoroughgoing in its purge of Buddhism; but there, too, several hundred temples were abolished.

Other areas in which particularly severe anti-Buddhist outbursts occurred included Tsuwano domain, which continued its pre-Meiji policies of abolishing minor temples and enforcing Shinto rituals, and Naegi *han*, where a domain council declared in 1869 that *kokugaku* should be the principal teaching in the domain and that all Buddhist temples should be abolished, their monks defrocked, and their lands confiscated.[28] In Toyama domain, all but 8 out of more than 1,600 temples were abolished. Temple bells and statues were brought to Toyama castle for smelting and conversion into weapons. Troops were mobilized to quell any resistance, and bounties were offered to monks and patrons who yielded property to the purge. There was, however, considerable local opposition. Pure Land devotees chanted the *nenbutsu* as statues were consigned to the flames. The head priests of the various sects complained bitterly to the government. Even the Jingishō itself was surprised by the severity of the Toyama enforcement and urged restraint. In 1872, in response to local and sectarian appeals, the Kyōbushō permitted the reopening of temples having more than seventy sponsoring families.[29]

The daimyo of Matsumoto domain, and many of the domain officials, were pro-Shinto, Mito-school Confucian scholars. In 1869, the daimyo, claiming that the Buddhist monks in his domain were lazy, greedy, disloyal to the emperor, and hostile to Shinto, took the lead and abolished all his family temples. Shinto rites were adopted and more than 140 temples closed. When temples were abolished, monks were paraded before the local villagers and questioned about Buddhism. Those who could not answer satisfactorily were publicly upbraided.[30] On the island of Sado, following the promulgation of the *shinbutsu bunri* edicts, the local official, Okudaira Kamesuke, declared that there were too many temples for the population of the island and that their monks were mostly ignorant and idle. He ordered that the 539 temples on Sado be reduced to 80, that more than one thousand monks be defrocked and returned to farming, and that temple property be confiscated. Buddhist proselytizing was forbidden, and burial with Shinto rites replaced cremation. In 1870 a new official replaced Okudaira; the number of temples permitted on the island was raised to 135, and a slow Buddhist recovery began.[31] On Oki

[27] Tsuji et al., *Shinbutsu bunri shiryō*, vol. 1, pp. 1019-1062, esp. p. 1020.

[28] Ibid., vol. 2, pp. 609-624.

[29] Ibid., vol. 1, pp. 785-812; vol. 5, pp. 491-522.

[30] Ibid., vol. 2, pp. 633-734; Shibata, *Haibutsu kishaku*, pp. 155-159; Tamamuro et al., *Nihon bukkyō shi*, vol. 3, pp. 285-286.

[31] Tsuji et al., *Shinbutsu bunri shiryō*, vol. 1, pp. 813-974.

island a young, reform-minded group of *kokugaku* and Confucian scholars and officials ordered the abolition of all Buddhist temples on the island, the destruction of Buddhist statues, paintings, and family altars, and the institution of Shinto funeral services. In 1867 there were 71 temples on the island. By 1875, not a single active temple remained, and all the monks had either returned to lay life or left the island.[32]

In Kyoto and Nara, too, there was a vigorous attack on Buddhism in the early Meiji period. The court itself was a focus for pro-Shinto sentiment. Buddhist ceremonies, such as those for Obon, that had traditionally been performed by Buddhist priests at the court were prohibited. Buddhist statues and books, together with the memorial tablets of deceased emperors and empresses that had been kept in the *okurodo* (a Buddhist sanctuary in the palace), were moved out of the court. Those members of the imperial family who had been installed as abbots (*monzeki*) in Buddhist temples were recalled to lay life.

Under the Kyoto official Makimura Masanao, dozens of small temples were closed; stone Buddhas were smashed, to be used as building materials for new primary schools. In some cases, it was rumored, statues were used in the thresholds of school toilets: teachers and students were required to step on them to demonstrate that no curse would befall those abusing Buddhist statues in this way.[33] In Nara, government officials zealously enforced anti-Buddhist policies. Many temples were abolished, their monks laicized, and their treasures sold or burned. The future for Buddhism seemed bleak. Within months of the Restoration, the community of the great Nara monastery of Kōfukuji, which had been wrenched apart from the Kasuga shrine, dissolved itself. The monks requested to be allowed to become Shinto priests at the nearby shrine. Kōfukuji was allowed to fall into ruins, and many of its buildings were destroyed in a bout of anti-Buddhist desecration in 1872. The five-story pagoda was saved from destruction only because local fear of fire prevented the dealer who had bought it for 250 yen from burning it down to retrieve its metal fittings.[34]

The Evidence of Meiji Census Statistics

The above are piecemeal examples, dramatic but clearly far from reflecting conditions throughout the whole country. It is fair to ask what was the overall effect of the Meiji government's *shinbutsu bunri* policy on

[32] Ibid., vol. 1, pp. 976-1004.

[33] Hayashiya Tatsusaburō et al., eds., *Kyōto no rekishi* (Tokyo: Gakugei shorin, 1974), vol. 7, pp. 524-545.

[34] Tamamuro, *Shinbutsu bunri*, pp. 167-175.

the Buddhist institution. How, for instance, did the scale of the institution in mid-Meiji compare with Buddhism under the Tokugawa? How many temples were closed; how many monks and nuns laicized? How many statues, paintings, texts, bells and other ritual objects were destroyed or sold? How much land was confiscated?

These questions are valid, but not easy to answer. A full accounting of the destruction and alienation of Buddhist property and images will probably never be made. Without question, tens of thousands (perhaps hundreds of thousands) of Buddhist sutras, paintings, statues, temple bells and other ritual objects were destroyed, stolen, lost, or sold during the years of disturbance and neglect. But records at the time were imperfect, many have since been lost, and others are still piled in disorder in prefectural archives. Some estimates have been made of the amounts of land recovered from Buddhist temples and Shinto shrines by the Meiji government; but these are almost certainly incomplete and do not take into account lands that, at the height of the attacks on Buddhism in the first few years of Meiji, had already been confiscated by domain governments. Under the land reclamation law (*jōchi rei*) of 1871, lands granted to Buddhist temples by the Tokugawa *bakufu*, lands granted by daimyo, and all the lands outside the central compounds of temples were to be returned to the government or local authorities. According to Toyoda Takeshi this amounted to 87,200 *chō* (213,640 acres) of shrine land and 52,800 *chō* (129,360 acres) of temple land.[35] Fukushima Masao gives a lower estimate: 70,670 *chō* (173,141 acres) of shrine land and 43,743 *chō* (107,170) acres) of temple land.[36] Much of this land was used to resettle laicized monks and their families and thus allow them to return to agriculture. Some of it, however, was granted to impoverished samurai and in this sense can be said to have helped finance the Restoration and relieve some of its social costs.

Reliable statistics for the number of temples, monks and nuns reduced during the transition from Tokugawa to Meiji are also hard to find. Late-Edo-period documents such as the *Suijinroku* (c. 1859) give figures of 460,000-500,000 temples throughout Japan. It is not clear whether these documents were based on actual surveys, however, so the figures must be treated with caution. A document compiled in 1871, in response to the Meiji government's demand for information about abandoned temples, gives a figure of 465,049 temples.[37] Again, this was probably based upon estimates by the various schools of Buddhism rather than on careful

[35] Toyoda, *Nihon shūkyō seido shi no kenkyū*, p. 187.

[36] Fukushima Masao, *Chiso kaisei no kenkyū* (Tokyo: Yūhikaku, 1962), p. 448.

[37] Included in Shūkyō shi kenkyūkai, ed., *Jiin honmatsu chō shozai mokuroku* (Tokyo: shūkyō shi kenkyūkai, 1965), vol. 1, pp. 105-106.

surveys. Since the document greatly overestimates the number of temples surviving in some schools—for example, 60,076 temples are claimed by the Ji school, whereas only 1,100 can be confirmed by analyzing actual temple records—its overall reliability cannot be accepted. Thus, it is impossible to say with any degree of precision how many temples were closed or destroyed in the first few years of Meiji.

From 1872, however, the Meiji government began to employ a Western-style national census. For the ensuing five years, Buddhist temples, monks, nuns, and their families were included in the census records for households. For these years, therefore, it is possible to trace the overall institutional decline of Buddhism and see the longer-range effects of the attacks on Buddhism.

Table 6.1 includes some of the national data relating to Buddhism.[38] According to the census data, nearly 18,000 temples were closed between 1872 and 1876 alone. More than 56,000 monks and 5,000 nuns, together with their families and many of their disciples, were returned to lay life. The large number of family members recorded in the census may seem surprising. The law encouraging the Buddhist clergy to marry and eat meat (*nikujiki saitai*) was issued in 1872. Prior to this, Jōdo Shinshū priests had married openly, and many monks and *yamabushi* of other schools had covert marriage arrangements. These were all made public in the census of 1872 and after.

It is very clear from Table 6.1 that the reduction of Buddhism was still proceeding in 1876 and that the outbursts of the early Meiji years described above were not, as is sometimes suggested, a sporadic or short-lived phenomenon. Behind the occasional local outbursts of destruction (*haibutsu*) was a less violent but quite determined government policy, aimed at a drastic reduction of the scale and influence of Buddhism in Japanese society. This involved the closure of many thousands of temples throughout the country. In general those that had few lay patrons, lacked an abbot, did not perform funeral services, or only offered magical prayer services (*kitō*) were the first to be closed.

Naturally, some schools of Buddhism were hit harder than others by

[38] Naimushō, ed., *Nihon zenkoku kosekihyō, Meiji 5–Meiji 9* (Tokyo: Nihon tōkei kyōkai, 1965 reprint). It may be argued that these census data are not necessarily accurate. Certainly there is no way of knowing whether every temple, monk, and nun in every prefecture or province was recorded. It is quite possible that the thoroughness of the census taking may have varied from place to place, or that the definition of "temple" or "monk" may have varied. Notwithstanding these possible distortions in the data, it must be stressed that these are the only "objective," nationwide data on the transformation of the Buddhist institution as a whole that I have been able to find for these critical years. I must express my thanks to Professor Akira Hayami for introducing this source to me.

TABLE 6.1

The Reduction of Buddhism in Early Meiji

	Edo Period	1871	1872	1873	1874	1875	1876
Temples	460,000-500,000 (?)	465,049 (?)	89,914	88,423	79,120	74,784	71,962
Monks	—	—	75,925	73,875	69,256	64,881	19,490
Family members of monks	—	—	98,585	97,372	95,434	90,230	38,711
Disciples of monks	—	—	37,336	36,422	33,745	26,918	8,229
TOTAL	—	—	211,846	207,669	198,435	182,029	66,430
(male)	—	—	(151,677)	(148,807)	(141,390)	(127,737)	(42,710)
(female)	—	—	(60,169)	(58,862)	(57,045)	(54,292)	(23,720)
Nuns	—	—	6,068	5,632	4,284	3,509	1,067
Family members of nuns	—	—	—	—	9	5	—
Disciples of nuns	—	—	3,553	3,694	3,423	2,672	646
TOTAL	—	—	9,261	9,326	7,680	6,186	1,713
(male)	—	—	—	—	(3)	(1)	—
(female)	—	—	—	—	(7,677)	(6,185)	—

SOURCES: For the Edo period, *Suijinroku* (c. 1859); for 1871, *Goshuin-tsuki jikakuchō*, vol. 87 of *Shaji torishirabe ruisan*, cited in *Jiin honmatsu chō shozai mokuroku* (Tokyo: Shūkyō shi kenkyūkai, 1965), vol. 1, pp. 105-106; for 1872-1876, Naimushō, ed., *Nihon zenkoku kosekihyō, Meiji 5–Meiji 9* (Tokyo: Nihon tōkei kyōkai, 1965 reprint).

Meiji government policies. Older monasteries, mainly Tendai and Shingon, that had held large grants of "red seal" or "black seal" land under the Tokugawa had most to lose economically. Temples that had relied on daimyo as exclusive patrons were also bereft. Many Rinzai Zen temples were in this category. Likewise, those schools such as Tendai, Shingon, and Sōtō Zen that engaged heavily in *kitō* were severely affected. On the whole, Jōdo Shinshū was least affected by the government's policies and was quickest to recover. It had not held extensive donated lands, but drew its strength from widespread popular support.

TRANSITION AND TRANSFORMATION

Although the full picture remains far from clear, the above examples, combined with the information provided by the early Meiji census data, should suffice to give us a fair idea of the extent, severity, and variety of the separation policy and its local enforcement. With Buddhism being wrenched away from Shinto; with many thousands of temples being closed, laid waste, or allowed to slip into dereliction; with tens of thousands of monks and nuns being laicized; with temple property being confiscated, sacred objects being burned in the streets, desecrated, or converted into weapons; with Buddhism being disestablished and demoted, Buddhist leaders like Fukuda Gyōkai can scarcely be accused of exaggeration in viewing *shinbutsu bunri* as a crisis of religious survival.

For the first few years of Meiji, the Buddhist clergy were stunned and unable to mount any very effective resistance to the tide of separation, destruction, and disestablishment. There were occasional scuffles between shrine monks and Shinto priests, and some Jōdo Shinshū priests were involved in local uprisings; for the most part, though, Buddhist monks and nuns could do little but acquiesce. Sir Harry Parkes commented without much surprise at the docility with which thousands of monks in Satsuma returned to lay life.[39] They had little choice. Government, central and local, was determined and had force at hand, if necessary. Three centuries of regulation within the Tokugawa system had inured Buddhism to compliance with political authority.

Moreover, there was a sense of demoralization among Buddhists of all

[39] "A singular instance of what in Europe would be regarded as gross religious apathy was afforded towards the close of the year by the abolition of Buddhism in Satsuma, which was accepted without a murmur, even by the Buddhist priests themselves. The purification of Shintō by eliminating Buddhist elements, which for some years formed a prominent feature of the new policy, met with little opposition." Quoted in S. Lane-Poole and F.V. Dickins, eds., *The Life of Sir Harry Parkes* (New York: Macmillan, 1894), p. 140.

schools. Shinto and Western studies were obviously the rising force. While most Buddhist priests probably remained convinced of the essential truth and validity of their beliefs and traditional practices, they found it hard to deny that there were too many temples, that many monks and nuns were ignorant, poorly trained, and not always punctilious in their observance of the *Vinaya*, and that Buddhism as an institution had sacrificed vitality for security under Tokugawa patronage. Not only did monks and nuns comply with docility; many asked to be allowed to become lay people or to be re-enrolled as Shinto priests. What resistance there was from the Buddhist clergy was mostly in the form of appeals to the court, to members of the government, or to domain officials—calls for restraint or protests against excessive violence. There were some monks, like the head monk of the daimyo's family temple in Naegi domain, who took quiet but pointed action to show their disapproval. When his temple was abolished this monk was allotted five servants and offered an appointment as instructor in the domain school—on condition that he promote a policy of laicization. Instead, he moved to a temple in Shinano, taking with him the daimyo family mortuary tablets and the principal images of the defunct temple.[40]

Lay resistance to *shinbutsu bunri* took a variety of forms. There were places, as in Toyama, where Buddhists protested in the streets. There were certainly many places, such as Satsuma, where Buddhists met in secret after severe anti-Buddhist policies had been enforced. And there were a few places in which local protest was violent or took the form of a religious uprising, or at least a protest in which opposition to *shinbutsu bunri* blended with hostility to the renewed threat from Christianity and to other aspects of the new government's program.

The most serious of these mass protests was that in the Kikuma domain, Mikawa, in 1871. Farmers' resentment at plans to reform village land and tax laws ran together with the frustrations of the True Pure Land clergy. As a result, some forty Jōdo Shinshū priests and a band of angry farmers took up arms against local officials trying to enforce *shinbutsu bunri* and other village reforms.[41] A large uprising in Fukui prefecture in 1873 rallied around hostility to Christianity, the crushing of Western trends, the protection of True Pure Land Buddhism, and farmers' demands for relief from government agrarian policies and the new land tax. Again, the uprising was quickly put down and the leaders imprisoned

[40] Tsuji et al., *Shinbutsu bunri shiryō*, vol. 2, pp. 618-619.

[41] Yoshida, *Nihon kindai bukkyō shi kenkyū*, pp. 19-80; Tsuji et al., *Shinbutsu bunri shiryō*, vol. 2, pp. 227-392; Shibata, *Haibutsu kishaku*, pp. 180-183; Tamamuro, *Shinbutsu bunri*, pp. 199-205.

or executed.[42] Other popular outbursts, directed at least in part against the anti-Buddhist religious policies, occurred in Shimane, Oita, and several other prefectures.

Although the whole first decade of Meiji was a difficult one for Buddhism, the most painful phase of the transition was the initial four or five years when the new government's promotion of Shinto was at its strongest, when the intellectual and physical attacks on Buddhism were most virulent, and when the pressure from foreign powers for the freeing of Christian missionary activity began to meet with success. During this crisis of transition a variety of overlapping responses, or sets of responses, became evident. Some of these looked inward or to the past for help in dealing with the priest crisis; others looked outward or forward. Together, they allowed Buddhism to make a partial recovery and helped Buddhists to re-examine their religion and redefine their place in Meiji society.

We find among these responses efforts at sectarian self-strengthening and mutual cooperation, pleas for a revival of religious discipline and spiritual regeneration, attempts to reach a wide following and encourage lay Buddhism, suggestions for renewal of the traditional protective (*chingo kokka*) alliance with the state, arguments in favor of a renewed Buddhist-Shinto-Confucian syncretism against Christianity, pleas for the freeing of Buddhism from Shinto domination, appeals for freedom of religious belief, and suggestions that Buddhists should engage in social reform or learn from the West in order to counter the Christian threat.

One strong and well-defined response was based on the acceptance of guilt: that abuses were prevalent; that these had invited the anti-Buddhist storm; and that, if only they could be eradicated and a traditional religious discipline and spirituality recovered, then Buddhism would be strengthened and survive. This response found active expression in the influential "back to the *Vinaya*" movement started by monks like Fukuda Gyōkai and Shaku Unshō from the early years of Meiji.

Another immediate response to the crisis was the encouragement of sectarian reform and inter-sect cooperation. Shinshū Honganji, for instance, was quick to promote organization reform and the improvement of education and training of its priests. By 1869, an inter-sectarian committee was meeting and had drafted a crisis agenda. Called for were renewed devotion to Buddhism, the study and countering of Christianity, the association of Buddhism with Shinto and Confucianism, closer study of the separate doctrinal traditions, elimination of abuses within the

[42] Tsuji et al., *Shinbutsu bunri shiryō*, vol. 5, pp. 458-479; Shibata, *Haibutsu kishaku*, pp. 186-190.

Buddhist sects, more effective training and promotion of good monks, and more active proselytization and public defense of Buddhism.

A third set of responses hinged on the question of alignment with the state. Those Buddhists who argued in favor of the traditional *chingo kokka* relationship, or one in which Buddhism supported Shinto in the protection of the state, and those who were active in cooperation with the Kyōbushō and the Daikyōin were merely seeking to maintain a long-standing arrangement of mutual benefit. Shimaji Mokurai, a Jōdo Shinshū priest who had originally been in favor of cooperation with the religious policies of the Meiji government, came to criticize the association of religion with politics. After observing the role of religion in Western societies, he appealed for the abolition of the Daikyōin and pressed for freedom of religious expression. The Kyōbushō was abolished in 1877, its functions transferred to the Naimushō. Freedom of religion was recognized in Article 28 of the Meiji Constitution. But Shimaji's ideas on the separation of religion and politics and on religious freedom were qualified. He was from Yamaguchi (Chōshū) and had close ties with Itō and Kido. In his successful campaign for religious freedom, Shimaji clearly used his political connections to achieve the limited tactical objective of freeing Buddhism from its subordination to Shinto.

Fourth, there were responses to Christianity and the West. For many Buddhists, the threatened resurgence of Christianity in Japan loomed as a greater menace than Shinto supremacy. Some Buddhist supporters even claimed that the attacks on Buddhism were inspired by Christianity. Regeneration of Buddhism through a reemphasis on the *Vinaya* was one way to meet this threat. Alliance of Buddhism with Shinto was another. But Hara Tanzan, the first lecturer in Buddhist studies at Tokyo University, was convinced, as were others, that Buddhists had to adopt some of the textual and scientific methods of Western religious scholarship in their own study and teaching, and that young Japanese monks should be sent to the West to study and observe. The Honganji was most active in sending priests to study abroad, but other schools of Buddhism soon followed suit. Some prominent Buddhists, affected by the mood of Civilization and Enlightenment (*bummei kaika*), organized lecture and discussion groups or started journals in which they could discuss the relationship of Buddhism to the social changes and drastically altered attitudes of early Meiji. A few Buddhists in this transitional period took a more active interest in social welfare work or in the politics of the Movement for People's Rights.[43]

[43] These social welfare activities are discussed in detail by Yoshida Kyūichi, *Nihon kindai bukkyō shakai shi kenkyū* (Tokyo: Yoshikawa kōbunkan, 1964), pp. 3-169.

By 1877, the year of the abolition of the Kyōbushō, the worst of the storm was passing. Although Buddhism as an institution had been severely reduced; although the centuries-old harmonious interrelationship with Shinto had been destroyed; although the relevance of Buddhism to the needs of the new political and social order had been called into question; although monks and nuns had been humiliated, and temples and religious objects subjected to desecration; and although Buddhism had been disestablished and demoted within the Meiji state and religious hierarchy, it was becoming clear that Buddhism would not, as Fukuda had feared, be eradicated. Nor would it remain totally subordinate to Shinto or be swamped by Christianity. Transformation and adjustment to the rapidly changing Meiji society would have to continue, but at least a transition had been made.

CHAPTER 7

THE MILITARY

BY D. ELEANOR WESTNEY

Military institutions were the leaders in the organizational transition from Tokugawa to Meiji. They were the first areas of major structural change, the first to adopt Western organizational patterns, and the first to hire foreign advisers. The army and the navy rapidly became the largest-scale organizations in Japanese society; and not only did their demand for resources act as a major stimulus in the development of other systems, from the centralized tax system to universal primary education, but they also served as powerful models for those systems.

One can identify three phases in the transition to a modern military organization. The first (1853-1870) was a relatively lengthy period of experimentation with new forms and involved wide variations among a large number of organizations—the military forces of the many domains of the *bakuhan* system. In the second phase (1870-1878) the central government established a single, highly centralized organizational model for the army and for the navy, and both institutions were absorbed in intensive organization building, focused on internal structures and processes. In the third phase (1878-1890), attention shifted to the ways in which the organizations interacted with the political and social environment, with respect to ensuring the supply of needed resources and increasing the military's professional autonomy and institutional effectiveness. For the army, this involved a switch to a new, Western model. How great was the transformation required by the development of a modern army and navy? This is best highlighted by a comparison of Japanese and Western military organization at the midpoint of the nineteenth century.

In the early seventeenth century, it can be argued, Japan could stand on equal terms with the Western military powers of the day. With the closing of the country in the 1630s, however, Japan entered a long period in which military organization and technology not only made no significant advance, but actually retreated. The long peace saw the ossification of what had been a flourishing industry of firearms manufacture; the prohibition on the construction of warships likewise ended a growing sector of the shipbuilding trade. Many domains continued to maintain one or more units armed with muskets, but their function became largely ceremonial.

Japan in the 1850s confronted the West with no navy and no standing army.[1] Despite the "warrior" lineage of the samurai, the long peace had eroded not only military skills, but military organization as well. The closest approach to full-time military organization was the large number of samurai units that performed guard duty and police functions; these were attached to civilian administrative offices, rather than being integrated into a comprehensive military structure. The Tokugawa retained the prerogative of exacting a levy of men and supplies from the daimyo. The result would be not a national force comparable to mid-nineteenth-century European armies, but a large number of units lacking the unified command, standardized structure, and professional leadership of a modern army.

While a number of guns remained in use, the basic weapons were the spear and the sword, weapons whose organizational implications for supply and support systems were very different from those of the artillery and rifles of the Western armies of the mid-nineteenth century. For one thing, the sword remained the property of the individual rather than of the organization; the logistics of ammunition supply, which necessitated elaborate support organization in the West, were largely missing. Over time, the differentiation among the samurai between high-status mounted warriors and lower-status foot soldiers had been largely reified into hereditary distinctions of rank and stipend, of which the horse itself became a relatively minor symbol. This provided at least one useful legacy for the new army: Japan escaped the aristocratic glorification of the cavalry that was endemic in many European armies.

All these features stood in marked contrast to those of European military forces. In the West, the nineteenth-century revolutions in military technology had created serious organizational problems: problems having to do with the coordination of increasingly specialized services, the greater training and discipline necessary for an effective fighting force, and the increased specialization and complexity of command. These problems could be solved only through the development of large-scale, centralized,

[1] Ernst Presseisen, *Before Aggression: Europeans Train the Japanese Army* (Tucson: University of Arizona Press, 1965), p. 2.

highly differentiated formal organizations—development that was closely linked with the expansion of the state. For example, the demand for literate soldiers spurred the provision of publicly financed universal education in Prussia; revelation of the appalling physical condition of conscripts stimulated many of the late-nineteenth-century developments in public health and sanitation. This close relationship between military organization and the state posed problems of formal articulation between military and other state subsystems that would continue unresolved in most societies well into the twentieth century. In the Tokugawa settlement of the early 1600s, the problem of the military and the state had been resolved by extending military organization to encompass the administrative tasks of the state, transforming the former in the process. The impossibility of rapidly reversing this process made major changes in both military and state organization inevitable in the event of sudden internal or external challenges.

That Japan had no military organization comparable to that of the Western powers did not mean that the society was without the resources to generate it. Indeed, for at least a decade and a half before the arrival of Perry, those resources had been slowly but steadily expanding. As news filtered through of the increasing European presence in Asia, and especially after China's defeat in the Opium War, a handful of students of Western military techniques urged the upgrading of Japan's defenses by means of current Western weaponry and organization. Even though the most knowledgeable and outspoken of these men was a *bakufu* official in Nagasaki, Takashima Shūhan, these petitions fell on deaf ears in Edo. In 1841, to render his arguments more convincing, Takashima imported some up-to-date Dutch field guns and rifles at his own expense, organized a model troop, and persuaded *bakufu* officials to allow him to present a demonstration exercise near Edo. Impressive as the exercise was to many domain officials and to several in the shogunate itself, conservatives in Edo, fearing the consequences of the radical changes entailed by the new weaponry, forced Takashima's arrest and imprisonment. He remained in confinement until after Perry's arrival in 1853; then, in one of the reversals of policy that made the careers of so many *bakumatsu* and early Meiji figures so volatile, he was made a military instructor of the *bakufu* forces in 1856.

In a centralized polity, the conservative reaction would have prevailed; in Tokugawa Japan, it was possible for the individual domains to pick up what the shogunate discarded. The officials of the great southwestern domains were closer to the sources of information in Nagasaki and were more exposed to the incursions of Western ships. In 1837, for example, an American ship had entered Kagoshima Bay, and the Satsuma shore batteries had proven utterly ineffective in driving it away. After that incident, Satsuma sent two of its young samurai to study under Takashima in Nagasaki.[2] Saga and Chōshū also dispatched retainers to study in Takashima's school, and experimented with the manufacture of larger cannon and newer models of firearms.[3] Satsuma and Saga by 1852 had each constructed reverberatory furnaces to provide the iron necessary for such weapons, and Satsuma and Chōshū both reorganized a substantial portion of their domain forces into gun-bearing troops. Meanwhile, Nagasaki-based military scholars, making use of imported books and conversations with the traders of Deshima, produced a growing stream of books on Western military practices and strategy.

By the early 1850s, there existed among the leaders of the *bakufu* and the domains an awareness of Western military technology, and the nucleus for the expansion of military industry in subsequent decades. It took the arrival of Perry and the ensuing internal unrest, however, to prod the *bakufu* and the domain authorities into utilizing these resources in new organizations that could make their effective use and expansion possible.

Phase One: Experimentation and Variation

The 1853 lifting of the formal prohibition on the construction or purchase of large-scale ships marked the beginning of nearly two decades of military mobilization and innovation at the domain level. Initially this was stimulated by Japanese fears of invasion by the Western powers. As the early panic receded in the late 1850s, however, internal conflicts over the handling of foreign policy and over access to the new resources of Western trade accelerated. Thereafter, military expansion was spurred by the anticipation of internal rather than external conflict, with a resulting change of emphasis from sea to land forces. The 1860s also witnessed five armed conflicts within Japan: two between Japanese and Western forces, three between *bakufu* and domain forces. Each of these stimulated further expansion of military organization, and not only among the participants. By 1870, therefore, the new central government faced the task of building a national military in a country whose military resources had been greatly increased by the varied innovations of the 1850s and 1860s, but in which

[2] Kurihara Ryūichi, *Bakumatsu Nihon no guntai* (Tokyo: Shinjimbutsu ōraisha, 1972), p. 28.

[3] Chōshū's observers at Takashima's demonstration were so impressed that they persuaded the domain to send three young men to study under him. Ibid., p. 77.

those resources had not yet been pulled together in the institutional framework of a modern army and navy.

In Japan, as in most of the non-Western world, the principal threat from the Western powers came from the sea. It was a threat to which Japan was especially—one might even argue, uniquely—vulnerable. It is hardly surprising, then, that the first major area of organizational development was in naval forces. They were the first organizations to emulate Western structures, to introduce formal training of specialized personnel by Western instructors, to adopt Western-style uniforms. A Western-style navy could be created in "a vacant niche": there was no existing organization performing that function which might resist attempts at transformation on a new model or oppose the creation of a rival organization.

In the land forces, by contrast, not only did elaborate organizational structures already formally exist, but models for incorporating Western technology into those structures had already been developed. Paradoxically, this acted as a barrier to an immediate resort to contemporary Western organizational models. The existing models involved the lowest-ranking samurai armed with guns, troops that remained part of the forces organized along traditional lines. The involvement of higher-ranking samurai in this low-status type of military unit, or in the even lower-status "dirty work" of using field artillery, met with strong resistance.

The longer life of traditional skills in land forces is illustrated by the contrast in two academies that the shogunate opened in 1855 to upgrade its capacity to respond to the Western military threat. The Naval Training Institute (Kaigun denshūjo) was set up in Nagasaki, with six Dutch instructors whose lectures covered gunnery, seamanship, naval strategy, engineering, and shipbuilding. In its eagerness to expand Japan's naval power, the *bakufu* admitted young men from the domains as well as its own retainers: 129 of the nearly 200 students were sponsored by their domains. In contrast, the Kōbusho, opened in Edo in the same year to improve land-based military skills, served only shogunate retainers of the rank of *hatamoto* or below. The subjects of instruction included traditional military arts such as swordsmanship and jujitsu as well as gunnery, and the instruction texts for gunnery were more than a decade old. No foreign instructors were thought necessary.

By the early 1860s, however, it was becoming apparent that incorporating the weapons of the West into the Japanese context involved more than the addition of the rifle to the weaponry of the individual samurai and the installation of larger cannon in existing shore batteries. The new weapons required radically different levels of specialization within military organization, new kinds of knowledge among those in positions of command, and new ways of drill and training. They also demanded new infrastructures of transport and supply: guns, unlike swords and spears, require reloading to be effective and one of the organizational effects of the newer, breech-loading rifles was to increase dramatically the amount of ammunition used. Further problems were encountered in recruiting men for the troops to be equipped with the new weapons. Some domains relied on forming new units composed of volunteers—in some cases resorting to commoners when the samurai proved reluctant.[4] Others, including the Tokugawa, relied largely on the conversion of existing units. Finally, officials faced difficulties in integrating the new units into structures of command in which traditionally armed and organized troops still predominated.

By the early 1860s, the new weapons were entering Japan at a rapidly accelerating rate. The increase in the number of Western merchants after the opening of the ports in 1859 gradually eroded control over the flow of arms into Japan. This was an important factor in the escalating military expansion of the 1860s. Both the imports and the large-scale initial investment required by domestic production facilities (arsenals, shipyards, iron foundries) were expensive, and this forced those domains bent on military expansion either to build up their resource base or to redirect existing resources. Some domains (Tosa being the primary example) resorted in the 1860s to expanding trade in order to finance arms purchases. Others, including the *bakufu* itself, relied on the reduction of expenditures in other areas—abolishing existing offices, cutting retainers' stipends, eliminating traditional financial obligations. The effect of such measures was to erode traditional administrative structures and to undercut the loyalty of the samurai to the established order—in short, to trigger processes of organizational disintegration that were an essential condition of the collapse of the old order.

The search for solutions to these problems, made urgent by the escalation of open conflict in the 1860s, led to increasing resort to Western models. In this area of change, the shogunate was unequivocally the leader. Its position as the titular government of Japan, at least in the eyes of the West, gave it privileged access to the flow of information from the Western powers and to the import of weapons. It used this advantage to good effect in its two major military reforms. The first, in 1862, drew on translated Western military manuals and the knowledge of its own military scholars to create a new command structure both for its land

[4] Commoners were often used in the more menial tasks associated with the new weapons: supply, maintenance, transport. The Tokugawa began to use commoners in rifle units in 1865. Some of the domains—most notably Chōshū—admitted commoners to the ranks of the units.

and its sea forces; the second, in 1867, was more far-reaching and engaged the expertise of French army advisers and English naval advisers.[5] Each reform drew more heavily on Western models, and each reached further beyond the structure of the military itself to generate the resources necessary to support it. The keynote of the 1867 reform was the opening of a training academy for the army in Edo, staffed by French army officers. The *bakufu* also used French technical advisers to help build a new iron foundry, an arsenal, and a shipyard. The shogunate, in the 1850s considerably behind the great southern domains in terms of military technology, was by 1867 reaching a position of leadership.[6]

The shogunate's military reforms, important as they were in providing a nucleus for future developments, were more impressive in design than in execution: they encountered major problems in implementation, in part because they involved such extensive changes and such high expenditures. The shortage of trained officers, the failure to develop an effective command structure at the top of the military pyramid, and the continuing shortage of funds all hampered development. The very scale of the changes meant that the *bakufu* was potentially at a short-term disadvantage, and time was the most critical shortage: the Keiō reforms, designed to remedy the worst of these problems, were initiated less than a year before the fall of the *bakufu*. In fact, the great potential of these reforms was an important factor in galvanizing the opponents of the Tokugawa into concerted action against it.[7]

Those opponents were domains that had continued to invest heavily in military expansion. Saga and Satsuma maintained their early lead in the development of naval forces. Chōshū, under attack from the shogunate in 1864 and again in 1866, had attained the most extensive mobilization of land forces, an achievement that had subsequent costs: the domain had grave problems with demobilization after the Restoration.

In terms of manpower, technology, and organization, it was the *bakufu* and the great southwestern domains which provided the most important base for military developments in the Meiji period. But these domains were by no means alone in the increasing resort to innovation on Western models; their example and a continuing flow of books and manuals expanded the information base available to other domains. The multi-

[5] Both reforms are described in careful detail in Conrad Totman's *The Collapse of the Tokugawa Bakufu, 1862-1868* (Honolulu: University Press of Hawaii, 1980).

[6] Miyazaki Fumiko, "Bakufu no sanbei shikan gakkō setsuritsu o meguru ikkōsatsu," in Kindai Nihon kenkyūkai, ed., *Bakumatsu: Ishin no Nihon* (Tokyo: Yamakawa shuppansha, 1981), p. 132.

[7] See Totman, *The Collapse*.

TABLE 7.1
Military Organization Changes in Seven Nagano-Prefecture Domains, 1850-1870

	Status and Size	Dutch-Style	English-Style	French-Style
Matsumoto	*fudai*, 60,000 *koku*	1866	—	1870*
Takatō	*fudai*, 33,000 *koku*	1856	—	1870*
Ueda	*fudai*, 53,000 *koku*	1850	1869	1870
Suzaka	*tozama*, 10,000 *koku*	1854	1865	1870
Iiyama	*fudai*, 20,000 *koku*	—	1866	1870
Tanoguchi	*fudai*, 16,000 *koku*	1861	—	1865
Iwamurata	*fudai*, 15,000 *koku*	1866	—	1867

SOURCE: Nagano ken, ed., *Nagano kensei shi 1* (Nagano: Nagano ken, 1971), p. 14.
NOTE: An asterisk means that the change was adopted prior to the central government's standardization decree of 1870.

plicity of political units in the *bakuhan* system provided opportunities for a variety of experiments and innovations, in which even relatively small domains were active. Table 7.1 charts the changes in the military organizations of seven relatively small domains in what is now Nagano prefecture; it demonstrates the variety in the timing and the models used even among neighboring domains. Six of the seven were *fudai* domains having strong military traditions and officials who were involved in the military debates within the *bakufu*; the seventh was a very small *tozama* domain. Such innovations were not just important in expanding the military resources of Japan; they also provide a graphic indicator of the eager emulation of foreign models, openness to change and experiment, and the flow of information across Japan—all of which were important in later years not only in the military, but in a range of activities from administration to commerce.

The Restoration itself did not halt military development. Both in terms of the national political situation and of intra-domain stability, conditions were sufficiently uncertain to encourage many domains to continue their military expansion and mobilization. The military school in Numazu, the domain to which the former shogun retired, carried on with the same curriculum and with many of the French-trained instructors from the military training institute set up in Edo.[8] Several domains continued to import weapons. Kii, for example, imported several thousand needle guns from Germany in 1870; these were accompanied by a German officer,

[8] See Miyazaki, "Bakufu no sanbei shikan gakkō," pp. 157-159.

who proceeded to instruct the domain retainers in their use and in the organization of units to use them effectively. Most domain schools expanded their instruction in Western military studies. The potential for increasing fragmentation of the country was very real, and the ongoing military mobilization provided a strong incentive for the center to move toward the early abolition of the domains.

From the viewpoint of the domains themselves, the military buildup was a two-edged sword. In many domains, the continued westernization of arms and organization was accompanied by the demobilization of more traditional forces and the consolidation and streamlining of the more modern units (in this latter process, one common element was the dismissal of the commoners who had been recruited to swell the ranks). This demobilization was not accomplished without difficulty; in Chōshū, for example, it provoked an extensive mutiny that had to be quelled by troops recalled from Kyoto. Domains that chose to avoid such stresses by not demobilizing on so large a scale faced another problem: heavy financial burdens. In short, the problems posed by reversing the expansion of the previous two decades of military mobilization were major factors both in the financial troubles and in the threat of internal unrest that were to induce domain officials' acquiescence in the 1871 abolition of the *han*.

Phase Two: The Emergence of a Dominant Model

The emergence of a "modern" national military in Japan is conventionally dated either from the 1871 formation of the Imperial Guard, the first military force directly under the control of the central government, or, more commonly, from the 1873 Conscription Edict. The base for both these actions was laid, however, in 1870, even before the abolition of the domains. In that year, the central government decreed that all domains adopt the French model for their land forces and the English model for their naval forces. In so doing, the government both asserted the principle of central jurisdiction over the military and took the first steps toward achieving a standardized national structure.

The legacy of the previous regime proved invaluable. The physical facilities for quartering and drilling the troops were provided by the castles of the regionally dominant castle towns chosen as headquarters for the major garrisons. The 10,000 troops of the Imperial Guard were drawn from the pick of the domain troops of Satsuma, Chōshū, and Tosa. The very models authorized by the new government, the French army and the English navy, were inherited from the *bakufu*. The English navy was the obvious model: it had been so for Satsuma and Saga as well as for the *bakufu*, and had no rivals then or later. Several voices in the new government were raised in favor of the German model rather than the French, but the argument that existing resources favored the latter proved decisive. The schools established by the *bakufu* provided a group of trained men familiar with the institutional patterns as well as with the language of the instructors, and the accumulated body of texts and manuals reinforced the strength of existing patterns. The Japanese government formally adopted the French model for the army exactly one month after the French were defeated by the Prussians at Sedan. But the widespread belief that the Japanese switched to the German army model because of the outcome of the Franco-Prussian War is a pleasant fiction. As Presseisen points out, central government leaders perceived France's defeat as the result not of weaknesses in military organization, but of a lack of popular support. Presseisen quotes a Japanese government statement of the time:

> After deciding to adopt the French system, if we changed our mind only because France was defeated, this would give a wrong impression to other countries that the Japanese Empire has no backbone and [is] unreliable, and eventually [it would] become a laughing stock among the nations. We must guard against this.[9]

Throughout this second phase of development, the principal tasks of the army and the navy were those concerned with building the infrastructure of their respective organizations: establishing the internal structures of coordination and control, setting up training and socialization programs, and expanding internal information links. For the army, however, concentration on these internal tasks was periodically interrupted by demands for intervention to suppress samurai and peasant uprisings, which flared intermittently during the first decade of the Meiji period. This necessitated a dispersal of military units throughout the country (there were forty garrisons in Japan) and the commitment of officers and men to tasks outside the purview of institution building. However, in a time of scarce government resources on which there were many urgent claims, this meant that the army was given virtually top priority.

One of the most urgent tasks facing the army and the navy was the development of an officer corps, one socialized into the patterns of the modern military and equipped with the skills adequate to the training of recruits and the effective use of the new weapons. The early 1870s wit-

[9] Presseisen, *Before Aggression*, p. 39. Presseisen gives the source as Enjoji Kiyoshi, ed., *Ōkuma haku sekijitsu dan* (Tokyo: Fuzambō, 1914), pp. 453-454.

nessed the establishment of a number of military schools in both services, built around a core of foreign military advisers but leaning heavily on the knowledge and experience of those trained in earlier schools and on young men returning from foreign study. Suspicious of French connections with the *bakufu* and unhappy over the high financial costs, the Meiji government rejected French offers to continue supplying military instructors. The first military training school under the new regime was set up in Kyoto in 1868, with a curriculum oriented to Western military studies but staffed by Japanese. By 1871, the Meiji government decided to reverse its policy, and in 1872 a mission of sixteen French officers arrived in Japan.[10] In 1875 these Frenchmen would provide the core staff for the first class at the military academy (Shikan gakkō). The resort to Western instructors was once again more rapid in the navy: the Meiji government's first naval school was opened at Yokohama in 1869, and in 1870 its first British instructor was hired. By 1873, thirty-four British instructors were employed in the naval schools.[11]

It was not until the late 1870s that sizable cohorts began to be graduated from these schools. For the first generation of officers, entrance into the new military was not through standardized formal professional training, but along two principal routes. One led through the domain troops and distinguished combat experience into the Imperial Guard; the second was through the acquisition of experience with Western military forces in the late 1860s. Those recruited through the first route came overwhelmingly from the three domains from which the troops of the Imperial Guard had been drawn; those recruited through the second were of more varied origin, although the former retainers of the shogun were heavily represented. The first group provided the bulk of the first generation of line officers. The second, whose loyalty was perhaps perceived as more equivocal and who had virtually no ascriptive ties to the earliest rank-and-file troops, provided staff officers for the army and navy ministries or technical instructors for the shools. The handful of men whose experience covered both categories (most notably Yamagata Aritomo and Saigō Tsugumichi) constituted the top-ranking architects of the new organizations.

The problem of the recruitment of rank-and-file soldiers was more vexatious than that of the officer corps. The introduction of conscription in Japan is now viewed as a natural and progressive step, in tune with the state-building ambitions of the Meiji leaders. Yet the inevitability that historical hindsight confers on the decision to build a conscript army disappears when the time frame shifts to the early 1870s.

[10] Ibid., pp. 33-45.

[11] Fukuchi Shigetaka, *Gunkoku Nihon no keisei* (Tokyo: Shunjusha, 1959), p. 35.

In Europe, the impetus for conscription was provided by the need to expand the size of the armed forces. No such necessity operated in Japan, at least in the 1870s. Even if fewer than half of the estimated 450,000 unemployed samurai were incorporated into a new army and navy based on Western models, their numbers would have exceeded the actual military strength mustered by Japan through the 1880s. Those who advocated a samurai-based professional force, at least as a transitional step, had a reasonable case. The Satsuma leaders were the strongest spokesmen for this approach, and Yamagata of Chōshū the most outspoken advocate of universal conscription, but the arguments by no means followed straight domain lines. Chōshū's Yamada Akiyoshi, an army officer, returned from the Iwakura mission convinced of the virtues of universal conscription; but he also believed that its introduction in Japan should be deferred until a nationwide system of compulsory education was turning out potential recruits who were both literate and socialized into new patterns of loyalty, obedience, and nationalism. Moreover, the experience of Chōshū in particular during the 1850s and 1860s would seem to have validated the principle of the volunteer rather than the conscript force.

The advocates of an early introduction of conscription triumphed; the justifications based on Japan's ancient tradition of peasant soldiers, the valiant performance of commoners in the domain troops, and prevailing trends in Europe were reinforced by economic and political calculation. A conscript force composed of men who were not heads of families was cheaper than a professional force, and that was by no means a minor consideration. By the early 1870s, moreover, it was clear that the principal opposition to the changes envisioned by the Meiji government would come from the samurai, and the potential danger of relying on a professional force of armed samurai for the defense of the new regime did not escape consideration.

The announcement of conscription late in 1872 and the Conscription Edict of 1873 were recognized as landmarks clearly indicating the government's commitment to building a modern nation-state on the Western model. The organizational reality was less clear-cut. Both the army and the navy continued to accept samurai volunteers; their exact number is uncertain, since official records made no formal distinction. In these early years, moreover, the number of conscripts actually inducted was very small: only about 3 percent of the men in the appropriate age cohorts actually served during the 1870s.[12]

Much has been made of the many loopholes in the Conscription Edict, which excused from service men who were family heads or who were

[12] Recruitment of conscripts was limited to Tokyo in 1873; in the following year, recruits were also inducted at Osaka and Nagoya.

heirs of farms or family businesses. This has been portrayed as reflecting a feudal emphasis on the continuity of the *ie*. In fact, though, these exemptions were virtually identical with those of the French conscription act on which they were based; the principal category added by the Japanese was that of *yōshi* (son-in-law adopted as family heir). The French rationale behind such exemptions was to avoid damage to the economy and to prevent conscription from being a significant burden on the individual family. The Japanese also copied the French provisions for purchasing exemptions, included in France to circumvent resistance to conscription from the influential middle classes.[13]

Developing the manpower of the military was only part of building the new organization. The range of tasks included consolidation of the scattered military industries of the *bakufu* and the domains; purchase of the necessary equipment from abroad until those industries could be expanded to meet the demands of the national forces; provision of transport and communications; decision on the optimum dispersion through Japan; and construction of suitable military installations. The center of these activities was the bureaucracy of the military ministries, beginning with the Hyōbushō (Military Affairs Ministry), set up in 1869.

The ancient *ritsuryō* system, on which the first Meiji central government structures were modeled, included no distinct administrative office for naval forces, there having been none in the eighth century. Consequently, breaking with both Tokugawa precedent and Western example, there was in the new government a single ministry for military affairs (containing two bureaus, one for each service). Even before the 1871 unification of the country, this ministry began the process of centralizing military resources: the arsenals and training facilities of the *bakufu* were put under its control, and in 1870 the various domain troops guarding Kyoto were placed, at least nominally, under its direction. As the early structures were modified, however, separate army and navy ministries were established, in 1872.

These military ministries played the key role in the formation of the new army and navy. Much more than their European counterparts, the Japanese armed forces were created by bureaucratic government departments that were integrated into the central administration and parallel in structure to the civilian ministries, with civil service categories assigned to military ranks. The key decision makers and leaders in these formative years were part of the central government bureaucracy: the upper-ranking officers of the Imperial Guard, for example, also held

[13] Eugen Weber, *Peasants into Frenchmen* (Stanford: Stanford University Press, 1976), p. 293.

appointments in the Hyōbushō. The military structures were part of the larger state decision-making apparatus, the Dajōkan, and were constructed on the emerging patterns of government bureaucracy.

In France and Germany, the military ministries had developed later than the military structures themselves and, in large part were attempts to integrate the armed forces into the administrative apparatus of the state. In turn, the armed forces devised strategies for maintaining their autonomy. In France, top-ranking military men avoided serving in the ministry, for the highest status and power accrued to the line commands.[14] In Germany, there was a long struggle to develop the General Staff into an autonomous agency of coordination and control above the jurisdiction of the ministry.[15] In Japan, largely as a consequence of the virtually simultaneous development of state administration and the modern military, it was the ministry, staffed by professional military officers, that was the locus of power for both services during this formative period.

Of the two services, it was the army that was undoubtedly the leader during this phase of development, despite the early pioneering role of the navy in previous decades. There are several reasons for the slower development of the navy. The early concern of the Meiji government with the maintenance of internal order favored the rapid expansion of the army. In the 1870s, fear of invasion from the West had subsided, and no immediate plans were being laid for foreign expansion; the navy suffered accordingly. The weakness of the internal industrial base for naval construction was also a major factor. The first Japanese-built warship was constructed under the shogunate; the second was not completed until 1876. However, the enormous expense of imported ships made the government reluctant to supplement its naval strength by extensive purchases abroad. Despite continued pleading by navy officials, the Meiji government ordered only six new warships before 1886: three from Britain and three from Japanese shipyards. The British-made ships did not arrive in Japan until 1878.

The navy suffered from political weakness. Many of the key figures in the naval ministry of the 1870s were drawn from the leading pre-Meiji naval power, the *bakufu*, and therefore lacked strong ties to the decision-making elites of the domain-based government. Rivalry within the Navy Ministry among former *bakufu* officials, Satsuma men, and Saga factions

[14] David Ralston, *The Army of the Republic* (Cambridge: The MIT Press, 1965), pp. 152-159.

[15] Gordon A. Craig, *The Politics of the Prussian Army, 1640-1945* (New York: Oxford University Press, 1964), pp. 219-232.

also hampered the development of effective policy making.[16] Before the late 1880s, many of the officials were men with little or no direct naval experience; some were former army officers, and many were civilians with administrative experience but no understanding of the navy.[17]

Finally, the development of a professional, Western-trained officer corps took longer in the navy than in the army. The average length of stay in the West for naval training was eight to eleven years,[18] and the first sizable groups of foreign-trained students did not begin to return to Japan until 1878. The advances made in the navy during this phase were important: the establishment of a number of naval academies and schools (one of which was a school of accounting, set up in 1874 with an American instructor); the dispatch of students abroad; and the consolidation of the Navy Ministry. But these were an investment in the future; with respect to the current development of the institution, the navy continued to lag behind the army.

Important advances in building a modern, Western-style army and navy should not be allowed to obscure the existence of a very different, traditional kind of military expansion: the *tondenhei* ("military colonists") of the northern island of Hokkaido. This program, initiated in 1874, had three purposes: to provide employment for samurai, to stimulate the economic development of Japan's northern frontier, and to provide a military defense against possible encroachment by the Russians. It also served to appease some of the Satsuma military men who felt that the initiation of conscription had been a betrayal of the government's obligations to the samurai. The program drew on traditional Satsuma precedents and was the brainchild of Kuroda Kiyotaka, one of the principal Satsuma army officers and head of the colonial office that administered Hokkaido. Samurai were provided with transportation to the island, a house, agricultural land and tools, and, at least initially, food subsidies for themselves and their families. The land was allocated in clustered military settlements; the recruits were to be farmers and part-time soldiers, with fixed obligations for military service.

Thirty-seven of these settlements were established, and the total military strength they provided came to 3,500 active soldiers and nearly 1,000 reserves, although to reach these numbers the program had to be opened to commoners as well as to samurai (the latter proving less than eager to become farmers in the unfamiliar territory of Hokkaido). Reflecting the traditional orientation of the program, commoners and sa-

[16] Yonezawa Fujiyoshi, *Yamamoto Gonnohyōe* (Tokyo: Shinjimbutsu ōraisha, 1974), p. 92.

[17] Fukuchi, *Gunkoku Nihon no keisei*, p. 91.

[18] Ibid., p. 34.

murai were settled in different villages. The program was a distinct anomaly: under the jurisdiction of the Hokkaido Development Office, rather than the Army Ministry, it looked to traditional rather than to Western models, and involved a reduction rather than an increase of military professionalism. However, it provided an outlet for the energies of some of the more traditionally minded military men, distracting them from obstructionism within the army. Moreover, its rapidly apparent inadequacy as a defense for Hokkaido supplied a convincing demonstration of the fundamental weakness of traditional models of military mobilization in the modern context.

The regular army, by comparison with the Western forces of the day, was hardly strong. By 1874, Germany had a total of 1.3 million soldiers, including reserves; France claimed even more. By 1878, the Japanese army had increased to just over 41,000 which represented a tripling of the national land forces since the end of 1871. This second phase of development, however, had seen enormous strides in military organization. It had witnessed the consolidation of scattered resources generated in previous decades; the creation of formal structures of coordination and control; the establishment of conscription; the emergence of the top leadership of the army; and the foundation of military schools for the training of a cadre of professional junior officers. It had also established the legitimacy of the new military, through its success in defeating the most serious challenge faced by the new regime, the Satsuma Rebellion.

The proximate cause of the 1877 rebellion was the attempt by the central government authorities to consolidate their control over the last remaining military supplies of the previous era, three ammunition depots in Kagoshima.[19] Apparently spontaneously, more than 1,000 samurai in that city mobilized to thwart the naval troops sent to take possession, and the incident expanded into a full-scale rebellion, centered on the samurai who had gathered in Satsuma around the former government leader, Saigō Takamori. Many standard accounts of the rebellion portray it as a dramatic conflict between the sword-wielding, tradition-wedded samurai and the modern, technologically advanced, commoner-based conscript army. In fact, the organization and training of the Satsuma force were probably superior to those of the army: many Satsuma officers and men were former members of the Imperial Guard, and a significant number had received extended training in Western military techniques. The force itself had two artillery units; most of the men were armed with

[19] The following account draws heavily on James H. Buck, "The Satsuma Rebellion of 1877—From Kagoshima through the Siege of Kumamoto Castle," *Monumenta Nipponica*, vol. 28, no. 4 (Winter 1973), pp. 427-446.

rifles. Moreover, not even four years had elapsed since the introduction of conscription, and the elite army academy, the Shikan Gakkō, with its complement of French instructors, had yet to graduate its first full cohort.

The central government's army, however, had, a critically important advantage: a much more extensive resource base. It could replenish its ammunition from government arsenals, its supplies from the central markets of Japan, its manpower from auxiliary organizations such as the police. Indeed, the defeat of the Satsuma force owed as much or more to the role played by the well-trained, samurai-based Tokyo police detachments (over 5,000 men) and to the units of samurai recruited on an emergency basis from northern and central Japan as it did to the "commoner" conscript army itself.[20] Overall, the active government forces outnumbered those of Satsuma two to one.

The suppression of the rebellion was publicly hailed as a triumph for the new conscript army. The top-ranking officers and many of their subordinates, however, recognized that the campaign had exposed serious organizational problems: a weak logistical system, inadequacies of command, as well as poor coordination and communications—all of which strongly suggested inadequate preparation for large-scale operations.[21] In part, this was a problem traceable to the orientation of the French, who in their instruction in 1867 as well as in the military mission of the 1870s emphasized basic drill and command in terms of the small-scale unit, on the grounds that the Japanese were not yet ready to deal with large-scale command logistics. The French system itself had revealed similar problems of supply, command, and coordination during the Franco-Prussian War.[22] The problem, however, was also attributable to the fact that as a result of rapid military expansion the army line officers were predominantly products of an older system, relying on personal qualities such as bravery and martial skills rather than on the technical expertise and attention to details of supply and coordination needed in large-scale military campaigns.

The dissatisfaction of the architects of the army with their handiwork was increased by the August 1878 mutiny in the Imperial Guard. The apparent cause had to do with disappointed samurai guardsmen who harbored tradition-based expectations concerning the distribution of rewards after the previous year's successful campaign. The spectacle of an elite unit of the army opening fire on government ministry buildings—in the immediate vicinity of the Imperial Palace and the foreign embas-

[20] Oikata Sumio, "Seinan sensō ni okeru 'junsa' no rinji chobo," *Nihon rekishi*, no. 363 (July 1978), pp. 50-67.

[21] Matsushita Yoshio, *Meiji no guntai* (Tokyo: Shibundo, 1963), pp. 49-51.

[22] Presseisen, *Before Aggression*, pp. 50-56.

sies—was an unlooked-for humiliation for the top leadership of the army, and it confirmed the view that their new organization required major changes if it was to provide the solid base for the Meiji state that its leaders expected.

Phase Three: Consolidation and Adjustment

The establishment in 1878 of an autonomous General Staff for the army—largely at the instigation of Katsura Tarō, a young army officer who had just returned to Japan after six years in Germany—was the first in a series of organizational changes that continued until the 1889 reform of the Conscription Edict, changes that were largely based on the German military model. These marked the emergence of a second generation of organizational leaders, whose more thorough professional training and deeper knowledge of Western systems led them to desire changes in the structures set up in an earlier phase of development. But these changes, too, would be presided over by the first generation of leaders.

The general goals behind the organizational changes in this third phase were strongly influenced by developments in the European forces of the day. Indeed, they were much the same: greater autonomy, more effective coordination and control, more secure access to needed resources. Likewise, the changes had very similar roots: increasing organizational size (and demand for resources) and growing military professionalism. This last was epitomized by the opening in 1883 of the Japanese Army War College, an elite educational facility to train upper-level staff officers; the model and two of the instructors were German.

The creation of the General Staff was a key element of the increasing autonomy of the top decision-making structures of the military, and it provides a case of Japanese anticipation of European developments. Throughout the 1860s and 1870s, the German army was growing restive over the ambiguous relationship between the War Ministry and the General Staff: the autonomy of command accorded the latter depended on the incumbents of the top positions within the General Staff itself, the ministry, and the government. The army urged that the General Staff should be responsible directly to the emperor; the politicians and many civilian bureaucrats insisted on its subordination to the ministry. The issue was not resolved in Germany until 1883, when the General Staff was formally freed from the war minister's jurisdiction and its chief given direct access to the emperor.

As Ernst Presseisen makes clear in his study of the influence of French and German military models on the development of the Japanese army,

Katsura, the principal force behind the creation of the Japanese General Staff, was familiar with this debate, and during his years of military study in Germany he had undoubtedly imbibed the army's point of view. In Japan, moreover, the way was much clearer for the creation of an autonomous General Staff, both because there was no elected national assembly to demand some form of accountability from the military and because the War Ministry itself was staffed with army officers.

In Meiji Japan the relationships among the line commanders, the service ministries, and the General Staff were clearer and less fractious than in Europe, both because of the timing of their development and because of the staffing of the ministries. In France and Germany, the service ministries had been set up to integrate the armed forces into the administration of the state and thus included a large number of civilians. In Japan, the ministries had been set up to create the modern military and were therefore staffed largely with professional officers.

The direct responsibility of the General Staff to the emperor was one of the first elements of the special relationship between the imperial institution and the military which was to be cultivated assiduously during this phase of development. The language of the 1882 Imperial Rescript to Soldiers and Sailors indicated the military's special status in the society, a status reinforced by symbolic observances: the emperor attended reviews and military exercises and, from the beginning of the 1880s, was either present at the graduation ceremonies of the army and navy academies or sent personal messages. Furthermore, much more in line with European practice than with Japanese tradition, members of the imperial family who entered public service after the very earliest years of the Meiji period did so in the context of the army or navy. The designation of the emperor as commander-in-chief in the Meiji Constitution formalized an already special relationship.

Although the language and symbolism in which this special relationship was expressed were distinctly Japanese, these developments paralleled similar efforts in Europe (most notably in Germany and Austria) to generate a special tie between the ruler and the armed forces. One effect was to enhance the special status of military organizations in the state and to strengthen their ability to obtain financial resources and manpower. Another was to increase the military's ability to resist any attempts at control or restriction from other state organizations. Finally, it was one of the elements that strengthened the organization's control over its members. The special duty of each soldier and sailor, officer and enlisted man alike, to the ruler was invoked purposefully: to justify the increasing isolation of the members of the armed forces from their environment (particularly restrictions on individual political activities); to reinforce the nationalism and sense of uniqueness that were intended to insulate the military from the currents of change and differentiation in Japanese society at large; and to hold up military men as models for that society.

In any society, the military seals its members into a comprehensive environment in which organizational roles encompass the individual's identity twenty-four hours a day and in which, ideally, all the activities and needs of its members are dealt with internally. Especially in the first two decades of their existence, the army and navy of Meiji Japan were even more separated from the general social environment than their Western counterparts. Shoes, tunics and trousers, beds, tinned food, bread, beer, and cigarettes were foreign, in every sense of the word, to the recruits, marking their military life as utterly distinct from their previous existence. These customs, by degrees, permeated society as increasing numbers of recruits underwent military training.

The autonomy of the military was reinforced by several measures taken in the early 1880s. One was the development of a more effective and autonomous mechanism for enforcing the Conscription Edict. Throughout the 1870s, the army had relied on village officials for reports on the number and identity of young men eligible in terms of age and physique for military service. Under this system, the opportunities for favoritism and for widespread evasion of conscription were extensive, and during the early 1880s the army replaced it. Army doctors would now be dispatched to county offices to conduct the physical examinations which determined whether or not a conscript was fit to serve. Other measures included the prohibition on political activities of members of the armed forces, controls on reading materials permitted in the barracks, and the creation of a separate military police, the *kempeitai* (which quickly became involved in civilian policing as an auxiliary political control force).

Military men also moved out of the army and navy into the regular police, bringing with them military patterns of internal control that would profoundly influence the police structure.[23] The 1880s witnessed the movement of top-ranking military officers into the ministerial portfolios concerned with education (Saigō Tsugumichi in 1878), production (Saigō Tsugumichi at the Nōshōmushō, 1881-1884), law (Yamada Akiyoshi at the Shihōshō 1883-1885), and internal administration (Yamada Akiyoshi and Yamagata Aritomo at the Naimushō)—all critical areas in terms of the required resources and task structures of the military. In fact, civilians did not form a majority of the cabinet until 1898; and during the Meiji

[23] See D. Eleanor Westney, "The Emulation of Western Organizations in Meiji Japan: The Case of the Paris Prefecture of Police and the Keishi-chō," *Journal of Japanese Studies*, vol. 8, no. 2 (Summer 1982), pp. 321-324.

period as a whole, military officers held 45 percent of the civilian cabinet posts.[24] At slightly less exalted levels, significant numbers of military officers moved into the police and the educational system, the latter when military training was made part of the curriculum in the nation's normal schools, in 1886; that same year a general, Yamakawa Isamu, was appointed principal of the Tokyo Normal School. The organizational model that such men took with them placed considerable emphasis on centralization, standardization, professionalism (including a very strong commitment to one's assigned position), predictability, and a clear hierarchy of authority. In these and other respects, the military led the way in changing Japanese society.

This outward movement of military personnel was obviously stimulated in large part by a desire to shape the relationship between the military and its environment to the advantage of the former: to increase the quantity and the quality of resources (this applies particularly to education), and to increase the predictability of the environment and protect the army from unplanned calls on its resources. This last was especially true with respect to the role of military men in the development of the police force and local administration, whose expansion dramatically reduced calls on the army to restore public order. Moreover, military officers provided a pool of men experienced in the administration of large-scale organizational systems, already assimilated into the system of civil service ranks, and highly unsympathetic to the Movement for People's Rights so feared by the Meiji statesmen.

The movement of officers into other organizational systems was also, however, partly response to internal pressures. The 1880s witnessed a clash of organizational generations that was common to most Meiji institutions, but that was earliest and most pronounced in the military. As noted earlier, the first generation of line officers was recruited through the domain troops; they shared a "feudal" culture of personal valor, legitimation of their position by virtue of combat experience, and a hard-drinking, anti-intellectual life style. Those members of this first generation who were attracted to study and technical knowledge were by and large drawn off into staff positions in the Army Ministry and the schools.

The graduates of the army schools, who began to enter line positions in large numbers after 1878, were oriented to formal training and professionalism, personal discipline, academic study, and technical expertise. Jōhō Yoshio quotes the autobiography of one of the early graduates of

[24] Roger F. Hackett, "The Military: Japan," in Robert Ward and Dankwart Rustow, eds., *The Modernization of Japan and Turkey* (Princeton: Princeton University Press, 1964), p. 345.

the military academy, going with high hopes and eager ambition to his first line command in Kumamoto, where he was dismayed and disillusioned to find his fellow officers spending much of their time drinking and reminiscing about old campaigns, and openly disdainful of his efforts to "shape up" the garrison.[25] These young graduates can be seen as the heirs to one aspect of the Tokugawa military tradition, that of the military scholars of the closing decades of that era, whose study-oriented tradition continued through the military academies of the *bakufu* and into the new army and navy schools. The first generation of line officers were heirs to another aspect of the tradition, that of the old-style samurai, the men of action and traditional *bushi* skills and life styles.

Moreover, there tended to be a regional as well as a cultural gap between the two generations: the first-generation men were overwhelmingly recruited from Satsuma and Chōshū; those of the second generation, although these two regions were still overrepresented, had much more varied origins. One young officer, who was graduated from the Shikan gakkō in 1878, described his own feelings and those of his fellow graduates of the early 1880s:

> We sincerely respected the achievements of both Satsuma and Chōshū in the Restoration, but the idea that because of this, today, more than ten years later, the necessary development of the military should be blocked by those factions was more than we could stand.[26]

The young man himself was from Chōshū, which is a further demonstration that the base of the anti-*hanbatsu* feeling was more generational than regional.

The tensions were exacerbated by the fact that the first generation had been elevated into positions of command in the new army at a very early age (in terms of conventional military careers). Therefore, although their professional skills and training rarely came close to those of later cohorts, they were likely to occupy their positions for some time to come, blocking not only what the younger generation defined as "the necessary development of the military," but also the upward mobility of their subordinates. Yamagata Aritomo played a major role in moving senior officers into institutions outside the army in the 1880s, thereby accomplishing several things at once: he relieved to some extent the internal generational pressures of the army; he developed an extensive network of men, to whom he had been connected personally and institutionally, in influential positions in the bureaucracy; and he removed from the army itself a

[25] Jōhō Yoshio, *Rikugunshō gummukyoku* (Tokyo: Fuyō shobō, 1979), pp. 122-123.
[26] Ibid., p. 125.

number of senior officers who might in time have threatened his own predominance. The Satsuma-Chōshū origin of these men, however, was as salient in these other institutions as it had been in the army—and attracted much resentment, since such men were outsiders and proponents of a hierarchical, centralized, "authoritarian" organizational model that imposed considerable restrictions on their subordinates.

Yet, the outward mobility of the first generation of officers by no means emptied the senior ranks. Indeed, there was greater continuity in the top leadership of the army than in any other Meiji state subsystem. One of the principal factors in this continuity was the army's ongoing structural differentiation. As major new organs of coordination and control were set up—in 1878 the General Staff and, in 1887, the Inspectorate (an agency to supervise and standardize army education and training, and which reported, like the General Staff, directly to the emperor)—the army's key organizational leaders stepped into their top positions.[27] This provided an extremely useful device for ensuring the control of the new, specialized agencies and for integrating them into the overall organization; it furthermore enabled the old guard to ensure continuation of their personal dominance. However, it also sowed the seeds of future problems, as it clearly made the three positions of army minister, chief of the General Staff, and inspector general equivalent in status and potentially in authority.

This continuity of leadership did not mean resistance to change. Those first-generation leaders who survived in the organization were not only men who possessed great political skill; they also recognized that the expansion of the army so dear to their hearts required structural adjustments as well as the infusion of resources from the state. The primary model for these changes was drawn from Germany.

The French army emphasized the role of army schools, the importance of the morale and nationalistic spirit of the officer corps, and the mastery of the fundamentals of commanding a small unit. After 1878, though, the French model proved less instructive. As one historian has noted, one of the chief problems facing the French army after 1871 was "the coexistence of a republican regime, increasingly democratic in form and spirit, and a large standing army, led by a caste of professional soldiers."[28] The integration of the army and the state in Japan posed very different problems, concerning which the French experience was largely irrelevant. Germany provided a much more suitable model: like Japan, the German

[27] The Chōshū and Satsuma leaders, Yamagata Aritomo and Ōyama Iwao, were the first two holders of those positions.

[28] Ralston, *The Army of the Republic*, p. 1.

state was a monarchy which had not instituted responsible government and in which the military was expected (or itself expected) to play an active role in consolidating a centralized, unified state. The reform of the French-modeled Conscription Edict along German lines was an example of the Japanese adoption of this German-style state-building role.

Conscription in the German system was seen as a comprehensive mobilization of the entire nation in the larger interests of the state, going beyond purely military considerations to encompass the control of social changes potentially antipathetic to the existing state system. The extensive exemptions permitted under the French-modeled system were drastically narrowed, and the German system of one year's active training for graduates of the middle and higher schools was introduced. Smethurst has described the effect of this second measure as follows:

> The educated landlords' sons served only one year on active duty and then returned home as second lieutenants. . . . By this innovation, Katsura aimed to identify the military's elite, the officer corps, with the village's, the landlord class, and thus increase army prestige and at the same time reinforce both military and social order.[29]

In the mid-1880s the government committed itself to an ambitious program of naval expansion, but navy organization continued to be much smaller in scale than the army's, and there was relatively little internal push for structural differentiation of administration and command. The navy did not follow the army's lead in 1878 in creating a separate command structure; rather, it continued to assign general staff functions to a bureau of the Navy Ministry, and resisted army pressures to bring the naval command structure into line with that of the other service. In order to improve coordination between the two services, Saigō Tsugumichi, one of the principal army generals, transferred into the navy to become the navy minister in the early 1880s. Presumably, his personal connections with the Satsuma faction in the navy and his close ties to leading government figures made him acceptable to navy officers. In 1886, the year after Saigō became navy minister, the army succeeded in creating a Joint Staff for the two services, headed by an imperial prince, whose appointment both reinforced the close ties between the imperial institution and the military and avoided the problems posed by choosing a career officer from one of the rival services. The structure was revised in 1888 to provide for the creation of separate army and navy general staffs under the direction of the Joint Staff; and in 1893 the Navy General Staff became,

[29] Richard Smethurst, *A Social Basis for Prewar Japanese Militarism* (Berkeley: University of California Press, 1974), p. 7.

like its army model, formally independent of the ministry, finally standardizing the command structures of the two services on the army model.

One source of the resistance by the navy to the army's plans was the ardent emulation of British patterns. Although these eventually gave way at the top level to a more continental command structure, the patterns of daily life on board ship and the culture of the officer corps remained oriented to the English model. Where the army tended to invoke the legitimation of Japan's samurai traditions, the navy favored images of Nelson and Trafalgar. The returning students who had spent eight to eleven years in English naval academies and on board English ships provided powerful role models for younger officers, and carried their Anglophilism throughout their careers. This cultural gap reinforced the isolation of the navy from society as a whole, an isolation greater even than that of the army, given the separation of the basic unit, the ship, from the normal social context.

In at least one respect, the navy had a considerable impact on Japanese society as a whole: it had a significant influence on the development of heavy industry through the naval shipyards at Tsukiji and Yokosuka. However, production from these shipyards did not rise significantly until the 1890s; in the 1870s and 1880s, the navy was bought, not made. Ships were ordered largely from the great English shipyards—reinforcing the naval identification with Britain.

The organization building of this third phase culminated in the Constitution of 1889, which formalized both the special status of the military in the Meiji state (with the emperor as commander-in-chief) and the autonomy of the two services (with the later requirement that the service ministers be military officers). By 1890, the Japanese army and navy had assumed the fundamental features that they were to maintain until the Pacific War.

Conclusion

The army and the navy were the agents by which many aspects of Western-originated technical and social developments were introduced into Japan. The building of the nationwide telegraph system in the 1870s; the fostering of heavy industry and an array of support industries such as canning, wool spinning, and bootmaking; the spread of consumption of such foodstuffs and artifacts as beer, cigarettes, bread, and even newspapers; the increase of functional literacy—all these were greatly spurred by the demands of military organization.

The military initiated the systematic, large-scale application of Western models, and many aspects of organizational development that were introduced by the military were adopted on a less systematic scale throughout Japanese society. Among the many important innovations in the context of the military—the employment of Westerners in what was to become the dominant mode for the employment of foreigners (as teachers and staff personnel, not in line positions); the introduction of pensions (in 1875); the systematic use of Western-style accounting (exemplified by the navy's 1874 accounting school)—perhaps the most important was the development of a model of "organizational professionalism." This was a pattern that enabled organizational systems to combine a high degree of centralization and standardization with a high degree of spatial dispersion. Several aspects of the Western notion of professionalism were involved: a highly developed ideal and rhetoric of public service; careful selection of recruits; extensive formal training; a comprehensive concept of the professional role; and the development of forums for information exchange and professional socialization, such as regular conferences and a specialized literature. On the other hand, control over certification, conditions of work and remuneration, and advancement remained in the hands not of the individuals or a body of professional peers, but of nationally centralized bureaucratic organizations in which the professional was employed. The development of this pattern marked the largest and most influential official organizations in Meiji Japan (the police, the school system, and the civil service as well as the military) and, in subsequent years, spread into the private sector.

Such an organizational professionalism owed something to the legacy of the Tokugawa period, although that legacy is less direct than portrayals of the "officer-as-samurai" might suggest. The military's use of the samurai past was traditionalistic rather than traditional: that is, it drew selectively on those elements of traditional samurai roles that were adaptable to the achievement of its organizational goals of coordination and control. The ideals of selfless loyalty, an all-consuming standardized organizational identity, and service to the "public good"—redefined as that of the nation-state—were important elements of the new organizational professionalism. This co-optation of the samurai tradition was facilitated by the fact that, in contrast to contemporary European countries whose armies also drew heavily on aristocratic traditions (Germany, Austria, England, France), the status referred to in Japan no longer had a concrete base. After the elimination of samurai stipends, the samurai no longer constituted a "class" in any sense of the term; they had no economic base. They therefore had little basis for common interests which could be in conflict with the larger interests of the organization; insofar as they can be seen as having a "class" interest, or a status-group interest, it was in the expansion of the new state structures in which so many had found employment.

This relates to another Tokugawa "legacy" whose importance has been overdrawn: the prestige that accrued to the modern military by virtue of its association with the samurai's monopoly of weapons. This may have been a factor in attracting young samurai into the officer corps; although the case can be made that the prestige of the samurai was the prestige of power, not of arms, and that it was inherited by the state structures in general, not only by the army and navy. Indeed, as Smethurst has pointed out, most of the early Meiji leaders were attracted to civilian administration rather than to military careers. Certainly, however, the prestige of the army did not seem to attract commoners in the early Meiji period. Peasants resisted military service as vigorously as they had resisted Tokugawa-period demands for manpower in the transport system. It was not until the mid-1890s, with the victory in the Sino-Japanese War and—more important—with the maturation of graduates from the standardized national educational system, that military service came to be accepted and even celebrated by the common people.

For the development of the modern military, the most important legacies of the Tokugawa era were the material resources generated by the military mobilization of the *bakumatsu* period. These provided an essential base for the organization building which produced the military victories of the Sino-Japanese and Russo-Japanese wars, and which so profoundly influenced the development of the Meiji state system.

CHAPTER 8

EDUCATION: FROM ONE ROOM TO ONE SYSTEM*

BY RICHARD RUBINGER

The most important organizational development in the history of Japanese education was the creation of a national system of schools by the end of the second decade of the Meiji period. Despite the epochal nature of the event, scholars have not yet adequately analyzed the continuities and changes in educational institutions, policies, and practices from the *bakumatsu* years (1853-1868) to the late 1880s.

This chapter focuses on three fundamental shifts: 1) from wide regional variation in the provision and quality of schooling to greater national standardization; 2) from officially sponsored schools that exhibited sharp class distinctions to an integrated system that fostered mobility based on talent; and 3) from a loose configuration of discontinuous and mostly private arrangements to a compulsory system having a clearly articulated structure controlled by public authority. Changes in educational policy did not, of course, occur in isolation; the administrative rationalization of education during the early Meiji years paralleled similar developments in many other spheres as the new government consolidated its power and sought to establish a unified, centralized state.

The periodization adopted depends upon which facet of the subject one cares to pursue. If the formulation of central government policy is the criterion, then the years 1872-1886 might be used. If, however, organizational change measured at the local level is to be traced, one is

* I should like to acknowledge a Japan Foundation grant, which made it possible for me to spend the academic year 1981/82 at Kyoto University, where this chapter was written. I am also grateful to Professors George Elison, Motoyama Yukihiko, Herbert Passin, Umihara Tōru, Edward Beauchamp, R.P. Dore, and Ms. Sophia Lee for reading the manuscript and offering helpful suggestions, many of which improved the final version.

justified in pushing back the beginning date about two decades, to the period immediately following the arrival of Perry in 1853. This is not so much because new institutions suddenly were set up (although some were) or because drastic changes were made in school policies (although some were), but primarily because the pace of change that was set in motion even earlier quickened and continued unabated after 1853. We begin, then, with the *bakumatsu* period.

Late Tokugawa Trends

Modern Portents

During the final decades of the Tokugawa period, all of the important types of school institutions—from *bakufu* and *han* schools for the samurai to the *gōgaku* (local schools), *shijuku* (private academies), and *terakoya* (parish schools) attended by samurai as well as commoners—increased dramatically. More than 4,000 schools were opened from 1854 to 1867 in the *terakoya* category alone.[1] Schooling had become an important part of the daily routine of most samurai and was widely available to commoners as well. This means that even before the modern system was established there were already large numbers of experienced teachers, numerous young people who had been exposed to at least the basics of reading and writing, and many families who had been introduced to a style of life that included schoolgoing for their children. School buildings, desks, writing implements and other paraphernalia were already available by the *bakumatsu* period; textbooks had become a distinct category of books. Although the content of the new learning would be quite different, the package it came in would be recognizable and to that extent more acceptable.

Some of the functions of modern schools had appeared, and many of the reform measures carried out in the 1870s had already been tried in the earlier period.[2] Particularly good examples of modern trends in Tokugawa schooling are to be found in the numerous independent *shijuku* during the *bakumatsu* years. These schools were privately run, usually in a scholar's home, and were supported by students' fees. The *shijuku*

[1] Ishikawa Matsutarō, "Terakoya kara kindai gakkō e no mei to an," *Chishiki*, no. 22 (Spring 1981), p. 159. For a chart showing the number of schools established at different periods, according to type, see Richard Rubinger, *Private Academies of Tokugawa Japan* (Princeton: Princeton University Press, 1982), p. 5

[2] This point is argued persuasively in Herbert Passin, *Society and Education in Japan* (New York: Teachers College Press, 1965), pp. 50-61.

covered a diverse array of institutional arrangements, from informal tutorial types like Yoshida Shōin's Shōka sonjuku, in Hagi, to large centers with elaborate administrative machinery like Hirose Tansō's Kangien, in Hita. Some perpetuated ancient practices by initiating students into a special body of knowledge and pledging them to secrecy, a transmission know as *hiden*. But more significant were those, like the Dutch schools, that provided specialized training above the level of basic Chinese studies. It was in these schools, which were outside the perimeter of official control, that advanced training in Western studies—Dutch language, Western military, medicine, navigation, and natural science—reached high levels. Such training enabled students to become competent specialists in technical fields at a time when the *bakufu* and *han* were recruiting men of talent.

The private academies, unlike the official schools of the *bakufu* and *han*, had no geographical or class criteria for entrance. They were the only schools that could attract a national constituency and provide advanced training opportunities to samurai and commoner alike. The combination of advanced training and open admissions enabled them to become agents of change from a traditional vocational pattern of hereditary succession to a more modern function of schooling—selecting and sorting students into occupational areas by ability and specialized training. They became escalators of talent into official bureaucracies, and mechanisms of increased upward mobility for commoners and lower samurai. Such functions became more pronounced in the Meiji period; they had roots going back to the *bakumatsu*-period *shijuku*.[3]

It was not only in the private schools that changes occurred. For most of the Tokugawa period the primary purpose of the *bakufu* and *han* schools was the moral training of a hereditary elite. The constituency of these schools was limited to the upper echelons of the samurai class, and the curriculum was narrowly based on the traditional combination of *bun* and *bu*, letters and the military arts. In response to the military danger posed by Perry's arrival, the *bakufu* and the domains made efforts to upgrade their defensive capabilities. An important part of these efforts was reform of the official schools where leaders were trained. The *bakufu* reorganized the central institution of Confucian orthodoxy, the Shōheikō, regularizing lessons and establishing grade levels. The status of a woefully neglected translation office was upgraded, and in 1856 it became a new center for Western studies, known as the Bansho shirabesho. By 1866, when it was reformed and named the Kaiseijo, it had become a leading

[3] Further details on the *shijuku* can be found in Rubinger, *Private Academies*.

center of Western studies and attracted many of the best students in the country.

Evidence from *han* school regulations show reforms instituted in a number of areas that anticipated developments in the modern system. A call for training of talent and ability (*jinzai*) became widespread, and was specified explicitly in 40 percent of *han* school edicts. Domains also developed programs for training talented students outside the domain at the Bansho shirabesho/Kaiseijo or in *shijuku*. Some 91 percent of all domains that recorded their policies had such *yūgaku* (travel study) programs, and most adopted strict merit criteria for the selection of these students. Also related to increasing the *han* talent pool were the compulsory schooling laws for higher ranks of samurai, adopted in some form in 200 of the 215 *han* that recorded their policies, and the admission of commoners to the *han* schools. With respect to the latter, some schools were very progressive. In Echizen, the Ōno domain school (Meirinkan) permitted commoners as early as 1857. In Echigō, the Shibata domain school (Dōgakudō) opened its doors to non-samurai in 1858, although not for military studies.[4]

Although the Confucian *Four Books* and *Five Classics* remained the center of the curriculum at almost all domain schools, there was a trend to incorporate new areas of knowledge and to increase the complexity of the administrative structure. National learning (*kokugaku*) is estimated to have been introduced in about one-third of the *han* schools, and Western learning—primarily medicine, military affairs, and shipbuilding—was adopted in varying degrees in about one-quarter of the schools. More diversified curricula and provisions for commoner attendance, together with the growing size of the schools, led to more rational systems of organization. The Kōriyama *han* school, for example, created lower, middle, and higher levels out of what had been a simple, uniform program of study. The *bakumatsu* years saw a big jump in the number of schools that devised complex systems of three, four, and even five levels.[5] Thus, rewards for merit and achievement, comprehensive curricula, and articulated school programs had already begun to appear before the modern system made such things the law of the land.

[4] The *han* edicts calling for talent are cited in Inoue Hisao, *Gakusei ronkō* (Tokyo: Kazama shobō, 1963), p. 42. Data on merit criteria for *yūgaku* are taken from Ishizuki Minoru, *Kindai Nihon no kaigai ryūgaku shi* (Kyoto: Minerva shobō, 1972), p. 118. The figure on compulsory school laws comes from *Nihon kindai kyōiku hyakunen shi*, 10 vols. (Tokyo: Kokuritsu kyōiku kenkyūjo, 1974), vol. 3, p. 90. Data on specific *han* are from *Nihon kyōiku shi shiryō*, 9 vols. (Tokyo: Mombushō, 1892), vol. 4, pp. 68, 275 (hereafter *NKSS*).

[5] *Nihon kindai kyōiku hyakunen shi*, vol. 3, pp. 94, 446-48; *NKSS*, vol. 1, pp. 8-9.

The Persistence of Traditional Patterns

Although innovation and experimentation in schooling marked the *bakumatsu* period, traditional patterns persisted. The character and pace of the educational transition, therefore, were determined not only by modern trends but also by patterns of long standing that tended to resist the thrust of the Meiji reforms. Among the latter were wide regional disparities in educational offerings, class and sexual discrimination at official schools, and a tradition of ad hoc and discontinuous private schooling.

The numerous schools established during the Tokugawa period were not evenly distributed throughout the country. *Terakoya* and *shijuku* did exist in farming communities and mountain villages, but they were concentrated in urban areas, particularly in Edo, and in regions of the country with longstanding traditions of enthusiasm for schooling, such as Nagano, Okayama, and Yamaguchi.[6] Generally, the more remote areas had far fewer institutions. The city *terakoya* were usually larger and more systematic, and attendance at them was more regular than in the country schools. Calculation on the *soroban* (abacus) and reading in materials of specific interest to the merchant class, such as *Shōbai ōrai* (a primer of terms, phrases, and ethical precepts useful in commerce), were often added to the basic reading and writing. By the *bakumatsu* period, cash payments for tuition at urban *terakoya* had been introduced on a fairly wide scale. The rural schools, in contrast, were small, averaging about ten to twenty students; and attendance at them was irregular, often seasonal to allow children to work in the rice fields. Payments were usually in the form of gifts of food or clothing. Reading materials differed from those of the city schools and featured passages on agricultural topics.[7]

There were also great differences among the domains in the availability, quality, and level of their domain school offerings. Some provided only the rudiments of learning, others only advanced study. Some *han* had no *han* school at all; others not only provided facilities, but made attendance compulsory. Western studies tended to be provided by the larger and more strategically placed domains, such as Chōshū, Tosa, Satsuma, Kaga, and Saga. Others were less enthusiastic. Kasama *han*, for example, specifically forbade Western-style calculation to be taught in its school.[8]

While some domain schools, like those in Ōno *han* and Shibata *han*, began admitting commoners in the 1850s, others, such as those in Aizu

[6] A map, charting locations of all *terakoya* and *shijuku* (through 1872) listed in *NKSS*, can be found in Rubinger, *Private Academies*, p. 4.

[7] Umihara Tōru, *Gakkō* (Tokyo: Kondō shuppansha, 1979), pp. 94-95.

[8] *Nihon kindai kyōiku hyakunen shi*, vol. 3, p. 448.

and Hikone, continued to forbid admittance to commoners.[9] In those schools where commoners were admitted, there was great variation in the kinds of facilities provided. Usually commoners were housed in separate facilities, and schedules were arranged so that mixing of social classes would not occur. Generally, the situation at the end of the Tokugawa period was probably like that in Koromo *han*: "In the spring of 1869 samurai and commoners were permitted entry to the *han* school for the first time. But because of old customs, children of commoners were reluctant to attend, and, in fact, none did."[10] Furthermore, the data on *han* sponsorship of schools or educational programs for women show that of 245 domains only 7 provided any such opportunities at all.[11] Nor were the *shijuku* for everyone. They required fees, and in the schools of Dutch learning (especially the better-known ones like Itō Gemboku's Shōsendō, in Edo, or Ogata Kōan's Teki juku, in Osaka) the fees could be high. Thus, the better academies of Western studies were out of reach for those without at least moderate means.

Differences in types of learning available in different regions persisted in *bakumatsu* Japan, as did differences in the degree to which the various classes took advantage of learning opportunities. Male members of the samurai class were probably fully literate; they attended school in systematic fashion and for extended periods of time, and in some places were required to do so. All studied the Confucian classics, and some were exposed to Western learning, either in the *han* school itself or, more likely, in one of the Dutch studies *shijuku*. Merchants in the cities made full use of opportunities provided by *terakoya*. While the leadership levels of the farming class tended to be well represented at both *terakoya* and *shijuku*, ordinary farmers saw little need for formalized schooling outside the home, and their children attended schools irregularly, if at all.

For most, education in the *bakumatsu* period was characterized by arrangements that were largely unsystematic. Initiatives rested not with public promoters of education, but with its private consumers—individual families and students. There were few explicit connections among the diverse types of schools that dotted the landscape. Only some high-ranking samurai were officially required to attend schools; and, in the absence of compulsory attendance laws, the great majority of people were free to arrange schooling for their children as they saw fit. The questions of where, when, and how much education should be obtained were individual matters. Teachers, like students, were unregulated, and followed no prearranged course of preparation. To a very large extent,

[9] For the Aizu *han* edict, see *NKSS*, vol. 1, p. 680; for the Hikone edict, see *NKSS*, vol. 1, pp. 373-374.

[10] *NKSS*, vol. 1, p. 168.

[11] Fukaya Masashi, *Gakureki shugi no keifu* (Nagoya: Reimei shobō, 1969), p. 27.

a school—particularly a *terakoya* or a *shijuku*—was perceived as a person (the teacher) rather than as an institution; in most cases, when the teacher left the school ceased to exist. As R.P. Dore has pointed out, personal discipleship rather than institutional affiliation remained the basic organizational principle even in *han* schools, despite the progress that the systematization of educational programs had made in the official schools by the end of Tokugawa.[12]

Thus, education in *bakumatsu* Japan was very much a patchwork of different teachers and various experiences, with the overall design stitched together to fit individual needs. For most commoners, formal schooling was not a part of career preparation, so apprenticeship or informal tutoring at home was seen as quite sufficient. *Terakoya* attendance was a supplement to vocational preparation and not seen as a necessity by many in rural areas. The more ambitious, on the other hand, could combine extensive travel with the availability of various kinds of *shijuku* to fashion highly individualized, innovative, and progressive sequences of schooling. The school career of Ōmura Masujirō (1824-1869) is illustrative of schooling patterns that were followed by many of the more successful in his generation. A commoner and the son of a physician, Ōmura began his studies of Dutch in a small *shijuku* near his home in Chōshū. Finding that Chinese was needed to read the translations of Dutch texts, Ōmura traveled to Kyūshū and entered Hirose Tansō's Kangien, in Hita. He then went to Osaka and enrolled in Ogata Kōan's Teki juku for further Dutch study. Because of his academic talent, Ōmura was recruited by the daimyo of Uwajima *han* and given a samurai stipend to consult on Western-style military defense. Later, he received a *bakufu* appointment to teach at the Bansho shirabesho but eventually returned to Chōshū to lead military forces against the shogunate. After the Restoration he was put in charge of military affairs by the new Meiji government.[13] As his case shows, at the end of the Tokugawa period, a motivated individual acting on his own initiatives, entirely outside the official school institutions, could put together sophisticated educational programs and advance into elite positions in the *han* and *bakufu* bureaucracies.

The educational developments of the *bakumatsu* period were both advantageous and detrimental to the movement to establish a modern school system after the Restoration. Facilities and personnel were abundant; Western studies had been introduced; merit systems, comprehensive curricula, and articulated administrative structures had been tried. At the

[12] R.P. Dore, *Education in Tokugawa Japan* (Berkeley: University of California Press, 1967), pp. 73-74.

[13] Summarized from Ōmura denki kankōkai, comp., *Ōmura Masujirō* (Tokyo: Hajime shobō, 1944). For the school careers of a sample of early Meiji leaders, see Rubinger, *Private Academies*, chap. 9.

same time, education in Japan was marked by particularity among different regions, distinctions among different classes, and discontinuity among institutions.

Initial Steps toward Systematization, 1868-1871

On September 2, 1871, four days after the abolition of *han* and the establishment of prefectures (*haihan chiken*), Dajōkan Order no. 361 called for the establishment of a Mombushō (Ministry of Education) with the responsibility of planning and implementing a national system of education. The preceding three and a half years from Restoration to *haihan chiken* had been marked by great confusion and turmoil. Yet, during this period, the Meiji government made decisions and set in motion changes that were to have great influence on its subsequent planning. In education, the period witnessed three important developments: the establishment of an early prototype for a university; attempts to regulate private schools; and experiments in systematization at the local level.

The University

The early Meiji leaders were clear and explicit about the need to create a new system of education in order to develop the Japanese people's talents and consolidate a national citizenry responsive to the goals of the central regime. They did not, however, agree about the means for accomplishing these objectives.[14] To be sure, there was little question that the government's first priority was to establish a system of higher education that would strengthen the leadership group with the best talent to be found in the country. But what form was this system to take? There is no better example of the conflicts and confusions in early Meiji educational policy than the serpentine twists and turns involved in setting up Japan's first modern university.

On March 15, 1868, even before the Restoration battles had ended, Iwakura Tomomi (1825-1883) had appointed a committee of *kokugaku* scholars to draft a proposal for higher education.[15] Although the Charter

[14] The often conflicting views of Iwakura, Kido, Ōkubo, and Itō are described in Motoyama Yukihiko, *Kindai Nihon no seiji to kyōiku* (Kyoto: Minerva shobō, 1972), chap. 1.

[15] The committee was made up of *kokugaku* scholars Tamamatsu Misao (1810-1872), Hirata Kanetane (1799-1880), and Yano Harumichi (1823-1887). The plan they came up with, known as *gakushasei*, called for a return to the ancient system of *daigakuryō* in the

Oath of April 6, 1868, had announced that "knowledge shall be sought throughout the world," and "all classes of people shall be allowed to fulfill their aspirations," Iwakura, two days earlier, took a step more in line with immediate political realities by reopening the Gakushūin (Peers' School) for the court nobility in Kyoto. This was the first educational institution opened by the new government. Iwakura's concern was to create support for the imperial government by training the *kuge* (court nobles) and placing them in important government posts. This, he believed, would lessen criticism of the new government as simply a revised form of the *bakufu* with the Satsuma-Chōshū clique dominating policy.[16]

These initial moves led to three years of bitter conflict that involved not only ideological disputes among specialists of Confucian, Shinto, and Western learning over the content and goals of higher education, but also regional rivalries between the authorities in Kyoto and Tokyo over the location of the new university. The details of the squabbling, though fascinating for the light they throw on the politics of educational decision making, need not concern us here. The outcome, however, was important.

With the change of the emperor's residence from Kyoto to Tokyo on September 3, 1868, plans to divide the university between the two cities were dropped in favor of a unified institution located at the seat of the central government, in Tokyo. Until the summer of 1870, plans called for combining Confucian and Shinto studies with Western learning in a single institution called the Daigaku. The Confucianists and the Shinto scholars were placed in the Daigaku honkō (Main School), which had both educational and administrative functions like the *bakufu*'s Shōheikō from which it sprang. The scholars of Western studies ran both the Daigaku nankō (South School) and Daigaku tōkō (East School), which developed out of the *bakufu*'s schools of Western and medical learning (Kaiseijo and Igakujo, respectively).[17] The rising power of the westernizers

Nara period. *Gakushasei*, however, proposed that the content of learning be based on Shinto and *kokugaku* rather than on Confucian thought. Kyōiku shi hensankai, comp., *Meiji ikō kyōiku seido hattatsu shi*, 12 vols. (Tokyo: Byūginsha, 1938), vol. 1, pp. 239-240.

[16] Motoyama, *Kindai Nihon no seiji to kyōiku*, p. 4.

[17] The lineages of the various sections of the university through 1870 can be summarized as follows:

Edo Period	*August 17, 1868*	*July 23, 1869* (Daigakkō)	*January 18, 1870* (Daigaku)	*August 8, 1870* (Daigaku)
Shōheikō →	Shōhei gakkō →	Daigakkō →	Daigaku honkō →	Closed
Kaiseijo →	Kaisei gakkō →	Daigakkō →	Daigaku nankō →	Daigaku nankō
Igakujo →	Igakkō →	Daigakkō →	Daigaku tōkō →	Daigaku tōkō

within the government, together with the continued bickering among the Confucianists and Shinto scholars, led to the closing of the Daigaku honkō on August 8, 1870. Thus Confucian domination of higher education was ended and Western scholars emerged triumphant, in uncontested control of the university. The central administrative function of the Daigaku honkō was also lost and did not reappear until the establishment of the Mombushō just over a year later.

With the ideological battles in the university over and the government itself firmly committed to a policy of westernization, the university became the government's central institution for assimilating advanced and practical knowledge from the West. Accordingly, foreign instructors were hired in large numbers, and students were sent abroad for study; these two programs alone claimed 32 percent of the central government's entire educational budget in 1873.[18] A *kōshinsei* system was set up whereby scholarships were provided to selected students from each domain for advanced study of Western subjects at the Daigaku nankō. Domains with assessed yields of 100,000 or more *koku* could send three students; those *han* with assessments between 50,000 and 100,000 *koku* could send two; and those assessed below 50,000 *koku* were to send one student. A total of 326 students came from all the *han*.[19] This program was strikingly similar to the Tokugawa-period practice of providing domain stipends for outstanding students to travel to Edo to study Chu Hsi Confucianism at the Shōheikō. Although the *kōshinsei* program lasted only about one year and was abolished along with the *han* in August 1871, it nonetheless played an important role in educating local leaders in Western studies.

Control of Private Schools

Although the government's main focus during the first four years of the Meiji period was on the university and its problems, there was also movement toward establishing a system of public schools. One indication of this was the attempt to bring private schools under public control. During the Tokugawa period there had been little regulation of the various *shijuku* and *terakoya*. But this began to change in 1871. On February 13, 1871, the Council of State (Dajōkan) ordered that any teacher planning to open a *shijuku* would first have to receive permission from a local government office. Furthermore, teachers were asked to keep enrollment records and information on the background of students who entered.[20]

[18] Nagai Michio, *Higher Education in Japan: Its Take-off and Crash*, trans. Jerry Dusenberry (Tokyo: University of Tokyo Press, 1971), p. 23.

[19] Karasawa Tomitarō, *Gakusei no rekishi* (Tokyo: Sōbunsha, 1955), p. 22.

[20] *Meiji ikō kyōiku seido hattatsu shi*, vol. 1, pp. 239-240.

On April 11, 1872, the Mombushō ordered an end to the use of public funds for students at *shijuku* in Tokyo. Within a month of this disposition, further orders went out to local government offices—to inspect curricula and teachers at private schools and to improve the local administration of central control over the opening of new schools. To what extent these orders were carried out is not known, but the record does not show any great outcry. One noteworthy critic, though, was Fukuzawa Yukichi (1834-1901), headmaster of Keiō gijuku in Tokyo, whose school stood to suffer from the new regulations; he attacked the new regulations in the pages of *Shimbun zasshi*, a popular Tokyo newspaper. Another critic was Seki Shimpachi (1839-1886), headmaster of Kyōritsu gakusha in Tokyo, who protested directly to authorities in Tokyo. Both men argued strongly for the continued independence of the private schools.[21] It may be, however, that the restrictions were not aimed primarily at the higher-level schools, such as Keiō, but were part of an attempt to bring the unregulated multitude of small, *terakoya*-like private schools within the public domain, as the basis for a new system of elementary schools.

Many petitions submitted by *shijuku* seeking permission to open have been preserved, most abundantly for Tokyo. Analysis of petitions for 1872 and 1873 shows that most of the schools were simple writing schools of the *terakoya* type, although schools of Chinese studies and Western studies appear as well. It is evident that patterns of schooling carried over from Tokugawa continued to be strong. By the end of 1872, 1,146 petitions had been filed in Tokyo alone, thus demonstrating the continued popularity of private schools. In Tokyo the schools continued to be larger than in rural areas; moreover, female attendance was greater, samurai attended in larger numbers, and Western studies were stressed more heavily.[22]

Early Systematization in Local Areas

Tentative government plans for a system of schools existed prior to the abolition of domains and the establishment of prefectures in 1871, but these lacked authority and often sent mixed signals to the prefectures. An early government regulation for the administration of the prefectures,

[21] Kambe Yasumitsu, "Meiji shoki ni okeru shigakunin no teikō," in Tōkyō shiritsu chūgaku kōtō gakkō shinkō kyōkai, ed., *Shigaku no seikaku ni tsuite no kenkyū* (Tokyo: Shigaku kyōiku kenkyūjo, 1966), pp. 231-245.

[22] Petitions for the opening of new schools in Tokyo for 1873 are available in reprinted form in *Kaigaku meisai-sho*, 7 vols. (Tokyo: Tōkyō tōsei shiryōkan, 1963). The petitions for Tokyo and rural Ishitetsu (Ehime) are analyzed and compared in Kaigo Tokiomi, *Meiji shonen no kyōiku: sono seido to jittai* (Tokyo: Hyōronsha, 1973), pp. 80-96.

issued on March 17, 1869, included an order to provide elementary schooling for all children. About one year later, on March 20, 1870, a comprehensive plan, known as *Daigaku risoku chū-shōgaku risoku* [Rules for the University and for Elementary and Middle Schools] was submitted to the Dajōkan. It envisioned an entirely different system, with elementary and middle schools designed to serve only the purpose of university preparation. The plan was never enacted, but it is notable for being the first to include middle schools, and for suggesting the outlines of a comprehensive preparatory curriculum leading to advanced Western training in a university.[23]

Local areas may have been influenced by these plans, but it is more likely that regional reform plans were made for reasons closer to home. The political and economic upheaval caused by the Restoration put some areas in advantageous positions with respect to educational reform. Numazu, a city in Shizuoka prefecture, is one such example. After the fall of the shogunate, the Tokugawa moved their Western military facilities and transferred many of their advisers, including some leading Western studies experts (such as Nishi Amane, Tsuda Mamichi, and Katō Hiroyuki) to Numazu. There, a Western-style military school, Numazu heigakkō, was established. In early 1869 an elementary school (*shōgakkō*) was attached to the military academy to provide a preparatory course including Western subjects. This school served as a model for other elementary schools that were established in nearby towns, and it is considered the first modern elementary school in Japan.[24]

The appointment of energetic governors in such places as Nagano and Aichi immediately following *haihan chiken* led to the establishment of quasi-public elementary schools on the model of the Tokugawa-period *gōgaku*, with some degree of public control over the curriculum and the appointment of teachers. In Aichi, these *gikō* (as such schools were called there) were so numerous that by the time a national plan was inaugurated, in 1872, two-thirds (or 428) of the 600 elementary schools mandated for the region had already been established.[25]

The earliest and most comprehensive local school system was established in Kyoto. In 1868, plans were made for a citywide system of school districts. By the end of 1869 it was fully implemented, and the city was divided into two middle school districts and sixty-four elementary school districts. Central guidance for curriculum, appointment of teachers, and

[23] *Gakusei hyakunen shi* (Tokyo: Mombushō, 1972), pp. 86-90.

[24] Kaigo, *Meiji shonen no kyōiku*, pp. 99-100.

[25] Ibid., p. 114.

administration of examinations was provided by the city. This system was made possible by advantages peculiar to Kyoto. For one thing, the emperor had left a special fund for the city when he took up his new residence in Tokyo. Part of the fund was divided among the school districts for educational use. For another, a Chōshū colleague of Kido Takayoshi, Makimura Masanao (1834-1896), had been appointed to an influential position in the Kyoto city administration. It is believed that he was appointed in part to experiment locally with the kind of school system Kido had in mind for the nation.[26] Makimura's efforts apparently were fruitful. Touring Kyoto in the spring of 1869, Fukuzawa Yukichi praised the Kyoto plan in a pamphlet entitled *Kyōto gakkō no ki* [An Account of Kyoto Schools] and noted its similarities to Western systems. Although the record is not clear, it is likely that through the efforts of Fukuzawa and Makimura the Kyoto model had some influence in the drafting of the national system.

During the years prior to the abolition of *han* and the establishment of prefectures in the summer of 1871, government efforts in education were concentrated on founding a university. Plans for a national school system were restrained by political instability, and patterns inherited from the Tokugawa period were still strong. Private schools continued to prosper and proliferate, as seen from the large number of petitions requesting permission to open, despite government attempts at regulation. Regional disparities increased as particular areas benefited from the political changes following the Restoration. Beginning in the summer of 1871, however, government efforts began to focus on creating a nationwide system of public elementary schools.

Setting the Foundation: Elementary Schools, 1872-1879

Soon after the Mombushō was created on September 2, 1871, plans were set in motion for a nationwide school system under its authority. In January 1872, a twelve-man committee, chaired by Mitsukuri Rinshō (1846-1897), was appointed to draft a comprehensive code. Mitsukuri was a scholar of French law, and several other members of the committee were also trained in Western studies. Thus Western, particularly French,

[26] Kyōto furitsu sōgō shiryōkan, comp., *Kyōto fu hyakunen no nempyō: kyōiku hen* (Kyoto: Kyōto fu, 1970), p. 2.

models of national school systems were carefully studied.[27] In addition, investigations of educational affairs were undertaken in different parts of Japan. These studies pointed to very wide gaps in both the quantity and the quality of educational offerings throughout Japan. The Mombushō also carried out experiments in regulating six elementary schools in Tokyo that were already under its direct jurisdiction.[28]

A draft plan for the nation was prepared during the spring of 1872, and on September 4 the Preamble (*Ōseidasaresho*) to the Fundamental Code of Education (*Gakusei*) was issued by the Dajōkan. On the same day, all schools in the country were ordered closed. They were to reopen according to detailed provisions of the code itself, copies of which were sent to the prefectures on the next day, the fifth.

The Preamble indicated that the goals of education under the new system would be quite different from the stress on Confucian morality found in the official schools of the Tokugawa period. Instead, there would be a thrust directed toward individual goals, equality among the classes, and self-improvement.[29] The Fundamental Code itself consisted of 109 articles (enlarged to 213 in 1873) that provided, for the first time, a comprehensive outline of a national school system. Japan was to be divided into university, middle school, and elementary school districts with 8 universities, 256 middle schools, and 53,760 elementary schools. Compulsory attendance was set at four years. Local supervisors were appointed to enforce attendance, construct new schools, and oversee the distribution of public funds.[30]

The larger significance of the Fundamental Code, however, does not lie in its specific provisions, many of which were adjusted when the code was replaced by the Education Law of 1879 (*Kyōikurei*). Its primary importance was in providing a basic design for a nationally unified system and in making it clear that, henceforth, education was to be a government enterprise. The new plan established a focal point around which public views could form, and a framework for change in subsequent years, as the Japanese wrestled with the complicated issues surrounding the creation of a modern school system. For a larger perspective on the meaning

[27] Inoue, *Gakusei ronkō*, p. 113. The prominence of Western scholars, both on the draft committee and within the Mombushō itself, stemmed from the earliest days of the Mombushō when the first director, Etō Shimpei (1834-1874), appointed many Western experts and set the westernizing tone to early Mombushō policies.

[28] The domestic educational survey is described in Inoue, *Gakusei ronkō*, p. 103; early control of Tokyo schools by the Mombushō is discussed in Kaigo, *Meiji shonen no kyōiku*, p. 112.

[29] An English translation of the Preamble appears in Passin, *Society and Education*, pp. 209-211.

[30] *Gakusei hyakunen shi: shiryō hen* (Tokyo: Mombushō, 1972), pp. 11-19.

of the code, it may help to look first at some of the symbolic changes it brought about, such as those in the architecture of school buildings and in the development of a terminology of modern school organization.

Architecture and Words

The architects of the new schools constructed in the 1870s, intent on making a clean break with an outworn past and bringing a new generation of children into an age of "civilization and enlightenment" (*bummei kaika*), created grand public buildings using explicitly Western models. The buildings were intended to be permanent and prominent symbols of the success of the centrally organized system. The fiction of the period suggests that they may have had the intended effect. The protagonist of Tokutomi Roka's *Omoide no Ki*, arriving at one of these schools, was impressed because it was "built from the start as a school, with a second storey . . . and windows all round which made the rooms almost dazzlingly bright, a playground, imposing black gates, with the school's name inscribed on the posts, and a flagpole. It *looked* like a school."[31] In Shimazaki Tōson's *Hakai*, another novel of this period, an observer looking out over his town observed, "If anything in the panorama had a modern air, it was the white-painted building of the primary school."[32]

Many of the new buildings were indeed imposing. They were large two-storied structures with porticos and ornate entranceways. Some had large cupolas or towers on their roofs. These buildings clearly provided superior facilities for some, but their importance went beyond schooling in the narrow sense. The towers usually housed bells or drums that not only sounded the beginnings and ends of classes, but served community functions as well. Such towers marked the hours of the day and night for the entire area and, since they offered the single best vantage point in the community, functioned as watchtowers for fires and other natural disasters. Evidently there were no sharp distinctions among types of public buildings in the early Meiji years, and schools were used as community centers, as station houses for police patrols, and as facilities for routine medical services such as vaccinations. The new buildings, then, came to play a new and important role in community life, and symbolized the central place that education would have in Meiji society. The Western-style architecture of some of the buildings heralded a new age when

[31] Tokutomi Roka, *Footprints in the Snow*, trans. Kenneth Strong (London: Allen & Unwin, 1970), p. 110.

[32] Shimazaki Tōson, *The Broken Commandment*, trans. Kenneth Strong (Tokyo: University of Tokyo Press, 1974), p. 3.

culture from abroad would be brought to remote towns and villages through their elementary schools.[33]

Also indicative of a fundamental shift in the way schools were thought of was the development of a new vocabulary of educational organization. In another context, George Sansom has written: "Indeed, it is one of the special features of early Meiji controversy that it was a battle about words, and about words that had only just entered the native vocabulary, to represent ideas new to most Japanese."[34] Sansom was referring to words connected to political disputes such as *minken* (people's rights), but the point is applicable to the educational world as well. Distinctions among the various school types that we now associate with the Tokugawa period—*bakufu* and *han* schools, *gōgaku, shijuku*, and *terakoya*—were not clearly made during Tokugawa itself. Nor, with the exception of *terakoya*, were the terms themselves commonly used. In fact, no generic term for "school" was in regular use, and no terminology for levels of schooling (in the modern sense of elementary, middle, and higher) existed. Education in Tokugawa Japan was a decidedly particular phenomenon; and schools, reflecting this, were known only by their names—Meirinkan, Shōka sonjuku, Kangien, and so on.

It was during the birth pangs of the modern school system in the early 1870s that new terms and categories came into use, and their meanings were worked out as the need arose to establish regulatory procedures for the new national system. Thus, in the early years of the Meiji period, school names changed to indicate not just the locale of the school, but its level within the system—elementary (*shōgakkō*), middle (*chūgakkō*), or university (*daigaku*)—as well as its status as private, public, or official.

Like the architectural design of the new schools, the choice of terminology for new educational entities symbolized important trends in the transformation of education. The word *gakkō* (school) provides an interesting example. Although the word was not new, it was seldom used before the Meiji period. It was certainly not used in the same sense it came to have in the 1870s, as a generic equivalent to the English "school" or the French "école."[35] According to Ishizuki Minoru, before the Meiji

[33] According to *Mombushō nempō* for 1875, of about 20,000 elementary schools in existence, 40 percent were housed in Buddhist temples and 33 percent in private homes; only 18 percent were in newly built structures. Naka Arata, *Meiji no kyōiku* (Tokyo: Shibundō, 1967), pp. 118-119.

[34] George B. Sansom, *The Western World and Japan* (New York: Vintage Books, 1973), p. 311.

[35] The term *gakkō* is believed to have been first used in the Kamakura-period Ashikaga gakkō. It was also used as a name in the well-known Shizutani gakkō, in Okayama *han*.

period the Chinese character read *kō* in *gakkō* had only infrequently been combined with the character for learning (*gaku*) to indicate a school institution. It was more often used to denote a sense of restriction, limitation, or conformity to a uniform standard. That being the case, the choice of characters for the modern word *gakkō*, Ishizuki suggests, was entirely appropriate, symbolizing a shift to a new kind of institution that was part of a larger system whose goals were fashioned by a central authority.[36]

Enrollment Patterns

Without better data on the Tokugawa period than are available at present, it is difficult to measure how enrollment patterns changed from late Tokugawa to early Meiji, if indeed they did change. Futhermore, few data have come to the fore since the mid-1960s to make it possible to adjust in any meaningful way the estimates made by Dore and Passin. On the basis of *terakoya* enrollment figures, they postulate approximately 40 percent of male children and 15 percent of female children getting some kind of formal schooling outside the home by the end of the Tokugawa period.[37] Both writers were careful to point out the paucity of the data with which they were working and the tentativeness of their conclusions. Subsequent authors have been less careful, and so some cautions are in order.

Recent studies reveal ever larger numbers of *terakoya* and *shijuku* during the Tokugawa period. However, to link increasing numbers of schools to higher rates of literacy is problematic for at least two reasons. First, schools in Tokugawa Japan opened and closed with great frequency, and students often flitted from one to the next, making the simple number of schools an unreliable guide to extended attendance. A second, not unrelated problem is the question of what level of literacy was reached in the *terakoya*. It may be that even when a student attended faithfully he did not gain much from the experience. A student who entered one of the new elementary schools, a converted Buddhist temple, in the summer of 1872 recalled that "although we were supposed to be doing penmanship [*te-narai*] we mostly just fooled around—painting each

---

Of 300 *han* school names checked by Umihara Tōru, only 20 used *gakkō*. Umihara, *Gakkō*, pp. 12-13.

[36] Ishizuki Minoru, "Nihon no kindaika to kyōiku," *Kyōiku to igaku* (January 1981), p. 78.

[37] Dore, *Education in Tokugawa Japan*, pp. 291-295, 317-322; Passin, *Society and Education*, pp. 47-49, 310-313.

others faces black with ink and playing ghost behind the Buddhist altar."[38] Apparently, then as now, one got out of schooling exactly what one put into it. Thus, even when the number of institutions that existed is known, there remain important questions about the quality of learning that took place and the level of literacy attained.

Beginning in 1873, enrollment figures become more reliable than those for the Tokugawa period, and one is also on stronger ground in linking enrollment with reasonably functional literacy.[39] To be sure, in the early Meiji period attendance beyond the first year was low and dropouts remained a problem. Nevertheless, once schooling became compulsory, measures to increase attendance began to be actively implemented at the local level. For most local officials, the essence of the new school law boiled down to establishing public elementary schools and increasing

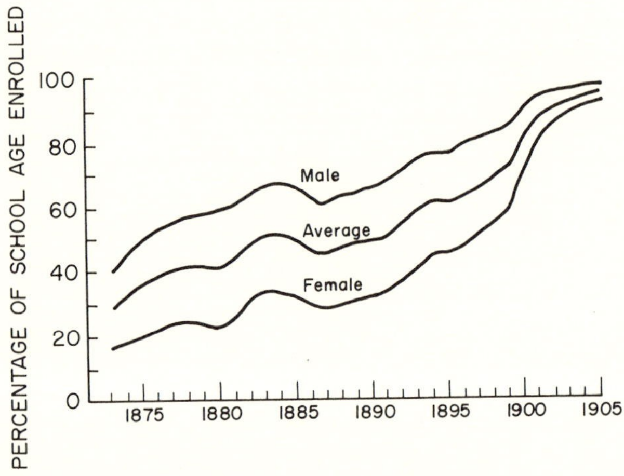

Figure 8.1. Elementary School Enrollment Rates, 1873-1905
Data from *Mombushō nempō*, in Umihara Tōru, *Gakkō* (Tokyo: Kondō shuppansha, 1979), "Educational Statistics" app., p. 32.

[38] Honda Seiroku, "Taiken hachijūgonen," *Sekai non-fuikushon zenshū* (Tokyo: Chikuma shobō), pp. 36, 310-313.

[39] Enrollment figures provided by *Mombushō nempō* beginning in 1873 are far more reliable than anything available for earlier years. They are not, however, without problems. Satō Hideo, in *Nihon kindai kyōiku hyakunen shi*, vol. 3, p. 613, has shown "actual attendance" in the 1870s to be about 30 percent below enrollment figures. On the other hand, official data do not record a large number of informal schools where basic literacy training was probably provided.

attendance in them. A wide variety of schemes was concocted to get students into the school and to keep them there. In Ōita, for example, all children of school age were made to wear wooden tags, which were then marked for attendance or truancy. Officials would periodically inspect the tags of each child and consult with parents if truancy persisted.[40]

Figure 8.1 shows the pattern of enrollment indicated by official records from 1873, when they first became available, through 1905, when rates reached nearly universal levels. Noticeable are the similarity in the patterns of male and female rates, the clear differentials between them until about the turn of the century, and the generally upward direction of both male and female enrollment rates—all continuous with what we know of Tokugawa enrollment patterns.

If we look beyond the national averages, however, to the local data from the prefectures, even more significant trends become apparent. (See Table 8.1.) The figures for 1874 show strong similarities with what we know of *bakumatsu*-period enrollment patterns. Not only is the wide geographical variance evident, but it is, for the most part, the same areas, in both late Tokugawa and early Meiji, that show the highest and lowest enrollment rates. What is striking, though, is the change that takes place over the next two decades. Over five-year intervals, the areas with highest

TABLE 8.1
Elementary School Enrollment Rates in Selected Prefectures, 1874-1894

		1874	1879	1884	1889	1894
HIGH	Nagano	66.0[a]	62.9	71.6	51.0	67.4
	Gifu	59.5	49.4	60.4	55.2	62.9
	Tokyo	57.8	60.1	40.5	48.5	62.1
	Kyoto	51.3	52.3	56.7	50.6	67.8
LOW	Kagoshima	7.1	32.1	27.9	32.6	52.0
	Aomori	12.4	31.1	35.2	34.5	46.7
	Akita	13.5	26.3	41.1	35.9	54.8
	Nagasaki	17.1	29.5	34.8	39.0	56.6

SOURCE: *Mombushō nempō.*

[a] This figure is for Chikuma, most of which became part of Nagano prefecture and a small part of which became part of Gifu in 1876.

[40] Ōita ken kyōiku iinkai, comp., *Ōita ken kyōiku hyakunen shi*, 2 vols. (Ōita: Ōita ken kyōiku iinkai, 1976), vol. 1, pp. 210-211.

early enrollment show fluctuations, but the rates in 1894 are not very different from those in 1874.[41] The areas with lowest early enrollment, in contrast, show dramatic increases. Even allowing for a margin of error in the figures themselves, the quadrupling of Kagoshima rates between 1874 and 1879 and the more than doubling of rates in Aomori during the same period are impressive. By 1894, the marked variation between the areas of highest and lowest rates had narrowed considerably.

The average national figures show a steady but gentle upward trend in enrollment during the early Meiji years. The regional figures, however, suggest much more dramatic success for the government's policy of providing greater uniformity in the availability of schooling and evening out the regional disparities inherited from the Tokugawa past.

Teachers and Textbooks

Once inside the new elementary schools, what did students learn? One cannot of course assume that what was in textbooks was taught and, if taught, learned. This is especially true for the early Meiji years, when many teachers were unprepared to teach the materials they had in front of them, and when attendance by students was often irregular. In October 1872, shortly after issuing the Fundamental Code, the Mombushō set out detailed guidelines for curriculum and textbooks for elementary schools, but adopted a laissez-faire policy with regard to implementation. Thus, in the early 1870s there was a considerable mix of materials used in the elementary schools—from the readers, vocabulary lists, and copybooks used at *terakoya* to the newer texts, based on Western translations, that were disseminated by the new publication offices within the Mombushō and the Tokyo Normal School (Shihan gakkō). Local compliance with curriculum guidelines was, at first, weak. Ōita, for example, did not immediately introduce geography or science in its schools, but instead put greater emphasis on ordinary reading and writing. Nagano prefecture did not at once provide Western-style calculation courses, but continued to print and disseminate its own text materials and teachers' guides.[42]

[41] It is difficult to account for the drop in Tokyo's rate between 1879 and 1884, or the falling rate in Nagano between 1884 and 1889. In Tokyo, it might have been the result of more stringent regulations for private schools; in Nagano, there was a reduction in the educational budget during the years in question. There might also simply be inconsistencies in the methods of compiling the data in *Mombushō nempō*.

[42] *Ōita ken kyōiku hyakunen shi*, vol. 1, p. 231; Nagano ken kyōiku shi kankōkai, comp., *Nagano ken kyōiku shi*, 16 vols. (Nagano: Nagano ken kyōiku shi kankōkai, 1979), vol. 4, pp. 93, 141.

The organization of the curriculum around basic reading, writing, and arithmetic did not change immediately, but the texts did become more comprehensive in coverage, and many added translated Western materials in history, geography, and science. A study of the contents of the ethics and language texts used during the 1870s and 1880s suggests that, at least in these areas, there continued to be a good deal of mixing of Western, Japanese, and Confucian values for some time. Thus, at no point during the first two decades of Meiji did any of these three main areas of thought—Western, Confucian, and Japanese nationalist—become eliminated entirely, and there remained considerable diversity in the content of learning.[43]

In the 1870s there began a transformation in teacher training. The *shijuku* and *terakoya* teachers had operated independently, and were without official status or authority, but nevertheless commanded personal respect and affection. While some of these teachers performed an important transitional function in the early Meiji schools, by the late 1870s they were by and large replaced, by a new breed trained at one of the increasingly numerous prefectural normal schools. A memorable characterization of the new, professionally trained teachers comes from the young boy in Tokutomi Roka's novel when he first sees his teacher, a young man "who parted his hair with great precision, and whose sole idea of education was that the Divinity of the Profession must be Maintained—a principle he lost no opportunity of impressing upon us."[44]

In the late 1880s, the training of teachers became the center of Mori Arinori's nationalist reforms of the education system. Military drill and uniforms became compulsory in the normal schools in order to instill in young teachers-to-be habits of soldierlike obedience to higher authority.[45]

In 1881, the Mombushō began to take steps to tighten its control over textbook use and published a list of texts considered appropriate. By 1883 a "permission system" required the prefectures to submit for approval lists of texts intended for use. Under Mori's Elementary School Law of 1886 (*Shōgakkō rei*) this procedure was fully implemented, setting up the first nationwide system for the standardization of textbooks. This was taken a step further in 1903, when the Mombushō eliminated selection altogether and required all elementary schools to adopt identical, state-approved texts.

[43] E. Patricia Tsurumi, "Meiji Primary School Language and Ethics Textbooks: Old Values for a New Society?" *Modern Asian Studies*, vol. 8, no. 2 (1974), pp. 247-261.

[44] Tokutomi, *Footprints in the Snow*, p. 61.

[45] Karasawa Tomitarō, *Kyōshi no rekishi* (Tokyo: Sōbunsha, 1955), pp. 41-42.

The Financing of Elementary Schools

From the view of the central government, the school plan of the Fundamental Code combined the best of two worlds—national control and local support. The principle that schools should be supported by those who used them was written into the document.[46] While the government's control over the content of curriculum and the training of teachers grew, its financial contribution remained comparatively small. After 1873, as the figures in Table 8.2 show, Mombushō support for elementary schools never went over 10 percent of total school income. In percentage terms, central support generally decreased during the period shown; by 1882, Mombushō support was entirely withdrawn.[47]

The various local regions developed a wide variety of schemes to provide support for mandated elementary schools. Proportions differed, but most areas relied on combinations of tuition charges, interest from endowments, private donations, and locally collected tax revenues. Tuition charges had been commonplace in Tokugawa *terakoya* and *shijuku*, except that payments were flexible and were often in the form of gifts of

TABLE 8.2
Income Sources of Public Elementary Schools, 1873-1881
(%)

	1873	1874	1875	1876	1877	1878	1879	1880	1881
Funds brought forward	0	13.2	22.1	13.5	15.2	17.7	18.8	18.9	14.8
Tuition	6.3	6.9	5.7	5.7	5.8	4.8	4.5	4.3	4.1
Contributions	19.1	24.8	18.3	16.6	10.6	10.8	7.4	6.6	7.9
Local district funds	43.3	33.3	30.1	36.5	40.1	41.9	42.2	41.1	46.1
Mombushō support	12.6	6.2	8.9	9.8	8.2	6.2	5.5	5.4	2.0
Interest on endowment	13.4	8.1	9.2	9.9	12.3	9.7	9.7	9.5	9.7
Other	5.3	7.5	5.7	8.0	7.8	6.7	6.0	4.7	4.2
Area tax	0	0	0	0	0	2.2	5.9	9.5	11.2

SOURCE: Murakami Shunsuke and Sakata Yoshio, eds., *Meiji bunka shi*, 13 vols. (Tokyo: Yōyōsha, 1955), vol. 3, p. 372.

[46] *Gakusei hyakunen shi: shiryō hen*, p. 17.

[47] *Nihon kindai kyōiku hyakunen shi*, vol. 2, p. 47.

food or clothing. When cash was used, it was disguised as a "gift" until Fukuzawa Yukichi decided to do away with pretense and openly began collecting tuition payments in cash at his Keiō gijuku in 1868. By 1876 more than half of all elementary schools were charging tuition, with amounts varying from as little as 2-3 sen per month in the provinces for the lower grades to as much as 50 or 75 sen per month in Tokyo for the upper grades of elementary school.[48]

Private donations were also a very important source of income for schools, especially in areas where traditions of public support were not strong. One school in rural Ōita prefecture has left a record of those who made individual donations to the school. Among them were samurai who contributed bonus money they had received for helping to quell peasant uprisings, housewives who donated money from their savings, local notables who made gifts, and poor families who gave small amounts.[49]

The lion's share of income came from taxes assessed on landholders. These assessments were usually made according to the amount and value of the land as well as the number of persons in the family. The financial burden was undoubtedly heavy, and it was one of the chief complaints raised about the new schools in the late 1870s. It was only in 1900 that tuition in the elementary schools was abolished, stimulating a sharp climb in enrollment to nearly universal levels. The pressures of local finance, however, had some positive effects. Villagers and townspeople began to engage in many activities on behalf of the new schools. Volunteers went from door to door to raise funds; interested citizens participated in numerous public meetings and assemblies convened by school support groups to encourage attendance. In the town of Beppu, in Kyūshū, an association of school supporters decided to purchase goods only from those who supported the elementary schools. This was an early form of consumer boycott, and it worked.[50] There were also those who contributed material and labor for the construction of new school buildings. As a consequence of this kind of participation, there was a subtle shift to greater public awareness and responsibility for the support of local schools. Thus, despite the crescendo of complaint that arose in the late 1870s, and despite the disappointing record that official figures showed for school attendance during the first decade of Meiji, it is nevertheless significant that the Japanese people for the first time had a school sys-

[48] At this time, 1.8 liters of rice (about the amount consumed by one person in four days) was equivalent to 4 sen. Fukaya, *Gakureki shugi no keifu*, p. 69.

[49] *Ōita ken kyōiku hyakunen shi*, vol. 1, pp. 221-223.

[50] Ibid., p. 203.

tem—a network of buildings, personnel, orders, and regulations—which began to take over the initiative in schooling.

Completing the System: Middle Schools in the Seventies and Eighties

The Private School Decade

The decade of the 1870s witnessed intensive efforts by the Mombushō at both the higher and lower levels of the school plan set out in the Fundamental Code of 1872. Tokyo University was established in 1877 for the advanced training of future leaders, and more than 20,000 elementary schools were hurriedly put in place throughout the country for lower-level mass education. As in the Tokugawa period, linkage between the two educational levels continued to be provided largely by a variety of independent institutions outside effective public control. These private schools offered diverse opportunities to those best able to take advantage of them: namely, former samurai and the local leadership classes. Although school institutions abounded, the organization of the public system throughout the decade lacked articulation between the two levels that had already been formed. So long as this situation persisted, possibilities for commoner mobility through the system remained limited. One prominent Meiji educator has described the structure of the system as follows: "The evolutionary stage of the public schools in the Meiji period resembled that of lower animals before they developed spinal cords or nervous systems—they were partly controlled by the head and partly by the tail, with each working independently of the other."[51]

The Fundamental Code had mandated a public middle school in each of Japan's 256 middle school districts. The prefectures, however, were already strapped financially with expenses for elementary schools and normal schools and, as a result, were not able to implement the law. As Table 8.3 clearly shows, the bulk of middle school education was undertaken in private institutions, and a disportionate number were located in Tokyo.[52] Furthermore, the thirty-one prefectural public schools listed

[51] Motoyama Yukihiko, *Meiji zenki gakkō seiritsu shi* (Tokyo: Miraisha, 1965), p. 8. The words are those of Izawa Shūji (1851-1917), who became president of the Tokyo Normal School and the Tokyo Music School.

[52] These data, from *Mombushō nempō*, are frequently cited by scholars. The figures are used here to indicate general trends only and, for a number of reasons, are probably not very accurate indications of actual numbers of schools, especially in the private sector. Many smaller schools were probably never recorded, and, in some cases, schools that lasted for only short periods were recorded. More important, this was a period before precise

TABLE 8.3
Number of Middle Schools, 1877-1879

	Total	Public	Private	Tokyo (public and private)
1877	389	31	358	209
1878	579	65	514	274
1879	784	107	677	319

SOURCE: *Mombushō nempō.*
NOTE: These figures are used to indicate general trends only. See fn. 52.

for 1877 were located in only nineteen of the thirty-eight prefectures at this time.[53] The middle schools were supported in large part by contributions from former daimyo. As might be expected, students came from the samurai class in the early years. Many early middle schools tended to show wide regional variation, as had the domain schools from which many of them originated. The change in the content of learning toward more Western-style curricula, however, was far more conspicuous here than at the lower levels. The texts used varied widely, but most followed a comprehensive course rather than a vocational course centered around Western science and foreign language. The curriculum, as set out by the Mombushō in *Chūgaku kyōsoku* [Rules for Instruction at Middle Schools] in October 1872, suggests that the purpose of these schools was to prepare students for the university. Even though the original concept of the Fundamental Code was that middle schools would provide general higher education as well as university preparation, the focus shifted to the latter very quickly.[54]

Whereas the *han* schools had used the Confucian classics, students at the new middle schools went from Willson readers to Francis Wayland's *Elements of Moral Science* and Peter Parley's *History of England*;[55]

distinctions were made between the various types of schools above the *terakoya* level—*semmongakkō* (special or technical schools), foreign-language schools, middle schools—and it is difficult to know what is being included in *Mombushō nempō* lists for any given year. Even for the same school, categorization is not consistent. Keiō, for example, was first listed as a foreign-language school, then as a middle school. It is clear, however, that private schools were predominant in this period. One scholar, looking at all middle schools, *semmongakkō*, and foreign-language schools in 1877, has calculated that 44 percent of all students were in private schools in Tokyo. Fukaya, *Gakureki shugi no keifu*, pp. 90-91.

[53] Fukaya, *Gakureki shugi no keifu*, p. 125.

[54] Motoyama, *Meiji zenki gakkō seiritsu shi*, pp. 18-23.

[55] The text by Francis Wayland (1796-1865) was translated into Japanese as *Shūshinron*; Peter Parley was the pen name of Samuel Griswold Goodrich (1793-1860), and his book was known in Japanese as *Bankoku shi*.

whereas students had earlier studied Chinese by *sodoku* (rote reading), they now struggled with English conversation. Since higher-level instruction was carried out for the most part in foreign languages (primarily English) during the 1870s, strong emphasis was put on language training in the middle schools. The emphasis by the Mombushō on providing high-quality foreign-language training is also evident in the establishment of special language schools, financed entirely by the national government as university preparatory institutions. Seven of these were set up from 1873 to 1874; in Tokyo, Osaka, Nagasaki, Aichi, Hiroshima, Niigata, and Miyaji. This concentration on language skills caused private language schools to pop up like mushrooms to prepare the students—a phenomenon not unknown in contemporary Japan.

A second look at the more than 1,100 *shijuku* petitions submitted to the prefectural government of Tokyo provides an overview of the types of private schools that flourished in the early 1870s. The petitions indicate that there was a very wide range of independent schools training students above the *terakoya* level, a carry-over from the Tokugawa period. It is apparent that there were still many schools for Chinese studies; calculation (*wasan*) and medical schools are also indicated. About one-hundred-fifty English-language schools were catering to over 6,000 students.[56] The great popularity of the English schools is also suggested by the numerous newspaper and periodical ads, many of them in *Shimbun zasshi*, that called attention to these schools in the 1870s.[57] Among the early English-language schools were those supported by Christian missions, which played an important role in the education of women in the early Meiji years.

Also appearing in the petitions were schools that provided comprehensive programs of Western studies, such as Fukuzawa Yukichi's Keiō gijuku, Kōgyokusha, run by Kondō Makoto (1831-1886), and Dōjinsha, run by Nakamura Masanao (1832-1891). Keiō was the most remarkable of the transitional *shijuku*. Begun in 1858 as a Dutch studies school, it became an English-language school before the Restoration. In the 1870s it developed into an institution of advanced Western learning and was competitive with the best of the government schools. Keiō's appeal during this period was its traditional *shijuku* character—close student-teacher relationships and an emphasis on independent and critical thought. The Tokugawa-period competitive technique for language teaching, known as *kaidoku* (group reading), was now practiced not with Dutch grammar or Chinese characters, as formerly, but with names and dates from world

[56] Fukaya, *Gakureki shugi no keifu*, p. 93.

[57] Kambe Yasumitsu, "Meiji zenki shijuku no shimbun kōkoku," *Shigaku kyōiku kenkyūjo kiyō*, no. 7 (April 1964), pp. 135-148.

history.[58] Keiō became an influential training school for teachers in public as well as private middle schools. In Kyoto, Osaka, Tokushima, and other areas, Keiō gijuku branches were set up; and 121 private schools adopted the "gijuku" title, possibly hoping to emulate the success of the original.[59]

By the middle of the 1870s, when government policies had begun to take shape, a group of politically oriented *shijuku* sprang up—attached to the political associations of the *jiyū minken undō* (Movement for People's Rights), which was pressing for a representative assembly and supported ideas of "natural rights," self-government, and autonomy for local areas. The curricula of these schools centered on English and French works on law, politics, and economics; included were the works of Spencer, Mill, Guizot, and Rousseau, as well as the Napoleonic Code. One of the best known of this type, Risshisha in Tosa, was called the "Western Keiō gijuku."[60] For a brief time in the late 1870s these schools were quite numerous, and students traveled from one to the next for debates and discussions, as their predecessors had in the Tokugawa fencing academies. The activities of these schools were a source of concern to government leaders—Motoda Eifu (1818-1891), the emperor's Confucian tutor, referred to such schools as "political discussion gangs"—in part, no doubt, because many elementary school teachers had become involved.[61] Whether from direct government pressure or from the waning of the *jiyū minken* movement itself in the 1880s, most of these schools were short-lived. Some leaders of the Risshisha, for example, were arrested and jailed in connection with their support for the Satsuma Rebellion of 1877.[62]

In addition, specialized schools of medicine, law, commerce, and agriculture provided opportunities for vocational training that were lacking in the public middle schools. In the days before there was great demand for highly trained specialists in these areas, schools remained informal—often run part time or at night, sometimes in rented rooms, with a teacher who was not paid. It was a period, moreover, before official and formal qualifications were set, and these informal private schools were able to

[58] Murata Shōji, *Kadono Ikunoshin Sensei jiseki bunshū* (Tokyo: Kadono Ikunoshin Sensei kaikyūroku oyobi ronshū kankōkai, 1939), pp. 129-130.

[59] Keiō gijuku, comp., *Keiō gijuku hyakunen shi* (Tokyo: Keiō gijuku, 1958), vol. 1, pp. 246-252.

[60] Motoyama, *Meiji zenki gakkō seiritsu shi*, p. 72.

[61] Katsuda Shūichi and Nakauchi Toshio, *Nihon no gakkō* (Tokyo: Iwanami shoten, 1964), p. 111.

[62] Tenkyō gijuku in Kyoto, another school of this type, was put up for sale when interest in the political movement died during the 1880s. It eventually became a public middle school. Tōō gijuku, in Aomori, was threatened with loss of support by its sponsors unless the curriculum dropped its strong political emphasis. It reformed in what one work has called a "sellout." Ibid.

compete with government offerings. In the field of law, for example, one could become a lawyer in the 1870s with just a general knowledge of the law and court system. Accordingly, law *shijuku* like Tōkyō hōgaku (later Hōsei University) sprang up to accommodate aspiring lawyers.

During the first decade or so under the Fundamental Code, a wide range of independent private schools continued to exist, and their numbers probably far exceeded those in the official records. Before a public school system was organized, these schools provided higher training to those interested in pursuing "enlightenment" (*bummei kaika*) as well as in more traditional areas of knowledge. Ambitious youth in the 1870s, on a path similar to that followed by Ōmura Masujirō a generation earlier, continued, largely on their own initiative, to combine travel and the available *shijuku* to fashion highly individualized sequences of advanced training. The school career of Tokutomi Sohō may be taken as illustrative.

Tokutomi was born in Minamata, in what is now Kumamoto prefecture, in 1863, so he was of school age at the time of the Restoration. He was the son of a village head and received considerable training at home in the Confucian classics. When the family moved to the city of Kumamoto, he continued his basic studies at a *shijuku*, then moved on to more advanced Confucian learning at the nearby school of Motoda Eifu. When Motoda was called to Tokyo as imperial tutor, Tokutomi changed schools. In 1871 he entered still another *shijuku*, where he stayed for two years. He began his Western learning under the retired American army captain Leroy Lansing Janes (1838-1909) at the Kumamoto yōgakkō (Western Studies School), where he became a member of a band of Christian converts. In 1876 he traveled to Tokyo for more advanced studies and entered Tōkyō eigo gakkō (Tokyo English School). Displeased by the formality of this government school, Tokutomi left Tokyo for the more gentle ambiance of Kyoto. He entered Dōshisha, the well-known Christian-mission-supported school run by Niijima Jō (1843-1890). Graduating in 1880, Tokutomi returned to Kumamoto and continued his *shijuku* activities as a teacher—first at Kyōritsu gakkō and then, in 1882, at his own school, Ōe gijuku, where he combined Japanese, Confucian, and Western learning of the *jiyū minken* variety.[63]

In seven years Tokutomi Sohō's studies had taken him to seven different schools—from Confucian studies to English language, advanced Western studies, and Christianity. With the exception of a brief period at Tōkyō eigo gakkō, his studies had been under private auspices. Tokutomi's school career is representative of that pursued by many of the most successful leaders of the middle Meiji period. He was, however, one of

[63] Tokutomi Iichirō, *Sohō jiden* (Tokyo: Chūō kōronsha, 1934), pp. 28-82.

the last who would follow a school pattern largely of his own making. Beginning in the 1880s, the organization of schools in Japan underwent a significant and lasting change.

The Eighties: Consolidating the Public Middle Schools

The Education Law of September 29, 1879 (*Kyōikurei*) superseded the Fundamental Code of 1872 and attempted to lessen some of the burdens imposed on local areas by the earlier law. It abolished the university district system, considerably reduced the duration of compulsory schooling (from four years to sixteen months), and decentralized educational control by turning supervisory responsibility over to the prefectures. Once pressures from the central government decreased, however, the unintended result was that people began to desert the public schools for the more informal arrangements characteristic of pre-Meiji years. The government responded in the early 1880s by reasserting central authority over the school system and redirecting the goals and content of learning away from what were perceived as the Western excesses of the 1870s. Since the prefectures demanded expanded facilities for the new generation that was coming out of the elementary schools, the central government began to pay particular attention to the most neglected segment of the system—the middle schools.

Though it was not the purpose of the 1879 Education Law to systematize the middle schools, it nevertheless had the effect of upgrading their status by establishing a new category of miscellaneous schools, known as *kakushu gakkō*. Many private schools that had previously been considered middle schools were reclassified to this lower status. Consequently, the number of private middle schools dropped drastically, as Table 8.4 shows.

A set of regulations enacted on July 29, 1881 (*Chūgakkō ryōsoku taikō*) began the process of standardizing the curriculum of the middle schools. The new curriculum specified courses in natural science, literature, *shūshin* (ethics), English, and economics, as well as bookkeeping, penmanship, chorus, and calisthenics. It put less emphasis on foreign language (courses were to be taught in Japanese by Japanese instructors) and more on traditional subjects like ethics and literature. The regulations of 1881 also set the middle schools into the overall system by providing a lower division for those coming out of the elementary schools and an upper division for university preparation. In actuality, however, many areas were not able to afford the cost of establishing the upper course.

On January 26, 1884, another regulation (*Chūgakkō tsūsoku*) set rigorous standards for middle schools. The qualifications of the teaching staff were considerably tightened, so that each school was required to

TABLE 8.4
Number of Middle Schools, 1879-1887

	Public	Private	Total
1879	107	677	784
1880	137	50	187
1881	158	14	172
1882	163	9	172
1883	166	6	172
1884	130	2	132
1885	104	2	106
1886	54	2	56
1887	43	5	48

SOURCE: *Mombushō nempō.*

have at least three teachers who had graduated either from the normal course at the middle school level or from the university. The law also required that any school which had the middle school designation would have to provide well-stocked libraries and expensive scientific equipment for the laboratories.[64]

Needless to say, few schools could meet such standards. In practice, the requirements were eased somewhat according to local conditions; but, even so, the result was a drop in the number of public middle schools, and a reduction of the private middle schools to almost zero. Although many students continued to be trained in the miscellaneous schools, the high standards of the public middle schools had begun to make them the important channel for anyone wishing to prepare for advanced studies at the university.

Efforts to reform the school system culminated in 1886 with a series of laws designed by Mori Arinori, the first minister of education. The goals and structure of the comprehensive school system that was erected by these statutes remained essentially unchanged until the post–World War II reforms. The new system was designed to serve the purposes of the state, and each segment was given a unique and vital role within the framework of the whole. Elementary schools were redesigned to inculcate proper character and patriotic loyalty; their pupils were to be guided by teachers trained in normal schools run along military lines, complete with uniforms and drills. The newly designed Imperial University was to train

[64] Motoyama, *Meiji zenki gakkō seiritsu shi*, pp. 34-36.

elites for government service, and although academic freedom was guaranteed, it was set within parameters defined by the national interest. Between the two, functioning as an elite sorting mechanism, were the middle schools. The Middle School Ordinance (*Chūgakkō rei*) conferred a dual structure on the middle schools: a five-year ordinary middle school (*jinjō chūgakkō*), for students from twelve to seventeen, as well as a two-year (later three-year) higher middle school (*kōtō chūgakkō*, which in 1894 became *kōtō gakkō*). Mori's intention was to provide both levels with a vocational course and a university preparatory course in law, literature, science, medicine, engineering, agriculture, and commerce—corresponding to the courses of study at the university. These could, however, also be terminal programs, intended to train middle-level professionals in such areas.[65] The ordinary middle schools were run by local prefectures without assistance from the national government, whereas the higher middle schools—limited to only five at first, then seven by 1887—were entirely separate institutions, financed out of the national treasury.

For the prefectures, the most significant part of the law was the requirement that each prefecture concentrate public funds in only one middle school. The prefectures responded to this in different ways. Some areas, such as Fukuoka, where a number of middle schools already existed, had to consolidate several schools into one; others, not having a middle school, had to create one, as Ibaraki did by splitting a new middle school off from a normal school.[66] One important consequence of the drastic reduction in the number of public middle schools—from 104 in 1885 to 43 in 1887—was a more even distribution of public middle schools. Another was the consolidation of curricula and practices within the schools under a standardized set of regulations.

If one thinks of the expansion of the elementary schools as movement outward toward greater numbers, the development of the middle schools may be thought of as movement upward toward greater mobility within the system. Once the middle schools provided articulation between the lower and upper levels of the system, the possibilities for commoners to advance to the higher reaches of schooling increased. This did not happen right away because the constituencies at the top and bottom of the system had for so long been different—samurai at the top, commoners at the bottom. But in 1890 the proportion of commoners in the ordinary middle schools went above 50 percent for the first time; by 1898, the commoner figure stood at 67.6 percent, and it continued to rise. The large increase

[65] *Gakusei hyakunen shi*, pp. 367-368.

[66] Fukaya, *Gakureki shugi no keifu*, pp. 167-168.

in the number of students at ordinary middle schools in the 1890s, from 11,180 in 1890 to 51,786 by 1898 was primarily among the commoner classes.[67] We do not have figures for the higher middle schools, but it is clear that commoner mobility into the higher levels of the system was advancing. The proportion of students of samurai origin at Tokyo University was 77 percent in 1879; by 1885, it had dropped to 51.7 percent. In the private medical and law schools, commoner representation was higher, about 75 percent by 1890. At Keiō the proportion of commoners went above 50 percent for the first time in 1880.[68]

It is well to remember that there were limits to this process. The ordinary middle schools did not accept girls, and since expenses were a factor, only boys who could afford to pay the fees could enter. The bottom 25 percent of the income scale was, in effect, excluded. Attendance, however, did not require great wealth, so the vertical expansion provided by the middle schools was important for educational mobility. The path may have been narrow, but it was no longer based on class. Once the path was open, talented boys of humble background could begin to make the climb to the national university.

The Fate of the Shijuku

Following the Education Law of 1879, the term *shijuku* was no longer used in official notices. Such schools were referred to as "miscellaneous schools" or by the more modern designation of "private school" (*shiritsu gakkō*). This change of nomenclature merely reflected the fact that educational functions dominated by the *shijuku*—extension of literacy, provision of advanced learning opportunities for commoners, and training men of ability—were steadily taken over by an expanding public system, first at the elementary level and then at the secondary level. Although even after 1886 private schools continued to carry out important functions at the secondary level—extending opportunities for women and providing vocational training, in particular—most of them carried the inferior designation of *kakushu gakkō* and came increasingly under public supervision.

[67] Kikuchi Jōji, "Kindai Nihon ni okeru chūtō kyōiku kikai," *Kyōiku shakaigaku kenkyū*, vol. 22 (1967), pp. 136-137.

[68] For data on students of commoner origin at Tōdai and at the private medical and law schools, see Kikuchi Jōji, "The Emergence and Development of a National Education System in Modern Japan," paper presented at a conference of the International Sociological Association on the origins and operations of educational systems, Paris, August 1980. For material on Keiō, see Nishikawa Shunsaku, "Seinan sensō infureki ni okeru Keiō gijuku to Fukuzawa Yukichi," *Mita shōgaku kenkyū*, vol. 24, no. 4 (October 1981), pp. 8-9.

In higher education, where the possibilities for private schools were greatest, the combination of a weak financial base and discriminatory policies by the government placed the private schools at considerable disadvantage with respect to the state system. Denied public funds, private schools had always had to attract students by their reputations, and these were subject to great change as the fads and fancies of students shifted. One Hiroshima school, called Meibindō is reported to have had an enrollment of 452 students in 1877, but only 40 the next year.[69] Even Keiō, despite its reputation for quality and its popular and well-connected headmaster, Fukuzawa, came close to shutting its doors in September 1880 owing to financial troubles.[70]

Quite naturally, the creation of a more prestigious public track aggravated problems the private schools already had. Dōshisha, for example, was plagued by high dropout rates in the late 1870s, partly the result of students leaving to enter the preparatory school (Daigaku yobimon) for Tokyo University.[71] New regulations denied the private schools special privileges available to the state schools, such as draft deferments and exemptions from government licensing examinations. Tokutomi Sohō's Ōe gijuku lost many students when, in 1883, draft deferments for private schools were lifted.[72] The many private law schools suffered in the early 1880s when only graduates of the state law schools were permitted to practice without passing qualifying exams. The private schools, which until then had competed equally, were forced to tailor their programs to prepare students for these tests. The very best of the college-level private schools were burdened with the inferior designation of *semmongakkō* (special or technical school) until 1918, when they were finally elevated to the status of university.

Most private schools, as a consequence of such problems, offered less expensive programs, hired less qualified teachers, and accepted almost any student willing to pay. There were notable exceptions—namely, Keiō, Waseda (Tōkyō semmongakkō until 1902), and Dōshisha—which managed to keep quality up and maintain an independent tradition. But by the late 1880s a "two-layer structure"—high-quality, expensive programs for selected students at the national university; lower-quality programs for larger numbers of students at the private schools—was already visible in Japanese higher education.[73]

[69] Fukaya, *Gakureki shugi no keifu*, pp. 98-99.

[70] *Keiō gijuku hyakunen shi*, vol. 1, p. 757.

[71] Fukaya, *Gakureki shugi no keifu*, p. 122.

[72] John D. Pierson, *Tokutomi Sohō, 1863-1957: A Journalist for Modern Japan* (Princeton: Princeton University Press, 1980), p. 104.

[73] The concept of a "two-layer structure" is discussed in Ikuo Amano, "Continuity and

Conclusion

By 1886 the outlines of a distinctive Japanese organization of schools had appeared. To be sure, the system was not yet fully mature. School attendance did not reach near-universal levels until the turn of the century; formalized vocational training was still in its infancy; opportunities for women lagged behind those for men; and there was only one officially recognized university until Kyoto Imperial University was created in 1897. The basic framework for a modern system was, however, in place.

Continuities from the Tokugawa past provided both advantages and disadvantages to the new system. The slow development of women's education, particularly beyond the elementary level, and the lack of demand for professional-level vocational training in commerce and agriculture were difficult inheritances from the past. The reluctance of much of the rural population to entrust the care of their children to public authorities, and the continued predominance of children of samurai origin at the higher levels of schooling, were also factors of long standing.

At the same time, though, the development of schools and schooling practices during the late Tokugawa period contributed significantly to easing the transition to a modern system. The categories of schools that made up the organization of the new system had each developed out of Tokugawa institutions. The university traced its beginnings to the *bakufu*'s Bansho shirabesho, the elementary schools had their origins in the *terakoya* and *gōgaku*, and the middle schools came out of the upper levels of *han* schools and the more advanced *shijuku*. This means that the modern Japanese school system was more a product of reorganization than of creation. Furthermore, the widespread availability of schools of many kinds during the *bakumatsu* period, the proliferation of books and text materials, the large number of teachers plying their trade, and the constant increase of families accustomed to the routines of schoolgoing ensured that the training of the generation that grew up in the Meiji years would not be sacrificed to the political confusion of the times.

During the opening decade of the Meiji period, continuities with Tokugawa were strong in the content of learning, in the textbooks used, and in the methods of teachers. Hence, the view that early Meiji education produced "radical cleavages between traditional and modern, Japanese and Western," and caused emotional stress among elites who sought Western learning, may be questioned.[74] Changes were more gradual and

---

Change in the Structure of Japanese Higher Education," in William K. Cummings, Ikuo Amano, and Kazuyuki Kitamura, eds., *Changes in the Japanese University: A Comparative Perspective* (New York: Praeger, 1979), pp. 10-39.

[74] This view is set forth in Kenneth B. Pyle, *The New Generation in Meiji Japan: Problems of Cultural Identity, 1885-1895* (Stanford: Stanford University Press, 1969), chap. 1.

the effects probably a good deal less wrenching than that. The education available after the Restoration was a mix of old and new. There was widespread institutional diversity, and opportunities for individual choice in matters of content and learning environment were considerable.

This is not to deny that fundamental shifts did take place over the period from the 1850s to the 1880s. Geographical disparities in the availability and content of learning diminished. Greater possibilities for commoner mobility through the system opened up. School arrangements that had been private and discontinuous changed to a public system that was uniform and centrally controlled.

Meiji leaders found the loose arrangement of Tokugawa schools clearly inadequate to the needs of nation building. They viewed uniformity as an essential value in the new system, not only because they sought to use the schools as primary agents of moral and political socialization, but also because they were intent on raising minimum standards of education and encouraging merit-based progress. Moreover, they planned to do so nationwide, eliminating the pernicious disparities that had characterized Tokugawa practice. National standardization undoubtedly yielded perceptible benefits by the end of the transition period. Access to schooling at all levels was widened, mobility through the system had increased, qualifications of teachers were raised, ability was rewarded along more impartial lines, and the inequities stemming from class and geographical location were lessened. Certainly, by the turn of the twentieth century it could be said that the new school system had succeeded remarkably in raising the general level of educational attainment, and in providing the country with the skills and knowledge required for modern political and economic development. These achievements, however, were not gained without cost.

By the late 1880s, educational professionals of the central bureaucracy in the Mombushō were making decisions that had formerly been in the hands of individual teachers. The Mombushō was determining curricula, selecting text materials, setting school hours and schedules, preparing examinations, deciding on teaching methods to be used, and so on. Teachers, who had been the focus of educational institutions in the Tokugawa period, were now mere parts of a larger, national apparatus. A clear sense of loss is expressed by the protagonist of *Omoide no ki*:

> There are few of these [single-teacher private schools] left now. The world has progressed: our teachers ride to brick-built schools in private rickshaws, students line up for military-style physical training, wear uniforms and caps—every activity is becoming splendidly organized, or regimented, to put it bluntly. Inevitably, therefore, the

> old-fashioned type of home school that depended entirely on the personality of one man is disappearing—and with it, unhappily, many of the qualities it fostered: the deep tie between teacher and students, the peculiar enthusiasms of moral and intellectual improvement, the sense of honour and integrity, the characteristic gaiety that naturally grew out of the life of such a small community.[75]

To be sure, not all the *shijuku* teachers were idealists like Yoshida Shōin, and the "sense of honour and integrity" and "characteristic gaiety" that are invoked by the author of these words, Tokutomi Roka, may be nothing more than sentimental delusions born out of faulty reminiscence on a time gone by. Yet if one can imagine Yoshida Shōin, hair parted with precision, riding to his brick schoolhouse in a hired rickshaw, one will have no trouble visualizing the ambivalences of Japanese schools in the time of transition from Tokugawa to Meiji.

The shift in the locus of educational authority from the one-room schoolhouse of the *bakumatsu* period to the centralized bureaucracy of the late 1880s inevitably brought with it diminishing possibilities for individual and local influence in the control and practice of education. As the public system was put in place under the guidance of the Ministry of Education—first the university, then the elementary schools, and finally the middle schools—functions that had earlier been carried out by individuals and private schools were gradually co-opted by the expanding public sector. Although the private schools continued to educate large numbers of students, those schools had lost their former independence. They no longer provided real alternatives to the public system as they had in the Tokugawa period, when they offered new areas of learning and innovative methodologies not found in the *han* schools. The private schools were no longer outside the system, but were appendages of it. Although the policy of creating a strong public system and of imposing uniform regulations from the top achieved some desirable results, it also tended to stifle individual initiatives and to overlook the special requirements of local areas. The result was a lack of flexibility in the system as a whole.

The process of standardization transformed not only the organization of the schools, but their purposes as well. With the establishment of the comprehensive system under Mori Arinori in the late 1880s, the school system became an effective instrument of national policy. As succeeding decades would make abundantly clear, once the schools became subject to uniform policy decisions their importance for the political goals of the national government increased.

[75] Tokutomi, *Footprints in the Snow*, p. 80.

CHAPTER 9

THE PRESS

BY ALBERT A. ALTMAN

A modernizing society requires channels through which those at the helm can provide information about their destination, and thus win over the mass of the population that must be drawn into the national endeavor. In Japan, the press provided such channels. But the press was also at the disposal of widening sections of the population, as a place to air their views and to mobilize others for attaining goals at variance with official ones. Because most Japanese were concentrated on the narrow coastal plains, it was relatively easy to reach them; high and growing literacy made it certain that the press would be used not only by the government, but also by its opponents.

The Japanese press began with Western initiatives in the treaty ports, but in less than a decade it had entered deeply into the mainstream of Japanese life. The speed with which a native press grew and spread beyond the foreign settlements illustrates just how quickly Western models were incorporated as part of the drive toward centralization.

Late Tokugawa

In Tokugawa Japan it was forbidden to publish information concerning government. Publications required licensing, and a censorship apparatus kept such knowledge out of print. Knowledge of the facts of government "belonged" to those holding bureaucratic office, and since the majority of samurai and all commoners were normally out of office, there were no grounds for considering diffusion of, or access to, official information. Still, popular gossip and scandal, and at times thinly veiled commentary on government, were spread by a variety of broadsides that were hawked, by colophons on prints, by popular storytellers, and even by the theater.

In *Shinjū ten no Amijima*, Chikamatsu's narrator announces the imminence of the lovers' double suicide by intoning, "Tomorrow the gossip of the world will scatter like blossoms the scandal of Kimiya Jihei's love suicide, and carved in cherry wood, his story to the last detail will be printed in illustrated sheets."[1] The ban on the publication of government news was paralleled by a ban on the publication of comment on the acts of the government or its officials. Most samurai, as Albert Craig has pointed out in the case of Chōshū, "were expected to obey without understanding the decisions made by the han's highest councils. Thus, a student at the school of Yoshida Shōin was warned by his father that it was unpardonable to discuss the political affairs of the han. . . . An even more stringent prohibition existed against discussion of the affairs of the nation, particularly those areas under the control of the Bakufu."[2] The superior was insulated from unanticipated approaches by the inferior. In mid-1864, even entrance into the offices of the Chōshū government building in Yamaguchi was strictly forbidden without official permission.[3]

The expression of one's opinion about political, economic, and social issues was a privilege that could be exercised only on request from a superior. There were even Confucian scholars (*jusha*) who believed that they were overstepping the bounds of their status if they discussed *keizai*, or the art of government, without a specific request from their superiors.[4] Kaibara Ekken, the seventeenth-century Confucianist put it succinctly when he wrote, "To criticize superiors—to criticize the country's administration—that becomes a serious breach of loyalty and piety."[5]

The appearance of Perry's flotilla in Edo Bay was quick to produce official as well as unofficial forms of communication. Officially, the *bakufu* found it necessary to consult its vassals, who just as naturally turned to theirs. The circle of those who knew, and of those who had opinions, whether welcome or not, grew steadily. Beyond the official world of memoranda and proposals, informal and often bitterly critical commentary began to circulate.

[1] Donald Keene, trans., *Major Plays of Chikamatsu* (New York: Columbia University Press, 1961), p. 418.

[2] Albert Craig, *Chōshū in the Meiji Restoration* (Cambridge: Harvard University Press, 1961), p. 299. Craig (p. 158) also quotes from the *Shōin zenshū* that "many parents say that Shōin is a criminal . . . and do not want their sons to attend his school. If [their sons] attend his school, they caution them saying that it is not objectionable to practice reading books, but that is unpardonable to discuss the political affairs of the han."

[3] Ibid., p. 224.

[4] J.R. McEwan, *The Political Writing of Ogyū Sorai* (Cambridge: Cambridge University Press, 1962), p. 20.

[5] Kaibara Ekken's *Kadōkun*, quoted in Dan Fenno Henderson, *Conciliation and Japanese Law* (Seattle: University of Washington Press, 1965), vol. 1, p. 401.

Unpublishable material, of course, had always circulated in manuscript, but the crisis guaranteed that such commentary would increase both in quantity and shrillness.[6] As was usual in periods of crisis, handwritten and covert forms of communication multiplied after the coming of Perry politicized first samurai and then commoner society. Lampoons commonly bunched together under the rubric of *rakugaki* or *rakusho*, usually unsigned, criticized officials and their policies in a manner by turns satirical, mocking, often insulting, and sometimes inflammatory. Such lampoons were posted in public places or scattered along roads and streets where they could be easily found, copied, and passed on secretly to others. We can no longer understand them without elaborate explanations often many times longer than the original squib, but contemporaries savored the peppery allusions to current happenings and leading personalities.

Clandestine comment of this sort was an outlet for feelings and ideas, and helped crystallize views on issues considered vital. The aggressiveness, intemperateness of language, and satirical tone that characterize many *rakusho* are also found in the Meiji political dialogue and journalism. There were even Meiji-period magazines that specialized in this type of writing.

The *bakufu*'s inability to keep political information within bounds is apparent from the broadsheets and pamphlets (*kawaraban*) dating from the arrival of the American ships until the end of the Tokugawa period. These writings, like all other printed matter, were forbidden from publishing political news or comment. But now prints appeared, showing the encampments of the daimyo summoned to man the coastal defenses; others illustrated the Americans' gifts and listed foreign words in several languages. Politicized broadsheets and pamphlets were printed off woodblocks in growing numbers alongside the profusion of lampoons and news-in-manuscript.[7]

With the opening of the ports in 1859, the presence of foreigners who had regular access to foreign news resulted in shogunal appropriation and even diffusion of some of that news. In the early days, the regular reports presented by the Dutch and Chinese had been sheltered carefully from all but those authorities having a need to know, but now it became

[6] Suzuki Hidesaburō, *Honpō shimbun no kigen* (Kyoto: Kuriosha, 1959), pp. 75-86. Ernest Satow also commented that "as nothing could be published without permission, any book that touched upon governmental matters had of old to circulate in MS." *A Diplomat in Japan* (Philadelphia: J.B. Lippincott, 1921), p. 68. Both Tokugawa and Meiji censorship are examined in Richard H. Mitchell, *Censorship in Imperial Japan* (Princeton: Princeton University Press, 1983).

[7] Ono Hideo, *Kawaraban monogatari* (Tokyo: Yūzankaku, 1960), pp. 224-295.

impossible to operate the control mechanism in the accustomed manner. Shortly after the negotiation of the "modern" treaty with Holland in 1857, the Dutch informed the *bakufu* that they would no longer file their regular report on world news as they had done in the past.

This decision ushered in a period of uncertainty about how to find a substitute. The *bakufu*, its sources of intelligence limited by a lack of diplomatic representation in the leading capitals and by isolation from the mainstream of world developments, decided to cull information from the foreign press to help keep abreast of changes abroad. Soon after Nagasaki and Yokohama were opened to foreign settlement in mid-1859, the settlement press was tapped for this purpose. The translation facilities in the Bansho shirabesho were expanded, and translations of English newspapers and of Chinese newspapers published by missionaries began appearing for use by officials.

From 1862 to 1864 the *bakufu* sponsored the commercial publication of three collections of news translations from the Western press, three reprints of missionary publications in China which contained news stories, and one collection of items from a Hong Kong newspaper. But this *bakufu* initiative was not followed up. The reason was not a dearth of material, for scholars in official employ were translating items from the Yokohama foreign press for senior officials.[8] There was a plan to release these translations to the general public in the fall of 1864, but it never came to fruition.[9]

The decision to make such information publicly available flowed from the *bakufu*'s growing inability to confine knowledge of state affairs to channels that bolstered Tokugawa rule. The wall of isolation was breached time and again. Official missions were going overseas, getting a first-hand picture of the outside world. Other Japanese were being sent abroad, or were stealing away in violation of *bakufu* regulations.[10] Perhaps most important, once foreigners were permitted to reside in Japan (from mid-1859), newspapers were published in the foreign settlements,

[8] These translations also circulated among the translators and their friends, who had organized a Society of Translators (Kaiyakusha) for that purpose with two dozen members. See Osatake Takeshi, *Shimbun zasshi no shōshisha Yanagawa Shunsan* (Tokyo: Takayama shoin, 1950), and *Bakumatsu Meiji shimbun zenshū*, 8 vols. (Tokyo: Taiseidō, 1934-1935 [vols. 1-5] and Sekai bunko, 1960-1961 [vols. 6-8]).

[9] The communication of the Kaiseijo authorities seeking the clearance of the *metsuke* for defense affairs and of the *Kanagawa bugyō*, with their approval, are reprinted in Nihon shiseki kyōkai, *Ibi nyūkō roku*, 2 vols. (Tokyo: Tōkyō daigaku shuppankai, 1967), vol. 2, pp. 197-199.

[10] *Osaka shōnin taiheiki (jō)*, vol. 9 of *Miyamoto Mataji chosaku shū* (Tokyo: Kōdansha, 1977), p. 151.

which themselves attracted Japanese seeking knowledge of the world beyond their islands.

Restoration and Civil War

While it is clear that the access to news of official importance increased steadily in the 1860s, nothing was done to regularize this, nor was there any sort of consistent policy thrust to legitimate the diffusion of such information. What was happening was that the shogunate was making a more concerted effort to inform itself at the same time that its control mechanisms to restrict the flow of information had collapsed. The January 1868 announcement of "Restoration" and the civil war that followed produced, for a brief period, an open situation in which publication was both possible and unrestricted in Edo and Yokohama.

In Kyoto, the seat of the new government until the defeat of the Tokugawa holdouts at Edo in July 1868, the authorities continued the 1862 *bakufu* policy of making news of state available to the public. But this time it was not news of foreign countries that was released, but information directly concerning Japan itself. The *Dajōkan nisshi*, which began appearing in March 1868, carried the texts of decrees, exhortations, and announcements of appointments plus other information concerning action taken by the government and its officers. The first issue, for example, opened with a description of the audience of the foreign envoys at the Nishi Honganji in Osaka. This publication was launched so that "high and low alike may respectfully receive the government's announcements and, with one mind, knowing the end at which they aim, give it practical expression."[11] The government originally intended the *Dajōkan nisshi* for certain official recipients. But persons not on the official list could also buy it, since the government, lacking its own printing facilities, had it published in both Kyoto and Edo by privileged bookdealers who, as was customary, were permitted to retain a number of copies for sale. (There was also a Chōshū edition.) The *Dajōkan nisshi* was the first of at least a dozen *nisshi* published by the central government during 1868 alone. Over the next decade, most government ministries issued their own.[12]

[11] Naikaku insatsukyoku hensan, *Naikaku insatsukyoku nanajūnen shi* (Tokyo: Naikaku hensan, 1943), p. 188.

[12] The *Dajōkan nisshi* was discontinued in January 1877, and it was not until July 1883 that the government started publishing an official gazette, the *Kampō*. Osatake Takeshi is one of the few historians to have appreciated the significance of the *Dajōkan nisshi*. See his *Meiji bunka sōsetsu* (Tokyo: Gakugeisha, 1934), p. 250.

On March 17, 1868 the first of the Edo newsbooks—the *Chūgai shimbun*—was published, one day after the first issue of the *Dajōkan nisshi* had appeared in Kyoto. A total of seventeen such unlicensed and uncensored newsbooks (these were octavo-size booklets) were being published in Edo and Yokohama before the new government's army could gain control during the first week of July and snuff them out. Before this, at Kyoto in mid-June, the Meiji government had reasserted the authority of the Japanese state to control printed matter.[13] During the same month, two newsbooks were issued in the Kansai area: one in Osaka, the *Ukiyo fubun*, which had only one number, and one in Kyoto, the *Naigai shimbun*, which lasted for seventeen. Sometime between mid-June and mid-July, a third newsbook, the *Tohi shimbun*, was issued in Kyoto, but it lasted for only eight numbers. The unlicensed newsbooks made significant contributions to the future development of the Japanese press. They kept alive the idea that newspapers had a positive social value—that ferreting out the news and publishing it was not simply, or only, a private idle curiosity, but rather an activity of considerable pragmatic and symbolic importance.

The short life of the civil war press in Edo belies its significance. A new mode of public communication, the newspaper, had stepped out of the foreign settlements into the main centers of Japanese life, leaving the foreign settlement press on the periphery of Japanese life and politics. Within less than a decade, in 1875, the Japanese gained complete control of the press by making it impossible for foreigners to publish newspapers.[14]

The civil war newsbooks in Edo had been an anomaly. The *bakufu* could no longer enforce its authority in Edo, and the Meiji government, its seat still in Kyoto, had not yet gained control of the city. In this power vacuum, the newsbooks printed uncensored news and opinion about the conflict. No sooner had the Meiji regime established its authority in Edo (soon to be Tokyo), than it asserted the right of the Japanese state to control publication by banning the newsbooks (July 1868). In April 1869, the government promulgated a set of regulations (*Shimbun shi inkō jōrei*), according legality to newspapers on condition that certain restrictions

[13] Dajōkan Decree no. 358, June 18, 1868; censorship was relegated to the *nisshi no tsukasa*. Okudaira Yasuhiro, "Shuppan keisatsu hōsei no rekishiteki kenkyū jōsetsu," *Hōritsu jihō*, vol. 39, no. 4 (1967), p. 55.

[14] J.E. Hoare, "The 'Bankoku shinbun' Affair: Foreigners, the Japanese Press and Extraterritoriality in Early Meiji Japan," *Modern Asian Studies*, vol. 9, no. 3 (July 1975). On the civil war press, see Albert A. Altman, "Shimbunshi: The Early Meiji Adaptation of the Western-style Newspaper," in William G. Beasley, ed., *Modern Japan: Aspects of History, Literature and Society* (London: Allen & Unwin, 1975), pp. 55-77.

be observed.[15] These regulations became the foundation of the legal structure within which the Japanese press developed. Thus, the Japanese press came into being almost simultaneously with the Meiji state.

April 1869 was a milestone. It now became possible to publish news and opinion on political questions—and the press was one of the channels. This was a period of change that produced new issues, and the press became a platform from which to propose answers and to seek support for them.

Early Meiji

Legality, by itself, resulted in the publication of very few newspapers. The great upsurge did not come until the abolition of the domains in August 1871. Within six years, newspapers (many of them still in book format) had been started within the boundaries of most present-day prefectures. They were expected to buttress the goals set by the country's new rulers. This purpose was enunciated clearly within five days after the new national framework had been announced. The object of newspapers, said a Dajōkan notice, "shall be to develop people's knowledge," and "developing people's knowledge means destroying the spirit of bigotry and prejudice, and leading [the people] to civilization and enlightenment." The instructions went on to emphasize that "compiling a newspaper shall be considered equivalent to composing the authentic records of the times. . . . [It] is forbidden to make something out of nothing, to turn falsehood into truth, to agitate men's hearts, or to deceive the public."[16] In other words, newspapers were to serve policy and not to be vehicles for the expression of discontent.[17]

Although the authority to decide what might be printed remained the exclusive prerogative of those in power, the exercise of that power was not absolute. Needing wider support than it enjoyed, the government both lifted the veil of secrecy that had shrouded politics from public view during the Tokugawa period and also permitted a limited expression of opinion. One of the first reasoned statements for making government

[15] *Junkan Chūgai shimbun*, no. 1 (April 18, 1969), in *Shimbun hen*, vol. 13 of Meiji bunka kenkyūkai hen, *Meiji bunka zenshū*, 32 vols. (Tokyo: Nihon hyōronsha, 1955-1969), p. 369.

[16] *Dai ippen, monjo mon, shuppan*, in Naikaku kiroku kyoku, ed., *Hōki bunrui taizen* (Tokyo: 1888-1894), pp. 405-406.

[17] Although these instructions were issued to the Kyoto authorities, they very likely had a general application throughout Japan. See Nishida Taketoshi, *Meiji jidai no shimbun to zasshi* (Tokyo: Shibundō, 1961), p. 38.

information available is that of Iwakura Tomomi, who in the fall of 1870 argued that details of the national budget should be revealed.[18] Better known is Kido's view, stated some four months later, in favor of newspapers and of permitting criticism of the government.[19] But it was not only domestic weakness that drew the government in the direction of greater openness. The end of isolation, the lifting of restrictions on travel abroad, and the official imprimatur given to seeking knowledge "throughout the world so as to strengthen the foundations of imperial rule" (in the words of the Charter Oath) opened the gateway to new ideas.

Newspaper publication during the early 1870s was intimately linked to government either, as in Tokyo, in the form of support extended by a highly placed patron (such as Kido's for the *Shimbun zasshi*, or Maejima Hisoka's for the *Yūbin hōchi shimbun*) or in the form of a combination of government and private initiatives, as was the case in most prefectures. Providing financial and other assistance in publishing newspapers, the authorities also made use of newspapers in a number of ways to give wider currency to their decrees and regulations. One such was to encourage the establishment of news reading rooms (*shimbun jūransho, shimbun etsuransho*, etc.), where newspapers were made available to readers, or read aloud and explained to villagers. By 1872, such rooms were found throughout the country. In a short while, in addition to those sponsored by the authorities or local elites for "enlightening" the population, some rooms were privately owned and charged fees; others were ventures by small groups of readers who shared the costs of subscribing to newspapers in which they were interested.[20]

Measures such as these supplemented the more formal official channels through which information flowed from Tokyo to the prefectures. One of these, inherited from the Tokugawa regime, was the system of public notice boards (which, however, went out of use in 1873).[21] Another was

[18] "Kokutai shōmei seitai kakuritsu ikensho," in Nihon shiseki kyōkai hen, *Iwakura Tomomi kankei monjo*, 8 vols. (Tokyo: Tōkyō daigaku shuppankai, 1968), vol. 1, p. 345.

[19] Ryusaku Tsunoda, William Theodore de Bary, and Donald Keene, comps., *Sources of Japanese Tradition* (New York: Columbia University Press, 1958), pp. 652-653.

[20] Hironawa Motosuke, "Shimbun jūransho shōran," *Toshokan kai*, vol. 25, no. 3 (1973), pp. 84-100, and no. 4 (1973), pp. 138-152. Hironawa presents data to show how expensive the newspaper was for most of the population. He points out that the news reading room was also used by the Movement for People's Rights to spread its message. Reading rooms in one part of Japan are discussed in Kamio Takenori, "Kenkyū nōto: Chiba ken no minken kessha to sono dōkō," in Wakamori Tarō Sensei kanreki kenen rombunshū henshū iinkai, *Meiji kokka no hatten to minshū seikatsu* (Tokyo: Kōbundō, 1975), pp. 151-156.

[21] *Meiji jimbutsu kigen*, vol. 29 of *Meiji bunka zenshū* (fn. 15, above), p. 64. The official

the Meiji version of the Tokugawa *rusui* system, whereby prefectural and *fu* representatives (instead of domain representatives, as formerly), stationed for the purpose in Tokyo, received communications from the national government for forwarding to their superiors. This system was abolished in 1873.[22]

In October 1873, the government split; and, in January 1874, the memorial demanding the establishment of a national assembly brought a political opposition and its press into being. Just as the government could not quash this opposition, neither could it outlaw its press. In the following years, repeated efforts were made to restrict and control opposition journalism as well as opposition politics; nevertheless, these were to become permanent features of Japan's political landscape.

A Confucian-derived philosophy helped draw the Western-style newspaper into the mainstream of Japanese life and, at the same time, also provided a justification for opposition. Government policy, it was claimed, had disrupted the natural harmony that characterizes relations between the emperor and his subjects. The emperor was no longer aware of his subjects' needs and problems; communications upward from the people to him had been blocked by his ministers. If the channels of communications were cleared of obstructions, the people's voice could be heard once more and harmonious relations restored. The press was a vehicle for conveying this voice to the emperor. Thus, the theory of social harmony in which initiatives lie with the superior did not prove to be an insuperable ideological obstacle to the creation of an opposition and its press. But the same theory also ensured that the political dialogue would encourage emphasis on nationalist symbols and appeals. Since government and opposition alike were committed to creating a strong Japan, this meant that criticism of the government would emphasize its "weakness" in the defense of national interests and demand "strong" (i.e. opposition) policies to ensure the protection of these interests.

The political crisis changed the Japanese press economically as well as politically. Until then, newspapers had been promoted by a combination of public and private interests, but after the crisis they became, and remained, private property. The government never published its own newspaper. It had other means, such as subventions (which some called bribes), to put its message across as well as legislation to restrict press freedom. The Meiji government came close to backing a newspaper in

---

reason for discontinuing the notice boards was that their contents were "well known"; in fact, though, this was a way of abolishing the anti-Christian notice board without appearing to yield to foreign pressure.

[22] Miyatake Gaikotsu, *Fuhanken seishi* (Tokyo: Natori shoten, 1941), pp. 155-156.

1881 when Itō, Inoue, and Ōkuma negotiated unsuccessfully with Fukuzawa toward that end; and in 1883 it started issuing the *Kampō*, a gazette in which official decisions were promulgated, local and foreign news reported, and the government's views enunciated.[23]

Newspaper proprietors in the following decades were a mixed lot: some were private investors; others, political clubs and parties, or other special interest groups. They shared a dependence on subscribers for their income and competed with each other. One result was that newspapers became more reader-oriented. It was no longer sufficient to have scholarly types using a newspaper to give currency to their views; more attention had to be paid to satisfying readers' curiosity about the latest developments at home and abroad, and to introducing features that appealed to a wide variety of tastes. More advanced printing technology made it possible to reduce printing time and to increase the press run; hence, more copies were available for sale at a lower cost per unit. The press as a whole was enjoying a growing readership. Nation-stirring events such as rebellions and wars pushed up circulations and accustomed people to look to the newspaper to find out what was happening; compulsory education added to the pool of potential readers. From the mid-1870s, therefore, newspapers soon abandoned the old printing technology based on woodblocks and adopted the Western printing press. By the end of the nineteenth century, the establishment necessary to handle the increased circulations had changed considerably from what it had been in the 1870s: multistoried Western-style buildings had replaced Japanese-style structures to house both the printing plant and the larger management and editorial/reportorial staffs. These called for larger outlays of capital. Starting a newspaper and operating it now demanded a considerable investment, especially in the case of the metropolitan dailies.

Ideals vs. Commerce

The years bounded roughly by the government split of 1873 or the 1874 memorial on a national assembly, on the one hand, and the collapse of the party movement in the late 1880s, on the other, are often looked upon in the standard histories of the Japanese press as a golden age of journalism. Journalists, we are told, then pursued their calling in the name of social ideals, very often suffering imprisonment and fines for what they wrote, their newspapers very often becoming the objects of repression. These journalists are seen as the "true" journalists, and these

[23] *Naikaku insatsukyoku nanajūnen shi*, pp. 195-198; also *Shimbun hen*, vol. 13 of *Meiji bunka shiryō sōsho* (Tokyo: Kazama shobō, 1959-1963), pp. 13-15, 118-173.

newspapers the "true" newspapers, by which others are to be judged. Their opposition stance is more "pure" because it was not self-serving; the penalties they paid—both material and personal—were the stigmata left by the repression they suffered.

The political crisis also brought tightened government control over the press. Along with other print media, the newspaper had been hedged about with restrictions from the very outset of the establishment of Meiji authority. The April 1869 regulations had conferred legality on newspapers, but they also enumerated the subjects that could be treated, stressing that "government shall not be irresponsibly criticized."[24] So long as there was no political opposition, however, these regulations do not appear to have been considered onerous. Indeed, no punishments for violations are on record, and from mid-April 1871, when the new national polity was established, newspapers basked in the warmth of a benevolent policy and in many cases were quasi-official.[25]

The emergence of a political opposition—the Movement for People's Rights—ended this mutually beneficial relationship. During the eight years between 1875 and 1883, the government erected an increasingly oppressive structure of restraints and punishments to diminish the likelihood that unfavorable news and opinion would appear in the press, and to stem the tide of opposition. It simultaneously restricted public assembly, political organization, and book and magazine publication. The instrument for implementing the press laws (as well as the others) was the Home Ministry (Naimushō). Created in 1873, the Home Ministry was given extensive administrative authority to keep the press in line, and by 1883 this authority had become crystallized in a form that remained substantially unchanged until the military defeat of 1945.[26]

This decade and a half of journalistic history is contrasted with what followed from approximately the late 1880s and early 1890s, when the press is said to have "gone commercial." The press of the latter period is found wanting: no longer did the press serve social ideals, authors say;

[24] See fn. 15, above.

[25] Suehiro Tetchō, "Shimbun keireki dan," in *Shimbun hen*, vol. 13 of *Meiji bunka zenshū* (fn. 15, above), p. 52. In the fourth section of his *Gakumon no susume*, published in December 1873, Fukuzawa Yukichi wrote that "regulations governing publishing are not usually severe; newspapers nevertheless do not carry anything at all that offends the government." See *Fukuzawa zenshū*, 21 vols. (Tokyo: Iwanami shoten, 1959-1964), vol. 4, p. 52. But four years later, Fukuzawa described how the Japanese press had changed. "Bunken ron," *Zenshū*, vol. 4, p. 252.

[26] Okudaira Yasuhiro, "Nihon shuppan keisatsu hōsei no rekishiteki kenkyū," *Hōritsu jihō*, vol. 39, nos. 4-10 (1967); Peter Figdor, "Newspapers and Their Regulation in Early Meiji Japan, 1868-1883," *Papers on Japan*, 6 vols. (Cambridge: East Asian Research Center, Harvard University, 1972), vol. 6.

newspapers had become business enterprises geared to the making of profit, and newspapermen no longer stood at the forefront of society, carrying the banners of idealism. The journalist no longer led. He followed the people, providing them what they wanted and not what he knew they *needed*. What they wanted is variously termed "amusement," "self-indulgence," "selfishness," "private profit"—all condemned in terms reminiscent of traditional, but still accepted, moral values.[27]

It would be foolish to deny that the press of the 1880s and 1890s was different from what it had been after the government crisis of 1873, but it is more useful to view this change as the continuation of a process that began in the mid-1870s. Indeed, the more significant turning point may well have been the mid-1870s, when the Japanese press severed ties with its official sponsors and began fending for itself in the marketplace. If so, then the virtues that have been discerned in the press of the "golden age" were compatible with commerce; contrariwise, the vices that have been discerned in the press of the 1890s have their beginnings in the "golden" 1870s.

The conventional periodization is based upon the changing fortunes of the politically engaged press, serving an elite (usually Tokyo) readership. It does not take into consideration the fact that two kinds of newspapers made their appearance in the early 1870s, each appealing to a different readership. One, just mentioned, was aimed at readers concerned about politics, doubtless from the population's more privileged sectors. Such papers clustered initially in Tokyo, and the characteristics they acquired became standard for the Meiji press as a whole.

The expression of critical opinions and views on a diverse range of subjects was more characteristic of the post–October 1873 press. This assumed two main forms: the editorial and the discursive article. Adoption of the editorial column gave the Japanese press an instrument that concentrated the reader's attention on the expression of opinion in a manner not previously done. The withdrawal of the explicit expression of opinion into its own compartment was part of an extensive change in the physical appearance of the Tokyo press during the early 1870s. The Western—and in contemporary Japanese estimation "advanced"—sheet format and printing from movable metal type were displacing the newsbook format and printing from woodblocks. The grouping of items under

[27] Even in the *bummei kaika* 1870s the authorities were giving cash prizes to exceptionally filial children. The press reported these awards, and the edifying stories were often collected and published in book form. *Hito no kagami*, for example, published by Ehime prefecture in 1883, is a collection of stories about local filial children and virtuous women from 1877 to 1881.

general rubrics was unknown in the civil war and earliest Meiji-period newsbooks; nor did the editors arrange an issue's contents in a sequence reflecting a judgment of significance. Rather, the sequence seems to have been determined by the order in which the items were received and then carved into the woodblocks; once carved, items could not be moved into a different position. Journalistic norms determining where items were to be placed soon became standard for the entire Tokyo press. The very top of page one reported the texts of official decrees as well as announcements from national and local authorities, this prominent placement reflecting a respectful attitude toward imperial rule. In the mid-1870s, such official material was typically followed further down on page one and on the inside pages by news stories (*zappō*), contributions from the paper's staff or from readers and, further along in the paper, lists of current commodity prices, other economic news, and advertisements.

The daily editorial made its debut in the Tokyo press in the December 2, 1874, issue of the *Tōkyō nichi-nichi shimbun*. By the early spring of 1875, most of the Tokyo quality press was publishing editorials almost daily. Before, these papers had run an occasional opinion piece or essay, dealing with timely questions and written either by a staff member or a guest contributor.[28] Now these newspapers prided themselves on their editorials and discursive articles, which became the touchstone of a paper's excellence. This emergence of the editorial into a position of prominence, which was given journalistic expression by the editorial's placement high on page one and by its length (sometimes continuing over several consecutive issues), brought with it a competition among newspapers for writers whose names would add luster and attract a following of loyal subscribers. The pre–October 1873 papers had worn a cloak of impersonality; now, in contrast, the premium was put on writers who could persuade readers not only by the cogency of their reasoning, but also by the distinction of their literary style. Aside from the texts of government decrees, there was hardly anything in such papers not produced by the staff or by guest contributors. And there was little that was also in other papers, for this was the age before domestic and foreign news services. (Most papers translated foreign news stories from the foreign-language press, few having their own foreign correspondents.)[29]

[28] James L. Huffman, *Politics of the Meiji Press: The Life of Fukuchi Gen'ichirō* (Honolulu: University Press of Hawaii, 1980), p. 88.

[29] The *Jiji shimpō*, which signed a contract with the Reuter's News Agency in 1893, was the first paper to get foreign news directly from abroad. For a brief survey of the history of Japanese domestic news agencies, see Okamoto Kōzo, ed., *Nihon shimbun hyakunen shi* (Tokyo: Nihon shimbun kenkyū remmei, 1961), pp. 696-708.

This dependence on "homemade"material enhanced the importance of the paper's own staff, particularly since the greater part of the revenue still came from sales, and provided opportunities for students with even a smattering of Western knowledge to gain fame or to earn money to support themselves.[30]

Alongside these prestigious quality newspapers, called by contemporaries the *ōshimbun* ("great," or perhaps "major" or "superior," newspapers), there very quickly appeared in Tokyo others appealing to a public for whom political debate was considered less compelling, perhaps because it had always been thought inappropriate to their low station. The heart of such newspapers, the *koshimbun* ("small," or perhaps "minor" or "inferior," newspapers), lay elsewhere. Their realm was what was known in the press jargon of the Meiji period as *zappō*, "miscellaneous reports" of current happenings, largely concerning sex, crime, and violence. The *koshimbun* also featured serialized fiction. The latter, known as *tsuzukimono*, was an outgrowth of the *zappō* human-interest stories and was partly fact, partly embellishment, combined in such a way that the news ingredient could not be distinguished from the imaginative elaboration, thus happily satisfying two needs simultaneously. Based, ostensibly at least, on actual events, *tsuzukimono* was "truthful" and hence less open to the charge of frivolity. On the other hand, it was written in a style meant to appeal to the literary tastes of its readers, enhanced by woodblock illustrations that were often spread over several columns—an indulgence rejected by the quality press.[31]

To a Meiji gentleman, emphasis on such news and fiction (which his Confucian culture had taught him to distrust) distorted the press's social purpose for the selfish pursuit of amusement. This is not to say that his favorite paper did not print such news stories as well. It did, but relegated them to the inside pages and used elevated, restrained language. In the Meiji gentleman's newspaper, such stories were like his concubine: a

[30] Ozaki Yukio, while still a student of 19 at the Kōgakuryō in 1876, was contributing articles to the *Tōkyō Akebono shimbun*, a People's Rights newspaper. See his *Minken tōsō 70-jūnen* (Tokyo: Yomiuri shimbunsha, 1952), p. 12. Ozaki was also writing for the *Yūbin hōchi shimbun*, as was Inukai Tsuyoshi, another Keiō student. Washio Yoshinao, ed., *Inukai Bokudō den*, 3 vols. (Tokyo: Tōyō keizai shuppansha, 1938-1939), vol. 1, pp. 70-75. Inukai achieved instant fame when that paper sent him to cover the Satsuma Rebellion while he was still at school.

[31] Ono Hideo, *Nihon shimbun hattatsu shi*, 6th ed. (Osaka: Osaka mainichi shimbunsha, 1924), p. 290; *Meiji hen*, in Takagi Takeo, *Shimbun shōsetsu shi* (Tokyo: Tosho kankōkai, 1974), pp. 19-21; and Itō Sei, *Nihon bundan shi*, 24 vols. (Tokyo: Kōdansha, 1953-1966), vol. 1, pp. 124-125.

pleasurable, socially approved, but discreet diversion from life's strenuous obligations.

The Newspaper as Education

Early in the history of the Japanese press, concerned intellectuals, invariably of samurai derivation, conceived of the press as mentor.[32] Some even tried publishing newspapers for their social inferiors. Perhaps the earliest attempt to produce such a newspaper was made in May/June 1869 by Hashizune Kanichi, an editor of several civil war newsbooks in Edo, who brought out the *Kaichi shimpō* in Tokyo. Its contents, the prospectus declared, would include articles on Western knowledge, and "in order that its origins may be easily grasped even by women and children [a euphemism for "uneducated"], the paper will add illustrations so that the principles involved may be comprehended at a glance." These civilizing aims notwithstanding, the paper failed to attract readers and was so ephemeral that all we know of it is the date of the first issue. Other attempts to reach a reading public considered insufficiently literate involved the elimination of Chinese characters (*kanji*), or almost so, from the letterpress in favor of a syllabary (*kana*). Two such ventures were launched in Tokyo in 1873, but both soon failed.

The *Yomiuri shimbun*, founded in 1874, was the first successful newspaper intended for a popular reading public. Financed by a yarn merchant and edited by men of samurai descent, the paper set out to educate its readers in values consistent with the policy of change on which the government had embarked. Instead of trying to reach such a public through a newspaper written entirely in *kana*, the *Yomiuri* used characters with *furigana* (phonetic) readings added as part of a literary style considered dignified though not learned. Instead of long essays on political and social problems, the *Yomiuri* carried mainly human-interest stories. Thus the first issue (dated November 2, 1874) contained the following items: several stories on filial behavior; a report on a farmer's wife who, according to rumor, recovered the use of her paralyzed arms through faith in the *kami* (deities); the number of silkworm cards destroyed by fire in Yokohama; the number of passengers and the volume of freight carried from October 19 to 26 on the railway leaving Yokohama station, as well as the revenue earned; news about a fire in Nagasaki; and a story about forty-eight persons bitten by mad dogs near Kuwayama, this last

[32] Altman, "Shimbunshi" (fn. 14, above), pp. 61-62.

being a transparent advertisement for a nostrum recommended for such complaints.

But, in addition, the *Yomiuri shimbun* offered information about government. It adopted a novel method of publishing official decrees and announcements to ensure their being understood. Such news was presented in the formal Japanese in which government documents were written—but with *furigana* and with a brief commentary, explaining some of the more difficult abstractions as well as crucial words and phrases. The first issue carried a Home Ministry decree instructing the population to observe decorum and show respect to the emperor during his progress through the streets of Tokyo the following day. *Yomiuri*'s commentary explained the meaning of the Chinese compound for imperial progression, *gyōkō gyōkei*, and told the readers in simple language how to behave when the imperial carriage approached. Connected with the imperial visit, which fell on Tenchō setsu, there was an article explaining the background of the festival and its significance. This format, with differences of emphasis and style, was adopted by other popular newspapers. It did not, however, become frozen: such newspapers soon began adapting features of the elite press, such as editorials and discursive articles, to the presumed interests of a popular readership.

The pattern set by the popular press was taken over by the political parties as a way of packaging their message for a larger readership than could be reached through the elite papers. By the mid-1890s, the elite press, too, had adopted the pattern. The impetus for this revamping of the quality press came initially from declining circulation and from the financial difficulties that elite papers suffered in the 1880s. (These problems were the result of economic stringencies induced by government policy, on the one hand, and the dissolution of the political parties, which deprived newspapers of patrons, on the other.) Once underway, the changes were spurred on by the profits to be made from satisfying the hunger for news from the front during the Sino-Japanese War. One consequence of the war was the disappearance of the old distinction between the "superior" and "inferior" press: in different degrees and combinations, most newspapers now shared a common body of content. Historians of the Japanese press have labeled the newspapers of the post–Sino-Japanese War period *chūshimbun*—neither *ōshimbun* nor *koshimbun*, but something in between that was meant for all. In these newspapers, may we not see the precursor not only of today's much maligned "middle brow" Japanese press, but also of the evolving Japanese culture of the present?

By the 1890s, a small number of giant newspapers were already standing head and shoulders above their contemporaries, and clustered around them was a larger number of smaller enterprises, thus foreshadowing today's division into national, regional, and local newapapers. The press was privately owned and competitive, and considerable capital was now needed to launch and operate a newspaper. Western-style printing technology had helped change printing from a craft to an industry and had moved printing from the workshop to the factory. Western-style buildings now housed these printing plants, and a much larger staff of managers, editors, and reporters was needed. Moreover, modern communications equipment, such as the telegraph and the telephone, meant additional expenses. Changes such as these are usually summed up in phrases describing the press as having become "capitalistic" and newspapers as having become "items of commerce." Accompanying this transformation was a change in the character of newspaper writers. Whereas formerly they had for the most part been men of samurai descent, who regarded journalism as a steppingstone to a life in politics, now these writers increasingly looked to journalism as their livelihood.[33]

The Japanese press had undergone many changes in about a quarter of a century. Not the least of these was the fact that the press was now part of a larger complex of public communications in print that included magazines—one that would soon be joined by another element, film. It is probably no coincidence that these changes were occurring roughly in the same period when the modern sector of the economy had reached "takeoff." Indeed, the changes in the press were part of a much larger modernizing phenomenon. Moreover, a vigorous, often disputatious, press was at hand to supply information about these larger changes in Japanese society and to provide a platform for those with opinions to voice and a desire to influence others.

[33] Nishida, *Meiji jidai no shimbun to zasshi*, p. 152. Also stating that these new journalists received a more systematic education than their predecessors, Nishida gives us examples of this new type: Tokutomi Sohō, Miyake Setsurei, and Kuga Katsunan.

CHAPTER 10

SHIPPING: FROM SAIL TO STEAM*

BY WILLIAM D. WRAY

The most visible characteristic of the transition in the shipping industry was the collapse of traditional commercial agencies and the rise of new, large companies backed by the Meiji government. Examples of these large-scale organizations are Mitsubishi, formed in the early 1870s and originating in the Restoration struggle itself, the Ōsaka Shōsen Kaisha (OSK), formed in 1884, and the Nippon Yūsen Kaisha (NYK), the result of a 1885 merger between Mitsubishi's shipping assets and a government-sponsored firm, the Kyōdō Un'yu Kaisha (KUK), established in 1882. This transition was accomplished in a short time; by the mid-1880s, large firms with their growing fleets of steamships were dominant. Even so, many Tokugawa shipping enterprises not only survived the Restoration, but continued to use the traditional Japanese sailing ship (*wasen*) into the 1880s. Some of these enterprises transformed themselves into sizable local organizations, while others remained basically family firms, owning or operating only a few ships.

Commerce in the Tokugawa period operated in diverse environments: some hostile to change; others, reflecting the vitality and competitiveness of the traditional economy, supportive of it within the confines of a country largely closed to the outside world. The needs of the Meiji government provided an environment different from Tokugawa pluralism. Whereas the *bakufu* needed shipping for the transport of tax rice and for the maintenance of the interregional trade upon which the commercial agencies licensed by it had come to rely, the Meiji government's dependence on shipping was defined more by the international environment

* For assistance in preparing this chapter I would like to thank Akira Hayami, Kitahara Itoko, Nakagawa Keiichirō, and Uekusa Masu.

and by the need to strengthen the political order against potential external and internal danger. Specifically, a new shipping enterprise would have to provide transport in wartime, facilitate national integration, and compete with foreign companies whose earnings from Japanese freight exacerbated the balance-of-payments deficit of the 1870s.

These functions demanded a large organization. Their institutional effects can be illustrated by the case of Mitsubishi. Government backing enabled Mitsubishi to purchase steamships, and made possible the firm's rapid expansion into a national organization having branch offices in the major ports. It led to increasing complexity in Mitsubishi's administrative structure because of the need for rapid communication between the branches and the head office in Tokyo.[1] New shipping organizations (often backed by subsidies) developed strategies of either large-scale horizontal merger (e.g. OSK) or diversification, i.e. activity in several fields of business. This latter strategy was characteristic both of the early Mitsubishi and of smaller operators with longer histories. By contrast, shipping enterprises that failed to survive the transition had persisted in the specialized operations they had earlier followed.

Though Mitsubishi realized advantages, defined mostly by speed, distance, and regularity of transport, until the 1880s the actual composition of its freight remained similar to that carried by the smaller shipping enterprises, which still used *wasen*. They retained the *wasen* primarily because the cost of a large steamship capable of voyaging from Yokohama to Shanghai was roughly 250,000 yen in 1875, a figure that probably exceeded the assets of all but a few firms at the time. Even the older and smaller steamships, fit mostly for coastal service, cost over 50,000 yen in the late 1880s. Yet the steamship offered immense advantages. The *wasen* usually took anywhere from thirteen to twenty days, depending on the winds, to reach Edo from Osaka. The modern steamship could make the same trip in two or three days.[2] The long process of replacing the *wasen* with the steamship had as its middle stage a period, between the late 1870s and the late 1880s, when the Western-style sailing ship became the most popular alternative for those who still lacked the capital to buy steamships.

Behind the rise and fall of particular enterprises lay transformations in the organization of normal business transactions. The changing relations between the shipper and the shipowner (and/or operator) led to fundamentally new patterns by which the latter received income from

[1] William D. Wray, *Mitsubishi and the N.Y.K., 1870-1914: Business Strategy in the Japanese Shipping Industry* (Cambridge: Harvard University Press, 1984).

[2] Makino Ryūshin, *Kitamaesen no jidai* (Tokyo: Kyōikusha, 1979), p. 169; *Chūō ku shi*, 3 vols. (Tokyo: Chūō ku yakusho, 1958), vol. 3, pp. 417-420.

carrying freight. A large portion of shipping in the Tokugawa period was conducted by "private carriers," i.e. transporters who carried their own goods or who purchased the cargo they carried instead of levying freight charges (*kaizumi*). The "common carrier," by contrast, levied freight charges on goods carried for any and all shippers (*unchinzumi*). The role of steamships in producing greater uniformity in the prices of goods throughout Japan led most enterprises to abandon both the *wasen* and the private carriers, a change that facilitated national integration. While the opening of Japan in the early 1850s provides a convenient starting point for the transition, we can define what marks the end of the transition by way of a discussion of this connection between national integration and transport. It is possible, also, to relate the end of the transition to a fundamentally new role for the large Japanese firms: namely, the move toward transoceanic lines.

Commercial Organization and Competition

Tokugawa Shipping

Shipping had been organized around a few primary routes, each dominated by one or a few groups of ship operators. Formally set up in the 1670s, the Western Circuit became the most famous of Tokugawa routes. On this circuit ships traveled from northern Japan, along the Japan Sea coast, through the Straits of Shimonoseki and the Inland Sea, and finally to Osaka. This route replaced the faster but more expensive network of transporting northern produce overland to Osaka via the Japan Sea ports of Tsuruga and Obama. The second major route, the Eastern Circuit, from Hokuriku through the Tsugaru Straits and down the Pacific coast to Edo, developed more slowly because of navigational hazards and a paucity of return cargo from the Kantō (usually processed goods from Edo). Even though from central Hokuriku to Edo this second route was shorter, in the 1670s it cost 50 *momme* of silver to ship 100 *koku* of rice from Kaga domain to Edo along the Eastern Circuit, compared with 38 *momme* along the Western Circuit.[3]

Two large shipping organizations came to dominate the country's prin-

[3] Yasuoka Shigeaki, "Bakuhansei no shijō kōzō," *Iwanami kōza Nihon rekishi* (Tokyo: Iwanami shoten, 1975), *kindai* vol. 2, p. 253; Furuta Ryoichi and Hirai Yoshikazu, *A Short History of Japanese Merchant Shipping* (Tokyo: Tokyo News Service, 1967), pp. 58-107. On the cost disadvantages of the overland route, see Furuta Ryōichi, "Higashi mawari kaiun oyobi nishi mawari kaiun no kenkyū," in *Nihonkai kaiun shi no kenkyū* (Fukui: Fukui kenritsu toshokan, 1967), pp. 41-45, and Makino, *Kitamaesen no jidai*, pp. 43-44.

cipal route, that between Osaka and Edo. The first of these, the *higaki kaisen*, began in 1619, shipping cotton, oil, sake, raw cotton, vinegar, and other commodities to Edo and returning with dried sardines and fertilizers. Later in the century, the *higaki kaisen* came under control of the ten major trade associations. Frequent accidents with sake shipments on the *higaki* line led to the emergence of a second organization, the *taru kaisen*, which began in the 1640s as a specialist in sake shipments, operating faster and safer vessels. Since the sake brewers offered guaranteed shipments, the *taru* line could afford to diversify its cargo by quoting lower rates for commodities normally carried by the *higaki* line. Beginning around 1700, this led to a century and a half of competition in which the *taru kaisen* got the best of its rival.[4] This competition was restrained by a series of agreements designed to preserve the *higaki* line's shipments by allocating specific cargo to each line. The frequency of the trade associations' ordinances, however, attests to how easily the *taru* line was able to evade them. In the 1770s the *higaki* line operated 160 ships, compared with the *taru* line's 106. By 1808 the *higaki* figure was only 38 ships. Thereafter the *higaki* line did sustain a partial recovery, chartering ships from groups of shipowners who were pressured by the *bakufu* and trade associations to come to its aid; yet, expenses remained high and profits were slight.[5]

The earlier growth of these two lines had been a function of Edo's dependence on Osaka imports. In the nineteenth century both enterprises declined, partly because the development of the Kantō region reduced the need for shipments from Osaka. The *higaki* line, which lacked the *taru* line's cargo guarantee, was the more vulnerable to such changes in trade patterns. While the number of the latter's ships traveling from Osaka to Edo also declined, their cargo capacity was increasing.[6]

Offering a contrast to the *higaki* and *taru* lines were the *kitamaesen* ("ships from the north"). Operating on the Western Circuit, these ships carried rice, soybeans, marine products, fertilizers, lumber, and tobacco to the Kansai region and returned north with tea, cotton, salt, paper, and sugar. Generally, the *kitamaesen* owners had more capital, ran their

[4] Fukuo Takeichirō, "Higaki kaisen tokumi tonya omotedana gumi seiritsu no zentei," *Nihon rekishi*, no. 164 (February 1962), pp. 2-8; Tsugawa Masayuki, "Tokumi shotonya to higaki kaisen," *Keizai ronshū* (Kansai daigaku), vol. 16, nos. 4-5 (December 1966), pp. 109-131; Yunoki Manabu, *Kinsei kaiun shi no kenkyū* (Tokyo: Hōsei daigaku shuppankyoku, 1979), pp. 24-71, 80-84; Sasaki Seiji, *Nihon kaiun kyōsō shi josetsu* (Kobe: Kaiji kenkyūkai, 1954), pp. 1-31.

[5] Yunoki Manabu, "Higaki kaisen to taru kaisen," in Toyoda Takeshi and Kodama Kōta, eds., *Kōtsū shi*, vol. 24 of *Taikei Nihon shi sōsho* (Tokyo: Yamakawa shuppansha, 1970), pp. 274-276; Yunoki, *Kinsei kaiun shi*, pp. 3-4, 91-100.

[6] Sasaki, *Nihon kaiun kyōsō shi*, p. 28; Yunoki, *Kinsei kaiun shi*, pp. 125-127.

businesses individually rather than as part of an umbrella organization, exercised more autonomous management, and operated bigger ships (sometimes over 2,000 *koku*, compared with a *higaki*-line maximum of 1,800 *koku*).[7]

The most fundamental distinction between the *kitamaesen* and the *higaki* and *taru* lines has to do with how they earned income from freight. The *kitamaesen* generally did not levy freight charges. Instead, they actually bought the cargo (*kaizumi*) and transported it (not necessarily to a destination prearranged with a shipper) to a market that could bring them the highest price for their goods. By contrast, the *higaki* and *taru* lines received freight income based on the amount of goods they carried for their shippers (*unchinzumi*). They were generally not common carriers in the modern sense, however; for they were controlled by their shippers, who often owned the ships and set the freight rates. The *taru* line did have more flexibility; it was able to act as a genuine common carrier for the cargo it transported in addition to sake.[8]

The aforementioned ship sizes show that the *bakufu*-imposed limit of 500 *koku* had long since been ignored, and that impressive growth had occurred both in national totals and in individual enterprises. In 1872, the total national capacity for *wasen* came to 3.3 million *koku*, compared with roughly 30,000 gross tons for steamships (11 *koku* = 1 gross ton). In 1871, the Ōie family, a *kitamaesen* based in Kaga, possessed fifteen ships of more than 1,000 *koku*, while in the late 1850s, owners of at least fifty-one ships of more than 1,000 *koku* had operated out of Ishinomaki.[9] These sizes, impressive by Tokugawa standards, were minuscule when matched against the Western steamship; those plying Japanese routes in the 1860s were in the 1,500-to-2,000-ton range. Moreover, the *wasen* was slow, could not operate on a fixed schedule, and was more threatened by the numerous navigational hazards along the Japanese coast.

Despite these disadvantages, the *wasen* held its own on certain routes. In the relatively calm Inland Sea some fast sailing ships could travel from Shimonoseki to Osaka in three and a half days.[10] Actually the *wasen*'s

[7] Makino Ryūshin, *Kitamaesen* (Tokyo: Kashiwa shobō, 1972); Makino, *Kitamaesen no jidai*; Yunoki, *Kinsei kaiun shi*, pp. 20-21, 332ff.

[8] Yunoki, *Kinsei kaiun shi*, pp. 1-22, 217-245, 419-435.

[9] Miwa Ryōichi, "Suijō kōtsū," in Toyoda and Kodama, *Kōtsū shi*, p. 481; *Shimonoseki shi shi*, 3 vols. (Tokyo: Meicho shuppansha, 1973), vol. 2, pp. 251- 252; *Ishinomaki shi shi*, 3 vols. (Ishinomaki: Dō yakusho, 1956), vol. 2, pp. 156-157. Government statistics were usually kept in net tons (6 *koku* = 1 net ton), those of private companies in gross tons. I have used the latter here for the sake of consistency.

[10] *Shimonoseki shi shi*, vol. 2, p. 247.

reputation, by dint of Ishii Kenji's careful study of a *wasen* captain's meticulously kept diary, has recently experienced something of a rehabilitation. This diary covers eighteen years (1842-1860) in the life of a 900-*koku wasen* owned by the Matsumae domain. A tramp ship, the *Chōja Maru* did not operate on a fixed schedule and could thus take maximum advantage of the winds. Indeed, there were occasions when it averaged more than 4 knots over 200-mile stretches. (Few of Mitsubishi's steamers in the mid-1870s could exceed 10 knots.) The captain's exhaustive knowledge of climate and weather conditions enabled him to sail for 70 percent of his planned navigation time (that is, he had to stop for adverse conditions only 30 percent of the time) and to attain an average speed of 1.27 knots (including stops) over nine years. Ships like the *Chōja Maru* may well have been more effective at handling wind than the Western-style sailing ship, and they were unquestionably superior in confined or shallow ports.[11] In short, the *wasen* was well suited to certain parts of the Japanese coast, and in these areas even the steamship found it hard to dislodge. *Wasen* owners could thus continue to operate at a comparative advantage until acquiring sufficient capital for steamships. This course was chosen primarily by the *kitamaesen*.

More vulnerable to the shocks of the transition period were the ship operators on the major Osaka-Edo trunk line. Even before the opening of Japan, the Tempō reforms had disrupted this route. By abolishing the exclusive privileges of the trade associations, which enforced the cargo agreements between the *higaki* and *taru kaisen*, the reforms brought to an end the special allocation formulas. The resulting chaos led to major changes in the management of shipping, changes that affected the *higaki* line more adversely. The new situation confronting *higaki* as well as *taru* was that they had to negotiate "free contracts" with shippers and could no longer rely on the formerly exclusive relations with trade associations. Only the *taru* line retained its stamp as an organization, primarily because of longstanding ties to the sake brewers. However, the effect of the Tempō reforms was to increase the power of the brewers. First of all, without the protective buffer of agents (*tonya*), the free contract system strengthened shipper control by the brewers over the *taru kaisen* operators. Secondly, the brewers supplemented their role as shippers by purchasing more ships. By 1851, brewers in the area around Nada (the center of the sake industry) owned 80 percent of the ships operated by *taru kaisen*.[12]

Though functioning as owners, the sake brewers, who shipped only

[11] Ishii Kenji, "Kinsei kōki ni okeru kaisen no kōkai," in *Nihon kinsei kōtsū shi kenkyū* (Tokyo: Yoshikawa kōbunkan, 1979), pp. 463-466.

[12] Yunoki, *Kinsei kaiun shi*, pp. 91-130, 428; Sasaki, *Nihon kaiun kyōsō shi*, pp. 25-31.

one commodity, lacked the commitment to diversified shipping that would be needed to cope with the next major shock: namely, the opening of Japan in the 1850s and the rescinding of the seclusion edicts with respect to ship purchases. This led to the purchase of Western ships by the *bakufu* as well as the domains, and represented a major threat to the *wasen* even though these Western ships were operated primarily for military purposes prior to the Restoration. Finally, the arrival of foreign steamship companies, which soon opened lines between western Japan and Yokohama, undermined the *taru kaisen* and exposed a marked weakness in Japanese operations on the country's most important line. This situation called for an urgent response from the *bakufu*, and then from the new Meiji government, to promote a new commercial organization that could compete with the foreigners. The arrival of the steamship was one of the most immediate and serious of the technological challenges to Japanese organizations. The response to it shows how existing as well as new commercial organizations dealt with the problems of transition.

Early Meiji Government Policy

In the early 1870s the government could not afford the luxury of a gestation period during which the shipping industry might build a new "model" organization, as had been attempted with some industrial enterprises. Instead, it had to begin immediately with what was already at hand. Not surprisingly, therefore, initial government attempts to promote shipping enterprises were dismal failures. The very instability of the government militated against a consistent implementation of policy, for it frequently shifted jurisdiction over shipping from one bureau to another and moved the bureaus from one ministry to another.

Early policy went through two stages. The first was an attempt to amalgamate existing shipping agents and courier services, with some financial backing from Mitsui, into a semipublic company known as the Kaisō Kaisha (Marine Transportation Co.).[13] Organized in late 1869, this followed an immediate Tokugawa precedent, for in 1866 the *bakufu* had issued instructions to an organization of couriers to establish a regular Osaka-Edo line using steamships.[14] Instructions given to the Kaisō Kaisha, however, were much more detailed, amounting in fact to a book-

[13] Miyamoto Mataji, *Meiji zenki keizai shi no kenkyū* (Osaka: Seibundō, 1971), pp. 98-111; Saitō Yoshihisa, "Meiji shonen no kaiun seisaku," *Dōshisha shōgaku*, vol. 22, nos. 5-6 (March 1971), pp. 67-70.

[14] One of the most famous instructions given to the Kaisō Kaisha, that it transport "peasants, townsmen, and women and children" as well as samurai families, was also given to this courier service by the *bakufu* in 1866. *Chūō ku shi*, vol. 3, pp. 414-415.

let on how to operate a steamship: establish three classes for passengers, charge passengers for using blankets, have foreigners bring their own food (since they will not eat Japanese style), and other minutiae.[15] Nevertheless, the Kaisō Kaisha suffered from too many old ships in need of repair and from an unwieldy managerial structure in which a government superintendent exercised joint administration with the fifteen heads of the private agencies. Within a year, large debts to the *kawase kaisha* (exchange companies, or protobanks) forced its dissolution.

The second stage of policy involved larger investments by the major commercial houses (Mitsui, Ono, Shimada, and Kōnoike) in a government-sponsored firm, the Nippon Seifu Yūbin Jōkisen Kaisha (Japanese Government Mail Steamship Co., or YJK). In the YJK, managers of the leading commercial houses had replaced the agency heads dominant in the Kaisō Kaisha. But these managers knew even less about shipping and were still primarily committed to their own firms. The YJK thus remained a specialized service, run by outsiders, rather than becoming an independent company possessing an identity of its own. Even though the YJK inherited larger ships from the domains, inconsistent government financial policy would lead it to ruin.[16]

The YJK's original supporters had espoused lofty ideals, but vicissitudes of policy, uncoordinated management, and inadequate financing led to its downfall. The YJK reflected the "cooperative" philosophy of Shibusawa Eiichi, who together with Inoue Kaoru had supported the idea of a government-initiated shipping company operated by private firms acting in cooperation. Essentially, Shibusawa tried to graft an imported idea (the joint-stock company as a model for cooperation) onto existing organizations (the Tokugawa commercial agencies). Ōkubo Toshimichi, whose establishment of the Home Ministry in November 1873 marked the first major step toward government stability, rejected both the cooperative approach and the idea of a government-managed company. Such a firm, he feared, would produce monopolistic abuses that would hinder private shipowners. Yet, he also opposed competition, arguing that by driving down freight rates competition impeded the financial health of the shipping industry. His solution—high rates and government aid to a single private firm—implicitly countenanced a private monopoly.[17]

Iwasaki Yatarō's firm, Mitsubishi, to which Ōkubo extended his favor

[15] "Ōkurashō enkakushi," in Tsuchiya Takao and Ōuchi Hyōe, comps., *Meiji zenki zaisei keizai shiryō shūsei*, 21 vols. (Tokyo: Kaizōsha, 1931-1934), vol. 3, pp. 269-272.

[16] Wray, *Mitsubishi and the N.Y.K.*, pp. 33-42.

[17] *Ōkubo Toshimichi monjo*, 10 vols. (Tokyo: Nihon shiseki kyōkai, 1927-1929), vol. 6, pp. 353-359, 383-384.

in 1875, originated in the 1860s. The domain agency from which Mitsubishi emerged was more capable of a flexible institutional response than were the agencies that had long existed within the highly structured world of *bakufu*-regulated commerce. Benefiting from this flexibility, Iwasaki used his leadership skills to transform his Tosa agency into Mitsubishi between 1871 and 1875.

Domain Organization and Mitsubishi

The domain agencies of the 1860s were more concerned with profits than were specialized organizations such as the *taru* and *higaki* lines. Their purpose, after all, was to raise money for domain finances, industrial development, and military forces. In the 1860s several domains, particularly Fukui, Satsuma, Chōshū, Hizen, and Tosa, established trading offices in Nagasaki.

Tosa had the most explicitly commercial orientation of these domains. In 1866 it set up an industry promotion agency called the Kaiseikan, which exported such domain products as camphor, dried bonito, paper, whale oil, tea, and sugar, and imported ships and weapons. The diversified operations of the Kaiseikan, ranging from military imports to whaling, provided a precedent for a later multifunctional organization. Iwasaki gained influence in the agency's key bureau, which was concerned with freight and industrial promotion. Between 1867 and 1869, heavy expenditures by the Kaiseikan and changing government commercial policies set the stage for transformation of Iwasaki's bureau into a private firm. Tosa's attempt in early 1869 to prohibit private trading in a wide range of its commodities greatly expanded the role of the Kaiseikan. However, a central government edict of 1869, prohibiting the operation of commercial monopolies by domains, undermined the now debt-ridden Kaiseikan and gave support to a retrenchment policy already advocated by some domain officials. To overcome these financial problems, Tosa leaders asked Iwasaki to form a new agency that would retain ties to the domain but that would be nominally separate from it.

These discussions led to the establishment in 1870 of the Tsukumo Shōkai, which became independent the following year upon the abolition of the domains. Even before that, however, Iwasaki had won considerable autonomy for the firm by assuming responsibility for the domain's debt (more than 400,000 *ryō* was owed to just one American firm, Walsh, Hall & Co.). In return, he received various domain properties, principally ships. Finally, in 1873, having severed his official ties to the new Kōchi prefecture, Iwasaki changed the firm's name to Mitsubishi.[18]

[18] Hirao Michio, *Tosa han* (Tokyo: Yoshikawa kōbunkan, 1965), pp. 51-56, and *Tosa*

The process leading to the establishment of Mitsubishi highlights several contrasts between the Tosa agency and its successors, on the one hand, and the earlier Tokugawa shipping organizations, on the other. Generally, the Tosa agency operated more as a multifunctional enterprise and differentiated among these functions in its organizational structure. Its management, at least after 1870, was more autonomous. Between 1870 and 1873 it rapidly transformed itself from a private carrier for the domain into a common carrier. Finally, it raised its own capital through Iwasaki's currency speculation and adroit use of foreign loans, which he repaid partly by selling distribution rights to the agency's camphor. Also, when the domains were abolished in 1871 and the central government incurred their debt, the Finance Ministry seems to have paid off at least some of Iwasaki's debt, previously assumed from the domain.[19] The diversified operations of the Kaiseikan and newly acquired copper mines also buttressed shipping operations, which had become the firm's main function.

The Impact of Subsidies and Foreign Competition

As Mitsubishi emerged as a common carrier it enjoyed increasing success in competition with the YJK, particularly in 1873. Its principal gain, however, came during the Taiwan expedition in 1874. After unsuccessful attempts to persuade foreigners to undertake military transport for the expedition, the government offered a transport contract to the YJK. Fearing loss of its domestic business to Mitsubishi if it became involved in military transport, the YJK refused this government request.[20] When Mitsubishi won the contract and successfully performed its "duties," the YJK quickly fell from official favor. The government then entrusted Mitsubishi with the large steamships (thirteen in all) that had been purchased, both for the expedition and for commercial purposes, later in 1874. Finally, in 1875, the government transferred formal ownership of these vessels to Mitsubishi on easy terms and began subsidizing it at an annual rate of 250,000 yen.

Thus began a new period of institutional change for Mitsubishi. The subsidy acted as a vehicle through which the Meiji government could shape Mitsubishi's organization. Throughout the subsidy negotiations of

---

han shōgyō keizai shi (Kōchi: Kōchi shiritsu shimin toshokan, 1960), pp. 222-230; Ōta Shūme, "Bakumatsu no Nagasaki to Iwasaki Yatarō," *Nagasaki dansō*, no. 44 (February 25, 1966), pp. 1-26; Nagasawa Yasuaki, "Iwasaki Yatarō to Mitsubishi no hasshō," in Miyamoto Mataji, ed., *Kamigata no kenkyū*, 5 vols. (Osaka: Seibundō, 1976), vol. 4, pp. 223-248; *Iwasaki Yatarō den*, 2 vols. (Tokyo: Denki hensankai, 1967).

[19] *Iwasaki Yatarō den*, vol. 2, pp. 680-681.

[20] Ibid., pp. 102-105.

mid-1875, Mitsubishi consulted closely with government officials as it implemented a major administrative reform that delineated the functions of the company's various departments. Also, the financial reports made necessary by the subsidy led to Mitsubishi's rapid adoption of Western accounting techniques. Mitsubishi had a good reputation among foreign businessmen and journalists for accepting Western practices, and many of its specific reforms benefited from consultants like A.R. Brown, a former navigator for the P & O (Peninsular & Oriental S.N. Co.) and adviser to the Japanese government. Clearly, Western influence on Mitsubishi derived not just from public initiative, but also from Iwasaki's careful channeling of outside advice to strengthen his own firm and enhance its autonomy. Iwasaki's rhetoric of one-man leadership had a dictatorial ring, but he was possibly the most effective businessman in early Meiji at recruiting skilled managers with a knowledge of English and at giving them specific administrative responsibilities—as department heads to oversee reform, as managers of subsidiary enterprises, and as branch office heads. The flow of information from the West therefore came not just from the top, but also through the middle echelons of the firm.

Foreign shipping companies operating in Japanese waters were also a crucial factor in the shaping of Japanese institutions throughout the two decades of transition from the 1850s to the 1870s. They quickened the decline of the Tokugawa shipping organizations, precluded profitable operations by the government-initiated firms of the early 1870s, and contributed to Iwasaki's sense of urgency during Mitsubishi's first decade.

Western companies carried virtually all of Japan's foreign trade between the late 1850s and the mid-1870s. However, since Japanese competition on transoceanic routes was still years away, the West's most immediate impact came in the coastal trade. The foreign share of the coastal trade, though not yet dominant, had reached alarming proportions by the Restoration. To take one example, though only eighteen foreign steamers entered the port of Niigata in 1869 (compared with 2,869 *wasen*), on a value basis they accounted for 26 percent of Niigata's imports from other Japanese ports. During the same year they also carried one-quarter of Niigata's rice shipments.[21]

The government had subsidized Mitsubishi in large part to meet this foreign threat, which had intensified by 1875. In the mid-1870s, Mitsubishi engaged in two decisive confrontations in coastal waters and on the Yokohama-Shanghai line it had opened in January 1875. Mitsubishi won on both occasions, first against the American Pacific Mail, in 1875,

[21] Yamaguchi Kazuo, "Meiji shoki no gaikoku kaiun to Mitsubishi Kaisha," in *Sekai keizai bunseki* (Tokyo: Iwanami shoten, 1962), pp. 124-125.

and then against the P & O in 1876. The latter competition especially led to further innovations in Mitsubishi's business organization.

Mitsubishi's tactics in the mid-1870s involved cutting out the middleman, i.e. the shipping agent, and dealing directly with the producer, i.e. the shipper. These tactics threatened such traditional organizations as the Nine Shop Union (*kutana*), which was formed in 1846 to bring order to shipments in the aftermath of the Tempō reforms and which was also the controlling force behind the *higaki kaisen*. In one of the more extraordinary alliances of early Meiji, the conservative Nine Shop Union agreed with the P & O to refuse to forward shipments to the government-backed Mitsubishi. This alliance recalls a principal argument against opening Japan in the 1850s. As one memorial to the *bakufu* had remarked, "All merchants are led astray by profits. . . . In a crisis, we cannot predict what they might not do in league with the enemy."[22] In response, Mitsubishi received government aid to establish an Exchange Bureau to finance shippers. This facilitated Mitsubishi's move into new business ventures, provided organizational support for the shipping enterprise, and decisively contributed to Mitsubishi's acquisition of a monopoly in certain coastal routes by 1880.

External forces—government guidance and foreign competition—provided the main impetus for Mitsubishi's organizational change in the mid-1870s. By the late 1870s, however, monopoly profits, an influx of funds from service in the Satsuma Rebellion, and the large subsidy gave Mitsubishi the financial wherewithal to adopt a more autonomous strategy. Thereafter, Mitsubishi's organization was shaped primarily by the firm's own business strategy. This fact had an enormous impact on the structure of the shipping industry, for Mitsubishi was using its funds to buy mines rather than ships. This investment strategy made Mitsubishi a more diversified firm, no longer dependent on shipping for its survival. It also prompted a degree of administrative decentralization in which subsidiary enterprises like the Exchange Office (upgraded from bureau status in 1880) and the mines (see Figure 10.1) kept their own accounts and gained some decision-making autonomy, within the bounds of capital allocations specified by the head office.[23] Finally, it led to government intervention and a reorganization of the industry, culminating in the formation of the NYK in 1885.

Government intervention, prompted by increased concern over deteriorating shipping services, national security, and military strategy, brought about closer supervision of Mitsubishi and the establishment of

[22] Maruyama Masao, *Studies in the Intellectual History of Tokugawa Japan* (Tokyo: Tokyo University Press, 1974), pp. 338-339.

[23] Wray, *Mitsubishi and the N.Y.K.*, pp. 108-122.

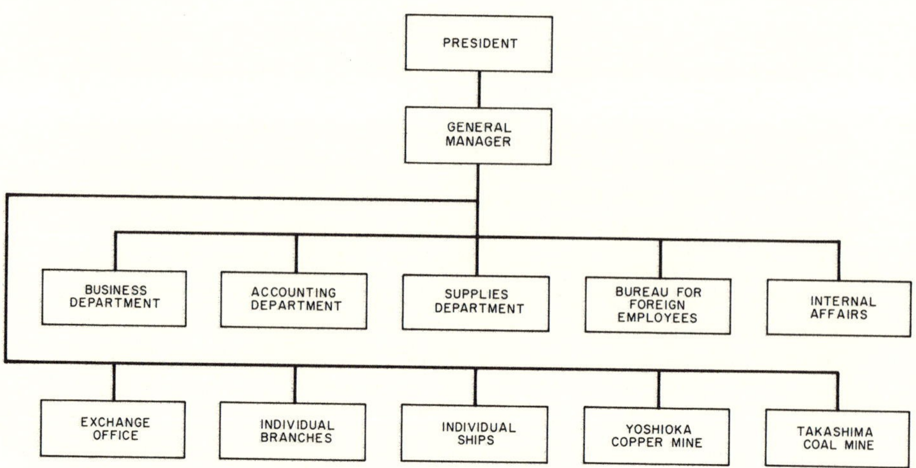

Figure 10.1. Mitsubishi Administrative Structure, 1882
Adapted from Nagasawa Yasuaki, "Shoki Mitsubishi no keiei soshiki—kaiungyō o chūshin ni shite," *Keiei shigaku*, vol. 11, no. 3 (March 1977), p. 35.

the Kyōdō Un'yu Kaisha in 1882. Despite Mitsubishi's obligation to provide transports for military emergencies and the benefits accruing to it from such services, the early government directives to the company contained remarkably little about military matters. By contrast, the KUK was regarded as virtually a naval agency. The first six of the seventeen articles in its directive dealt with the navy, which was also the nominal owner of the company's ships.[24] The KUK, however, was a short-lived exception in the industry. When it became part of the NYK in 1885 the obligations remained, but without the legal ties to the navy. In general, the military had an undeniably strong influence on shipping in that its needs provided one of the chief motivations for subsidizing the industry. The military impetus for the building of telegraphs also facilitated the expansion of Mitsubishi's administrative domain. Yet the military still had little direct impact on the internal organization of shipping companies.

Some Long-Term Trends

Another military-related issue, the buildup of Western-style sailing ships and steamships during the *bakumatsu*, has left the impression of discon-

[24] *Shibusawa Eiichi denki shiryō*, 56 vols. (Tokyo: Ryūmonsha, 1957-58), vol. 8, pp. 49-50.

tinuity, of sudden new developments, in the shipping industry. Nevertheless these ships had a rather ambiguous legacy for commercial shipping. Expensive to run and often in need of repairs, they undermined the finances of early companies and were often the first to be sold or wrecked. Their main positive contribution lay in the managerial experience they offered Iwasaki prior to his acquisition of larger steamships during the Taiwan expedition. Generally, an accurate picture of the transition is best achieved not by focusing on the discontinuity represented by these ships, but rather by examining the continuing strategies of firms with respect to three issues: the type of ship normally employed; the routes on which they operated; and the business functions the firms performed.

Taru Kaisen

Until the early 1870s the *taru kaisen* continued to use only *wasen* on its sole route, the Osaka-Edo line. The tenacity with which it clung to its specialized tradition as an operator but not shipowner explains the *taru* line's demise as an organization in early Meiji. Despite the shocks of the *bakumatsu*, it had at least retained its sake shipments. But in 1871, when rumors circulated that sake shippers were about to switch to steamships, this line had to plead with the shippers' union to keep its allegiance. Of the twelve major shippers in the union, four agreed to the request, but only because there were still not enough steamships to handle all the sake shipments. This compromise soon broke down, for in the summer of 1871 the *taru* line lost 3,000 barrels of sake in two major accidents at sea (the premodern version of the oil spill). Later in the decade, it enjoyed a very brief recovery when the steamships carrying sake were requisitioned for the Satsuma Rebellion. Soon thereafter, though, the shippers adopted Western-style sailing ships which overwhelmed the *wasen*. Then, in the early 1880s, in order to ward off competition from other companies, Mitsubishi offered the sake shippers rebates and won an exclusive contract. By that time, the *taru* line had ceased to exist as a separate organization.[25]

In the late 1870s some of *taru*'s individual members had made the switch to Western-style sailing ships. Generally, however, they did not take the next step of adopting the steamship; thus, few became prominent in the later shipping industry. An important exception was a group led by the Tatsuuma family of Nishinomiya, which set up a company in 1887 to try to recapture some of the sake transport then dominated by the NYK. Tatsuuma himself was a sake brewer with close capital ties to some

[25] *Chūō ku shi*, vol. 3, pp. 417-420. At their peak capacity of 1,800 *koku*, the *taru* ships could carry 3,000 barrels of sake. Yunoki, *Kinsei kaiun shi*, p. 126.

members of the *taru kaisen*. These special ties, which blurred somewhat the usual distinction between shipper and operator, constitute the key variable between the Tatsuuma experience and that of most *taru kaisen* operators.[26]

Kitamaesen

In contrast to *taru*, the *kitamaesen* were less hampered by structural constraints and thus were able to survive the Restoration. During the Tokugawa period, the *kitamaesen* had been shipowners as well as operators, and using the Western Circuit they had more flexibility, plying the many subroutes of the circuit around the Inland Sea and Kyūshū. Most important, they engaged not only in shipping, but in such business ventures as warehousing, trading, and agency activity. Some have considered the *kitamaesen* simply as Hokuriku regional firms and have seen them as modernizers of the industry, owing to their shift in the 1880s from private to common carriership and from *wasen* to steamship (after a limited adoption of Western-style sailing ships in the late 1870s).[27] By contrast, Yunoki Manabu, who favors a more inclusive definition of *kitamaesen*, sees this stress on the modernization of the Hokuriku shipowners as unrepresentative of the experience of many *kitamaesen* during the Tokugawa-Meiji transition. Many, he argues, actually withdrew from shipping before going beyond the *wasen* stage and then settled permanently in the major ports between Osaka and Hokkaido. There they used their shipping-acquired capital to make substantial contributions to the local economy—acting as commercial agents, financing new business ventures, and investing in land.[28]

The very variety of *kitamaesen* suggests that they evolved in different periods. The best known, though, seem to have gone through the following stages. Among those who began as boatmen on ships of the Ōmi merchants, some had become prosperous enough by the late eighteenth century to begin chartering out ships to those merchants, who had declined in influence with the decreasing use of the overland route to Osaka via Tsuruga. By the nineteenth century, *kitamaesen* had established ties with the Osaka market, and during the *bakumatsu* many, especially those from Hokuriku, moved from employment as junk masters for Osaka shipowners to full independence as *kitamaesen* owners. Their rapid in-

[26] Matsumoto Ichirō, "Tatsuuma kaiun 150 nen keiei shi," *Kaiji kōtsū kenkyū*, vol. 8 (1972), pp. 9-79; Yunoki, *Kinsei kaiun shi*, p. 11. Tatsuuma is a predecessor of today's Yamashita-Shinnihon, one of Japan's top six shipping firms.

[27] Sasaki Seiji, *Nihon kaiungyō no kindaika* (Kobe: Kaibundo, 1961), pp. 165-221.

[28] Yunoki, *Kinsei kaiun shi*, pp. 354-358, 373-378, 420-430.

crease as *kaizumi* operators may also have been facilitated by the declining regulatory power of some domains. Finally, by the early Meiji period a few, such as Hiroumi Nisaburō, the most famous of the Hokuriku "Big Five," had moved their base of operations to Osaka.[29]

Those who became prominent in the shipping industry during the Meiji period followed two courses of action. First, many remained independent family firms and continued their diversified business enterprises, the profits from which enabled them to buy steamships in the late 1880s. By the end of the century, however, some of these firms had retreated from ship operation to ownership.[30] Secondly, the 1880s saw a move toward horizontal merger among some *kitamaesen*. For example, in 1881 some of the leading Hokuriku *kitamaesen* formed the Etchū Sailing Ship Company. The following year, this firm joined the KUK, established through an alliance between the government, large trading firms like Mitsui, and small local shipowners.[31]

The abandonment of *wasen* by major ship operators came in two stages. In the late 1870s, first of all, sailing ships fell in price as many Western companies sold them off while converting to steam, thus enabling Japanese to buy. Then, in the 1880s, the fierce steamship competition within Japan drove freight rates down so far that the *wasen* no longer enjoyed such a comparative advantage. In 1885 the government tried to speed up the shift away from *wasen* by prohibiting construction of vessels larger than 500 *koku*. The growth of smaller owners, however, kept the national capacity of *wasen* at around 3 million *koku* through the end of the century.[32]

The staying power of the *wasen* is attributable to the continued use of sea transport for bulk cargo and to the role of *kaizumi* operators, which used *wasen*. A good example of this is the *noma kaisen*, a shipping agency based in Owari, near Nagoya, which had acted as a *kaizumi* operator on the Osaka-Edo route since the 1790s. *Noma kaisen* specialized in bulk cargo, such as salt and rice. Essentially it was a speculator, often making 30 to 40 percent profit in early Meiji on the purchase, transport, and sale of salt. Rice, because its price did not vary as much, generated profits under 10 percent. By the 1890s, however, the increasing

[29] Ibid., pp. 21, 418.

[30] Nakagawa Keiichirō, *Ryōtaisenkan no Nihon kaiun*, vol. 1 of *Nihon kaiun keiei shi* (Tokyo: Nihon keizai shimbunsha, 1980), pp. 47-53, 67-68.

[31] Kaji Teruyoshi, "Kyōdō Un'yu Kaisha no setsuritsu," *Kaiun keizai kenkyū*, no. 8 (1974), pp. 14-15; *Fushiki-kōshi* (Takaoka: Fushiki-kō kaiun shinkōkai, 1973), pp. 223-255; Takase Tamotsu, *Kaga han kaiun shi no kenkyū* (Tokyo: Yūzankaku, 1979), pp. 518-525.

[32] *Shimonoseki shi shi*, vol. 2, pp. 743-745; Makino, *Kitamaesen no jidai*, pp. 59-60.

transport of salt by steamship and the dissemination of market information by telegraph had brought greater price uniformity, thereby lessening speculative opportunities. In 1891, the *noma kaisen* split into two groups, each of which incorporated itself. One became successful as a common carrier using steamships. The other, retaining the *noma* name and the tradition of carrying its own cargo in *wasen*, went bankrupt within ten years.[33]

Ports, Regional Transport, and National Integration

The *wasen* continued to play a major role during the 1870s. For one thing, new port development occurred mainly along the arterial Osaka-Tokyo route, thus leaving the *wasen* free to dominate shorter, connecting routes (especially in western Japan) and to maintain their influence in many outlying areas. In early Meiji, expansion of the ports of Kobe (previously Hyōgo), near Osaka, and Yokohama, near Tokyo, were the two most important developments. These became Japan's chief international ports. But this expansion did not dramatically alter the structure of the domestic trade routes. Kobe continued to be the center of the intense *wasen* traffic of the Inland Sea. Nevertheless, some new trading patterns did emerge along the Western Circuit.

Chōshū was one domain whose ports underwent change between the *bakumatsu* and early Meiji. Chōshū benefited from the *kitamaesen* traffic on the Western Circuit. Some idea of the extent of this traffic can be seen from the fact that in 1857, 60 percent of the marine products exported from Hokkaidō were shipped down the Japan Sea coast as far as Shimonoseki and beyond to Kansai.[34] This is just one example of the trade that provided business opportunities for Chōshū's warehouse lending agency (*koshinigata*). *Kitamaesen* stopped not only at Shimonoseki, but also at smaller Chōshū ports on the Inland Sea. When the domain expanded the *koshinigata* in the 1840s, it set up branch offices in these ports and made loans to ship operators, using their freight as collateral.[35]

The fact that the *kitamaesen* purchased the goods they carried gave

[33] Suenaga Kuninori, "Kinsei kōki ni okeru shio no ryūtsū to kaisen shōgyō katsudō" and "Meijiki zairai kaiungyō no suii," *Keizaigaku ronsō* (Dōshisha), vol. 20, no. 6 (January 1973), pp. 1-40, and vol. 21, nos. 1-2 (May 1973), pp. 1-38; Murase Masayuki, "Bishū-Sanshū ni okeru Meiji zenki no kaiungyō," *Kaiji shi kenkyū*, no. 30 (April 1978), pp. 1-14; Murase Masayuki, *Kinsei Ise wan kaiun shi no kenkyū* (Tokyo: Hōsei daigaku shuppankyoku, 1980).

[34] Makino, *Kitamaesen*, p. 135.

[35] Kobayashi Shigeru, "Nishi mawari kōro to Chōshū han," in Fukuo Takeichirō, ed., *Naikai sangyō to suiun no shiteki kenkyū* (Tokyo: Yoshikawa kōbunkan, 1966), pp. 163-165.

them the freedom to utilize their freight for their own purposes, and facilitated business dealings with Chōshū's *koshinigata*. If they had been common carriers, probably a larger portion of their freight would have been transported under contract with a shipper to customers in Kansai. This would have meant fewer stops in Chōshū ports and fewer deals with the *koshinigata*. As it was, although some of the new shipping companies established branch offices in Shimonoseki, *kitamaesen* calls at Chōshū ports dropped off precipitously in the mid-1870s as more northern cargo was shipped direct to Kansai.[36] This change probably resulted from the introduction of Western ships and the beginnings of common-carrier-style operations.

In areas of the country where steamships could have made major changes in trade routes, port planning and development proceeded slowly. For example, Ishinomaki in Tōhoku had become a major regional port in the Tokugawa period. Its importance grew after the opening of Japan, as an increasing amount of Sendai exports flowed through Ishinomaki. Even in the *bakumatsu*, however, the navigational problems of sailing north along the Pacific coast prevented Sendai from becoming a big import center. Instead, most Sendai-bound goods were shipped from Kansai through the Straits of Shimonoseki to Sakata, and then carried overland to Sendai. Though there were some direct shipments from Edo to Ishinomaki, these would have increased through greater use of steamships.[37] However, Ishinomaki was not designated as a major port in the 1870s because the Kitakawa River caused too much silting in the harbor. Instead, the government chose Nobiru, just west of Ishinomaki, as the site for a major Tōhoku port. With support from Ōkubo, construction began in 1878 only to be halted in the 1880s (after an expenditure of 678,000 yen) because of technical errors and a feeling that rapid development of the region was unlikely even with government investment in a port.[38]

There were two prerequisites besides regional development for the extension of steamship services and the replacement of *wasen*. These were the upgrading of ports and the building of railways to connect inland centers to those ports. Work on these projects, however, was delayed until the late 1880s and early 1890s. Consequently, as Table 10.1 shows, steamship ownership in 1887 was still overwhelmingly concentrated in Tokyo and Osaka. Tokyo's monopoly of large ships reflects

[36] Ibid., p. 195; *Shimonoseki shi shi*, vol. 2, pp. 246, 273.

[37] *Ishinomaki shi shi*, vol. 2, pp. 144-145; *Miyagi ken shi*, 34 vols. (Sendai: Miyagi ken kankōkai, 1960), vol. 5, pp. 623-624.

[38] *Miyagi ken shi*, vol. 5, pp. 624-627; Teratani Takeaki, *Nihon kōwan shiron josetsu* (Tokyo: Jichōsha, 1972), pp. 17-42.

the dominance of the NYK. If we eliminate from Table 10.1 the figures for Shiga (whose ships were lake vessels), Tokyo and Osaka possessed 51 percent of the small steamships. The figures for Kanagawa and Hyōgo are low because major port construction, even on the international ports of Yokohama and Kobe, did not begin until the 1880s and because the most frequent users of these ports were registered in Tokyo and Osaka.[39] Nevertheless, the figures in Table 10.1 were compiled on the eve of the shift to steamships by many *kitamaesen*. This switch had a profound effect on concentration levels in the industry. Between 1887 and 1894, the combined share of national steamship tonnage held by the NYK and OSK fell rapidly from 72 to 40 percent.[40] Reflecting the continuing vitality of the *kitamaesen* tradition, Kansai and Hokuriku were the main beneficiaries of the dispersal of new tonnage.

Construction of regional ports, which proceeded slowly, was funded not only by direct government expenditures, but also by development banks and shipping companies. Before World War I, for example, the NYK had more than a million yen invested in port projects at Osaka, Nagasaki, Hakodate, and Otaru. With regard to railways, during the 1880s Mitsubishi and the NYK developed a strategy of "service integration." Mitsubishi, in addition to its holdings in the NYK, became Japan's second largest stockholder in railway companies. An NYK president explained Mitsubishi's motivation as follows: "Land transport and shipping are like the two wheels of the same vehicle. . . . We can say for sure that if overland rail traffic becomes heavy, it will give rise to prosperous trade in regions which until now have not had means of transport, and these regions will quickly be able to transport their products overland to the ports. As a result, railways will lead to more and more traffic on sea routes and bring increasing vigor to maritime enterprises."[41]

Railways, however, had a dual effect on shipping. They helped when they connected inaccessible inland centers to ports, but they hurt when they ran parallel to the major Yokohama-Kobe line. This development of trunk railway lines cut deeply into the profits from coastal trade and forced large steamship companies to look overseas for future prospects. Their place in the local sea lanes was gradually taken by the small shipowners, many of them former *kitamaesen*, who could compete with the railways by offering tramp services. By changing the role of the large

[39] Teratani Takeaki, "Yokohama chikkō no keiei," *Keiei shigaku*, vol. 10, no. 3 (March 1976), pp. 22-41.

[40] These figures were compiled from statistics that exclude steamships under 20 gross tons. See Wray, *Mitsubishi and the N.Y.K.*, tables 41 and 49.

[41] NYK kabunushi sōkai gijiroku, December 15, 1887 (NYK Archives, NYK Legal Department).

TABLE 10.1
Regional Distribution of Steamships, by Prefecture, June 1887

Region	Prefecture	Number of Ships	
		Over 500 HP	Under 500 HP
Hokkaidō		1	10
Tōhoku	Iwate	0	3
	Miyagi	0	7
	Fukushima	0	2
Kantō	Ibaraki	0	4
	Chiba	1	14
	Tokyo	51	91
	Kanagawa	3	9
Chūbu	Niigata	3	22
	Toyama	1	2
	Ishikawa	1	3
	Fukui	0	2
	Shizuoka	1	10
	Aichi	0	4
Kinki	Shiga	1	29
	Mie	0	6
	Wakayama	0	2
	Kyoto	0	6
	Osaka	6	83
	Hyōgo	0	5
Shikoku	Kōchi	0	3
	Ehime	0	3
Chūgoku	Shimane	0	5
	Okayama	0	1
	Hiroshima	0	2
	Yamaguchi	0	8
Kyūshū	Fukuoka	0	2
	Ōita	0	1
	Kumamoto	0	2
	Kagoshima	1	6
	Saga	0	1
	Nagasaki	4	20
Okinawa		1	1
TOTALS		75	369

SOURCE: Rikugunshō sōmukyoku dai ikka, ed., *Chōhatsu bukken ichiranhyō, 1887* (Tokyo: Yanagihara shoten, 1979), pp. 21-32.

NOTE: Omitted from this table are prefectures that had no steamships.

steamship companies, the establishment of a better integrated national transport network brings to an end the transition period.

Conclusion

The Meiji government, for reasons of economic and military security, urgently needed a large shipping enterprise. Prerequisites included technical skill in steamship operation, expertise in business management and administrative organization, the flexibility to adopt Western practices, and the capacity to undertake common-carrier transport. For various reasons, enterprises formerly tied to the *bakufu* commercial order failed to meet these standards. The old Tokugawa agencies on which the early Meiji government tried to impose a cooperative order were incapable of delivering the streamlined management required to perform new functions. Mitsubishi emerged as the new strategic enterprise. The original spur to the organizational innovation of its predecessor came from the Tosa domain's concern with strengthening itself financially and militarily, a concern analogous to that of the Meiji government.

Continuity can be seen in attributes that Mitsubishi shared with the *kitamaesen*: namely, managerial autonomy and diversified business. Yet the *kitamaesen* never became candidates for government aid. Why? A first, and perhaps sufficient, reason was that *kitamaesen* generally came from domains not affiliated with Restoration forces, and thus lacked political ties to the new Meiji government. Second, though they were diversified in function, organizationally the *kitamaesen* remained small, like family firms. They lacked the bureaucratic structure of the Tosa agency which, with its administrative divisions and branches, proved more transformable into a national organization. Third, the Tosa agency was still too young to have more than a very limited range of commercial transactions and business clients. As such, its existing business ties did not get in the way of organizational change. The *kitamaesen*, by contrast, though free of the constraints imposed on groups like the *taru kaisen*, had deep roots within the most vibrant sector of the traditional economy. Their diversified operations afforded them the flexibility to shift assets from one field to another—thereby avoiding risk, exploiting the most profitable opportunities available, and remaining free from the need to perform a standard set of functions. This strategy, though effective for survival—and for continued prosperity—in the 1880s, did not lend itself to large-scale organization in the shipping industry of the early 1870s. The *kitamaesen* carried "their own goods" because they had purchased them, not because they had some connection with their production. They bought cargo not to "deliver" it, but rather to "sell" it where the market was good. In this sense, as Yunoki Manabu suggests, the *kitamaesen* were not primarily shipping firms, simply because their shipping was collateral to their overall trading activity.[42] The decline in such speculative transport is relevant to the transition because of the way that national integration (aided by the more uniform prices made possible by the telegraph and rapid steamship service) rendered *kaizumi*-style operations unprofitable.[43]

The business of distributing, handling, insuring, and storing goods was a much more developed and differentiated process in the area between Edo and, say, Okayama than it was along the Japan Sea coast.[44] The shipping enterprises on the Osaka-Edo route, then, tended to become specialized, whereas on the Japan Sea coast the shipowner found it necessary to perform all these functions himself. In contrast to the flexibility of the *kitamaesen*, shipping on the Osaka-Edo route was characterized by shipper dominance. *Taru* and, particularly, *higaki* lines were not genuine common carriers because their dealings were restricted by, and often confined to, the associations that controlled them. How did Mitsubishi respond to these Tokugawa shipping practices? Iwasaki's attack on the Nine Shop Union, which had allied with the P & O and which formerly had controlled *higaki*, is instructive. His criticism of the union for what he called two hundred years of backward customs equated morality with freedom from shipper control. As Mitsubishi grew stronger during the latter half of the 1870s, it tried to break up the specialized, differentiated trading practices of the previous era. It then began to perform many of these functions itself. Mitsubishi's tactics facilitated national integration through overall coordination and more rapid distribution. By operating as a common carrier, with steamships and on a national scale, Mitsubishi both contributed to and benefited from the decline in the power of shippers during early Meiji. That decline was also the result of more general upheavals in the economy. By the 1880s, on the other hand, as the economy grew, larger trading firms and national industrial associations began to form more powerful shippers' groups.

[42] Yunoki, *Kinsei kaiun shi*, p. 217. I have commented on the possible connection between the *kitamaesen* and early trading companies like Mitsui in "NYK and the Commercial Diplomacy of the Far Eastern Freight Conference, 1896-1956," in Yui Tsunehiko and Nakagawa Keiichirō, eds., *Business History of Shipping: Strategy and Structure* (Tokyo: Tokyo University Press, 1985), pp. 279-311.

[43] Note Imazu Kenji's comment that "Japan is probably the only nation to have had a complete telecommunications network at the start of industrialization." "Modern Technology and Japanese Electrical Engineers," in Okochi Akio and Uchida Hoshimi, eds., *Development and Diffusion of Technology* (Tokyo: Tokyo University Press, 1980), p. 127.

[44] Yunoki, *Kinsei kaiun shi*, pp. 217, 219.

Interestingly, local shipping enterprises, many of them former *kitamaesen*, aligned themselves with these shippers' groups to challenge Mitsubishi's monopoly. The constant interaction during early Meiji between the large organizations and the small firms suggests a symbiotic relationship. For instance, though their organization and ships differed, during the 1870s they carried much the same freight. There were even some financial ties, most notable in the case of the Hiroumi Nisaburō firm (the former *kitamaesen*), which later became one of the largest stockholders in the OSK.[45] Falling freight rates, moreover, caused by competition among steamship companies, was a factor in the shift from *wasen* to steamship. And, in the late 1880s, the small firms provided a market for older steamships that the large firms, in order to consolidate their finances in the wake of mergers, wished to sell. To cite just one case: in 1889 the Toyama-based Baba Steamships, one of the former Big Five Hokuriku *kitamaesen*, purchased a twenty-year-old vessel from the NYK and began rallying other shipowners to protect themselves against NYK dominance.[46] Steamship purchases like this enabled the smaller firms to expand their tramp services, functions which differed from the liner operations offered by the large firms but which, in many parts of Japan, eventually made the small enterprises competitive with the large ones. Like the large enterprises, the small ones were also switching to modern (albeit old) steamships and were revamping their organizational structure in response to new market opportunities. In this way, within a span of barely two decades, numerous commercial organizations in Japan, earlier threatened by foreign competition, recovered much of their influence in domestic markets, even though they received little or no government aid.

[45] *Ōsaka Shōsen Kabushiki Kaisha 50-nen shi* (Osaka: ŌSKK, 1934), pp. 487-489.
[46] Takase, *Kaga han*, p. 523.

PART THREE

CITIES AND POPULATION

INTRODUCTION TO PART THREE

BY GILBERT ROZMAN

In recent decades, social scientists have been groping for a term to apply to changes that precede modern economic growth and help make it possible. They have proposed such labels as "sprouts of capitalism," "preconditions of modernization," and "proto-industrialization." Whatever the choice of terminology, specialists have increasingly drawn attention to four concerns that figure importantly in the chapters that follow: 1) the use of statistical records; 2) the examination of local and regional variations; 3) the differentiation of short-term and long-term fluctuations; and 4) the investigation of decision making at the household level, as reflected in aggregate data. Two of the central fields in the social science literature that bring together these four concerns are demography and urban studies. Those who seek to apply these fields to historical periods have developed measures for analyzing population growth and urbanization. Drawing on statistical data that show variations across space and over time, specialists have identified important regularities in the ways societies change. They have shown the value of analyzing data revealing the number of births, deaths, and migrants—as measures of decisions made by households in response to the conditions and opportunities that face them. Before discussing how these concerns figure into studies of the Tokugawa-Meiji transition, let us consider how demographic and urban research enters into studies of Japan in the preceding and following periods.

Previous research has pointed to the extraordinary changes in urban and demographic rates during the Tokugawa era and again in twentieth-century Japan. Here I list five generalizations, which reveal some of the most striking features of Tokugawa urbanization. First of all, by premodern standards, Japan was highly urbanized. In the eighteenth century, only England and perhaps a few much smaller countries managed clearly to exceed the 16-17 percent of Japan's population living in cities of 3,000 or more inhabitants.[1] Second, a tremendous urban spurt occurred, which was seen as a consequence of government policies directed at reordering society. Over approximately 150 years until 1720, the urban population at least quadrupled—in response to the concentration of samurai in castle towns, the regularization and intensification of taxation, the expansion of commerce, the growth in agricultural productivity, and so on. Third, Japan boasted what was probably the world's largest city prior to England's Industrial Revolution: Edo, renamed Tokyo following the Meiji Restoration, had more than 1 million residents. In addition, there was a cluster of cities in the Kinai region (including Osaka, Kyoto, and Sakai) that at their peak, and coterminous with Edo's great size, together comprised close to 1 million inhabitants. Fourth, across the settled valleys and plateaus of Japan there was a remarkably even distribution of cities, the nucleus of which was formed by a network of more than 200 castle towns, each housing roughly 10 percent of the population in its domain.[2] Fifth, the dynamism of urban expansion was increasingly shifting to smaller towns and regional ports, reflecting a diffusion of urban functions and tastes to places in close proximity to village life.[3]

The substantial and widespread urban presence, demanding as it did considerable rural-urban migration and massive shipments of rice and other products, exerted a transformative impact on household decisions. The large-scale and closely regulated migration to and from Edo, as part of the *sankin kōtai* system of alternate residence, together with the meager movement from castle towns of urban residents who were assigned a place in the established order of their domain, were distinctive features of Tokugawa urbanism. Less distinctive, but of great consequence in breaking down local isolation, was the active involvement of rural households in the migration and marketing that sustained the local economies of late Tokugawa.

The social classes of the Tokugawa era were unevenly distributed in the cities. A policy of separation of cities, and of areas within cities, by social class and type of activity remained the ideal. With respect to samurai, the ideal was closely adhered to; this favored class concentrated in Edo and the castle towns, where stipended households were grouped by

[1] Gilbert Rozman, *Urban Networks in Russia, 1750-1800, and Premodern Periodization* (Princeton: Princeton University Press, 1976), p. 245.

[2] John W. Hall, "The Castle Town and Japan's Modern Urbanization," in John W. Hall and Marius B. Jansen, *Studies in the Institutional History of Early Modern Japan* (Princeton: Princeton University Press, 1968), pp. 169-188.

[3] Thomas C. Smith, "Pre-Modern Economic Growth: Japan and the West," *Past and Present*, no. 60 (1973), pp. 127-160.

rank into separate residential areas.[4] The townspeople crowded together in the densely populated wards outside of the main samurai residential areas, and large numbers lived in other types of cities, large and small. Over time, the separation of townspeople by initial status and activity broke down. Most peasants lived in their native villages; yet, contrary to announced restrictions, many moved at least temporarily to cities, in search of work as hired laborers. Rural-rural migration also became pronounced. The intensification of commercialized agriculture and rural crafts (by-employments) contributed to an influx of peasants into the cities and a diffusion of urban activities into small towns and the countryside.

Urbanized areas and places where the urban impact was great led the way in demographic changes that eventually reached far across Japan. Family life was altered by a steep decline in average household size until the late eighteenth century, a drop in birth rates caused at least in part by delayed or forgone marriage, and a reduction in sex ratios roughly to normal levels. Individuals could expect to live longer in smaller households and with more women present. The population continued to grow—but slowly and not in the east, which suffered from chronic bad weather, nor in the hinterlands of the largest cities, where crowded conditions contributed to death rates in excess of birth rates. In his chapter, Akira Hayami is concerned with the relationship between population growth and economic development. He distinguishes the eastern and western regions of Japan. Whereas the former areas fared badly into the nineteenth century, in western Japan, where peasant handicraft industries were spreading, there were increased jobs, improved living standards, and population growth.

Turning to the twentieth century, we find an unmistakable record of massive transformation at a rate unprecedented among major countries of the world. Within several decades, especially from the 1920s to the 1960s, Japan achieved a high level of urbanization;[5] its rapidity was perhaps as unusual as that of premodern urbanization—of course, at a much lower level—three centuries earlier. As before, Tokyo and its megalopolis developed into the largest urban entity in the world. As urbanization proceeded, there was also a sharp drop in birth rates, especially from 1949 to 1957.[6]

[4] James L. McClain, *Kanazawa: A Seventeenth-Century Castle Town* (New Haven: Yale University Press, 1982), pp. 35-37, 76-84.

[5] Norman J. Glickman, *The Growth and Management of the Japanese Urban System* (New York: Academic Press, 1979), pp. 11-16.

[6] Hiroshi Ohbuchi, "Demographic Transition in the Process of Japanese Industrializa-

The chapters that follow focus on urbanization, Tokyo's growth, and birth rates, not at the time of the rapid transformations already examined, but during the transition away from patterns characteristic of mid- or late Tokugawa and after the reforms of the Meiji Restoration. This period of transition links the earlier and later periods of extraordinary transformation. Until now, little attention has been given to examining the local data that show just how the basic patterns of population growth and urbanization changed during this transition.

An obvious common concern in these chapters is to use the statistical records of nineteenth-century Japan. This is possible only because of the extensive records that have been preserved. For most other nineteenth-century countries, including China, comparable studies of local data on a national and regional scale would be impossible: the record-keeping system was not as developed elsewhere. To be sure, there are problems with the Tokugawa and Meiji data; e.g. time series are incomplete, and records for some areas are not as comprehensive as for others. For the years 1846-1872 demographic and urban population data become scarce. Yet, what does exist is remarkable—a sign of both the high levels of literacy in local areas and the longstanding concern of officials to acquire detailed and accurate information for everything from population to food intake. The data are also testimony to the speed with which the new Meiji government achieved a centralized record-keeping system.

The following chapters draw from statistical materials that make it possible to ascertain a great deal about local and national conditions: the population growth rate, the birth and death rates for some areas, the age composition, the population in cities, the percentage of the population who were samurai, the number of in-migrants and out-migrants in an area, and more. In the transition period, as in the mid-Tokugawa and the late twentieth century, Japan can be characterized, in comparison with countries at a similar level of development, as an unusually statistically oriented society. The possibilities are open for research based on demographic and urban data—possibilities that are by no means exhausted in this book.

A second concern here is with local and regional variations. Henry Smith's chapter differentiates areas of Tokyo—especially the wards of the townspeople and the land long assigned to samurai estates—and comments on the role of nearby Yokohama. The other chapters divide Japan into regions, attaching major importance to the differences observed between eastern and western Japan. Assertions about national

tion," in Hugh Patrick, ed., *Japanese Industrialization and Its Social Consequences* (Berkeley: University of California Press, 1976), pp. 329-361.

population stagnation in the first half of the nineteenth century and urban stagnation until the 1880s, we propose, should be qualified by attention to regional variations. Our claim is not simply that greater detail is preferable, but that contradictory developments in areas each encompassing roughly half of Japan shed a markedly different light both on the nature of change and on the reasons for it.

A third concern is with variations in local and regional trends over time. Some national policies, e.g. the abolition of the *sankin kōtai* system, enter into the explanations offered. The foreign impact is also mentioned, in discussions of rapidly growing ports and improved sanitation. But the principal explanations focus on changing domestic commerce and crafts, especially the impact of inland Japan's expanding sericulture, silk reeling, and textile industries, which accompanied a change in the terms of trade in favor of silk and against rice. In conjunction with this shift, which was influenced by Japan's integration into world trading networks, regional disparities in rates of population growth and urbanization were largely reversed. These chapters converge to show a major regional turnaround in the locus of growth during the transition period. Data that might identify the exact timing of this changeover are missing, but each chapter uses the available records to differentiate among short-term periods.

Fourth, we are concerned with decisions made at the household level. The statistics for cities and prefectures aggregate the decisions of thousands of households, and thus may appear quite removed from the day-to-day decision making within the home. But, as the fields of demography and urban studies have long established, such aggregate figures reflect with great accuracy the behavior of masses of people. People who move or who marry late are responding to changing opportunities, often associated with regional variations in expanding crafts and trade. The Meiji government's efforts at centralization and standardization were among the important influences that are reflected in local statistics concerning household behavior.

In the Meiji era, Tokyo gained increased importance as the leading city of Japan. As urban population data indicate, Tokyo's (Edo's) central position had been strengthened over the previous centuries even though Japan continued to be divided into some 260 domains, each with a high degree of autonomy in its internal politics. Beginning in the 1870s, this city solidified its role in the political, economic, and cultural spheres. Samurai and commoner households responded differently during this period of readjustment; the greater disruption occurred in the lives of the samurai, many of whom left the city or at least moved within it.

Taking account of these differences, Smith's chapter is the first study of this city's transition from Edo to Tokyo.

Whereas the unit of decision making in Part One was mostly local and national administration and in Part Two was formally constituted organizations involving large numbers of households, the unit in Part Three is primarily the *ie*, or Japanese household. Changes in the *ie* are the subject of an extensive literature. Sometimes these studies have also considered the important place of the community in local decision making: e.g. in establishing rules or expectations about the formation of new households that alter household behavior with regard to marriage, migration, and childbearing.[7] An unusual degree of community solidarity created an environment in which villagewide objectives could be formulated and conformity elicited from local households. Above all, scholarship on the *ie* points to its persistence as a corporate body concerned with self-perpetuation and its status in the community. The emphasis is on the flexibility of the *ie* in response to new conditions, both in the later Tokugawa and in the Meiji period. This flexibility was manifested in the easy acceptance of adoption and in the diverse options considered for placing surviving sons apart from the one selected as heir. Kin outside the *ie* generally made few demands; the Japanese language was unusual among premodern societies for its limited range of kinship terms.[8] In the late Tokugawa, a fluid labor market as well as stable (and gradually expanding) marketing opportunities gave households the confidence and the incentives to plan in new ways for the future.

By the 1850s, household decisions were quite different from what they had been two centuries earlier. This is shown by various social indicators whose pattern increasingly resembled that in modern societies. The Japanese were relatively mobile and literate, lived in small households, had sex ratios close to unity, and could anticipate fairly long lives. Explanations for these changes center on urbanization, commercialization, rising incomes, and a labor shortage, on the one hand, and on the character and durability of the *ie* and of community and government organizations, on the other. The peculiar nature of the Japanese household is clearly a factor to keep in mind as we examine statistics on population growth and migration during the transition years.

In the early Meiji there was no sudden spurt in population growth, no expansion of Tokyo beyond its earlier population size. In contrast to the immediate reorganization of Japan's administrative system and the de-

[7] Susan B. Hanley and Kozo Yamamura, *Economic and Demographic Change in Preindustrial Japan, 1600-1868* (Princeton: Princeton University Press, 1977), pp. 260-266.

[8] Robert J. Smith, *Ancestor Worship in Contemporary Japan* (Stanford: Stanford University Press, 1974).

liberate establishment of new, large-scale organizations, the Tokugawa legacy was more enduring in the dimensions considered here. Households decided where to live and when to marry. The chapters that follow examine these decisions, and discuss some of their causes and consequences. Through the analysis of statistics, they show some responses of the Japanese people to the changing conditions of the transition period.

Other nineteenth- and twentieth-century transformations that preceded high levels of modernization were mainly reflected in falling death rates and expanding treaty ports and primary cities. Japan's urban and demographic transitions were different. As the analysis by Akira Hayami indicates, Japan's birth rates were rising long before death rates had fallen substantially. And as Rozman's chapter on castle towns shows, small urban centers were leading the way in urbanization decades before Tokyo and Osaka expanded much beyond their earlier sizes. The 1850s-1880s transition in Japan was a time of tremendous structural change and regional reversals. The regions that had suffered population and urban decline in the preceding period were suddenly among the leaders in growth. Changes in urban land use and in social class residential patterns, as Smith points out for Tokyo, occurred with great speed. At present, we lack for the changes of the transition the sort of widely recognized comparative framework that has shed so much light on the extraordinary nature of Tokugawa and Shōwa dynamism; however, there is no reason to suspect that what was occurring in Japan during the transition period was not also extraordinary.

From the 1860s to the 1880s Japanese responded to a relaxation of restrictions and, in some areas, to an expansion of opportunities. Because large numbers of households already had experience with migration and had the skills and knowledge that made mobility possible, the changes that occurred should not come as a surprise. The fact that demographic and urban changes were widely noticeable in local areas, far from the few treaty ports or large cities, indicates that Japan was not merely duplicating the experience of foreign penetration observed in much of the Third World. Indeed, the major trends of rising birth rates and expanding small towns predated Perry's arrival. With the Meiji period came increased geographic mobility and greater ease in choosing one's future. Although there was more freedom of movement and occupation in the Tokugawa period than is often suggested, given the status-bound nature of that society, it was only after 1868 that the restrictions associated with fixed classes, castle towns, and hereditary rights to land ownership crumbled together. Prepared for the new opportunities, many Japanese shifted their residence and their activities in ways that brought a more efficient allocation of the society's resources.

CHAPTER 11

POPULATION CHANGES*

BY AKIRA HAYAMI

A careful study of Japan's population on the eve of industrialization will help resolve the longstanding debate over which came first—population growth or modern economic development. It should shed light on the crucial problem of how the demographic indices of a premodern society, such as general population trends, birth and death rates, average age at marriage, and average life expectancy, can affect that society's subsequent industrialization. Finally, it should even allow us to determine which indices contributed to industrialization, and to what extent, so that we can posit population as an independent variable against economic development. One of the essential steps toward these goals is to decide whether population increase stems from a rising birth rate or a falling death rate, which indicates whether or not the demographic transition theory holds true for a given society. Yet even this basic question has not been answered for Japan. Despite an obvious need to clarify the nature of Japan's demography from *bakumatsu*[1] to mid-Meiji, on the eve of industrialization, we have surprisingly few such demographic studies. In this chapter I seek to show that by re-examining the data of the 1820-1850 and 1870-1910 periods, together with other evidence on the transition decades themselves, it is possible to clear up many uncertainties about population change in Japan.

Japan is blessed with an unusually rich store of source materials for the historical study of its population: *bakufu* and *han* population surveys based on village or town religious-investigation registers (*shumon ara-*

* The author gratefully acknowledges the contribution made by Bob Tadashi Wakabayashi, not only for his patient translation work, but also for many helpful comments and suggestions made during the preparation of this chapter.

[1] We shall here consider the *bakumatsu* era to be 1843-1868.

tame cho)[2] allow us to obtain precise figures for such demographic indices as long-range population trends and changing patterns of birth, death, and marriage. Furthermore, the establishment of the local administrative system in the 1890s and the appearance of fairly reliable demographic statistics for the first decade of the twentieth century mean that good data, on both the regional and the national level, are available for part of the Meiji period. But we lack national population data for the period from 1846, when *bakufu* population surveys ended, to 1872, when Meiji surveys began, and there is confusion about demographic rates over the following decades. We do have a national population figure for 1872 (33.1 million) based on data obtained from the domicile registration system (*koseki seido*) established by the Meiji government. The early Meiji population, however, has been the subject of much controversy. In 1930 the 1872 figure was revised upward to 34.8 million by the Cabinet Statistics Bureau (Naikaku Tōkeikyoku), which added the estimated number of persons missed in the registration process.[3] Yet, doubts persisted and re-estimates were made. The nation's population in 1875 was estimated variously as 35.3 million by the Cabinet Statistics Bureau, 34.8 million by Akasaka Keiko, and 37.2 million by Okazaki Yōichi.[4] The differences are not very great in absolute numbers, but as Umemura Mataji has shown, they assume critical significance when we attempt to determine the *rate* of population growth during that era.[5]

This problem is central to the mid-1960s Okazaki-Umemura debate over early Meiji population growth rates, a debate well known among Japanese economic historians. Okazaki's position was that since the early Meiji population was relatively large to begin with, its subsequent rate of increase should be interpreted as low. Umemura, on the other hand, while noting that his own view was still a "hypothesis," opposed Okazaki's assertion from the standpoint that population increase preceded modern economic growth. Because an understanding of this debate is crucial to the problem at hand, we must examine the positions adopted by these two scholars in some detail.

[2] The *bakufu* conducted twenty-two national population surveys from 1721 to 1846, at six-year intervals. Of these surveys, twelve break down aggregate national figures province by province.

[3] Naikaku tōkei kyoku, ed., *Meiji gonen ikō waga kuni no jinkō* (Tokyo: Tokyo tōkei kyōkai, 1930).

[4] See Umemura Mataji, "Meijiki no jinkō seichō," in Shakai keizai shi gakkai, ed., *Keizai shi ni okeru jinkō* (Tokyo: Keiō tsūshin, 1969), pp. 118-141.

[5] Ibid. See also Okazaki Yōichi, "Meiji jidai no jinkō: toku ni shusshōritsu to shibōritsu ni tsuite," *Keizai kenkyū*, vol. 16, no. 3 (1965), pp. 207-213; Umemura Mataji, "Meiji jidai no jinkō ni tsuite: kommento" and Okazaki Yōichi, "Umemura Mataji-shi no kommento ni taisuru kaitō," both in *Keizai kenkyū*, vol. 16, no. 4 (1965), pp. 356-359.

First, Okazaki dismissed the birth and death rates published in the early Meiji period as being incredibly low. Instead, he used the first modern census of 1920 to project life tables backward and estimate birth, death, and growth rates for each time frame within the Meiji period. Using these tables, he estimated that Japan's population was 36.3 million in 1870 and 37.2 million in 1875. His results indicated that the Meiji birth rate remained at the level of thirty-five to thirty-seven per thousand, that it did not decline until after the turn of the century, and that the death rate fell almost continuously from the figure of thirty-one per thousand recorded at the start of the period. In short, Okazaki found that Meiji population increases stemmed solely from a decline in the death rate.

Akasaka's estimates, used by Umemura, were also derived from the 1920 census. Akasaka had projected these figures backward to obtain vital statistics, and her results were similar to the figures obtained in 1930 by the Cabinet Statistics Bureau—34.8 million in 1875. This figure was 2.4 million, or about 7 percent, lower than Okazaki's. But a more important difference was that, according to Akasaka, the birth rate jumped greatly, from twenty-six per thousand to thirty-five per thousand. These figures argued that Meiji population increases should be attributed solely to a rise in the birth rate. Umemura noted that Okazaki's findings conformed to the demographic transition theory, and he suspected that this conformity was more than coincidental. According to the demographic transition theory, a nation's population changes during modernization by stages: high birth rates and high death rates, then high birth rates and low death rates, and finally low birth rates and low death rates. Umemura argued that this theory was untenable, citing the example of the Scandinavian countries as well as Akasaka's figures for Meiji Japan. The astounding increase in Meiji Japan's birth rate noted by Akasaka, he asserted, could not be left unaccounted for.

The more important and relevant of Umemura's findings are as follows. First, he held that the decline in the death rate in an industrializing society often reflects an income level that rises owing to endogenous factors—the increased scope and wider distribution of that society's aggregate production. Thus, rising income levels lead to increased personal expenditures and then to a declining death rate. Population growth, when it is achieved in this manner, conforms to the theory that economic growth produces population increase. But—and this is of immense importance—a declining death rate does not always stem from endogenous economic betterment. In much of the Third World today, the death rate has been lowered by importing advanced technology and hygiene already developed in the industrialized nations, and this exogenously induced decline in the death rate actually *obstructs* economic growth and improvement of living standards.

In regard to the birth rate, Umemura wrote that so long as the death rate remains high, a desire to ensure the survival of offspring will prevent people from taking steps to reduce the birth rate to a level below that of the death rate. But after the death rate has fallen and people no longer feel a compelling need to ensure the survival of offspring, they will lower the number of births out of a desire to raise their standard of living. Moreover, when income levels are on the rise and seem likely to continue to do so indefinitely, forces that once held down the birth rate become relaxed, and an increasing birth rate may accompany or even precede modern economic growth.

Of course, Umemura's views presuppose that the increase in modern Japan's birth rate began in the *bakumatsu* and Restoration era, prior to large-scale industrialization or economic growth. Some form of the theory that population increase produces economic growth, he hypothesized, may hold true for Japan, where factors during the Tokugawa period probably had worked to raise the birth rate.

Umemura's hypothesis has been neither confirmed nor refuted by later Japanese scholars studying the historical demography of Japan. For one thing, intensive research on the Tokugawa period can be conducted only at the village-survey level. Second, vital statistics for the early Meiji period are unreliable. And third, there is a dearth of economic statistics in contrast to the wealth of population statistics available.

Even so, we who specialize in Tokugawa economic and demographic history look with envy upon the national population data available for the early Meiji era, since the *bakufu* surveys upon which we must rely are less reliable as quantitative sources. For example: population figures for samurai households are omitted; statistics for certain domains or provinces do not contain child populations; and domain surveys were not conducted in a uniform, consistent manner. *Bakufu* surveys yield figures that are significantly lower than actual population levels, but we do not know how much lower;[6] nor do we have firm evidence to deter-

[6] Sekiyama Naotarō has gone over these materials with the utmost care, and probably for that reason they are known to foreign researchers as "the Sekiyama data." His estimates, though not precise, place the unreported population count at between 4.5 million and 5 million. See Sekiyama Naotarō, *Kinsei Nihon no jinkō kōzō* (Tokyo: Yoshikawa kōbunkan, 1969), p. 117. However, we should note that Sekiyama's estimate was made by "logically linking" a national population figure based on the 1846 *bakufu* survey with early Meiji government statistics. These early Meiji statistics are themselves by no means reliable. Moreover, given the fluid social and political conditions that did so much to reduce *bakufu* and daimyo authority in the late Tokugawa period, Sekiyama's estimate should not be accepted as an absolute of the highest accuracy. We must take into consideration regional

mine whether or not underreporting continued at the same rate and in the same numbers throughout the Tokugawa. Hence, these imperfect source materials pose many pitfalls.

Regardless of such pitfalls, we continue to use *bakufu* survey data to plot Tokugawa demographic trends.[7] Indeed, these surveys are the only quantitative source materials available that indicate national population levels and break them down province by province.[8] Without them, our understanding of Tokugawa society certainly would be much more limited than it is now. Thus, the early Meiji population data that have been virtually ignored (particularly by demographers) for being statistically flawed appear, to Tokugawa specialists, as a hitherto undiscovered Treasure Island awaiting exploitation. Their value in clarifying the nature of that momentous transition from Tokugawa to Meiji must be immense.

In the late Tokugawa and early Meiji, modernization had yet to be pursued in earnest; accordingly, population changes that accompanied it were still of minimal importance. This is not to ignore the rapid development of port cities, the appearance of export-oriented industrial areas centered on raw silk production, the opening of Japan to foreign trade and diplomatic intercourse, the changes in politics and military organization that accompanied the Meiji Restoration, and the modern means of transportation imported soon after that event. There have been many demographic changes produced by these developments, but prior to the Matsukata deflation policy of 1881 and the establishment of railroad networks and new political institutions in the early 1890s, Japan's population composition and distribution were not drastically altered. True, the early Meiji government did introduce vaccination and other public health measures but many of these policies had already been initiated in the *bakumatsu* era, and their effects on Japan's population were therefore gradual rather than sudden and disruptive. Thus, early Meiji population data, although they do not reflect late Tokugawa demographic conditions as accurately as modern statistics might, nonetheless present a picture that is remarkably clear—there was no radical disjunction between *bakumatsu* and early Meiji population structure and composition.

Many of the demographic statistics published in the early Meiji period

---

variations in the source materials that yielded his figures as well as periodic fluctuations in them.

[7] For example: Hayami Akira, "Tokugawa kōki jinkō hendō no chiikiteki tokusei," *Mita gakkai zasshi*, vol. 64, no. 3 (1971); Umemura Mataji, "Tokugawa jidai no jinkō to keizai," in Umemura et al., eds., *Sūryō keizai shi ronshū: 1, Nihon no keizai hatten* (Tokyo: Nihon keizai shimbunsha, 1976), pp. 3-18; Susan B. Hanley and Kozo Yamamura, *Economic and Demographic Change in Preindustrial Japan, 1600-1868* (Princeton: Princeton University Press, 1977), pp. 38-68.

[8] Surveys by the *bakufu* and a few of the domains, often listing little more than population figures by sex, constitute the exception.

are given in units of the old Tokugawa-period "provinces" (*kuni*) as well as in the newly established "prefectures" (*fu* or *ken*).[9] A problem with the prefectures of this period is that their boundaries changed frequently. On the other hand, although the old Tokugawa provinces officially ceased to exist as administrative units, they were clearly defined geographic entities. Even if statistics using these provinces as units were not published, we can still produce figures for them by first finding data for the subadministrative units of *gun* (counties) and *ku* (large cities or their wards) that constituted the provinces, and then adding these subtotals together. This is possible because the *gun* units themselves did not change (except to be appended to, or detached from, one or another prefecture).

It would be wonderful if we could treat early Meiji "province" figures as simple extensions of Tokugawa province figures, but so uncritical a use of source materials is not permissible. Tokugawa province statistics were compiled from *han*-gathered data, and the gathering process differed from domain to domain. For example, the 1846 figure for Satsuma, which contained a high proportion of unenumerated samurai, stood at 242,000. But the total for Meiji-period Satsuma "province" came to 549,000—a jump of 227 percent, which is utterly implausible even in light of the 23 percent increase registered for the nation as a whole during that same period.[10] Yet, despite this shortcoming, a comparison of Tokugawa and Meiji general population *trends* is permitted: if the historian is not overly rigid in his attitude toward the limitations and imperfections found in early Meiji demographic data, they can be employed with great profit.[11]

[9] Published demographic statistics on the early Meiji are to be found in Naimushō, ed., *Nihon zenkoku kosekihyō* (1872-1876) and *Nihon zenkoku kokōhyō* (1877-1878). These two works are available in reprint editions: Nihon tōkei kyōkai, ed., *Tōkei kosho shiriizu*, vol. 4 (Tokyo: Nihon Tōkei Kyōkai, 1965); Naimushō kosekikyoku, ed., *Nihon zenkoku gun-ku bun jinkō hyō* (Tokyo: Naimushō kosekikyoku, 1879) and *Nihon zenkoku jinkō hyō* (Tokyo: Naimushō kosekikyoku, 1880-1885).

We are able to use these early Meiji statistics with confidence owing to the splendid annotated bibliography compiled by Hosoya Shinji, *Meiji zenki Nihon keizai tōkei kaidai shoshi* (Tokyo: Hitotsubashi daigaku keizai kenkyūjo, 1974-1980). Professor Hosoya, of the Nihon Keizai Tōkei Bunken Center at Hitotsubashi University, has listed the legal basis, statistical genealogies, and contents of individual records. In addition, the Sōrifu Tōkeikyoku has published (Tokyo: 1976) *Sōrifu Tōkeikyoku hyakunen shi shiryō shūsei*; vol. 2, pt. 1, "Population," lists laws, regulations, and other legal documents that bear on population studies. Thanks to these two works, we can approach early Meiji statistics in an orderly fashion and can utilize a particular set of data with secure knowledge of its relationship to other kinds of data.

[10] See the "Kunibetsu jinkōhyō," in Sekiyama, *Kinsei Nihon no jinkō kōzō*, pp. 137-138. Between 1846 and 1872, there were extremely high jumps—150 percent or more—in the provinces of Kaga, Etchū, Hizen, Hyūga, Osumi, Satsuma, and Tsushima. In these areas, populations were systematically underreported in the Tokugawa period.

[11] One promising avenue of future research is to use the *gun* or *ku* units (of which there were over 700) as a framework to set up manageable or appropriate-size populations for

Before discussing the results of my research, I should explain my basic assumption about the nature of the "population" that emerges from Tokugawa and Meiji statistics. As discussed above, *bakufu* statistics suffer from a variety of imperfections—omission of samurai households, non-standardized methods of census taking by the various domains, occasional double counting of individuals or groups, and so on. Absolute figures obtained from Tokugawa population surveys, then, are not always reliable. To skirt the pitfalls involved, I adopted the following strategy. I have considered the population given for each province to be an index, and from the annual provincial or regional population, I sought to determine changes for every era under consideration. Assuming that there were no variations in survey methods within each domain throughout the Tokugawa period—and there is a good possibility that there were none—the figures derived should then be amenable to statistical treatment.

As far as Meiji populations are concerned, the registered population after the 1872 registration (*jinshin koseki*) became the basis of my calculations, and I added or deleted changes in the register from that year until 1885. The allowances made for births, deaths, and entries (by marriage and adoption) into and deletions from the register are known as "legally domiciled population" (*honseki jinkō*). Those who left their place of legally registered domicile, resided in one place for ninety days or more, and followed legal procedures to declare themselves to be living in a temporary domicile are known as "temporary-resident population" (*kiryū jinkō*). Finally, the "resident population" (*genjū jinkō*) is calculated from the "legally domiciled" population: registered temporary incoming residents are added, and temporary outgoing residents subtracted, to obtain the "resident populaton." This "resident population," then, is a purely theoretical calculation and is different from the resident population counted in Japan's truly modern censuses, which begin in 1920. In those censuses, the census takers actually met the people they counted.[12] Yet the Meiji population counts derived by this method are still much more accurate than those available for the Tokugawa period.

One noteworthy fact is that surveys conducted from domicile registers produce cumulative distortions in population statistics; in other words, population figures based on domicile registers become progressively more divorced from reality. In the early Meiji period, there may have been

---

investigation in conjunction with other statistics, say of prices or production (though these are even less reliable than demographic data). Detailed studies of early Meiji demographic and economic history can be undertaken in this manner.

[12] This is discussed by Osamu Saitō, "Migration and the Labour Market in Japan, 1872-1920: A Regional Study," *Keiō Economic Studies*, vol. 10, no. 2 (1973), p. 48.

omissions in the registers, but the inaccuracies they produce are not blatant. Instead, our chief problem is how to determine the true size of the migrating population. The number of out-migrants should theoretically equal that of in-migrants—at least in the domestic sphere. But in almost all cases, the recorded population of the latter group was greater than that of the former. Many migrants terminated their domiciled residence in one area and re-migrated to another without duly reporting the fact. Because of this, and given the natural increase in the proportion of in-migrants that accompanied urbanization and rising population-mobility rates, it eventually becomes impossible to determine the resident population. In 1908, the difference between in- and out-migrating populations reached 2,420,000—about 4 percent of Japan's total population. Earlier in the Meiji period the discrepancy was less serious: the first statistics available on a nationwide scale for migrating populations (in 1884) show that there were 230,000 more out-migrants than in-migrants, and this accounted for 0.7 percent of the national population.

I have noted conspicuous flaws that skew statistical data derived from early Meiji domicile registers. Nevertheless, we must recognize that these and other Meiji data *are* amenable to quantitative analysis, and we should make full use of them to clarify conditions in nineteenth-century Japan.

The Debate among American Scholars

National population statistics derived from *bakufu* population surveys, which are extant for the years 1721-1846, seem to provide quantitative evidence of population stagnation. Some have even described the situation as a Malthusian trap. In 1721, the population was 26.1 million; in 1846, 26.9 million. The highest figure recorded in these surveys is 27.2 million; the lowest, 24.9 million. We get a mean figure of 26.0 million for the period, plus or minus 1.2 million (or 4.6 percent).

Scholars who emphasize the dark side of Tokugawa society, particularly those who consider population to be a dependent variable of the economy, are quick to interpret such population "stagnation" as resulting from economic stagnation. Then again, those who attribute a lack of Tokugawa population growth to abortion and infanticide resorted to by commoners find in these figures just what they are looking for—proof of the poverty and despair that plagued Japanese society in that "feudalistic" era. But are such perceptions accurate?

Recently, certain American specialists on Tokugawa demographic and economic history have published important studies that shed light on these issues. In one such work, by Susan B. Hanley and Kozo Yamamura, it is argued that 1) because of relatively low birth rates in Tokugawa Japan, the concept of "demographic transition" is not applicable and 2) in most cases, death rates approximately equaled birth rates, resulting in a stable population. The authors found a slight increase in Japan's population after the Tempō mortality crisis of 1837-1838, an increase that continued throughout the Meiji period but did not begin with it. In addition, they saw "a remarkable similarity with pre- and early-industrial population trends in Europe and no similarity at all between Tokugawa Japan and the other nations of Asia today."[13]

In another study, Thomas Smith put forth the following conclusions about one village located in central Japan:

> Both mortality and fertility . . . were low to moderate in Nakahara as compared to eighteenth-century European parishes. . . . [T]here can be little doubt that one of the reasons for low registered fertility was the practice of infanticide. . . . What is surprising is that the practice does not appear to have been primarily a response to poverty. . . . In short, it gives the impression of a kind of family planning.[14]

From the overall tone of Smith's book, we may infer his position: 1) at least during the eighteenth century, steps taken by peasants to maintain families at a certain size held down population increase; 2) this presents a marked contrast to Ch'ing China, where the population is believed to have doubled between 1749 and 1819; and 3) this contrast may have much to do with Japan's earlier and more rapid economic development. Smith notes:

> If population was held in check by deliberate controls over fertility, we should have in some respects a functional equivalent of the European marriage pattern [late marriage and high celibacy]. But if population was checked mainly by famine, as some historians believe, we should have reason to doubt the economic expansion and consequent rise in per capita income after 1721.[15]

James Nakamura and Matao Miyamoto also believe that in contrast to Ch'ing China, which experienced a tremendous population increase during roughly the same period, Tokugawa Japan's basically "stagnant" population created relatively higher per capita income, paving the way for Japan to industrialize successfully and achieve high economic growth.

[13] Hanley and Yamamura, *Economic and Demographic Change*, p. 318.

[14] Thomas C. Smith, *Nakahara: Family Farming and Population in a Japanese Village, 1717-1830* (Stanford: Stanford University Press, 1977), p. 147.

[15] Ibid., p. 5.

Nakamura and Miyamoto stress differences in social and political institutions between Tokugawa Japan and Ch'ing China. For example, the Japanese *ie* (household) system "that tied the Japanese to a fixed vertical structure of mutual obligations and responsibilities and impartible inheritance" was in direct opposition to the family system of Ch'ing China. "In Japan," they write, "this took the form of population control and long-run investment, both of which tended to cause per capita output to rise."[16]

Of course these scholars do have differences of opinion. But they all agree that 1) the Tokugawa population did not increase; 2) this nonincrease resulted from the "rational" behavior of Japanese peasants who sought to maintain or improve their standard of living; and 3) these factors help explain Meiji Japan's rapid and "successful" modernization, in contrast to that of late Ch'ing China.

One American scholar, however, takes exception to these views. Carl Mosk, in a recent article, wrote:

> They [Hanley and Smith] argue that peasant families in Tokugawa Japan deliberately kept family size small through infanticide to maintain a relatively comfortable standard of living. To the contrary, I suggest that fecundity was low and the chances of infant survival poor, so parents were forced to adopt strategies about the sex of the births they would permit to survive in addition to eliminating many weak and sickly offspring soon after birth.[17]

Mosk estimated statistical data on food consumption and physical characteristics and discovered that, between 1874 and 1877, daily food consumption per individual was no more than 1,530 calories and 47.4 grams of protein, levels that subsequently rose along with per capita income. From these findings, he argued that "during the Tokugawa period *desired* fertility exceeded actual for the bulk of the population and this negative gap closed during the Meiji era."

Mosk's statement contradicts the findings of Hanley and Yamamura, Smith, and Nakamura and Miyamoto. "The concept of a demographic transition is applicable to Japan," Mosk suggested:

> If we think of demographic transition theory as explaining why *desired* fertility falls from relatively high levels prior to and in the

[16] James I. Nakamura and Matao Miyamoto, "Social Structure and Population Change: A Comparative Study of Tokugawa Japan and Ch'ing China," *Economic Development and Cultural Change*, vol. 30, no. 2 (1982), p. 262.

[17] Carl Mosk, "The Decline of Marital Fertility in Japan," *Population Studies*, vol. 33, no. 1 (1979), p. 37.

> early period of modernization to low levels as modernization spreads, it is my contention that Japanese demographic history does not deviate from the main lines of demographic transition theory. . . . [T]he Japanese demographic transition experience conforms in its essential features to the experiences of Europe, North America, Australia, and New Zealand.[18]

Mosk's challenge is clearly relevant to the Okazaki-Umemura debate on population trends in Japan. According to Mosk, the demographic transition theory once refuted by Umemura may hold true for the Tokugawa period after all—if we can certify that physical reasons made fertility lower than *desired* fertility and that this low fertility stemmed from inadequate food consumption and malnutrition. (Of course Mosk did not deny that abortion and infanticide were practiced.)

It now appears certain that new debates will emerge over why fertility was low in the Tokugawa period and what this fact means to the historian. Before those debates can be resolved, we must accumulate many regional studies—each based on reliable source materials that have been subjected to rigorous demographic and economic analysis, performed with the aim of determining the general standard of living and the actual steps taken to alter it, if any.[19] Mind-boggling amounts of time, money, and energy will doubtless be required to complete this task, but I believe it can be done.

The Latter Half of Tokugawa

Assuming that a useful purpose can be served now by viewing overall population trends before seeking out detailed demographic indices, I will look at provincial and regional data, derived mainly from *bakufu* and domain surveys in the Tokugawa period, and will attempt to link these figures to early Meiji population statistics for corresponding geographic areas.[20] *Bakufu* population surveys, which are extant from 1721 to 1846,

[18] Carl Mosk, "Fecundity, Infanticide, and Food Consumption in Japan," *Explorations in Economic History*, vol. 15, no. 1 (1978), pp. 269-289.

[19] I have published a book-length regional study of Tokugawa population in Suwa county, Shinano province: *Kinsei nōson no rekishi jinkō gakuteki kenkyū* (Tokyo: Tōyō keizai shuppansha, 1973). A similar study on Owari and Mino provinces is in preparation.

[20] Province-by-province Tokugawa population figures are available for 1721, 1750, 1786, 1792, 1798, 1804, 1822, 1828, 1834, 1840, and 1846. The figures for 1792 are published in Minami Kazuo, "Kansei yonen no shokoku jinkō ni tsuite," in *Nihon rekishi*, no. 432 (May 1984), pp. 42-47, and those for 1840 are published in Minami Kazuo, *Bakumatsu Edo shakai no kenkyū* (Tokyo: Yoshikawa kōbunkan, 1978), pp. 164-185. Figures for the other years can be found in Sekiyama, *Kinsei Nihon no jinkō kōzō*, pp. 137-139.

contain various noteworthy characteristics and problems. First, although absolute national population figures show stagnation, regional variation was pronounced: in some areas the population rose continuously, while in others it fell. These increases and decreases offset each other to give the overall appearance of "stagnation," or a lack of aggregate population growth. Generally speaking, in the Kantō and Tōhoku areas, population decline was the rule; in Kyūshū, Shikoku, and Chūgoku, increases predominated; and in central Japan, there was a slight population decrease in the Kinki region and an increase in Hokuriku. Map 11.1 shows that Tokugawa Japan's "demographic center of gravity" moved across Lake Biwa from east to west, as eastern areas decreased in population and western areas rose.

In 1721, the three northern Kantō provinces of Kōzuke, Shimotsuke, and Hitachi as well as the six Sanyō provinces of Bizen, Bitchū, Bingo, Aki, Suō, and Nagato both had populations of 1.8 million. But by 1846, the Kantō region had lost 0.5 million while the Sanyō area had gained the same number, so that the total difference in population was roughly 1 million. Thus, the aggregate population count for these two areas shows an undeniable, yet purely accidental, form of "stagnation" that disguises the sharply contrasting regional population changes which actually took place.

Tokugawa peasants were not tied to the land, notwithstanding what we are told in most high school textbooks: they were free to migrate as individuals, and they moved from village to city in surprisingly large numbers to look for work.[21] However, their geographical mobility was not limitless. Such movement was generally restricted to a hundred-mile radius of towns and cities within a specific region, such as Edo in the Kantō, or Kyoto and Osaka in the Kinki.[22] Population increase in western Japan and population decline in eastern Japan *just happened*: these contrasting trends did not result from economic rationality—the migration of peasants in search of work—as asserted by Yamamura in his two-region model of Tokugawa Japan.[23]

Instead, I propose the following explanation. In the eighteenth century,

[21] Akira Hayami, "Labor Migration in a Pre-Industrial Society: A Study Tracing the Life Histories of the Inhabitants of a Village," *Keiō Economic Studies*, vol. 10, no. 2 (1973), pp. 1-18. In the same issue, see also Susan B. Hanley, "Migration and Economic Change in Okayama during the Tokugawa Period," pp. 19-36, and W. Mark Fruin, "Farm Family Migration: The Case of Echizen in the Nineteenth Century," pp. 37-46.

[22] For Edo, see Minami, *Bakumatsu Edo shakai no kenkyū*; for Kyoto, Hayami Akira, "Kyōto machikata no shumon aratamechō," in *Kenkyū kiyō Shōwa 55–nendo* (Tokyo: Tokugawa rinsei shi kenkyūsho, 1981).

[23] Hanley and Yamamura, *Economic and Demographic Change*, pp. 28-37.

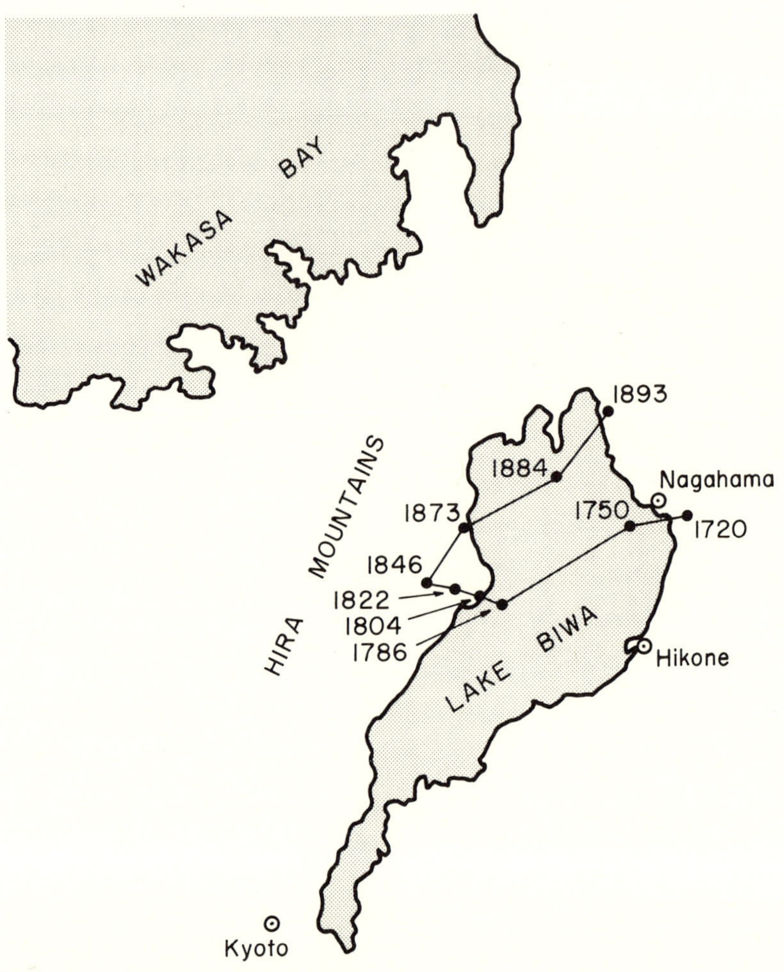

Map 11.1. The Shifting Demographic Center of Gravity, 1720-1893
Redrawn from *Nihon rettō ni okeru jinkō bumpu no chōki jikeiritsu bunseki* (Tokyo: Shakai kōgaku kenkyūsho, 1974), p. 125.

eastern Japan suffered from chronic bad weather which produced a long-term drop in agricultural production, but western Japan was largely unaffected.[24] Owing to the high death rate in cities, which teemed with workers who had migrated from the depressed countryside, the Kantō and Kinki regions (which included Edo, Kyoto, and Osaka) were subject to the negative-feedback function and their populations stagnated.

The long-term decline of northeastern Japan's population in the eighteenth century can be understood better by examining the annual domain-population surveys of Yonezawa and Aizu *han*. As shown in Figure 11.1, these two domains enjoyed population growth throughout the seventeenth century; but from the start of the eighteenth, decline set in, and owing to the calamitous Hōreki and Temmei famines of 1756 and the 1780s, their populations fell precipitously to a level two-thirds that of their seventeenth-century peak. In Yonezawa *han*, the population had not quite recovered to its earlier peak level even by *bakumatsu* times, which means that this *han* contained more people in the late seventeenth century than in the mid-nineteenth.

These facts suggest that the eighteenth-century decline in eastern Japan's population was not a result of short-term famines—however devastating—during the 1750s and 1780s. Instead, the decrease was a long-term trend that was probably caused by chronic bad weather, which lowered agricultural output throughout the century. Although the population increase in western Japan during this same era was but 0.2 to 0.3 percent annually, it could not have occurred apart from the development of peasant by-employments, particularly in handicraft industries.

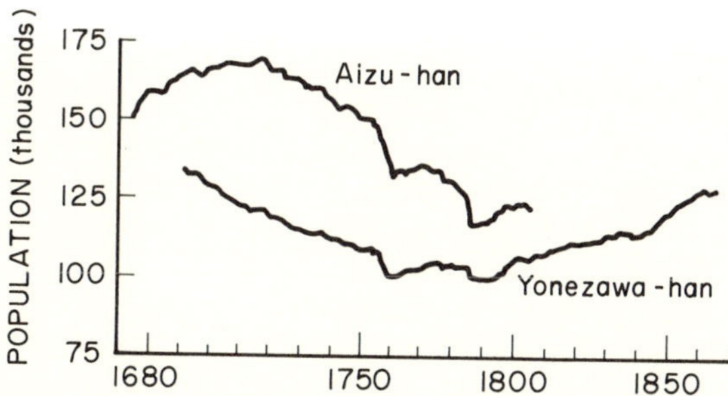

Figure 11.1. Population Trends of Aizu *Han* and Yonezawa *Han*, 1680-1850
Data for Aizu *han* from Takahashi Bonsen, *Nihon jinkō shi no kenkyū* (Tokyo: Sanyūsha, 1941), pp. 208-217; for Yonezawa *han*, Yoshida Yoshinobu, *Oitama minshū seikatsu shi* (Tokyo: Kokusho kankōkai, 1973), pp. 113-118.

[24] From 1732 to 1733, however, western Japan did suffer from famines caused by pests, which bred in massive numbers and inflicted damage on rice plants.

One conspicuous example is Chōshū *han*, where about half of the peasant's income was earned from by-employments and nonagricultural activities, a fact that offers persuasive evidence of economic development having produced population growth in this period and area.[25]

In sum, by discussing Japan's population in the latter half of the Tokugawa period solely in terms of aggregate numbers, and then summarily labeling it "stagnant," we preclude an appreciation of its complexities and regional variations. Only through more detailed studies that account for geographic differences and changes over time can we attain a meaningful historical understanding of "Tokugawa Japan" as a whole.

A second problem has to do with the lack of *bakufu* survey statistics after 1846.[26] If the *bakufu* had continued conducting national surveys as usual up to the Restoration, population statistics for 1852, 1858, and 1864 would be available; but domestic and foreign crises left *bakufu* leaders with little time or inclination to conduct censuses. Since no further national population figures are available until 1872, when the new Meiji government instituted its registration system (*jinshin koseki*), we have a statistical blank space of twenty-six years—from 1846 to 1872. This mid-nineteenth-century era cannot be interpreted either as one of "stagnation" or as a simple continuation of eighteenth-century demographic trends.

To begin with, as shown in Map 11.1, the nation's "demographic center of gravity" during the period under consideration was furthest west in 1846, but by 1873 it had moved northeastward at considerable speed. Of course, Tokugawa and Meiji population statistics are not of uniform quality or accuracy, so the speed of this shift cannot be plotted with precision; but *general trends* can be determined. Clearly, Japan's "demographic center of gravity" had been moving westward at a rapid pace prior to 1846; this speed slackened considerably in *bakumatsu* times, and by the beginning of Meiji, the center of gravity was moving eastward swiftly. We may conclude, then, that the eastward shift in Japan's population distribution had already begun by the *bakumatsu* and Restoration era.

Next, as shown in Figure 11.1, the population of Yonezawa *han* (in present-day Yamagata prefecture) began to rise after the start of the nineteenth century, and by *bakumatsu* times it had just about recovered

[25] Thomas C. Smith, "Farm Family By-employments in Pre-Industrial Japan," *Journal of Economic History*, vol. 29, no. 4 (December 1969), pp. 397-423; Shunsaku Nishikawa, "Productivity, Subsistence, and By-employment in Mid-Nineteenth-Century Chōshū," in *Explorations in Economic History*, vol. 15, no. 1 (1978), pp. 69-83.

[26] Prior to the first *bakufu* survey of 1721, Japan's early Tokugawa population increase had already tapered off, but a discussion of that era lies beyond the scope of this study.

the population losses incurred during the eighteenth century. Hence we need to reconsider whether or not the general trends of rising population in the west and falling population in the east hold true for the nineteenth century. Fortunately, national population statistics, though flawed in some respects, do exist for every sixth year during the twenty-four-year period from 1822 to 1846; by using these data in a discriminating manner, we gain valuable information with which to solve this problem.

Finally, it should be noted that Japan suffered a disastrous mortality crisis triggered by nationwide epidemics in 1837 and 1838. Osaka, for example, lost 11 percent of its population during these two years. The disease in question remains unknown, but in the Owase area (of present-day Mie prefecture) it evidently was accompanied by high fever and diarrhea.[27] According to the death registers (*kakochō*) of a farm village near Hida-Takayama, seventy-three persons starved to death in 1837 alone; in addition, forty-nine children and twenty-three elderly persons died from the illness, and thirty-seven others died from acute infectious diseases. Infectious diseases took their greatest toll in lives during the sixth and seventh months of that year.[28]

The Tempō mortality crisis, then, stemmed not just from famine-induced starvation, but also from infectious diseases—probably ailments of the intestinal tract and/or measles. Here again, a cause-and-effect relationship in history is hard to determine. Were the deaths from infectious disease caused by weakened resistance, the result of poor harvests that reduced food consumption and brought on malnutrition? Or did the poor harvests stem from widespread disease that was produced by some new, virulent strain of virus that sapped peasants of the strength to farm? The resolution of this problem will have to await identification of the culprit disease.

In any case, the immensity of this Tempō mortality crisis is beyond doubt. According to *bakufu* statistics, a 4.2 percent decline in Japan's total population occurred between 1834 and 1840. This was the second largest rate of decline for any six-year interval on record from 1721 to 1846; it was exceeded only during the 1780s. Between 1834 and 1840, only eight of Tokugawa Japan's sixty-eight provinces registered a population increase, while twenty-seven showed a decrease of 5 percent or more.

The area of most precipitous decline stretched from Tōhoku to Hokuriku, and traces of the decimation can be found in Meiji records.

[27] Hayami Akira, "Kishū Owase-gumi no jinkō sūsei," in *Kenkyū kiyō Shōwa 43–nendo* (Tokyo: Tokugawa rinsei shi kenkyūsho, 1969).

[28] Suda Keizō, *Hida "O" jiin kakochō no kenkyū* (private printing, 1973), pp. 154-155.

Statistics compiled in 1884 are the first for which quinquennial age structure is known.[29] From these data we find that, in fifteen of the nation's forty-three prefectures, the number of 45-to-49-year-olds[30] (born between 1836 and 1840, the five-year interval in which the Tempō mortality crisis occurred) was lower than the number of 50-to-54-year-olds (born in the preceding five-year interval, from 1831 to 1835). Furthermore, those fifteen prefectures were all on the Japan Sea coast stretching from Tōhoku to Hokuriku. More detailed analysis reveals the following. Statistics in 1886, the first year for which the national one-year age structure is known,[31] show that the age-49 population (born in the crisis year 1837) was 16 percent less than those age 50 (born in 1836). In theory, the higher up in the age structure, the smaller the population should be, since it normally is reduced to a greater degree through death by natural causes—barring large-scale out-migration from a certain area, of course. The above facts, then, mean either that there were few births in the crisis year of 1837 or that the infant death rate was extremely high. These Meiji data are many years removed from the crisis year; moreover, we must take into account regional variations in the adult death rate. Even so, regional statistics derived from *bakufu* surveys and Meiji source materials match beautifully.

One more short-term population change remains to be discussed—the cholera epidemic that struck Japan right after the opening of the treaty ports. During the nineteenth century, there were several worldwide cholera pandemics; the third just happened to coincide with *kaikoku* (the opening of the country).[32] The disease raged throughout Japan, starting at Nagasaki in 1858. Though there is no accurate record of how many people died or suffered from it, its imprint, like that of the Tempō mortality crisis, was left indelibly on Meiji records. For example, there were relatively few births in 1861, when the pestilence hit its peak. The 1884 records giving quinquennial age structure show that, in forty-one out of forty-three prefectures, the number of 20-to-24-year-olds born in the five-year interval including 1861 was lower than the number of 25-to-29-year-olds born in the previous five-year interval (a national average of 93.2 percent). The one-year age-structure figures for 1886 reveal that the

[29] Naimushō kosekikyoku, ed., *Nihon zenkoku jinkōhyō* (surveyed January 1, 1884; date of publication unknown).

[30] Throughout this chapter "year-old" will refer to *sai* in the Japanese method of reckoning ages.

[31] Naikaku tōkeikyoku, ed., *Nihon teikoku daishichi tōkei nenkan* (surveyed December 31, 1886; published in 1888).

[32] Tachikawa Shōzō, *Byōki no shakai shi* (Tokyo: Nihon hōsō shuppan kyōkai, 1971), pp. 180-223.

national population born in 1861 was 12 percent less than that born in 1860. Statistics show that the epidemic raged most furiously in the Tōkai, Kinki, Chūgoku, and Shikoku areas, and that the greatest loss of life occurred in the five central prefectures of Aichi, Gifu, Mie, Nara, and Wakayama. In those prefectures, the number of persons born in 1861 fell to less than 80 percent of those born in 1860.

Thus, the mortality crises of the late 1830s and early 1860s were nationwide in scope and had brutal effects on Japan's population. Figure 11.2 shows one-year age structures for males and females at the end of 1886, plots their age backward, and shows changes in the population for each structure. This graph indicates that the Tokugawa population declined sharply on four separate occasions: the Tempō mortality crisis of 1837-1838; in 1846;[33] in 1851; and from 1859 to 1862. It is quite conceivable that either the birth rate was extremely low, or the infant death rate was extremely high for these years.

What we must keep in mind, however, is that such abnormal conditions were of short duration and were caused mainly by communicable diseases

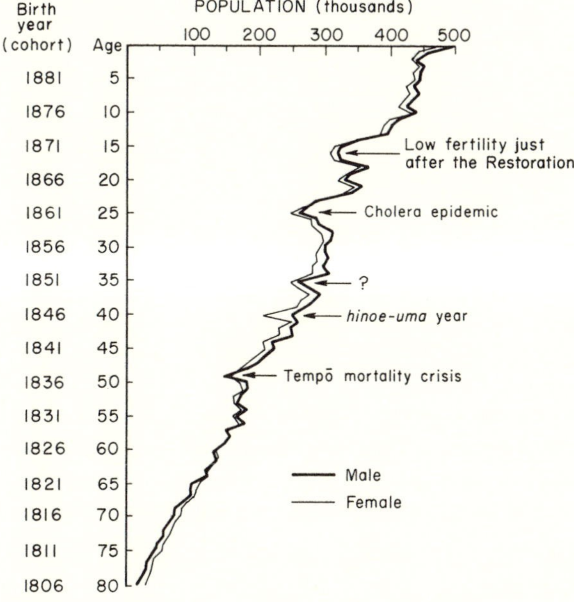

Figure 11.2. Age Composition in Japan, December 31, 1886

[33] This was the year *hinoe-uma*, considered to be an inauspicious year for females to be born. Therefore, the "population decline" observed in statistics for that year actually stems from nonregistration of female births and, presumably, infanticide.

having little connection with national economic conditions. In sum, from the beginning of the nineteenth century down to the Restoration, exogenous short-term factors worked to hold down population increase on a few occasions; what is more, there took place pronounced regional variations in population change that cannot be ignored. The Tempō mortality crisis and *bakumatsu* cholera epidemics were most devastating in areas where population was on the rise (except for Tōhoku); the *bakumatsu* epidemics, in particular, wrought their greatest havoc in Japan's economically advanced regions.

Before we can sort out the cause-and-effect relationship between population growth and economic development in Tokugawa Japan, we must discount such short-term, exogenously induced negative effects on population change. The lack of population surveys broken down by province for the *bakumatsu* era prevents us from measuring the precise impact that the cholera epidemics had on Japan's population, but existing statistics do shed some light on the Tempō crisis. The twenty-four years from 1822 to 1846, for which surveys were taken every sixth year, can be divided up into four intervals of six years each. When we disregard the 1834-1840 interval (in which the Tempō mortality crisis occurred) we obtain a picture of long-term, overall national population trends on a province-by-province basis. During the other three six-year intervals, the population increased 5.2 percent, and of the sixty-seven provinces for which reliable data exist,[34] all but eleven showed an increase. Without a doubt, this means that Japan's early-nineteenth-century population was growing.

More detailed analysis of provincial figures for those three six-year intervals reveals that in thirty-five provinces the population showed some growth in all three intervals. Furthermore, among these thirty-five provinces, Echigo, Hōki, Izumo, Bingo, Aki, and Sanuki enjoyed a population increase of more than 2 percent in all three intervals. Thus, in the first half of the nineteenth century, most of Japan's provinces were enjoying steady population growth. Chūgoku, Shikoku, and northern Kyūshū, areas that enclose the Inland Sea, displayed continuous growth, as did certain provinces in the Tōhoku, Hokuriku, and Tōsan regions. By way of contrast, Kantō and Kinai—the core areas of Tokugawa Japan and the economically most advanced—failed to grow. (See Maps 11.2 and 11.3.)

We may summarize the significance of these observations on late Tokugawa population as follows. In the first half of the nineteenth century, western Japan (particularly areas surrounding the Inland Sea) enjoyed

[34] This excludes Shimōsa, where records are poor.

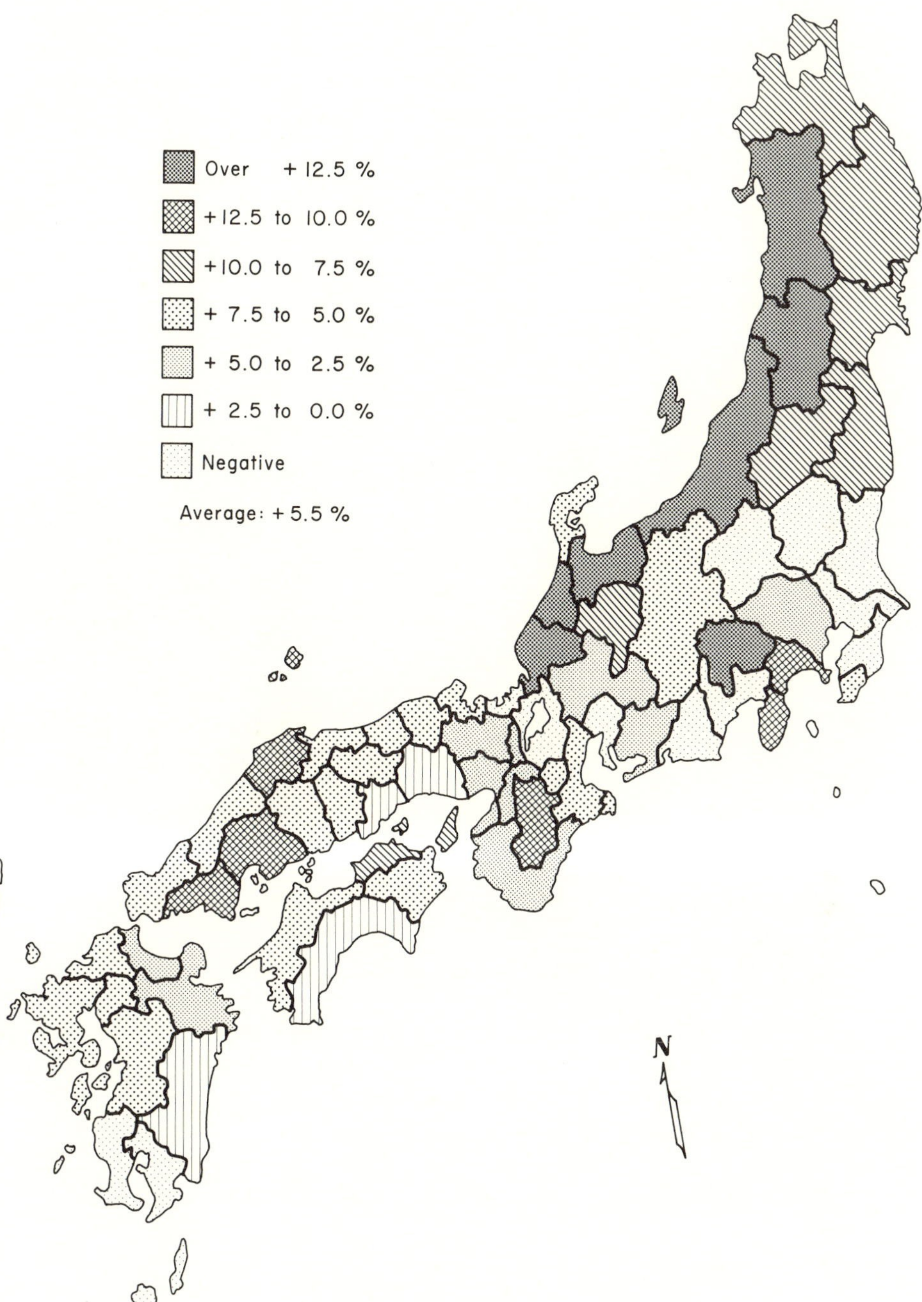

Map 11.2. Population Change in Japan, 1822-1846 (Except 1834-1840)

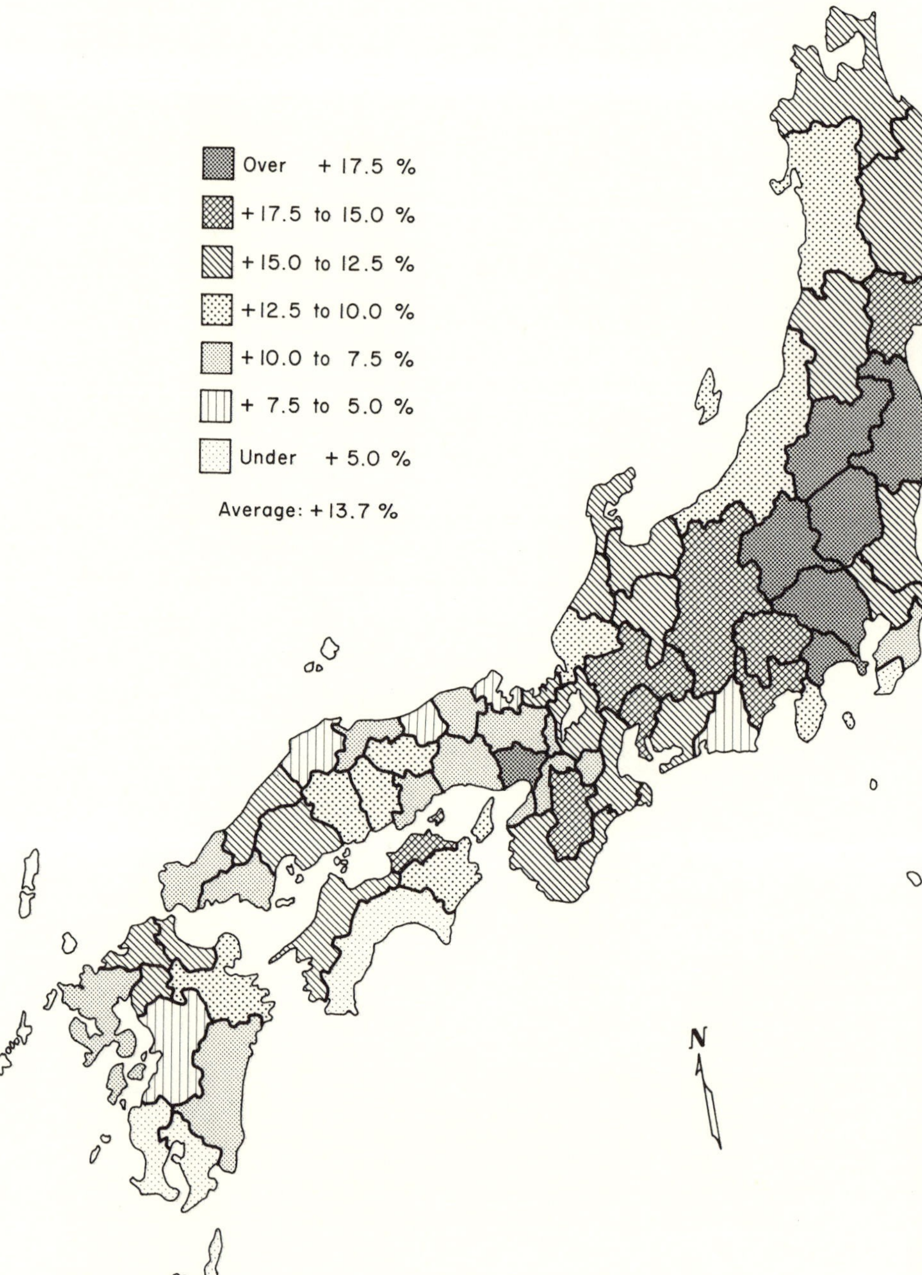

Map 11.3. Population Change in Japan, 1872-1885

steady population growth. Such growth, though to a lesser extent, also took place in other parts of the country—even in Tōhoku. Japan's population was on the upswing, and this increase continued throughout the *bakumatsu* era; although temporarily checked by the Tempō mortality crisis, late Tokugawa population growth soon resumed. Why was it that the areas around Edo, Kyoto, and Osaka—the nation's heartland—enjoyed no large population increases, while western Japan and Tōhoku, whose population had been decimated in the eighteenth century, did? One reason may lie in the high death rate found in all preindustrial cities; but the real answer, I think, should be sought outside of population structure, in economic development. In the Inland Sea area, village industries and peasant by-employments were developing during this period, and sericulture and the silk-reeling industry were beginning to emerge in Tōhoku. But the Kantō and Kinai, in contrast to these "developing" areas, were already "developed." The divergent forms of population change that occurred in these two types of regions conform precisely to phenomena that characterize periods of proto-industrialization. Yet until we obtain detailed regional and, if possible, village-level studies, the question of whether population growth engendered economic development or vice versa will remain unsolved.

The Early Meiji

The first national population statistics available for post-Restoration Japan date from 1872, and are derived from the new Meiji government's domicile registration system. From this time on, Japan's population continued to rise each and every year. The average annual growth rate was, it is true, less than 1.0 percent during the period under consideration, but it is nevertheless important to emphasize that national statistics show sustained growth in the Meiji population. Modern medicine and sanitation were implemented to prevent epidemics of typhoid fever and cholera, which had taken a great toll in lives during the Tokugawa period. Consequently, acute short-term fluctuations in Japan's population were eliminated. (See Figure 11.3.)

But when we examine regional population growth trends and the reasons for population change in early Meiji Japan, we find clear differences from the Tokugawa period. Map 11.3 indicates that southern Tōhoku, northern Kantō, Kai and Shinano, Tokyo, and Osaka enjoyed the greatest population growth in early Meiji; yet most of these areas were *not* growing in the first half of the nineteenth century or in the latter half of the Tokugawa period. (See Map 11.2 for Tokugawa trends.) Thus, the na-

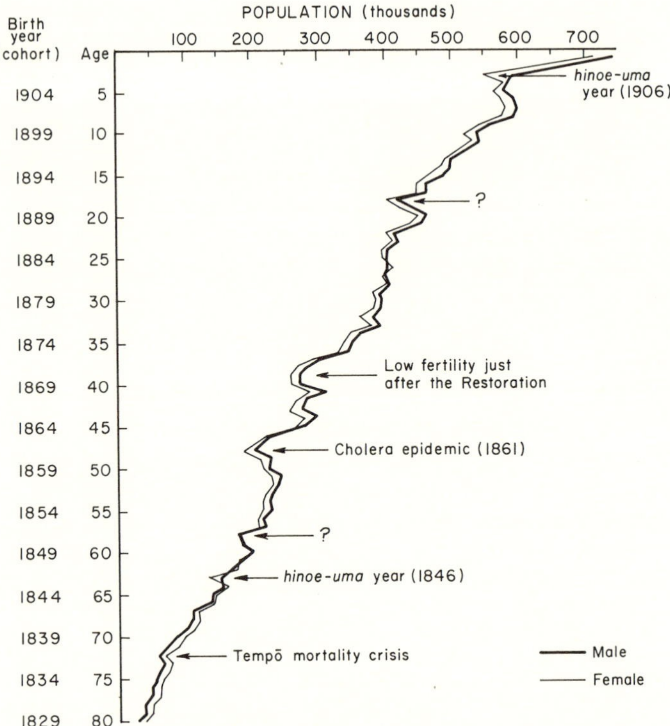

Figure 11.3. Age Composition in Japan, December 31, 1908
Data from Naikaku-tōkeikyoku, *Nihon zenkoku jinkō seitai tōkei* (1911).

tion's population was definitely increasing during the early Meiji era, and the regions that spurted ahead to take the lead in this increase were those that had been "also-rans" during the late Tokugawa.

Figure 11.4 shows the relationships between various types of population change from 1822 to 1846 and from 1872 to 1885 in fourteen regions. (Note, however, that I have omitted changes from 1834 to 1840 in order to minimize the effects of the Tempō mortality crisis.) In late Tokugawa, we see that the population was rising in all regions except northern Kantō. Hokuriku and the side of the Tōhoku region along the Japan Sea showed the highest growth; Tōkai, Kinai, and the areas surrounding Kinai had little growth. The figure for southern Kyūshū is surprisingly low, probably because of the dubious, misleading counting methods employed by Satsuma *han*: population growth in this region was most likely much greater. In early Meiji, eastern Japan (from Hokuriku and Tōkai eastward) recorded a higher growth rate than western Japan; and, surprisingly enough, the region of greatest increase was north-

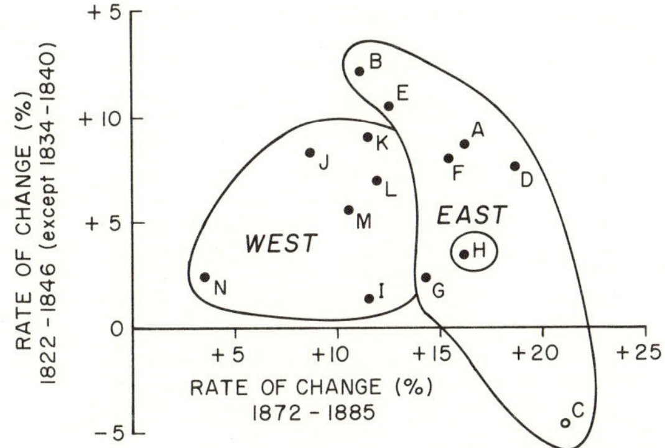

Figure 11.4. Comparison of Population Change, by Region, 1822-1846 and 1872-1885

KEY:

A. East Tōhoku: Mutsu (in 1868 divided into Mutsu, Rikuchū, Rikuzen, Iwaki, and Iwashiro)
B. West Tōhoku: Dewa (in 1868 divided into Uzen and Ugo)
C. North Kantō: Kōzuke, Shimotsuke, and Hitachi
D. South Kantō: Musashi, Sagami, Kazusa, Shimoosa, and Awa
E. Hokuriku: Sado, Echigo, Etchū, Noto, Kaga, Echizen, and Wakasa
F. Tōsan: Kai, Shinano, and Hida
G. Tōkai: Izu, Suruga, Tōtōmi, Mikawa, Owari, and Mino
H. Kinai: Yamashiro, Yamato, Kawachi, Izumi, and Settsu
I. Peripheral Kinai: Ōmi, Iga, Ise, Shin, Kii, Awaji, Harima, and Tanba
J. San'in: Tango, Tajima, Inaba, Hōki, Oki, Izumo, and Iwami
K. Sanyō: Mimasaka, Bizen, Bitchū, Bingo, Aki, Suwō, and Nagato
L. Shikoku: Awa, Sanuki, Iyo, and Tosa
M. North Kyūshū: Chikuzen, Chikugo, Hizen, Iki, Tsushima, Buzen, and Bungo
N. South Kyūshū: Higo, Hyūga, Osumi, and Satsuma

ern Kantō which had been declining at the most precipitous rate in the nation during the latter half of the Tokugawa period. Next came southern Kantō and the Pacific coast of Tōhoku. From 1872 to 1885, Japan's greatest population growth occurred precisely in those areas where it had failed to increase significantly from 1822 to 1846.

During the early Meiji era, the regions in eastern Japan that enjoyed the fastest growth in population were those in which sericulture, silk reeling, and textile industries were the most developed; the regions that showed the least growth were those in which rice was the most important single agricultural product. These two facts lead us to believe, as independent evidence confirms, that the terms of trade shifted in favor of silk and against rice. In fact, the eight provinces that displayed the greatest population increase between 1872 and 1885 (over 18 percent) were Shimotsuke, Kōzuke, Musashi, Iwaki, Sagami, Settsu, Iwashiro, and Mino, in that order. Except for Settsu, which includes the metropolis of Osaka, all were located in eastern Japan; moreover, all were centers of sericulture. Kai and Shinano, the nation's most important sericulture centers, both enjoyed more than a 15 percent increase. (See Map 11.3.) Hokuriku and the Japan Sea coast of Tōhoku became the areas of least population growth in eastern Japan.

As for western Japan, population increase did continue in early Meiji, but at a low rate. Map 11.3 shows that except for Settsu (Osaka), no western province is included in Cluster I, which denotes a 17.5 percent rate of increase or higher. Furthermore, Cluster II contains only the four western provinces of Yamato, Kawachi, and Izumi (which surround Osaka) and Sanuki (in Shikoku). The low figure for southern Kyūshū may be the result of casualties suffered in the Satsuma Rebellion of 1877. In western Japan as well, Kinai, which had a rather low rate of population increase from 1822 to 1846, enjoyed the highest growth rate in early Meiji. This turnabout probably can be explained by improved urban living conditions in Kinai, one of the nation's two highly urbanized areas. Improved hygiene no doubt lowered the high mortality rate that had afflicted this urban region in Tokugawa days.

All of this means that Japan's "demographic center of gravity" moved eastward during the Tokugawa-Meiji transition (see Map 11.1).

Figure 11.4 shows "eastern" Japan as everything eastward from Hokuriku and Tōkai and "western" Japan as everything from Kinki westward. After the beginning of Meiji, eastern Japan's rate of population increase outstripped that of western Japan. The relationship between rates of population change in the east for these two periods shows that regression is negative and that the correlation coefficient is quite high ($r = -.745$). By way of contrast, the dotting is scattered in the west, and the correlation coefficient is not at all significant. Our problem is to determine precisely when this "turnabout" in rates of increase between east and west took place and to discover what caused it.

Japan's national population began to rise after the start of the nineteenth century. As previously noted, if we disregard the short-term Tempō mortality crisis, we find that the population in about 80 percent of the Tokugawa provinces was growing during the first half of that century. Later, in the *bakumatsu* era, there is strong evidence to indicate that an onslaught of cholera lowered the population for a short time, especially in central Japan. But pestilence did not halt the general trend of national population increase. The emergence of export-oriented industries such as raw silk, textiles, and tea meant increased opportunities for employment in the regions where those industries flourished, and this new economic development did much to alter demographic conditions in Japan.

By emphasizing the trend of population growth in nineteenth-century Japan, we should not lose sight of the short-term negative factors which lessened that growth. We have already mentioned one of those negative factors—the cholera epidemics of the 1860s. But Figure 11.3 shows that another fairly sharp drop in the number of births occurred from 1869 to 1872. This latter decrease can be accounted for partly by undercounting, but a more important cause lies in the warfare and social disorder that occurred during and immediately after the Restoration. Combined with the cholera epidemics of the same decade, then, two significant decreases in the number of births took place during this ten-year *bakumatsu*-Restoration era, which may mean that the national population fell for a short time in this period. By 1872 or 1873, the causes of this short-term decrease clearly were eliminated, and Japan's sustained population growth began. Yet we must remember that the latent potential for this continued growth had existed from the 1820s.

The Satsuma Rebellion may have affected regional population change in southern Kyūshū, but the number of casualties was relatively small when viewed on the level of national population statistics. Of greater consequence were the cholera epidemics of 1879 and 1886, for on both occasions more than 100,000 people died. By the late 1870s, however, the Meiji government was moving to eliminate cholera, infectious diseases of the intestinal tract, typhoid fever, and venereal disease, all of which had hitherto taken a great toll in lives. This stepped-up government program to eliminate disease and improve hygiene is overshadowed by its larger goal—to achieve "national wealth and strength"—and, indeed, some scholars interpret modern medicine and hygiene as having been *sacrificed to that end*.[35] This is clearly untrue. Modern medicine and hygiene were essential means to attain that end, and the Meiji government actively sought to disseminate them throughout society. The police were mobilized to combat cholera, and vaccination against smallpox became obligatory, though not everywhere in Japan. Between 1874 and 1882, the construction of hospitals increased tenfold.[36] Medical schools were established at a fast clip. Of course, these measures did not prove effective overnight: it took time to lower the death rate for normal years, but infectious diseases and typhoid, which had decimated Tokugawa populations, virtually disappeared. Not counting the two cholera epidemics already mentioned, no plague resulted in 100,000 or more deaths. Such improvements in hygiene and medicine raised the reproductive capacities of urban populations, which had suffered from high death rates during

[35] Tachikawa, *Byōki no shakai shi.*

[36] Ibid.

the Tokugawa period: the negative feedback function between urbanization and population increase was definitely eliminated at some point in the early Meiji.

Thus far, we have outlined the factors behind post-Restoration national population growth. We should now discuss the problem of regional variation, particularly with respect to geographic areas in which Meiji population trends represented turnabouts in relation to Tokugawa trends.

In the first half of the Meiji period, the two areas that displayed the highest rate of population increase were 1) southern Tōhoku, northern Kantō, and Tōsan, where the sericulture and silk-reeling industries flourished; and 2) the cities of Tokyo, Yokohama, Osaka, and Kobe, where modern industry and the military establishment produced population growth. The former regions had the highest growth rate for rural areas in Japan, and the latter regions, the highest for urban areas. By province, Shimotsuke, Kōzuke, Musashi, Iwaki, and Sagami led the nation in that order; and all of these provinces lay in the east. Moreover, the major centers of Japan's export-oriented industries—sericulture, silk reeling, and tea—were also located in the east. Statistics for the twelve provinces of Iwaki, Iwashiro, Uzen, Kōzuke, Musashi, Sagami, Kaga, Kai, Shinano, Hida, Mino, and Tajima show that in 1882 the per-villager production of raw silk and silk thread accounted for 20 percent of the total value of agricultural output. Except for Tajima, all twelve lay in the east.[37]

By comparing these eleven eastern silk-producing provinces and the eleven provinces that lay in the Sanyō and Shikoku regions, we get markedly different pictures of population change. In nine of the eleven Sanyō and Shikoku provinces, the value of ordinary agricultural products (rice and other foodstuffs) per person accounted for more than 75 percent of total agricultural output. Table 11.1 shows the rates of population change for the two regions between 1872 and 1885 as well as their respective per capita values for silk-related production and ordinary agricultural production (cereals and foodstuffs). We should keep in mind that the statistics for agricultural production used here are by no means highly reliable and that they do not include the villagers' earnings from nonagricultural by-employments. Nevertheless, it is clear that in the silk-producing provinces, not only did the value of silk production account for a much greater percentage of total agricultural output than in Sanyō

[37] On the value of agricultural production, see Nōmushō nōmukyoku, ed., *Meiji jūgonen nōsanhyō* (Tokyo: Meiji bunken shiryō kankōkai, Meiji zenki sangyō hattatsu shi shiryō, 1965 reprint of 1882 ed.), *bessatsu* 5. For village population, I have used Sambō Hombu, ed., *Kyōbuseihyō Meiji jūninen*, 2 vols. (Kyoto: Yanagihara shoten, 1978 reprint of 1879 ed.). I considered every administrative unit of 5,000 persons or more to be an "urban area" or "city" (*toshi*) and subtracted these urban populations in my estimates for each province.

TABLE 11.1
Population Growth and Per Capita Agricultural Production, 1872-1185

Province	Growth Rate	Food Production %	Food Production yen	Silk Production %	Silk Production yen
SILK-PRODUCING AREAS					
Iwaki	22.0	66.6	8.80	26.5	3.51
Iwashiro	18.3	54.7	9.63	41.0	7.22
Uzen	12.6	74.8	8.82	25.0	2.95
Kōzuke	24.8	31.7	6.83	65.4	14.08
Musashi	23.9	68.7	12.05	21.9	3.85
Sagami	19.3	70.5	8.04	23.0	2.63
Kaga	12.8	67.4	10.86	22.1	3.57
Kai	17.1	61.4	9.48	33.9	5.23
Shinano	15.0	53.4	9.30	42.6	7.43
Hida	14.6	66.3	19.44	32.6	9.56
Mino	18.0	67.0	6.67	23.0	2.29
AVERAGE	18.0	62.0		32.5	
(Average income per capita)	(16.47)		(9.99)		(5.67)
SANYŌ AND SHIKOKU					
Mimasaka	11.9	82.9	6.36	1.3	0.10
Bizen	7.5	78.5	10.95	0.3	0.05
Bitchū	12.8	83.9	6.83	0.9	0.08
Bingo	14.2	77.8	6.61	0.2	0.02
Aki	13.9	76.5	6.59	0.1	0.01
Suō	9.9	76.2	6.98	0.3	0.03
Nagato	8.5	93.0	8.52	0.2	0.02
Awa	11.9	65.1	7.49	3.0	0.35
Sanuki	15.3	74.3	9.12	—	—
Iyo	14.5	84.5	5.95	0.7	0.05
Tosa	4.8	81.0	7.57	1.2	0.12
AVERAGE	11.4	79.5		0.7	
(Average income per capita)	(9.57)		(7.54)		(0.07)

and Shikoku, but the per capita value of food production was also higher than in Sanyō and Shikoku.

To a certain extent this contrast stems from the spread in food prices between these two regions, since interregional differences in rice prices were great during the 1880s. In the silk-producing provinces as a whole, the average price of rice per *koku* was 7.4 yen; in the six Kantō and Tōsan provinces, it was as high as 8.4 yen. But in Sanyō and Shikoku, the price averaged 6.4 yen. In the Japan Sea coastal provinces, the price was roughly 4.2 yen per *koku*; in consuming areas of the Pacific coast, it was 7 to 8 yen. Given these regional price variations, it seems that the higher cost of food products in the silk-producing regions was related not only to proximity to the Tokyo market, but also to increased demand caused by rapid population growth and by growing purchasing power.

These investigations allow us to draw the following tentative conclusions. First, sometime between 1846 and 1872, the rate of population increase for eastern Japan surpassed that for western Japan. Second, this spurt in population growth rates was most pronounced in eastern silk-producing provinces.

A Regional Comparison

In this section we will compare the early Meiji demographic development of two selected areas that had displayed significantly different patterns of population change during the Tokugawa period, particularly in the eighteenth century. Of course, comparative analyses of this type must be conducted for many other areas as well, but limitations of time and space force us to focus on these two regions of marked contrast.

One area, Kōzuke and Shimotsuke provinces, lies in northern Kantō and constitutes the modern prefectures of Gumma and Tochigi; the other area, Bingo and Aki provinces, is located in the Sanyō region and forms present-day Hiroshima prefecture.[38] I chose these two areas because 1) both had roughly the same size population at the beginning of the nineteenth century—852,000 for Kōzuke-Shimotsuke and 889,000 for Bingo-Aki—according to the *bakufu* survey of 1804; 2) these eastern and western areas displayed contrasting patterns of population change in the Tokugawa and Meiji periods, as shown on Maps 11.2 and 11.3; and 3) provincial and prefectural boundaries coincide in both areas, which allows us to link their respective Tokugawa and Meiji statistics.

Between 1721 and 1846, the population of Kōzuke-Shimotsuke fell a full 29 percent, from 1,130,000 to 807,000—an annual decrease of 0.2 percent. During the same period, in contrast, the population of Bingo-Aki rose 34 percent, from 682,000 to 915,000—an annual increase of more than 0.2 percent.[39] As noted earlier, the population loss in Kōzuke-

[38] These areas are abbreviated "KS Area" and "BA Area," respectively, in Figures 11.5-11.8 and Table 11.2.

[39] On source materials for the Tokugawa period, see fn. 20, above.

Shimotsuke, the area of greatest population decline in the nation, was caused by bad weather in the eighteenth century and by heavy out-migration to Edo. Even within the limited interval of 1822-1846, Kōzuke-Shimotsuke suffered a 5.3 percent population loss, while Bingo-Aki enjoyed an 8.9 percent gain. As revealed in Figure 11.5, the population of the BA Area was definitely on the upswing and, if not for the Tempō mortality crisis of 1837-1838, would have grown 0.4 percent annually during this interval, which is a fairly high sustained growth rate for a preindustrial society.[40]

But from 1872 on, the wide spread in population figures for these two regions rapidly began to close.[41] Between 1872 and 1885, Bingo-Aki registered a population increase of 14 percent, or 0.9 percent annually—which is by no means low, even when early Meiji underregistration is taken into consideration. On the other hand, Kōzuke-Shimotsuke recorded an astounding 25.6 percent increase, or 1.7 percent annually, during the same period. According to *bakufu* surveys, the Bingo-Aki population had overtaken that of Kōzuke-Shimotsuke sometime between

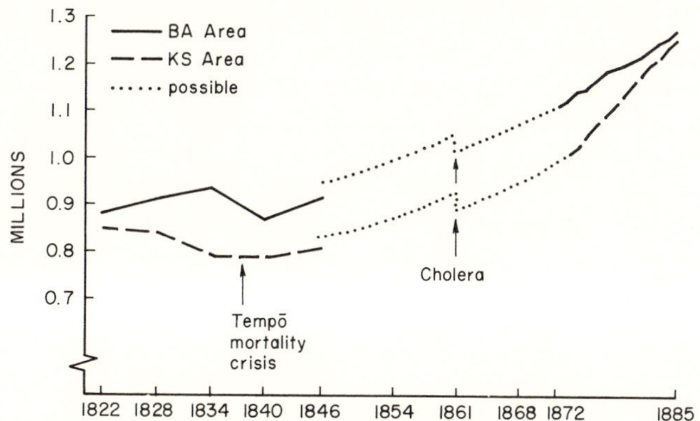

Figure 11.5. Population Trends in KS (Kōzuke-Shimotsuke) and BA (Bingo-Aki) Areas, 1822-1885

[40] Any direct linkage of the figures for 1846 with those for 1872 (see Figure 11.5) is purely speculative. To do this, I added the estimated unreported population to the 1846 figure, and arbitrarily set the death rate from the 1861 cholera epidemic at 5 percent. The estimates of unreported population for 1846 were derived from statistics compiled by status (*mibun*) in 1881; these amount to 4 and 5 percent, respectively, for the Kōzuke-Shimotsuke and Bingo-Aki areas. I also assumed that there was no change in their rates of population increase between 1846 and 1872 except for the year 1861. Of course, these presuppositions must be verified by future town- and village-level studies, but population age-structures (to be discussed below) lend credence to such assumptions.

[41] On source materials for the Meiji period, see fn. 9, above.

1804 and 1822; yet we now see that by 1885 the two areas had roughly the same number of inhabitants. And if figures for migrating populations (discussed below) are added, Kōzuke-Shimotsuke has clearly overtaken Bingo-Aki once again.

Precisely when did this unusual population growth in Kōzuke-Shimotsuke begin? Statistics for 1885, the first year for which province-by-province quinquennial age structures are known, provide a clue, for they permit us to compare population age-structures in the two areas. (See Figure 11.6.) The decrease in 46-to-50-year-olds and 21-to-25-year-olds in Bingo-Aki indicates the damage inflicted by mortality crises in 1837-1838 and 1861. Although there are no pronounced drops in the Kōzuke-Shimotsuke age structures, the KS Area has higher (by 1.3 percent) component ratios than Bingo-Aki for 6-to-10-year-olds and 1-to-5-year-olds. If we assume that there was no great difference in child mortality rates between the two areas, this last discrepancy points to the emergence of a high birth rate in Kōzuke-Shimotsuke, beginning from about 1875.

As mentioned earlier, provincial and prefectural vital statistics are available from 1877, but their reliability is by no means great. Figure 11.7 drawn up from those vital statistics, shows that although there clearly was a difference in crude birth rates between the two areas, their crude death rates were not far apart. But these figures are inconceivably low, to be sure. To obtain more precise statistics on births, I compiled ratios of the number of females of childbearing age to the number of births for the respective areas, which also permitted me to address general fertility. Unfortunately, age differentials for 1880-1883 are different from those for 1884-1885, so I could not obtain consecutive statistics. Therefore, I

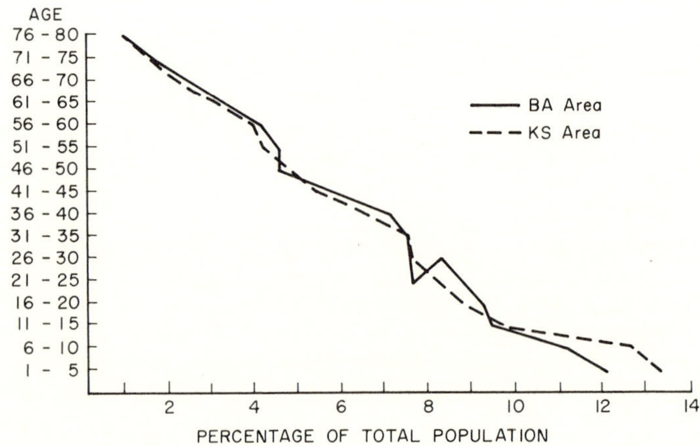

Figure 11.6. Age Components in KS (Kōzuke-Shimotsuke) and BA (Bingo-Aki) Areas, 1885

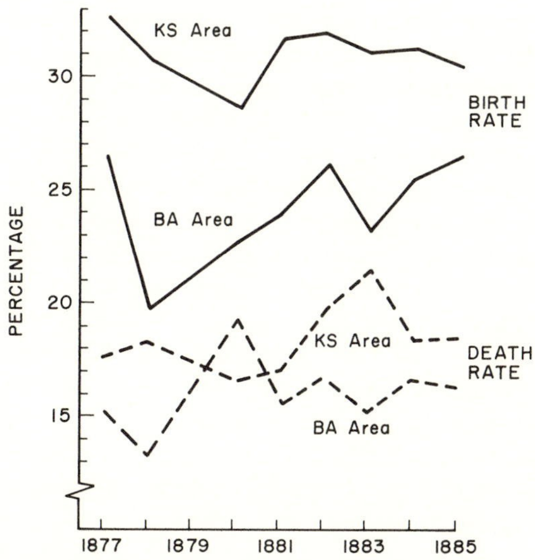

Figure 11.7. Crude Birth and Death Rates in KS (Kōzuke-Shimotsuke) and BA (Bingo-Aki) Areas, 1877-1885

sought to determine ratios of the number of females aged 20-49 to the number of births for the period 1880-1883, and of the number of females aged 20-39 to the number of births for 1884-1885. The averages for 1880-1883 were 0.158 for Kōzuke-Shimotsuke, 0.124 for Bingo-Aki, and 0.125 for the nation as a whole. Averages for 1884-1885 were 0.216 for Kōzuke-Shimotsuke, 0.177 for Bingo-Aki, and 0.178 for the nation as a whole. Thus we see that Bingo-Aki averages were virtually the same as national averages, but that those for Kōzuke-Shimotsuke were 26 and 21 percent higher, which shows that fertility clearly was high in the KS Area.

One further factor behind population change—a social factor—should be discussed. This has to do with in-migrating and out-migrating populations as they appear in domicile registers. Needless to say, when one area has a greater number of register entries and in-migrants than it has register deletions and out-migrants, that area in theory should be taking people away from other areas. But in actuality, the number of out-migrants never equals that of in-migrants as they should when national totals are made from register counts. For example, on January 1, 1884, there were 520,000 in-migrants and 290,000 out-migrants. But there was little difference in the register entries and register deletions—both were about 110,000. We should not lose sight of this statistical shortcoming when assessing the social changes in population shown in Table 11.2.

Note that there were more register entries and legally recognized in-migrants coming into Kōzuke-Shimotsuke than there were persons leaving that area. For Bingo-Aki, on the other hand, out-migration was greater than in-migration. But we should note that the population turnover thus produced was not of significant size: it was less than the turnover produced by natural causes. Thus, there was not much difference between the "legally domiciled population" (*honseki jinkō*) and the "resident population" (*genjū jinkō*) in this period. Yet, as Table 11.2 shows, when we compare "resident population" figures for the two areas, we find that Kōzuke-Shimotsuke had already surpassed Bingo-Aki by the beginning of 1884.

The reader no doubt has already guessed the causes of this rapid population increase in the Kōzuke-Shimotsuke area. According to agricultural output statistics for both areas in 1882, the per capita value of agricultural output in Kōzuke was 21.5 yen; in Shimotsuke, 10.6 yen.[42] When we consider that the national average for this year was 11.9 yen

TABLE 11.2
Population Indices for Kōzuke-Shimotsuke (KS) and Bingo-Aki (BA) Areas, 1884

	KS Area	BA Area
Legally domiciled population	1,246,151	1,262,561
Births	39,043	32,142
In-registered	5,338	2,325
Deaths	23,088	21,271
Out-registered	4,411	3,634
Total entries	45,417	36,227
Total deletions	27,830	25,326
SUBTOTAL	+17,587	+10,901
In-migration	27,338	2,745
Out-migration	9,966	6,159
SUBTOTAL	+17,372	−3,774
Resident population	1,263,523	1,258,787

NOTE: All changes occurred in 1883. "Legally domiciled population" = *honseki jinkō*; "resident population" = *genjū jinkō*.

[42] See fn. 38, above.

(s.d. + 3.8 yen), we see that, in contrast, Kōzuke's figure is extremely high. Moreover, the figure for Kōzuke, when broken down, shows that the value of ordinary agricultural production (mainly cereals and other foodstuffs) was 6.8 yen, or 32 percent of the total, while that for specialized agricultural production (raw materials for industry) was 14.7 yen, or 68 percent of the total. Of these specialized products, the value of silk thread and raw silk output was 14.1 yen, accounting for 65 percent of total agricultural output. No similar example can be found elsewhere in Japan.

By way of contrast, in Bingo-Aki the average per capita value of agricultural output was 8.6 yen. Ordinary agricultural production accounted for 77 percent of total output, specialized agricultural production, 23 percent. Rice made up approximately 60 percent of the former production figure and comprised 49 percent of total agricultural production in the area. In Kōzuke, the price of rice was 8.6 yen per *koku*; in Aki, 6.1 yen. In Kōzuke, the amount of rice produced per farmer was 0.53 *koku*; in Aki, 0.69 *koku*; and on the national average, 0.99 *koku*. The value of rice production per farmer, however, was another matter, with Kōzuke showing 4.6 yen to Aki's 4.3 yen.

Figure 11.8 shows trends in sex ratios for the two areas.[43] In 1750, the first year for which figures are available, the sex ratio for Kōzuke-Shimotsuke was 123.5 (females = 100), but by 1846 it had dropped sharply, to 106.5. On the other hand, the sex ratio for Bingo-Aki increased slightly, from 104.8 to 106.5, during the same period. In Kōzuke-Shimotsuke, population decline was combined with a lowering of the sex ratio: the male population fell to approximately 67 percent of its original

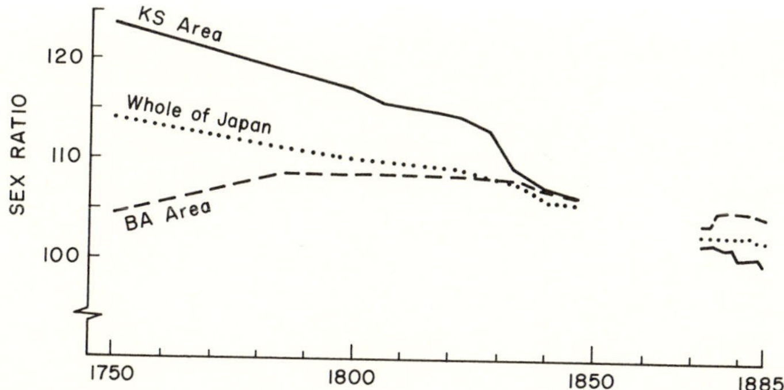

Figure 11.8. Sex Ratio Trends in KS (Kōzuke-Shimotsuke) and BA (Bingo-Aki) Areas, 1750-1885

[43] Statistics for sex ratios derive from source materials listed in fn. 20, above.

size during this period; the decline in the female population was limited to about 20 percent.

At present it is impossible to ascertain just what caused this decline. In general, the sex ratio for central Japan during the late Tokugawa period remained at a normal level, while in the Kantō and Tōhoku regions, and in Shikoku and Kyūshū, it fell from a high to a normal level.[44] No single factor can explain the changes that occurred in the Tokugawa sex ratio as well as the diverse population changes that took place simultaneously thoughout Japan. Rather, the answer lies in the changing position of women in society and in the family, in the rising value of women's labor, and in the declining mortality rate for females during pregnancy and childbirth. These changes, moreover, took place according to regional time lags during the Tokugawa period—beginning and taking hold earliest in central Japan, and extending to remoter areas by the early eighteenth century. These changes then spread to all parts of the nation more or less evenly after the period when population data became available.

Sex ratios in the early Meiji era for our two areas are as follows. In 1872, Kōzuke-Shimotsuke had a ratio of 101.9 and Bingo-Aki 104.1; the national average was 103.0. In 1885, the Kōzuke-Shimotsuke ratio was 100.0; Bingo-Aki's was 104.9; and the national average was 102.4. During the twenty-six year statistical gap from 1846 to 1872, then, there was a turnabout in the sex ratios for the two areas. Figure 11:8 shows that in 1750 the sex ratios for the two areas were far apart—one far above and the other far below the national average. But like the original difference in population size between these two areas, this wide divergence in sex ratios gradually narrowed. By 1830, both were about the same as the national average, and by the early Meiji era, both were slightly below it. All of this indicates a turnabout in the relative standings held by the two areas with respect to sex ratios. Perhaps most impressive is the rapid decline of the sex ratio in Kōzuke-Shimotsuke after 1828. Most likely the sex ratio of surviving babies had become balanced a few decades before that year; or there may have been a lowering of the death rate in women (which had been high until 1828). In any case, something important must have occurred to lower the sex ratio. At this point, I can offer only the following observations. The sex ratio in Kōzuke-Shimotsuke became moderate completely apart from any change in population size. If we are to interpret this fact as resulting from the "rational"

[44] See Hayami Akira, "Tokugawa kōki jinkō no chiikiteki tokusei," *Mita gakkai zasshi*, vol. 64, no. 8 (1971), pp. 67-80. Recently, Thomas C. Smith, Susan B. Hanley and Kozo Yamamura, and Carl C. Mosk have entered the debate on changes in the Tokugawa sex ratio.

behavior of peasants, who made up the vast majority of Japan's population, we must first come up with an explanation as to why the balancing of the sex ratio was a "rational" occurrence.

CONCLUSION

We have come to see that Japan's national population began increasing from the start of the nineteenth century and that, after the 1820s, this trend of stable growth held true for virtually all localities. The mortality crises of 1837-1838 and 1861 cannot be overlooked; yet, despite these temporary setbacks, the population grew at an annual rate of 0.3 to 0.4 percent.

Regional variations did exist; but on the whole Japan's population continued to rise during the statistical gap from 1846 to 1872. Toward the end of this quarter-century, those regions where the sericulture and silk-reeling industries had developed recorded an annual population growth on the order of 1 percent. This growth probably stemmed mainly from an increased birth rate; but a lowered sex ratio or, in other words, a higher percentage of females to males (beginning in the 1830s) may also have been a contributory factor.

What do these findings tell us about the relationship between population and the economy, a problem introduced at the beginning of this chapter? No firm conclusions can be arrived at until many, many more empirical studies have been conducted; at this time, I can submit the following very tentative answer.

During the Tokugawa period, there was moderate population growth in the nation's most economically advanced region—the west—particularly in areas surrounding the Inland Sea, where opportunities were plentiful for nonagricultural by-employments in cottage industries. The Hokuriku area, where rice was cultivated successfully as a cash crop, also enjoyed moderate growth. The apparent "stagnation" in aggregate national population figures was a purely chance occurrence caused by exogenously induced population decreases in Tōhoku and northern Kantō that offset gains in western Japan and Hokuriku. The nation's most highly urbanized areas—southern Kantō and the Kinai—failed to grow, or even declined slightly in population, owing to the negative feedback function. Considered together, these facts suggest that economic development and population increase in Tokugawa farming villages went hand in hand: population stagnancy was definitely *not* a precondition of economic development.

I wish to reserve judgment as to whether or not the demographic transition theory applies to the period under examination, since the early Meiji birth rate did in fact rise in those regions where export-oriented industries developed. Even so, no proper conclusion can be drawn until we take into consideration the period after 1890, when industrialization began in earnest—and such an inquiry lies beyond the scope of this study.

Japan's population increase, which began at the start of the nineteenth century and picked up speed after the 1850s, stemmed mainly from a rising birth rate. Yet this does not necessarily mean that the death rate did not fall. In many of the villages that I have surveyed, mortality did in fact decline after the 1840s.[45] However, empirical studies are too few to be able to draw any definite conclusion on this matter, and in any case, the short-term death rate jumped abnormally during the mortality crises of 1837-1838 and 1861. Japan was free from the horrors of pestilence only after the 1870s, when it imported modern science and hygiene from the West. Prior to that, Japan's population increase was interrupted by exogenously induced crises on a few occasions, but the latent potential for increase surfaced undeniably in the nineteenth century.

What phrase should we use to describe the pattern of population increase that took place in nineteenth-century Japan—an increase whose causes have yet to be identified fully? Western Japan's population had been growing at approximately 0.2 percent annually since 1822; it did not begin increasing suddenly in the nineteenth century. So it was for the nation as a whole. Japan's national population was on the upswing during the late Tokugawa period; this increase only accelerated in the nineteenth century. I believe that the emergence of the stem family as the unit of agricultural production in Tokugawa Japan provided Japan with the potential for population growth. Therefore, growth was *to be expected* in the Tokugawa population; indeed, the *absence* of population increase would have required explanation. When we consider the low ratio of urban population and the impressive rural economic expansion that took place in areas where population increased, we cannot but conclude that moderate population growth in farming villages went hand in hand with economic development in this preindustrial society. During

[45] In Yokouchi village, Shinano province, the crude death rate was 19.5 per thousand from 1826 to 1850, and 17.5 per thousand from 1851 to 1871. In Nishijo village, Mino province, the death rate fell from an average of 21 per thousand before 1830 to 16 per thousand after 1845-1850. See Akira Hayami, "Demographic Aspects of a Village in Tokugawa Japan," in Paul Deprez, ed., *Population and Economics* (Winnipeg: University of Manitoba Press, 1970), pp. 109-125, as well as Hayami Akira, "Nōshū Nishijō mura no jinkō shiryō," in *Kenkyū kiyō Shōwa 47–nendo* (Tokyo: Tokugawa rinsei shi kenkyūsho, 1973). From just two village surveys, of course, nothing can be said about Tokugawa Japan as a whole. Scores of similar studies must be accumulated.

the statistically desolate quarter-century from 1846 to 1872, this combination of moderate population increase accompanied by economic development spread throughout Japan, spurred on by irreversible domestic commercial advances plus the appearance of export-oriented industries after the opening of the treaty ports. After 1872, this trend became the sustained population growth that continues to our day.

CHAPTER 12

CASTLE TOWNS IN TRANSITION

BY GILBERT ROZMAN

What happened to the castle towns (*jōkamachi*)? Apart from the question of what happened to the samurai, there is probably no more obvious question to ask about the transition away from the Tokugawa social order. A planned spatial distribution of settlements and, within them, of social classes had been essential to the Tokugawa system. The end of that system brought the inevitability of change. Study of the changes that were taking place in urban networks and urban land use can tell us a good deal—both about the decisions of large numbers of families in the wake of reform and about the adaptability of the old order for modern urban growth.

In the middle of the nineteenth century, Japan was unique among major countries in having a large network of administrative cities, each built around a castle and founded on two principles that are strikingly incompatible with modern urban development. First, each of these castle cities under the protection of its daimyo enjoyed a *monopoly position* within its hinterland, which was artificially separated from surrounding territories. For each domain, except some of the smallest which lacked a city of their own, there was one castle town. Second, the internal land use of each city, extending out from the lord's castle and surrounding moats, reflected the *planned segregation* of social classes. The samurai, located according to their rank, occupied large tracts of land including estates in close proximity to the castle, while the townsmen (*chōnin*) were crowded into separate wards.

Joining these 200-odd castle towns were three great central cities (Edo, Osaka, and Kyoto) and hundreds of local and regional port cities, post towns, and small commercial and craft centers. The castle towns were intermediate between these other two types; they flourished as the core of Japan's urban system during the two and one-half to three centuries of their existence. Their continued dependence on such restrictive principles must have appeared to outsiders as a medieval holdover in contrast to the efficient organization of space in cities elsewhere, geared to the unrestricted movement of people and goods. When the Meiji Restoration recognized new freedoms and the domains were abolished in 1871, the two principles—monopolies for designated cities and planned segregation of social classes—were abandoned. Table 12.1 shows the chronology of reforms. Castle towns were transformed under the impact of market forces.

What was the nature of the transformation for these distinctive cities during the decades of the Tokugawa-Meiji transition, especially after their

TABLE 12.1
Chronology of Reforms Affecting Japanese Cities, 1859-1889

1859	Ports opened to international trade
1862	Revision of *sankin kōtai* system, reducing residence requirements in Edo
1868	Charter Oath granting all people the right to pursue their own calling
	Imperial edict proclaiming Tokyo (Edo) the capital of Japan
1868/69	Abolition of barriers (such as highway checkpoints) to free movement
1869	Emperor Meiji takes up residence in Tokyo (formerly Edo) Castle
	Daimyo return lands to central administration, but retain posts
1871	Castles taken over by central government; new administrative divisions (*ken* and *fu*) chosen
	City land tax exemptions ended
1872	First railway built, connecting Shimbashi (Tokyo) to Yokohama
1873	End of grain storage system used by *han* in Osaka
1875/76	Readjustment of *ken* boundaries, bringing further consolidation
1876	All samurai stipends canceled
1878	Consolidation of local administration
1888/89	Revision of local administration based on local autonomy; new qualifications to form a city (*shi*); consolidation of villages
1889	Tokyo-Kobe railroad complete, linking Kantō and Kinai

special status was ended and samurai were able to disperse? The answer to this question does not require us to take much account of the modern forces of urbanization that have been so conspicuous over the past century. Prior to 1885 there was little railroad construction, buildup of factory production, or granting of municipal self-government. All these factors became important in the next period, when urbanization quickened. During the transition years, different forces were at work. Some changes in city populations resulted from the development of foreign trade and the designation of new administrative centers (*fu* and *ken*). Other changes reveal the fate of cities shorn of their privileges and their exclusive samurai residential districts. One might expect the castle towns to have fared poorly under the new competitive conditions, but we shall see that castle towns survived to form a large part of Japan's modern network of cities. The castle towns proved that they were not primarily parasites, and they provided a solid foundation for modern urban development.

Much has been written, primarily in Japanese, about castle towns in their earlier stages of development: 1) the formative sixteenth-century decades[1] when settlements developed around the lord's castle; 2) the large-scale seventeenth-century expansion[2] within the Tokugawa system; and 3) the gradual maturation, without major transformation, over more than one and one-half centuries.[3] Unlike these three earlier periods of development, the fourth period, in which castle towns gave way to modern cities, has yet to be broadly examined. No one book has yet been devoted either to Meiji cities or to the continuities between late Tokugawa and early Meiji urban change. There exist only scattered articles or chapters, all in Japanese, on selected aspects of the urban transition.[4]

[1] Harada Tomohiko, *Nihon hōken toshi kenkyū* (Tokyo: Tokyo University Press, 1957); Toyoda Takeshi, *Nihon no hōken toshi* (Tokyo: Iwanami shoten, 1968); Matsumoto Toyotoshi, *Jōkamachi no rekishichiri gakuteki kenkyū* (Tokyo: Yoshikawa kōbunkan, 1967).

[2] Nishikawa Koji, *Nihon toshi shi kenkyū* (Tokyo: Nihon hōsō shuppan kyōkai, 1972); Nakabe Yoshiko, *Kinsei toshi shakai keizai shi kenkyū* (Tokyo: Kōyō shobō, 1974); Nakabe Yoshiko, *Jōkamachi* (Kyoto: Ryūhara shoten, 1978); Wakita Osamu, "Kinsei shoki no toshi keizai," *Nihon shi kenkyū*, no. 200 (April 1979), pp. 52-75; James L. McClain, *Kanazawa: A Seventeenth-Century Japanese Castle Town* (New Haven: Yale University Press, 1982).

[3] Yamori Kazuhiko, *Jōkamachi* (Tokyo: Gakuseisha, 1972); Yamori Kazuhiko, *Toshi puran no kenkyū* (Tokyo: Ōmeido, 1970); Fujimoto Toshiharu, *Kinsei toshi no chiiki kōzō: sono rekishichiri gakuteki kenkyū* (Tokyo: Kokon shoin, 1976); Matsumoto Shirō, "Kinsei kōki no toshi to minshū," *Iwanami kōza Nihon rekishi*, vol. 12, *kinsei* no. 4 (Tokyo: Iwanami shoten, 1976), pp. 89-146.

[4] Examples include Fujioka Kenjirō, ed., *Nihon rekishichiri sōsetsu: kindai hen* (Tokyo: Yoshikawa kōbunkan, 1977); Morikawa Hiroshi, "Meiji shonen in okeru Hiroshima ken no toshi to sono kinō," *Shigaku kenkyū*, no. 99 (March 1967).

One reason for the neglect of this period of urban development is the dearth of data, in comparison to the proliferation of statistics for more recent periods of Japanese history, and the extraordinary records (for a premodern society) that are preserved from the preceding era. Nevertheless, the penchant for gathering statistics is also evident in the early Meiji; there exist valuable materials for examining both the distribution by size and the plans (including social structure) of cities.[5] Japanese scholars have already analyzed some of the urban statistics and maps.[6] Further analysis of available data and review of the existing scholarship make it possible to go beyond their efforts and draw general conclusions about the fate of the castle towns.

URBANIZATION

What changes occurred in the urban population of Japan during the years of transition to the mid-1880s? Before focusing on this brief period in the history of cities, let us consider the long-term trends of urbanization on either side of the transition. The second half of the Tokugawa period was a time of gradual deurbanization in which castle towns as well as Osaka and Kyoto were the primary losers. Thomas Smith and Nakabe Yoshiko have compiled data showing that the number of townspeople in most castle towns was in decline.[7] Of thirty-seven cities for which they have found records, twenty-seven declined, six remained stable, and only four grew appreciably in population. There was a shift of population toward smaller cities and cities with other primary functions, principally local commercial and handicraft centers (known as *zaigōmachi*) and regional ports. Nonetheless, Japan remained relatively urbanized. I have estimated that 16-17 percent of the population in the late Tokugawa resided in cities of 3,000+. The largest eighty cities (two-thirds of these

[5] Urban population statistics are to be found in Sambō Hombu, ed., *Kyōbuseihyō* (Tokyo: 1875 and 1880); Naimushō kosekikyoku, *Nihon zenkoku kokōhyō* (Tokyo: Naimushō kosekikyoku, 1884); and *Tofumeiyū kokōhyō* (Tokyo: Naimushō chirikyoku, 1884).

[6] On population data, see Morikawa Hiroshi, "Meiji shonen no toshi bumpu," *Jimbun chiri*, vol. 14, no. 5 (1962), pp. 45-63; Kurosaki Chiharu, "Meiji zenki no toshi ni tsuite," *Shakai keizai shigaku*, vol. 39, no. 6 (1974), pp. 94-113; Hayami Akira, "Kinsei kōki chiikibetsu jinkō hendo to toshi jinkō hiritsu no kanren," *Tokugawa rinsei shi kenkyūsho kenkyū kiyō* (March 1975), pp. 230-244; and Hayami Akira, "Tokugawa kōki jinkō hendo no chiikiteki tokusei," *Mita gakkai zasshi*, vol. 64, no. 8 (August 1971), pp. 67-80. On maps, see Yamori, *Jōkamachi* and *Toshi puran no kenkyū*.

[7] Thomas C. Smith, "Pre-Modern Economic Growth: Japan and the West," *Past and Present*, no. 60 (1973), pp. 127-160; Nakabe, *Jōkamachi*, pp. 306-310.

were castle towns) exceeded 10,000 residents each and comprised 12-13 percent of the country's population.[8]

Japan's modern spurt in urbanization was clearly visible by the period 1893-1898; from that time, the annual rate of city growth averaged more than 3 percent, except for rare interruptions, until the slowdown in urbanization during the second half of the 1970s. During the preceding period, 1889-1893, growth averaged slightly under 2 percent.[9] Prior to that, although there was recovery in the late 1870s and 1880s from a decade or so of urban decline, the levels of late Tokugawa urbanization were probably not surpassed. As seen in Table 12.2, in 1886 the percentage of Japan's population in cities of 10,000+ was roughly the same as the estimates for the early nineteenth century. A massive redistribution of urban population into several Pacific coast megalopolises became pronounced only after the transition years.

Sandwiched between these two long periods of continuous trends—first gradual deconcentration, then rapid concentration—is the transition from one pattern to the other. Comparisons in Table 12.2 of the number and population of cities of various sizes shed some light on this period. Prior to 1875 there was a marked decline in residents of the largest cities (130,000+) and a notable increase in the population of small cities (3,000-9,999). The decline was in the three central cities of Tokyo, Osaka, and Kyoto, and the increases occurred in hundreds of small towns, perhaps a reflection of continuous growth over the previous half-century or longer. Castle towns were not in the forefront of urban population changes to 1875 unless one considers (as I do not) Edo, with its huge samurai population, to have been a city of this type. It was the central cities, not the castle towns, that lost out in the 1860s and early 1870s.

By the late 1870s, city populations were clearly growing again, although boundary realignments that occurred by the mid-1880s may account for some of the growth indicated for larger cities. From 1879 to 1884, according to Itō Shigeru, the population of seventy-seven large cities rose by 1.6 percent annually.[10] In Table 12.2 Fujioka Kenjirō's data for 1886 indicate that the three largest cities had recovered their peak population, cities of 10,000+ had collectively once again reached 12-13 percent of the national population, and smaller cities had achieved a more substantial presence than in the Tokugawa era. Tokyo had re-

[8] Gilbert Rozman, *Urban Networks in Ch'ing China and Tokugawa Japan* (Princeton: Princeton University Press, 1973).

[9] Itō Shigeru, "Kenkyū nōto: senzenki Nihon no toshi seichō" (pt. 1), *Nihon rōdō kyōkai zasshi*, vol. 24, no. 7 (July 1982), p. 28.

[10] Itō Shigeru, "Kenkyū nōto: senzenki Nihon no toshi seichō" (pt. 2), *Nihon rōdō kyōkai zasshi*, vol. 24, no. 8 (August 1982), p. 31.

TABLE 12.2
Distribution of Cities, by Size, Late Tokugawa–1886

	Late Tokugawa*		1875†		1878‡	1886§	
	No. of Cities	Population (millions)	No. of Cities	Population (millions)	No. of Cities	No. of Cities	Population (millions)
130,000+	3	1.8	3	1.358	3	3	1.8
50-129,999 }			7	.552	7	9	.708
	20	1.0					
30-49,999 }			17	.619	15 }		(1.15)
						115	
10-29,999	60	1.0	62	.999	74 }		(1.15)
5-9,999 }			134	.919		154	1.072
	250	1.3					
3-4,999 }			244	.920		305	1.159
	333	5.1	467	5.367		586	(7.1)
Total population (millions)		30-32		33.007			38.541
% in cities 10,000+		12-13		10-11			12-13
% in cities 5,000+		—		13-14			15-16
% in places 3,000+		16-17		16			18-19

SOURCES: * = Gilbert Rozman, *Urban Networks in Ch'ing China and Tokugawa Japan* (Princeton: Princeton University Press, 1973); † = Sambō Hombu, ed., *Kyōbuseihyō* (Tokyo: 1875); ‡ = Fujimoto Toshiharu, *Kinsei toshi no chiiki kōzō: sono rekishichiri gakuteki kenkyū* (Tokyo: Kokon shoin, 1976), p. 135; § = Fujioka Kenjirō, ed., *Nihon rekishi chiri sōsetsu: kindai hen* (Tokyo: Yoshikawa kōbunkan, 1977), p. 182, and Kurosaki Chiharu, "Meiji zenki no toshi ni tsuite," *Shakai keizai shigaku*, vol. 39, no. 6 (1974), pp. 99-102.

NOTE: Numbers in parentheses are estimates.

covered to 1,120,000; and Osaka (310,000) and Kyoto (250,000) were little changed from their late Tokugawa population totals, although well below their eighteenth-century peaks. Thus the new circumstances of the Meiji era accelerated two long-term trends: deurbanization and redistribution from large to small cities.

In this time of transition, policy changes appear to have produced countervailing effects in castle towns. As Henry Smith's chapter in this book shows, Tokyo's (Edo's) population declined sharply after 1862, in large part because many samurai returned to their domains after relaxation of the alternate-residence requirements. Further decline in Tokyo occurred at the time of the Meiji Restoration. In large measure, the samurai were returning to the castle towns. In 1884, after large numbers of commoners had migrated to the city, only 93,637 of Tokyo *fu*'s 1,020,411 people were registered as samurai—a far cry from estimates of 40 percent or more for the late Tokugawa.[11] Of course, many castle towns experienced a degree of depopulation too—in some domains, this decline may have begun with penalties of a reduction-in-area imposed for active support of the Tokugawa;[12] elsewhere, it may have come after domains were abolished or, later, after samurai status and stipends were eliminated. The statistics from 1875 on do not establish the short-term trends that preceded. But if we examine the 1875 statistics in relationship to the production figures for domains in the Tokugawa era, we may be able to distinguish how castle towns of different sizes and regions fared.

City Size and Domain Production

John Hall suggests a rule of thumb that the population of a castle town equaled one-tenth of the *kokudaka*, or *koku* rating, of its *han*.[13] Supportive of this hypothesis are data that show that more than 200 former castle towns had a combined population exceeding 2.2 million in 1875 while their *han* registered more than 22 million *koku* (according to the *uchidaka*, an upgraded and more accurate measure of production, not necessarily the original assessment, or *omotedaka*). As seen in Table 12.3, the 212 former castle towns or, in a small number of cases, substantial *jin'ya* (subadministrative centers staffed by *daikan*) averaged 10.1 *koku* per city resident. Hall's rule of thumb holds up remarkably well except

[11] Naimushō kosekikyoku, *Nihon zenkoku kokōhyō*, pp. 3-4.

[12] For information on changes in the holdings of each domain, see Kōdama Kōta and Kitajima Masamoto, eds., *Hanshi sōran* (Tokyo: Shinjinbutsu shoraisha, 1977).

[13] John W. Hall, "The Castle Town and Japan's Modern Urbanization," in John W. Hall and Marius B. Jansen, eds., *Studies in the Institutional History of Early Modern Japan* (Princeton: Princeton University Press, 1968), pp. 169-188.

TABLE 12.3
Populations of Former Castle Cities, 1875

City Size	No. of Cities	Combined Population	Production of Domains (*uchidaka*)	Production Ratio (*koku*/city population)
50,000+	6	488,000	4,654,000	9.5
30-49,999	13	486,000	5,439,000	11.2
10-29,999	36	626,000	5,830,000	9.3
5-9,999	49	352,000	3,367,000	9.6
3-4,999	38	155,000	1,575,000	10.2
3,000–	70	137,000	1,770,000	12.9
	212	2,244,000	22,635,000	10.1

Regional Variations in
Production Ratio (*koku*/city population)

LOW		INTERMEDIATE		HIGH	
Kinai	7.0	Shikoku	8.5	S. Kyūshū	12.7
Tōkai	7.3	Hokuriku	8.7	Sanyō	13.0
San'in	7.8	Tōsan	8.8	N. Kyūshū	15.5
W. Tōhoku	7.9	Peripheral Kinai	9.3		
		E. Tōhoku	10.1		
		N. Kantō	11.7		
		S. Kantō	11.9		

SOURCE: Sambō Hombu, ed., *Kyōbuseihyō* (Tokyo: 1875). Production figures are from the *Hanshi sōran* (Tokyo: Shinjinbutsu shoraisha, 1977).

in the small *han* (below 30,000 *koku*), which could not be expected, without the presence of supplementary interdomain functions, to achieve the autonomy necessary for a castle town's development to its full potential.[14] There were 50 *han* with at least 100,000 *koku* (and 55 castle cities over 10,000), 101 *han* with at least 50,000 *koku* (and 104 cities with 5,000+ residents), and 143 *han* of 30,000+ *koku* (matched by 142 cities of 3,000+).[15] Since, on average, the *uchidaka* figure approx-

[14] Places having fewer than 1,000 residents are omitted from the 1875 population records in the *Kyōbuseihyō* and, therefore, from the list of 212 former castle towns drawn from it. This means that some of the small domains (those having a meager 10,000-20,000 *koku*) do not have their castle towns recorded.

[15] Data on domain production (*kokudaka*) are from *Bakumatsu kohan no ummei* (Tokyo: Takano chō, 1977).

imates the total population of a late Tokugawa *han*, it is correct to conclude that about 10 percent of the population in the areas involved (more than three-quarters of Japan) resided in former castle towns and that, together, these cities comprised more than 40 percent of Japan's urban population.

In his analysis of the 1875 data, Hayami Akira divides Japan into fourteen regions.[16] In Table 12.4 and Map 12.1, I present Hayami's findings by ordering the regions into five levels of urbanization; in Table 12.5, I display data from the *Kyōbuseihyō*, by city size and according to these same fourteen regions. Of course, the greatest urbanization is seen in the Kinai (Osaka and Kyoto) and in South Kantō (Edo). The three central cities still comprised a quarter of Japan's urban total. It is also clear that northeastern areas along the Japan Sea (Hokuriku and West Tōhoku) had high urbanization, while the southwest (including all of Kyūshū and Shikoku) had low urbanization, as did a belt of three adjacent northern areas, Tōsan, North Kantō, and East Tōhoku.

At the bottom of Table 12.3 are the ratios of domain production to the combined 1875 populations in the former castle towns within each of Japan's fourteen regions.[17] The regional differences in the ratio are considerable—much greater than the differences associated with domain size. The highest ratios are found in the southwest, especially in North Kyūshū where low urbanization is associated with castle towns that were small in relation to the agricultural production of their domains. Low ratios are found along the Japan Sea (including West Tōhoku, San'in, and, to a lesser extent, Hokuriku) and in central Honshū (Tōkai and, to a lesser extent, Tōsan). Areas of the Kinai and Kantō having numerous small domains and the diverse impact of cities not part of any domain vary widely in this ratio.

Figure 12.1 and Table 12.6 show the relationship between domain production (*kokudaka*) and city size for cities of the largest *han*. Low ratios of 3.6 and 6.1 *koku* per resident appear in Toyama and Takada

[16] Hayami, "Kinsei kōki chiikibetsu jinkō hendo to toshi jinkō hiritsu no kanren."

[17] In using these regional ratios, it is important to note that *kokudaka* were not consistently updated for all domains. For Japan as a whole *kokudaka* registered an increase of 9,263,729 from 1645 to 1873. The records of the *Bakumatsu kohan no ummei* fail to reflect all these gains. For example, Sendai (East Tōhoku) is credited only with its original seventeenth-century production figure, which, according to Ōtsuka Takematsu, *Hansei ichiran* (Tokyo: Nihon shiseki kyōkai sōsho, 1928), undercounts the domain's actual production by more than 200,000 *koku*. Some domains may be credited with too high a production figure; Hagi (Sanyō) is a likely candidate. If corrections in *kokudaka* per region were incorporated into the analysis, I suspect that the inverse relationship between the ratio of production to castle-town populations in Table 12.3 and regional urbanization in Table 12.4 would be strengthened.

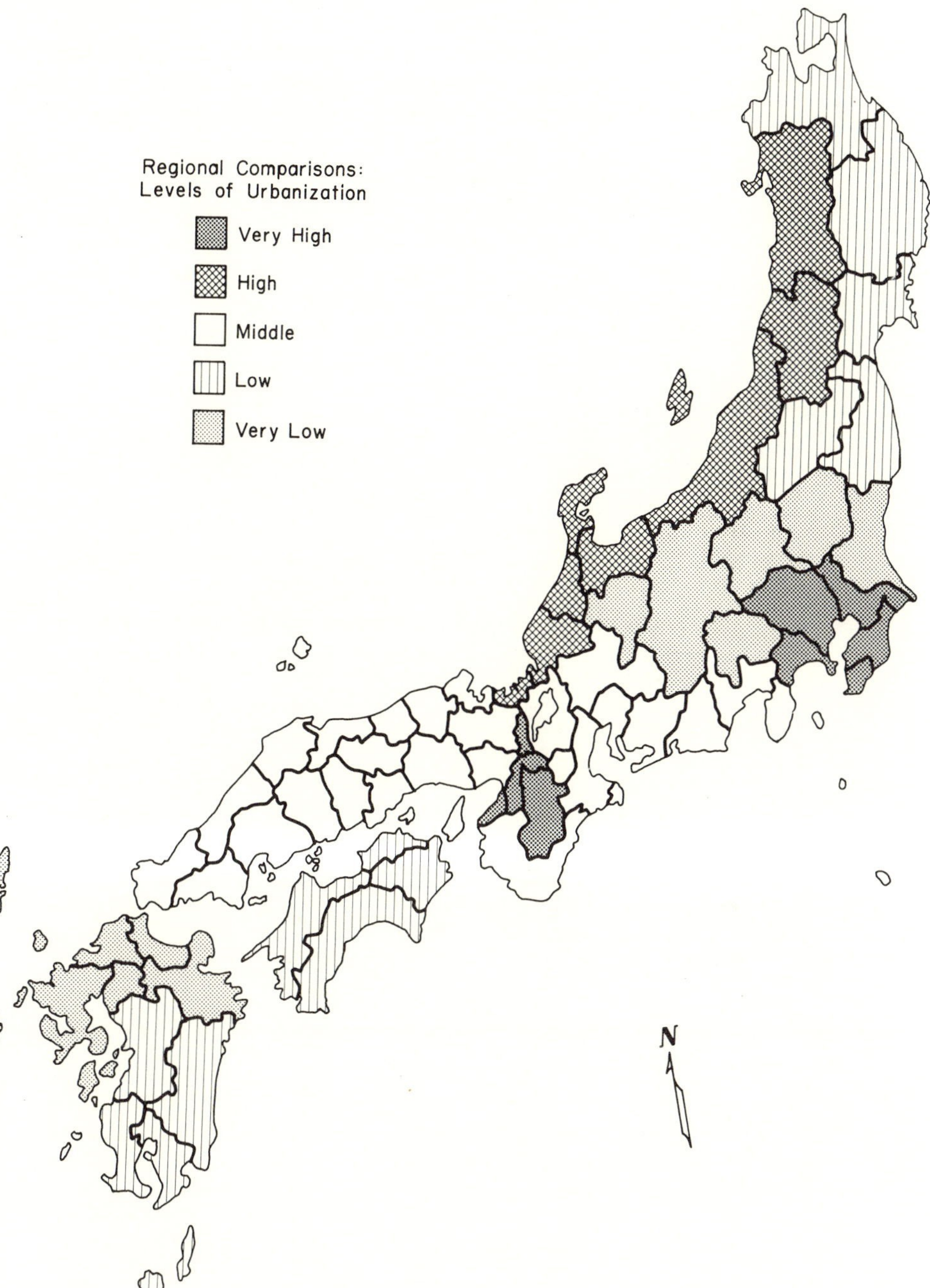

Map 12.1. Urbanization in Japan, by Region, 1875

TABLE 12.4
Regional Levels of Urbanization, 1875
(% population in places of 5,000+)

Level	Region	Percentage Urban	Provinces
Very High	Kinai	32.7	Yamashiro, Yamato, Kawachi, Izumi, Settsu
	S. Kantō	27.8	Musashi, Sagami, Shimōsa, Kazusa, Awa
High	Hokuriku	16.0	Sado, Echigo, Etchū, Noto, Kaga, Echizen, Wakasa
	W. Tōhoku	14.5	Uzen, Ugo
Intermediate	Tōkai	10.8	Izu, Suruga, Tōtōmi, Mikawa, Owari, Mino
	Peripheral Kinai	10.3	Ōmi, Iga, Ise, Shima, Kii, Awaji, Harima, Tamba
	Sanyō	9.8	Mimasaka, Bizen, Bitchū, Bingo, Aki, Suō, Nagato
	San'in	9.7	Tango, Tajima, Inaba, Hōki, Izumo, Aki, Iwami
Low	Shikoku	8.8	Awa, Sanuki, Iyo, Tosa
	E. Tōhoku	8.6	Iwaki, Iwashiro, Rikuzen, Rikuchū, Mutsu
	S. Kyūshū	8.5	Higo, Hyūga, Osumi, Satsuma
Very Low	N. Kyūshū	7.7	Chikuzen, Chikugo, Buzen, Bungo, Hizen, Iki, Tsushima
	N. Kantō	6.3	Kōzuke, Shimotsuke, Hitachi
	Tōsan	5.2	Kai, Shinano, Hida

SOURCE: Hayami Akira, "Kinsei kōki chiikibetsu jinkō hendo to toshi jinkō hiritsu no kanren," *Tokugawa rinsei shi kenkyūsho kenkyū kiyō* (March 1975), p. 238.

respectively (both in Hokuriku). Here cities were larger than predicted. High ratios of 33.5 and 17.6 are found in Saga and Kumamoto respectively (both in North Kyūshū). Why were these castle towns unexpectedly small? It may be important that leading domains in the Meiji Restoration were characterized by castle towns that were small, both in relation to their production capacities and to the high revenues they realized through domain monopolies. With a normal ratio of 9.7, Kagoshima (Satsuma) appears to be the exception in comparison to Hagi, Saga, and Kōchi, but it is necessary to consider that the *kokudaka* for Satsuma did not reflect its profitable trade with China. A large surplus not committed to vast

TABLE 12.5

Regional Distribution of Cities, by Size, 1875

(no. of cities, population in 000s)

City Size	Hokkaidō		E. Tōhoku		W. Tōhoku		N. Kantō		S. Kantō		Hokuriku		Tōsan		Tōkai	
130,000+									*1*	860						
50,000+			*1*	52					*1*	63	*1*	110			*1*	110
30-49,999			*1*	33	2	68			*0*		*3*	103			*1*	38
10-29,999	2	45	*5*	90	*3*	60	*4*	61	2	32	*8*	136	*3*	43	*8*	98
5-9,999	*1*	5	*10*	61	6	45	*5*	37	*11*	81	*25*	179	*4*	30	*11*	72
3-4,999	*1*	3	*26*	98	9	35	*13*	48	*28*	105	*28*	108	*7*	26	*26*	95
TOTAL		53		334		208		146		1,141		636		99		413
(Regional Population)*	(175,000)		(2,347,507)		(1,195,120)		(1,549,276)		(3,708,538)		(3,360,285)		(1,391,740)		(2,803,578)	

TABLE 12.5 (cont.)
Regional Distribution of Cities, by Size, 1875
(no. of cities, population in 000s)

City Size	Kinai		Peripheral Kinai		San'in		Sanyo		Shikoku		N. Kyūshū		S. Kyūshū		Totals	
130,000+	*2*	498													*3*	1,358
50,000+			*1*	61			*1*	67					*1*	89	*7*	552
30-49,999	*2*	72			*2*	74	*2*	62	*2*	82	*1*	42	*1*	45	*17*	619
10-29,999	*5*	82	*9*	158	*1*	10	*3*	58	*5*	97	*4*	74	*0*		*62*	999
5-9,999	*4*	27	*14*	93	*7*	51	*12*	83	*7*	39	*12*	83	*5*	38	*134*	919
3-4,999	*11*	42	*17*	70	*8*	31	*18*	64	*14*	55	*19*	73	*19*	70	*244*	920
TOTAL		721		382		166		334		273		272		242	467	5,367
(Regional Population)*	(2,093,500)		(3,032,366)		(1,341,044)		(2,880,989)		(2,459,214)		(2,815,219)		(2,028,402)		(33,006,778)†	

SOURCE: Sambō Hombu, ed., *Kyōbuseihyō* (Tokyo: 1875).

NOTE: Number of cities is shown in italics; populations are in roman type.

* Not in 000s.

† Excluding Hokkaidō.

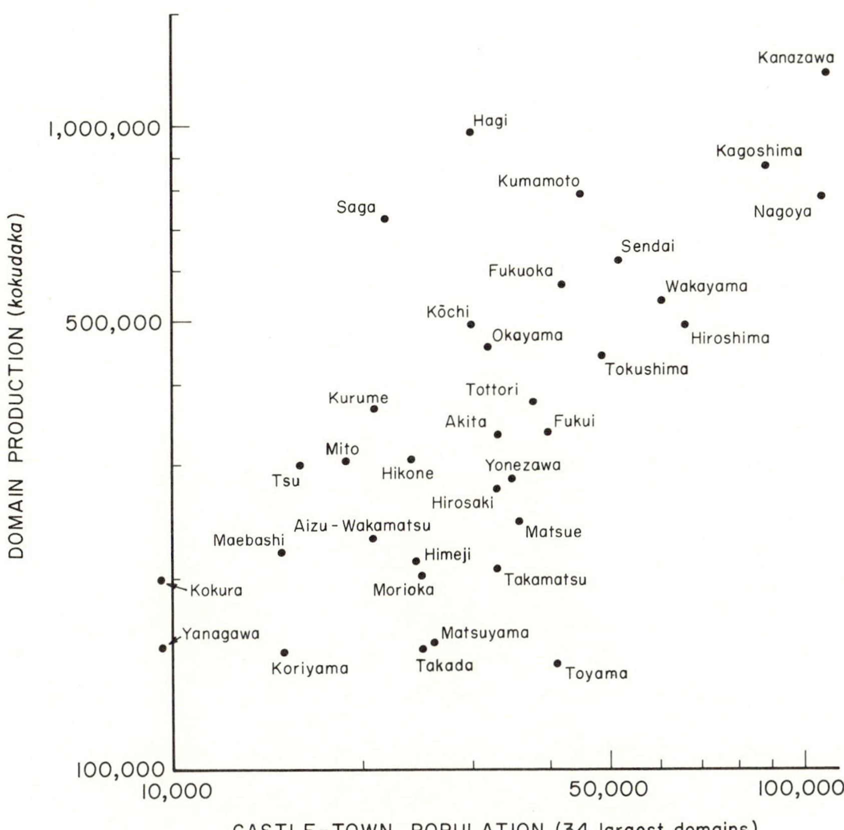

Figure 12.1. Domain Production and Castle-Town Population, 1875

samurai populations in the castle town may have facilitated the mobilization of resources in these domains in the 1860s. A less likely possibility is that these cities had declined considerably by the time of the 1875 enumeration, owing to the exodus of many residents for jobs with the new Meiji government in Tokyo. In either case, that these cities did not prosper after 1868 shows the lack of regional favoritism and the intense centralization pursued by the leaders from these areas.

On the basis of the old measure of production (*omotedaka*) and the 1878 population figures reported by Sekiyama Naotarō,[18] Fujimoto Toshiharu has also found sharp regional disparities in the ratio of production to castle-town population.[19] He suggests that the more commercialized

[18] Sekiyama Naotarō, *Kinsei Nihon no jinkō kōzō* (Tokyo: Yoshikawa kōbunkan, 1958).
[19] Fujimoto, *Kinsei toshi no chiiki kōzō*, pp. 38-42.

TABLE 12.6

Taxes, Stipends, and City Populations for Large Domains, Late Tokugawa

	A *han koku* (000s)	B city pop. (000s)	C ratio A/B	D *han* tax rate (%)	E *koku/bushi*	F stipend/*bushi*	G ratio E/F
Kanazawa	1,353	110	12.3	33.0	72.3	14.3	5.1
Hagi	988	30	32.8	23.6	94.5	8.0	11.8
Kagoshima	870	89	9.7	36.1	18.0	2.9	6.2
Kumamoto	786	45	17.6	41.9	92.3	14.3	6.5
Nagoya	779	110	7.1	34.5	71.2	9.8	7.3
Saga	725	22	33.5	29.5	64.8	5.1	12.7
Sendai	(625)	52	12.0	—	86.2	—	—
Fukuoka	571	42	13.6	41.0	79.6	10.7	7.4
Wakayama	539	61	8.8	50.9	50.4	7.3	6.9
Kōchi	495	30	16.8	39.0	62.3	10.8	5.8
Hiroshima	488	67	7.3	53.0	34.6	6.9	5.0
Okayama	454	32	14.0	39.5	69.4	9.2	7.5
Tokushima	443	49	9.1	43.6	59.7	13.9	4.3
Tottori	374	38	9.9	49.9	54.1	11.9	4.5
Kurume	366	21	17.7	32.3	107.4	12.8	8.4
Fukui	336	40	8.5	33.0	68.9	13.0	5.3
Akita	332	33	10.0	54.0	48.3	12.8	3.8
Mito	307	19	16.0	18.8	80.1	5.0	16.0
Hikone	304	24	12.5	(46.1)	(64.2)	8.2	7.8
Tsu	299	16	18.8	41.5	153.7	15.1	10.2

TABLE 12.6 (cont.)

Taxes, Stipends, and City Populations for Large Domains, Late Tokugawa

	A *han koku* (000s)	B city pop. (000s)	C ratio A/B	D *han* tax rate (%)	E *koku/bushi*	F stipend/*bushi*	G ratio E/F
Yonezawa	285	35	8.2	21.1	47.7	5.2	9.1
Hirosaki	274	33	8.3	51.5	63.6	10.4	6.1
Matsue	245	36	6.8	59.2	64.4	14.7	4.4
Aizu	(230)	21	11.2	—	—	—	—
Maebashi	218	15	14.5	25.0	87.8	12.4	7.1
Himeji	211	24	8.7	39.4	68.0	9.6	7.1
Takamatsu	205	33	6.3	51.5	47.3	8.0	5.9
Kokura	203	7	27.2	43.5	52.3	9.9	5.3
Morioka	(200)	25	6.3	42.8	90.8	14.4	6.3
Matsuyama	157	26	5.9	70.5	38.0	16.4	2.3
Yanagawa	155	8	18.6	43.0	57.1	10.7	5.3
Takada	154	25	6.1	31.4	78.8	11.2	7.0
Kōriyama	153	15	10.3	38.9	79.8	11.5	6.9
Toyama	146	41	3.6	45.3	41.1	9.6	4.3

SOURCE: Kōdama Kōta and Kitajima Masamoto, eds., *Hanshi sōran* (Tokyo: Shinjinbutsu shoraisha, 1977). City population figures are from the 1870s, as reported in the *Kyōbuseihyō* (1875).

NOTE: Numbers in parentheses are estimates. For columns C and D, $r = -0.41$, $P = .05$.

southwest had larger domains with relatively small castle towns because of greater urban development elsewhere in the domain. Even so, as Table 12.4 shows, nonadministrative centers did not fully compensate for the smaller-than-expected castle towns in their regions.

Regional Variations in City Growth

In the second half of the Tokugawa era, castle towns in the commercialized southwest were declining. This was not the case, however, in the largely monocultural economies of northeastern Japan. Did this regional contrast persist after 1868? Two books, by Fujioka Kenjirō, ed., and Fujimoto Toshiharu, look at regional variations in urban development.[20] The Fujioka work points to the stagnation and decline in Hokuriku; its largest city, Kanazawa, slipped from 123,763 in 1871, 107,878 in 1878, and 106,659 in 1883 to 94,209 in 1889. The 1886/1878 population ratios for large castle cities in this region reveal similar or greater losses: Toyama, 92:100; Fukui, 90:100; Ogaki, 81:100; and Takaoka, 71:100.[21] Cities in Tōkai also stagnated during these years: the ratio in Hamamatsu, for instance, was 95:100. Not until 1885 did cities along the Pacific Coast begin to revive, led by Nagoya. Crucial to urban growth were a secure place in the emerging transport networks along the Pacific Coast and retention of administrative and military functions via selection as the capital of a new prefecture or, at least, of a subadministrative *gun*. These advantageous factors became more decisive toward the end of the century.

Kurosaki Chiharu compares the registered population in 1886 to the actual number of residents (including information on migrants) in former castle towns as an indication of population change.[22] He finds a general pattern of stagnation: the figures for 138 cities were within 5 percent, while 44 cities grew and 66 declined. Small castle towns particularly declined; 17 of 38 in the categories 1,000 – and 2,000 – lost more than 5 percent of their population. Centralization of government weakened these small centers, where the ratio of production (*koku*) to urban population was already relatively high (probably a sign of little diversification). The rapidly increasing number of small cities both in the second half of the Tokugawa and in the early Meiji meant that rival local centers were positioned to vie for service functions. The smaller the castle town, the more vulnerable it was to the increased competition of the Meiji era.

Analysis of 1883 statistics for 173 former castle towns shows that 60 such were relatively stagnant, with a net migration below one hundred

[20] Fujioka, ed., *Nihon rekishichiri sōsetsu*; Fujimoto, *Kinsei toshi no chiiki kōzō*.

[21] Fujioka, ed., *Nihon rekishichiri sōsetsu*, pp. 185-186.

[22] Kurosaki Chiharu, "Meiji zenki no toshi ni tsuite," pp. 104-108.

persons; 40 were growing, with in-migrants in excess of out-migrants by one hundred or more; and 73 were declining, with a negative migration of at least one hundred persons.[23] Table 12.7 shows the sharp regional differences in these figures. If one excludes the North Kantō and Tōsan regions, where small castle towns managed to take advantage of the expanding silk industry, only 24 of 94 castle towns with a net change of one hundred or more experienced a positive net migration. Many of the declining cities were attracting few migrants. In as many as 63 of the 173 settlements, the number of in-migrants was no more than one-half the number of out-migrants. The growth of other cities helps explain the decline in some areas. In the South Kantō, Yokohama (with a net in-migration of 16,000) as well as Tokyo (86,000) served as magnets to migrants. In Kinai and its vicinity, Osaka, Kyoto, and Hyōgo (Kobe) together attracted a net gain of more than 70,000 migrants. The prox-

TABLE 12.7

Regional Variations in Castle-City Growth, 1883

	No. of Former Castle Cities Identified	No. of Cities in Rapid Short-Term Decline*	Ratio of Cities Growing to Those Declining†
E. Tōhoku	14	5	3:7
W. Tōhoku	10	6	1:5
N. Kantō	16	1	12:2
S. Kantō	13	6	0:9
Hokuriku	14	9	0:11
Tōsan	8	1	4:1
Tōkai	13	3	3:4
Kinai	3	1	1:1
Peripheral Kinai	26	11	3:10
San'in	9	5	1:6
Sanyo	13	6	3:5
Shikoku	8	0	5:2
N. Kyūshū	17	5	3:7
S. Kyūshū	9	4	1:3
	173	63	40:73

SOURCE: *Tofumeiyū kokōhyō* (Tokyo: Naimushō chirikyoku, 1884).
*Ratio of in-migrants to out-migrants ≤ 1:2.
†Net change > 100 persons.

[23] *Tofumeiyū kokōhyō* (1884).

imity of Hokkaido, where Hakodate (11,000) and Sapporo (7,000) led in growth, may have contributed to the high rates of decline in Tōhoku. Nagasaki's growth (6,000) in Kyūshū and, to a lesser extent, Niigata's (3,000 in Hokuriku) exerted a more limited impact. Thus we see the inverse relationship between the growth of new ports and frontier cities, on the one hand, and population change in former castle towns, on the other. The small number of rapidly expanding cities lured migrants from the once protected urban centers. Of these growing cities, some were smaller ones that succeeded in being designated as prefectural capitals. For example, the former castle town of Fukushima in East Tōhoku experienced a net gain of almost 1,000, bringing its total to 9,908.[24]

A longer-range perspective on the development of former castle towns can be found in the work of Fujimoto Toshiharu. Looking at population changes from 1878 to 1920, he classified four types (I have relabeled them) of cities:

A = a large booming city, with more than 10,000 residents in 1878 and at least a fivefold increase by 1920;
B = initially smaller but also a booming city, with fewer than 10,000 residents in 1878, yet sufficient growth to be designated a municipality (*shi*) after that category was introduced in 1889;
C = a slowly growing city, with more than 10,000 residents in 1878, but insufficient growth to qualify as a municipality before 1920;
D = a stagnant city, with more than 10,000 residents in 1878, but a rate of growth so low as to fall below that of the national population.

Types A and B were cities that thrived in the Meiji era, benefiting from commerce, industry, administration, or military functions, and often from a combination of these. Castle towns were numerous in these categories, but they were not nearly so dominant as they were in the C and D categories.

Of the nineteen Type C cities, all but two had been castle towns. Included are Kanazawa, Wakayama, and many of the former centers of domains with 100,000-300,000 *koku*.[25] These cities fared badly because they were mostly from relatively self-sufficient domains. When the domains were abolished, the cities lost their monopoly privileges. Moreover, new prefectural boundaries cut across the old domains so that their designation as prefectural administrative centers (and, even more, the failure of some to win that designation) meant a loss of centrality. Hikone,

[24] Ibid., p. 18.

[25] Fujimoto, *Kinsei toshi no chiiki kōzō*, p. 346.

Tottori, and Hagi actually lost population during this period, while by 1920 some cities had barely recovered from early Meiji losses. The Type C cities had relied on tax rice from administered agricultural areas for consumption and transshipment. Many were in grain surplus regions of Tōhoku, Hokuriku, and San'in. When samurai lost their stipends drawn from tax revenues, these places could not easily attract as much of the grain production. It is noteworthy that those regions which largely avoided castle-town decline during the second half of the Tokugawa were also the least successful in revitalizing their former castle towns after 1878. Castle towns in these regions were not so well integrated into expanding commercial networks as castle towns elsewhere.

While Type C cities were large enough to maintain substantial administrative, military, and commercial functions in the Meiji era, the twenty-nine Type D cities were too small in the 1870s to be able to count on continued importance as local centers in a competitive environment. Located in domains with no more than about 100,000 *koku*, they were numerous in the Kinki and Kantō regions and in between, i.e. in the leading regions of urbanization and industrialization where new cities prospered into the early twentieth century. Unable to capitalize on new functions, they could not compensate for lost castle-town functions. Their populations stagnated or experienced little growth.

Fujimoto concludes that castle towns were generally not well suited for the transition to industrialization. Especially in the northeast, they lacked capital and relied excessively on an agricultural base. From Tokyo to North Kyūshū, where the largest cities developed after the Meiji Restoration, other cities having better access to a diversified economy rose to prominence while former castle towns did not.

Fujimoto finds evidence by the late 1880s of an increasing concentration of cities, rather than the relatively even dispersal of cities across Japan that was characteristic of the late Tokugawa. Nonetheless, the legacy of the castle towns continued to provide a spread of sizable cities throughout the country. Apart from the Kinai and South Kantō regions, which strengthened their primacy as highly urbanized areas in the Meiji era (from 1878 to 1886, Kobe grew by 82 percent and Yokohama by 46 percent), regional variations in urbanization were diminished.

The Samurai Impact on Castle Towns

The fate of castle towns depended in part on the continued delivery of tax revenues and the continued presence of former samurai with substantial incomes. How did dependence on these factors vary in the late Tokugawa? Based on data in the *Hanshi sōran*, Table 12.6 shows (for the thirty-four largest domains) the tax rate, the amount of *koku* per samurai on stipend, and the average amount of stipend.[26] Smaller than expected cities (high ratios in column C) are associated in some cases (Hagi, Saga, Kurume, Mito, and Maebashi) with low rates of taxation (column D) and in some cases (Hagi, Kurume, Mito, Tsu, and Maebashi) with small samurai populations in relation to grain production (high values in column E). Relatively large cities (low ratios in column C) may be associated with high rates of taxation (column D) and numerous samurai (low values in column E), as in the case of Matsuyama. Samurai stipends may be low, as in Saga and Mito, which presumably reduces the movement of resources flowing into the castle town. Yet, low stipends may be counterbalanced by numerous samurai (as in Kagoshima, where large numbers resided in rural areas), which keeps the ratio of *koku* to castle-town population close to the expected level.

Calculating the ratio of the two samurai-related factors (*koku*/samurai and stipend/samurai), I have identified in column G an index of the samurai impact on castle-town size relative to domain production. Despite great variation in columns E and F, most values of the index listed in column G fall within a fairly narrow range of 5.1 to 8.0. Ratios higher than 8.0 tend to be in underurbanized domains such as Hagi, Saga, Kurume, Mito, and Tsu (the only exception is Yonezawa). Ratios lower than 5.1 tend to be in overurbanized domains such as Hiroshima, Tokushima, Matsue, Matsuyama, and Toyama (again, the exception is in West Tōhoku, the city of Akita). In other words, where there was only a slight accumulation of revenues for samurai, domains supported smaller castle towns than predicted. This extends the correlation noted earlier between *kokudaka* and city size to *kokudaka* and samurai numbers. Where there was a large accumulation for samurai, cities were relatively large. This is what one would expect, and it offers a statistical approach to the samurai impact on *jōkamachi* size. Note, however, that in some cities this factor does not account for the variation from the expected size; e.g. Kanazawa is somewhat smaller than expected despite a rather low index of 5.1, and Nagoya is larger than expected despite a moderate index of 7.3. In particular, the small size of the cities of Kokura and Yanagawa in North Kyūshū cannot be accounted for either in terms of their ratios of 5.3 each or in terms of their unexceptional rates of taxation (around 43 percent). In such cases, one expects that the explanation for city size must focus not on the samurai population and its multiplier effects, but on commercial functions. The calculations in Table 12.6

[26] Kōdama and Kitajima, eds., *Han shi sōran*, pp. 425-431.

should be taken as no more than suggestive, since the data on *kokudaka* and taxes are of inconsistent quality.

Summary

By the eighteenth century, the more than 200 castle towns gave Japan an evenly dispersed and relatively concentrated distribution of local urban populations. On this foundation modern urbanization accelerated rapidly, with only modest readjustment in city populations until the 1880s. The readjustments prior to the Tokugawa-Meiji transition were nonetheless important, for they enhanced the survival of these cities by strengthening their commercial functions and bolstering their ties to dynamic local centers. In the northeast, where retrenchment of castle towns was least in evidence, the abolition of domains and of the special status of their long-term centers brought on chronic stagnation. In contrast, those castle towns—preponderantly in the southwest—which were least dependent on tax revenues and samurai stipends, and which had already readjusted to expanded local commercial networks, weathered the first part of the transition with little population loss and, in the decade after 1875, were well along the path of growth.

The urban record of the transitional period demonstrates the durability of the *jōkamachi*. To be sure, the new treaty ports led the way in urban growth, and many castle towns were smaller in the mid-1880s than they had been a century earlier. But what is striking is that cities established on the premise of the forced migration of stipended samurai into large agglomerations survived, on the whole, with scarcely any short-term losses visible in 1875, after the abolition of samurai status and stipends. Centralization of government, equalization of legal status, and freedom of movement did not greatly disturb the population size of these cities. Clearly they were not parasitic growths fit mainly for consumption. By the 1880s, following the gradual deconcentration of the second half of Tokugawa and the more rapid readjustments of early Meiji, these cities formed the nuclei for local urban networks capable of servicing the accelerated modernization of Japan.

Land Use

What changes in the urban plan had occurred in former castle towns by the mid-1880s? To answer this question, it is again helpful to take into account variations among cities and their patterns of change in the late Tokugawa. Although castle towns had much in common, studies by

Yamori Kazuhiko manage to differentiate the various types of land use found in them.[27] Numerous maps of these cities in the Tokugawa era show the position of the castle, the network of moats around it, as well as the size and shape of areas assigned to samurai (*yashiki*) and of commercial districts (*machi*) that doubled as residential areas for merchants, artisans, and hired labor. The amount of detail in some of the maps is extraordinary, even indicating the frontage and ownership of individual lots. Examining how the parts of the city fit together, Yamori concludes that the period of a city's origin and, secondarily, the size of the city and its primary functions account for many of the observed variations. Large, multifunctional cities (particularly late-developing cities) show the most deviation from the early blueprints for a castle town.

The evidence reveals changes in castle towns during their period of gradual decline from the eighteenth century: the breakdown of occupational segregation by *machi*, accompanied by the weakening of commercial monopolies and guilds; the dispersal of stores and of residents to the city outskirts (an urban sprawl that may have contributed to the undercounting of city populations in fixed boundaries); the development of cottage industries in residential districts set aside for lower samurai; and even the establishment of branch stores by *machi* residents within areas formerly reserved for samurai.[28] Some mixing of samurai and townspeople took place; the *machi* and the lower-samurai neighborhoods exhibited the greatest deviation from the original forced residential segregation by social class. Nevertheless, the basic plan remained essentially intact. The castle persisted as the military and administrative fortress, and the exclusive preserve of samurai estates was scarcely penetrated.

Population Density and Samurai Land Area

Combining Yamori's figures on the area of seventy-three cities[29] with the above-cited population data from 1875 permits calculation of citywide population density. The range is roughly between 25 and 400 persons per *chō* of land (about 1,500- 24,000 persons per square kilometer). Cities with many samurai and few townspeople tended to have low densities. E.g. Yonezawa (West Tōhoku) had just 74 persons per *chō*, while Saga (North Kyūshū) and Tōyama (Hokuriku) reserved most of their land for townspeople and maintained high densities of 235 and 234 per *chō*, respectively. The big cities having both a high percentage of land assigned to samurai and prosperous commercial districts supported rather

[27] Yamori, *Toshi puran no kenkyū* and *Jōkamachi.*

[28] Yamori, *Toshi puran no kenkyū*, p. 257.

[29] Ibid., pp. 297-300.

high densities: e.g. 216 per *chō* in Kanazawa (Hokuriku), 177 in Nagoya (Tōkai), and 151 in Tokushima (Shikoku).

Both regional variation and domain size must be figured into any sound explanation of samurai land allotments or citywide population density. In the northeast, castle towns had low population densities (the range in West Tōhoku for six cities was 124-172 per *chō*). In contrast, four of six cities in the San'in region and two of three in Sanyo exceeded 200 persons per *chō*. More pronounced than regional variation are differences by domain size. An analysis of this relationship shows that half of all small and medium domains having less than 100,000 *koku* granted no more than 45 percent of their land to samurai.[30] The larger the domain, the larger the proportion of land allotted to samurai.[31] Nevertheless, sizable *han* also realized high population densities; their compact commercial districts were densely populated. The castle town which boasted the largest population in each region typically also had the highest urban density, or close to it.

One finds a downward progression: the percentage of the city land occupied by samurai averages thirteen points higher than the percentage of the population that was samurai, and the latter in turn averages twelve points more than the percentage of all buildings in the samurai areas.[32] Thus, an average city with 60 percent of its area set aside as samurai land would have counted 47 percent of its population and 35 percent of its buildings in that area. Nakabe Yoshiko estimates that the samurai population was frequently about 70-80 percent of the *chōnin* population, although in some large cities where samurai land constituted as much as four-fifths of the city total (such as Sendai in East Tōhoku and Kagoshima in South Kyūshū) the late Tokugawa samurai total exceeded the *chōnin* population by as much as 3 to 1.[33]

Cities with a high percentage of their land reserved for samurai residences and with low to moderate population densities were understandably more vulnerable to the land use changes of the Meiji period. These "political" cities, disproportionately located in the northeast, depended heavily on samurai consumption and on daimyo authority for the accumulation of domain grain surpluses. With the reforms, decline was difficult to fend off. In the 1870s and early 1880s, the greatest impact on land use occurred in the castle area and in residential districts of

[30] Ibid., p. 303.

[31] Fujimoto Toshiharu, in Fujimoto Toshiharu and Yamori Kazuhiko, eds., *Shiro to jōkamachi* (Kyoto: 1978), p. 191.

[32] Yamori, *Toshi puran no kenkyū*, pp. 302-303.

[33] Nakabe, *Jōkamachi*, p. 305.

upper- and middle-level samurai, not in the *machi* and the outlying lower-samurai areas.

The Samurai Population

The questions of what happened to the samurai and what happened to the castle cities both demand information on how many samurai were living in each city at the end of the transition period. This information also can contribute to our understanding of land use changes, for the percentage of samurai in the population and the rate of decline in that figure were important determinants of the city plan.

With Professor Hayami's assistance, I have found statistics on the ex-samurai population in 1883 for nineteen large cities.[34] Table 12.8 separates figures for castle cities, other cities, and selected wards of Tokyo. It shows a continuing high level of ex-samurai presence in the relatively stagnant cities of Sendai (Tōhoku) and Kanazawa (Hokuriku). Whereas persons of samurai descent made up 5.5 percent of the national popu-

TABLE 12.8
Percentage of Samurai in the Urban Population, 1883

Castle Cities*		Other Cities		Selected Wards of Tokyo†	
Sendai	43.8	Sapporo	14.6	Ushikomi	30.1
Kanazawa	41.1	Hakodate	3.4	Akasaka	25.2
Okayama	30.0	Yokohama	3.2	Yotsuya	22.0
Kumamoto	27.0	Kyoto	3.0	Azabu	17.6
Hiroshima	23.3	Kobe	2.7	Hongō	17.4
Fukuoka	23.0	Shimonoseki	2.3	Shiba	12.3
Nagoya	22.7	Osaka	1.5	Kanda	9.5
Wakayama	22.4	Nagasaki	1.4	Asakusa	7.9
		Niigata	1.2	Shinagawa	6.7
		Sakai	0.6	Kyobashi	4.6
				Nihonbashi	3.3
				E. Tama	0.8

SOURCE: Naimushō kosekikyoku, *Nihon zenkoku kokōhyō* (Tokyo: Naimushō kosekikyoku, 1884).

* National total, urban and rural = 5.5%.

† Tokyo total = 9.2%.

[34] Naimushō kosekikyoku, *Nihon zenkoku kokōhyō*.

lation, ex-samurai in these cities continued to comprise more than 40 percent of the population (maintaining the high levels typical of the Tokugawa era). Ex-samurai in the six castle towns in or near western Japan (from Kumamoto and Fukuoka in North Kyūshū to Nagoya in Tōkai) made up 22-30 percent of the population.

Except for Tokyo and Sapporo, other cities counted just 0.6-3.4 percent of their inhabitants as samurai descendants. New cities, especially Sapporo, had more persons in this category than such long-established commercial centers as Sakai. Migrants to the frontier cities of Hokkaido included a fair number of samurai in accord with government policy. Yokohama's somewhat elevated figure may have resulted from the migration of samurai from nearby Tokyo. In any case, what is striking about Table 12.8 is the very slight presence of ex-samurai in places that had not served as castle towns. There was no widespread equalization of class background among cities.

The figures for Tokyo reveal the continued existence of residential areas whose populations had strikingly different class backgrounds. The wards west and southwest of Edo Castle, such as Akasaka, where samurai had long predominated, had 22-30 percent of their inhabitants from this background. The wards east of the castle, in contrast, such as Nihonbashi, which had long been the commercial centers, had few samurai. Areas in Tokyo *fu* that remained rural, such as East Tama, had scarcely any samurai at all.

Changing Land Use

Prior to the late 1880s, in regions throughout Japan, the evidence seems to show that not growth, but sudden decline followed by reorganization, produced many of the major changes in urban land use. Frequently the castle grounds did not offer inviting prospects for military headquarters; and the castle, which along with other castles was handed over to the military in 1871, was quickly turned into a park or given over to temples and shrines. In some cases, the land was even turned to residential use or to farming. Moats, initially the outer one and then the inner one, were filled in (in fifty-seven of ninety-six cities they had been filled in by 1934 and many others had been partly filled in).[35] In the case of small cities and cities with little commercial growth, the moat areas were frequently used for agriculture. In big cities they were more likely to be converted to residential use or to roads.

The large samurai area was the main site of the decline. Samurai

[35] Yamori, *Toshi puran no kenkyū*, p. 369.

resettled, often outside the castle town, and land values were much lower than in the more stable *machi* and in the lower-samurai districts that had already been converging with the *machi* during the late Tokugawa. Wakayama dropped from 64,582 persons in 1873 to 49,699 in 1892; a map of 1886 shows much vacant land where samurai estates had formerly been.[36] Similar decline occurred in large numbers of former castle towns.

Public buildings exerted an increasing impact on the redevelopment of these areas. Administrative offices and by the 1880s schools, in some cases, occupied the castle grounds. Such construction also led in the revitalization of portions of the old samurai districts. It should also be noted that the earliest factories, perhaps built with government support, helped fill in the samurai districts where land was relatively plentiful and cheap. Of course, the commercial districts also expanded into some former samurai districts. In the late 1880s and 1890s, railroad stations were constructed in numerous former castle towns, often causing a relocation of the central business district. Whereas the districts nearest the castle had originally prospered, the reorientation away from dependence on daimyo and samurai consumption was already underway in Tokugawa. The mid-Meiji shifts in intercity transportation brought a further readjustment in land values.

Summary

In the decade after the Meiji Restoration, urban land use changed in some ways that were not anticipated in the late Tokugawa and in other ways that were. Whereas late Tokugawa urban population decline centered in the *machi* (which had the effect of narrowing differences in population densities) early Meiji decline centered in the samurai residential areas. Modernization in Japanese cities began as it may have nowhere else—with a huge, centrally located area opened up for new uses at low prices.

CONCLUSION

The principles of Meiji and Tokugawa urban life were diametrically opposed. The Tokugawa system was restrictive. Castle towns were founded on the basis of forced migration and obligatory residential segregation according to a rigid ideal of land use. Their population totals have been perceived as artificially bloated by a localism based on feudal

[36] Suida Giichi, in Fujimoto and Yamori, eds., *Shiro to jōkamachi*, p. 96.

prerogatives, their rural relations as feeding like parasites on vast revenues that were wasted on samurai consumption, and their land use as an inefficient barrier to market forces. In contrast, Meiji cities stood for centralization, for urban competition through market forces, and for freedom of movement and occupation. What continuities could be expected between two systems founded on such contradictory principles?

In fact, the continuities were great in both the urban network and the plan. Together the gradual trends of the second half of the Tokugawa era and the surprisingly untraumatic adjustments of early Meiji better oriented Japan's cities to the needs of the new age. They preserved a high level of urbanization, a broad distribution of sizable cities across the country, and densely settled commercial areas. Rather than withering away, the castle towns maintained their populations at about 40 percent of Japan's urban total during the 1880s and made possible the national integration that gave meaning to Meiji centralization. Despite, especially in the southwest, some late Tokugawa population losses to local cities and, in the northeast primarily, early and mid-Meiji decline, these same cities continued to link local areas and the center. Urban administrative and commercial services retained their vitality. These cities served as educational centers and as local trade centers. It was not the negation of castle towns, but their streamlined existence after Tokugawa restrictions were ended that facilitated modern development.

The fate of individual cities depended on a great number of circumstances and decisions by separate households and organizations. The Meiji government's selection of administrative seats during the successive reorganization of *ken* in the decade after 1871 was a major factor. Entire regions were affected by changing transportation networks such as the decline of the Western Circuit route around Honshū from the Japan Sea to Osaka. From the mid-1880s, the railroads' right of way became another powerful determinant of city prosperity. Soon thereafter, industrial functions began to take their place along with services as a primary force behind urban population growth.

In the transition from castle city to modern metropolis, more was at stake than the fate of individual cities. As in other countries, political interests vigorously and sometimes nefariously competed to gain for their cities designation as administrative centers as well as other plums that the central government handed out. Such actions mattered. These decisions helped determine where individual households set up their businesses or located their residences. But, seen macroscopically, it is unlikely that these decisions register strongly on nationwide patterns. The cumulative effect is seen in the spatial reorganization of the entire network of cities of varying size and across different regions. It is seen in the general reallocation of urban land to changing functions and groups. In turn, these overall outcomes can be seen to create a foundation for subsequent government actions and business decisions, not to mention their consequences for modern development.

We lack the means to weigh the importance of various periods of urban change in creating the foundation for modernization that existed in Japan by the late 1880s. It seems likely that the results of each of the first three stages of castle-town development were important and built upon the achievements of the preceding stage. By the early seventeenth century, Japan possessed a broadly dispersed network of cities whose land use reflected the local concentration of administration and commerce. By the early eighteenth century, the remarkable growth of these cities produced a highly urbanized network and a highly centralized distribution of nonagricultural functions. Then gradual changes until the mid-nineteenth century reoriented castle towns toward emerging local centers and away from segregated land use dominated by services to the samurai. The fourth stage examined in this chapter rejected the principles that had governed the preceding three centuries of development. In just a quarter-century, there were many reforms consistent with modern cities, and their consequences for population change and land use could be discerned. In both of these dimensions, the changes of the fourth stage of castle-town decline appear necessary but not sufficient for the establishment of a modern urban foundation. While Tokugawa principles were rejected, population concentrations and land uses were only gradually transformed. The result was more an adjustment than an overturning of Japan's rich urban heritage.

CHAPTER 13

THE EDO-TOKYO TRANSITION: IN SEARCH OF COMMON GROUND

BY HENRY D. SMITH II

No city in Japan was so profoundly affected by the collapse of the Tokugawa regime as its political capital. In the space of less than seven years, Edo lost half of its population of more than 1 million, with a final exodus of more than 300,000 in 1868 alone. The decision on September 3 of that year to make Edo the capital of the new imperial regime, however, meant that the 1868 disaster was a momentary nadir, from which recovery was swift and sustained. By 1890, Tokyo had recaptured the dimensions of Edo, both in population and settled area. It is this pattern of precipitous decline and speedy recovery that sets the basic contours of the Edo-Tokyo transition.

The years around 1868 have tended to be treated as a historical no man's land, setting a comfortable distance between two distinct cities known as "Edo" and "Tokyo." Over the past two decades, Japanese scholars have produced much new and original research on the history of the city, but 1868 remains the great divide—between those historians for whom it is a beginning and those for whom it is an end.[1] It is easy enough to preach the need for a "common ground" between Edo and Tokyo, but the practical difficulties are considerable, given the discontinuity of most surviving primary materials. This chapter takes the initial

[1] For Edo, see Minami Kazuo, *Edo no shakai kōzō* (Tokyo: Hanawa shobō, 1959) and *Bakumatsu Edo shakai no kenkyū* (Tokyo: Yoshikawa kōbunkan, 1978); and Nishiyama Matsunosuke, ed., *Edo chōnin no kenkyū*, 5 vols. (Tokyo: Yoshikawa kōbunkan, 1972-1978). For Tokyo: Ishizuka Hiromichi, *Nihon shihon shugi seiritsu shi kenkyū—Meiji kokka to shokusan kōgyō seisaku* (Tokyo: Yoshikawa kōbunkan, 1973) and *Tōkyō no shakai keizai shi* (Tokyo: Kinokuniya shoten, 1977); Ogi Shinzō, *Tōkei shomin seikatsu shi kenkyū* (Tokyo: Nippon hōsō shuppan kyōkai, 1979).

steps: first, considering the transition from Edo to Tokyo in terms of the city's changing function within both a regional and national context; then venturing into the city itself, exploring the social dynamics leading into and out of the vortex of the 1860s.

Edo Centrism

Edo's unique character and extraordinary size derived from the superimposition of two political functions. On the one hand, it was the castle city of the *bakufu* domain—in a class by itself, given the pre-eminent size and strategic location of the shogunal realm. Purely as castle city, Edo would certainly have had a population exceeding half a million, several times greater than Kanazawa or Nagoya, the largest of the domain capitals. But the function that pushed Edo's population much higher was the *sankin kōtai*, that peculiar institution of national political control by which the daimyo were required to maintain large establishments in Edo for their hostage families, and to reside there themselves in alternate years to attend the shogun.

In contrast to Edo's direct administrative role, the *sankin kōtai* spared the *bakufu* the need of providing civil and military services for the nation as a whole. Its effect was to give the city a high degree of centrality, by dictating the systematic and extensive requisition of population and wealth from beyond its own administrative realm and economic hinterland. The initial impact of the Meiji Restoration on the city was thus paradoxical: in replacing the centralization enforced by the *sankin kōtai* with a more direct form of centralization, Edo lost population, and probably wealth as well, in the transition to Tokyo.

The heavy concentration of power and wealth in Edo made it a center of consumption previously unknown in Japan, working over the course of the Tokugawa period to stimulate the economic changes that form the backdrop of the transition. The *sankin kōtai* served as a vehicle for the regular transfer of a large share of domain income to the city of Edo. An undetermined amount of this was in the form of direct supply of the Edo mansions from the domains, serving in effect to bypass the Edo market and thus constituting a kind of autarkic system.[2] But the domains were necessarily dependent on the local Edo market for many needs, including fresh fish and produce, lumber, menial labor, and any bulky, low-value items that could not be economically supplied from the domains.

[2] I am grateful to Kitahara Itoko for this suggestion.

The combination of the demands of the domain establishments with those of the indigenous samurai population was so great that Edo could not possibly be supplied by its natural hinterland, but was forced to rely heavily on Osaka, the center of distribution of western Japan. Indeed, the provisioning of Edo was itself a major and continuing stimulus to the commercial development of Osaka. This dependence on the Osaka market emerged in the mid-Tokugawa period as a matter of profound concern for *bakufu* authorities, who in a variety of reforms sought to encourage the development of Edo's own immediate hinterland in the Kantō Plain (the so-called *jimawari*), typically at the expense of Osaka.[3] One scholar has coined the term "Edo centrism" to describe this policy orientation.[4] Whatever the efficacy of the policies themselves, the regional hinterland of Edo did in fact develop, and rapidly so. Reliance on the Osaka market remained heavy in such processed goods as lamp oil, sake, and cotton fabrics; but in other basic commodities, such as rice and soy sauce, Edo came to be supplied with little or no dependence on the Osaka market.

This development meant that by the time of the Tokugawa-Meiji transition, Edo had become the center of a unified regional marketing sphere, encompassing the Pacific coast of eastern Japan and extending west as far as the provinces of Ise, Mino, and Owari. The demand created by Edo and its large population was the critical force in stimulating and unifying this region, which was to become the leader in national population growth during the transition period.[5]

The Passing of the Sankin Kōtai

The first truly traumatic change in the basic social structure of the city of Edo came with the *bakufu* decree of October 15, 1862, which drastically relaxed the regulations of the *sankin kōtai*. The measure was taken to relieve the daimyo of the great expense of attendance in Edo, and thereby to encourage efforts to strengthen coastal defenses. The time that the daimyo were required to spend in Edo was effectively reduced by 82

[3] Itō Yoshiichi, *Edo jimawari keizai no hatten* (Tokyo: Kashiwa shobō, 1966); William B. Hauser, *Economic Institutional Change in Tokugawa Japan—Osaka and the Kinai Cotton Trade* (London: Cambridge University Press, 1974), chap. 3.

[4] Herman Ooms, *Charismatic Bureaucrat: A Political Biography of Matsudaira Sadanobu, 1758-1829* (Chicago: University of Chicago Press, 1975), p. 88. In Japanese-language scholarship, it seems more common to conceive of "Edo-centered" policies as those which favor Edo City wholesalers versus rural Kantō merchants.

[5] See Akira Hayami's chapter in this book.

percent—to one hundred days every three years—and permission was given to return the hostage families to the domains.[6]

The pace and extent of the exodus that followed is not known. Totman indicates that the *fudai* lords remained in the city as a show of support for the *bakufu*, although "a good many" sent their family members back to the domains.[7] The *tozama* daimyo appear to have withdrawn in large numbers. Chōshū is even reported to have disassembled most of the buildings in its several estates and packed them back to Hagi.[8] In almost all cases, however, the daimyo mansions in Edo remained inhabited and kept in repair; it is only from 1868 that eyewitness accounts report widespread decay and disrepair of the daimyo quarters. A survey made by the new government in June 1868, suggests that about 50,000 persons still remained in the daimyo estates.[9] Figure 13.1 reflects my estimate that the population of the daimyo establishments dropped by about one-half (to 130,000) within a year after the 1862 relaxation, then continued to decline to perhaps 80,000 by late 1867, with a final decrease to under 30,000 by the end of 1868.[10]

Contemporary accounts make it clear that the departure of the daimyo greatly depressed the economy of the city. Some were far more directly affected than others. Those merchants who catered exclusively to daimyo clientele were hardest hit—from the elite privileged purveyors of cloth and confections down to the peculiar trade known as the *kenzan'ya* ("dealers in leftover gifts"), whose job it was to buy up, refurbish, and resell the lavish gifts that were ritually exchanged among the daimyo and privileged *chōnin* (townspeople).[11] But the resulting depression was pervasive and was compounded by the mounting inflation.

The most immediate social consequence of the daimyo exodus was the dismissal of large numbers of servants who had been employed on term

[6] Toshio G. Tsukahira, *Feudal Control in Tokugawa Japan: The Sankin Kōtai System*, Harvard East Asian Monographs, no. 20 (Cambridge: Harvard University Press, 1966), pp. 134-137.

[7] Conrad Totman, "Fudai Daimyo and the Collapse of the Tokugawa Bakufu," *Journal of Asian Studies*, vol. 34, no. 3 (May 1975), p. 583.

[8] Tōkyō to, ed., *Tōkyō hyakunen shi*, 7 volumes (Tokyo: Tōkyō to, 1973-1980), vol. 1, p. 1556.

[9] Tōkyō to, ed., *Meiji shonen no bukechi shori mondai* (Tokyo: Tōkyō tosei shiryōkan, 1965), pp. 28-31.

[10] I have accepted Sekiyama Naotarō's estimate of 180,000 for the domain samurai population (of whom 150,000 were in permanent residence, 30,000 in alternating attendance), plus 50,000 for their servants. *Kinsei Nihon no jinkō kōzō* (Tokyo: Yoshikawa kōbunkan, 1958), p. 228.

[11] Nishiyama Matsunosuke, ed., *Edogaku jiten* (Tokyo: Kōbundō, 1984), pp. 220-221; Maeda Isamu, ed., *Edogo no jiten* (Tokyo: Kōdansha, 1979), p. 368.

contract. Particularly troublesome were those hired as military guards—in effect, rent-a-samurai. Numbering in the tens of thousands, this population of unmarried men had long been in disrepute as rowdy, unreliable, and given to drinking and gambling.[12] Their dismissal was therefore of great concern to the *bakufu*, which just one week after the *sankin kōtai* reforms issued an edict offering allowances to any contract soldiers who would return to the countryside. The employment agencies that handled such workers even petitioned the *bakufu* to take on 5,000 of them as foot soldiers, but the plan never materialized.[13] At any rate, we hear no more about the problem after 1862.

In spite of the clear indications of distress resulting from the daimyo departure, it is puzzling that the impact was not greater. The enumerated *chōnin* population of Edo, for example, showed a decline of only 20,000 persons between 1860 and late 1867, less than 4 percent of the total. We can only hypothesize that the dependence of the city of Edo on the patronage of the daimyo was considerably less than might be expected from the sheer volume of resources expended in the *sankin kōtai.* I have already suggested that the daimyo establishments may have been supplied as much as possible directly from the domains, avoiding any involvement with the Edo market. It is also plausible that the domains had already been reducing their Edo expenses as far as possible in order to deal with their mounting financial crises in the last decades of the Tokugawa period. In other words, there might already have been a certain weaning of the Edo economy from the breast of the daimyo coffers.

The significance of the *sankin kōtai* for Edo, particularly with respect to the Edo-Tokyo transition, may have lain primarily in its *physical* aspect—in the vast area that the daimyo occupied and in the mansions and gardens that they maintained. Most accounts of Edo emphasize the imbalance between a samurai population occupying 70 percent of the urban area versus a *chōnin* population of roughly the same size, squeezed into a mere 15 percent of the land. (Shrines and temples accounted for the remainder.) This overlooks the majority of the "samurai" population (perhaps one-fourth of which was made up of servants), living in cramped barrack quarters no better than those of average *chōnin.* In addition, a good part of the land occupied by the daimyo estates scarcely qualified as urban, and would have made no economic sense as *chōnin* settlements anyway.

Still, a large number of the domain establishments were located on

[12] Minami, *Edo no shakai kōzō*, pp. 167-262.

[13] Tōkyō to, ed., *Tōkyō hyakunen shi*, vol. 1, p. 1557; Conrad Totman, *The Collapse of the Tokugawa Bakufu, 1862-1868* (Honolulu: University Press of Hawaii, 1980), p. 22.

land in or near the center of the city—land, we have seen, that was of great utility to the Meiji government in setting up the new regime in Edo. In short, the negative impact of the withdrawal of domain samurai from Edo may in the end have been counterbalanced by the legacy of developed land that they left behind.

Finally, it should be noted that the daimyo exodus was not for good. In the complex process of the disposition of domain lands following the Restoration, most of the daimyo (the exceptions being "enemies of the court," mostly *fudai* and *shimpan*) were permitted to keep at least some of their former holdings in the capital.[14] Then, in 1871, following the abolition of the *han*, all of the former daimyo, together with the members of the Kyoto court aristocracy, were required to take up residence in Tokyo. This measure, not a little reminiscent of the *sankin kōtai*, does not seem to have met with much protest; remember that one consequence of the *sankin kōtai* itself had been to ensure that virtually all daimyo were born and bred in Edo. Ex-daimyo thus became fixtures in Meiji Tokyo. The majority were reduced to modest means and hence were of little consequence, but a number survived as prominent members of the new urban aristocracy and as powerful landholders. In 1878, for example, former daimyo accounted for one-half of the fifty largest landholders in Tokyo (those holding more than 10,000 *tsubo*, or 8.3 acres). Three decades later, in 1906, ex-daimyo still made up one-third of this group.[15]

The Yokohama Connection

"Edo centrism" also continued in the *bakumatsu* period as a powerful *policy* orientation that favored the independent economic development of Edo within its natural hinterland. This way of thinking was strongly reflected in the two most critical political decisions of the Edo-Tokyo transition: the opening of Yokohama in 1859 and the designation of Edo as the new imperial capital in 1868. The choice of Yokohama was the outcome of negotiations between Townsend Harris and the key *bakufu* representative, Iwase Tadanari.[16] Yokohama had not even been on the list of ten possible ports submitted to the *bakufu* by Harris when treaty negotiations opened in late 1857, and the weight of foreign opinion strongly favored Osaka. Iwase shared with all other *bakufu* officials a determination to keep foreigners out of the three major cities, particularly Kyoto, for fear of interference in domestic politics.

[14] Tōkyō to, ed., *Meiji shonen no bukechi shori mondai.*

[15] Ishizuka, *Tōkyō no shakai keizai shi*, p. 116.

[16] Yokohama shi shi henshū shitsu, ed., *Yokohama shi shi*, 30 vols. (Yokohama: Yūrindo, 1959-1982), vol. 2, pp. 157-166.

But beyond this, Iwase contended on *economic* grounds that the new international port should be near Edo rather than Osaka. Osaka, he argued revealingly, was blessed with a prime location and was already the beneficiary of "70 to 80 percent of the profits of the entire nation." Edo, by contrast, with little natural transport advantage, had "built its prosperity completely by human effort [*jinryoku*]." By locating the international port in Yokohama, he claimed, Edo merchants would prosper greatly, and the profits of the entire nation would accrue to the *bakufu* realm. In much the same language that would launch the Meiji Restoration a decade later, Iwase proclaimed that a "restoration" (*chūkō isshin*) of the *bakufu* would result from the opening of Yokohama, "laying the foundation for a rich nation and strong military [*fukoku kyōhei*]."[17]

Iwase's skilled diplomacy carried the day, and the opening of Yokohama in July 1859 may be taken as the real start of the Edo-Tokyo transition. The hopes of concentrating foreign trade in Yokohama were fully realized. Within one year, the new port had outstripped Nagasaki as Japan's center of foreign trade, and even after the opening of Hyōgo (Kobe) in 1867, Yokohama maintained an average annual share of 71 percent of all overseas trade until 1887. The gap then narrowed, and after 1895 Yokohama and Kobe each handled about the same volume of trade through the remainder of the Meiji period.[18]

The actual economic relationship between Edo and Yokohama, however, did not work for the "restoration" of the shogun's capital (and hence regime) in the way envisioned by Iwase. His initial plan was to entrust the entire Yokohama trade to Edo wholesalers, but he failed to overcome Harris's commitment to free trade. After the 1859 opening, a number of Edo merchants did set up Yokohama branches, dealing primarily in porcelains and other craft items. They suffered a severe handicap, however, in competition with rural merchants for the silk, tea, and oil that soon came to form the bulk of the export trade. Distressed at this turn of events, the *bakufu* intervened with a decree on May 9, 1860, requiring that five items (grain, oil, wax, cloth, and raw silk) all pass through Edo on the way to export. The decree proved unenforceable, though, and rural merchants continued to ship directly from the tea- and silk-producing areas.[19]

[17] The quotations are from Iwase's memorials of December 21, 1857, and circa January 4, 1858 (ibid., pp. 158-160). A partial translation of the second memorial appears in W.G. Beasley, trans. and ed., *Select Documents on Japanese Foreign Policy, 1853-1868* (London: Oxford University Press, 1955), pp. 174-176.

[18] Yokohama shi shi henshū shitsu, ed., *Yokohama shi shi*, vol. 3, p. 558; vol. 3 *ge*, p. 197; vol. 4 *ge*, p. 8.

[19] Ibid., vol. 2, pp. 337-369.

In time, however, Yokohama worked to the advantage of Edo (and later Tokyo) by the stimulation of the capital's hinterland, particularly the silk regions of North Kantō. It was this "silk road" traffic, for example, that was a major determinant of the early Kantō rail network, which had Tokyo as its hub.[20] Tokyo also became particularly important as a distribution node for foreign goods entering through Yokohama. According to a 1878-1879 survey, 70 percent of all Yokohama imports (which themselves accounted for 77 percent of the national total) went directly to Tokyo; and of this share, two-thirds were then forwarded to other markets, primarily within Tokyo's eastern Japan marketing region.[21]

Also important was Yokohama's cultural impact on the Edo-Tokyo transition. The port served as the major gateway for foreign influence in early Meiji Japan, generating intense public interest in Western customs and establishing Tokyo as the primary point of diffusion of Western culture to the rest of the country. The opening of Yokohama in 1859 led to a boom in "Yokohama pictures," woodblock prints produced in Edo primarily for the Edo market and depicting foreign manners. From this point on, Western influence began to leave a visible mark on the city—in decorative innovations of architecture, in restaurants offering meat dishes, in photographic studios, and in many other ways.

Yet, at the same time, the twenty miles that separated Yokohama from Edo-Tokyo (though travel time was greatly shortened by the railroad after 1872) served as a sort of cultural and political buffer between the capital and the West, as had been the earnest hope of *bakufu* officials in negotiating the commercial treaties. Tokyo was finally opened as an international market (as opposed to a port) in late 1868, six years behind the schedule stipulated by treaty. Even then, few foreign merchants actually settled in the capital. The Tsukiji settlement, at its peak in 1890, had only about 175 foreign residents, compared with nearly 5,000 in Yokohama.[22] Even taking into account missionaries, diplomats, and government-employed experts, the foreign population in the capital during the transition period was far less conspicuous than foreign cultural influence. The separation of Yokohama from Tokyo thus obviated the common Asian pattern by which a semicolonial foreign settlement within a traditional city created a clear barrier between the "old" native city and the "new" modern city. In early Meiji Tokyo, "new" and "old,"

[20] Ishizuka, *Tōkyō no shakai keizai shi*, pp. 98-100.

[21] Yokohama shi shi henshū shitsu, ed., *Yokohama shi shi*, vol. 3 *ge*, pp. 268-279; Ishizuka, *Tōkyō no shakai keizai shi*, p. 33.

[22] Ishizuka, *Tōkyō no shakai keizai shi*, pp. 35-36; Tōkyō to, ed., *Tōkyō hyakunen shi*, vol. 2, pp. 109-132.

"foreign" and "indigenous," were far more interwoven than elsewhere in Asia.

The Choice of an Eastern Capital

Of even greater consequence for Edo than the opening of foreign trade was the decision in 1868 to make that city the new imperial capital. In retrospect, the military realities probably left no alternative. The fledgling government still faced determined opposition in Tōhoku, and realized that an eastern base would be necessary to pursue what might be a prolonged campaign. There was, nevertheless, an extended debate in 1868 over the site of the new capital, and the arguments put forth were particularly revealing of official attitudes toward Edo.[23]

Kyoto had never been a candidate as capital in the minds of the Restoration leaders, who were determined to break free of the entrenched aristocratic interests of the ancient imperial city. It was rather Osaka that was initially proposed as the new capital, by Ōkubo Toshimichi. In a memorial of February 16, 1868, he stressed the need for a fresh start, nearer to "the people" and to an international port. Behind the rhetoric apparently lay the urgent need for financial support from Osaka merchants, and the emperor actually paid a six-week visit to the city from mid-April. In the meantime, however, former *bakufu* retainer Maejima Hisoka in a memorial of April 2 proposed that Edo would be a more sensible choice. His most practical observation—one that impressed Ōkubo—was the availability of broad tracts of land vacated by the daimyo, lands that could serve as convenient sites for the offices and institutions of the new regime. Osaka, by contrast, was densely settled, with narrow streets and a generally unimposing topography.

Maejima also raised economic arguments in favor of Edo, arguments that harked back to those of Iwase in 1857-1858. As a merchant city, noted Maejima, Osaka would survive the political transition easily, whereas Edo was in great distress owing to the loss of so much of its samurai population. This theme was reiterated even more forcefully in the compromise scheme of May 22, 1868, put forth by Ōki Takatō and his Saga colleague Etō Shimpei. The nature of the compromise was a "two capital" plan whereby the emperor would alternate residence every other year between his "Western Capital" (Saikyō) in Kyoto and the new "Eastern Capital" (Tōkyō) in Edo. In fact, the plan was never realized and, after May 1869, the emperor never returned to Kyoto. But the

[23] Tōkyō to, ed., *Edo kara Tōkyō e no tenkai—Tōkyō sento no keizaishiteki igi*, Toshi kiyō, no. 1 (Tokyo: Tōkyō to, 1953), pp. 36-63.

interest is rather in Ōki and Etō's argument in favor of Edo. Basically, they observed, Edo was like "a babe snatched from the breast," utterly without self-supporting skills in the absence of daimyo patronage—in contrast to "multiskilled" Kyoto, which could survive as a city of artisans, or Osaka with its commercial wealth. Hence it was necessary, for the good of the nation, to save Edo from desolation by making it the imperial capital.

These arguments fall clearly within the established pattern of "Edo centrism," the policy of building up the economy of Edo in order to counter the commercial power of Osaka. One crucial difference, however, is that what was traditionally advocated as a matter of *bakufu* advantage was now construed in the *national* interest. In short, the underlying structure of an economically advantaged western Japan versus a politically advantaged eastern Japan was consciously perpetuated in the Edo-Tokyo transition.

Breathing Space

Edo's designation as the new imperial capital was no instant guarantee of recovery, and the political uncertainties of the first two or three years after the Restoration meant rather a brief lull between the exodus of 1868 and the beginning of new growth. From about 1871, however, the population of the city grew rapidly at an annual rate of about 3.6 percent throughout the remainder of the Meiji period.[24] (See Figure 13.1.)

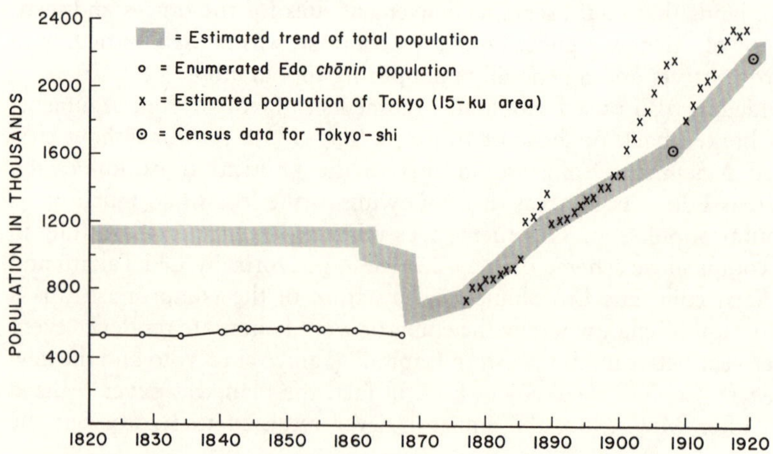

Figure 13.1. Population Change in the Edo-Tokyo Transition, 1820-1920

[24] This average is based on the two most reliable figures for the population of Meiji

NOTE: The surviving quantitative data consist of—

a) a sexennial series for the enumerated *chōnin* population of Edo until 1840. See Kōda Shigetomo, "Edo no chōnin no jinkō," *Shakai keizai shigaku*, vol. 8, no. 1 (April 1938), reprinted in *Kōda Shigetomo chosakushū*, 7 vols. (Tokyo: Chūō kōronsha, 1972-1974), vol. 2, p. 263.

b) a series for the enumerated *chōnin* population of Edo, classified by Kōda as "Type 1" (based on primary town-magistrate sources); see Kōda, chart facing p. 248. The graph shows only figures for enumerations made in the ninth month, and includes data for 1849 and 1853 from Nishiyama Matsunosuke, ed., *Edo chōnin no kenkyū*, 5 vols. (Tokyo: Yoshikawa kōbunkan, 1972-1978), vol. 1, p. 534.

c) Tokyo population figures estimated from changes in household registration statistics. These were calculated annually by Tokyo prefecture from 1877 until the first national census in 1920; see Tōkyō fu, ed., *Tōkyō fu shi, gyōseihen*, vol. 1 (1935), pp. 117-119. These figures show a cumulative tendency to overestimation, described by Ogi Shinzō, *Tōkei shomin seikatsu shi kenkyū* (Tokyo: Nippon hōsō shuppan kyōkai, 1979), as "duplication of temporary [*kiryū*] residents" (p. 34), probably caused by underreporting of out-migrants (*de-kiryū*). This error was corrected in 1890 and again after the 1908 Tokyo city census, but it continued to accumulate thereafter in each case. The overall curve attempts to minimize this systematic error by limiting the points to 1877, 1890, 1908, and 1920.

d) true census figures, which are available from the Tokyo city (Tokyo *shi*) census of 1908 and the first national census of 1920; see Tōkyō tō, ed., *Tōkyō hyakunen shi*, 7 vols. (Tokyo: Tōkyō to, 1973-1980), vol. 4, p. 60.

For an estimation of the total population of late Edo, I have made two adjustments to the officially enumerated *chōnin* population. First, I have added a figure of 85,000 for non-enumerated *chōnin*, consisting of residents of the shrine and temple lands (*jishachi*), the Yoshiwara and the outcaste communities; here I have relied on Naitō Akira, "Edo no toshi to kenchiku," supplementary volume to Suwa Haruo and Naitō Akira, *Edo zu byōbu* (Tokyo: Mainichi shimbunsha, 1972), p. 25. I have assumed that this figure remained constant until 1867. Second, I have accepted Sekiyama Naotarō's estimate of the samurai population of Edo, including dependents and servants, as 500,000; see Sekiyama, *Kinsei Nihon no jinkō kōzō* (Tokyo: Yoshikawa kōbunkan, 1958), p. 228. I have represented the decline of the samurai population in the 1860s in three stages: a sudden drop of 100,000 following the relaxation of the *sankin kōtai* in 1862; then a more gradual decline of 50,000 domain samurai until early 1868; and finally a precipitous decline of 300,000, some two-thirds of which were shogunal retainers, in the course of 1868. The winter of 1868/69 was the nadir for the total population of the city, which I estimate then to have been about 650,000—based on an 1869 *chōnin* enumeration of 504,000 (see Ogi, *Tōkei shomin seikatsu shi kenkyū*, p. 34), plus a continuing non-enumerated *chōnin* population of 85,000 and a samurai remainder of 60,000.

This sustained population growth was of course a reflection of the impact of the reforms of the Meiji government: centralizing national administration, freeing the movement of goods and people, encouraging modern industry, and consequently stimulating the growth of the urban

---

Tokyo: for 1877 (from Ogi, *Tōkei shomin seikatsu shi kenkyū*, p. 37), when the cumulative distortions in the household registration (*koseki*) statistics were least; and for 1908 (from Tōkyō to, ed., *Tōkyō hyakunen shi*, vol. 3, p. 658), when a true census was first conducted. See *Tōkyō hyakunen shi*, vol. 4, pp. 58-59, for the problem of inaccuracies in *koseki* statistics.

sector. Whereas Edo's immense population had been sustained primarily by political mechanisms and only secondarily by the economic growth of its regional hinterland, in Meiji Tokyo more of a balance was achieved between the two. It is true that Tokyo's function as national capital was crucial to its rapid recovery from the trauma of the 1860s, but this function was less critical than it had been for Edo.

The political arrangements of the *bakuhan* system, particularly the *sankin kōtai*, had worked over time to prime a pump of economic development in eastern Japan that was self-sustaining by the time of the Edo-Tokyo transition.[25] For the first two decades of the Meiji period, Tokyo's growth was more regionally oriented than it would be after the 1890s, with the completion of the national rail network and the beginning of modern economic growth. This was in part because of the capital's decreased dependency on the Osaka market following the collapse of the *sankin kōtai*, and in part a reflection of the continued growth in the traditional economy of eastern Japan.[26] In certain respects, the strong pull of Tokyo as the paramount city of eastern Japan worked in the Meiji period to enhance its competitive advantage versus Osaka, as seen clearly in the 1880s reorientation of the Hokuriku rice market from Osaka to Tokyo.[27] In this sense, Meiji Tokyo was the fulfillment of "Edo centrism."

The shape of Figure 13.1 insistently reminds us, though, that early Tokyo remained a lesser city than Edo. It was only after two decades of sustained growth that the limits of Edo, both in population and in settled area, would be surpassed; and still another two decades would be required before Tokyo could match Edo's share of the national population (somewhat under 4 percent). Nor was the rate of Tokyo's growth in any way exceptional: the 90 percent population increase that the capital experienced in the 1878-1897 period was the exact average of the net increase in population for the twenty cities of more than 30,000 persons.[28]

Those cities which most conspicuously outstripped Tokyo in rate of growth were the international ports—and Osaka. The obvious relevance of foreign trade to urban growth reminds us of the importance of Yokohama both in stimulating the growth of the Kantō region and in cush-

[25] The pump-priming metaphor is from Albert Craig, *Chōshū in the Meiji Restoration* (Cambridge: Harvard University Press, 1961), p. 30.

[26] See the Hayami chapter in this book.

[27] Kazuo Nakamura, "Eastern and Western Japan," in Association of Japanese Geographers, ed., *Geography of Japan* (Tokyo: Teikoku shoin, 1980), pp. 190-191; Kurosaki Chiharu, "Tō-zai daishōken to sono henbō," *Rekishichirigaku kiyō*, vol. 6 (1964), pp. 23-40.

[28] Calculated from figures in Takeo Yazaki, *Social Change and the City in Japan—From Earliest Times through the Industrial Revolution*, trans. David L. Swain (Tokyo: Japan Publications, 1968), pp. 312-313.

ioning the impact on Tokyo, essentially diverting population that might otherwise have accrued to the capital. The more rapid growth rate of Osaka is a reflection of the higher level of economic advancement of the Kinai region. Tokyo, by contrast, had a less developed industrial hinterland, and its indigenous artisan population was largely dedicated to the small-scale production of handmade items for daily use. In the early Meiji period, Tokyo's artisan production was often Western in form (leather shoes, cloth umbrellas, trousers, and so forth) but rarely in mode of production.[29] The government set up several model factories in Tokyo, but these were typically in the suburbs and had little impact on the city as a whole.

The Meiji half of the transition period might thus be interpreted as a sort of breathing space for Tokyo, which had declined in relative population far more than other cities. Tokyo did of course catch up, and proceeded from the turn of the twentieth century to resume a pattern of centralizing momentum that recalled Edo. But this was the product of developments that lay beyond the limits of the transition period: the completion of the nationwide trunk-railway network in the 1890s, the increased political centrality of the capital under the Meiji Constitution, and the impact of modern industrial growth in the capital region.[30] The breadth of Tokyo's political and economic reach over twentieth-century Japan was in effect a convergence of two vectors: that of the "Edo centrism" of the latter half of the Tokugawa period, and that of the policies of the Meiji state which came into full force in the early twentieth century. In between lay the transitional "breathing space."

In the city of Tokyo itself, vacant daimyo estates provided the new government with ample space for its offices and choice residential lots for its followers, many complete with buildings.[31] Indeed, the space was more than enough, and in a curious transitional scheme (in 1869) large areas were set aside for the cultivation of tea and mulberry. The plan failed. Neither crop did very well in Tokyo, and the hopes for a booming export industry in tea and silk were dashed.[32] However quixotic, the "tea and mulberry policy" reveals the amplitude of space in early Meiji Tokyo.

The Meiji government was spared the need of devoting energy and resources to the construction of an appropriate capital, and in the end

[29] Ishizuka, *Nihon shihon shugi seiritsu shi kenkyū*, pp. 345-351.

[30] Sugiura Yoshio, "Innovation Diffusion and Urban System in Japan during the Meiji and Taisho Era, 1868-1926," *Geographical Report* (Tokyo Metropolitan University, Department of Geography), vol. 13 (1979), p. 38.

[31] For details of the disposition of samurai land, see Tōkyō to, ed., *Meiji shonen no bukechi shori mondai.*

[32] Ibid., pp. 70-94; Ogi, *Tōkei shomin seikatsu shi kenkyū*, p. 53.

merely made a few relatively simple adjustments in Edo's plan and infrastructure: widening and straightening streets to accommodate the onslaught of wheeled traffic, upgrading the water supply to control epidemic disease, and sponsoring fireproofing projects to protect Tokyo from the "flowers of Edo." As a physical resource, Edo needed only to be adapted rather than replaced, establishing continuities of form that have survived to the present.[33] The "breathing space" of the transition made this leisurely accommodation possible.

Edo-Tokyo Residents and Their Culture

Bakufu *Retainers in the Edo-Tokyo Transition*

The direct retainers of the shogun, the so-called *jikisan*, constituted a segment of the Edo population roughly the same size as that of the domain samurai—but one very different in its implications for the culture of the city as a whole and, in particular, for the dynamics of the transition to Tokyo. Consisting of about 25,000 households, the *hatamoto* and *gokenin* were a wholly indigenous population within Edo; and despite their scattering in 1868 and their generally inconspicuous presence in Meiji Tokyo, it is likely that they functioned as a critical pivot in the Edo-Tokyo transition, in ways that have yet to be fully explored.

The shogunal retainers differed sharply from the domain samurai in their close integration with the commoner city, both culturally and economically. They depended on the Edo merchant class for all of their needs, and contact between the two was constant. Moreover, the increasing poverty of the *jikisan*, it has been argued, meant that the *gokenin* majority was for all intents and purposes becoming more and more like *chōnin*.[34] The covert sale of *gokenin* status was becoming increasingly frequent in the *bakumatsu* period, and many engaged in domestic by-employments, such as making umbrellas or other handicraft items, while others were permitted to build rental apartments and let them out.[35] Many of the lower-ranking *jikisan* themselves lived in barracks little different from the back-street tenements of the commoner districts.

[33] Fujimori Terunobu, *Meiji no Tōkyō keikaku* (Tokyo: Iwanami shoten, 1982), p. 272.

[34] Kozo Yamamura, *A Study of Samurai Income and Entrepreneurship* (Cambridge: Harvard University Press, 1974), p. 133.

[35] Kodama Kōta and Sugiyama Hiroshi, *Tōkyō to no rekishi* (Tokyo: Yamakawa shuppansha, 1969), p. 251; Matsumoto Shirō, "Kinsei toshiron—Hairyō machi yashiki no keisei to hatten o chūshin ni," in Fukaya Katsumi and Matsumoto Shirō, eds., *Bakuhan shakai no kōzō*, vol. 3 of *Kōza Nihon kinsei shi* (Tokyo: Yūhikaku, 1980), pp. 109-146.

Culturally, too, it is perhaps best to see *chōnin* and samurai in Edo as complementary rather than opposed. The popular culture of Edo that emerged in the last century of Tokugawa rule is inevitably described as *chōnin*, or "plebeian," but this is misleading. Samurai writers were conspicuous in the formative phrase of Edo popular literature in the 1770s and 1780s; and among the early *edokko* ("Edo-born") were the *fudasashi*, merchants whose job was to broker the rice stipends of the *jikisan*, a profession that was in no way "plebeian" and involved daily contact with samurai.[36] In the early nineteenth century, direct samurai involvement in the creation of popular culture declined, but they remained among its avid consumers. It was this symbiotic relationship between *chōnin* and samurai in Edo culture, for example, that accounts for the increasing resemblance of speech patterns of the two classes. By the mid-nineteenth century, the everyday language of the *gokenin* was little different from that of the *chōnin*.[37]

As a class, nevertheless, the shogunal retainers were still the political elite of Edo, and hence potentially of great significance as a force for continuity in the transition to Tokyo. This role was greatly undermined, however, by the extensive dispersal of the *bakufu* retainers in 1868. Following the defeat of the Shōgitai at Ueno on July 4, many die-hard shogunal loyalists fled north to continue their resistance. But far more moved later that year to the newly created 700,000-*koku* Tokugawa domain of Shizuoka; the figure of 14,000 families given by Katsu Kaishū as the size of this group would account for well over half of the total retainer band.[38] Others left the city and faded into the countryside, as the new regime encouraged them to do.

A minority of the *bakufu* retainers, however, proclaimed their loyalty to the new regime and remained in Edo. Their numbers must have been small. A survey from early 1871 records an ex-samurai (*shizoku* and *sotsu*) population of only 66,000 for all Tokyo *fu*, under 10 percent of the total.[39] Even if we assume two-thirds of this group to be former *bakufu* retainers (a generous assumption in view of the domination of the new regime by domain samurai), they would amount to no more than six or seven thousand families, less than 30 percent of their former number.

The greatly diminished numbers of ex-*bakufu* retainers in Tokyo, however, may belie their importance in the transition process. Apart from

[36] Nishiyama Matsunosuke, *Edokko* (Tokyo: Yoshikawa kōbunkan, 1980).

[37] Matsumura Akira, *Edogo Tōkyōgo no kenkyū* (Tokyo: Tōkyōdō, 1957), p. 16.

[38] Katsu Kaishū, ed., *Suijinroku* [1890], 2 vols. (Tokyo: Hara shobō, 1968), vol. 2, p. 327.

[39] Tōkyō to, ed., *Tōkyō shi shikō* (Tokyo: Tōkyō to, 1911–), *shigaihen* 51, p. 794.

such prominent figures as Katsu Kaishū and Enomoto Takeaki, it is likely that the former shogun's men performed critical transitional functions at the middle and lower levels of the central government during the early Meiji period. Their influence was probably even greater in the Tokyo city and prefectural bureaucracies, since they possessed a fund of expertise on the city and its traditional governance. In contrast to those who chose to serve the Meiji government was a vocal minority who acted rather as critics of the regime—men such as Narushima Ryūhoku and Fukuchi Ōchi. Whatever their loyalty, however, the ex-*bakufu* retainers seem to have shared an orientation that might be interpreted as cosmopolitan rather than provincial, national rather than clannish. If such an interpretation is valid, this characteristic certainly relates to the nature of late Edo as increasingly a truly national capital, its culture increasingly the common culture of Japan as a whole.

The spoken language of the city of Edo-Tokyo provides some particularly interesting suggestions about the role of the shogunal retainers in the broader cultural transition. When James Hepburn, in the preface to the second (1872) edition of his famous Japanese-English dictionary, noted that "one conversant with Yedo dialect will have no difficulty in being understood in any part of the country, amongst the educated classes," he was probably referring to "proper Edo" (*hon'Edo*), the relatively polite version of Edo dialect spoken by the *hatamoto* and *gokenin*.[40] In short, the language of Edo, particularly as spoken by the *bakufu* retainer class, had by the end of the Tokugawa period become a "common language" for all Japan.

After the Meiji Restoration, the speech of the shogunal retainers became the nucleus for the emerging standard language of modern Japan. Edo language had developed as an amalgam of various dialects and had already been diffused through the alternating residence patterns of the *sankin kōtai*. In the third (1886) edition of his dictionary, Hepburn observed that a critical change had taken place: "The language of Kyoto, the ancient capital of the country, . . . has been considered the standard and of highest authority; but since the restoration and the removal of the capital to Tokyo, the dialect of the latter has precedence."[41] In other words, the Edo dialect that had been a "common" language was transformed into a "standard" language. The culture of the *bakufu* retainer class served as the point of departure for the transformation of Edo as a provincial culture into Tokyo as a national culture.

The course of this transformation inevitably meant a widening gap

[40] See Matsumura, *Edogo Tōkyōgo no kenkyū*, pp. 13-16.

[41] Ibid., p. 58.

between "Edo" and "Tokyo." In language, for example, what emerged as "standard" Tokyo speech showed many influences from outside, both from provincial Japan and from foreign languages as well. As in so many other ways in the latter part of the transition period, the perception of "Edo" and "Tokyo" as two contrasting entities gradually emerged, the one increasingly "traditional" and the other increasingly "modern." The establishment, in the 1890s, of this sense of *opposition* between "Edo" and "Tokyo" marks the end of the Edo-Tokyo transition. Those who most publicized this contrast and lamented the passing of "Edo" were none other than former *bakufu* retainers, in such magazines as Annals of the Edo Society (*Edo-kai shi*, 1889–) and The Old Bakufu (*Kyūbakufu*, 1897–).[42]

Cultural Continuity

The most provocative approach to the Edo-Tokyo transition in recent scholarship emerges from Ogi Shinzō's highly original and meticulously detailed study of daily life in early Meiji Tokyo.[43] Ogi sees the period from the Meiji Restoration until about 1889 as a distinct and unique era in the history of the city, one characterized by the underlying continuity and stability of Edo commoner culture in the face of traumatic political events that transformed the elite city. Ogi seizes upon "Tōkei," the common early Meiji reading of the characters for "Eastern Capital," as a rhetorical device to suggest the special character of these two decades. Ogi interprets "Tōkei" as a city in which the disappearance of the old samurai elite cleared the way for a culture that was predominantly "commoner" (*shominteki*) in tone—"more Edo-like than Edo," as Ogi would have it.[44]

Ogi carefully documents the essential continuity from Edo to Tokyo in daily life style, showing that the diet, clothing, and housing of the great majority of the citizenry remained unchanged through the 1880s. This perspective is a healthy corrective to the common depiction of Meiji Tokyo as a hotbed of westernizing "civilization and enlightenment," which had little real impact on the lives of most of the residents of Tōkei. In the area of popular entertainment, as well, such characteristic late Edo

[42] Ogi, *Tōkei shomin seikatsu shi kenkyū*, pp. 17-21; Mizue Renko, *Edo shichū keisei shi no kenkyū* (Tokyo: Kōbundō, 1977), pp. 38-41.

[43] *Tōkei shomin seikatsu shi kenkyū*. Ogi has also written a short, popular version of much the same material: *Tōkei jidai: Edo to Tōkyō no hazama de*, NHK Bukkusu, no. 371 (Tokyo: Nippon hōsō shuppan kyōkai, 1980).

[44] Ogi, *Tōkei shomin seikatsu shi kenkyū*, p. 2.

forms as *rakugo* and Kabuki enjoyed continuing if not increased popularity in early Meiji Tokyo.[45]

Indeed, as a way of grasping the Edo-Tokyo transition, it seems preferable to expand Ogi's exclusive focus on early Meiji to envision the entire era from Bunka-Bunsei (1804-1830) through the 1880s as the final great flowering of Edo culture. Spanning the Edo-Tokyo transition, this era was characterized by the establishment of Edo popular culture as wholly distinct from that of Osaka and Kyoto, and by the permeation to the great middle range of Edo society of a wide variety of popular pastimes. Nishiyama Matsunosuke has developed the concept of *kōdō bunka*, perhaps best translated as "a culture of movement and performance," encompassing sightseeing, pilgrimages, flower arranging, tea ceremony, and theatrical and musical performances of every kind: all were practiced in nineteenth-century Edo-Tokyo to an extent previously unknown.[46]

One particularly important reflection of this era was rapidly rising literacy among all classes. The spread of "temple schools" (*terakoya*) continued from late Edo into Meiji Tokyo with virtually no interruption, while *terakoya* textbooks constituted one of the most flourishing sectors of the publishing market in the *bakumatsu* period.[47] The characteristic forms of late Edo fiction continued to be widely read, if not written, in the early Meiji period.[48] But nineteenth-century Edo-Tokyo culture was not communicated in books alone. Although often denigrated as "decadent," this was in fact the great era of the color woodblock print, the Edo *nishiki-e*, which in quantity, in the skill of the artisans, and in the literacy of its content reached levels that far outstripped the "classic" era of the late eighteenth century. The final capitulation of woodblock printing to lithography, photography, and movable type in the 1890s serves clearly to mark the end of an era.

One enduring, indeed defining, characteristic of Edo culture was a strong spirit of opposition to Osaka and its customs. This was the cultural counterpart of "Edo centrism," a sense of the need to enhance Edo's independence of western Japan.[49] Such a tone was central to the image

[45] Ibid., chap. 3.

[46] Nishiyama Matsunosuke, "Edo bunka to chihō bunka," *Iwanami kōza Nihon rekishi*, vol. 13, *kinsei 5* (Tokyo: Iwanami shoten, 1964), pp. 183-186.

[47] Ogi, *Tōkei shomin seikatsu shi kenkyū*, p. 457; Konta Yōzō, *Edo no hon'ya-san—Kinsei bunka shi no sokumen* (Tokyo: Nippon hōsō shuppan kyōkai, 1977), p. 189.

[48] P.F. Kornicki, "The Survival of Tokugawa Fiction in the Meiji Period," *Harvard Journal of Asiatic Studies*, vol. 41, no. 2 (December 1981), pp. 461-482.

[49] Nishiyama, *Edokko*; Sofue Takao, *Kenminsei—Bunka jinrui gakuteki kōsatsu* (Tokyo: Chūō kōronsha, 1971), p. 123.

of the *edokko*: proud, fast-talking, easy-spending, and contemptuous of the cautious, penny-pinching ways of the stereotypical Osaka merchant. This attitude may be traced directly through the transition period, and explains both the pride of the Edo citizenry at being residents of the new "imperial capital" and, at the same time, their haughty contempt of the new elite from western Japan.

Patterns of Immigration

The broad perspective of a basic continuity between the culture of late Edo and early Tokyo, as revealed both in daily life and popular culture, is highly suggestive. One danger, however, particularly as the concept is applied by Ogi Shinzō, is the neglect of the parallel process of *change*. Edo culture was not merely surviving, it was evolving—in new directions and in response to major changes in the social structure of the city.

One important way of analyzing the process of change is in terms of spatial differentiation *within* the city, especially in terms of the familiar distinction between *shitamachi* (the low-lying and densely settled eastern sector of the city) and *yamanote* (the hilly upland area to the west). But it would first be useful to consider some basic indicators of social change within the city as a whole, and the ways in which these relate to cultural evolution. Ogi's own explanation for the eventual demise of "Tōkei" focuses on such changes: basically, he sees a huge increase in the proportion of immigrants as undermining the foundations of the traditional urban culture, working particularly to destroy the solidarity of neighborhood society. He dates this process from 1889, his own terminal date for "Tōkei."[50]

What was the basic pattern of immigration in the Edo-Tokyo transition? Edo, like any premodern city, required a constant flow of immigrants to maintain its population. In the seventeenth century, when the city was growing rapidly, Edo was overwhelmingly a city of immigrants, the majority of them male. From the early eighteenth century, however, the population stabilized and the flow of immigration slowed. Available statistics confirm two predictable consequences of a stable population: an equalization of the sex ratio and a declining percentage of those born outside the city.

The sex ratio figures are shown in Figure 13.2. Bearing in mind that the Edo figures exclude samurai and priests (which would tend to raise the overall sex ratio), note that this graph suggests that the unique interlude is not, as Ogi proposes, early Meiji (which appears merely as the

[50] Ogi, *Tōkei shomin seikatsu shi kenkyū*, pp. 583-588.

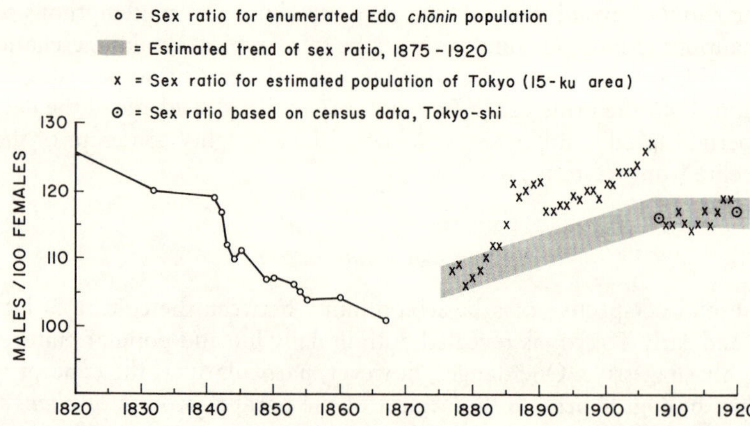

Figure 13.2 Edo-Tokyo Sex Ratios, 1820-1920

NOTE: Data for Edo (until 1867) from Kōda, "Edo no chōnin no jinkō" (see Figure 13.1, above), chart facing p. 248; the projected value for 1798 (135 M/100F) is from Tōkyō fu, ed., *Tōkyō fu shi, gyōseihen*, vol. 1 (1935), p. 92. For Tokyo, the figures have been calculated from Ogi Shinzō, *Tōkei shomin seikatsu shi kenkyū* (Tokyo: Nippon hōsō shuppan kyōkai, 1979), p. 34, and *Nihon chiri taikei* (Tokyo: Keizōsha, 1930), vol. 3, p. 382. The values for the Tokyo city census of 1908 and the national census of 1920 are from Tōkyō to, ed., *Tōkyō hyakunen shi*, 7 vols. (Tokyo: Tōkyō to, 1973-1980), vol. 4, p. 60.

The Meiji figures prior to the 1908 census show an evident tendency to progressive exaggeration of the sex ratio, with a partial correction as a result of the 1890 adjustments in the *kiryū* population. The exaggeration presumably results from the same cause—underreporting of out-migrants—that caused the overestimation of the total population in the same years (see Figure 13.1). In other words, the unreported out-migrant population was closer to equality of sex ratio than was the total reported population. The "estimated trend" line attempts to compensate for this error.

start of a new upward trend in the sex ratio), but rather the period of the Edo-Tokyo transition itself (which shows as a distinctive trough).[51]

What about more direct indicators of change in the pattern of immigration to Edo-Tokyo? Enumerations of *chōnin* after 1832 provide a breakdown of "native born" (*tōchi shusshō*) versus "elsewhere born" (*tasho shusshō*).[52] These show the latter group rising from 24 percent in 1832 to a peak of 31 percent in 1843, and then declining gradually to a low of 22 percent in 1867. Clearly this indicates a decline in immigration to Tokyo after the Tempō period, a decline that is confirmed by a few

[51] Ibid., pp. 287-317.

[52] Kōda Shigetomo, "Edo no chōnin no jinkō," *Shakai keizai shigaku*, vol. 8, no. 1 (April 1938), reprinted in *Kōda Shigetomo chosakushū*, 7 vols. (Tokyo: Chūō kōronsha, 1972-1974), vol. 2, pp. 244-265.

detailed neighborhood studies available from the 1860s.[53] After 1868, however, with the rapid growth of Meiji Tokyo, the flow of immigrants swelled. Even with a decline in urban mortality rates, the great bulk of the average annual increase of 3.6 percent must have been immigrants, whose numbers in annual increment and hence in total share of the city population rose steadily.

The pattern of migration appears to have changed little in the course of the Edo-Tokyo transition: migrants continued to be predominantly male, and to come from the same regions as in the past. The Hokuriku region, for example—Echigo province in particular—emerged in the late Tokugawa period as a disproportionately large source of Edo immigrants, a function that continued unabated into the twentieth century.[54] On these grounds, we would predict that the pattern of immigration was a source of stability in the transition. This is particularly true if we project backward from the twentieth century White's finding that urban immigrants tended to be relatively well prepared for the urban milieu, and did not necessarily constitute a segregated and oppressed subclass, as much Japanese scholarship has suggested.[55]

The changing ratio of "native born" versus "elsewhere born" is suggested in Figure 13.3, which is based on a direct (and hence approximate) comparison of the late Tokugawa *chōnin* enumerations with those of the 1920 census and which assumes a regular rate of increase in the percentage of "elsewhere born" within the city.[56] By this projection, the size of the immigrant population surpassed that of the "native born" in about 1909. If one considers only the adult population, however, then immigrants became a majority about two decades earlier, in 1889. This tends to support Ogi's concept of the period from the 1890s on as a new era in which the immigrant population was now dominant—as it had been two centuries earlier at the crest of the city's first great period of expansion.

[53] Minami, *Bakumatsu Edo shakai no kenkyū*, pp. 3-120.

[54] Sofue, *Kenminsei*, pp. 17-19; Minami Kazuo, "Toshi ryūnyūmin," in Toyoda Takeshi, Harada Tomohiko, and Yamori Kazuo, eds., *Kōza Nihon no hōken toshi*, 3 vols. (Tokyo: Bun'ichi sōgō shuppan, 1982-1983), vol. 2, p. 339; Tōkyō to, ed., *Tōkyō hyakunen shi*, vol. 4, pp. 49-50.

[55] James W. White, "Internal Migration in Prewar Japan," *Journal of Japanese Studies*, vol. 4, no. 1 (Winter 1978), pp. 81-123.

[56] Ogi, *Tōkei shomin seikatsu shi kenkyū*, pp. 41-42, uses the Meiji statistics for "legally domiciled population" (*honseki jinkō*) and "temporary-resident population" (*kiryū jinkō*) as equivalent to the native-born and immigrant populations; but this is unacceptable, since (among other problems) the *kiryū jinkō* was greatly overreported in Meiji Tokyo, as reflected by the periodic attempts to correct the registers.

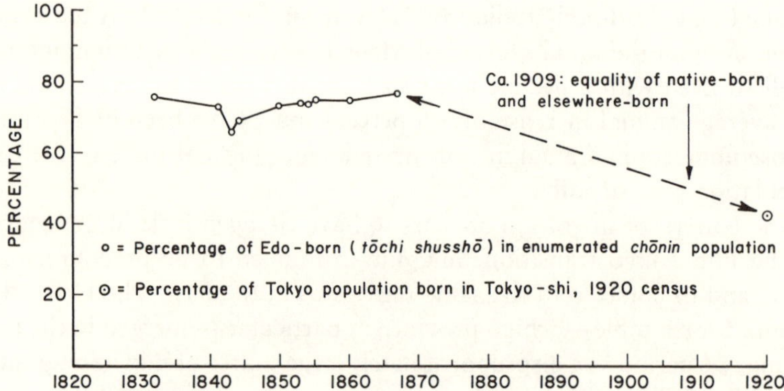

Figure 13.3 Native-Born Population in Edo-Tokyo, 1830-1920
Data from Kōda, "Edo no chōnin no jinkō" (see Figure 13.1, above); Nishiyama Matsunosuke, ed., *Edo chōnin no kenkyū*, 5 vols. (Tokyo: Yoshikawa kōbunkan, 1972-1978), vol. 1, p. 534; and Tōkyō to, ed., *Tōkyō hyakunen shi*, 7 vols. (Tokyo: Tōkyō to, 1973-1980), vol. 4, p. 47.

Neighborhood Solidarity

In Edo, the fundamental unit of urban life above the household was the *machi*, an administrative unit that typically consisted of the lots along both sides of a block-long street. The *machi* were essentially modular, enclosed by gates that were always guarded and closed at night. They were governed through a peculiar and pivotal class of "superintendants." Called by a variety of names—*ienushi* formally, *ōya* colloquially, and *yamori* noncommitally—these men wore two hats. Their basic roles were as caretakers and rent collectors for the landlord class. At the same time, they came to be assigned functions of political control, passing on official directives from the city magistrate's office to their tenants and assuming responsibility in five-man groups for any offenses their tenants might commit. The *yamori* (as I shall call them) numbered about 13,000 in Edo, and they emerge in the literature of the Edo-Tokyo transition (particularly in *rakugo* storytelling) as mediating father figures, watching over and yet protecting their "house children" (*tanako*).

The collapse of the traditional system of local administration in 1868 posed a severe threat to neighborhood stability. The new regime consciously aimed at uprooting the entrenched local authorities and replacing them with functionaries designated by the new national bureaucracy.[57]

[57] The details of local administrative reform are to be found in Tōkyō to, ed., *Kusei enkaku* (Tokyo: Tōkyō to, 1958). A good summary appears in Tōkyō to, ed., *Tōkyō hyakunen shi*, vol. 2, pp. 151-164.

The primary targets were the headmen (*nanushi*), the 260-odd officials who stood between the neighborhood *yamori* and the three hereditary city elders. By late Edo, the headmen had become entrenched hereditary powers, and they were replaced in early Meiji by appointees of Tokyo prefecture. At first, it was difficult not to rely on the former headmen, but over time their numbers were reduced, and the "ward heads" who replaced them (*chū-toshiyori*; later, *kochō*) came to be civil servants fully incorporated into the centralized prefectural bureaucracy.

Below the new ward heads, however, at the neighborhood level, the new government chose to leave most matters to informal and semiformal structures, which in effect meant the continued dominance of the *yamori*. This course of action was not evident from the start. On the contrary, the earliest edicts of the new government seemed intended to uproot the *yamori* as well as the headmen. They were even barred from any sort of administrative function in the new system, and the very word *ienushi* was legally banned in November 1869, to be replaced by (*chisho*) *sahainin* ("[land] superintendant").[58] But thereafter the government seems to have been content to let governance at the neighborhood (*machi*) level go its own way. In early 1870, some of the *sahainin* were permitted to undertake *machi* business without pay, and eventually a paid position of *machi* secretary (*chōyō kakari*) was established; typically, it was filled by a *sahainin*.

More important than this tenuous administrative continuity, though, was the uninterrupted role of the landlords and their *yamori* agents as the de facto holders of power in neighborhood Edo-Tokyo. There had been far fewer restrictions on land dealing in Edo than conventional wisdom would allow, and the liberalization by the new regime served largely to confirm what had long been practice. The city remained one in which landed power was restricted to a stable elite, and the majority of residents were renters.

Those scholars (principally Edo specialists) who depict the class structure of the city as a fundamental opposition of landlord and tenant also mislead.[59] On the contrary, neighborhood society in nineteenth-century Edo-Tokyo was highly differentiated, with not one but many lines of opposition. The *yamori* himself occupied an ambiguous middle ground between landlord and tenant: he held no property, but received housing as a fee for his services. Another peculiarity of Edo-Tokyo property holding that complicated the social hierarchy was the widespread practice

[58] Murata Shizuko, "Meiji ninen Honkokuchō nichōme koseki shitagaki ni tsuite," *Nihon rekishi*, no. 218 (July 1966), p. 45.

[59] For example: Matsumoto Shirō, "Bakumatsu ishinki ni okeru toshi no kōzō," *Mitsui bunko ronsō*, no. 4 (March 1970), pp. 105-164.

of leasing land upon which to build one's own house. This distinction between landowning and houseowning probably had its roots in the short life expectancy of houses in fire-susceptible Edo, but it has survived in Tokyo until the present.

The very complexity of organization at the neighborhood level may have been a critical factor in the stability of urban society at its base. The upward shift in the lowest level of official bureaucracy in the Meiji reforms meant that neighborhood control was left to the informal mechanisms of local power. We may assume that in early Tokyo these traditional mechanisms proved adequate to assimilate the new immigrants flowing into the city. In time, however, strains emerged, as the proportion of immigrants increased. New types of organization emerged to cope with the strains, and these may be taken as marking the effective end of the transition period.

One of these was the *chōnaikai* (neighborhood association), which numbered a mere 39 in 1897 but rose to 452 on the eve of the 1923 Kantō earthquake. While diverse in origin, the *chōnaikai* were essentially a means of sustaining local community solidarity in the face of rapid population turnover.[60] Parallel with these were the prefectural clubs (*kenjinkai*), which sought to offer comradeship to immigrants of common origin. The *kenjinkai*, like the *chōnaikai*, were basically products of the twentieth century and as such mark the end of the transition period, during which the traditional mechanisms of neighborhood solidarity continued to function with little need for new organizations.[61]

"Edo" and "Tokyo"—Two Cities or One?

Ogi Shinzō's concept of the "Tōkei era" helps focus attention on two useful distinctions for analyzing Meiji Tokyo: the "provincial city" versus the "imperial capital," and the *shitamachi* versus the *yamanote*. Ogi argues that in the first two decades of Meiji, Tokyo was essentially provincial and dominated by the commoner culture of the *shitamachi*.[62]

Tokyo, of course, *was* the "imperial capital" as of late 1868, but it

[60] Henry D. Smith II, "Tokyo as an Idea: An Exploration of Japanese Urban Thought until 1945," *Journal of Japanese Studies*, vol. 4, no. 1 (Winter 1978), p. 66.

[61] Sofue, *Kenminsei*, pp. 12-14, shows roughly equal proportions of contemporary Tokyo *kenjinkai* to have been founded in three periods: in Meiji; between the end of Meiji and the Pacific War; and in the postwar period. I assume that the majority of the Meiji group were founded in the twentieth century.

[62] Ogi Shinzō, "Tōkei saiken," in Ogi Shinzō and Maeda Ai, eds., *Tōkyō 1*, Meiji Taishō zushi, no. 1 (Tokyo: Chikuma shobō, 1978), p. 143.

did not take on a look appropriate to the grand term "Teito" until the 1890s. The offices of the early Meiji government were located in an ad hoc manner in and around the grounds of the former Edo Castle, whose surviving walls and crumbling gates were still the city's grandest monuments, an ever-present reminder of the *bakufu* city. The Imperial Palace, which had been moved into the old Nishinomaru of Edo Castle, went up in flames in 1873, and was not rebuilt until 1888; its very absence is an appropriate symbol of the transition era. It was only in the 1890s that the two characteristic districts of Tokyo as a modern imperial capital took shape: the central business district of Marunouchi and the national government center of Kasumigaseki. Both stood clearly and grandly apart from the old center of Edo to the east, and a strong sense of opposition between the two was established.

During the early Meiji period, however, "provincial" Edo and "national" Tokyo were far more interwoven, and one draws a distinction between the two at the peril of missing the essence of the transition. The true monument of Meiji Tokyo was the Ginza district, reconstructed in brick after a disastrous fire in 1872. The initiative for the project came from the central government, in no small part because such leading figures as Ōkuma Shigenobu and Yuri Kimimasa, who then lived in the downtown area, had lost their homes in the fire. The project was also construed as a means of impressing foreigners with Japan's modernizing vigor. But the Ginza area was an old artisan district, and the merchants who moved into it were mostly local, Edo-style *chōnin* eager to adapt to new ways. The end result was an astonishing amalgam of national and provincial, indigenous and Western, "Edo" and "Tokyo." Often judged a failure in terms of the grand intentions of its planners, who had envisioned a Regent Street in the center of Tokyo, the resulting Ginza was in practice a great success, setting patterns of merchandising, display, and architectural form that continue to the present.[63]

Less well known than the Ginza was a similar blending of the old "Edo" and new "Tokyo" in what constituted the modern business district of early Tokyo. Located southeast of Edobashi in the very belly of the *shitamachi*, on a mix of both *chōnin* and samurai land, was an assortment of buildings of diverse and often eclectic style, housing a variety of leading Meiji banks, insurance companies, newspapers, commercial associations, and—the only survivor today—the Tokyo Stock Exchange. Put together under the entrepreneurial aegis of Shibusawa Eiichi, this area combined the feel of riverside Edo with such Tokyo-like amenities as gas streetlamps

[63] On the failure of the Ginza see, for example, *ibid.*, p. 140; on its success, see Fujimori, *Meiji no Tōkyō keikaku*, chap. 1.

and the first electrical generating plant. It was one of those early Meiji phenomena that could be understood only as neither "Edo" nor "Tokyo," as the two would come to be distinguished.[64] Not so with its successor, the uniform rows of brick buildings that Mitsubishi constructed in Marunouchi after 1896. The Marunouchi business district, like the grand baroque plans for Kasumigaseki which were being laid at the same time, served to set "imperial" Tokyo apart from the old commoner districts to the east that were increasingly being perceived as the realm of "Edo." Although the Kasumigaseki plan was realized only in part, it did become the nucleus of a coherent national government district, a visible "imperial capital" that sets late Meiji clearly apart from the transition era.

The division of the city as a whole into two mutually opposed cultural zones, the "plebeian" *shitamachi* to the east and the "elite" *yamanote* to the west, similarly tends to restrict our understanding of the Edo-Tokyo transition. The *shitamachi/yamanote* distinction is an old one, dating back to the first century of Edo's history, but one that continued to change with the city itself.[65] In late Tokugawa, the distinction seems to have been between center and periphery. *Shitamachi* was clearly the "downtown" area centered around Nihonbashi; there is no evidence that the conception extended to the eastern flatlands of the city as a whole. *Yamanote* was geographically vaguer, referring to the hilly western uplands in general. The cultural sense of *yamanote* in late Edo is difficult to document, since the term does not appear frequently in the surviving literature, but it appears to have suggested rusticity, in opposition to the urbanity of the center.[66]

It is reasonable to assume that this same conceptual structure dominated the early Meiji period, although the dynamics of the transition launched a critical transformation. Particularly important was the enforced removal in 1871 of the (ex-)daimyo and the imperial aristocracy to Tokyo. They were settled primarily on the lots of ex-*bakufu* retainers around Kōjimachi and in the former daimyo villas of Aoyama, Azabu, and elsewhere. It was their residential style, of detached houses set back behind gated walls and surrounded by gardens, that would in time become the *yamanote* ideal. But the formulation of that ideal awaited a critical development that began only near the turn of the century: the emergence of a modern middle-class culture and its residential concentration in the *yamanote*. One factor in this transformation was probably

[64] Fujimori Terunobu, "Ushinawareta 'Shibusawa Shōgyōgai,' " *Bunka kaigi*, no. 135 (September 1980), pp. 26-33.

[65] Takeuchi Makoto, "Edo no chiiki kōzō to jūmin ishiki," in Toyoda et al., eds., *Kōza Nihon no hōken toshi*, vol. 2, pp. 302-309.

[66] Ibid., pp. 304-305.

the residential model of the foreigners, perched high in the hills above Kobe and Yokohama; it is hard to find a precedent for this practice in an agricultural society that generally reserved the low-lying, watered areas for the elite, relegating the poor and the holy to the hills.

This revised sense of *yamanote* was paralleled by an even more sweeping redefinition of *shitamachi*, which came to be seen not as the city center, but rather as an eastern hemisphere set in mutual opposition to the *yamanote* to the west. The key development in this change was the industrialization of the city beginning in the 1880s, a process that for reasons of locational advantage was centered in the low-lying areas. The result was a new and distinctively modern *shitamachi*—more a periphery than a center, and in general poorer and less middle class than the western side of the city.

Critical to this transformation of the *shitamachi/yamanote* distinction was the incorporation of a historical dimension, by which the one became equated with "Edo" and the other with "Tokyo." In the process, the distinction would broaden further into a characteristic array of ideal-type dichotomies: *shitamachi* as old, traditional, unchanging, artisanal, indigenous, plebeian, and emotional; versus *yamanote* as new, modern, changing, imperial, bureaucratic, elite, and intellectual. From this framework, it is a logical progression to the conception of the Edo-Tokyo transition as envisioned by Ogi Shinzō and, more recently, by Edward Seidensticker, both of whom see the period after 1868 in terms of the *replacement* of "Edo" by "Tokyo."[67]

The *shitamachi/yamanote* distinction thus became increasingly "real" in the twentieth century, both conceptually and as an objective description of the urban ecology. As such, it has appeared as a familiar distinction in the writings of social scientists interested in Tokyo, although most seem aware of its limitations. Ronald Dore's skillful concept of "Shitayamachō" (that is, a neighborhood which is both "*shita*machi" and "*yamanote*") is the classic example.[68] But the distinction is far less adequate for the transition period, prior to industrialization and the emergence of a modern middle class.

In short, the sense of *opposition* between "Edo" and "Tokyo" emerged

[67] Edward Seidensticker, *Low City, High City—Tokyo from Edo to the Earthquake* (New York: Knopf, 1983).

[68] R.P. Dore, *City Life in Japan—A Study of a Tokyo Ward* (Berkeley: University of California Press, 1958), chap. 2; Robert J. Smith, "Pre-Industrial Urbanism in Japan: A Consideration of Multiple Traditions in a Feudal Society," *Economic Development and Cultural Change*, vol. 9, no. 1, pt. 2 (October 1960), pp. 241-257; James W. White, *Migration in Metropolitan Japan* (Berkeley: Institute of East Asian Studies, University of California, 1982).

only after the transition period, beginning in the 1890s. In the process of the transition itself, the "two" were rather a constantly changing "one," separated largely by a somewhat capricious change of name in 1868. The real tensions were not between "Edo" and "Tokyo," but rather between the center of the city and its many peripheries: subcenters, suburbs, the port of Yokohama, the domains and prefectures, and indeed the very nation of Japan. In sorting out the complex dynamics of these interactions, we will be able to free ourselves of the picture of a "dying" Edo versus an awkwardly maturing "Tokyo," and establish a broad middle ground where Edo and Tokyo overlap, interact, and produce syntheses that are neither one nor the other.

PART FOUR

RURAL ECONOMY AND MATERIAL CONDITIONS

INTRODUCTION TO PART FOUR

BY KOZO YAMAMURA

In 1880 about 70 percent of the gainfully employed in Japan were engaged in agriculture on a full-time basis, producing nearly 47 percent of the gross domestic product and paying approximately three-quarters of all taxes. Japan in the transition period was predominantly rural and agrarian. Thus, an understanding of how village life changed during the transition period is of utmost importance in better comprehending the reasons for—and the character of—the political, social, and economic changes that occurred through the *bakumatsu* years and the first years of the Meiji period.

However, in carefully examining both English and Japanese literature that deals with the various aspects of rural Japan during this period, one finds that many important and basic questions remain unanswered. Or perhaps it would be more accurate to say that the answers offered to date by some scholars are still subject to serious challenge by others. Such questions are of fundamental importance: the answers to them can and do substantively affect one's interpretation of the character and significance, for example, of the various protest movements, the land tax reform, the changes in landholding patterns, and the increase in rural by-employment and market activities during the Meiji period as well as one's interpretation of the nature of the Meiji Restoration itself.

Among the most important questions are these: Was the living standard of the rural population rising or falling? Or was it rising only for some, while falling for most? Did the patterns of income distribution change—and, if so, why? Did the number of tenant farmers increase (and if so, why)? How did various policies adopted by the Meiji government and the growth of market activities affect the economic lot of the villagers? Did the real tax burden increase or decrease because of the Meiji land tax reform? Did the effective tax burden increase because of the local taxes imposed after the reform, or did it decline as a result of increases in agricultural productivity (throughout the Meiji period) and increases in the price of rice (until the Matsukata deflation)? Did an increasing number of opportunities for by-employment and alternative employment raise the wage level? How, and to what extent, did the day-to-day lives of the villagers change during the period? Conflicting answers to these important questions are being offered by two broad groups of scholars. The answers offered by each of the two groups can be summarized as follows—with the caveat that many scholars in each group would qualify or modify the summary offered for their own group.

One group of scholars argues that the economic lot of most Meiji farmers deteriorated because the real tax burden rose and because the growth of the market benefited only a small minority among them. For these scholars, increasing economic hardship was the reason that tenancy rose rapidly and that "surplus" agricultural labor sought work in industry during the decades following the Restoration. In sharp contrast, the other group, which includes neoclassical economists, believes that the real income level of most villagers rose because the gains from increasing agricultural productivity and market activities were appreciable and because the real tax burden did not increase, and may even have declined. This group argues that the rate of increase in tenancy directly attributable to the land tax reform was small, and that many who moved out of the village did so in order to obtain better-paying work, i.e. to increase their income.

Why do the foregoing answers differ so sharply? First of all, there is a difference in methodology between Marxists (and those who implicitly accept the basic framework of their analysis) and neoclassical economists. A second reason relates to the quality of the quantitative evidence available. For the Tokugawa period, the few aggregate-data series that exist are highly suspect, and the disaggregated (i.e. local-level) data are all too often of little use to economists because of incomparability and unreliability. The data for the early Meiji decades are not much better. Many official data series that might be useful in answering some of the above questions do not begin before the mid-1880s, and the types of data series that would enable us to answer with some confidence the question of how living standards changed are available only from the early 1920s. While in comparison to other premodern societies there is a substantial amount of useful data, the statistics do not meet the requirements of most quantitative economic analysis.

There is an additional factor that contributes to the difference in views held about the transition period. With rare exceptions, Japanese and Western historians alike specialize in one or another period of Japanese history that is distinguished by a major political event, and it appears that Japanese historians are especially reluctant to cross self-imposed demarcation lines in choosing their research topics. This means that studies of the transition period tend to remain disjointed, and the period as a whole receives little scholarly attention.

Economists, too, again with a few exceptions, are reluctant to cross their own demarcation lines and venture back into a study of the Tokugawa period. In their case, the reasons are a lack of interest, the significant "entry cost" of studying the Tokugawa period, and/or the knowledge that their analytic arsenal is not very well equipped to deal with the data-scarce premodern period. For Japanese neoclassical economists, moreover, there is still another reason for staying away from the Tokugawa period. Why get entangled with the Tokugawa economy, which has long been the domain of Japanese historians whose methodology is incompatible with one's own? It is far more rewarding for such economists to focus their research efforts on one of many topics of the post-1868 period that remain yet uninvestigated. As a result, few economists have studied the transition period as a whole, thus leaving many questions unanswered.

There are signs that the current state of research on the transition period may be improving. One such was the establishment in 1972 of the Quantitative Economic History (QEH) group in Japan. From a dozen or so members, this group has grown in size to almost forty economists and historians. Though consciously emphasizing the use of quantitative evidence in its research, the group's methodology is not limited to neoclassical economic analysis, and the questions asked are broadly conceived to include social and political implications.

The major QEH publications to date are Umemura Mataji et al., eds., *Nihon keizai no hatten* [The Development of the Japanese Economy] (Tokyo: Nihon keizai shimbunsha, 1971); Shimpō Hiroshi et al., eds., *Sūryō keizai shi nyūmon: Nihon no zenkōgyōka shakai* [An Introduction to Quantitative Economic History: The Preindustrial Society of Japan] (Tokyo: Nihon hyōronsha, 1975); and Yasuba Yasukichi and Saitō Osamu, eds., *Puroto-kōgyōkaki no keizai to shakai* [Economy and Society in the Proto-Industrialization Period] (Tokyo: Nihon keizai shimbunsha, 1983). Currently, the collective research goal of the QEH group is a thorough re-examination of nineteenth-century Japan, with an emphasis on the economic changes that occurred during that century. As in the past, the group's goal is broadly defined to include analyses of sociopolitical changes that affected, and were affected by, economic change.

Another important historiographical development of recent years, one that can also be regarded as a hopeful sign, is the growing interest shown by an increasing number of Japanese historians in *minshū*, or "people's," history, which studies the thought, culture, and life styles of the nonelites, among whom cultivators constituted a large majority. The importance of this development in increasing our knowledge of rural Japan, both in the premodern and the modern period, has been made evident by Carol Gluck in her article "The People in History: Recent Trends in Japanese Historiography," *Journal of Asian Studies*, vol. 38, no. 1 (November 1978) and by Keiji Nagahara in his "Reflections on Recent Trends in Japanese Historiography," *Journal of Japanese Studies*, vol. 10, no. 1 (Winter 1984).

To be sure, the work of the QEH group and of historians interested in *minshū* history is not likely to overcome either rapidly or completely the problems—paucity of reliable data, methodological differences, specialization by political period—that are responsible for the conflicting views we have of rural Japan in the transition period. Nevertheless, progress is being made toward answering the questions posed above. Even if progress remains slow, scholarship has progressed from the "Debate on Japanese Capitalism" that was waged between the rōnō-ha and the kōza-ha during the Taishō and the early Shōwa years to Takafusa Nakamura's *Economic Growth in Prewar Japan* (Tokyo: Iwanami shoten, 1971 in Japanese; and Yale University Press, 1983 in English). Nor is there any reason not to expect further analytic progress in reaching less conflicting and more integrated views of the economic and social history of Japan.

The four chapters that follow represent the efforts of three economists and one historian toward the same goal. My own essay examines the reasons for the land tax reform of 1873 and the specific form it took, and analyzes the economic effects of the reform. A few bold hypotheses are offered in the hope of enticing others either to support or refute them.

Susan Hanley has contributed an exploratory study of life styles and material culture. Despite the importance of her topic, it has not attracted the attention it deserves from Western specialists of the Tokugawa and Meiji periods. Hanley finds a relative stability in the life styles and material culture of the transition. If these findings on stability can be confirmed, then the historians and economists who now argue that the standard of living was rising during the period and those who argue to the contrary must take them into account. As did a recent study by Neil L. Waters, "Local Leadership in the Kawasaki Region from Bakumatsu to Meiji," *Journal of Japanese Studies*, vol. 7, no. 1 (Winter 1981), Hanley's work invites attention to the importance of studying what did *not* change in order to better understand the turbulent decades that we call the transition period.

Osamu Saitō and Shunsaku Nishikawa, members of the QEH group, are among those rare Japanese economists who are contributing important works on the economic history and development of both the Tokugawa and the modern period. Saitō's contribution is an important one. He offers a rigorous, critical re-examination of the thesis that the more rural economic life was penetrated by market forces, the more wage labor moved from the agricultural into the industrial sector. This, of course, is part of a more general view that Japanese industrialization was made possible by the existence of a reservoir of surplus labor, which in turn was the result of increasing economic difficulties that caused the villagers to become tenant cultivators. Saitō also questions the view of some Japanese and American economists who believe that the process of Japanese industrialization can be analyzed by means of the well-known Lewis model, which assumes the existence of a pool of underemployed workers in the agricultural sector.

Saitō's central finding is that no large "reservoir" of unemployed and underemployed existed in Meiji Japan, and that this is demonstrated by the fact that the supply price of labor (the lowest wage that labor will accept) was high until the 1920s because of the income that could be earned from sericulture and various cash crops. This fact cannot be ignored either by historians holding a Marxist view of the Meiji rural economy or by economists still using the Lewis model to analyze Japanese industrialization. For those not familiar with the pertinent literature, I should add here that the historiographical and analytical significance of Saitō's contribution will be much more readily appreciated if Professor Yasukichi Yasuba's "Anatomy of the Debate on Japanese Capitalism," *Journal of Japanese Studies*, vol. 2, no. 1 (Autumn 1975) is read first.

Nishikawa's essay on grain consumption in Chōshū is based on his long-term and painstaking study of the changing condition of that region's economy during the 1840-1880 period. It is a significant contribution toward our understanding of the economic history of the transition. The quantitative evidence marshaled by Nishikawa casts doubt on the oft-made assertion that many Tokugawa and Meiji peasants lived on an inadequate diet, doing little better than subsisting. As Hanley found with respect to a more broadly defined material culture, so does Nishikawa discover a long-term stability in the living standard of most Japanese during the transition. These findings of "stability" are significant for the study of the transition period; if they should hold up over time, their implications for any analysis of the larger sociopolitical change that took place during the second half of the nineteenth century will be impossible to ignore.

CHAPTER 14

THE MEIJI LAND TAX REFORM AND ITS EFFECTS

BY KOZO YAMAMURA

The Meiji land tax reform, which some scholars believe was "the single most important reform of the Meiji Restoration,"[1] was begun in July 1873 and was virtually complete by the end of 1876. What the new government accomplished was by any standard a major feat. By determining the monetary value (tax base) of 85.44 million parcels of rice paddies and all other types of land, and issuing 109.33 million certificates of land ownership, the nascent government had replaced the complex and inequitable Tokugawa tax system with a significantly more equitable and efficient land tax system that was essential to meet the political and fiscal needs of the emerging modern state.[2] No less significantly, the effects of the reform were profound and lasting. No one can deny the fact that the political, social, and economic changes that occurred in Meiji Japan and even in the subsequent interwar years were substantively affected by the reform.

This brief chapter has three modest goals. The first is to add to what has already been written in English a few observations concerning the reasons why the reform was adopted and why the Meiji officials chose to adopt the specific form they did. The second is to present some evidence showing that the reform succeeded in achieving one of its principal goals: to replace the complex and inequitable Tokugawa tax system with a more efficient and equitable land tax system. And the last is to offer brief

[1] Yujiro Hayami, *A Century of Agricultural Growth in Japan* (Minneapolis: University of Minnesota Press, 1975), p. 47.

[2] An authoritative Japanese source containing detailed discussions of the reform is Fukushima Masao, *Chiso kaisei no kenkyū* (Tokyo: Yūhikaku, 1974), which is an expanded version of the 1962 edition. There are numerous books in Japanese on this subject.

discussions of the effects of the reform that I believe significantly affected Japan's economic as well as social and political history for several decades following the reform.[3]

ADOPTION AND IMPLEMENTATION OF THE REFORM

For the first few years after the Restoration, the full attention of the new government was absorbed by the political, administrative, and fiscal exigencies that had to be solved in order to establish a functioning polity. As a result, even by late 1872, the government had not been able to undertake a land tax reform and was continuing to rely on the Tokugawa land tax system to obtain necessary revenue.

But following the adoption in 1871 of the *haihan chiken* (discussed in Chapter 4 by Michio Umegaki), the need for adopting a new land tax system had become an urgent political necessity. Those taxpayers who had been paying more land tax than others under the Tokugawa system found little reason to go on doing so after the *chiso kaisei* created new districts and prefectures out of the former domains and land that had been directly administered by the *hatamoto* and the *bakufu*.[4] The government could ill afford to continue to collect taxes using the Tokugawa system if it wished to prevent the discontent of the taxpayers over such disparities, substantial in some cases, from adding fuel to the politically costly uprisings that were occurring.[5] Many taxpayers believed that the land tax being collected in their region was higher than that paid in other parts of Japan, and this was another reason that the government wanted to adopt a new land tax system as soon as possible. Furthermore, under the new government, centrally administered in the name of the emperor, this equality of the tax burden, as a matter of principle befitting a modern

[3] Put differently, the basic intent of this essay is to take a small step toward filling the large gaps now existing in the English literature on the reform and its effects. The very limited discussion of the reform that we have—in a few monographs and in several college textbooks of Japanese history—does not provide 1) sufficiently detailed discussions, backed up by evidence, of the reasons for the reform; 2) analyses of the changes (equalization) in the tax burden that occurred as a result of the reform; or 3) quantitative evidence that can more directly demonstrate the economic effects of the reform. Several English sources that discuss the reform and its effects, either briefly or more extensively, are cited below.

[4] This is well known. Fukushima's *Chiso kaisei*, pp. 111-116, contains numerous examples gathered by Meiji officials.

[5] That the Meiji officials were acutely aware of the political inadvisability of continuing to use the Tokugawa system is evident in Ōuchi Hyōe and Tsuchiya Takao, eds., *Meiji zenki zaisai keizai shiryō shūsei* (Tokyo: Kaizōsha, 1933), vol. 1, p. 12 et passim. Hereafter, this source will be referred to as *MZS*.

state, had to be achieved as soon as practicable. As Smith has noted, "local variations in the rate of taxation were repugnant to the unifying nationalist spirit of the new regime."[6]

The government, engaged in an increasing number of the undertakings of a modern state, had fiscal reasons as well in wanting to carry out a land tax reform; its need for a reliable, fixed annual revenue was rapidly growing. The annual revenue obtained from the Tokugawa system changed from year to year, affected both by harvest conditions and by changes in the market price of rice. Furthermore, continued reliance on the cumbersome Tokugawa tax system was costly in time as well as effort.

Despite these evident political and fiscal necessities, the Meiji government, still in the process of solidifying its political and administrative foundations, was not able to undertake land reform quickly. Unlike other political and administrative measures it had successfully adopted, the land tax reform directly affected the economic interest of most of the population. Reform had to be approached with extreme caution and skill, for a misstep could easily trigger a political crisis and threaten the foundation of the young government.

Evolution of the Reform Proposals

Immediately following the Restoration, many former daimyo advocated maintaining the status quo and urged the new government to continue to use the Tokugawa system. Other former daimyo and samurai-turned-officials proposed various revisions to the Tokugawa tax system. One of these proposals called for substantial tax increases on urban residents, merchants, and others so that the land tax paid by peasants could be reduced; another called for a new cadastral survey, principally to eliminate the interregional disparities in the tax burden existing under the Tokugawa system.[7] These and other proposals might be termed "conservative" in that at most they suggested mere modifications of the Tokugawa system.

One proposal, however, made in 1869 by Kanda Takahira, a high official in the new government, was drastically different. As should perhaps be expected of a former *rangaku* (Dutch studies) scholar of the Tokugawa *bakufu* (he had translated a Dutch version of an English book

[6] Thomas C. Smith, *Political Change and Industrial Development in Japan: Government Enterprise, 1868-1880* (Stanford: Stanford University Press, 1955), p. 79.

[7] An excellent summary of these views is found in Fukushima, *Chiso kaisei*, pp. 20-43.

on Ricardian political economy), his was a "radical" proposal[8] that in effect "initiated a real discussion"[9] concerning the specifics of the reform. The essence of his proposal can be paraphrased in the following four points:[10]

1) Land is to be bought and sold freely.
2) For each parcel of land, the government is to issue a certificate of ownership on which the monetary value of the parcel, as reported by the owner, is indicated. This value, which is to reflect the market value of the parcel, is to be used as the tax base. If the reported value is believed to be below the fair market value, the government will establish the market value by subjecting the parcel in question to competitive bidding by potential purchasers. In establishing the tax base, this procedure, by making use of the market, should eliminate the need for cumbersome and costly cadastral surveys.
3) The tax is to be paid in cash. This will eliminate the cost and effort of collecting the tax in rice and then selling it. Cash payment of tax will also reduce the opportunities for corruption and simplify accounting procedures. Also, the annual budget can be predetermined because the tax revenue, collected entirely in cash, can be fixed in advance.
4) The amount of the total tax to be collected in cash (i.e. the rate to be applied to the tax base) can be determined by calculating the average cash value of the tax collected in kind over the past twenty or thirty years.

It is important to note that Kanda made his proposal in 1869, three years before the Meiji government issued a decree permitting unrestricted sales of land, in preparation for the land tax reform it finally decided to adopt. Even assuming that the right to alienate land would soon be granted to all landowners, Kanda's proposal raised several questions. To list the most obvious: Was it likely that bidders would be available to raise the price of the undervalued land of the largest landholders in a village, so that the price would reflect the real productivity of the land? How would the government "create" a land "market" if some villagers colluded to undervalue their land? And, given the complexity of the prevailing Tokugawa tax system, under which tax payments were being made in varying combinations of rice, other agricultural products, and

[8] For a biographical description of Kanda (1838-1898), see Fukushima, *Chiso kaisei*, pp. 45-46.

[9] Arimoto Masao, "Chiso kaisei to chihō seiji," in *Iwanami kōza Nihon rekishi*, vol. 14, *kindai* 1 (Tokyo: Iwanami shoten, 1975), p. 171.

[10] *MZS*, vol. 7, pp. 301-303.

cash, how would the average cash value of the taxes that had been paid during the past twenty to thirty years be determined?[11]

Because the Meiji government was still preoccupied with immediate problems, and because of the questions that the Kanda proposal left unanswered, a proposal advanced by Mutsu Munemitsu in 1872 became the basis for the land reform as it was formally adopted.[12] However, as is evident in comparing Mutsu's proposal with Kanda's, Japanese specialists are correct in assuming that Mutsu benefited substantially from Kanda's ideas. The proposal made by Mutsu, who as governor of Settsu prefecture had considerable experience in tax collection and local administration, was more realistic than Kanda's. In essence, Mutsu proposed to levy the land tax on the "real value" (*jikka*) of the land, as determined by its *productivity*. To the extent that productivity was the principal factor determining the market price of land, the basic intent of the Mutsu proposal did not differ from that of Kanda.[13] The crucial difference was that the success of Mutsu's proposal did not rely on the market to determine productivity. Instead, it more realistically advocated that, however cumbersome, the value of land should be determined by examining each parcel for its productivity.

Because Mutsu made his proposal in 1872, when the urgency of initiating a land tax reform had become evident, and because his was a realistic proposal, it quickly won the backing of Inoue Kaoru, then the highest official of the Ministry of Finance. Mutsu's proposal was approved in principle in June 1872. The Ministry of Finance then immediately organized a working group to refine the proposal, and Mutsu was asked to come to the ministry to head the Tax Bureau. From the summer of 1872, earnest deliberations began to solve the numerous difficult problems involved in implementing the Mutsu proposal.[14]

Even confining our attention to rice paddies, we can see that the problems faced by the Tax Bureau were substantial.[15] To mention only the most important: since the existing land registers invariably included a large number of paddies with under- or overassessed yields (vis-à-vis real productivity), the government had to reassess the productivity of all

[11] Also, Kanda's proposal, which was publicly debated in the early press had little to say about land worked by tenant farmers.

[12] *MZS*, vol. 7, pp. 310-311. For a biographical sketch and analysis of the role played by Mutsu (1844-1897) during the transition period, see Marius B. Jansen, "Mutsu Munemitsu," in A.M. Craig and D.H. Shively, eds., *Personality in Japanese History* (Berkeley: University of California Press, 1970), pp. 309-334.

[13] According to several Japanese specialists, however, none of Mutsu's writings refers specifically to Kanda's proposal.

[14] Fukushima, *Chiso kaisei*, pp. 100-154.

[15] There were also many complex problems relating to residential land, mountains, forests, and so on.

paddies, measuring the size and establishing the "normal" yield of each. The same had to be done for all paddies that, either because they had been hidden or because they had been tax-exempt, had not been taxed previously. The cash tax to be paid by the landowners of paddies worked by tenants had to be determined in such a way that the tax burden on these paddies would, as a rule, be the same as that levied on land worked by the landowners themselves.

In carrying out the difficult task of coping with these and many other problems, officials also had to do their best to meet two fundamental conditions. One was that the total tax revenue to be collected under the reformed system was to be no larger than that being collected under the Tokugawa system. However fiscally strapped the new government was, it was politically in no position to increase the tax burden on landowners and tenants who were hoping—indeed, assuming—that the new government would reduce their taxes. In the early 1870s, the government was already facing frequent uprisings of farmers protesting what they regarded as high taxes.[16] And, as might be anticipated from our earlier discussion of the results of *haihan chiken*, the second condition was that the officials determining the tax burden (i.e. assessing the value of the land) were also to attempt to equalize the tax burden within as well as across newly created district and prefectural boundaries.

These two conditions made the work of the officials who had to carry out the reform extremely difficult. The principal reason for the difficulty was that, in assessing the tax burden, officials had to satisfy three goals *simultaneously*: 1) the total tax burden of each administrative unit was to be raised or reduced in order to eliminate the inequality that existed under the Tokugawa system; 2) the tax burden of each parcel was to correspond, as closely as possible, to its real productivity; and 3) the total revenue to be obtained was to come as close as possible to the amount that was collected before the reform. To satisfy these goals, which were at times conflicting, officials were often forced to adopt many ad hoc measures and/or arbitrary assumptions as well as to resort to expedient compromises.[17]

In practical terms, the Meiji officials attempting to reconcile these goals adopted the following well-known formulas: (1) for the landowners and (2) for the tenant farmers.[18] As discussed below, these were "model" formulas from which officials were allowed to deviate:

[16] An authoritative source on the peasant uprisings and the reasons for them is Tsuchiya Takao and Ono Michio, *Meiji shonen nōmin sōjōroku* (Tokyo: Keisō shobō, 1953).

[17] For a useful and detailed discussion, see Fukushima, *Chiso kaisei*, pp. 123-198, 285-306.

[18] Readers interested in further discussion of the procedures adopted should read James

$$(1)\ \text{Value of owner-cultivated land} = \frac{PQ - 0.15PQ - [0.03V + 0.01V]}{0.06}$$

$$(2)\ \text{Value of tenant-worked land} = \frac{0.68Q - [0.03V + 0.01V]}{0.04}$$

In the above, P is the market price of rice, Q is the assessed rice output, and V stands for the value of land (i.e. the tax base). As seen in Formula 1, the value of land cultivated by the landowner was determined by dividing, or capitalizing, the numerator (i.e. the market value of the total rice output minus 15 percent of PQ allowed for seed and fertilizer costs, and minus the sum of 3 percent of the value of the land for land tax plus 1 percent of the value of land paid as village tax) by 0.06, which is the interest rate used to capitalize the value of the numerator. For the land worked by tenants, the value of the output in the numerator was calculated at 68 percent of total output (i.e. the amount of rent in kind received by the landowner). The rate used for capitalizing the value of output is 0.04, lower than that used in Formula 1 applying to owner-cultivated land. The lower interest rate in Formula 2 was adopted principally because it made the values (thus, the tax burdens) of owner-cultivated and tenant-worked land identical. (See Table 14.1, which presents the model calculations provided to the officials by the Tax Bureau.)

It is evident that the models contain several arbitrary assumptions the officials were forced to make. For example, the deduction of 15 percent of the total market value for seed and fertilizer was most likely an underestimate; the assumed 68 percent for land rent was unrealistically high in many cases; and the labor cost allowed for tenanted land (0.816 yen, i.e. the difference between the net income from owner-cultivated and tenanted lands) was too low.[19] But, without involving ourselves in a lengthy analysis of the ad hoc measures adopted and the assumptions made, what is important for our purpose here is the fact that the Meiji officials using these two models were able to deviate from them and meet the two politically essential conditions: maintaining the tax income that prevailed in the late Tokugawa period and making significant progress toward reducing interregional disparities in the tax burden.

First, we can show that the total tax collected in 1875, the first year taxes were collected under the new system, was quite similar in magnitude to that collected during the 1871-1874 period. In 1875, total revenues

I. Nakamura, *Agricultural Production and the Economic Development of Japan, 1873-1922* (Princeton: Princeton University Press, 1966), app. A, pp. 177-196.

[19] All of these assumptions must be carefully examined. These examples are mentioned merely to indicate the types of arbitrary procedures officials had to adopt in carrying out the nationwide reform in such a short time.

TABLE 14.1
Model Calculations of Land Value, 1873

	Yen	Notes
OWNER-CULTIVATED		
Gross income	4.800	1.6 *koku* × 3 yen (per *koku*)
Allowance for seed, fertilizer	0.720	15% of gross income
Land tax	1.224	3% of value of land
Village tax	0.408	1% of value of land
Net income	2.448	4.800 − [allowance + taxes]
Value of land	40.800	capitalized at 6%
TENANTED		
Gross income*	3.264	rent = 1.088 *koku* (i.e. 68% of 1.6 *koku*) × 3 yen (per *koku*)
Land tax	1.224	same as owner-cultivated land
Village tax	0.408	same as owner-cultivated land
Net income	1.632	3.264 − taxes
Value of land	40.800	capitalized at 4%

SOURCE: Ōuchi Hyōe and Tsuchiya Takao, eds., *Meiji zenki zaisei keizai shiryō shūsei* (Tokyo: Kaizōsha, 1933), vol. 7, pp. 328-329.

* Income to landowner.

from the land tax were 49,462,946 yen, which was equivalent to 11,819,913 *koku* of rice when calculated at 4.185 yen per *koku*, the average selling price of the rice the government received. Since the total tax rice received in the preceding years was 12,545,354 *koku* in 1871 (excellent harvest), 12,135,195 *koku* in 1872 (good harvest), 11,239,718 *koku* in 1873 (mediocre harvest), and 10,745,983 *koku* in 1874 (poor harvest), it is evident that the tax collected in 1875, a mediocre year, met the condition that the total tax burden remain the same. Put differently, in monetary terms, the 49,462,946 yen received in 1875 was only slightly less than the 51,224,000 yen that the officials expected to collect for that year, assuming a marginally better harvest. The same can also be said for 1876, the last year before the tax rate was reduced from 3 to 2.5 percent (reducing 1877 revenues by 16.7 percent from the 1876 level) under strong pressure from the farmers.[20]

Second, it is evident that officials consciously and effectively reduced regional disparities in the tax burden. Calculation by prefecture of the

[20] See *MZS*, vol. 7, p. 79, and Fukushima, *Chiso kaisei*, pp. 456-464.

TABLE 14.2

Post-Reform Mean Prefectural Effective Tax Rate

Region/Prefecture	%	Region/Prefecture	%
TŌHOKU		KINKI	
Aomori	25.14	Mie	25.27
Iwate	24.88	Shiga	25.10
Miyagi	26.88	Kyoto	25.87
Akita	25.00	Osaka	25.59
Yamagata	26.05	Hyōgo	25.44
Fukushima	25.66	Wakayama	25.69
HOKURIKU		CHŪGOKU	
Niigata	24.72	Tottori	27.84
Ishikawa	26.44	Okayama	25.57
Fukui	25.41	Hiroshima	25.56
		Yamaguchi	28.97
KANTŌ			
Ibaragi	25.40	SHIKOKU	
Tochigi	25.50	Tokushima	25.50
Gumma	25.50	Ehime	25.50
Saitama	25.47	Kōchi	25.66
Chiba	25.41		
Tokyo	25.56	KYŪSHŪ	
Kanagawa	25.48	Fukuoka	25.46
TŌSAN-TŌKAI		Nagasaki	25.50
Yamanashi	28.97	Kumamoto	25.25
Nagano	24.06	Ōita	25.47
Gifu	26.59	Kagoshima	25.76
Shizuoka	25.50		
Aichi	25.30		

SOURCE: Ōuchi Hyōe and Tsuchiya Takao, eds., *Meiji zenki zaisei keizai shiryō shūsei* (Tokyo: Kaizōsha, 1933), vol. 7, table 8.

NOTE: Data are for the year in which the reform was carried out in each prefecture; the source offers no comment about those cases in which more than one year was required to carry out the reform. The source showed the paddy price per *tan*, the price of rice, and total rice output (all by prefecture). Therefore, the effective tax rate was calculated as follows: 0.03 yen (i.e. price of land) ÷ (rice price × total rice output).

effective tax rate—the ratio of the tax paid over the total income from the paddies (i.e. total rice yield multiplied by the price of rice)—yields the results presented in Table 14.2. The most remarkable facts to be noted are that the interprefectural variance in the effective tax rate was quite small and that the rate for a large majority of prefectures was about 25.5 percent.[21] In short, there is little doubt that Meiji officials were successful in accomplishing much of their intent to reduce the interregional variations in tax rates. (The implications of this reduction in interregional variations will be discussed in the final section of this chapter.)

As noted, the officials carrying out the reform faced numerous and extremely difficult problems. This is evident from the fact that they frequently faced strenuous resistance and even uprisings by landowners protesting official yield assessments, as well as strong tenant protest against low allowances for labor costs. These problems, which many Japanese scholars have described in detail,[22] were overcome (though with great difficulty in some instances) within a rather short period of time. What is significant is that, despite these difficulties, the enormous task of the reform was virtually complete within three years, and the Meiji government was able to put a quick end to the disturbances and uprisings resulting from it.

Some Effects of the Reform

Because of its scope and the fundamental changes it brought about, the reform had several important economic effects that could not but affect the course of Japan's social and political history—not only during the Meiji years, but during the subsequent Taishō and Shōwa decades as well. In this section, I present brief discussions of the four effects I believe to be most significant.

First, because the reform imposed a fixed cash tax, and because the amount was reduced in 1876 (as will be described below), all farmers working their own land had a strong incentive to increase productivity of land by increasing capital investment (for example, by acquiring more

[21] Though I believe that the data presented in Table 14.2 are basically reliable, and strongly suggest significant changes, they should be seen only as first approximations of the degree of interregional equality in the effective tax rate achieved by the reform. The rates presented in Table 14.2 were calculated assuming that the officially reported data were accurate—that the amount of the tax actually collected in each prefecture was as reported. However, it is quite possible that the real tax burden may have been higher in some prefectures and lower in others. Thus, for various reasons, we can be reasonably certain that the amount of tax actually collected in Yamaguchi was appreciably lower than that shown in Table 14.2 (i.e. closer to the national average). See, for example, Fukushima, *Chiso kaisei*, p. 472. Yamaguchi prefecture's total tax burden, it should be noted, declined as a result of the reform.

[22] See fns. 16 and 17, above, as well as Inoue Kiyoshi, *Meiji ishin*, vol. 20 of the Chūō kōron *History of Japan* series (Tokyo: Chūō kōronsha, 1966), pp. 430-436.

costly but more efficient agricultural implements, using more fertilizer, and investing more in irrigation and drainage). As a result, quantitative evidence accumulated by Japanese and Western economists unequivocally establishes that agricultural capital investment increased rapidly over the remainder of the Meiji period, and that the increased investment played an important role in raising agricultural productivity.[23]

Second, the reform contributed significantly toward making Meiji agriculture more market-oriented and, consequently, more efficient in the use of resources (land, manpower, and capital). Put differently, the reform that caused farmers to participate in market activities more than they ever had in the past (as direct sellers of rice, as increasingly active investors in land, and in other capacities) was no less an important factor than the fact that land could now be bought and sold freely and that regional markets were becoming steadily better integrated throughout the Meiji period. Moreover, increasing market activity was important to economic efficiency, for farmers now had more economic information to help them make the best economic decisions possible. However difficult it might be to assess quantitatively, few economists would question the significant contribution that this information boom made to greater efficiency in the use of resources—i.e. to the growth of Meiji agriculture.[24]

Third, an important effect of the reform was to change—depending on the market price of rice prevailing each year—the real tax burden on the landowners, and thus the revenues received by the government. When the price of rice rose, as it did during the years 1877-1881 and again in the 1890-1898 period, it greatly benefited the taxpayers at the expense of the government. In some of these years when the rice price was high, the fiscal crisis faced by the government was extremely acute. Thus, for example, in 1880 when the price of rice reached 10.49 yen per *koku* (compared to 5.01 yen in 1876), the government was forced to consider reassessing the value of land (i.e. increasing the tax base) and reinstituting tax payments in rice, either wholly or partially. Neither of these methods to increase tax revenue was adopted, however. The consensus reached by the government leadership was that the adoption of either would rekindle taxpayer revolts against the land tax system.[25] For taxpayers,

[23] For literature supporting both of these observations, see, for example, Kazushi Ohkawa, "Phases of Agricultural Development and Economic Growth," in Kazushi Ohkawa, Bruce F. Johnstone, and Hiromitsu Kaneda, eds., *Agriculture and Economic Growth: Japan's Experience* (Princeton: Princeton University Press, 1970), pp. 3-36, and the sources Ohkawa cites on pp. 35-36.

[24] See Appendix, below.

[25] An excellent analysis of the pros and cons of changing the cash tax system in effect and/or increasing the assessed value of paddy fields is presented in Inoki Takenori, "Meiji zenki zaisei seiri ni okeru ichi sōwa," *Gendai keizai*, no. 47 (Spring 1982), pp. 93-105.

these years of high prices were years in which "the living standard of farmers rose" and the "import of luxury goods was greatly stimulated" because of the great demand for such goods by farmers.[26]

In contrast, when the price of rice declined, as it did during the 1882-1888 period (including and following the Matsukata deflation), the real tax burden rose, benefiting the government. But we should note that between 1873 and 1899, the seven years from 1882 to 1888 were the only ones during which the rice price declined; and, even in 1888, when the price of rice reached its lowest level since 1873, it was still 4.91 yen per *koku*, compared to 4.81 yen in 1873.[27]

All of the above suggests that the real tax burden was most unlikely to have risen in the Meiji period. This observation can be stated even more strongly if we take into account the fact that the tax rate was reduced in 1876 (from 3 percent to 2.5 percent of the assessed tax base) and that agricultural productivity was steadily rising owing to increasing capital investment as well as to the gains resulting from a growing domestic and international trade in agricultural products.[28] In the final analysis, of course, this increase in the real income level was possible because the Meiji state during these decades possessed neither the political power to withstand the farmers' demand for a reduction in the tax rate nor the political strength to share in the gains resulting from increases in the rice price, productivity, and trade—gains that were being captured by the agricultural taxpayers.

The last significant effect of the reform was that the changes in the effective tax burden, when closely examined, are found to fit the following pattern: the tax rates in the poorer, less productive eastern regions tended to be raised, substantially in some areas; in the richer, more productive western regions, however, rates either were raised less than in the eastern areas or were reduced appreciably. Before discussing what I believe are the historically important implications of this effect, let me first present some quantitative evidence and then offer my analysis and explanation of the pattern described above.

In comparing the pre- and post-reform tax burden by district and prefecture, we find that the increases in the tax burden resulting from the reform tended to occur in the Tōhoku, Hokuriku, Kantō, and Tōsan-Tōkai regions, rather than in the western regions of Kinki, Chūgoku,

[26] Ibid., p. 102.

[27] For the price of rice, see Bank of Japan, *The Hundred Year Statistics* (1966), p. 90.

[28] The gains realized by Japanese producers of agricultural exportables (such as raw silk and tea) were very large. For a quantitative analysis, see J. Richard Huber, "Effects on Price of Japan's Entry into World Commerce after 1858," *Journal of Political Economy*, vol. 79, no. 3 (May/June 1971), pp. 614-629.

Shikoku, and Kyūshū.[29] To be more specific, post-reform changes in the amount of tax paid by each prefecture on paddies and other types of land are as shown in Table 14.3. Though the data must be interpreted carefully—principally because taxes included those levied on upland and residential plots and because the area of taxable paddy changed—they unmistakably indicate the contrasting (west vs. east) pattern of changes in the tax burden.

An obvious question arises. If the increase in the tax burden in most prefectures of the Kantō region, especially in Tokyo, is to be explained by the fact that these prefectures had a large proportion of *tenryō* and upland plots (only lightly taxed or even tax-exempt in the Tokugawa period, but taxable according to productivity after the reform), then why did the tax burden increase in many other eastern parts of the nation where paddies were generally less productive than those in the west? One possible reason is that the observed east/west contrast is itself not significant, and that what must be explained is why the tax burden in each district and prefecture changed as a result of the reform. In short, the Tokugawa tax rates for each district and domain must be seen as outcomes of complex political, economic, and geographic factors that were specific to each district or domain.[30]

Another possible reason is that the Tokugawa land tax functioned, in part at least, as a quasi-income tax and was not merely a land tax. In the more productive and commercialized western domains, that is to say, the tax on paddies was higher than can be explained only in terms of higher productivity, for the amount of tax levied on land included, as it

[29] What is described in the text is the product of a preliminary study using the data for some districts and all prefectures, as well as historical maps of the Tokugawa period that identify the administrative and geographic characteristics of these districts and prefectures before they were created by the *haihan chiken*. The primary sources for the data are *MZS*, vol. 7, pp. 82-120 and table 8; Fukushima, *Chiso kaisei*, pp. 466-469. The historical maps used are from Nishioka Toranosuke and Hattori Shisō, eds., *Nihon rekishi chizu* (Tokyo: Zenkoku kyōiku tosho K.K., 1956), pp. 180-197, 258. The map on p. 258 shows whether or not the tax rate in each prefecture (and in some districts) rose or fell as a result of the reform.

[30] For example, it is well known that the tax burden in those districts which included a significant amount of land that had once belonged to the *hatamoto* was *reduced* (because the *hatamoto* tended to levy considerably higher taxes on paddies than the daimyo) and that the tax burden in those districts and prefectures which included, either wholly or in significant part, the small former domains was *reduced* (because the small domains were financially the hardest pressed and had levied taxes almost as high as those levied by the *hatamoto*). These observations are hardly controversial; most Japanese specialists have said much the same thing using somewhat different terminology. See Susan B. Hanley and Kozo Yamamura, *Economic and Demographic Change in Preindustrial Japan, 1600-1868* (Princeton: Princeton University Press, 1977), pp. 91-198.

TABLE 14.3
Post-Reform Changes in Tax Burden, by Prefecture
(as % of pre-reform tax)

Region/Prefecture	Change	Region/Prefecture	Change
TŌHOKU		KINKI	
Aomori	2.4	Mie	−10.4
Iwate	38.4	Shiga	−12.6
Miyagi	11.1	Kyoto	−8.4
Akita	−3.4	Osaka	−9.0
Yamagata	−15.2	Hyōgo	−13.6
Fukushima	5.3	Wakayama	−13.9
HOKURIKU		CHŪGOKU	
Niigata	14.1	Tottori	−3.1
Ishikawa	−24.4	Okayama	6.4
Fukui	−8.8	Hiroshima	0.4
		Yamaguchi	−17.3
KANTŌ			
Ibaragi	−5.0	SHIKOKU	
Tochigi	9.1	Tokushima	−8.7
Gumma	10.0	Ehime	−15.3
Saitama	21.6	Kōchi	−36.5
Chiba	−16.3		
Tokyo	71.2	KYŪSHŪ	
Kanagawa	6.5	Fukuoka	−26.9
TŌSAN-TŌKAI		Nagasaki	−22.7
Yamanashi	2.1	Kumamoto	−18.7
Nagano	3.4	Ōita	−16.0
Gifu	2.2	Kagoshima	−4.1
Shizuoka	6.6		
Aichi	0.4		

SOURCE: Ōuchi Hyōe and Tsuchiya Takao, eds., *Meiji zenki zaisei keizai shiryō shūsei* (Tokyo: Kaizōsha, 1933), vol. 7, pp. 80-120.

NOTE: The "subtotals," in the terminology of the source use, of pre- and post-reform taxes paid by prefecture include the land taxes paid on uplands, residential and other "city land," plus a few other categories of land. However, as an examination of the raw data readily reveals, the dominant part of the "subtotals" of the taxes paid by each prefecture was the tax paid on rice paddies; the taxes paid on other types of lands were quite small in a very large majority of prefectures. The taxes levied on mountains, forests, uncultivated fields, and several other types of land were reported separately and were not included in the "subtotals" used in the above calculations. Ideally, only the pre- and post-reform taxes on rice paddies alone should be used in making such calculations, but this is not possible. Unfortunately, the post-reform data, unlike those provided for the pre-reform period, are given only in the "subtotals" as described above. Depending on when the reform was carried out in each prefecture, the exact date of the data differs by prefecture; however, the dates can be presumed to be mostly 1871 and 1872 for "before" the reform and 1873, 1874, and 1875 for "after" the reform.

were, taxes on income that peasants were able to earn through by-employment. In other words, the tax on paddies in the west was appreciably higher than that in the east because the domains faced difficulties in assessing and collecting taxes on nonagricultural economic activities.

On the other hand, in the eastern regions of Japan, peasants had significantly fewer by-employments and commercial opportunities. As a result, the land tax in the east may not have been as high as the tax levied on paddies of comparable productivity in the western regions. For the eastern domains, to tax at a rate that was "justified" (after adjusting for the lower productivity) was to reduce further the relative standard of living that the eastern peasants felt entitled to maintain—especially by the late Tokugawa period—vis-à-vis that being enjoyed by their counterparts in the west. Thus, for Meiji officials to reduce interregional inequality in the tax burden, the tax rate had to be raised in the east and lowered in the west.

Whatever may ultimately explain the pattern of changes in the tax rate that occurred as a result of the reform, the second reason offered—that the Tokugawa land tax functioned as a quasi–income tax—is to some extent valid. One can, I believe, argue that the reform was responsible for the two well-known facts: 1) in the eastern regions, tenancy rose more rapidly than it did in the western regions during the Meiji years, and 2) tenant-landlord disputes occurred more frequently in the eastern regions during the Meiji and Taishō-Shōwa periods in comparison to the west during the same periods.[31] This is to say that Meiji officials, in their desire to equalize the interregional tax burden, may have played an important role in depriving small eastern landowners of the economic margin they needed to overcome hardships imposed on them by periodic declines in the price of rice and by the relative "backwardness" of the regional economy.

Conclusion

In this brief space I have been able to offer little more than a glimpse of a complex subject: the land tax reform of 1873 and its effects. My hope is that this essay may aid in enticing other Western students to continue to re-examine the reasons for and the consequences of the reform, as

[31] See Matao Miyamoto and Kozo Yamamura, "Ryōsenkanki kosaku sōgi no sūryō bunseki e no ichi shiron," in Takafusa Nakamura, ed., *Senkanki no Nihon keizai bunseki* (Tokyo: Yamakawa shuppansha, 1980), pp. 389-425.

well as important questions closely relating to the reform. One research theme that immediately comes to mind is how the economic lot of the farmers, both the landowners and the tenant cultivators, changed because of the "positive" and "negative" effects of the reform. The "positive" effects I have described in this essay: i.e. the growth in capital investment that resulted from increased economic incentives; the boom in economic information that resulted from increased market activities; and the apparent declining trend of the land tax burden on landowners throughout the Meiji years. By "negative" effects, I refer to those effects of the reform that are so often presented in the works of Japanese and Western historians: i.e. increases in tenancy, "high-rent landlordism," and various socioeconomic manifestations of changes that are said to have occurred in the pattern of income distribution among agricultural households.[32] Finally, there is a closely related question that needs to be pursued: How valid is my suggestion that the reform, by ending the quasi-income-tax functions that the Tokugawa land tax performed, played a role in shaping the economic as well as the social and political history of the Meiji and post-Meiji decades?

Only by addressing such questions can we increase our understanding of the real intent of the reform and the effectiveness of the Meiji officials in carrying out their intent, the relationship between the reform and the political and economic history that unfolded following the reform, and the character of the Meiji state that both shaped and was shaped by the process of one of the most crucial transitions in Japanese history.

Appendix: Increased "Market-Orientedness" of Meiji Agriculture

Though at best indirect, quantitative evidence of increased "market-orientedness" during the Meiji period can be presented. For example, when a regression equation is calculated for the 1874-1899 period, using the price of land (P_L) as the dependent variable and the quantity of rice yield (R), the price of rice (P_R), and capital stock per *tan* of land (K/L) as independent variables, we obtain the following (numbers in parentheses are standard errors):

[32] On "negative" effects, see J.K. Fairbank, E.O. Reischauer, and A.M. Craig, *East Asia: The Modern Transformation* (Tokyo: Charles E. Tuttle Co., 1965), p. 236; W.G. Beasley, *The Meiji Restoration* (Stanford: Stanford University Press, 1972), pp. 399-400; and Ann Waswo, *Japanese Landlords* (Berkeley: University of California Press, 1977), p. 21.

$$\log P_L = \underset{(1.126)}{16.541} - \underset{(-1.14)}{0.567} \log R + \underset{(3.90)}{0.707} \log P_R + \underset{(1.47)}{7.400} \log (K/L)$$

$$R^2 = 0.86;\ DW = 1.156;\ n = 26$$

Though we can interpret this equation in various ways, the most evident fact is that the land market was able to reflect in the price of land the productivity change resulting from capital investment. Note that the equation is calculated in logarithmic form; thus, the large positive coefficient (7.4) for K/L is the elasticity, indicating that the land price (P_L) was highly elastic (i.e. responsive) to the amount of investment (K/L) made to improve the productivity of land. This is to demonstrate that market forces were at work creating conditions in which investment in land was being encouraged, both to increase the productivity of land that the owners intended to continue working by themselves and to increase the market value of land the owners held as assets. Note also that, in the above equation, R (total yield of rice) has a small negative coefficient and P_R (price of rice) has a positive coefficient of less than unity. These coefficients indicate that annual changes in rice output and rice price were not nearly as important as capital investment in determining the market value of land.

Another example of the findings from this statistical study is the following:

$$\log P_R = \underset{(-4.95)}{-3.968} + \underset{(1.23)}{0.384} \log R + \underset{(4.77)}{1.345} \log CPI$$

$$R^2 = 0.84;\ DW = 1.37;\ n = 26$$

In the post-reform market, the price of rice was determined much more significantly by the changes in the general consumer price index (CPI) than by changes in the output of rice (R). In contrast to what happened in the Tokugawa period, during which the rice yield determined the price of rice, which in turn exerted a dominant influence on the price levels of all other consumer products, the price of rice following the reform was significantly influenced by the *CPI*. What occurred was that, as market activity increased, integrating the agricultural and industrial sectors of the economy, the price of the principal agricultural product, rice, reacted sensitively during the Meiji years to changes in the prices of many consumer products.

Although I shall not present the results of the statistical analyses that were made, I should add here that a comparison of cross-sectional regression and covariance analyses for 1874 and 1890 (using data obtained for forty-seven prefectures) shows, not surprisingly, that the market was functioning more efficiently in 1890 than it was in 1874. The sources of the time-series data used in these calculations are K. Ohkawa et al., *The Long-Term Economic Statistics* (Tokyo: Tōyō keizai shimpōsha, 1967), vol. 8, for R (p. 166), K (p. 212), and L (pp. 216-217); Bank of Japan, *The Hundred Year Statistics of the Japanese Economy* (Tokyo: Bank of Japan, 1966), for P_R (p. 90) and P_L (p. 474); and other, supplementary sources.

CHAPTER 15

THE RURAL ECONOMY: COMMERCIAL AGRICULTURE, BY-EMPLOYMENT, AND WAGE WORK*

BY OSAMU SAITŌ

It is now widely accepted that many peasants in the *bakumatsu* period were already familiar with the market in various forms—through cash cropping, silkworm breeding, side businesses, paid jobs at home, or wage work during the slack season—[1] and rising tenancy rates are sometimes regarded as a symptom of expanded market ties. The land tax reform of 1873, once reckoned the great divide in agrarian history, simply furthered this trend.[2] In the decades that followed the reform, growing industry—not only factories in the modern sector, but workshops in the indigenous sector—relied heavily upon labor from peasants who already had a cash network. Given these facts, historians have postulated, though sometimes implicitly, a causal linear relationship between the two phenomena: the more market forces penetrated into rural economic life, the more wage

* The research on which this chapter is based was supported by grants from the Japanese Ministry of Education and Keio University.

[1] Readers not familiar with the Japanese-language literature may consult Thomas C. Smith, *The Agrarian Origins of Modern Japan* (Stanford: Stanford University Press, 1959); id., "Farm Family By-employments in Preindustrial Japan," *Journal of Economic History*, vol. 29, no. 4 (1969), pp. 687-715; E.S. Crawcour, "The Tokugawa Heritage," in W.W. Lockwood, ed., *The State and Economic Enterprise in Japan* (Princeton: Princeton University Press, 1965), pp. 17-44; and William B. Hauser, *Economic Institutional Change in Tokugawa Japan: Osaka and the Kinai Cotton Trade* (New York: Cambridge University Press, 1974), chap. 6.

[2] See Kozo Yamamura's discussion in this book.

labor was supplied from the farming sector, whether in the form of a paid job at home, going out to work on a temporary basis (*dekasegi*), or leaving the farm with one's family. This presumed relationship is often associated with the view that Japan's industrialization in its early stages was able to tap a reservoir of surplus labor in the countryside, a surplus resulting from farm fragmentation and other forces that drove peasants into tenancy.

The purpose of the present essay is to re-examine this view and its implications. To do so, it is necessary to determine how commercial agriculture, one important aspect of the commercialization of rural economic life, interacted with the supply of peasant labor to outside employment opportunities. This chapter begins with a brief but critical review of the conventional framework, then proceeds to survey three types of activity undertaken by peasants on a part-time basis and to examine how these activities interacted with one another in relation to the effect of tenancy. Finally, suggestions are made about the differential impact of the opening of foreign trade in 1859. While the country's entry into world trade greatly increased involvement by the peasants of eastern Japan in the commercial production of silk and silk-related goods, it was unlikely—even in western Japan, where cotton was hit hard by imported goods—that this forced farm households to retreat into a subsistence economy or to increase their labor supply at lowered rates. At the national level, therefore, despite a growing market economy and despite slowly but steadily rising tenancy rates, depopulation of the rural area did not take place; nor did the rural sector suffer from a disguised unemployment syndrome during the Meiji period. Contrary to a widely accepted view, commercialization of agriculture did not lead to a large expansion of peasants leaving for outside employment.

The Conventional Framework Reconsidered

When reading works on Tokugawa and Meiji agrarian history, one often encounters a stylized account of how the money economy penetrated into the countryside, and how this process affected rural economic life.[3] According to such a view, one consequence of the growth of the market was a proliferation of nonagricultural economic activities and the production of agricultural specialties. This change, however, did not always result in an improvement of the peasant's well-being, for profits from

[3] This account is exactly what Yamaguchi Kazuo puts into his textbook, *Nihon keizai shi* (Tokyo: Chikuma shobō, 1976), pp. 52-62.

such activities often went into the hands of wholesalers, middlemen, or other merchants (who were sometimes wealthy farmers as well). Thus the peasantry, supposed to have been homogeneous at one time, could no longer be kept intact. The number of small tenant farmers increased, which in turn forced them to take up more by-employment and wage work to supplement their produce from a small plot of land. In some industrial villages, this led to the emergence of de facto wage laborers, such as women and children engaged in spinning or weaving and those who temporarily left the village to work elsewhere (*dekasegi*).

It is probably not difficult to detect in this regard two different, though mutually related, types of argument. The first relates the incidence of by-employment and wage work directly to the rise of the market. This is a simple idea shared by many historians and can be traced back to the Meiji era. As early as 1907, for instance, Hanabusa Naosaburō, then director of the Cabinet Bureau of Statistics, drew attention to the fact that a strikingly large number of farmers were listed under dual occupations (i.e. as having a side occupation) in the 1879 pilot census of Yamanashi prefecture (formerly Kai province). Having stated that the autarkic farm household produced almost all kinds of goods, he remarks: "As time goes on, such productive activities break off from the system of the isolated household economy and become social. . . . In one stage of this process, therefore, many productive activities take the form of a dual occupation."[4] By "social" Hanabusa no doubt meant "market-oriented" in our terminology. Clearly he sees increased by-employment as a change corresponding to an intermediate stage of development. More recently Arlon Tussing, in an article using the same source material as Hanabusa's, observes:

> Rapidly increasing production of agricultural specialties, such as cocoons and tea, fruits and vegetables, each having its peak labor demand at a different time of the year, absorbed much of the slack time of the farm population. In addition, as the demand for nonagricultural goods and services increased, former side occupations became primary occupations, first of individual members of farm households. Later individuals might become entirely committed to nonagriculture, "going-out" (*dekasegi*) to work for long periods of time, and farming might fall from the primary occupation of the household as a whole to the status of a side occupation. None of these patterns was uncommon even in pre-Meiji society.[5]

[4] Hanabusa Naosaburō, "Meiji jūninenmatsu no Kai no kuni," *Tōkei shūshi*, nos. 314, 316, 319, 320, 321 (1907). The quotation is from no. 320, p. 491.

[5] A. Tussing, "The Labor Force in Meiji Economic Growth: A Quantitative Study of Yamanashi Prefecture," *Journal of Economic History*, vol. 26, no. 1 (1966), p. 62.

Here commercial agriculture, as well as rural industry and commerce, is specified as a separate but important variable. Tussing, too, sees the increase in the supply of labor to nonfarm employment opportunities and the emergence of nonagricultural households in the rural context as a consequence of a larger process in which the growth of the market played a significant part.

There is one factor that Hanabusa and Tussing did not take into consideration, but that nonetheless occupies an important place in the historiography on Tokugawa and Meiji agrarian society: the differentiation of the peasantry, readily seen in increasing tenancy rates. The second line of reasoning stresses this factor, and suggests that nonfarm employment among the peasants increased not merely because the market expanded, but because increasing tenancy rates meant more unequal income distribution in terms of disposable income, a phenomenon that in turn forced smaller peasants to seek nonfarm employment even under unfavorable terms. A logical consequence of this process, it is contended, was a decrease in households engaged solely in farming, an event that did indeed prelude a dissolution of the peasantry. The Marxian thesis on the pattern of labor supply to the expanding industrial sector during the post-Restoration period is well known. Yet the differentiation-of-the-peasantry thesis is applicable not only to industrial labor, but also to the growth of by-employment in general. Thus Araki Moriaki was able to show that in a majority of prefectures in 1886 the proportion of tenant farm households with a side activity of any kind was distinctly higher (37.4 percent) than that of owner-farmers (31.1 percent).[6]

Since the differentiation of the peasant class itself was a product of the market penetration process, this second line of argument also assumes a linearity in the relationship among the growth of the market, increases in by-employment and wage work, and the shrinkage of the agricultural sector. One thing that distinguishes the second argument from the first, however, may be pointed out. The second line of reasoning often stresses that the penetration of market forces into rural life and the differentiation of the peasantry would have tended, even without the mounting population pressures, to create "surplus" labor in the rural sector. Thus W.W. Lockwood, writing about the period after the 1873 land tax reform, notes that, as a result of the growing numbers of small peasants driven into tenancy—an event he considers one of the "social ills attending the unregulated commercialization of agriculture" after 1873—"the mounting surplus of farm population had to find em-

[6] The difference between these two mean figures is statistically significant at the .01 level. Calculated from Araki Moriaki, "Jinushisei no tenkai," *Iwanami kōza Nihon rekishi*, vol. 16, *kindai* 3 (Tokyo: Iwanami shoten, 1962), p. 93.

ployment increasingly outside agriculture. Those families which remained on the farm also sought supplementary income, either through part-time employment in local industries, or through putting their reluctant daughters into the textile factories of the towns and cities."[7] When, and only when, the "surplus" of farm population is absorbed in the process of industrialization, one may add, the number of farm households should start declining.[8]

As a matter of fact, however, this did not happen in the pre–World War II period. Indeed, one salient feature of the agrarian history of that period is that the total number of farm households did not decrease, but remained almost constant at about 5.5 million. Admittedly "constancy" should not be overemphasized here. There was a regional difference: the number increased in the east while decreasing in the west.[9] Yet the decrease in the west was not substantial, the annual rate of decrease being only 0.1 percent during the period from 1880 to 1920.[10]

Why did the number of farm households not decrease as the industrial sector grew? Does this mean that a reservoir of surplus labor remained in the countryside? Those historians who pursue the second line of reasoning tend to think so. From early Meiji on, peasant families became more and more involved in the market economy; population was already on the increase. Hence there was a sustained, if not marked, upward trend in the tenancy rate until the 1930s. There must have been, it is argued, a continuous flow from the tenant farmer class into a rural reservoir of cheap labor, and symptomatic of this were *dekasegi* migration and by-employment in cottage industries.

This viewpoint, however, has difficulty accounting for some important anomalies. First of all, the slow but sustained increase in the tenancy rate in the rural west, where by-employment was widespread and migration frequent, was not accompanied by a fragmentation of the farm. Farm

[7] W.W. Lockwood, *The Economic Development of Japan: Growth and Structural Change, 1868-1938*, expanded ed. (Princeton: Princeton University Press, 1968), p. 99.

[8] The notion of a labor surplus economy has been applied by various scholars to explain Japan's modern economic development. See, for instance, C.H. Fei and G. Ranis, *Development of the Labor Surplus Economy: Theory and Reality* (Homewood, Ill.: Richard D. Irwin, 1964) and Ryoshin Minami, *The Turning Point in Economic Development: Japan's Experience* (Tokyo: Kinokuniya, 1973). One Marxist school, *kōza-ha*, also employs this approach. For an interpretation of the *kōza-ha* model in terms of modern economics, see Yasukichi Yasuba, "Anatomy of the Debate on Japanese Capitalism," *Journal of Japanese Studies*, vol. 2, no. 1 (1975), pp. 63-82.

[9] Umemura Mataji, *Chingin, koyō, nōgyō* (Tokyo: Taimeidō, 1961), pp. 123-127, and Takafusa Nakamura, *Economic Growth in Prewar Japan* (New Haven: Yale University Press, 1983), pp. 114-125.

[10] Calculated from Umemura Mataji et al., *Agriculture and Forestry*, vol. 9 of *Estimates of Long-Term Economic Statistics of Japan* (Tokyo: Tōyō keizai shimpōsha, 1966), p. 218.

size was already very small in the late Tokugawa period. In the 1840s and 1850s two-thirds of the farm households of villages sampled in Kinai and other advanced regions had holdings of less than half a *chō*,[11] and more detailed data for ten villages in Izumi province show that 61 percent of the farm households there had a sown area of less than half a *chō*.[12] Moreover, the tendency in the Kinai and its adjacent prefectures from 1897 to 1909 was against both the smallest and the largest farm categories.[13] Second, silk-producing areas in the east were characterized by high proportions of farm households with dual occupations—in turn associated with an increase, not a decrease, in the total number of farm households. Those areas had sericulture as well as silk reeling and weaving.[14]

Such considerations lead us to re-examine the conventionally assumed relationship between the growth of the market, the spread of by-employment, and the increasing supply of cheap labor in and from the rural areas. Moreover, there were various types of activity in which peasants were engaged as a side occupation. Some of these activities were not most prevalent among small tenant farmers, and these activities must have interacted with one another. Particularly neglected, it seems, is the effect of the commercialization of agriculture on the supply of labor to wage and by-employment opportunities, which sometimes acted as a factor holding the processes of peasant class differentiation and rural depopulation in check. We shall begin with a typology of the side activities of farm households, and then look at how each type was associated with landholding.

A Typology of Peasant Activity

Tokugawa peasants were engaged not only in cereal production, but also in one or another of the various activities known as side occupations. Such side occupations were undertaken in most cases for cash income; they were auxiliary and supplementary for the farm household. Many

[11] Yamaguchi, *Nihon keizai shi*, p. 60.

[12] Calculated from Nakamura Satoru, *Meiji ishin no kiso kōzō* (Tokyo: Miraisha, 1968), p. 77.

[13] Watatani Takeo, "Shihon shugi no hatten to nōmin no kaisō bunka," in Tōbata Seiichi and Uno Kōzō, eds., *Nohon shihon shugi to nōgyō* (Tokyo: Iwanami shoten, 1959), pp. 195-197. Even for the late Tokugawa period, the possibility of the *coexistence* of downward and upward mobility should not be dismissed. On this, see Yasuba Yasukichi's survey: "Another Look at the Tokugawa Heritage, with Special Reference to Social Conditions," Discussion Paper no. 104 (Center for Southeast Asian Studies, University of Kyoto: February 1979), pp. 15-16.

[14] Umemura, *Chingin, koyō, nōgyō*, p. 124.

of them were nonagricultural occupations, but some were agricultural. Many were done at home, but some were not. In the Tokugawa era there was a single expression, *nōkan yogyō*, for this array of peasant side activities. But it is possible to classify *nōkan yogyō* into three categories: 1) by-employment that was nonagricultural and residential; 2) industrial crop cultivation and sericulture; and 3) wage work.[15]

With respect to the first category, Nomura Kanetarō (using a sample of late Tokugawa village records largely from the Kantō area) found that on average 20-25 percent of the village population were engaged in part-time commercial and handicraft activities.[16] Fujita Teiichirō reports that in the Egawa *gumi* (which consisted of twenty villages) of Wakayama *han* there were ninety-seven craftsmen and ninety-nine merchants, almost all of whom held at least a piece of land and were thus assumed to practice such nonagricultural activities on the side. This comes to about five part-time craftsmen and five part-time merchants per village. Also interesting is that the average *kokudaka* of the part-time craftsmen was 2.48 as against 6.40 for the part-time merchants, while the average income from the side occupation was 262 *momme* (or 4.09 *koku* in rice) for the former group as against 3 *kan*, 325 *momme* (51.95 *koku*) for the latter. This suggests that farmers engaging in commercial side activity were wealthier than those working in handicrafts. In fact, some merchants were extremely rich both in terms of *kokudaka* and in earnings from their side activity. Outstanding were sake brewers and dealers of twisted cotton yarn and timber, both of which were staple commodities of this domain and were exported to Osaka. They had on average 25.52 *koku* of land and earned 16 *kan*, 587 *momme* (259 *koku* in rice) from their side businesses; other part-time merchants, in contrast, had only 2.48 *koku* of land, almost the same as the part-time craftsmen, and earned 575 *momme* (8.9 *koku*), or twice that earned by craftsmen.[17] This pattern is also revealed in some of the Nomura materials, from which Furushima Toshio showed that sake brewing, pawnbroking, and grain trade as side activities attracted many village officials.[18]

This pattern should not be taken to suggest that upper-class farmers

[15] Despite frequent use of the term *nōkan yogyō* (or *nōkan tosei* or just *yogyō*), I know of no attempt to develop a systematic typology, except for the very short but useful essay by Fukaya Katsumi, "Edo jidai no nōmin to 'kengyō,' " *Sekai*, no. 399 (February 1979), pp. 23-26. My own classification is somewhat different from Fukaya's.

[16] Nomura Kametarō, *Mura-meisaichō no kenkyū* (Tokyo: Yūhikaku, 1949), chap. 5.

[17] Fujita Teiichirō, "Tokugawa kōki Hidaka-gawa ryūiki ni okeru shakaiteki bungyō no tenkai," in Andō Seiichi, ed., *Kinsei Wakayama no kōzō* (Tokyo: Meicho shuppan, 1973), pp. 292-308.

[18] Furushima Toshio, *Kinsei Nihon nōgyō no tenkai* (Tokyo: Tōkyō daigaku shuppankai, 1963), pp. 244-246.

were more likely to have a side occupation. Such documents as Nomura and Fujita utilized virtually ignored other kinds of by-employment (e.g. spinning, reeling, and weaving), taken up by women and children, but only rarely by adult men.[19] And it is women and children of lower-class peasant households who supplied labor to these industrial activities. Uda Ōtsu *mura*, Izumi province, for instance, was one of the Tokugawa villages most deeply involved in the money economy and in rural industry. In 1843, 32 percent of its 277 households were nonagricultural, and as many as 44 percent combined nonagricultural activities with the tilling of an area smaller than 4 *tan*. A considerable proportion of such side activities falls in the wage-work category. But there were industrial by-employments too. Of 277 households, 58 had at least one member spinning cotton at home, with none supplying wage labor. Twenty-three of these 58 were nonfarm households headed by a female or a sickly person, the rest having on average a farm of just 2.2 *tan*.[20] It is evident that in this village spinning was a by-employment for poor peasants and the landless. Indeed, such cotton-related by-employment was widespread in the rural area around Osaka in the late Tokugawa period.[21]

It is difficult to tell a priori just how by-employments were connected with landholding. The relationship depended on how much capital a certain side activity required and on who provided it. It seems clear that the side activity of women in rural industry was related negatively to landholding, while that of men was not necessarily so. Also clear here is that the figures Nomura and Fujita present undoubtedly underestimate the extent to which Tokugawa peasants engaged in by-employment of various kinds. Indeed, this is what is suggested in works by Thomas Smith and Nishikawa Shunsaku on the Chōshū *han* economy of the 1840s. They found a strikingly large gap between the percentage of farm households and the percentage share of agriculture in the total *han* income; farm family by-employments account for this gap.[22]

A second category of peasant side activity includes the cultivation of industrial crops (such as cotton, indigo, and rapeseed) and sericulture. This may sound strange, as these are agricultural activities. Significantly, however, contemporaries drew a dividing line between grain growing and

[19] See my "Kindai zen no Yamanashi ken," *Keizai semina* (September 1980), pp. 22-28, and my article "Meiji shonen nōka setai no shūgyō kōzō," in *Mita gakkai zasshi*, vol. 78, nos. 1 and 2, especially sec. iii (1985).

[20] Nakamura, *Meiji ishin no kiso kōzō*, p. 51, and Tsuda Hideo, "Bakumatsuki no koyō rōdō ni tsuite," *Tochi seido shigaku*, vol. 2, no. 4 (1960), pp. 13-44.

[21] See Hauser, *Economic Institutional Change*, pp. 136-140.

[22] Smith, "Farm Family By-employments," and Nishikawa Shunsaku, *Edo jidai no poritikaru ekonomi* (Tokyo: Nihon hyōronsha, 1979), chap. 1.

other productive activities, rather than between agriculture and nonagriculture. They regarded the cultivation of industrial crops and sericulture as auxiliary and supplementary. Even in early Meiji statistics, industrial crops and cocoons were classified along with manufacturing goods as "special goods" (*tokuyū bussan*). As late as 1911, when Hiroshima prefecture conducted a survey of farm family side activities, fruits, tea, tobacco leaves, and ramie were included in one group with cocoons and industrial goods.[23] Sericulture remained in the side-activity category in the successive censuses that began in 1920. The persistence of this classification scheme probably reflects a varying commercialization among farm products that persisted even in the Meiji era. According to Yamaguchi Kazuo's estimates for the years before the land tax reform, the proportion commercialized was 15-20 percent for rice, 5-10 percent for other grains, and 80-90 percent for *tokuyū* products.[24] Another estimate, by Nakamura Satoru, for the years after the reform suggests that the percentages stood at 48, 24 and 77 respectively.[25] Even if the effect of the reform, notably in converting taxes in kind to cash, is taken into account, these two sets of estimates do not agree. Nevertheless, it is clear that the "specialness" of industrial crops and cocoons lies in their high degree of commercialization. Of course, rice must have been commercialized to a greater extent in the Kinai and other advanced regions, but it is nonfood farm products that were of prime importance to the commercialization of agriculture and rural economic life as a whole. This was particularly so in the silk-producing areas of the east; according to the Nakamura estimates, the proportion commercialized for *tokuyū* farm products in those areas was almost as high as that for the Kinai, whereas the percentage for rice in those areas was lower than the national average.[26]

Finally, wage work was also considered a type of peasant side activity. This is clear from a description in one of the Nomura materials. The village record of Hanbara *mura*, Sagami province, notes: "Our village being located in a hilly area, men gather firewood in the off-season or go to work in Edo or its vicinity by day."[27] This is a case of seasonal *dekasegi*. However, the form of wage work ranged from work for other

[23] "Hiroshima ken ni okeru nōka fukugyō no chōsa," *Hiroshima ken naimubu kangyōka* (August 1911), reprinted in Hiroshima ken, *Hiroshima ken shi, Kindai gendai shiryō hen*, vol. 2 (Hiroshima: Hiroshima kenchō, 1975), pp. 352-361.

[24] Yamaguchi Kazuo, *Meiji zenki keizai no bunseki* (Tokyo: Tōkyō daigaku shuppankai, 1956), pp. 53-59.

[25] Nakamura, *Meiji ishin no kiso kōzō*, pp. 150-160.

[26] Ibid., pp. 156-157.

[27] Nomura, *Mura-meisaichō*, p. 512.

villagers to going to work outside the village; and from day work to seasonal, one-year, or longer-term service. For example, in Misayama Gōdo *mura*, Suwa county, twenty-two people went to Edo as seasonal *dekasegi* migrants in 1827 when the village had 151 households. They were all men, probably adults who headed a household. And all of them came from the low 0-3 *kokudaka* class.[28] While day-work and off-season *dekasegi* were typical of adult men, live-in service was the job of unmarried children. Akira Hayami has found that in Nishijō *mura*, Mino province, more than 50 percent of those who were born in the village from 1773 to 1825 experienced *dekasegi* service at least once in their lifetime. This is a strikingly high proportion, and it becomes even higher if the *kokudaka* class of 0-2 is singled out: 63 percent for men and 74 percent for women. In Nishijō *mura* there was a shift in the destinations to which farm children, especially females, were sent: from large cities, such as Nagoya and Kyoto, to country towns where cotton weaving was thriving.[29] This shift seems to indicate that in some areas during the *bakumatsu* period rural industry increased the demand for labor in the form of wage work.

In this respect, the best documented region is probably northern Senshū. Uda Ōtsu *mura*, to which I have referred above, had thirteen households (or 5 percent of the total) headed by day laborers. More numerous were non-householders engaged in wage work by the day. Eight clothiers of the village employed thirty-seven loom workers and ten live-in servants, of whom only two weavers and four servants were males. Since there were twenty-eight households with at least one member working on looms in the clothier's workshop, this implies that there were nearly ten *dekasegi* weavers coming in from other villages. Of these twenty-eight households, sixteen (nine of which were headed by women) had no farm to run; the other twelve tilled on average only 0.3 *tan* of land, and only one of these owned at least part of the land.[30] It is interesting to note here that such weavers were called *chinbata hiyatoi*. *Hiyatoi* means a person hired by the day, while *chinbata* indicates a weaver working on rented loom *at home*. It might well be, therefore, that cotton weaving in this village had formerly been a domestic, part-time activity of the peasants, on a piecework basis, but that there then occurred a concentration of looms in workshops, thus turning farm family by-employment to wage

[28] Nōson shiryō chōsakai, *Kinsei nōson no kōzō* (Tokyo: Yamakawa shuppan, 1952), pp. 45-47.

[29] A. Hayami, "Labor Migration in a Pre-Industrial Society: A Study Tracing the Life Histories of the Inhabitants of a Village," *Keio Economic Studies*, vol. 10, no. 2 (1973), pp. 1-17.

[30] Tsuda, "Bakumatsuki no koyō rōdō."

work. If so, this would suggest that by-employment in rural domestic industries as well as wage work were regarded by contemporaries as belonging to the same category. At any rate, it seems that the association among the differentiation of landholdings, the fragmentation of the farm, and the incidence of wage work is well documented. Indeed, Nakamura Satoru has contended that by the early Meiji period the village societies around Osaka entered a stage characterized by the increased "social division of labor," high tenancy rates, and the existence of a substantial number of nonagricultural wage-earning households.[31] His argument is based on a survey of late Tokugawa evidence and on early Meiji regional statistics. Later, I shall discuss the accuracy of Nakamura's synthesis and interpretation.

The evidence presented thus far indicates a negative correlation between peasants having a side occupation in wage work or engaging in by-employment in rural domestic industry, on the one hand, and being landholders, on the other. However, this observation should not necessarily be taken to lend support to the dissolution-of-the-peasantry thesis. First of all, that thesis claims that the process was an irreversible, one-way movement. Yet, as the observed negative correlation is no more than a functional relationship, one would expect that when a tenant farm household increased its disposable income for any reason and acquired land, the probability of that household's members being engaged in by-employment or wage work would *de*crease. Second, the blanket concept of *nōkan yogyō* covers such a wide variety of activities that, as is shown above, not every type of side activity exhibited a negative relationship with landholding. Nor is it likely that one type of side activity had no repercussions for another. Indeed, as early as 1721, Tanaka Kyūgyū wrote: "Cotton spinning, weaving, etc., all these employments have more than doubled in these days, so it is easy now to earn a livelihood. Widows, girls, and even men have a dislike for uncomfortable live-in service, and rather like to earn a living by renting a parcel of land or a shop, and by taking up employment at home."[32] Tanaka clearly saw by-employment opportunities as having a negative effect on the supply of live-in servants. Such an effect of rural industrialization on out-migration has been confirmed with Meiji regional statistics.[33] Equally important is the introduction of cotton (and other industrial crops) and sericulture. In this respect, the only suggestive evidence thus far has come from Ōguchi

[31] Nakamura, *Meiji ishin no kiso kōzō*, pp. 104-112.

[32] Tanaka Kyūgū, *Minkan shōyō*, reprinted in Takimoto Seiichi, ed., *Nihon keizai sōsho* (Tokyo: Nihon keizai sōsho kankōkai, 1914), vol. 1, p. 328.

[33] Osamu Saitō, "Migration and the Labour Market in Japan, 1872-1920: A Regional Study," *Keio Economic Studies*, vol. 10, no. 2 (1973), pp. 47-60.

Yūjirō, who shows that after the 1810s the growing production of silkworm eggs in the village of Kami-shiojiri, Shinano province, led to an expansion of medium-size landholding groups.[34] Unfortunately no comment is made about how such a change affected household labor supply, but Ōguchi's finding does suggest that the number of peasants working for wages as a side occupation declined.

Case Studies

Yamanashi Villages in 1879

It is necessary to bring the effects of landholding as well as commercial agriculture into focus.[35] The 1879 pilot census returns for four Yamanashi villages provide us with interesting data in this regard.

All four villages are located in one purely agricultural area, with sericulture being the most important side activity of the farm households. It was women, especially married women, who took responsibility in breeding silkworms. While 12 percent of males aged 10 and older were engaged in sericulture, 55 percent of females in the same age group, and as many as 78 percent of married women, bred silkworms. More interesting is the fact that the percentage for females varied positively, not negatively, with the landholding status of the household (see Table 15.1).

There were 103 villagers working for wages, either as the primary or as a side occupation. The proportion of those in wage work was over all not very high (7 percent for males, 4 percent for females), but for the nonagricultural and landless classes it was quite significant. More than half of the males and females in wage work came from these marginal classes, more than one-third from the tenant farmer class, and none from the owner-farmer or landlord class (except for one son of a landlord).[36] For wage work, therefore, the relationship with landholding was negative.

As for the first category of peasant side activity (i.e. nonagricultural

[34] Ōguchi Yūjirō, "Bakumatsu ni okeru sanshugyō no hatten to nōson kōzō," *Tochi seido shigaku*, vol. 5, no. 3 (1963), pp. 38-54.

[35] This section summarizes my article in *Mita gakkai zasshi* (see fn. 19, above). The 1879 pilot census was conducted by Sugi Kōji and his associates. Its original returns were long believed to have been destroyed, but recently I discovered that for some villages there remain duplicates. Those analyzed here are for the villages of Masuda, Kita Yatsushiro, Minami Yatsushiro, and Oka, all of which are now part of Yatsushiro *machi*, Higashi Yatsushiro *gun*, Yamanashi prefecture.

[36] This is probably explained by the fact that not all "landlords" held sufficient land to be *rentiers*. Some may have had to lease their holdings because of ill health. In this case, it would not be surprising that their sons had a strong incentive to work for wages.

TABLE 15.1
Social Class of Population Engaged in Side Activities in Four Yamanashi Villages, 1879

Social Class of Household	No. of Persons	% engaged in* Seri-culture	Wage Work	Nonwage, Nonagricultural Work
MALES				
Landlord	56	2	2	59
Owner-farmer	214	21	0	11
Part-owner–farmer	225	11	1	9
Tenant farmer	376	9	6	12
Farm laborer	29	3	100	0
Nonagricultural	30	0	30	67
TOTAL	930	11	7	15
FEMALES				
Landlord	45	62	0	9
Owner-farmer	223	57	0	13
Part-owner–farmer	249	60	1	20
Tenant farmer	395	50	4	22
Farm laborer	17	0	76	0
Nonagricultural	31	10	23	19
TOTAL	960	53	4	18

SOURCE: *Kai no kuni genzai ninbetsu shirabe iebetsuhyō* for four Yatsushiro villages, Yamanashi prefecture, 1879.

* Because some were dually occupied, there can be cases where the three percentage figures total more than 100 percent.

by-employment) the pattern was not simple. There were marked differences between the sexes as well as between landholding classes. These can best be revealed if the landlord class is compared with the tenant farmer class. For the former, it was adult men, especially household heads, who had a side occupation in nonagricultural activity; in most cases, they were merchants, brewers, or pawnbrokers (in all, 77 percent of the married males in this class were engaged in these activities on a part-time basis). Adult males in the tenant farmer class were also engaged in petty trade, but they were craftsmen as well (in all, 18 percent of the married males). On the other hand, it was quite rare for women to take up an occupation in trade and commerce. Their nonagricultural side activity other than wage work was confined to spinning, weaving, and (if available) reeling. The probability of their being engaged in these activities was far higher for the tenant farmer class (31 percent of the unmarried and 14 percent of the married) than for the landlord class (none of the unmarried and just 4 percent of the married). As a result, the proportion working in this kind of side activity was higher for females than for males in the tenant class, whereas the reverse was the case for the landlord class. In other words, women's by-employment was negatively related to landholding, but men's was not.

More than three in four married women, we have seen, were in sericulture, but the percentage for tenant farmers was about ten points lower than for other classes: 72 percent, as against 83 percent for both part-owner and owner farmers and 85 percent for landlords. This means that there was a small but recognizable group of tenant farm households with no member engaged in sericulture. It will be interesting, therefore, to look at how the probability of involvement in other types of side activity varied according to whether or not the tenant farm household could combine sericulture with cereal production. Table 15.2 shows the results. These clearly show that the lack of sericulture exerted a marked influence on the supply of wage work: when the household had no one working in sericulture, the probability of being engaged in wage work was six times higher in the case of males (18 percent) and nearly three times higher in the case of females (8 percent) than otherwise. As for nonagricultural by-employments, the influence was at first glance not so marked. If, however, married women are singled out, the difference between the two groups of tenant farmers turns out to be equally significant.

TABLE 15.2

Sericulture among Tenant Farmer Households and Their Side Activities in Four Yamanashi Villages, 1879

Tenant Household Characteristics	No. of Persons	% engaged in	
		Wage Work	Nonwage, Nonagricultural Work
MALES			
At least one member in sericulture	299	3	11
None in sericulture	77	18	14
FEMALES			
At least one member in sericulture	307	3	19
None in sericulture	88	8	33

SOURCE: See Table 15.1.

In fact, when breeding silkworms, only 8 percent of the married women took up nonagricultural by-employment—no greater than the percentage for those of part-owner farmers—whereas the percentage stood at as high as 34 for those of the non-silkworm-breeding tenant farm households.

Thus, it is quite clear that sericulture had a countervailing effect against the "push" of tenancy with respect to the supply of wage work by both men and women as well as the probability that women will engage in industrial by-employment. One should therefore *not always* assume that the more market forces penetrated into the countryside, the more *dekasegi* labor was supplied and the more women were engaged in "proto-industrial" activity.[37]

The Osaka Region in the Early Meiji Period

Some readers might consider the foregoing analysis applicable only to the silk-producing areas of eastern Japan. It is therefore important to see whether my conclusions hold up in the case of the Osaka region, which has been regarded as an ideal-typical case for the dissolution-of-the-peasantry thesis.

Nakamura Satoru has provided us with a measure of the emergence of wage-earning households in the countryside: viz. the proportion of nonfarm households for each locality. Using *bakumatsu* village examples and early Meiji *gun* statistics, Nakamura asserted that high proportions of nonfarm households were found among villages or *gun* having rural industry and commerce, *or* among those growing cash crops such as cotton and rapeseed.[38] However, scrutiny of the data he presented, particularly the Osaka *gun* statistics, reveals that this simply was not so. Figure 15.1 shows the proportion of nonfarm households in 1888, as well as cash-crop production (viz. cotton and rapeseed) in 1877 as a share of gross agricultural product, for twenty-six *gun* of Osaka prefecture. The scatter appears to indicate a positively sloped relationship. But the correlation is very weak. Moreover, if we omit the three *gun* adjoining the great city of Osaka whose figures for the proportion of nonfarm households were distinctly high, then the positive correlation disappears. If, furthermore, the rest of the *gun* are divided by the share of rice in total agricultural production, then a *negative* correlation emerges. Nakamura named six *gun* as "most advanced" in terms of rural economy,

[37] On this concept and its application, see Osamu Saitō, "Population and the Peasant Family Economy in Proto-Industrial Japan," *Journal of Family History*, vol. 8, no. 1 (1983), pp. 30-54.

[38] Nakamura, *Meiji ishin no kiso kōzō*, pp. 93-112.

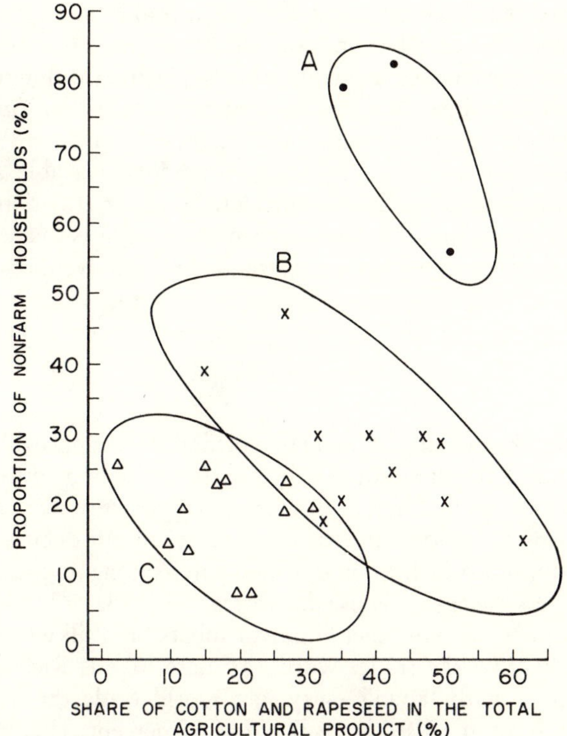

Figure 15.1. Nonfarm Households and Cash-Crop Production, 26 *Gun* of Osaka Prefecture, 1870s and 1880s

A. *Gun* adjoining city of Osaka
B. Proportion of rice below 60 percent
C. Proportion of rice 60 percent or more

Data from Nakamura Satoru, *Meiji ishin no kiso kōzō* (Tokyo: Miraisha, 1968), p. 110.

commercialization and tenancy rates. Thus, controlling for the influence of this factor (as a 0-1 variable), and for that of the share of rice, one may regress the proportion of nonfarm households on the share of industrial crops, and the result turns out to be statistically significant.[39]

[39] The estimated regression is as follows:

$$Z = 131.1 - 1.064X_c - 1.292X_r + 15.08D$$
$$(3.86) \quad (-2.67) \quad (-3.33) \quad (2.20)$$
$$R^2 = 0.524; \quad \text{d.f.} = 23;$$

where Z is the proportion of nonfarm households in 1888, X_c and X_r are the shares of cotton and rapeseed and of rice, respectively, in the gross agricultural product in *yen* for 1877, D is a dummy variable (1 if one of the "most advanced" *gun*), and the figures in

This confirms that cash cropping acted as a brake on the tendency for small farm households to become nonfarm households. It does not follow, of course, that the tenancy rate had no bearing, since the dummy variable included had a positive effect on the dependent variable. This becomes clearer if the percentage change in the tenancy rate from 1883 to 1887 is added into the regression equation: the added variable also had a positive, statistically significant coefficient.[40] Greater attention should be given to the finding that the effect of cash cropping was to keep peasants on the land, because this does not fit well with the conventional wisdom.

Conclusion

The impact of the opening of Japan to world trade was particularly strong in two sectors of the domestic textile industry—silk and cotton—though the effect was entirely different in each case.[41] Western demand for Japanese silk was so sudden and strong that in silk-producing regions of eastern Japan, not only local middlemen and Yokohama merchants, but local producers—farmers whose daughters reeled silk at home as well as farmers whose wives and other family members bred silkworms—gained tremendously from the trade. Worthy of note here is Richard Huber's suggestion that with Japan's entry into world trade the nation's real income may have increased by as much as 65 percent. This figure, however, even if accurate, should be taken to apply only to the situation in eastern Japan, since Huber's estimate was based on wage data for Edo, not for Kyoto or Osaka.[42] At any rate, this income gain in turn led to

parentheses are *t*-values. The result is, in a sense, remarkable because the coefficients of both X_c and X_r are significantly identified despite a very high correlation of -0.906 between the two logically related variables.

[40] The result is as follows:

$$Z = \underset{(3.34)}{110.7} + \underset{(2.11)}{0.713GT} - \underset{(-2.23)}{0.858X_c} - \underset{(-3.20)}{1.170X_r} + \underset{(2.99)}{20.62D}$$

$$R^2 = 0.604; \quad \text{d.f.} = 22;$$

where *GT* denotes the percentage change in the tenancy rate from 1883 to 1887. Other variables are the same as in fn. 39, above.

[41] For a general account, see Yokohama shi, *Yokohama shi shi* (Yokohama: Yokohama shiyakusho, 1959), vol. 2, pp. 337-345, 526-546, and Yamazaki Ryūzō, "Bakumatsu ishin ki no keizai hendō," *Iwanami kōza Nihon rekishi*, vol. 13, *kinsei* vol. 5 (Tokyo: Iwanami shoten, 1977), pp. 125-171.

[42] R.J. Huber, "Effect on Prices of Japan's Entry into World Commerce after 1858," *Journal of Political Economy*, vol. 79, no. 3 (1971), pp. 614-628.

increases in the number of silk-reeling and cocoon-producing farm households, as well as more articulated regional specialization.

By contrast, Japanese cotton was not competitive in the world market. But the impact of Western trade was not so sudden as in silk, and responses to the influx of foreign cotton goods were more complex. Overall, the weaving sector was least affected. In the first decade after the opening of the ports, it is true, cotton cloth was imported; soon, however, many weaving centers throughout the country began to substitute imported yarn for the domestic product, so that they could survive. With demand growing, foreign yarn flooded Japan from the Restoration period onward. As a result, the domestic spinning industry was destroyed, and it had to be re-established in the late 1880s and 1890s as a new, urban factory industry based on Western technology. Domestic cotton cultivation, too, was wiped out after the 1890s; but until then its responses to the impact of foreign imports varied by region and decade. At first, Japan exported ginned cotton, which ceased to be exported as thread imports increased. Nevertheless, output of domestic raw cotton did increase marginally up to the late 1880s. Furushima Toshio attributed much of this increase to an expansion of land under cotton into areas where cotton cultivation before 1859 had hardly been extensive. On the other hand, "advanced" areas like parts of Osaka prefecture, where cotton was largely grown in paddy fields at the expense of rice, saw an earlier contraction in cotton fields, which were converted to rice paddies again. This switch was possible because, given soil and technological conditions, rice cultivation there could also be commercially profitable.[43] Domestic cotton cultivation started to decline in the 1890s, when new, urban-based cotton mills began to turn to imported materials. Thus, albeit with a time lag, most regions where cotton was still grown (usually in upland fields) finally switched from cotton to cocoons. And such a fate was not confined to cotton. As Yamazaki Ryūzō writes, "cash crops, which had so colorfully characterized eighteenth-century agriculture, declined in the end, except for sericulture and tea growing."[44]

Probably Yamazaki oversimplified the change that took place during the transition period, but it is certainly true that eastern Japan gained, whereas the west lost, from the country's entry into world trade. Thus—given the mechanism that commercial cropping and sericulture acted as a brake on the dissolution of the peasantry, and that their disappearance became an incentive for peasants to leave farming—it is logical to suppose

[43] Furushima Toshio, *Shihonsei seisan no hatten to jinushisei* (Tokyo: Ochanomizu shobō, 1963), pp. 431-462.

[44] Yamazaki, "Bakumatsu ishinki no keizai hendō," p. 167.

that more peasant labor was supplied to nonfarm activities in the west after the transition period than before, whereas more peasants clung to the land in the east. This supposition is consistent with the data we have on changes in the number of farm households in the west and east.

There is some supportive evidence for this. First, Itō Shigeru has recently found that although the sex ratio of migrants into cities in the Meiji period was generally high, in the west even more men went to the cities.[45] In other words, relatively more eastern men stayed in their villages than did westerners, and this is certainly consistent with the above supposition. A second piece of evidence comes from the silk-producing prefecture of Nagano in the mid-Meiji period. Recent work by Satō Masanori suggests that despite the apparent lack of correlation between *gun* out-migration and sericulture, a net *gun* out-migration from 1888 to 1898 was negatively related to an increase in earnings from sericulture over the same period (for all *gun* in the prefecture except Suwa, where the "pull" from the growing silk-reeling industry was overwhelmingly strong).[46] Finally, there is evidence having to do with cotton mill recruits around the turn of the century. According to a survey conducted by the Federation of Japanese Cotton Manufactures, each mill had its own "recruitment territories" from which its factory girls were constantly and exclusively recruited. Quite interestingly, the list of these "territories" does not include such major silk-producing prefectures as Nagano and Yamanashi, but does include Inland Sea regions where cotton had been widely grown until the early Meiji.[47]

One should not conclude from the above, however, that a pool of surplus labor was formed owing to the demise of cotton and other cash-crop cultivation in the western countryside. Rural impoverishment was not the only consequence of the change that occurred during the transition. As noted, some western areas with fertile soil switched to market-oriented rice cultivation, while other areas, most of which had tried to introduce or expand cotton cultivation after the opening of Japan, turned gradually to sericulture. For instance, when Shimane prefecture drew up its second "ten-year economic plan" in 1909, it noted that production of cocoons had soared upward at 8 percent annually in the preceding decade, and it predicted an even higher rate of 14 percent for the next

[45] Itō Shigeru, "Meiji Taishōki no toshi nōson kan jinkō idō," in Morishima Ken and Akino Masakatsu, eds., *Nōgyō kaihatsu no riron to jisshō* (Tokyo: Yōkendō, 1982), pp. 55-74.

[46] I am grateful to Mr. Satō for making his unpublished findings available to me.

[47] Kajinishi Mitsuhaya, ed., *Sen'i, jō*, vol. 11 of *Gendai Nihon sangyō hattatsu shi* (Tokyo: Kōjunsha, 1964), p. 199.

ten years.[48] In Hiroshima prefecture, too, the aforementioned 1911 survey of farm family side activities noted that sericulture in the prefecture was making great progress, so that it was "most promising" as a side activity for Hiroshima farm households.[49] These responses do not suggest a substantial expansion of disguised unemployment in the countryside. The rural west suffered from the change that took place during the transition period, but the result was not necessarily either a swelling reservoir of cheap labor or a depopulation of the countryside.

Perhaps the foregoing argument should suffice to warn against an assumption that farm families in the Meiji era were underemployed and thus ready to take industrial employment as industrialization occurred. The observed tendency for farm households not to decrease in number cannot be evidence for the claim that Meiji Japan enjoyed an unlimited supply of peasant labor. That tendency was a product of various forces operating in different directions. Growing population, a burgeoning money economy, rising tenancy rates, and increasing labor demand from the industrial sector—all are regarded as functioning as accelerators, while rising peasant income acted as the brake. Among the factors affecting peasant income, an increase in the productivity of grain cultivation was probably very important. Yet, in this essay I have stressed sericulture and industrial agriculture, particularly the former. This is because sericultural output grew far more rapidly than the output of rice and other grains during the Meiji period.[50] More important, though, is the fact that sericulture, especially in relatively backward regions of eastern Japan, was a principal agent in the commercialization of the rural economy—a change that, with rising tenancy as one of its ills, is generally considered an accelerator of the dissolution of peasant society. In other words, the growth of sericulture from the opening of the ports on kept the peasants' supply price of labor higher than it would have been otherwise, not only by augmenting household income, but by counterbalancing the ill effects of rural commercialization itself.[51]

Only when an increase in farm income was no longer possible did

[48] Shimane ken, *Shinshū Shimane ken shi, shiryō hen: kindai chū* (Matsue: Shimane kenchō, 1966), pp. 684-685.

[49] *Hiroshima ken shi* (fn. 23, above), p. 356.

[50] From 1880 to 1920, sericulture grew at an annual rate of 4.3 percent; rice output increased at 1.3 percent. Kazushi Ohkawa and Shinohara Miyohei, eds., *Patterns of Japanese Economic Development* (New Haven: Yale University Press, 1979), p. 87.

[51] Note that even in the late Tokugawa period the supply price of peasant labor was not very low. According to Shunsaku Nishikawa's estimates for Chōshū in the 1840s, marginal labor productivity in agriculture was not lower than a postulated subsistence level. See his "Productivity, Subsistence, and By-employment in the Mid-Nineteenth-Century Chōshū," *Explorations in Economic History*, vol. 15 (1978), pp. 69-83.

farm family members come under great pressure to lower the price for their labor. Such a situation did not occur on a large scale until the 1920s, when the output of rice stopped increasing *and* the production of silk cocoons started to contract. Prior to that time, as our case studies show, commercialization and growth of agricultural production led the way in improving labor conditions in rural areas.

CHAPTER 16

GRAIN CONSUMPTION: THE CASE OF CHŌSHŪ*

BY SHUNSAKU NISHIKAWA

To know something about the food consumed in a given nation can be the basis for a knowledge of that people's standard of living as well as a key to understanding social conditions. This is especially true for Japan in the period from the *bakumatsu* to the decades after the Meiji Restoration. Notwithstanding, there has been little research on this topic, and it is widely believed that the peasantry lived at a mere subsistence level during the last years of the Tokugawa period. The Meiji Restoration of 1868 brought in its wake many changes that might have affected the diet. Thus, the focus of this chapter is on the level and adequacy of the Japanese diet in the 1840s and 1880s, and on dietary changes that may have occurred.

In 1922 Ono Takeo obtained some revealing answers to a series of questions about farm life during the Tokugawa period, from fifty elderly farmers in twenty prefectures around the country. At the time of the survey, most of the respondents were 60-70 years of age; but a few were older, even over 90, and a few others were in their early fifties. Thus, they talked from their own experience about the general picture at the time of the *bakumatsu*. According to Ono's summary, "What common people had to eat was simple. First, it was considered excellent if a day's three meals consisted of 3 parts *kome* [rice] and 7 parts *mugi* [barley and wheat] or *awa* [foxtail millet]. Generally, the morning meal was mostly *mugi* or *awa* and only a little *kome*, though sometimes *mugi* or

* I acknowledge the assistance and suggestions given by the following: Arai Hidenao, Robert Evans, Jr., John M. Freeman, Fujisawa Masuo, Fukushima Yasuto, Hiramatsu Kiyoko, Ishibe Shōko, Kumagaya Mitsuhisa, Kurosaki Chiharu, Ōtsuka Tsutomu, Takamatsu Nobukiyo, Ronald Toby, and Umemura Mataji.

awa meal, with *miso* soup and pickles, as supplementary food, was considered to be a good meal. In some places *mugi* or *awa* gruel mixed with *kome*, or the powder of *kibi* [proso millet] simply kneaded in hot water and eaten, sufficed in the morning."[1] The author emphasized the low proportion of rice. Whether it really was that low in the past is one of the points to be examined in this chapter.

In the Meiji period, the Ministry of Agriculture and Commerce and the Japan Federation of Farmers undertook a survey of the "Proportion of the People's Staple Food" (hereafter PSF) in 1880 and 1886, respectively.[2] For those years, the proportions of rice in the diet were 53 percent and 51 percent, respectively; barley and wheat combined were 27 percent in both years, while millets were 14 percent and 13 percent, respectively; and sweet potatoes and other staples were 6 percent and 9 percent of the staple diet, respectively. These figures were derived simply by averaging the results by prefecture. The proportions were based upon volume, and it is not known how sweet potatoes were converted into millet equivalent. The reader should also observe that the proportion of rice was twenty percentage points or more higher than the figure given by Ono. The surveys included cities and towns. Since it is known that the proportion of rice in city and town diets was higher than in villages—for example, the proportion of rice in the *ku* (densely populated wards) was 91 percent in 1880 and 86 percent in 1886—the national proportion was presumably higher than Ono's, which covered only villages. Even excluding the *ku*, the national average is more than 10 points higher than Ono's average.[3] Had the proportion of rice in the diet increased?

The defect that all three surveys share is that absolute figures are not given. Without knowing the quantities of the various food crops, it cannot be said that the people's diet was improved by a mere increase in the proportion of rice. For example, if the consumption of nonrice crops decreased as rice consumption remained unchanged, the proportion of rice could be increased without any improvement to the diet. Though rice was the favored food, even in 1886 half of the staple food intake (grain) consisted of other crops. To place too much emphasis on the consumption of rice is as unjustified as to concern oneself only with meat in studying Western food consumption today.

It is difficult to know the precise output of grain, apart from rice,

[1] Ono Takeo, *Tokugawa jidai no nōka keizai* (Tokyo: Ganshōdō, 1925), p. 28.

[2] *Dai niji nōmu tōkeihyō* (1881) and *Nōji tōkeihyō* (1888). In the latter, the data are labeled "Staple Food by Kind, and Demand for and Supply of Rice and Barley."

[3] For these national and prefectural data, see Umemura Mataji et al., *Chōki keizai tōkei 13: Chiiki keizai tōkei* (Tokyo: Tōyō keizai shimpōsha, 1983), pp. 246-251. Hereafter *Chōki keizai tōkei* is abbreviated *CKT*.

because the daimyo and samurai had scant interest in crops that were left for farmers' consumption. The domains kept good records on rice, but not on nonrice crops. Fortunately there is a censuslike survey of Chōshū—called *Bōchō fudo chūshin-an* (hereafter *chūshin-an*)—that was carried out beginning in 1841 at the order of the *han* government. It contains an accurate estimate of the output of staple food crops as well as a great deal of other socioeconomic data.[4] Moreover, we are fortunate that the 1886 PSF data for each *gun* in Yamaguchi *ken* are preserved in the *Yamaguchi ken daiyonkai kankyō nempō* (1889). From these *gun*-by-*gun* data, it is possible to derive estimates for 1886 comparable to those available for Chōshū in the 1840s in the *chūshin-an*. (The four branch *han* were incorporated with Chōshū to form Yamaguchi *ken* in the fall of 1871.)

Grain Output during the 1840s and 1887

Chōshū, located at the southwestern end of Honshū, consisted of two provinces, Suō and Nagato. Their area was approximately 6,000 km^2, two-thirds of which was in the possession of Chōshū *han*. The remaining one-third of the land had been ceded to four branch domains (see Map 16.1). Chōshū *han* is well known as one of the domains that brought about the Meiji Restoration.[5]

One may ask whether Chōshū/Yamaguchi can be a good sample for the study of changes in national food expenditures and consumption. First of all, it is likely that this area's level of per capita production at the end of the nineteenth century was equal to the national average, or slightly lower.[6] Second, on the basis of the 1886 survey, the proportion of rice in the staple diet in Yamaguchi was only 1 percentage point lower than the national average. While the proportion of barley was 3 percentage points above the national average, the figures for millet and sweet

[4] The *chūshin-an* is a collection of village reports compiled by village headmen. It contains quantitative data (such as arable area, output on which taxes are based, taxes in kind and in money, population, occupational distribution, number of draft animals, costs in both agriculture and other industries, and nonagricultural income) as well as descriptions of village geography, a calendar of village life, and a history of shrines and temples in the village. It was edited by the Yamaguchi *ken monjokan* and published by Yamaguchi *ken* (1962) in 21 volumes.

[5] Albert M. Craig, *Chōshū in the Meiji Restoration* (Cambridge: Harvard University Press, 1961).

[6] Nishikawa Shunsaku, "Chōshū/Yamaguchi ken no sangyō hatten," in Shimbo Hiroshi and Yasuba Yasukichi, eds., *Kindai ikōki no Nihon keizai* (Tokyo: Nihon keizai shimbunsha, 1979), pp. 29-48.

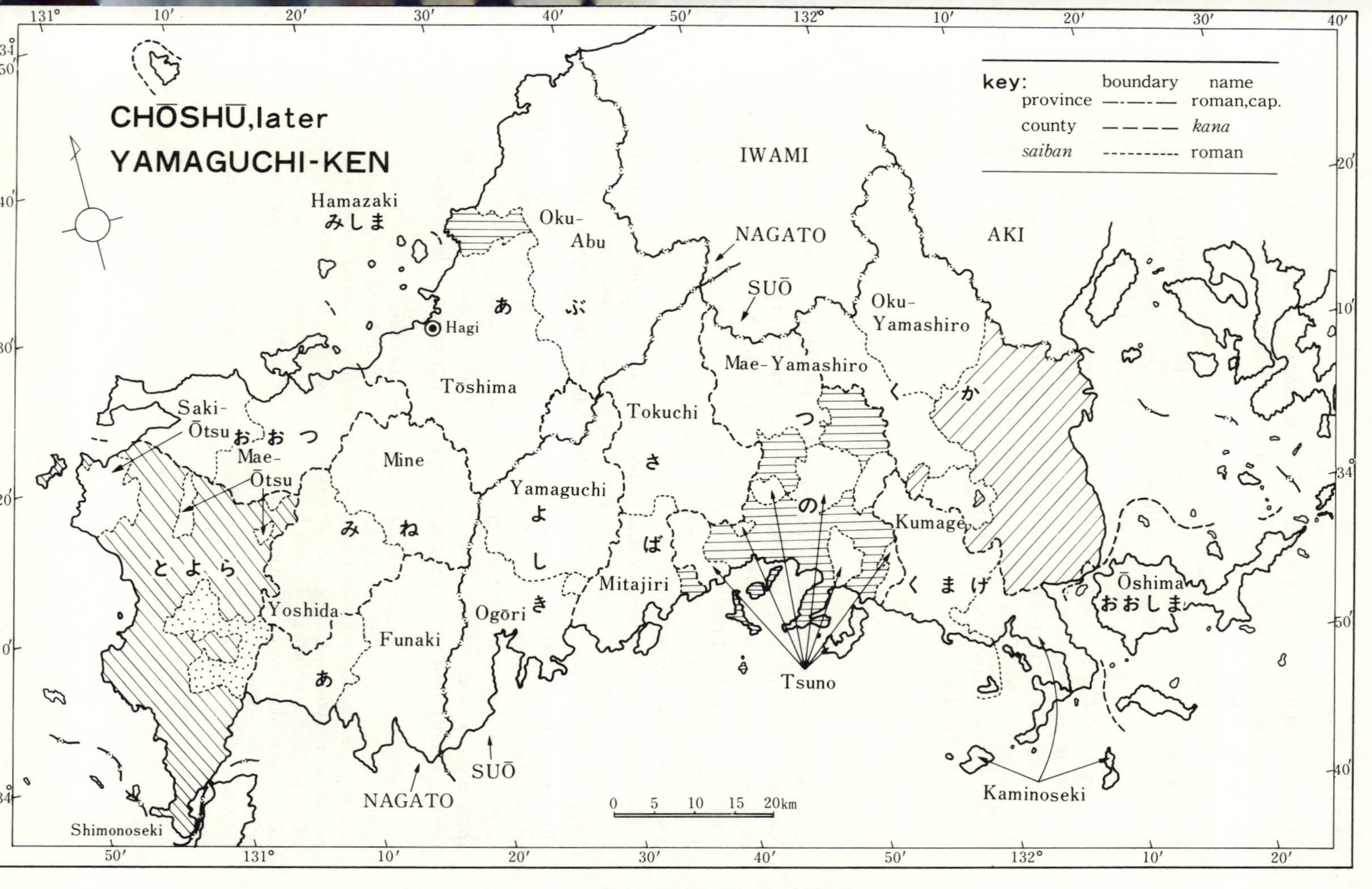

Map 16.1. Chōshū (Later Yamaguchi *Ken*)

potatoes, respectively, were no more than 1.2 and 0.6 percentage points from the average.[7] We have no comparable data for other domains in the 1840s, and it is difficult to make comparative judgments. The evidence, mostly impressionistic, that does exist indicates a level of material production similar to that found elsewhere; so Chōshū/Yamaguchi can be considered reasonably representative.

Table 16.1 shows the output and supply of grain in the 1840s and in 1887. The official announcement of the *chūshin-an* survey was in 1841, and over the next few years many villages compiled reports, some dated as late as 1845. The figures on output were to represent "the three-year average between good and bad harvests." The figures for 1887 were taken from the *Daiyonji nō-shōmu tokeihyō* (1890). Data for 1886 would have been more desirable, because of the PSF data from that year; however, since the production of several crops other than rice is unknown for that year, it is preferable to use the 1887 data. When comparing the figures for the 1840s and 1887, one must keep in mind that geographic area differs slightly: the 1840s figures cover only Chōshū *han* itself, while the latter figures include the branch *han*. Thus, direct comparison of output would lead to an erroneous result. This caution also applies to the population shown in Table 16.1. Accordingly, figures adjusted by population are given for comparison. Note that there was a less than 10 percent growth in per capita output during the half-century. The greater part of this expansion was based on an almost 14 percent growth in per capita rice production, from a little less than 1 *koku* to 1.14 *koku*. Grain production other than rice did not expand as quickly.

The lowermost panel of Table 16.1 shows the per capita and per day rice supply—output less the rice exported from Chōshū or used for seed and sake brewing. The supporting evidence and estimating procedures for these three components, stated briefly in the footnotes to the table, are so scant and rough that the estimates presumably have some margin of error. The rice export figure for 1887, in particular, is based on insufficient evidence. The sharp decline of seed reserve per output, as well as the substantial increase in rice used for sake brewing, stand out. The former reflects technical progress in rice cultivation, while the latter reflects the elimination of the old rice tax in kind and the free disposition of rice output. Nonrice crops were also used for seed and other purposes. According to the *chūshin-an*, *hie* (barnyard millet) was used for animal fodder during the cultivating season. Since there is hardly any reliable

[7] The national figure for grain supply in 1887 was computed as 3.9 *go* per capita daily. Data are from the *Nihon teikoku dai hachi tōkei nenkan* (1889). Red beans were not included.

TABLE 16.1

Output and Supply of Grain in Chōshū/Yamaguchi, 1840s and 1887

	1840s[a]		1887[b]	
	Output (*koku*)	(%)	Output (*koku*)	(%)
Rice	519,389	65.1	1,026,430	67.2
Barley and wheat	195,915	24.6	403,407	26.4
Millet[c]	26,479	3.3	19,671	1.3
Buckwheat	29,289	3.7	31,725	2.1
Soy and red beans	27,003	3.4	45,312	3.0
TOTAL	798,075	100.0	1,526,545	100.0
Population	520,000		902,600[d]	
Per capita grain output				
per year	1.534 *koku*		1.691 *koku*	
per day[e]	4.2 *go*		4.6 *go*	
Rice exported	100,000 *koku*[f]		200,000 *koku*[g]	
Rice used for sake	40,000 *koku*[h]		100,000 *koku*[i]	
Rice used for seed[j]	30,000 *koku*		40,000 *koku*	
Per capita grain supply				
per year	1.208 *koku*		1.375 *koku*	
per day	3.3 *go*		3.6 *go*	

[a] Aggregated from *chūshin-an*, 21 vols.

[b] Includes the territories of not only Chōshū *han*, but also four branch *han*. Output, except for *hie* (barnyard millet), from *Yamaguchi ken dai yonkai kangyō nempō* (1889); output of *hie* from *Dai yonji nō-shōmu tōkeihyō* (1890).

[c] Sum of *awa*, *kibi*, and *hie*.

[d] Population for 1886 in *Meiji 20-nen chōhatsu bukken ichiranhyō* (1889).

[e] Calculated on basis of 365 days per year.

[f] Estimated from Miyamoto Matao, "Kinsei chūkōki no Osaka ni okeru ryōshumai ryūtsū," *Kokumin keizai zasshi*, vol. 125, no. 6 (June 1977), pp. 53-84, table 1.

[g] Misaka Keiji, *Yamaguchi ken no rekishi* (Tokyo: Yamakawa shuppansha, 1971), p. 249.

[h] Estimated from sake tax revenue, in Akimoto Hiroya, "Hagi han zaisei shūshi to keizai seisaku," *Shakai keizai shigaku*, vol. 42, no 2 (February 1977), pp. 341-364.

[i] Estimated from both sake output and sake tax revenue, in *Yamaguchi ken tōkeishō, Dai nikai* (1884) and *Dai sankai* (1891).

[j] Arashi Kaichi, *Kinsei inasaku gijutsu shi* (Tokyo: Nō-san-gyoson bunka kyōkai, 1975), fig. 6-1 (for 1840s) and table 6-4 (for 1887).

information on this, no adjustment has been made. Accordingly the estimate of personal consumption in this chapter may have a slight upward bias. The amount shown in Table 16.1 is what the people, including samurai and their families in the 1840s or *shizoku* (former samurai and their families) in 1887, were able to consume.

Real Consumption of Rice and Other "Grain" in the 1840s

Per Capita "Grain" Consumption in the chūshin-an

The total number of villages (including fishing villages and a few towns but not Hagi, the domain capital) came to approximately 320. An explicit account of grain was calculated in 80 percent of the village reports. Rice was the first crop of calculation, then barley and wheat, millets (*awa, kibi*, and *hie*), buckwheat, soybeans, red beans, and so forth. First, the supply of food grain was computed as rice output (less rice tax) and other grain output. Second, the necessary quantity of food was computed as the amount needed per capita per day multiplied by the population and the number of days in a year—set as 360 days in most cases. Third, supply and demand were compared, to obtain the degree of correspondence.

One finds indications of a shortage in almost 70 percent of the villages. This seems to conform to the long dominant view that people in the Tokugawa period were forced to live on a "starvation," or minimum subsistence, level because of a heavy tax burden. Nonetheless, such a view should be tested by a more careful examination of the data by *saiban* (small administrative units), as shown in Table 16.2.[8] The basis for the calculation of minimum need (column 2) ranges from 3 to 5 *go* (1 *go* = 1/10 *shō* = 1/1000 *koku*). It is apparent that the *han* government assigned no specific amount. Presumably it was the village headmen who chose these specific amounts, for they knew well the living standard of their villagers, as well as the supply of foodstuffs in the village. The basis for calculation is obviously a kind of estimate, and might vary with the supply of food in each village. Some headmen might have chosen a subsistence level, others a somewhat higher quantity. There is the possibility that some headmen might have wanted to emphasize a shortage,

[8] The *saiban* was the local administrative division of Chōshū. It was governed by a magistrate and his officials, and village headmen assisted in administration. In the *bakumatsu* period, there were eighteen *saiban*; however, the *chushin-an* for Hamazaki *saiban* (later Mishima *gun*) has not been found.

TABLE 16.2

Supply of "Grain" by *Saiban* in Chōshū, 1840s

	(1) Population	(2) Basis for Calculation[a]	(3) Rice Output (*koku*)	(4) Tax Ratio[b] (%)	(5) Rice after Tax (*koku*)	(6) Paid and Purchased Rice (*koku*)	(7) Disposable Rice[c]
Ōshima	56,556	4	21,651	56.8	9,350	5,160	14,510
Oku-Yamashiro	16,878	4.5	8,181	45.1	4,495	3,274	7,769
Mae-Yamashiro	16,724	3	8,292	44.9	4,570	1,382	5,952
Kaminoseki	36,955	4	25,709	61.1	10,013	2,114	12,127
Kumage	33,156	—	29,340	63.2	10,800		10,800
Tsuno	23,436	2.9	22,620	73.9	5,905		5,905
Mitajiri	33,270	4	45,541	48.9	23,292		23,292
Tokuchi	20,376	—	18,111	66.0	6,161	5,250	11,411
Yamaguchi	25,480	4	45,770	47.5	24,015		24,015
Ogōri	38,843	—	48,588	50.0	24,294		24,296
Funaki	31,361	3.7	50,597	54.9	22,841		22,841
Yoshida	24,540	3.6	43,884	65.8	14,987		14,987
Mine	16,014	4.1	27,464	54.5	12,495		12,495
Saki-Ōtsu	24,585	—	31,858	50.0	15,929		15,929
Mae-Ōtsu	17,902	5	25,916	50.7	12,771		12,771
Toshima	24,991	5	25,005	53.4	11,659		11,659
Oku-Abu	29,129	5	40,902	60.0	16,344		16,344
TOTAL	470,196	4.1	519,389	55.7	229,921	17,180	247,101

TABLE 16.2 (cont.)

	(8) Barley and Wheat (*koku*)	(9) Millet and Buckwheat (*koku*)	(10) Soy and Red Beans (*koku*)	(11) Sweet Potato (*koku*)	(12) Grain Supply[d] (*koku*)	(13) Per Capita Per Day[e] (*go*)
Ōshima	21,252	2,498	2,063	13,884	54,167	2.6
Oku-Yamashiro	6,115	4,344	1,331	2,271	21,830	3.5
Mae-Yamashiro	4,815	4,603	1,742	1,505	18,617	3.1
Kaminoseki	12,817	2,670	2,177	3,954	33,745	2.5
Kumage	8,762	2,967	1,640	726	24,895	2.1
Tsuno	8,860	3,112	1,681	521	20,079	2.3
Mitajiri	19,756	1,398	1,311		45,759	3.8
Tokuchi	7,509	1,529	909	(22)	21,358	2.9
Yamaguchi	14,404	1,203	955		40,577	4.4
Ogōri	18,060	2,356	2,625	(149)	47,335	3.3
Funaki	12,379	3,421	2,005		40,646	3.6
Yoshida	9,758	4,614	1,932		31,291	3.5
Mine	9,590	5,463	1,336		28,884	4.9
Saki-Ōtsu	14,668	3,395	1,892		35,884	4.0
Mae-Ōtsu	5,786	2,355	635		21,547	3.3
Toshima	10,959	2,643	732		25,993	2.9
Oku-Abu	10,425	7,196	2,028		35,993	3.4
TOTAL	195,915	55,767	26,994	22,821	548,598	3.2

SOURCE: *chūshin-an*, 21 vols.

NOTE: Figures in parentheses are not included in the totals.

[a] Per capita per day.

[b] Column 4 = [1 − (column 5 ÷ column 3)] × 100.

[c] Column 7 = columns 5 + 6.

[d] Column 12 = columns 7 + 8 + 9 + 10.

[e] Column 13 = column 12 ÷ (365 × column 1).

choosing a higher basis for the purpose of tax evasion. If so, no explanation can be found as to why smaller amounts were used by a number of *saiban*. Possibly the figures that are whole numbers were either assigned by the magistrate or agreed on after a discussion among the headmen. Little is known about how and why these specific values were chosen as the basis for calculation.

The components of food supply are given by each *saiban* in columns 3 through 11. The ratio of the tax to output is shown in column 4; it ranges from 45 percent to 74 percent. Generally the main tax was 40 percent of the *kokudaka*, but an additional tax of some 10 percent was levied in most domains. Since fields and residential plots that produced no rice were included in the assessment of *kokudaka*, though at a reduced rate, the ratio of the tax to the real rice output often reached 60-70 percent, and even more, in villages where paddies were relatively scarce. Mae- and Oku-Yamashiro, Ōshima, and Kaminoseki are examples of such areas. Some were upland *saiban*, where the peasants produced paper for the domain monopoly during the slack season. The price of paper, undoubtedly lower than it would have been in a free market, was set in terms of rice equivalents. The purchase of rice was also authorized by the *han* government in two *saiban*, Ōshima and Kaminoseki, which consisted of densely populated islands and/or peninsula where cultivation was extremely poor. Paid and purchased rice are consolidated in column 6.

One additional component, the sweet potato, is shown in column 11, and is included in the total food supply (columns 12 and 13). As can be seen, sweet potato was produced mainly in Ōshima and Kaminoseki, where food shortages were severe. In the *chūshin-an* of both *saiban*, even *daikon* (long radish) and sake dregs were included. All these commodities were usually measured by weight (*kan* = 3.75 kg). The village headmen in these *saiban* then converted them into millet equivalents, as follows: sweet potato, 10 *kan* = 7.5 *shō; daikon*, 10 kan = 5 *shō*; sake dregs, 10 *kan* = 10 *shō*. These conversion ratios are conventional and reflect the experience of the times, but their accuracy is dubious in the light of current scientific knowledge.[9] Nevertheless, Table 16.2 follows the contemporary practice of including sweet potato in the food supply. *Daikon*

[9] Computed in terms of calories, the conversion ratios are as follows: sweet potato, 10 *kan* = 11.5 *shō; daikon*, 10 *kan* = 2.4 *shō*; sake dregs, 10 *kan* = 20 *shō* of millet. Sweet potato and sake dregs, then, were overvalued, while *daikon* was undervalued in the traditional Chōshū conversion ratios. Caloric values for each item are provided in Kagaku gijutsu-chō, Shigen chōsakai, *Santei-ho: Nihon shokuhin hyōjun seibunhyō* (Tokyo: Ōkurashō insatsukyoku, 1978-1979).

and sake dregs, however, are excluded because the former has little nutrition and the latter were negligible in amount.

The level of supply per capita per day (column 13) was more than 3.5 *go* in most *saiban* of Nagato province (the bottom seven *saiban*), where hardly any sweet potato was produced.[10] The amount of daily grain per capita was as high as 4.9 *go* in Mine. On the other hand, the "grain" supply, including paid or purchased rice and sweet potato, was approximately 2.5 *go* in Suō province (the top ten *saiban*). While it was 3.8 and 4.4 in Mitajiri and Yamaguchi, it was only 2.1-2.3 *go* in Kumage and Tsuno. The higher tax rate was one reason why such a low level of food supply was found in Tsuno. This tax rate was the result of a peculiar counting procedure used there; if we apply the procedure used in other *saiban*, the rate may be adjusted to 65 percent, the same as in Ōshima and Kumage.[11]

The Rice Market and Nonagricultural Income

The next question to be considered is whether the people in the *saiban* of Suō (except for Mitajiri, Ogōri, and Yamaguchi) had to get by on only 3 *go* or less of grain each day. Examining the *chūshin-an* of these *saiban* more carefully, I have concluded that this population was able to eat 3.3 *go* or more daily. Although a "shortage" of rice remained, the people were able to buy quantities of rice in addition to the special paid rice in upland areas and the authorized-purchase rice in island or peninsular areas by using cash obtained through various nonagricultural activities.

The total regional income in upland Mae-Yamashiro was estimated as

[10] Tōshima, Oku-Abu, and some other *saiban* reported sweet potato in units of *furi* and *ka*, which represent quantities a man could handle or transport on his shoulder. Since the precise quantity in either weight or volume is not known, these figures must be omitted. The omission, however, seems not to distort the larger picture.

[11] Nine villages, just half of the villages in the *saiban*, counted *shi-ina* (poor-quality rice not suitable for tax payment) as part of their millet production figures. In these nine villages, if we count this *shi-ina* as rice, then 13.8 percent of these villages' rice output was *shi-ina*. In another five villages, rice was counted by a measure augmented by 10 percent. The *han* government forced the use of such a measure in order to make up for rice lost during inspection and in transit. Since other villages and *saiban* did not record taxed rice in this way, it is appropriate for the sake of comparison to subtract this additional amount from the tax and add it to the peasants' disposable rice. These adjustments yield the rate of approximately 65 percent noted in the text.

Peasant disposable rice in other *saiban* (Table 16.2) is overestimated since the augmented measure was also used to count taxed rice. As we shall see in Table 16.3, however, the taxed rice exceeds the amount used for export, for sake, and for consumption by samurai and their families. This excess was undoubtedly eaten by commoners and is therefore to be ignored in Table 16.2

2,060 *kan* in terms of domain notes,[12] 740 *kan* having been earned by paper manufacture. Taxes in kind and in money were 610 *kan*; thus, the disposable income was approximately 1,450 *kan*. The estimated value of grain in Table 16.2 (excluding sweet potato) reached 930 *kan*. Village headmen in the *saiban* estimated that 290 *kan* was spent for salt, clothing, lamp oil, bowls and dishes, and house repairs. Accordingly, 230 *kan* of the money was left over. If it is reasonable to assume that the price of nonrice food was 55 *momme* (10 *momme* = 1/100 *kan*) per *koku*, then that amount of money should have sufficed to purchase 0.7 *go* of such food daily per capita for all the people in the *saiban*. Adding this to 2.8 *go* in Table 16.2 (excluding the sweet potato equivalent of 0.3 *go*), the total comes to 3.5 *go* per capita per day.

Ōshima provides a more striking example. The *saiban* consisted of one big island and several uninhabited small islands, and population density was as high as 404 per km². Islanders worked as fishermen, sailors, and salt makers. These were all male occupations, and work was often available off the island: whaling in Ōtsu and Oku-Abu, salt manufacturing in Mitajiri and Kaminoseki, and sailing and shipping elsewhere pulled migrants out of Ōshima. The number of emigrants was approximately 3,400 in the *chūshin-an*, a figure equal to 12 percent of the adult males on the island. Such seasonal out-migration, usually extended over six months each year, obviously reduced the food demand on Ōshima. If these migrants are excluded when counting "grain" consumption, the average can be increased by 0.1 *go* per day per capita for the remainder of the population. Wives and daughters also wove cotton cloth: each adult female averaged 16 *tan* of cloth annually. The weaving was done through a system called *wata-gae*, by which 25 percent of the output was paid as the wage. Since the mean household size was a little higher than five, the islanders would have consumed 1 *tan* or less of cloth per year per capita.[13]

Profits from sake and salt manufacturing, and incomes from other occupations such as carpentry and thatching, were estimated to have

[12] *Kan* was originally a unit of measurement equivalent to 3.75 kg. Thus, sweet potato was generally measured in terms of *kan* in the *chūshin-an*. Silver money was also valued by weight. Domain notes issued by the *han* government and circulated within Chōshū were paper money representing silver. In the 1840s such a note was valued at 80 percent of silver money, while 1 *ryō* of gold was equivalent to both 61-64 *momme* (1 *momme* = 1/1,000 *kan*) of silver and 1 *koku* of rice in Osaka. Therefore, rice was priced at 75-85 *momme* in terms of domain notes.

[13] One *tan* denotes the amount of cloth used for making an adult's kimono. Cotton cloth is estimated to have been priced at 10 *momme* per *tan*. It should be kept in mind that the annual expenditure for clothing in Mae-Yamashiro was approximately 10 *momme* per capita.

been 1,700 *kan*. Adding in the profits of shippers and merchants, and the remittances of out-migrants, the total of these nonagricultural incomes was estimated at close to 3,000 *kan*.[14] On the other hand, nonstaple food expenditures on Ōshima were estimated by village headmen to be about 1,400 *kan*. Subtracting this from nonagricultural income leaves a 1,500-*kan* surplus. The authorized quantity of rice purchases was approximately 5,000 *koku* (Table 16.2), which cost only 500 *kan* even if the price of rice is assumed to have been 100 *momme* per *koku*—a price presumably higher than the contemporary price level (see fn. 12). Even the islanders, having 1,000 *kan*, could have bought 10,000 *koku* of rice; and even if they bought only 5,000 *koku*, the islanders' "grain" consumption per capita would have been 2.9 *go* per day. Thus, the proportion of rice would have been 33 percent, rather than the 27 percent in Table 16.2.

Finally, at least 10,000 and 4,000 *koku* of rice in Yamaguchi and Mine, respectively, were sold. Moreover, the people working and living in the salt-producing villages of Mitajiri were reported to have eaten exclusively rice "imported" from elsewhere in northeastern Japan. Thus, domestic and/or imported rice was supplied to the people in Chōshū who had enough money to buy it.

The rice market was well developed in Chōshū. Consequently, even the people in the *saiban* of Suō, seemingly in a state of food shortage, had access to at least 3.3 *go* of "grain" per day. Table 16.3 gives estimates for the amount of rice possibly available for food consumption by the people of Chōshū as well as for other uses. (Round numbers are used for the sake of simplicity.) Column A shows that 200,000 *koku* of rice remained on hand for farmers after deducting the annual rice tax (290,000 *koku*) and seed rice (30,000 *koku*). Column B shows a surplus of 90,000 *koku* after deducting rice exports (100,000 *koku*), samurai stipends (60,000 *koku*), and sake-brewing rice (40,000 *koku*) from the tax rice. The sum of the two balances, or 290,000 *koku*, remains as the quantity that could have been consumed by commoners.

The total number of samurai, vassals, rear vassals, and their families was approximately 50,000.[15] Samurai of low rank do not seem to have

[14] The significance of *nōkan yogyō* (part-time by-employment) is discussed in Osamu Saitō's chapter in this book. Particularly for Chōshū see Thomas C. Smith, "Farm Family By-employments in Preindustrial Japan," *Journal of Economic History*, vol. 29, no. 4 (December 1969), pp. 687-715, and Nishikawa Shunsaku and Ishibe Shōko, "1840 nendai Mitajiri saiban no keizai keisan," *Mita gakkai zasshi*, vol. 68, nos. 9 and 10 (September and October 1975), pp. 663-684 and 707-732.

[15] As of 1869, vassals and rear vassals numbered 5,700 and 6,200 respectively. Assuming that the mean family size was 4.25, i.e. the same as that for commoners, the total number of samurai and their family members becomes approximately 50,000.

TABLE 16.3
Possible Consumption of Rice by Commoners in Chōshū, 1840s
(10,000 *koku*)

	A	B	
Output[a]	52		
Tax[b]	−29	→ 29	
	23[b]	−10	Exported[a]
Used for seed[c]	−3	19	
	20	−6	Consumption by samurai and their families[c]
		13	
		−4	Used for sake[a]
		9	
Possible Consumption by Commoners[d] (20 + 9)	29		

NOTE: Numbers are rounded. See discussion in text.
[a] From Table 16.1.
[b] From Table 16.2.
[c] See text.
[d] Includes both paid and purchased rice. See Table 16.2.

been able to eat three meals of rice daily. Presumably there was not a large difference in food consumption between farmers and samurai in rural areas; barley and millet were mixed in with rice.[16] It is assumed here, however, that samurai consumed 60,000 *koku* of rice, eating 3 *go* per capita daily, since they were principally resident in the castle town, where rice eating is considered to have been prevalent.

[16] Samurai who failed to maintain their household in the castle town were permitted to live in rural districts in order to recover their economic health. Such samurai numbered about 900 in the 1840s. Also, a considerable portion of the 600 *ashigaru* (the lowest-rank samurai) and 3,600 rear vassals lived elsewhere, not only in the vicinity of Hagi but in other rural areas, for their service. Altogether, the samurai living in rural districts amounted to nearly one-third of all samurai at the time of the *chūshin-an*.

Inoue Kaoru's house was of the rank of 103 *koku*, and so his stipend was slightly more than 40 *koku* of rice. His de facto income, however, would have been about 20 *koku*, because 50 percent used to be "borrowed" by the daimyo. In his biography it is written, "the normal breakfast of Chōshū samurai was rice porridge with vegetables, lunch was [rice and] soup and pickles, and supper was [also rice and] soup and cooked vegetables. Fish on the table was seen only on the first, fifteenth, and twenty-eighth of the month." *Segai Inoue-kō den* (Tokyo: Hara shobō, 1968 reprint), vol. 1, p. 10.

If we assume that the remaining 90,000 *koku* in column B of Table 16.3 was consumed by commoners, as is likely, then the additional rice added to per capita consumption would raise the average value of 3.2 *go* in Table 16.2 to 3.7 *go* (including other crops). The figure of 3.7 *go* is larger by 0.4 *go* than the figure computed in Table 16.1, a difference stemming from the deletion of sweet potato in Table 16.1, the exclusion of samurai and their families, and rounding.[17] More precise calculation would yield a figure of 3.4 *go* or more, as shown in Table 16.8.

Calories and Nutrition in the 1840s and in 1887

Calories Per Capita Per Day and Protein Intake

Table 16.4 shows the amount of "grain" available for consumption in the 1840s and in 1887. The rice figure at the top is the amount remaining

TABLE 16.4
"Grain" Consumption in Chōshū/Yamaguchi, 1840s and 1887

	1840s		1887	
	Total[a] (metric tons)	Per Capita Per Day (*go*)	Total[a] (metric tons)	Per Capita Per Day (*go*)
Rice[b]	53,008	279	102,965	312
Barley and wheat	27,036	142	55,670	169
Millet	2,477	13	2,065	6
Buckwheat	3,310	17	3,585	11
Soybeans	2,663	14	4,387	13
Red beans	915	5	1,628	5
Sweet potato[c]	11,410	60	44,093	134

[a] Except for sweet potato, tonnage is converted from volumes shown in Table 16.1, according to the ratios in Umemura Mataji et al., *CKT 9: Nōringyō* (Tokyo: Tōyō keizai shimpōsha, 1966), app. table 1, p. 250.

[b] Excluding exported rice and rice used for seed or sake (see fn. 18).

[c] Converted from *kan* into metric tons.

[17] In Yamaguchi town, only barley was regarded as the staple food of the people. Also, in Shinden *mura* (which produced salt exclusively), Mitajiri, it is reported that the people ate rice imported from northeastern Japan. Chōshū *kaisen* (ship merchants) imported rice and exported salt and other products. The *han* itself earned profits and interest from short-

after export, seed, and sake brewing—what people could actually put into their stomachs.[18] The amounts for the other items are simply the weight equivalents of output shown in Table 16.1. Table 16.4 also shows consumption per capita per day. Note that the amount of rice increased from 279 to 312 g, an increase of about 12 percent. The rate of increase of barley and wheat was higher, 19 percent. In contrast, consumption of millet decreased. Soybeans remained relatively constant. Sweet potatoes doubled; however, the growth in sweet potato consumption shown here should be thought of as an overestimate since some output in the 1840s was excluded (see fn. 10).

Table 16.5 shows the caloric and nutritional value of the staple foods consumed per capita per day. The growth from 1,664 kcal in the 1840s to 1,902 kcal in 1887 is 14 percent. A growth in protein intake of more than 10 percent, from 45.3 to 49.9 g, can be seen. Particularly worthy of note is that 80 percent of that protein was obtained from rice, barley,

TABLE 16.5

Caloric and Nutritional Intake Per Capita Per Day from Staple Foods in Chōshū/Yamaguchi, 1840s and 1887

	1840s	1887
Calories (kcal)	1,663.7	1,902.3
Protein (g)[a]	45.3	49.9
Fats (g)	16.2	17.3
Carbohydrates (g)[b]	343.5	395.3
Ash (g)	8.2	9.5

NOTE: The caloric values and nutritional components are from *Nihon shokuhin hyōjun seibunhyō* (see fn. 9).

[a] In 1840, 35.7 g came from rice, barley, and wheat; in 1887, 41 g.

[b] Excluding fiber.

run commercial credit and warehouse business related to the *kaisen* (see William Wray's chapter in this book). If rice imports were substantial, then grain consumption by the people of Chōshū could well have exceeded 3.2 *go*. The amount of rice imported, however, is unknown.

[18] The amount of rice used for sake brewing in the 1840s is estimated to have been from 36,000 to 40,000 *koku*. I show the round figure of 40,000 *koku* in Table 16.1, but take the lower estimate, 36,000 *koku*, in this calculation, as I feel that the smaller amount is more plausible. Thus the volume of 353,389 *koku*, rather than the 349,389 *koku* derived from Table 16.1, is converted into weight equivalent in Table 16.4.

and wheat. The amount of protein from soybeans (not shown in Table 16.5) was far less than expected—5.9 g in the 1840s and 5.6 g in 1887. It is not likely that *tōfu* (bean curd) was imported from other domains or prefectures; nor is there any indication that soy sauce or *miso* (soybean paste) was imported in significant quantity. Soy, then, was consumed in the form of domestically produced *miso* and *tōfu*. But clearly the protein intake from rice, barley, and wheat was of utmost importance during the middle of the nineteenth century. It is conjectured that any deficit was made up by protein from fish. Intake of animal protein is not known, but that quantity is assumed to have been small, judging from what we know of the Meiji period. Finally, the 10 percent growth in protein intake means that there was a slight "improvement" in the makeup of staple foods consumed.

Carl Mosk and Simon Pak, using the annual series (1874-1940) of per capita consumption of twenty-two food items in *CKT* 6, computed for all of Japan the daily intake of calories, protein, and vitamins.[19] Table

TABLE 16.6

Caloric and Protein Intake in Japan, 1874-1892 (five-year average)

	1874-1877[a]	1878-1882	1883-1887	1888-1892
Calories (kcal)	1,530	1,699	1,811	1,948
Protein (g)	47.4	54.4	57.5	60.9

SOURCE: Mosk, "Fecundity, Infanticide, and Food Consumption in Japan" (see fn. 19), table 1.

[a] Four-year average.

[19] "Food Consumption, Physical Characteristics, and Population Growth in Japan, 1874-1940," *Working Paper* no. 102 (Berkeley: University of California, Department of Economics, 1977). The data are summarized in Carl Mosk, "Fecundity, Infanticide, and Food Consumption in Japan," *Explorations in Economic History*, vol. 15, no. 3 (July 1978), pp. 269-289, table 1 and app. Mosk saw a positive correlation between the crude birth rate, the Japanese physique, and nutritional intake, arguing that slow population growth in the Tokugawa period was an outcome of low fertility due to poor nutrition. As Akira Hayami notes in this book, Mosk criticizes the view that the slow population growth resulted from family limitation aimed at improving the standard of living.

The Mosk-Pak estimate does not cover the period before 1874; nor is any comparable evidence on nutrition presented for the Tokugawa years, or even for the *bakumatsu* period. My estimate for the 1840s seems identical to the Mosk-Pak 1878-1882 estimate with respect to calories, and roughly equals their 1874-1877 estimate with respect to protein. If this

16.6 shows the five-year average of calorie and protein intake during the relevant period. Since only "grain" was taken into account in my computation, larger differences might have been expected between the two sets of intake values; but Mosk and Pak's 1883-1887 estimates are not very different from my own, shown in Table 16.5. The Mosk-Pak estimate of caloric intake is lower than mine by 90 kcal (about 5 percent), while their estimate of protein intake is higher by about 8 g (15 percent). This comparison suggests that "grain" was the staple food for the people of Yamaguchi as well as for Japan generally, and that their supplementary food was quite limited both in quantity and in quality. In order to confirm this assertion, the caloric value of the "national" consumption of grain has been computed (see fn. 7). That figure comes to 1,894 kcal, though if sweet potato were added, consumption would exceed 2,000 kcal. There may be some overestimation owing to our ignorance of the quantity of nonrice crops reserved for seed, however.

Comparison of the Meiji Estimate with Military Rations

The next step is to compare the 1887 figures obtained in the foregoing section with data on army rations. The latter were studied by Mori Ōgai, an army doctor and an accomplished author as well.[20] According to Mori's survey, the actual rations at the Army Officers' School in Tokyo, in September/October 1883, were as follows: 643.3 g of rice and 107.3 g of fish and vegetables per day. Table 16.7 shows his calculations of the nutritional components of those rations. For the purpose of comparison, I have recomputed (Table 16.7) the nutritional components of 643.3 g of polished white rice on the basis of the nutritional content of modern rice. With the exception of the fat component, the nutritional value of the staple is almost in agreement with Mori's calculations, differing less than I had expected. The chief purpose of Mori's work, by the way, was

comparison were construed to mean that the people of Chōshū consumed the same amount and kind of staple foods—and accordingly experienced the same level and pattern of nutrition—from the 1840s to 1880, then both 1,600-1,700 kcal and 45-47 g of protein might seem to be the "critical values" for zero population growth. Nevertheless, the rate of population growth in Chōshū, including the territory of the branch domains, averaged 3 percent per decade from 1721 to 1846, the highest rate of all the provinces, while the national rate was a mere 0.3 percent.

[20] Mori Rintarō (Ōgai), "Nihon heishokuron tai-i," *Iji shimbun* (May 5, 1886) and "Japanische Soldaten Kost vom Voit' schen Punkt," *Archiv für Hygiene*, Bd. V (1886), S. 334u. ff., are reprinted in *Ōgai zenshū* (Tokyo: Iwanami shoten, 1974), vol. 28, pp. 11-18 and 560-577. "Heishōhen," *Kōshū iji*, vol. 3, nos. 4 and 5 (May 25 and June 25, 1897) is also reprinted in *Ōgai zenshū*, vol. 33, pp. 299-325. The pages referred to hereafter are those in the *Ōgai zenshū*.

TABLE 16.7
Caloric and Nutritional Intake
Per Capita Per Day from Military Rations, 1883

	Rice (643.3 g)		Supplementary Food (107.3 g) (Mori)	Total (Mori)
	Recomputed	Mori		
Calories (kcal)	2,264.4	—	—	—
Protein (g)	43.7	48.25	34.82	83.07
Fats (g)	8.4	2.10	11.57	13.67
Carbohydrates (g)	485.7	586.88	35.56	622.44
Fiber (g)	1.9	2.99	5.53	8.52
Ash (g)	3.9	3.08	19.86	22.95

NOTE: The data under "Mori" are from Mori Rintarō, "Nihon heishokuron" (see fn. 20). The recomputed figures are based on the caloric values and nutritional components in *Nihon shokuhin seibunhyō* (see fn. 9).

to oppose a change from the "indigenous" ration, based on a traditional Japanese diet, to one of Western-style food. He particularly stressed the fact that the actual amount of rice served in the Army Officers' School mess was always less than the daily ration of 6 *go* (approximately 1 kg) prescribed in the Military Ration Rule.

According to "Heishōhen," 643.3 g of rice is approximately 4.5 *go* since 144.3 g equals 1 *go* of rice.[21] If 6 *go* of rice had actually been served, that would have amounted to 1/20 of a soldier's body weight; for that much rice would have weighed 2.5 kg when boiled, as Mori noted in "Nihon heishokuron." The soldiers would soon have become obese. Mori's assertion was that 4.5 *go* of rice per day together with some suitable supplementary food was an adequate meal for the average Japanese soldier 162 cm in height and approximately 50 kg in weight.[22]

[21] Mori, "Nihon heishokuron," p. 16, where the following is written: "The amount of rice in the meals at the Army Officers' School does not reach 6 *go* because such dry weight is 643.3 g, which weighs 721.5 g before being cooked." The latter part of the sentence, however, should read: "which weighs *1,752 g after* being cooked." In "Japanische Soldaten," p. 570, Mori states: "Reis gekocht—1750 (584 × 3) frisch g—643.3 g getrocknet g" (but "1750" should read "1752"). There is a further explanation: "Die Menge des gekochten Reises betrug in either Mahlzeit (Mittel aus 10 Mahlzeiten) 584 g, und der Wassergehalt desselben (im Mittel vom 11 Untersuchungen) 63.24%."

[22] The height is clearly stated as 162 cm in "Japanische Soldaten," p. 577n, but the weight is not. This is assumed to be 50 kg on the basis of the description in "Nihon heishokuron," p. 16. However, data on "soldier physique" for 1888, in *Nihon teikoku*

His plan was to combine 650 g of rice with 220 g of fish, 200 g of *tōfu*, and 60 g of *miso*, as well as some vegetables, seasoning, and tea as the basis for a standard ration.

Mori writes in "Nihon heishokuron" that besides 6 *go* of rice, a cash allowance of 6 sen (100 sen = 1 yen) per day for enlisted men, 8 sen per day for cadets, was given for the purchase of "supplementary food" (i.e. protein sources and vegetables to be eaten with the "staple food," rice).[23] These figures were the basis for calculating a cash allotment to each military unit, whose mess officer actually purchased rice, vegetables, soy sauce, etc. from local merchants. Mori Ōgai's "Heishōhen" (1897) reports that the nutritional value of the daily ration at the Tokyo barracks was 2,580 kcal, 84.8 g of protein, 14.8 g of fats, and 533.7 g of carbohydrates (pp. 299-300), but he does not make clear what proportion of this was derived from the "staple" and how much from the "supplementary food." If we assume that the 1897 ration contained the same 643.3 g of rice as the 1883 ration, and that the caloric content of that rice was 2,264 kcal (Table 16.7), then the remaining 316 kcal must have been derived from the "supplementary food" purchased with the cash allowance, and with the cash left over because the mess actually served only 4.5 *go* of rice to each man—freeing 25 percent of the rice ration for the purchase of "supplementary food." At the average 1897 market price of 1.1 sen per *go*, this would yield an additional 1.65 sen per man per day for the purchase of "supplementary food." Even though this money plus the cash allowance for "supplementary food" also had to help pay for fuel for cooking and for heating bathwater, the remainder

---

daiku tōkeinenkan (1890), put average height and weight at 162 cm and a little over 60 kg. Because Mori states elsewhere that daily food intake is enough if it weighs from 1/20 to 1/25 of a man's body weight, then 60 kg seems correct. In any event, there is no change from the conclusion that 6 *go* of rice is too much.

According to the data from the draft medical examination to which Mosk refers in table 1 of his 1978 article (see fn. 19), the average height of the examinees was nearly 157 cm, which is 5 cm less than the average height of a soldier. A significant portion of the nation's youth (20 years old) were shorter than 156 cm and were therefore not conscripted.

[23] The first (ad hoc) "Rules of Military Salary and Rations"—applied to *han* troops in the Imperial Army during the Restoration War—prescribed 6 *go* of rice and one *shu* (1/16 of one *ryō*) of cash for "supplementary food." Later, the salary schedule was revised several times up to the 1880s, and the rations were changed slightly. See *Gunsei kōryō* and *Rikugunshō enkaku shi* in Yoshino Sakuzō et al., eds., *Meiji bunka zenshū*, vol. 23 (Tokyo: Nihon hyōronsha, 1930), pp. 25-93 and pp. 103-196. If 1 *ryō* costs 1 yen, then 1 *shu* costs 6.25 sen. I do not know why Mori ignored the quarter-sen in "Nihon heishokuron," p. 11. In "Heishōhen," p. 299, he states that the cash allowance in 1897 varied from 5.1 sen to 7.2 sen, depending on the location of the barracks; however, he does not give the exact amount prescribed to the men in the Tokyo barracks.

could have been spent to provide the additional 316 kcal per day per man.[24]

It is hard to believe that supplementary food for soldiers was so plentiful in the military diet. According to the weekly menus of the Fifth Artillery Division in Hiroshima, for November and December 1891, the supplementary food furnished was as follows: *miso* soup and pickles for breakfast; something boiled, broiled, or steamed at lunch; and something boiled, curry soup, or curry stew at night.[25] "Something boiled" refers to vegetables and potatoes cooked with soy sauce and sugar, known as *nikorogashi*. The "something broiled" was probably fish. It is recorded that some beef was included either as a side dish at supper or in curry soup or stew, but this cannot have amounted to much. Thus, the ingredients of curry rice must have been mostly potatoes and onions, basically the same as what is served in today's student cafeteria. Ōtsuka Tsutomu points out that according to the *Shokkō jijō* (1903) and Hosoi Wakizō's *Jokō aishi* (1925), the menu at the factory workers' dormitory at the end of the nineteenth century was much worse. For the most part, the supplementary food served to the factory workers consisted of pickles for breakfast and of "something boiled" or *miso* soup for supper. Rarely, dried fish was also served. Moreover, the factory worker's staple food was "Nanking rice," imported from Korea and China, which was not as appealing to the Japanese palate as native Japanese rice. Thus, the three meals a day of native white rice that the army provided must have seemed much better to the farmer-soldiers than their diet at home, or the diet of their contemporaries in the factories of mid-Meiji Japan.[26] The nutritional value of supplementary food—in the military, in the factory, even in the home—must have been quite low, however.

The caloric and nutritional ingredients obtained for 1887 do not include supplementary food. Even if some supplementary food were added, to judge from the above evidence, what the people of Chōshū had to eat then would have amounted to roughly 2,000 kcal per day per capita. The daily protein intake could not have been much better than 50 g. Was this really "sufficient"? Against Mori's standard of 2,580 kcal per day,

[24] Ōtsuka Tsutomu, "Heiji heishoku kō: Itaku keiri hōshiki o chūshin to shite," *Toita joshi tanki daigaku kenkyū kiyō*, no. 11 (1982), pp. 5-11.

[25] Ōtsuka Tsutomu, *Shoku ni okeru Nihon no kindaika*, UN University Project "Ningen to shakai no kaihatsu," Program Report HSDRJE-82J/UNUP-406 (Tokyo: Ajia keizai kenkyūsho, mimeo., 1982).

[26] Ōtsuka Tsutomu quotes a farmer in Nagatsuka Takashi's novel *Tsuchi* [The Soil] as evidence that the farmer could enjoy a better meal (i.e. more rice) in the military: "Guntai zu tokoro wa ii mon da de ganshita [Being in the military was good]." *"Shoku" no kindai shi* (Tokyo: Kyōikusha, 1981), p. 23.

it was insufficient by 500-600 kcal. This deficiency, of course, might increase up to as much as 1,000 kcal at times of heavy activity in wartime. Peasants, too, probably needed more calories, perhaps 3,500 kcal.[27] Moreover, the reader should remember that the estimates have been obtained by averaging all categories—old and young, women and children. The average number of calories consumed daily by a Japanese in the period 1911-1915 was 2,124 kcal; during 1970-1974, it was 2,500 kcal.[28] However, since the average size of a Japanese has increased rapidly since the end of World War II, the 2,500 kcal represent the average daily consumption of a larger person than in the 1911-1915 period. Taking everything into consideration, 2,000 kcal per day per capita was not a low nutritional standard in 1887. Further, the survey data do not include consumption of unrefined sake, consumed by farmers, which could have provided additional calories needed for hard labor.[29]

Comparisons of Food Consumption over Time

Table 16.8 shows a comparison of my estimates with the PSF data, both in terms of volume. The figures in column A are for an area comparable to Chōshū, excluding Toyora *gun* and Akamagaseki *ku* (present-day Shimonoseki), which were under branch *han* before 1868, as well as Mishima *gun*. The figures in column B are for all of Yamaguchi prefecture, which includes both Toyora and Akamagaseki. Columns A and B can be compared with the averages for the 1840s and 1887, respectively.[30]

[27] For 3,500 kcal per capita per day needed in wartime, see "Heishōhen," p. 306. For additional calories needed by cultivators, see Kōshū eisei shingikai, *Nihonjin no eiyō shoyōryō: Shōwa 54-nen kaitei* (Tokyo: Kōseishō, 1979), "Table of Additional Requirement by Work Intensity."

[28] Kagawa Yoshiko et al., "Nihonjin no eiyō," in Nōsei kenkyū sentā, ed., *Shōwa 55-nen shokuryō hakusho* (Tokyo: Tōkyō kansho fukyū K.K., 1980), table 1-1-10.

[29] Shinohara Miyohei, *CKT 6: Shōhi shishutsu* (Tokyo: Tōyō keizai shimpōsha, 1967), suggests this possibility. Shinohara refers to what Kamiya Keiji heard from an elderly farmer in the Tōhoku (northeastern Japan), viz. that he used to supplement his caloric intake with unrefined sake, particularly during hard labor such as plowing. Mosk and Pak include sake (refined) among their twenty-two food items, estimating that sake contributed about 2 percent to caloric intake throughout the late nineteenth century. See their *Working Paper* (fn. 19, above). It is said that unrefined sake had much more caloric value than refined sake, and some portion of the rice consumed in the commoner household presumably was used to brew unrefined sake.

[30] The correspondence between *gun* (county) and *saiban* is rather crude. Roughly speaking, one *gun* comprises two *saiban* (see Map 16.1). Mishima *gun* (Hamazaki *saiban* in the old days) is excluded from the 1886 data in Table 16.8. Logically, Mishima should be included in the 1886 data when these are compared with the data for 1887, which include

TABLE 16.8
Comparison of Staple Food Proportions in Chōshū/Yamaguchi, 1840s and 1886-1887
(%)

	1840s[a]	1886[b]		1887[a]
		A	B	
Rice	54.0	51.5	53.6	53.8
Barley and wheat	29.9	31.0	29.7	31.6
Millet etc.[c]	12.6	11.3	10.8	7.6
Sweet potato etc.[d]	3.5	6.2	6.0	6.9
Volume per capita per day[e]	(3.44 *go*)	—	—	(3.87 *go*)

NOTE: Column A (Chōshū) omits Toyora *gun* and Akamagaseki *ku* (present-day Shimonoseki) which were branch *han* until 1868, as well as Mishima *gun*. Column B (Yamaguchi) includes both Toyora *gun* and Akamagaseki *ku*, but omits Mishima *gun*. Figures for 1886 and 1887 preserve rounding errors found in the original data, and thus do not total 100 percent.

[a] Same sources as Table 16.1.

[b] From *Yamaguchi ken daiyonkai kangyō nempō* (1889).

[c] Buckwheat, soy, and red beans included.

[d] Seaweed is included in the 1886 figures, but the quantities are very limited.

[e] For 1840s, rice and barley constitute 2.89 *go*; for 1887, 3.30 *go*.

Between the 1840s and 1886 (column A) the proportion of rice decreased by about 2 percent, whereas the proportion of sweet potato increased by the same amount. But the output of sweet potato in the *chūshin-an* is somewhat undervalued (see fn. 10). Comparing 1886 and 1887, one sees a 3-percentage-point decrease in "millet etc."—possibly because the *hie* (barnyard millet) output for 1887 was half that for the 1840s (or the 1887 output statistics may be in error).[31] Sweet potato proportions are approximately the same: 6.2 percent in 1886 and 6.9 percent in 1887. These two comparisons tell us that the PSF data were

Mishima. (The proportions for Mishima were as follows: rice, 10%; barley, 30%; millet, 20%; sweet potato, 30%; and seaweed, 10%.) If these were included, however, the 1886 figures would be skewed, since the 1886 figures are only simple averages over counties. The 1887 figures, on the other hand, are the weighted averages by population of each county. But since Mishima had a population of only about 2,000 in 1880, the 1887 figures are not seriously skewed.

[31] According to the *chūshin-an*, some portion of *hie* was used for fodder, especially during the plowing season. However, even if we exclude *hie* from our calculation of the human diet, a small discrepancy remains between the data for the 1840s and those for 1887.

calculated in terms of volume, with sweet potato converted into millet equivalent by some "traditional" ratio.[32]

It is not surprising to see that the proportions in 1886 (column B) and 1887 resemble each other; they are for consecutive years. That the proportions in the 1840s and in 1886-1887 are very similar, however, is surprising. The rice proportions are in agreement with each other at the high level of 54 percent—high, that is, when compared with the 30 percent estimate by Ono Takeo for the late Tokugawa period (see fn. 1). Since that survey did not concern itself with Chōshū, a direct comparison may be unwarranted; however, the 1886 national average was 53 percent. If Chōshū was close to the average then, there is reason to expect that its remarkable stability from the 1840s to 1886-1887 also applied to the nation as a whole.

From the 1840s on, the proportion of rice, along with the proportion of meat, increased steadily. It is estimated that by 1925 the proportion of rice eventually went beyond 70 percent of all grain consumption.[33] This being the case, recollections of the situation during the *bakumatsu* period, as reported in Ono's survey, might well exaggerate its misery. The proportion of rice estimated by Ono was significantly lower than the level that actually existed. If rice actually consumed had been at about 30 percent, there would have been a surplus, and rice would have piled up year after year. Another explanation—the one I find most plausible—for this difference of more than 20 percent might be that Ono had asked about the contents of the respondent's "usual" diet. People used to have rice or rice cakes as a "special" diet during village shrine festivals, temple pilgrimages, weddings and funerals, and *sekku* holidays such as New Year's Day and Children's Day, as is noted in the calender of village life in the *chūshin-an*. An alternative explanation is that Ono's survey covered only the diet of peasants and tenant farmers.

Diet Adequacy and the Timing of Its Improvement

Nowadays, no one would consider the diet of a nineteenth-century Japanese to be adequate. According to the 1980 White Paper on Food[34] the 1972-1974 intake of calories and protein in India was 1,971 kcal and

[32] Similar (though probably not identical) traditional ratios might have been used in other prefectures.

[33] This figure is an average over 1892-1924, showing the proportion of the caloric intake from rice to the total caloric intake from all "grain." *Shōwa 55-nen shokuryō hakusho* (see fn. 28), table 1-1-9.

[34] Ibid., table 1-1-1.

48.1 g per capita per day, respectively, while the per capita national income was only U.S. $135 in 1976. Comparable figures in Japan (for 1974) were 2,490 kcal, 79.5 g, and U.S. $4,478. Obviously, the higher the per capita national income, the better the food and nutrition. Even so, it is misleading to argue, by extrapolating this relationship backward, that in the nineteenth century the Japanese people were pressed below the subsistence level. The proportion of rice in the diet was clearly more than 50 percent by volume. In the early twentieth century, rice would supply 70 percent of the caloric intake from grain. As far as protein intake is concerned, it amounted to 57.6 g per capita per day in 1911-1915 and grew to 68.5 g in 1920-1924, remaining constant (or declining slightly) until 1960-1964. It was not until after World War II that the Japanese began to eat many dairy products and a great deal of fish. Until that time, most of their protein had been obtained from rice, barley, and wheat, rice being the favorite food. A diet providing 1,700-1,900 kcal and 45-50 g of protein might keep the physique of the Japanese people within certain limits, but was not insufficient for the Japanese of that era.

Something should be said about the timing and the reasons for the 240-kcal increase in caloric intake. An earlier investigation suggests that per capita material product in Chōshū/Yamaguchi from the 1840s to 1874 did not change and may even have declined a little.[35] It began to grow, at the earliest, in 1874 (probably later). The annual rate of growth of per capita material product in Yamaguchi prefecture was only 1.5 percent during 1874-1909, which was lower than the national figure (1.7 percent). Growth in Yamaguchi *ken* was produced by growth in agriculture, not by industrialization. In particular, it was the result of improvement in rice cultivation. During 1881-1896 the land under cultivation and the output of rice grew at a rate of 2.2 percent and 4 percent per annum, respectively; the corresponding rates were only 1.1 percent and 2.4 percent during 1894-1910. This made it possible for grain consumption to increase in the 1880s. In 1873, the land tax reform was undertaken. The governor of Yamaguchi prefecture, Nakano Goichi—once a *hatamoto* (Tokugawa vassal) and chosen by Inoue Kaoru as the right person to manage Chōshū's delicate state of affairs—launched the project early, according to Inoue's suggestion, and finished the reform in advance of other prefectures.[36] Nakano set a lower land tax than elsewhere, thereby stimulating investment in agriculture.

[35] Nishikawa, "Chōshū/Yamaguchi ken no sangyō hatten" (see fn. 6).

[36] Misaka Keiji, *Yamaguchi ken no rekishi* (Tokyo: Yamakawa shuppansha, 1971), pp. 237-239. For a discussion of the land tax reform, see Les Mitchnick, "Traditional and Transitional Tax Systems duing the Early Modern Period: A Case Study of Chōshū Han, 1600-1873" (University of California, Los Angeles, Ph.D. diss., 1972), chaps. 4-6.

The opening of Japan and the inauguration of foreign trade brought some unfavorable influences to the Chōshū/Yamaguchi economy and its industrialization. Neither tea nor cocoons, not even silk, was produced, and Chōshū/Yamaguchi farmers tended to rely on rice as their sole cash crop. Shimonoseki was not opened for overseas trade, and this oriented the economy exclusively toward domestic trade. The shogunate's devaluation of silver (against gold) in 1859—in order to stop an outflow of gold immediately after the opening of the ports—triggered galloping inflation. The daimyo had kept at least 60,000 *kan* of money in his storehouse, more than 70 percent of which was "transferred" to the Meiji government at the time of *haihan chiken*. The remaining money was kept in the prefectural coffers, yet those assets had been so substantially depreciated that they were later inadequate for investment in industry.[37]

The exodus of such talented individuals as Inoue Kaoru, Itō Hirobumi, and Yamagata Aritomo to the central government, and of other persons to business and commerce outside of Chōshū/Yamaguchi, was still another deterrent to industrialization in Yamaguchi *ken*. Inoue, Itō, Yamagata, and others would have liked to see the local economy develop, but they were more concerned with the national economy. Instead of building a state enterprise, military arsenal, or dockyard in this area, the central government placed them in Hiroshima *ken*, which is next to Yamaguchi *ken*. Slower industrialization meant slower growth of the prefectural economy and slower improvement in the standard of living. It is likely that both food consumption and nutrition in Yamaguchi *ken* lagged behind progress in the nation as a whole during the following years.

In the 1840s and 1880s, this area of Japan probably did not lag much behind other areas with respect to diet, but it was most likely not ahead of them either. Above all, what the foregoing analysis of local data shows is the adequacy of the diet and its long-term stability over a critical half-century of transition.

[37] Shunsaku Nishikawa, "Protoindustrialisation in the Domain of Chōshū in the Eighteenth and Nineteenth Centuries," *Keio Economic Studies*, vol. 18, no. 2 (1981), pp. 13-26.

CHAPTER 17

THE MATERIAL CULTURE: STABILITY IN TRANSITION

BY SUSAN B. HANLEY

The changes that occurred in the first few decades after the Meiji Restoration were so profound that they led one foreign observer to introduce his book on Japan with the statement: "To have lived through the transition stage of modern Japan makes a man feel preternaturally old; for here he is in modern times . . . and yet he can himself distinctly remember the Middle Ages."[1] What struck the foreign observers, the Japanese themselves, as well as later historians, about Meiji Japan were the developments that portended tremendous change for all Japanese—not only in the political, economic, and social spheres, but also in everyday life. We are left with the overwhelming impression that life in the Meiji period was very different from life just a few decades earlier before the fall of the Tokugawa *bakufu*.

But how much change did the ordinary Japanese face in his everyday life? Did a farmer or even a city resident find his life style transformed within a few decades as did virtually all Japanese in the quarter-century following the end of World War II? The emphasis in nearly all studies of the Meiji period is on change—political, economic, intellectual, institutional, technological, and cultural. These studies, and textbooks too, infer that such change occurred in every other aspect of life as well. Is the generalization accurate? Or does the lack of research and information on everyday life signify that most Japanese experienced a smooth transition from one way of life to another? Does it mean that life changed very little for most families during the transition years, despite rapid changes in other spheres of life?

[1] Basil Hall Chamberlain, *Things Japanese*, p. 1; reprinted as *Japanese Things* (Rutland, Vt.: Charles E. Tuttle, 1971).

Implicit in this question of whether life styles were changing is whether the standard of living was rising. This is a far more controversial question, and one more difficult to answer. Corollary to the question of the standard of living is that of quality of life, whether living conditions were improving and life was getting better in ways that would not be reflected in the standard of living. While one cannot avoid discussion of quality of life and standard of living in analyzing life styles, the focus of this chapter will be on changes in the way of life, particularly as measured in the material goods used in daily life—ranging from small domestic items in the home, including food and clothing, to consumer durables such as housing and furniture, to the utility derived from capital goods such as rickshaws and streetcars. Taken together, these constitute the material culture of a society. A study of the history of material culture is roughly comparable to what the Japanese consider *seikatsu shi*, of which the primary components are *i-shoku-jū*, or clothing, food, and housing.

Here, in an attempt to take a first step toward evaluating what life was like for most Japanese in the transition years from *bakumatsu* through the end of the nineteenth century, I will first examine the material culture of Japan. Then, I will point out evolving new life styles and briefly try to assess the standard of living and quality of life. In conclusion, I will look at what significance the changes or lack of change held for the Japanese who lived through the transition years.

Before proceeding, however, an important caveat is in order. Owing to space limitations and the analyses offered elsewhere in this book (notably the Hayami, Nishikawa, and Yamamura chapters), I have strictly limited the focus of this essay. Those who study material culture and life styles, and all their ramifications, find that it is nearly impossible to delimit these topics. The demographic aspects, changing levels of real income, changes in the sectoral composition of the economy, annual fluctuations in economic performance, social structure, and values, as well as a host of other subjects, ideally should be covered in dealing with life styles and the standard of living, but of necessity I leave these for the future.

The Material Culture of Japan, 1850-1900

The material culture at the starting point of this transition period was clearly that of the late Tokugawa period prior to any significant influence resulting from the renewed foreign contacts. The end date is halfway between the Sino-Japanese and Russo-Japanese wars of late Meiji. Neither 1850 nor 1900 has any significance in itself in terms of life style; rather, each represents two to three decades on either side of the Restoration. The starting point is far enough back in time to be representative of life before any significant changes occurred that could be associated with the Restoration, and the end date is far enough into the Meiji period to be able to analyze changes that had occurred since the Restoration.

We will begin by analyzing the three elements—housing, food, and clothing—and then move on to other aspects of the material culture relevant to these years. Among the major components of material culture, housing is certainly the item that changed least during the transition years.

Housing

A house is the most expensive good most families acquire, and in Japan a typical wooden house is considered to last about a generation. Thus innovations in housing would be only very slowly diffused throughout society, and people would be cautious about adopting new building styles and techniques that would be expensive and difficult to modify. By the same token, any small change in housing can be considered significant and noteworthy. Also, any shift in the quality or style of housing during the half-century under study should have been evident by 1900.

Early Meiji architecture clearly reflected Tokugawa styles. There were three major types of housing prevalent in the Tokugawa period: 1) samurai housing that grew out of the *shoin-zukuri* style; 2) farmhouses, with wide regional differences but all having the same basic functions; and 3) townhouses built for artisans and shopkeepers in the densely populated cities.

Farmhouses were the most numerous, for probably 80 percent of the population lived in farm villages or hamlets. Most were built of wood with thatched roofs, but types varied regionally according to climatic differences, availability of building materials, and styles dating from centuries back. By the Tokugawa period, houses in western Japan, especially in the warmer regions, tended to be single-family dwellings, usually from two to four rooms in size. In contrast, houses in the colder, northern regions tended to be large and to house servants and animals as well as the family. It is the larger, grandiose farmhouses that have tended to be preserved, but these can by no means be considered typical housing for the average Japanese. It is the atypical, special item that is preserved for the future, not the things of everyday life that are considered ordinary or that wear out quickly. This bias must be kept constantly in mind when studying the artifacts of material culture.

The various regions of Japan are proud of their unique architectural styles, particularly roofing, but to the foreigner who is not an expert in architecture, housing is seen to be part of a larger pattern and, in fact, is similar in many aspects to farmhouses of Germany, Austria, Switzerland, Italy, and the Balkans.[2] This is not to deny the importance of the regional variations, but to stress the common features of Japanese farm dwellings.

All farmhouses had a dirt floor area (*doma*) to the front or one side for use as a work area and as a kitchen. This area was often the location for the toilet and the well, and was also used for storage, for bathing, and as the entryway to the rest of the house. The family horse might be stabled in a room in this part of the house. Originally, the entire Japanese house was at ground level; but by the Tokugawa period many farmers had flooring (either boards or tatami or a combination of both) in the rest of the house. How prevalent flooring was is not known, since people either added floors when they had the funds to do so or rebuilt. Even up to World War II, it was still possible in remote villages to find houses in which there was no raised flooring. In such houses, the division between the *doma* and the sleeping area was a high sill, which kept the husks and other materials used on the floor from spilling over into the dirt area. On top of the husks and straw were straw mats, and this area was used for sitting and sleeping. Although the use of tatami dates from medieval Japan, in a village in Bitchū (Okayama) during the *bakumatsu* years more than 60 percent of the houses had no tatami—and this in an area famous for its rush! But by this period all houses in this village had at least one room with a raised wooden floor.[3]

A second type of house was the townhouse, built on a long and narrow lot, and typically three rooms deep (or six rooms, in twos side by side). Frontage on the street for access to customers was at a premium, which accounts for the shape of the lots. The room on the street served as the shop, and the two rooms behind it were for entertaining guests and for family life. To the side of these rooms ran a narrow, dirt-floored passage from the street through to the back, where there was often an open space for work and a building for storage. The kitchen was located in this passage. The most common pattern seems to have been to have a half-story on top of the first, used either for storage or as a place for servants to sleep. There were regional variations, but the pattern was similar.

The third and best-known type of Tokugawa housing was that of the samurai. These were detached houses whose lots and size befitted the status of the owner. Samurai housing always had both a formal entrance

[2] Bruno Taut, *Houses and People of Japan* (London: John Gifford, 1937), pp. 106-107.

[3] Fujisawa Shin, "Bakumatsuki nōson ni okeru kaisōbetsu jūtaku kōzō ni tsuite," *Okayama daigaku kyōiku gakubu kenkyū shūroku*, vol. 21 (1966), p. 54.

leading to the guest rooms and a service entrance into the dirt-floored work area, used primarily as the kitchen. Family rooms were often in between these two areas. Guest rooms had tatami flooring and overlooked gardens, however small. Samurai housing grew out of the *shoin-zukuri* style of architecture, and there was usually at least a *tokonoma* in even the smallest house. Other than the foregoing, there was usually no set pattern of rooms inside the structure as there was with farmhouses and townhouses.

Features common to samurai housing by the late Tokugawa period were *engawa* (a wooden extension of the floor under the eaves and overlooking garden areas), tatami in all the main living areas, *fusuma* (sliding paper doors) between rooms, and *shōji* (translucent, paper-covered sliding doors) at the sides of rooms to let in the light. Formal reception rooms for guests could be entered from outside and used without impinging on or disclosing family quarters or work areas.

There were obviously other kinds of housing, such as the long, one-story city tenements (*nagaya*) or huts belonging to the rural poor; but architects are not interested in these, and few examples have been preserved. In the *nagaya*, which opened off into back alleys, a family lived in one small room, with a small dirt-floored entry that served as a kitchen. Wells and toilets were shared by the tenants. These "apartments" were so tiny that much of one's life must have been lived outside the house, especially in the open space between buildings. Their size also accounts for the popularity of cheap entertainment in urban areas, both in the Tokugawa and the Meiji periods, because families would have been too cramped to spend much time together in the single room.

The new, Western-style buildings constructed in Tokyo and other cities during the Meiji period attracted much attention, but these were few in number and were considered more of an exotic import than an example to be followed in domestic architecture. The brick buildings of the Ginza were damp, and their closed fronts were considered bad for business. The Iwasaki family of Mitsubishi built a splendid mansion in Hongo, but this was primarily for show, and the family lived in a Japanese-style section. Only the very rich built Western-style rooms in the Meiji period; a house with a Western parlor was the rare exception until the Taisho period.

Changes in housing during the Meiji period were of two major types: diffusion of innovations from the Tokugawa period, or earlier, and modification of traditional housing styles by using modern materials (e.g. glass instead of paper). Since architectural history emphasizes innovation, it is easy to forget that the development of a new style or technique does not mean that it will necessarily be adopted throughout the population.

The middle- and lower-level samurai pattern of housing was adopted by the growing number of salaried workers in the Meiji period and later. In fact, the samurai style was adopted intact; not only was the *tokonoma* incorporated, but often the *chigaidana* (uneven decorative shelves) and the *tsukeshoin* (built-in desk).[4] This meant that government officials and a wide variety of white-collar workers, none of whom had to live at or near their place of work, were building houses and living like samurai. Naturally, many in this group must have been former samurai.

It is difficult to estimate how prevalent the various types of housing were in the nineteenth century, but an 1871 survey of 24,446 houses in Kanazawa shows that 20.2 percent had a *genkan* (formal entry), 18.8 percent were entered through a *doma* (and were therefore basically of farmhouse-style), and 61 percent were of the long, narrow type with a side passageway to the rear. This would represent the proportion of houses of each type in the *bakumatsu* years for a major castle town. A much smaller sample of Kanazawa houses, built later in the Meiji period, indicates that 28.9 percent had *genkan*, only 12.6 percent were of farmhouse style, and only 51.8 percent were now built with a *tōriniwa* (passage).[5]

While the urban middle classes were switching to samurai-style housing as their occupations and life styles gradually changed, other Japanese were also gradually adopting various features from the elite housing of the Tokugawa period. As people in the countryside could afford to do so, they built wooden floors where there had previously been dirt, or installed tatami where previously there had been wood. The open hearth near the center of the house had served as the only source of heat, both for cooking and for protection against the cold, and sometimes was the only source of light in the house. With the development of ceramics hard enough to serve as hibachi and with an increased supply of charcoal, other rooms could be used for living space in the winter months, in particular for receiving guests. New sources of light in the Meiji period were kerosene and oil lamps, which gave off better light to work or read by than rapeseed oil.

The *engawa*, developed in the Tokugawa period, became an increasingly common feature of Meiji housing, and this extended the living space, provided another area for talking to visitors without having to receive them formally into the house, and resulted in lighter interiors. Now inner rooms were completely free from rain, even with the outside wooden

[4] Hirai Kiyoshi, *Nihon jūtaku no rekishi* (Tokyo: Nihon kōsō shuppan kyōkai, 1974), p. 174.

[5] Shimamura Noboru, *Jūtaku kan no rekishi sei/fūdo sei ni kansuru kenchiku keikakuteki kenkyū* (private printing, 1979), p. 65. What type the other 6.7 percent were is unknown.

doors removed, and yet protected from the direct rays of the summer sun. But what really lightened houses was the increased use of shoji and the development of glass "shoji." Many people who could not afford glass or new paper, covered the frames with used paper, and even in the 1980s—to the horror of historians—documents from the Meiji period and even earlier are used to paper shoji in the countryside.

A major feature of commoners' houses in the Tokugawa period was that they were dark and dirty. The *doma* was simply a packed dirt floor; the smoke from the hearth was let out of the house through a hole or holes in the roof, but much of it became soot attached to the roof beams and walls. There was little daylight in the house, particularly if the family could not afford shoji, for whatever light there was came through sliding wooden doors that could be opened up on good days. Townhouses, crowded in closely and using every inch of space, were especially dark. Since there was so little light in the house (almost none in some of the inner rooms) dirt was not apparent, and the custom of cleaning thoroughly once or twice a year was often more of a ritual than what Westerners think of as spring housecleaning. If the sleeping and sitting area of the house was composed of mats on top of hulls or straw, there would have been no satisfactory way to clean without taking everything out and putting in fresh materials. People used the innermost room (the *nando*)[6] both for sleeping and for storing household goods, and it must have been the darkest room in the house. It must also have been very unsanitary—according to Yanagita,[7] who usually put the best interpretation he could on Japanese customs—particularly after Japanese started using cotton for bedding, which would get damp, musty, and sweaty and, being stuffed with cotton batting, would be impossible to clean thoroughly without taking it apart.

Thus, any change in Meiji toward creating lighter houses, raised off the ground, would result in cleaner houses, better sanitation, and more sunlight for occupants who were not working in the fields all day long.[8] But these developments were slow in coming and were not the result of

[6] The innermost room was called the *nema* (sleeping room) or *nando* (storage room). Although origins are obscure, the use of both terms to designate the same room suggests that it served a dual function.

[7] Yanagida [Yanagita] Kunio, comp. and ed., *Japanese Manners & Customs in the Meiji Era* (Tokyo: Ōbunsha, 1957), p. 60.

[8] It was discovered in the outskirts of Ashikaga *shi*, Tochigi *ken*, after World War II that people who lived in houses that did not face south had a significantly higher rate of lung disease, including bronchitis and tuberculosis. Gradually, these houses were rebuilt on lower ground to allow more sunlight to penetrate the rooms.

Western imports or Meiji innovations; they are explained instead by the wider diffusion of what had been developed during the Tokugawa period.

Food

Contrary to expectation, it is extraordinarily difficult to determine exactly what or how much people were eating during either the Tokugawa or the Meiji period. Although it is possible to find out the kinds of foods people consumed, there is no way of knowing how much of each kind was eaten or what the daily caloric intake was. People do not make note of the obvious. Thus, there are few accurate records, and none representative, of what people ate on a daily basis. As Nishikawa has demonstrated in his chapter in this book, asking the elderly what they ate when they were young does not yield information that can in any way be considered accurate.

Clearly the staple in the diet was grain. As Kitō Hiroshi has pointed out, there are two common beliefs regarding the role of rice in the diet that are basically contradictory: one is that rice has been the staple in the Japanese diet since the Yayoi period; the other is that the common people in the Tokugawa period were too poor to eat rice.[9] The truth probably lies somewhere between these two bits of common wisdom. Using rice output and population, Nishikawa (see Chapter 16) estimates that in Chōshū during the 1840s and in 1886-1887, rice constituted 54 percent of the staple, the rest having been composed of barley, wheat, millet, and sweet potatoes. This is just above the national average of 53 percent for 1886. Kitō would put the proportion of rice in the diet for the second half of the Tokugawa period at 60 percent. But clearly this does not mean that everyone ate a mixture of 60 percent rice and 40 percent other grains for every meal. Consequently, who ate how much rice is still open to question.

Clearly the elite was eating rice. The fourteenth shogun, Iemochi, died in 1866 at age 21, and his wife died eleven years later at age 32. Both are said to have died of beriberi. It is clear that the diet of the shogun and his family was not well balanced. Not only was white rice their staple food item, but because of various superstitions and erroneous information on their part, they refrained from eating such foods as onions, seaweed, and apples.[10] However, ordinary people did not have the money to be choosey about what they ate; the common wisdom was "Hara fukure-

[9] Kitō Hiroshi, "Edo jidai no beishoku," *Rekishi kōron*, no. 89 (April 1983), pp. 43-39.

[10] Watanabe Minoru, *Nihon shoku seikatsu shi* (Tokyo: Yoshikawa kōbunkan, 1964), p. 227ff.

reba, koto tareri" (All that matters is to have a full stomach).[11] But clearly the preference was for polished rice. As people obtained more money, they increased the proportion of rice in their diet; for those who could not afford to eat it on a daily basis, rice became a treat reserved for special days and festivals.

During both the Tokugawa and the Meiji period, the staple consumed varied by region. In the westernmost parts of Japan, people ate a higher proportion of *mugi* (wheat and barley) and sweet potatoes, while people in the mountainous areas ate more millet and *hie* (deccan grass). Only on the plains lying along the Japan Sea coast—Akita, Yamagata, Niigata, Toyama, Ishikawa, etc.—was rice the staple.[12] Although Nishikawa's evidence indicates that rice constituted about the same proportion of the diet in the 1840s as in the 1880s, it is likely that more people were eating polished rice as the technology to polish rice became available. Evidence for this comes from a rise in the incidence of beriberi, the cause of which was not known until the early twentieth century. The Japanese thought that the increased incidence of this disease during the late nineteenth century was related to the influx of people from the countryside to the urban centers, that these migrants brought whatever caused it with them and spread it to their new neighbors. The incidence of beriberi was highest in the largest cities and in the areas surrounding them. Obviously, in retrospect, the cause was an increase in the eating of polished rice, resulting in thiamine deficiencies. Ironically, the new technology and the higher standard of living necessary to support a diet of polished rice resulted for beriberi victims in a lower quality of life and a shortened life expectancy.

Despite the attention given to the new custom of eating meat and to the foreign-style restaurants that were opened in the Meiji period, for most Japanese the diet varied little from that of the Tokugawa period. One reason for the lack of change is that housewives, who were responsible for both the purchase and the preparation of food, ate out very seldom and therefore had little opportunity to learn what the new foods were; or if they did hear of them, they had no idea how to prepare them. Conversely, most of the dietary changes during the early Meiji years had their origins in the Tokugawa period.

Most striking was the transition from a vegetarian diet to one that included some meat. Although meat was reintroduced into the diet in the nineteenth century, most Japanese ate very little meat until after World War II. Here it should be noted that while the reintroduction of meat

[11] Ōtsuka Tsutomu, "*Shoku*" *no kindai shi* (Tokyo: Kyōikusha, 1979), p. 112.

[12] Watanabe, *Nihon shoku seikatsu shi*, p. 283.

into the Japanese diet was the result of Western influence, it did not stem from the coming of the Westerners in the *bakumatsu* years, but rather from the recommendations of scholars studying the West at least half a century earlier. Sumo wrestlers, outcastes, and undoubtedly others were consuming meat throughout the Tokugawa period, but those who did were by and large at the bottom of the Tokugawa social order.

Meat began to appear in specialty shops in the early years of the nineteenth century, having been promoted by scholars of Dutch learning as beneficial to the health. But the kinds of meat sold were wild boar, deer, badger, and monkey,[13] all of which would be considered gamey by even the most ardent of meateaters in the West; and, even considering its scarcity, it must have been eaten because it was a fad, rather than because people liked it. Although during the Rokumeikan period it was said that one could not really be cultured unless one ate meat, it is clear from the recipes developed that the Japanese did not really like the taste. It is virtually impossible to taste the meat in curry rice. Soy sauce camouflages the taste of beef in sukiyaki, and again very little meat is needed for this dish.

Among the Tokugawa changes in the Japanese diet that were most widely diffused during the Meiji period were increases in the drinking of tea, the eating of fruit, the use of sugar and soy sauce, and the custom of dining out. Mixed, unpolished grain has more flavor than white rice, and through the Tokugawa period, *miso* (along with pickles) was generally sufficient as a seasoning, as well as serving as a source of protein and other nutritional essentials. But with increased use of polished rice, the demand for soy sauce rose. (The progenitor of soy sauce was a sauce developed in the late Muromachi period and is considered to have been Western in origin.) During the Tokugawa period, there was no clear distinction between *hishio* (a kind of *miso*) and *shōyu* (soy sauce).[14] Thus Yanagita asserts that soy sauce is a Meiji development,[15] although what really occurred was a gradual change in processing.

Many of the new food items associated with the modernization of Japan were first introduced long before the Meiji period. The Dutch were responsible for introducing the Japanese to many new plants, some of which were food items or seasonings, in the eighteenth and early nineteenth centuries. These included asparagus, lima beans, and marjoram in the eighteenth century, and peppermint and sage in the nineteenth.

[13] Ibid., p. 268.

[14] Ibid., p. 202.

[15] Yanagida [Yanagita], *Japanese Manners & Customs*, p. 38.

Lemons were brought to Japan in the *bakumatsu* years, certainly before 1864, but Japan was never able to grow these as successfully as the United States, from which they were imported. Red kidney beans were also introduced during the *bakumatsu* years, but they were used for food only in the north; in the warmer west, the plants would not bear fruit and so were cultivated for their flowers. These introductions, however, did not become an integral part of the Japanese diet in the nineteenth century and were more a curiosity than anything else.[16]

Thus, in the Meiji period, as in the decades and centuries preceding it, the dietary staple was grain, rice being the preferred grain. The purpose of side dishes was to enhance the taste of the staple grain; they were not considered basic foods themselves. A meal was often referred to as *gohan*, or rice; and even today rice is considered the center of the meal as meat is in the United States, even though today the nutritional balance of a meal in Japan may be similar to a Western one. The staple was either a mixture of rice with some other grain, rice alone, or one or more grains other than rice, though it seems from various references and diaries that the first possibility was probably the customary everyday meal for both commoner and lower-level samurai households.

The pattern for ordinary meals was often referred to as *ichijū issai*, which means one soup and one vegetable, and which in fact would most likely refer to a meal consisting of rice, *miso shiru* (bean paste soup), and pickles. This type of meal was eaten by the samurai class in the Kamakura period; then the richer merchants adopted it and, after them, the townspeople in general, including laborers. Ōtsuka Tsutomu argues that this level of diffusion was reached in the Tokugawa period, and it was only during the Meiji period that most Japanese, including farmers, commonly ate such a meal. Just when additional soups and vegetable dishes were added is not known, as the new combination was still often referred to as *ichijū issai*.[17]

It can be said that what we think of as "traditional" Japanese cuisine started with the dishes known as *sakana*, which were created to go with sake.[18] Lists of what was served in the late Tokugawa and early Meiji periods sound very much like what is considered traditional Japanese cuisine today. One official of the *bakufu* kept a diary while on an official tour of the Kantō in 1856.[19] At the places he stopped, breakfast might

[16] On these new food items, see Adachi Iwao, *Nihon shokumotsu bunka no kigen* (Tokyo: Jiyū kokuminsha, 1981), pp. 333-417.

[17] Ōtsuka, *"Shoku" no kindai shi*, p. 14.

[18] Ibid., p. 35.

[19] Hayami Akira, "Bakumatsuki 'Kimi nikki' ni miru tabiyado no shokuji," *Rekishi kōron*, no. 73 (December 1981), pp. 80-87.

consist of rice, *miso* soup, *daikon, tōfu*, omelet (*tamagoyaki*), and *miso*-pickled *daikon* (*misōzuke daikon*). The menus this official jotted down tended to comprise a number of dishes, always including rice, a soup, and some kind of protein plus various vegetables and pickles. The protein was almost always *tōfu* or eggs, with only the occasional side dish of fish. The foods were sufficiently varied and interesting, though, for this gourmet to take the trouble to list them in his diary, and in fact the menus sound much like those found at Japanese inns today.

In his study of Tokyo in the first couple of decades after the Restoration, Ogi Shinzō found an essentially rice diet, with the middle and upper classes eating rice and the rest of the population eating rice extended with other grains.[20] With their staple, people were eating *miso* soup for breakfast, *okazu* (which could be a variety of things) for lunch, and a boiled dish (*nimono*) or clear soup (*tsuyumono*) for dinner. A list of the most popular foods, compiled in Tokyo in 1884, begins with dishes whose main ingredients are *tōfu*, sweet potatoes, eggplant, and lily bulbs, in that order. The list includes a wide variety of vegetables, seaweed, and sea products, but most of the protein comes from *tōfu*, and only a few fish are mentioned (including tuna served as sashimi and *misōzuke*). There is really no evidence of any transition to a diet including new types of Western-influenced foods.

Ogi examined the numbers and kinds of Tokyo shops selling foods to see if he could identify trends in changing food patterns during the first couple of decades after the Restoration. He found that there was a conspicuous decline in the number of small shops that sold only one item, such as salt, *miso*, vinegar, or various kinds of flour, but that the number of shops selling *katsuobushi* and *tsukudani* remained at about the same level. From the 1880s to 1900, there was an increase in shops selling rice, raw fish, and vegetables, owing to the population increase of the city, as well as an increase in the number of shops selling the new foods, such as milk, meat, and bread.[21] The slight increase in shops selling chicken eggs can be taken as a sign that these were sold in some quantity before the Restoration. There is a sharp increase in the number of shops selling sweets, which may be an indication of both availability of sugar and large enough incomes to permit the purchase of small luxuries. Some of the more indicative figures are shown in Table 17.1.

Although the new "Western foods" could be found in Tokyo, foreign visitors to Japan in the early Meiji period discovered that they had to

[20] Ogi Shinzō, *Tōkei shomin seikatsu shi kenkyū* (Tokyo: Nihon hōsō shuppan kyōkai, 1979), p. 149.

[21] Ibid., pp. 147-148.

TABLE 17.1
Number of Shops in Tokyo, 1881, 1891, and 1900

Goods Sold	1881	1891	1900
Rice	2,197	1,874	2,746
Other grains		241	247
Sake	1,418	824	2,128
Western liquors		246	335
Milk		239	452
Sweets	1,016	4,247	4,183
Chicken	30	121	160
Eggs	185	233	234

SOURCE: Ogi Shinzō, *Tōkei shomin seikatsu shi kenkyū* (Tokyo: Nihon hōsō shuppan kyōkai, 1979), p. 148.

carry food with them or have it shipped if they were going to outlying areas and expected to eat anything but traditional Japanese food. Tokyo did not even have a Chinese restaurant until the Kairakuen was established in Nihonbashi in 1883. Even those Japanese who did occasionally eat imported cuisine at restaurants ate traditional food at home.

The major change in diet during the early Meiji decades was a change in direction of the upper-class diet of the Tokugawa period. Increasingly the staple was rice, and since polished rice is blander than mixed, unpolished grain, people demanded more seasoning. Small pots and pans became more readily available, and even small families in the city could now cook the traditional side dishes that the upper classes had been eating. In the countryside, the diffusion of the *kama* for cooking rice continued, and more people were now enjoying the type of steamed rice that the Japanese still eat today, in contrast to rice cooked in an iron pot over a fire in the open hearth, or *irori*, found in the traditional house of a commoner.[22]

What really began to change the pattern of food consumption in Japan was the Russo-Japanese War and World War I. During the Meiji period, food served in the army remained traditional, despite the fact that the army was quickly westernizing in other ways. It was only after the Japanese became involved in foreign wars that a need was felt to adopt new kinds of foods and methods of preparation. For soldiers on the march or in battle, it was difficult (if not impossible) to stop and boil or steam

[22] Ekuan Kenji, *Daidokoro no rekishi* (Tokyo: Shibata shoten, 1976), p. 171ff.

a staple food, and the army command also became aware that soldiers fed on white rice were liable to develop beriberi. Biscuits were introduced during the Sino-Japanese War and, after the Russo-Japanese War, were produced in large quantity. The army also introduced beef, calling it *yamato-ni* (beef stew *à la Japonais*) to overcome the negative associations red meat would have for soldiers from the country. Beer, first brought in from England in 1868, was produced in Japan within a decade and consumed by bureaucrats and military alike.

After serving in the army, country boys returned home with a taste for new foods and cooking methods, and this more than anything else is what began to transform the dietary habits of the ordinary Japanese.[23] But all of this occurred after the turn of the century, and the Japanese diet did not really change until Taishō. Even then, so-called Western foods were exotic and extremely hard to find outside metropolitan areas. A rich merchant family in Hyōgo prefecture decided to import a cook skilled in French cuisine to give their daughter lessons. This was an expensive undertaking and much to-do was made about the lessons. In her old age the student thought it all enormously funny, for the only thing she was taught how to make was an omelet![24]

Significant changes in the diet of the ordinary Japanese came in the Taishō period, particularly with the economic boom that accompanied World War I. It was then that Japanese adopted curry rice (called rice curry in the Kansai) as a major dish in their diet. The mass consumption of milk, meat, and bread also dates from the Taishō years. The Japanese version of Worcestershire sauce became a commercial good in Japan around the time of the Sino-Japanese War, but Bulldog sauce was created only in 1926. Japanese cutlets, the most famous of which are the pork *tonkatsu*, became familiar only after World War I, and hamburgers remained a luxury item until well after World War II.[25]

Thus, the most striking change in the food culture of the Japanese during the *bakumatsu* and early Meiji years was the introduction of foreign foods and the establishment of restaurants that sold Chinese, Western, or meat dishes. But the shift in the diet that affected the majority of Japanese was a gradual, continued diffusion of a diet pattern that first the samurai class, then gradually the wealthier merchants and urban dwellers, adopted in the Tokugawa period. Rather than a westernization of the diet, then, the Meiji period witnessed the development of a more uniform, "indigenous" diet throughout Japan, a phenomenon that was

[23] Ōtsuka, "*Shoku*" *no kindai shi*, p. 80ff.

[24] Personal communication by Professor Wakita Haruko of Tachibana joshi daigaku, Kyoto.

[25] Adachi, *Nihon shokumotsu bunka no kigen*, pp. 333-417.

aided by the development of the transportation system and new forms of communication.

Clothing

Basic clothing did not change significantly for most Japanese during the second half of the nineteenth century, notwithstanding the great popularity of Western goods in the large cities. Even in the cities, work clothing and garments worn at home were traditional both in style and material. For even if Western-style clothing had been readily available, the full skirts fashionable in the West during this period would have been most impractical in Japanese housing—and impossible to manage in Japanese toilets. Western shoes were not much used because they had to be removed when entering a Japanese building, and the high-button styles of this period were difficult to put on and take off. Footgear did change in the Meiji period, but again the changes were the result of a diffusion of Tokugawa styles. Increasingly footgear was adopted: many people switched from straw sandals (*waraji*) to *geta* (wooden clogs) or from going barefoot to wearing straw sandals. More women began to wear obi, again a Tokugawa innovation, but even this was not widely worn until after 1900.

Probably the most noticeable changes in the Meiji period were in hair styles and cosmetics. Men soon began to wear Western haircuts, and as early as 1869 some 13 percent of the men in Tokyo had cut their hair; by 1890, it was hard to find a man in the cities with a traditional hair style.[26] Women, too, changed their look: as early as 1873 the empress appeared in public with her red eyebrows and unblackened teeth; but, even so, the traditional styles lingered on for decades in the countryside.

A number of new items that were worn or carried did come into common use during the Meiji period. When men cut their hair short, they began to wear caps and hats. They also carried Western-style umbrellas and watches, but their basic garb was still the kimono. Imported wool began to come into use for clothing. Men wore wool coats or cloaks, even over kimono, and women began wearing woolen shawls in winter. Eventually a special kind of coat worn over the kimono and obi was developed and popularized. Clearly, people sought greater comfort during the cold months, but Western materials and garments were adapted to traditional Japanese dress. Nonetheless, the use of wool was extremely limited until the twentieth century: imported wool was expensive, and

[26] Yanagida [Yanagita], *Japanese Manners & Customs*, p. 28.

the only important producer of woolen goods until after the turn of the century was a mill at Senjū in Tokyo.[27]

The government elite began to wear Western suits early in the Meiji period. Even the emperor appeared in Western dress in 1870. However, suits were worn by men during business hours or on special occasions; at home, they quickly changed back into Japanese garments, a custom that continued until very recently. The widespread use of Western clothing began when the military and other groups adopted uniforms. Women continued to wear kimono, even in the Taishō period, though by that time they too had adopted Western hair styles. Even the uniforms of school girls in the Meiji period were based on the kimono. Indeed, given Western styles for women up until about 1920, combined with the Japanese tradition of sitting on the floor, Western dress would have been most impractical for Japanese women in the Meiji and Taishō years.[28]

Thus, styles changed for men and women alike during the transition years, but the Western items adopted were mostly in the realm of accessories; new fabrics and new technology for producing fabrics were by and large adapted to the traditional types of clothing. And the new textile industry combined with a healthy traditional industry meant that consumers were able to afford more clothing and better quality fabrics, such as cotton and wool.

The Development of New Life Styles

Although a more widespread diffusion of material goods from the Tokugawa period was the primary direction of the changes experienced in the early Meiji years, some genuine changes in life style did occur in the decades immediately following the Restoration—developments that would eventually transform life for all Japanese. Many Western items were adopted, first by the urban elites (who were the first to learn about the new goods and who had the money to purchase them) and then gradually by other groups of Japanese, particularly through the influence of the military. These items ranged all the way from Western uniforms and clothes for businessmen, officials, and students to food. The eating

[27] See Keiichirō Nakagawa and Henry Rosovsky, "The Case of the Dying Kimono: The Influence of Changing Fashions on the Development of the Japanese Woolen Industry," *Business History Review*, vol. 37, nos. 1-2 (Spring/Summer 1963).

[28] For a discussion of dress, as well as other aspects of life style, see Mine Yasuzawa, "Changes in Lifestyle in Japan: Pattern and Structure of Modern Consumption," in Henri Baudet and Henk van der Meulen, eds., *Consumer Behaviour and Economic Growth in the Modern Economy* (London: Croom Helm, 1982), pp. 179-205.

of meat became socially sanctioned, and the Japanese gradually acquired a taste for it. From the West, they adopted such dishes as curry, omelets, rolled cabbage, and various beef dishes such as sukiyaki and *gyūnabe*; and from China, *anpan*, steamed buns filled with sweet bean paste.

Japanese also began adapting Western technology to their material culture, and this too began to transform their life styles. The first electric light service was provided in Tokyo in 1887. By 1893, in the area between Shimbashi and Nihonbashi, there were 164 houses with oil lamps, 113 with electric lights, and only one that still used rapeseed oil for lighting.[29] The new kinds of lighting quickly spread to all cities and gradually began to change the way people lived. Now it was possible to read at night, so people not only stayed up later, but family members began to sleep in separate rooms.

Modern transportation also came to Japanese cities early in the Meiji period. The rickshaw is thought to have been invented in Tokyo in 1869, though the origins are obscure. Japanese no longer had to rely on transport by water or on foot, and within a few years there were as many as 50,000 rickshaws in Tokyo. Next came horse-drawn transportation; the emperor had his first carriage ride in 1871. Horse-drawn buses and then trolleys were used in Tokyo; these were quickly followed by electric trolley cars, first in Kyoto (1895) and then in Tokyo (1903). As it became easier for people to move about the city, it became possible for people to live some distance from their place of work; the suburbs were gradually developed, making possible the building of samurai-style housing, which required more space than narrow townhouses.

The first railroad was built from Shinagawa (in Tokyo) to Yokohama, with service first provided in the summer of 1872. By 1891, there was railway service to Aomori from Ueno (in Tokyo). Although only the well-to-do could afford daily train commuting at first, railway use quickly widened. By 1903 more than 15,000 people a day were using Shibuya Station in Tokyo. Clearly the Japanese people became more mobile during the Meiji period, and they had not been nontravelers in earlier centuries; rather, the pace of travel quickened.[30] Note, however, that the general use of modern forms of transportation, as well as the accompanying changes, date from near the turn of the century and not from early Meiji.

As barriers between regions were removed through the establishment of a central government and through national communications systems (e.g. the telegraph), rural Japanese began to produce handmade goods

[29] Yanagida [Yanagita], *Japanese Manners & Customs*, p. 54.

[30] Edward Seidensticker, *Low City, High City* (New York: Knopf, 1983), portrays the changes in Tokyo from the end of the Tokugawa period until the 1923 earthquake in a very vivid manner.

for the market, people who used to make daily consumption goods at home began to buy them, and people who used to purchase expensive items used only for occasional ceremonial purposes began to rent them. The trend toward buying items of daily use (*miso, shōyu*, oil, cotton, indigo, etc.) which had begun in the Tokugawa period, rose during the Meiji period.

If there is a pattern in the new developments mentioned above, it is that they affected city dwellers primarily and had only a marginal effect on villagers. While it is true that making *zōri* and tatami for the market created by-employment for people who might not have had it before—though such side work provided much of the household income during the Tokugawa period as well—and that the linking of all parts of Japan through the installation of the telegraph would be felt in the countryside, it still changed the daily lives of most people very little. Rather, those Japanese who commuted each day by train, wore Western clothes, and ate meat on occasional meals out, who now lit their houses with electricity, and so on, lived in large cities.[31]

Living Standards versus Quality of Life

Abundant quantitative data exist for the Meiji period, but they are difficult to evaluate. Even though national averages indicate that real income rose, albeit very slowly, averages are by definition not useful for ascertaining the pattern of income distribution. With the political transition and the accompanying economic changes, some people were able to increase their real income substantially while others suffered a real decline in the standard of living. Thus one can find evidence for diverse socioeconomic interpretations of the Meiji period. It is not difficult to understand why the compilers of one excellent local history gave up providing any analysis whatsoever when they came to the Meiji and Taishō periods,

[31] Irokawa Daikichi, in his *Meiji no bunka* (Tokyo: Iwanami shoten, 1970), writes in beautiful prose of the changes in the countryside during the Meiji period—how it blossomed with color when the sumptuary laws were lifted and when flowers, whose seeds had come from the West, were planted (pp. 33, 39). Unfortunately, he does not offer the socioeconomic evidence that a historian demands. This kind of poetic longing for the past points up the problems inherent in researching the history of daily life, for there is no way of knowing how prevalent such changes were. From our knowledge of Taishō Japan, however, it seems unlikely that there was much change; what little color there was must have been striking because of its absence in the past. In any case, the kind of change described by Irokawa substantiates the view that much of the change in Meiji Japan was not basic, but involved fashion. Irokawa's book is available in translation as *The Culture of the Meiji Period* (Princeton: Princeton University Press, 1985).

saying: "Interpretations concerning social and economic changes differ by scholar, and we were unable to edit this section systematically in such a way as to reflect accurately the transformation of the economy."[32]

Nevertheless, most scholars would conclude that on balance the standard of living rose, if only slightly, in the latter half of the nineteenth century. Changes in the material culture support this assessment. The diffusion of goods once available only to the well-to-do of the Tokugawa period indicates that a larger proportion of the population was able to afford higher-quality goods. More people could afford to eat rice, and housing gradually improved.

We should not, however, emphasize changes in life style. Improvements in nutrition came about very slowly. According to statistics on the height of 20-year-old recruits for the military, going back to the 1880s, the average height for recruits was 156.7 cm for 1883-1887, 156.5 cm for 1888-1892, 156.5 cm for 1893-1897, 157 cm for 1898-1902, and 157.6 cm for 1903-1907; this figure grew at about 0.5 cm per five-year period from then on.[33] Thus, the height of recruits remained about the same until the turn of the twentieth century. Naturally the significance of these figures depends upon whether the sample from which the recruits were drawn remained the same; on the surface, though, they suggest that the height of Japanese men did not show any improvement in the diet until very late Meiji, which would mean a slow improvement in diet possibly from the late 1870s.

The Japanese were spending the greater portion of their incomes on food, and they continued to do so through the Taishō period. During early Meiji, fully two-thirds of personal income was spent on food alone. This proportion fell only very slowly from 67.5 percent in 1874-1883, to 63.7 percent in 1896-1906, and 58.9 percent in 1917-1926. It was only during the depression decade of 1931-1940 that the percentage spent on food fell to just barely below 50 percent.[34] This means that as incomes grew, Japanese continued to spend almost the same proportion on food, and thus spent more real income on eating. It also means that the Japanese had little disposable income to spend on anything other than the necessities of life during the Meiji period.

One might argue whether the continuity of traditional life styles was a preference of the Japanese or whether it was a function of income.

[32] Ninohe gun, *Ninohe gun shi* (Morioka: Ninohe gun, 1968), p. 463.

[33] Carl Mosk, "Fecundity, Infanticide, and Food Consumption in Japan," *Explorations in Economic History*, vol. 15 (1978), p. 279.

[34] Miyohei Shinohara, *Personal Consumption Expenditures*, vol. 6 of the *Estimates of Long-Term Economic Statistics of Japan since 1868* (Tokyo: Tōyō keizai shimpōsha, 1967), p. 5.

Certainly few people could afford the faddish new Western goods or to build other than traditional houses. Countries in the twentieth century with low per capita income, possibly lower than Japan experienced in the Meiji period, show food expenditures of between 55 and 63 percent.[35] On the other hand, income elasticities for food were low in Japan, not only in the 1878-1922 period, but between 1922 and 1940. This meant that changes in food demand in response to growth in income were small.[36] Thus, the Japanese preference for traditional foods, combined with only slow rises in income, which did not permit radical changes in consumption patterns, proved fortuitous to industrialization in the Meiji period. People continued to live much as they had, permitting a high savings and investment rate, with little income funneled off into the purchase of consumption goods, domestic or foreign.

All of the above data are averages, cloaking what was happening to individuals. And although these averages indicated gradual rises in the standard of living, what should not be forgotten is the fact that life was far from tranquil during the transition years. Japan experienced one of its three great famines of the Tokugawa period in the late 1830s, political unrest and governmental crisis from the 1840s on, severe earthquakes in Edo in 1854 and 1855, large-scale crop failures in 1866 and 1869, the Meiji Restoration in 1867-1868 along with the establishment of a new form of government and drastic socioeconomic change, and then the Matsukata deflation of the 1880s. The samurai as a class lost their monopoly over government as well as their sinecures, however meager these may have been for many by the 1860s. Although some samurai are known to have been reduced to dire poverty in the Meiji years, many others found secure positions at all levels of the bureaucracy, which paid, by the standards of the day, good salaries. They were thus better off than they had been under the Tokugawa regime. The new Meiji tax systems adversely affected farmers in some parts of the country, but resulted in a lighter tax burden in other areas. Many farmers found themselves very well off in the 1870s, but suffered under the Matsukata deflation. The overall effect of the new system on farmers is still disputed.[37]

Just as it is difficult to assess the changes in the standard of living, so

[35] Simon Kuznets, "Trends in Level and Structure of Consumption," in Lawrence Klein and Kazushi Ohkawa, eds., *Economic Growth: The Japanese Experience since the Meiji Era* (Homewood, Ill.: Richard D. Irwin, 1968), pp. 226-227.

[36] Hiromitsu Kaneda, "Long-Term Changes in Food Consumption Patterns in Japan," in Kazushi Ohkawa et al., eds., *Agriculture and Economic Growth: Japan's Experience* (Princeton and Tokyo: Princeton University Press and University of Tokyo Press, 1969), p. 426.

[37] See the chapter by Kozo Yamamura in this book.

is it equally hard to ascertain whether or not the quality of life improved during the late nineteenth century. Japanese were subject to cholera epidemics for the first time during this period, and as Tokyo grew after the first decade following the Restoration, the traditional sewage disposal methods were not able to cope with the growing volume of human wastes. Some suspect that the incidence of tuberculosis may have risen after the Meiji Restoration, and certainly that disease was prevalent during the Meiji period.[38] On the other hand, the new trends in housing, toward more light and more open space, combined with clothing that was warmer (wool) and more washable (cotton) were clear improvements in the quality of life.

CONCLUSION

Studies of the Meiji period focus almost entirely on what was new, borrowed, "modern," and innovative. This fact, combined with the establishment of a completely new government and national goals, has led scholars to overlook or play down the continuity to be found in the material culture, the way of life, and the standard of living during the nineteenth century, from well before the Restoration until several decades after it. The study of life styles, consumption patterns, and material culture are important to our knowledge of the transition from Tokugawa to modern Japan: these things indicate how quickly the transition took place, how widespread the changes were, and how long it took for the new technologies, new goods, and new ideas to be diffused. Even this short survey of the material culture of the transition years, I believe, reveals much about the impact of the Meiji Restoration on the Japanese people and about how the transition worked at the grass-roots level.

All evidence points to a stability in life styles over the half-century of transition from the late Tokugawa to the turn of the twentieth century. Any real changes in life style (housing, food, clothing, patterns of leisure, etc.) began to occur only after the turn of the century, from the Russo-Japanese War into the Taishō years. The changes that did occur during the early Meiji period—carrying Western umbrellas or wearing Western shawls with traditional kimono, substituting glass for paper in the home—were primarily those of style and in no way constituted radical cultural shifts. New foods, such as bread and meat, were luxuries and not an integral part of the diet. In no case were the changes as dramatic

[38] Rene and Jean Dubos, *The White Plague: Tuberculosis, Man, and Society* (Boston: Little, Brown, 1952), p. 189ff. and app. B.

as those following World War II, when the life of nearly every Japanese was transformed within a couple of decades to a more "modern" or Western style, accompanying a dramatic rise in the standard of living.

Because life styles remained traditional, so did consumption patterns. Increases in the standard of living resulted by and large in a greater demand for traditional goods. This helped stabilize the economy; it meant that the producers of traditional goods were not suddenly out of work or technologically obsolete. A good example of this is the textile industry. The new, large-scale textile factories produced cloth that was too wide for kimono, so that at the same time that they contributed to an increase in the consumption of cotton cloth, they also enabled the survival of the traditional industry which produced the material for kimono.[39] Furthermore, consumer preference for traditional goods meant that the country did not spend its valuable foreign currency on consumption goods during the early stages of industrialization. This was particularly important for Japan, which not only set upon industrialization with a much lower per capita income than had the Western nations, but was also nearly a century behind England when it began.

The impetus for the eventual diffusion of new life styles and of a preference for the new goods can be attributed to the military. Just as the Sengoku wars transformed life in the sixteenth century, it was the Sino-Japanese and Russo-Japanese wars at the turn of the twentieth century that transformed life in the Meiji period. The adoption of cotton for military use by the Sengoku daimyo led to its diffusion among the population as the favored material for clothing. So, too, did the soldiers' contact with Western uniforms and food help create a demand for such goods when the troops returned home after the wars with China and Russia.

The introduction of new life styles and consumption goods can be dated from the early years of the nineteenth century, with a quickening of interest after the Meiji Restoration. But it was not until the turn of the twentieth century that many Japanese made things Western a part of their daily lives, and the most significant change in life style came only after the economic boom of World War I. In neither case was the nature or the pace of change anything like that following World War II. Instead, during the turbulent transition from the Tokugawa to the Meiji government, nearly all Japanese had at least one important element of stability in their lives: their everyday life style.

To restate, what may have been more significant for Japanese in the nineteenth century than any amount of change in their lives was the

[39] See the essays cited in footnotes 27 and 28, above.

continuity of their material culture and life style. Toffler believes that people handle rapid change most effectively when there is a strong element of stability in their lives.[40] Meiji Japanese faced change in everything from government to the economy to education, as well as in many other aspects of their lives. What most Japanese did not have to face was change in their daily home lives. Just as Fukuzawa Yukichi held to traditional family values and the Japanese system of arranged marriage even while serving as a proponent of so much that was Western, the Meiji bureaucrats in their Western dress could retreat by modern transportation to their traditional homes, change into kimono, and enjoy a Japanese meal while viewing their gardens.

It might be hypothesized that continuity in the daily life of Japan provided a stable base that enabled the Japanese people to deal with the political, economic, and cultural change that confronted them—a base that allowed them to adopt and adapt what they wanted, rather than be overwhelmed by all that was new. This stability might provide a clue as to why the Japanese were able to modernize and industrialize effectively when so many other countries were not. Life styles did change over the course of the transition years, but most of the changes cannot be regarded as substantive. Only in the prewar decades of the twentieth century did a transformation in the life style of the ordinary Japanese occur, and it is suggestive that these were the very years whose events led to World War II.

[40] Alvin Toffler, *Future Shock* (New York: Random House, 1970).

ABOUT THE CONTRIBUTORS

Albert A. Altman, Senior Lecturer in Japanese History at the Hebrew University of Jerusalem, is the author of many studies of the early Meiji press.

Martin Collcutt is Professor of Japanese History and Chairman of the Department of East Asian Studies at Princeton University. His publications include *Five Mountains: The Rinzai Zen Monastic Institution in Medieval Japan* (1981) and other studies in the institutional history of Japanese Buddhism.

Albert M. Craig is Professor of History, Director of the Harvard-Yenching Institute, and Director of the Japan Institute at Harvard University. His publications include *Chōshū in the Meiji Restoration* (1961), *Personality in Japanese History* (ed. with Donald H. Shively, 1970), *Japan: A Comparative View* (ed. 1979), and other studies in Japanese history.

Andrew Fraser, of the Australian National University, is investigating political developments in Tokushima prefecture during the Meiji period. He is the author of many studies, among them *National Election Politics in Tokushima Prefecture, 1890-1902* (1972).

Susan B. Hanley is Associate Professor of Japanese Studies and History at the University of Washington and Managing Editor of the *Journal of Japanese Studies*. Her publications include *Economic and Demographic Change in Preindustrial Japan, 1600-1868* (with Kozo Yamamura, 1977), *Family and Population in East Asian History* (ed. with Arthur P. Wolf, 1985), and "A High Standard of Living in Nineteenth-Century Japan: Fact or Fantasy?" (*Journal of Economic History*, 1983).

Akira Hayami is Professor of Economics at Keiō University. He is the author of numerous studies of population and economic development in early modern Japan, among them *Kinsei nōson no rekishi jinkōgakuteki kenkyū* (1973) and *Sūryō keizai shi nyūmon* (1975).

Marius B. Jansen is Professor of Japanese History at Princeton University. His publications include *Sakamoto Ryōma and the Meiji Restoration* (1961) and *Studies in the Institutional History of Early Modern Japan* (ed. with J.W. Hall, 1968). He is a General Editor of the

Cambridge History of Japan and Editor of vol. 5, *The Nineteenth Century* (forthcoming).

Shunsaku Nishikawa is Professor of Economics, Faculty of Business and Commerce, at Keiō University. His publications include "Productivity, Subsistence, and By-employment in the Mid-Nineteenth-Century Chōshū" (*Explorations in Economic History*, 1978) and *Edo jidai no poritikaru ekonomi* (1979).

Gilbert Rozman is Professor of Sociology at Princeton University. His publications include *Urban Networks in Ch'ing China and Tokugawa Japan* (1973), "Edo's Importance in the Changing Tokugawa Society" (*Journal of Japanese Studies*, 1974), *The Modernization of China* (ed. 1981), and *A Mirror for Socialism: Soviet Criticisms of China* (1985).

Richard Rubinger is Associate Professor of Japanese at the University of Hawaii–Manoa. He is the author of *Private Academies of Tokugawa Japan* (1982) and is currently investigating literacy in nineteenth-century Japan.

Osamu Saitō, formerly of Keiō University, is Associate Professor at the Institute of Economic Research, Hitotsubashi University. His publications include "The Labor Market in Tokugawa Japan" (*Explorations in Economic History*, 1978) and "Population and the Peasant Family Economy in Proto-Industrial Japan" (*Journal of Family History*, 1983).

Henry D. Smith II teaches Japanese History at the University of California–Santa Barbara. His publications include *Japan's First Student Radicals* (1972) and *Learning from Shogun: Japanese History and Western Fantasy* (ed. 1980). His current research focuses on the culture of the city of Edo/Tokyo.

Michio Umegaki, of Georgetown University, is a specialist in Japanese government and is writing a detailed account of early Meiji politics entitled "Japan after Restoration."

D. Eleanor Westney holds the Mitsubishi Career Development Chair in International Management at the Alfred P. Sloan Institute of Management, Massachusetts Institute of Technology. Her publications include "The Emulation of Western Organizations in Meiji Japan: The Case of the Paris Prefecture of Police and the Keishi-chō" (*Journal of Japanese Studies*, 1982).

William D. Wray, Associate Professor at the University of British Columbia, is a specialist in Japanese business history. His publications include *Mitsubishi and the N.Y.K., 1870-1914: Business Strategy in the Japanese Shipping Industry* (1984) and *Eibun shiryō*, vol. 20 of *Shōwa zaisei shi: shūsen kara kōwa made* (ed. with Hata Ikuhiko, 1982).

Kozo Yamamura is Professor of Asian Studies and Chairman of the Japanese Studies Program at the University of Washington. His publications include *Economic and Demographic Change in Preindustrial Japan, 1600-1868* (with Susan B. Hanley, 1977), *A Study of Samurai Income and Entrepreneurship* (1974), and other studies in Japanese economic history.

INDEX

abortion, 287-290
adoption, 278
Aichi prefecture, 206, 220
Aizawa Seishisai, 41, 145, 147, 148
Aizu han, 42, 146-147, 199, 293; opposition to imperial forces, 33, 48, 67, 77, 80, 94-95
Akasaka Keiko, 281-282
American Civil War, 80
American Pacific Mail, 258
American Revolution, 10
Ansei purge, 42, 69
Aoki Shūzō, 83
Aomori prefecture, 214
Araki Moriaki, 403
architecture, 209-211, 355, 371-372, 449-451
artisans, 24, 340, 356, 359, 364, 371, 373, 449
Awa han (Tokushima or Myōdō), 32, 113-130; economic reform in, 100, 114-118, 124, 127-130; educational reform in, 121-123, 221; population in, 111

Baba Steamships, 270
bakufu: administration, 30, 37; economic reforms, 75, 136; educational reforms, 75, 196-202; military reforms, 30, 75, 79-80, 168-176
bakumatsu, definition of, 7
banks, 86, 133, 371
Bansho shirabesho (Kaiseijo), 197-198, 201, 203, 228, 234
Beasley, W. G., 79, 81
Beppu, 217
beriberi, 454-455, 460
Bizen han, 54
bonds, samurai pension, 84, 86-87
Bolitho, Harold, 64
Boulding, Kenneth, 133-135
Brown, A. R., 258
Buddhism: bakufu's position regarding, 4, 134, 144-150; Meiji government's position regarding, 19, 49-50, 143, 150-167; role of kuge in, 72; Jōdo Shinshū (Pure Land), 145, 149-150, 158, 161, 163-164, 166; Nichiren, 145, 149; Rinzai Zen, 163; Shingon, 163; Shinshū Honganji, 165; Sōtō Zen, 163; Tendai, 163
Bummei kaika, 25, 166, 209, 222
Bunkyū reforms (1862), 73
Bunsei reforms, 29
Burks, Ardath, 82
business tax (eigyōzei), 116

cabinet system, 62, 87-88
Capron, Horace, 20
castles, 17, 23, 34, 102, 116, 119, 158, 318, 340-344
censorship of printed matter, 231-233, 236-237, 241
censuses, 108, 286, 301
Charter Oath, 3-4, 20, 25, 47, 76, 96, 202-203, 238, 319
chihōzei (prefectural tax), 116-118, 120, 127-128
Chikamatsu Monzaemon, 232
China trade, 12, 30, 328
Chinese Revolution, 10
Ch'ing China, 16, 18, 40, 59-60, 62-63, 170, 276, 288-289
chinshōfu, 45
chiso kaisei (land tax reform): implementation of the reform, 4-5, 18, 34, 59-60, 382-397, 445; post-reform prefectural tax rate, 390, 395; reform proposals, 384-386
cholera, 296-298, 301, 304-305, 467
chōnaikai (neighborhood associations), 370
chōnin (townspeople), 275, 318, 341, 350-351, 360-361, 366-367, 371

chōshi and chokunin (court appointed officials), 88, 99

Chōshū (Yamaguchi prefecture): administration in, 12, 103, 350; anti-Buddhism in, 149-151, 157-158; civil war in, 30, 36-37, 43-44; economic reforms in, 30, 78; education in, 199; military reforms in, 44, 52, 171, 174; participation in Meiji government, 12, 46-48, 54-56, 61, 89, 104-105; peasant by-employment in, 294, 430, 432, 446; population statistics for, 328, 331, 337-338; role in Restoration, 30, 42-45, 93, 96-97

Christianity, 21, 144, 146, 149, 151, 153-155, 164-167, 220, 222, 234, 354

class relations, 6, 15, 17, 24

clothing, 26, 81, 363, 448, 461-464, 467

Confucianism, 20-21, 41, 144-146, 158-159, 197-198, 200, 203-204, 208, 215, 219, 221-232, 239

conscription, and Conscription Edict of 1873, 4, 17, 24-25, 60, 140, 176, 178-180, 183-185, 187, 191, 194

corvée (buyakugin), 116

cotton production, 407, 409-410, 416-418, 432, 462, 468

Council of Local Officials (1875), 19

Daigaku (honkō, tōkō, and nankō), 203-204

daimyo, post-Restoration status, 8, 12, 47, 49-50, 56-57, 60, 77, 83, 98-99, 352

Daishū Tetsunen, 154

Dajōkan (Council of State), 49-51, 56, 71, 87, 99, 151, 153, 181, 204, 206, 208

Dajōkan nisshi, 102, 235-236

dajōkansatsu (government paper currency), 100

dekasegi (temporary work outside the home), 401-402, 404, 408-409, 414

demographic changes: age composition of society, 296, 310-311; average age at marriage, 275, 277, 280-281; average household size, 275, 277-278; average life expectancy, 278, 280; birth-death rates, 275-276, 279-283, 288, 296-297, 305, 316; "demographic center of gravity," 304; demographic transition theory, 282, 316; in castle towns, 23, 274-275, 279, 318-346; regional variations in population, 6, 22, 274-277, 279, 291, 293-298, 301-304, 306, 308-309, 314-316, 322, 326-328, 331, 334, 345; sex ratios, 275, 278, 313-315, 365-367

Department of Rites (see also Ministry of Rites), 151, 154

de Tocqueville, Alexis, 36-38, 40, 63

devaluation of 1859, 446

diet (see also grain consumption and meat eating), 363, 421, 426-446, 454-461, 465

Disaster Savings Law (1880), 124

disease and epidemics, 282, 295-298, 301, 304-305, 316, 467

Dōgakudō, role of in education, 198

domain monopolies, 7

Dore, R. P., 201, 211, 373

Dōshisha University, 222, 227

Dutch studies, *see* Rangaku

earthquakes, 466

Eastern Circuit shipping route, 250

Echigō han, 198, 367

Echizen han, 198

Edo (Tokyo): becomes imperial capital, 12, 22-23, 48-49, 203, 319, 347, 352, 355-356, 358; castle, 343, 371; concept of "Edo-centrism," 277, 349, 352, 358-359, 364; distinction between shitamachi and yamanote, 365, 370-373; population statistics for, 22-23, 274-275, 306, 322-324, 335, 342-343, 347-348, 350-351, 356-359, 360, 365, 367

edokko (Edo-born), 361, 365

Education Law (1879), 208, 223, 226

electricity, 372, 463

Elementary School Law (1886), 215

emperor, concept of, 21-22, 40-41, 49, 90, 94

English Revolution, 10

Enomoto Takeaki, 11, 362

eta (outcastes), 78, 456. *See also* class relations

Etchū Sailing Ship Co., 263

Etō Shimpei, 31, 45, 51, 59, 137, 154-155, 355-356

factories, 344-345, 359, 468

feudal order, differences between Japan and Europe, 75-76
Fifteenth National Bank, 86
Fillmore, President Millard, and the opening of Japan, 68
fires, 209, 360, 371
foreign currency, 468
foreign influence: American influence, 20, 137; English influence, 20, 137, 174, 176-178, 192, 221; French influence, 20, 137, 139, 174-178, 180, 184-185, 190-191, 207, 221; German (Prussian) influence, 20, 114, 139, 175, 177, 185-186, 190-191; on the army, 137, 139, 174, 176-177, 184-186, 190-191; on education, 20, 137, 207, 221; on the legal system, 20, 137; on the navy, 174, 176-178, 192; on technology, 20, 137, 141
foreign language study, 137, 197, 201, 219-220, 223. *See also* Rangaku
foreign loans, 61, 81
foreign study, 84, 182, 234
foreign threat, 4, 6-8, 15, 18, 68, 93, 135, 171-172
foreign trade, 39, 136, 171, 173, 175, 258, 353-354, 358, 401, 446. *See also* opening of the ports
foreign (unequal) treaties, 4, 6, 8, 40-41, 71, 95, 135, 234, 352-353
Four Books and Five Classics, 198. *See also* Confucianism
Franco-Prussian War, 80, 177, 184
French civil code, 20
French Revolution, 36, 46, 63
fudai han, 19, 39, 63, 69, 73, 74, 175, 350, 352
Fujimoto Toshiharu, 331-332, 336-337
Fujioka Kenjirō, 334
Fujita Teiichirō, 406-407
Fujita Tōko, 41, 145, 147, 148
fukoku kyōhei (rich nation, strong military), 353
Fukuba Bisei, 148-150
Fukuchi Ōchi, 362
Fukuda Gyōkai, 143, 163, 165, 167
Fukui, 106, 164, 334
Fukumoto han, 101
Fukuoka, 57, 225, 342-343
Fukuoka Takachika, 96
Fukushima, 336
Fukushima Masao, 160
Fukuzawa Yukichi, 74, 82, 205, 207, 217, 220, 227, 240, 469
Fundamental Code of Education (1872), 208, 214, 216, 218-219, 222-223
furniture, 448
Furushima Toshio, 406, 417

gaikoku bugyō, 16, 135
gakkō (school), origin of the word, 210-211
Gakushūin (Peers School), 85, 203
gambling, 351
genrō, 88
Giseikan, 48
gisō (reserve granaries), 124
Gluck, Carol, 380
gōgaku (local schools), 196, 206, 210, 228
gokenin, 360-362
Go Mizunoo tennō, 73
gosanke, 69, 73
gosankyō, 73
Gotō Shōjirō, 55-56, 59, 70
governors, appointment of, 50, 77, 83, 98, 108, 206
grain consumption: and the concept of the Proportion of the People's Staple Food (PSF), 422-423, 425, 442-443; in Chōshū, 423, 425, 435-438, 441, 454; in factories, 441; and Military Ration rule, 438-441. *See also* standard of living
Griffis, William Elliot, 57, 86, 91
Guizot, François Pierre, 221
gunken and hōken government, distinction between, 65, 98
Gyōseikan, 48

Hachizune Kanichi, 245
Hagi city, 337-338, 350, 427
Hagi rebellion, 53, 60
haibutsu kishaku (eradication of Buddhism), 143-167
haihan chiken, 4, 18, 31, 57, 78, 91, 98, 100-103, 106-110, 112, 136, 176, 202, 204-207, 237, 319, 339, 352, 383, 387, 446
hairstyles, 26, 152, 215, 230, 461
Hakodate, 47-49, 266, 336, 342

Hamada (Tsuruta) han, 102
Hanabusa Naosaburō, 402-403
handicraft industries, 275, 293, 406. *See also* artisans and zaigōmachi
hankō (domain schools), 136, 197-201, 219, 228, 230
hanseki hōkan, 48-49, 53, 66, 77, 83, 96-99, 103
Hara Kei, 85-86
Hara Tanzan, 166
Harootunian, Harry, 79
Harris, Townsend, 41, 68, 71, 352-353
Hashimoto Jitsuryō, 156
Hashizune Kanichi, 245
hatamoto, 172, 361-362, 383, 445
Hayashi Razan, 144
Hayashi Yūzō, 82
Hepburn, James, 362
Hereditary Peerage Finance Law (1886), 86
higaki kaisen, 251-253, 256, 259, 269
Hikone, 200, 336
Hirano Gitarō, 86
Hirata Atsutane, 145, 148-149, 157
hired labor, 275, 340, 349-351, 450
Hirosawa Saneomi, 50, 54-55, 64
Hirose Tansō and the Kangien, 197, 201, 210
Hiroshima, 36, 220, 227, 338, 342, 408, 419
Hiroumi Nisaburō, 263, 270
hiyatoi (day labor) and chinbata (putting out), distinction between, 409. *See also* dekasegi and hired labor
Hokkaidō, 22, 26, 182, 264, 336, 343
Hokkaidō Development Office, 183
holidays, 444
Holland, 234. *See also* Rangaku
Homma family, 33
Honjō Eijirō, 37
Hōreki famine, 293
Hōsei University, 222
Hoshi Tōru, 88
Hoshina Masayuki, 145-146
Hōshū Kōson, 154
Hosoi Wakizō, 441
Household Residence Registry (1871), 108
household taxes, 116
House of Peers, 11, 62, 83-84, 88
housing, 363, 448-454, 467
Huber, Richard, 416

Ibaraki prefecture, 225
ie (household), 278, 289, 469
igakujo (school of Western medical learning), 203
Ii Naosuke, 42, 69
Iiyama han, 175
Ikeda Mitsumasa, 146-147
Imperial Diet of 1890, 19, 35, 70
Imperial Guard, 56, 104-105, 176, 178, 180, 183-184. *See also* sanpan kenpei
Imperial Household Ministry, 84-86, 88, 90
Imperial Rescript on Education, 21, 25
Imperial Rescript to Soldiers and Sailors, 21, 186
Industrial Revolution, 133, 274
infanticide, 287-290
Inland Sea shipping route, 252, 264
Inoue Kaoru, 56, 105-106, 240, 255, 386, 445-446
Inoue Kowashi, 123
Ishida Baigan, 145
Ishinomaki, port of, 265
Ishizuki Minoru, 210-211
Itagaki Taisuke, 12, 55-59, 64, 80, 87, 105, 107
Itō Gemboku and the Shōsendō, 200
Itō Hirobumi, 21, 36, 44, 51, 56, 58-59, 61, 64, 84, 85, 166, 240, 446
Itō Myoji, 84
Itō Shigeru, 418
Iwai Tadakuma, 86, 88
Iwakura mission, 3, 20, 58, 80-81, 83, 179
Iwakura Tomomi, 47, 50, 54-59, 70, 72, 80, 84-85, 86, 105-106, 150, 202-203, 238
Iwamurata han, 175
Iwasaki Yatarō, 255-258, 261, 269, 451. *See also* Mitsubishi
Iwase Tadanari, 352-353, 355

Janes, Leroy Lansing, and Meiji education, 86, 222
Japanese Army War College, 185
jikisan (direct retainers of the shogun), 360-361

jiyū minken, *see* Movement for People's Rights
Jōhō Yoshio, 188
Jūge Shigekuni, 156

Kabayama San'en, 64
kabuki, 364
kabunakama (merchant guilds), 136
Kaga han, 199, 252
Kagoshima, 43, 53, 149, 214, 338, 341. *See also* Satsuma han
kagyō (house specialties), 72
Kaibara Ekken, 232
kaigun bugyō, 16
kaigun denshūjo (naval training institute), 172
Kairakuen, 459
Kaiseikan, 256-257
Kaisō Kaisha (Marine Transportation Co.), 254-255
kaizumi, 250, 252, 263, 269
Kamei Koremi, 148-150
Kanazawa, 334, 336, 341-343, 348, 452
Kanda Takahira (Kōhei), 384-386
Kansei reforms (1790s), 20, 75
Kasama han, 199
Katō Hiroyuki, 206
Katsu Kaishū, 11, 361-362
Katsura Tarō, 185-186, 191
Kawamura Sumiyoshi, 56, 64
Kawasaki, 33-34
kawase kaisha (exchange companies), 255
kazoku class, 77, 79, 83-84, 86
Kazoku Kaikan, 84
Kazu no Miya, 73. *See also* kōbu-gattai
Keiō University (gijuku), 205, 217, 220-221, 226-227
Keiō reforms (1867), 174
kempeitai (military police), 187
kenjinkai (prefectural clubs), 370
kenzan'ya (dealers in leftover gifts), 350
kibetsu (registry unit), 114, 118, 122
Kido Takayoshi (Kōin), 3-4, 12, 44, 47, 50-60, 65-67, 80-81, 83-84, 97, 99, 103-106, 166, 207, 238
Kii han, 145, 175
Kikuma han, 164
Kita Ikki, 85
kitamaesen, 251-253, 262-266, 268-270
Kitō Hiroshi, 454
Kobe (Hyōgo), 16, 95, 264, 266, 306, 335, 337, 342, 353
Kōbu-gattai, 19, 37, 48, 70
Kōbusho, 172
kōdō bunka, 364
Kokinshū, 25
kokudaka, compared to city size, 324-326, 331-333, 338
kokugaku, 145, 148, 157-159, 198, 202
Komatsubara Eitarō, 88
Kondō Makoto and the Kōgyokusha, 220
Korean expedition (1873) and Seikanron, 6, 58-59, 61, 65, 81-82, 107
Kōriyama han, 198
Koromo han, 200
koseki seido (domicile registration system), 78, 108, 281, 301
koshinigata (warehouse lending agency), 264-265
kōshinsei (scholarship system), 204
kuge: and Meiji educational system, 203; participation in the Restoration, 50, 72; ranking of, 71-72, 77, 79, 83; required residence in Tokyo, 352
kuni, definition of, 26, 38-39
Kumamoto, 60, 102, 106, 328, 342
Kumazawa Banzan, 144, 146
Kurile islands, 26
Kuroda Kiyotaka, 61, 182
Kurosaki Chiharu, 334
Kuwabara Takeo, 9
Kyōdō Un'yu Kaisha (KUK), 248, 260, 263
Kyōikurei, *see* Education Law (1879)
Kyoto: anti-Buddhist incidents in, 159; and Chōshū coup d'état attempt, 36, 43; court nobility at, 44, 49, 70-71, 203; emperor's move from, 22-23, 49, 203, 207; and Meiji school system, 203, 206-207, 221; as a political center, 16, 22, 45, 47, 70, 355; population statistics for, 23, 274, 321-322, 324, 335, 342; the press in, 235-236
Kyoto Imperial University, 228

language standardization, 245, 362-363
law schools, 221-222, 225, 227
Lewis model of industrialization, 381
Lincoln, Abraham, 80

literacy rates, 13-14, 126, 179, 192, 200, 211-212, 278
Lockwood, William W., 403

machi (wards or neighborhoods), 114, 117, 340, 342, 344, 368-370
Maebara Issei, 50, 53, 64
Maeda daimyo, 86, 145
Maeda Renzan, 47
Maejima Hisoka, 56, 238, 355
Makimura Masanao, 159, 207
Mariyama han, 101, 103
Marugame han, 101
Marxist scholarship on Japan, 7, 378, 403
Matsudaira Katamori, 77
Matsudaira Sadanobu, 20
Matsukata deflation, 5, 7, 18, 60-61, 116, 130, 284, 377, 393, 466
Matsumae han, 253
Matsumoto han, 158, 175
measles, 295
meat eating in Meiji period, 152, 354, 455-456, 460, 463, 467
medicine, 197-198, 203, 220-221, 225, 284, 301, 305
Meibindō, 227
Meiji absolutism, 7, 70
Meiji Constitution, 8, 19, 61-62, 69, 166, 186, 192, 359
Meiji Emperor: as commander-in-chief, 186, 192; and Confucianism, 221; as symbol of state, 10-12, 21-22; tennō shinsai (personal rule by the emperor), 17, 50, 82
Meiji Restoration: contrasts with foreign transition-revolutions, 9-13, 58, 63-64; definition of, 8-9, 13; as an organizational revolution, 133-134
Meirinkan, 198, 210
Meisho, Empress, 73
merchants, 24, 200, 340, 350, 353-354, 371. *See also* chōnin
meritocracy, 4, 90, 198
migration, rural-urban, 16, 274-279, 287, 291, 293, 296, 311-312, 325, 336, 365-367, 404, 409-410, 418, 432, 455
Mill, John Stuart, 221
Minié rifles, 43
Ministry of Agriculture and Commerce, 422
Ministry of the Army, 183
Ministry of Education (Mombushō), 122, 137-138, 202, 204-205, 207-208, 214-216, 218-220, 229-230
Ministry of Finance, 33, 45, 51-52, 56-57, 67, 81, 108, 257, 386
Ministry of Home Affairs, 26, 50, 100, 125, 137-138, 151, 166, 241, 246, 255; and the Meiji police, 17-18, 24, 120, 139
Ministry of Justice, 100, 137-138
Ministry of Military Affairs (Hyōbushō), 180
Ministry of the Navy, 181-182
Ministry of Religion, 50
Ministry of Rites, 149, 153-154, 158
Ministry of Rites and Education (Kyōbushō), 153-155, 158, 166-167
minshū (people's) history, 379-380
Mito, 37, 146-149, 338
Mitogaku, 145, 158
Mitsubishi, 30, 248-249, 253, 255-261, 266, 268-270, 372, 451
Mitsui, 254-255, 263
Mitsukuri Rinshō, 207
Miyagi prefecture, 140
Miyamoto Matao, 288-289
Mizuno Tadakuni, 29
moats, 343
Mombushō, *see* Ministry of Education
moral training, 197, 208, 215, 223-224, 229
Mori Arinori, 123, 215, 224-225, 230
Mōri Motonari, 87
Mori Ōgai, 438-441
Morioka han, 100-101
Mosk-Pak theory, 289-290, 381, 437-438
Motoda Eifu, 21, 221-222
Motoori Norinaga, 145
Movement for People's Rights, 17-18, 69, 83, 90, 107, 128, 130, 166, 188, 210, 221-222, 241
Murata Seifū, 149
Mutsu Munemitsu, 386

Nada, 253
Naegi han, 158, 164
Nagahara Keiji, 380
Nagano, 33, 175, 199, 214, 418
Nagaoka han, 100-101

Nagasaki: and kaigun denshūjo, 170-172; and Meiji school system, 220; population statistics for, 336, 342; as a port city, 234, 256, 266, 353
Nagoya, 334, 341-343, 348
Nakabe Yoshiko, 321, 341
Nakae Tōju, 144
Nakamura, James, 288-289
Nakamura Masanao and the Dōjinsha, 220
Nakamura Satoru, 408, 410, 414
Nakamura Takafusa, 380
Nakano Goichi, 107, 445
Nakaoka Shintarō, 80
Nakatsu han, 74, 82. *See also* Fukuzawa Yukichi
Napoleonic Code, 221
Nara, 159
Narushima Ryūhoku, 362
National Police Officers Training Institute, 140
Nelson, Admiral Horatio, 192
Niigata, 220, 258, 336, 342
Niijima Jō, and Dōshisha, 222
Nine Shop Union (Kutana), 259, 269
Ninomiya Sontoku, 145
Nippon Seifu Yūbin Jōkisen Kaisha (YJK), 255, 257
Nippon Yūsen Kaisha (NYK), 248, 259-261, 266, 270
Nishi Amane, 206
Nishiyama Matsunosuke, 364
Nobiru, 265
nōkan yogyō (by-employment), 306, 315, 360, 396, 400, 402, 406-407, 410
noma kaisen, 263-264
Nomura Kanetarō, 406-408
Norman, E. H., 86
Numazu heigakkō, 175, 206

Obama han, 103
Oda Nobunaga, 72, 144
Office for Shinto Affairs, 49
Office of the Great Teaching (Daikyōin), 153
Office of Proselytizers (Senkyōshi), 153-154
Office of Rites, 152. *See also* Ministry of Rites
Ogata Kōan and the Teki juku, 200-201
Ōgi Shinzō, 363-367, 375, 458
Ōguchi Yūjirō, 410-411
Ohkawa Kazushi, 399
Ōita prefecture, 165, 213-214, 217
Okayama han, 95, 97, 100, 146-148, 199, 342
Okazaki-Umemura debate on population growth, 281-283, 290
Okazaki Yōichi, 281
Oki Takatō, 355-356
Ōkubo Toshimichi, 12, 31, 44-45, 47, 50-51, 53-60, 63, 65-66, 80, 99, 104-106, 109, 255, 265, 355
Okudaira Kamesuke, 158
Ōkuma Shigenobu, 50-51, 53, 55-59, 61, 67, 240, 371
Ōkuni Takamasa, 148
Ōmi merchants, 262
Ōmizo han, 101
Ōmura Masujirō, 44-45, 54, 64, 66-67, 201, 222
Ōno han, 198-199
Ono Takeo, 421-422, 444
opening of the ports (kaikō), 4, 8, 135, 173, 233, 254, 296, 317, 319, 352, 355, 401, 416, 446
Opium War, 39, 170
Osaka: and the choice of treaty ports, 352-353; cotton-related by-employment in, 407, 414; and the Meiji school system, 220-221; population statistics for, 23, 274, 295, 306, 321-322, 324, 335, 342, 358-359; as a source of commodities for Edo, 349, 358; and the "two capital plan," 355
Osaka-Edo shipping trade, 22, 249, 251, 253-254, 261, 263-264, 269, 349, 358
Ōsaka Shōsen kaisha (OSK), 248-249, 266, 270
Otaru, 266
Ōtsuka Tsutomu, 441
Owari han, 37, 106
Ōyama Iwao, 64

Pak, Simon, 437-438
Parkes, Sir Harry, 163
Parley, Peter, 219
Passin, Herbert, 211
Peninsular & Oriental S.N. Co. (P & O), 258-259, 269

Perry, Commodore Matthew, 7-8, 16, 19, 24, 29, 38-39, 42, 68, 75, 170-171, 196-197, 232-233, 279
political parties, creation of, 25
Peerage Law (1884), 84-85
Presseisen, Ernst, 177, 185
Privy Council, 88, 90
Pulitzer, Joseph, 36
Pusan, 26

Quantitative Economic History (QEH) Group, 379-380

railroad, development of, 86, 125, 265-266, 284, 319-320, 344-345, 354, 358-359, 463
Rakugaki (also rakusho), 233
rakugo, 364, 368
rangaku (Dutch studies), 39, 148, 197, 200-201, 220, 384, 456
Regulations for Prefectural Assemblies (1878), 35
Reischauer, Edwin Oldfather, 65
revolution, defined by R. R. Palmer, 12
rickshaws, 448, 463
rikugun bugyō, 16
Risshisha, and the Meiji educational system, 221
Rōnō-ha–Kōza-ha debate, 380
Rousseau, Jean Jacques, 221
Rules for Instruction at Middle Schools (1872), 219
rules for the university and elementary and middle schools (1870), 206
Russian Revolution, 10
Russo-Japanese War, 18, 21, 89, 194, 448, 459-460, 467-468
Ryūkyū islands, 12, 30

Saga: and arms manufacture in the bakumatsu period, 171, 174; and educational reform, 199; and haihan chiken, 48; participation in the Meiji government, 55, 61, 181; population statistics for, 328, 331, 338, 340
Saga rebellion, 12, 60
Saigō Takamori, 31, 44, 47, 51-60, 64-65, 80, 82, 105-107, 154, 178
Saigō Tsugumichi, 187, 191
saisei itchi (union of rituals and government), 50, 153
Sakai: anti-foreign incident in, 54, 95; population statistics for, 274, 342-343
Sakamoto Ryōma, 70
sake, 116, 253, 261, 349, 406, 430, 432, 442, 457
sakoku (seclusion), 3, 37, 42, 168, 254
samurai: activism and terrorism, 8, 42, 54, 61, 69, 90; distinction between shi and sotsu, 38, 74, 80-81; post-Restoration rebellion, 11-12; post-Restoration status, 26, 31, 51, 57, 78-84; rank consciousness of, 82, 85; stipends abolished, 17-18, 31, 56, 59-60, 80-81, 83, 86-87, 102, 319, 324, 337, 339, 466
Sanjō Sanetomi, 45, 47, 50, 54-55, 57, 70, 72, 84-86, 105
sankin kōtai (alternate residence system), 22, 29-30, 39, 42, 274, 277, 319, 324, 348-352, 358, 362
sanpan kenpei, 104-105. *See also* Imperial Guard
Sanshoku (Three Offices), 46, 87, 99
Sansom, George, 210
Sapporo, 336, 342-343
Sasaki Takayuki, 55, 100
Satō Masanori, 418
Satsuma han: administrative reforms, 53; anti-Buddhist policies in, 149-150, 157, 163-164; economic reforms, 30, 53, 78; education in, 199; military reforms, 53, 171, 174; participation in Meiji government, 12, 46-48, 54-56, 61, 89, 103-105, 181; population statistics for, 285, 302, 328, 331; role in Restoration, 30, 37, 42-45, 96
Satsuma Rebellion, 8, 11-12, 31, 60-61, 69, 81, 107, 183-184, 221, 259, 261, 304-305
Sayama han, 101
Seidensticker, Edward, 373
seika, *see* kuge, ranking of
Seitaisho, 46-47, 49, 65, 87, 99
Sekigahara, Tokugawa victory at, 13, 64, 73
Seki Shimpachi and the Kyōritsu gakusha, 205
Sekiyama Naotarō, 331
sekke, *see* kuge, ranking of
Sendai, 265, 341-343
Sengoku period, 468
Senjū Woolen Mill, 462

sericulture, 22, 277, 284, 301, 303-304, 306-308, 325, 335, 354, 381, 400-401, 405, 407-408, 411-414, 416-420
sesshō (regent), abolition of the position, 83
Settsu prefecture, 386
Shaku Unshō, 165
Shibata han, 198-199
Shibusawa Eiichi, 51, 56, 67, 141, 255, 371
shijuku, 121-122, 196, 199-201, 204-205, 210-211, 215-216, 220-222, 226, 228, 230
shikan gakkō, 178, 184, 189
Shimaji Mokurai, 154, 166
Shimane, 165, 418-419
Shimazaki Tōson, 209
Shimazu Hisamitsu, 44, 47, 51, 53, 56, 65, 104
Shimazu Nariakira, 149
Shimonoseki, 43, 264-265, 342
shimpan, 29, 69, 73, 352
Shimpō Hiroshi, 379
shinbutsu bunri (separation of Shinto and Buddhist deities), 50, 143-167
shinshoku-uke (registration at shrines), 146, 148
Shinto, 41, 144-167, 203-204
shishi (men of spirit), 54, 70, 75, 78
Shizuoka, 361
Shōbai ōrai, 199
Shōheikō, 197, 203-204
Shōnai han, 33
Shōwa Constitution, 3
shrines, 37, 48, 77, 147-157, 159-160, 343, 351, 444
shugendō (mountain asceticism), 157
shumon aratame cho (religious investigation registers), 280-281
shūshin (ethics), 21, 223
"silk-road" traffic, 354
Sino-Japanese War, 18, 21, 89, 194, 246, 448, 460, 468
smallpox, 305
Smethurst, Richard, 191, 194
Smith, Thomas, 288, 321, 384, 407
social mobility, 4, 75, 89-90, 195, 197, 218, 225-226, 229
Soejima Taneomi, 50-51, 55, 59
sonnō jōi movement, 41-42, 54, 93-94
Spencer, Herbert, 221
Spencer rifles, 43
statistical analysis, 5-6, 378-379
Stinchcombe, Arthur, 135-136
sumptuary laws, 16, 23
Sun Yat-sen, 63

Tadotsu han, 101
Taihō code, 51
Taiping Rebellion, 62-63
Taiwan expedition (1874), 257, 261
Takamatsu han, 94-95
Takane Masaaki, 89-90
Takashima Shūhan, 170-171
Takasu han, 100-101, 103
Takasugi Shinsaku, 36
Takatō han, 175
Takehashi mutiny (1879), 84
Tanaka Kyūgyū, 410
Tanakura han, 97
Tani Kanjō, 12
Tanoguchi han, 175
taru kaisen, 251-254, 256, 261-262, 268-269
Tatsuoka han, 101
Tawara han, 74
taxes, on commodities, 116
tea and mulberry policy, 353, 359
telegraph, 136, 192, 247, 264, 463
Temmei famine, 293
temples, 144-152, 155-161, 163-164, 167, 343, 351, 444
Tempō mortality crisis, 288, 295-298, 301-302, 304, 309-310, 315-316, 466
Tempō reforms, 7, 16, 29, 253, 259
tenancy, 15, 18, 369, 378, 397, 400-404, 410, 414-416
tenants, urban, 368-370, 448
tenryō, 17, 30, 98, 100, 394
terakoya, 121-122, 196, 199-201, 204-205, 210-211, 215-216, 220, 228, 364
tera-uke (registration and temples), 146, 148
"tiger band" at Aizu-Wakamatsu, 77
Toba-Fushimi, battle at, 43-44, 64, 94
Toffler, Alvin, 469
Tokugawa Hidetada, 73
Tokugawa house after 1868, 11, 93-95
Tokugawa Iemochi, 73, 454
Tokugawa Ieyasu, 64, 72-73
Tokugawa Keiki (Yoshinobu), also known

Tokugawa Keiki (Yoshinobu) (*cont.*)
as Hitsotsubashi Keiki, 11, 37, 70, 76, 94-95
Tokugawa Keishō, 37
Tokugawa Mitsukuni, 146-148
Tokugawa Nariaki, 147-148
Tokutomi Roka, 209, 215, 230
Tokutomi Sohō, 25, 222, 227
Tokuyama han, 101, 103
Tokyo, forced residence in, 57, 83, 85, 91, 352, 372. *See also* Edo
Tokyo Governor's Conference (1875), 109, 127
Tokyo University, 166, 218, 224-227
tondenhei (military colonists), 182
Torio Koyata, 105
Tosa (Kōchi) han: anti-Buddhist policies in, 157; and Dajōkansatsu, 100; economic reform, 30; education in, 199; military reform, 173; and Mitsubishi, 30, 256-257, 268; participation in Meiji government, 48, 55-56, 82, 104-105; population statistics for, 328, 331; role in Restoration, 12, 30, 37; samurai status in, 70, 78, 81
Totman, Conrad, 69, 73, 350
Tottori, 337
Toyama, 158, 334
Toyoda Takeshi, 160
Toyotomi Hideyoshi, 65, 72, 144
tozama han, 19, 29-30, 39, 63, 69, 73-74, 175, 350
Trafalgar, battle of, 192
treaty ports, 16, 22, 105, 231, 234, 279, 284, 296, 317, 339, 352-353, 358
Trotsky, Leon, 43
Tsuda Mamichi and the Numazu heigakkō, 206
Tsukiji shipyard, 192, 354
Tsukumo Shōkai, 256
Tsushima han, 26
Tsuwano han, 100-101, 148-150, 158
tsuzukimono (serialized fiction), 244
tuition, 199, 216-217, 226
Tussing, Arlon, 402-403
two capital plan, 355-356
typhoid fever, 305

Ueda han, 175
Umemura Mataji, 281, 379
unchinzumi, 250, 252
university, 202-204, 206-207
urban-rural differences, 199
urbanization, degree of, 273-275
Uwajima han, 201

vaccination, in Meiji period, 209, 284, 305. *See also* medicine
venereal disease, 305

Wakayama, 336, 342, 344
Walsh, Hall & Co., and Iwasaki Yatarō, 256
Waseda University (Tokyo semmongakkō), 227
wasen, 248-250, 252-253, 258, 261-265, 270
Washington, George, 80
Washington, D.C., 3, 20
Watanabe Kazan, 74
Watarai Nobuyoshi, 145
Waters, Neil, 33, 380
Wayland, Francis, 219
weather, effect on crop production, 275, 293
Webb, Herschel, 41, 72
Western Circuit shipping route, 250-251, 262, 264, 345
Willson readers, 219
women, opportunities for, 82, 200, 205, 211, 220, 226, 228, 412-414
woodblock prints, 244, 354, 364
World War I, 459-460, 468
World War II, 460, 468

Yamada Akiyoshi, 179, 187
Yamagata Aritomo, 56, 64, 91, 105-106, 178-179, 187, 189, 446
Yamaguchi Kazuo, 408
Yamakawa Isamu, 188
Yamanashi prefecture, 402, 411-414, 418
Yamauchi Toyonori, 85
Yamauchi Yōdō, 51-52
Yamazaki Ansai, 144, 146
Yamazaki Ryūzō, 417
Yamori Kazuhiko, 340
Yanagita Kunio, 456
Yasuba Yasukichi, 379, 381
Yokohama: naval school in, 178; population statistics for, 306, 335, 337, 342-

343; as a port city, 16, 22, 234, 254, 264, 266, 352-354, 358-359, 374; the press in, 236
Yokohama-Shanghai shipping route, 249, 258
Yokoi Shōnan, 54
Yokosuka shipyard, 192
Yomiuri shimbun, 245-246
Yonezawa han, 293-295, 338, 340
Yoshida Kiyonari, 80
Yoshida Shōin, 42, 197, 210, 230, 232
Yoshii han, 100-101, 103
Yoshikawa Koretaru, 145
yūgaku (travel study), 198
Yuri Kimimasa, 96, 371

zaigōmachi (handicraft centers), 321
zappō, in Meiji newspapers, 243-244

LIBRARY OF CONGRESS

CATALOGING-IN-PUBLICATION DATA

Main entry under title:

Japan in transition, from Tokugawa to Meiji.
Includes bibliographical references and index.
1. Japan—History—19th century. 2. Japan—History—Meiji period, 1868-1912. 3. Japan—Social conditions—1868-1912. I. Jansen, Marius B. II. Rozman, Gilbert.
DS881.4.J36 1986 952'.025 85-16775
ISBN 0-691-05459-2 (alk. paper)